FLIGHT
of the
WASP

FLIGHT
of the
WASP

THE RISE, FALL, *and* FUTURE *of*
AMERICA'S ORIGINAL RULING CLASS

MICHAEL GROSS

Grove Press
New York

FIRST EDITION

Published simultaneously in Canada
Printed in the United States of America

First Grove Atlantic hardcover edition: November 2023
First Grove Atlantic paperback edition: April 2025

Library of Congress Cataloging-in-Publication data is available for this title.

ISBN 978-0-8021-6187-1
eISBN 978-0-8021-6188-8

Grove Press
an imprint of Grove Atlantic
154 West 14th Street
New York, NY 10011

Distributed by Publishers Group West

groveatlantic.com

25 26 27 28   10 9 8 7 6 5 4 3 2 1

When we are planning for posterity, we ought to remember that virtue is not hereditary.

—THOMAS PAINE, *COMMON SENSE* (1776)

CONTENTS

AUTHOR'S NOTE

The subjects of this book are the northwestern Europeans who colonized the North American continent, beginning in the early seventeenth century, and then became its privileged ruling class. They are commonly called WASPs—white Anglo-Saxon Protestants—and I use that term freely, but it requires clarification.*

While they were all white and Protestant, the term "Anglo-Saxon" is geographically problematic, as the people it literally describes, who inhabited and ruled Britain between the end of Roman occupation in the fifth century and the Norman Conquest in the eleventh century, actually came from Germany, Denmark, and the Netherlands. And British culture was also heavily influenced by the Celts, Romans, and Norman French.

Later, those we now think of as WASPs emerged from the Reformation, which began as a religious movement in Germany but added a political dimension as it spread across Western Europe and then America. There it brought together English Calvinists, the Puritans among them, who settled New England and parts of America's Mid-Atlantic coastline; English-born Anglicans, who first colonized Virginia and Maryland; French Huguenots, who were scattered all

---

* E. Digby Baltzell has often been credited with coining the term "WASP" in his 1964 book *The Protestant Establishment*, in which he used the acronym in tables, he would later say, in order to save space. In a 2012 letter to the editor in the *New York Times*, Fred Shapiro, editor of *The Yale Book of Quotations*, took issue with that, citing a 1957 reference to WASPs in a scholarly article by sociologist Andrew Hacker and a 1948 article in New York's *Amsterdam News*, a Black-oriented newspaper, that used the term while criticizing WASPs for "ganging up" on minority groups.

along the Atlantic coastline from South Carolina to Maine; Dutch Reform church members, who settled Nieuw Amsterdam; and the Quakers of Pennsylvania. Many gravitated to the Episcopal Church after it was born in 1789 at Christ Church in Philadelphia, where George Washington had a pew and Robert Morris, John Penn, Payton Randolph, James Biddle, and Benjamin Franklin would be buried.

In the years since, statisticians have divided American Protestants into two distinct groups. One encompassed the "mainline" or "mainstream" establishment Protestants who colonized the north and east of the American continent and, as this book's subtitle puts it, invented America and became its economic and cultural gatekeepers. The other was a catchall for the born-again, evangelical, or conservative congregants who arrived later, gravitated south and west, and worshipped at Presbyterian, Lutheran, Baptist, Pentecostal, and other churches. This book focuses on mainstream Protestants, but it is not about any of their religious sects as such; rather, it will look at their followers as a sociocultural force defined by the status they gained, the economic and political power they exercised, and the good and bad they did as America's elite from the eighteenth century until today.

INTRODUCTION

Two generations ago, my family came to New York from the Jewish ghettoes of eastern Europe, almost certainly fleeing prejudice, violence, and oppression rather than seeking liberal democracy. My parents were born in America in the early twentieth century. Theirs was not the America of this book.

In ancient Rome, society was divided between elite patricians and common plebeians—and beneath both, current and former slaves. France had its three estates, the clergy, the hereditary nobility, and common people. American society was supposed to be different. We didn't have classes; no one was better than anyone else—or so I was taught at school. But for most of our history, we have had a patriciate, an aristocracy, a hereditary oligarchic upper class.

Where I grew up, in a suburb on Long Island, it was quite possible to be oblivious to the existence of the white Anglo-Saxon Protestants who first colonized that island, as well as the surrounding region from Virginia to Maine, and then initiated the American national experiment. I know that as a child I lacked any consciousness of America's original upper class. Rockville Centre was mostly white, but neither Anglo-Saxon nor Protestant. In school, where I learned about America's founding Pilgrims and Puritans and assumed their strict sects were long defunct, my white classmates seemed to me to be half Roman Catholic (the town was the seat of a diocese), half Jewish. If there were any members of what would later be known as Our Crowd, the wealthy German Jewish families who were the financial, if not quite social, equals of the WASP elite, in our little town, I didn't know about them.

Rich Jews lived a few towns away, and I vividly recall visiting one such family to frolic in their in-ground pool—luxury!—but though we had to drive through patrician towns like Old Westbury en route to that oasis, we never stopped in any of them or discussed who lived down the long driveways and past the sweeping lawns visible from the road. On the rare occasions when I ventured farther afield to visit Long Island's old-money North Shore, it was to attend bar and bat mitzvahs at new-money country clubs. I'd never heard of their WASP counterparts, Piping Rock or Seawanhaka—or heard Locust Valley lockjaw. I don't even know if I'd met a WASP before I went to college (Vassar, class of 1974), and even then I looked down on their campus representatives as khaki-clad, Weejuns-wearing, beer-chugging throw-backs of no consequence or relevance to my life in what already seemed more diverse, multicultural times.

I would later learn that one of my best friends at Vassar was a full-fledged member of the WASP elite whose family had sailed from old to New Amsterdam aboard the *Spotted Cow* in 1663. But we bonded over LSD, Little Feat, and the New York Dolls, not Sea Breezes or his Huguenot bloodlines. After college, I made a number of friends who came from colonial American families, and the more I saw of them, the more I thought they were trying to crawl out of the rubble of a collapsed culture, not understanding that their mothers and fathers, acutely aware of a changing world, if not quite accepting it, had pur-posely gone to ground in the hope of protecting and retaining the (as it turned out not inconsiderable) privileges WASPs had accumu-lated, while their children tried somehow to assimilate into the by then much broader and vital population that had overflowed their parents' world. We were a lot more fun.

Though none of these (to me) exotics indulged in braggadocio—indeed, they exuded practiced nonchalance and seemed more em-barrassed than chuffed by their heritage—this book was inspired by them. As hints of their notable families' stories emerged, an anthro-pological curiosity was piqued, and in the mid-1980s, as the rich had a revival under Ronald Reagan, I took my first tentative journalistic steps into the society they came from—and came to see that reports of the death of old money were exaggerated. I wrote several books that peripherally examined this phenomenon, including *740 Park,* about a New York City cooperative apartment house that was an establishment redoubt, and *Rogues' Gallery,* the story of the financial backers of the Metropolitan Museum of Art, and discovered that while WASPs hadn't given up the ghost, many of them would have preferred that the rest of us think they had.

Quite the contrary; with stubborn persistence and a surprising knack for adaptation, they've survived, even if they no longer prosper in comparison with hedge fund, infotainment, and tech money. Turns out they got a piece of that, once they sold their Park Avenue apartments, Palm Beach mansions, Adirondack camps, and shingled Atlantic cottages to the newly enriched. So they still sat near, if not at, the top of America's socioeconomic pyramid in summer 2019 as I began writing this book. But that imposing edifice was under attack from both ends of the political spectrum.

That reckoning, inevitable perhaps, indispensable for sure, is ongoing, and it is my hope that this warts-and-all look at those who designed, erected, and guarded the pyramid will contribute in some small way to an understanding of the complex legacy of American WASPs, their huge accomplishments, and their egregious lapses, from slavery and genocide to deadly exceptionalism. To be glib, it is my belief that a clear-eyed portrait of those currently seen as the perpetrators of great wrongs might help us reach even-handed conclusions about the past and better face the future. For we would all benefit if the traits WASPs idealized, like humility, responsibility, simple civility, and lack of pretension, which seem endangered in the world today, were revived and again revered.

The story of the WASPs is, for better and for worse, the story of America. The star-crossed settlers who came to Jamestown in 1607 were WASPs. The Pilgrims who landed off Massachusetts in 1620 were WASPs. The buyers of the first American slaves at Port Comfort near Jamestown in 1619 were WASPs, as was George Washington, and every president until 1961. Many of the brave men and women who supported the abolition of slavery before the Civil War were members of the northern WASP elite. The industrialists and financiers who built and ran America, men like Cornelius Vanderbilt, J. Pierpont Morgan, and Henry Ford, and the lawyers who protected them? WASPs. Until the third decade of the twentieth century, just about every person with power and influence in the United States was a WASP—or else a convert. Into the 1980s, the upwardly mobile wanted to wear the same clothes, go to the same schools, join their clubs, and move on up to their exclusive neighborhoods.

That can't be said anymore. The Anglo-American elite has drifted from American centrality to the periphery. States have been run by Jewish and Catholic governors throughout American history, beginning with Thomas Dongan, who was appointed governor of the Duke of York's Province of New York in 1683. The first Catholic governor of one of the United States was Thomas Sim Lee, who took over the Maryland statehouse in 1779 and returned in 1792. David Emanuel, a Jew, became the acting governor of Georgia in 1801. Edward Salomon was appointed governor of Washington Territory in 1870. Washington Bartlett, elected governor of California in 1887, was born Jewish but converted to Christianity before taking office. Simon Bamberger was elected the head of Utah in 1896.

Since 1961, we've had both non-Protestant and nonwhite presidents. But WASPs persist. The Episcopalian forty-first president, George H. W. Bush (Andover, Yale, Skull and Bones, CIA), appointed his fellow religionists James Baker (The Hill School, Princeton) as his secretary of state and David Souter (Harvard, Rhodes scholar, Harvard Law) as his first choice for the traditionally all-WASP Supreme Court, and later added Clarence Thomas (College of the Holy Cross, Yale Law) to that court. Thomas was born a Catholic but married an Episcopalian, and both he and his wife attend a charismatic Virginia Episcopal church.[1] Still, from 2010, when Justice John Paul Stevens retired and was replaced by Elena Kagan, until 2017, that illustrious bench was filled exclusively with Catholics and Jews.[2] When the WASP Neil Gorsuch (Georgetown Prep, Columbia, Harvard Law) was elevated to the high court that year, he was the WASP exception.

Congress is also a counterexample to the relentless advance of WASP diminishment. In 1965, the House of Representatives included 54 Episcopalians, 69 Methodists, and 56 Presbyterians. In 2021, those numbers had dropped to 23 Episcopalians, 31 Methodists, and 15 Presbyterians. There were 15 Episcopalian senators in 1965 (vs. 7 in

2021), 22 Methodists (vs. 7 in 2021), and 11 Presbyterians in both 1965 and 2021.[3] However, in 2021, the 117th Congress was still 55.4 percent Protestant, compared to only 43 percent of American adults. And Presbyterians, Episcopalians, and Methodists were all overrepresented when compared to their numbers in the general population.*

As late as 1916, the baseline economic power of mainline Protestants persisted, as demonstrated by the value of property and parsonages owned by Protestant religious groups. They owned real estate worth $1.177 billion versus $441 million for Catholics, $185 million for Black Protestants, $151 million for evangelicals, and $31 million for Jews. Of the mainline Protestant denominations, northern Methodists, Episcopalians, and Presbyterians held the most property, with over $100 million each. Jewish congregations were slightly richer; each Jewish congregation member's individual share was valued at $87, but the per capita wealth of individual mainline Protestants was only slightly less at $76, while conservative Protestants lagged far behind at $28. In urban areas, the same trend held true, with per capita wealth the highest among Jews, mainline Protestants lagging only slightly, and others well in the rear. At the time, census data indicated how many recent immigrants were part of those religious cohorts, because as many as 96 percent of American Jews were still worshipping in a foreign language, as opposed to 49 percent of Catholics, 17 percent of conservative Protestants, and only 10 percent of mainline Protestants.[4] But by the early twentieth century, the prescient could see that the forces of immigration would soon threaten WASP hegemony.

Statisticians measure status and social mobility through three socioeconomic indicators (or SEIs): income, wealth, and education. The earnings of contemporary white evangelical Protestants are 73 percent less than those of mainline Protestants, who hold twice as many bachelor's degrees as conservative Protestants. Conservatives,

---

* Congress in 2021 was 29.8 percent Catholic (against 20 percent of the adult population) and 6.2 percent Jewish (while only 2 percent of U.S. adults identified as Jews). Of the Protestants, 66 identified as Baptist, 35 as Methodist, 26 as Anglican/Episcopal, 24 as Presbyterian, 22 as Lutheran, 13 as members of other sects, and 108 as nondenominational or unspecified, according to the Pew Research Center's study "Faith on the Hill: The Religious Composition of the 117th Congress."

in turn, have earned a quarter as many bachelor's degrees as white Jews. So it's not surprising that between 1990 and 2016, according to the General Social Survey conducted by NORC, a nonpartisan research organization at the University of Chicago, white Jews, particularly members of the more liberal Reform denomination of Judaism, had the highest mean income and mean SEI scores (which rank prestigious occupations by the education they require and the earnings they generate) among Americans. Among mainstream Protestant denominations, Episcopalians and Quakers rank highest in mean income, with Congregationalists and Presbyterians close behind them. And those four denominations also have the highest SEI scores among all Protestants. Conservative Protestants score considerably lower by both measures.

Americans with more education, income, and professional prestige "are 50 percent more likely to be Mainline Protestant than Evangelical Protestant or Catholic," according to one analysis of this data, which concludes that despite their declines relative to the entire American population, and particularly Jews, Unitarians, and educated American Hindus, today's mainline Protestants still have considerable socioeconomic advantages.[5]

Another study of the Protestant establishment, comparing the religious affiliation of people listed in the 1930 and 1992 editions of *Who's Who in America,* found that despite some slippage in their position—and the marked rise of a Jewish and Catholic elite after World War II—Episcopalians, Presbyterians, and Congregationalists remained "overrepresented among both cultural and power elites."

In 1930, the three primary mainline Protestant sects still accounted for 53.5 percent of all listed bankers, businessmen, politicians, judges, lawyers, military officers, educators, scientists, doctors, engineers, social workers, religious figures, and cultural leaders such as editors, authors, artists, and actors. That majority shrank to 35.1 percent in 1992, although Episcopalians were more likely to have hung on in the upper tiers of society, and were even more prominent in 1992 than in 1930, rising from about 6 percent of the elite to just over 7 percent, with a notable presence in the realms of business and public policy.

In those sixty years, the overall representation of Episcopalians in *Who's Who* shrank from 21.94 to 18.04 percent, Presbyterians from 20.32 to 13.91 percent, and Congregationalists from 11.29 to 3.19 percent, the last an almost 72 percent drop. The number of those with no religious affiliation listed rose from almost 44 percent to 65.66 percent.[6] In contrast, Jews were more prominent despite being underrepresented in all but cultural occupations, rising from 1.31 percent of all those listed in *Who's Who* to 12.32 percent, and Catholics rose from 4.45 percent to 23.12 percent.

Those figures do not, however, reflect the waning importance of religious identification among younger Americans, another indicator of the decline of America's traditional ruling class. In 2020, 70 percent of Americans identified as Christian whether they were actively religious or not (vs. 1 percent as Jews), 42 percent as white (i.e., non-Hispanic Caucasian) Christians, and 16 percent as white mainline Protestants. Between 2006 and 2020, the percentage of the American population identifying as conservative Protestants dropped from 23 to 14 percent. Large numbers of white Christians, particularly younger ones, have stopped identifying as such. Between 1986 and 2020, the number of white Christians aged eighteen to twenty-nine who identify as religiously unaffiliated has risen from 10 to 36 percent.[7] If many American Protestants feel themselves under siege today, it is, at least statistically, understandable in a society steadily abandoning regular religious worship.

Diversity is refreshing, an unequivocal good. It has come as a belated and forced antidote to WASP hegemony, to WASP culture's advocacy of slavery, the genocide of the American Indian, white privilege, tribal exclusion, accumulation, isolationism, nativism, inequality, racism, sexism, austerity, cruelty, and prejudice. The WASPs ruled America as aristocrats. But there's something else. Their rule also promoted an American ideal. WASPs have certainly pushed back against the increasing inclusion of "others," be they Catholics, Jews, Muslims, people of color, or women. But honor, duty, tradition, leadership, modesty, restraint, stoicism, service, moral authority, courage, grace, noblesse oblige, and cultivation were still given lip service within (and even out-side) the WASP milieu—even if sometimes in the breach.

At its best, WASP culture was authoritative, not authoritarian. From the C-suite to Washington, D.C., its better qualities are deeply missed. In that context, the forty-fifth president, Donald Trump (New York Military Academy, Fordham, Wharton), descended from a Ger-man Protestant who came to America in 1885 and a Presbyterian by birth, represented the clan's nadir—a repudiation of the tattered remains of WASP virtue. His successor was a man defined by de-cency, America's second Catholic president, Joe Biden (University of Delaware, Syracuse Law). Nonetheless, a selfish, narcissistic, tribal, atomized nation might still look to WASPs for a restorative exam-ple of America's civic conscience: its rectitude, chivalry, sense of moral duty, collective purpose, and community.

The decline into irrelevance of the white Anglo-Saxon Protestant, first posited by WASPs, has been a generally accepted trope since 1960, when Cleveland Amory (Milton Academy, Harvard) published *Who Killed Society?* In the final pages of *The Protestant Establishment: Ar-istocracy and Caste in America,* E. Digby Baltzell (St. Paul's School, University of Pennsylvania, Columbia, Harvard) described his 1964 classic as "an attempt to analyze the decline of authority in America," an authority personified by the WASP elite, who "may still be deferred to and envied" but were "no longer honored in the land."[8]

A few years later, outright mockery superseded serious inspec-tion. *WASP, Where Is Thy Sting?* was the title of a 1977 book by the WASP humorist Florence King. In 1980, the Jewish humorist Lisa Birnbach's bestselling *The Official Preppy Handbook* ("Look, Muffy, a book for us") turned what some thought tragedy into farce. The people that invented America had become a joke.

In 1992, Joseph W. Alsop, the late political columnist and, by his own description, a "minor member of this now-vanished group," attempted to fine-tune, and narrow, the definition of the living-dead WASPs in his memoir, *I've Seen the Best of It.* Alsop proposed the pri-macy of a smaller and highly self-conscious subset of the species, which he called the WASP Ascendancy. Defined by "the right kind of origin and the right kind of name," it was led by both colonial families and those with fortunes made "just a little further down the line, like the Astors." It was, he wrote, "an inner group that was recognizable as a group . . . that was, on average, substantially richer and enjoyed substantially more leverage than other Americans." These WASPs served as role models to others "who were on their way up in the world." Typically Episcopalian, they were "highly recognizable" by, in Alsop's own order of precedence, their "fairly extreme but regional New England/ New York accent," odd pronunciation (*tomahtoes*), and use of "the earliest English name for anything" (WASPs had curtains, not drapes, and died rather than passed); their ownership of family summer homes, "large rural tribal dwellings" that smelled of beeswax and fresh-cut flowers; a strict dress code; a "high tolerance for eccentricity"; a snobbishness based primarily in lineage; a tendency toward conservatism and even intolerance; and "a certain provincialism and an all-too-common hostility to the intellectual life."[9] They were still America's elite, its haves, solid, established, decorous, and enviable, as opposed to its have-nots and the vast throng of in-betweens, who either didn't care about their place in the national hierarchy or were still engaged in striving accumulation.

If that was the opinion of a member of the clan, it's no wonder that WASP-bashing remains a mass-market bromide. The *National Review*'s Richard Brookhiser, a German Catholic, began his 1991 book *The Way of the WASP* recounting how the campaign that elected his former boss George H. W. Bush president in 1988 set off a wave of WASP abuse, and he concluded that we now live in "the post-WASP world."[10] In his review of that book in the *New York Times*, Christopher Lehmann-Haupt, who would shortly discover his own hidden Jewish roots, stated flatly, "A WASP renaissance is not going to happen."[11] In 2000, David Brooks observed that WASP culture, once "so powerful" and now "so dated," had been "crushed" by a new, highly educated meritocracy.[12]

Obituaries of America's former ruling class, whether melancholy or celebratory, stay evergreen in this century. In 2014, *Politico* published "The Death of the WASP," an essay premised on the notion that "the New England WASP has all but disappeared from its natural habitats—gone, almost, from the region's 12 Senate seats, van-

ished from its six governor's mansions." Rhode Island senator Sheldon
Whitehouse (St. Paul's, Yale, Virginia Law) was cited as the exception
that proved the rule of "extinction . . . retreat . . . departure."[13] And
in spring 2019, in "A Farewell to the WASPs," Rich Lowry, the editor
of the *National Review*, used a memorial service for Barbara Bush
(Rye Country Day School, Smith), wife of the aforementioned forty-
first president and mother of the forty-third, as his news hook, declaring, "The days of the WASP power brokers are gone."[14]

＞

WASPs dominated America for its first 350 years, but the ruling class
wasn't the monolith many imagine they were and George Washington hoped they would be. The predecessors of Alsop's WASP Ascendancy led the American Revolution and wrote the Constitution, but
by the time Thomas Jefferson was elected the third president in 1800,
WASP cohesion had fractured, the urban-centered Federalist Party
that had formed around Alexander Hamilton was failing, and the
agrarian Democrats who supported Jefferson were rising, supported
by the South and the West.

That didn't mean Alsop's top WASPs abandoned power, even as
they were slowly edged out of national political leadership in the late
twentieth century; in the Industrial Revolution, after the Civil War,
they pulled the levers of law and finance, and "retained a strong grip
not so much on industry itself, but on the banking and financial system on which industry depended for credit." Then, Alsop continued,
corruption led to an inevitable downfall due to their "grossly selfish
mismanagement of the nation's credit structure in the 1920s." Though
WASPs still won elections and stalked the corridors of power throughout his lifetime, and the powerful columnist, a relative of Theodore
Roosevelt, began his career during the WASP Franklin Roosevelt's
presidency and died just after the WASP George H. W. Bush was inaugurated, Alsop ultimately came to believe that "the whole view of the
world, and of history, the personal culture and the private manners
that produced these men, have all gone by the board."[15]

But there are many ways of looking at the American WASP, and
they are *not* merely the wealthy, powerful members of the Episcopal
Church who formed Alsop's inner circle. The Protestant Reforma-

tion churches that were their cradle encompass both mainline churches, which emphasized ceremony, rich vestments, rituals, sacraments, and clerical authority, and so-called conservative churches, which, ironically, took a freer, less structured, more evangelical approach to worship, focusing on the congregation more than the clergy. While the first families of America came from both traditions—the Anglicans of Virginia, for example, representing the most mainstream of churches, and the Puritans of Massachusetts, taking a more conservative approach—their religious differences would fade into the background by the time of our Revolution, and be overshadowed by socioeconomic distinctions.

Strictly speaking, WASPs were descended from the Germanic peoples who settled the British Isles; they usually worshipped either as members of the Church of England or as Presbyterians. But though Dutch and English colonists were, in the main, America's first families, to reflect the national reality its founding WASPs should be defined more broadly. As noted, they included those Puritan and, later, Congregationalist first families of Massachusetts; the Separatist Pilgrims of the Plymouth Colony;* the so-called New Puritans of Rhode Island and Connecticut; the English-born Anglicans of Virginia and Maryland; Swedish Lutherans, who became the first Scandinavians to settle in America when they established New Sweden in 1638 after landing near what is now Wilmington, Delaware; Dutch Reformed church-goers who dominated Nieuw Amsterdam; the French Protestants known as Huguenots and their French-speaking Belgian counterparts, Calvinist Walloons, who fled religious suppression, first in the Netherlands and England and then in several American colonies; and the Quakers of New Jersey and Pennsylvania. Many of those colonists, who dominated social and political life in early America, would ultimately join the Episcopal Church, a new, American religion formed in large part as a political repudiation of the unacceptably royalist Anglican Church.†

---

* The Puritans hoped to change the English church, while the Pilgrims chose to leave it. Instead, in 1692, the Pilgrims joined the Puritan-led Massachusetts Bay Colony when it absorbed their Plymouth Colony.

† Those who didn't become Episcopalian typically wound up as Presbyterians, Congregationalists, or Unitarians.

But there were also the Methodists (who split from the Anglican Church in 1784), Lutherans, and Baptists. Unlike the mainstream WASPs of northwest European origin, many of these more conservative WASPs came to the Western Hemisphere somewhat later, often from the borderlands between Scotland and England, from Ireland, and from Germany, and were more likely to head to what were then backwoods on the American frontier than its more settled, sophisticated, and urbanized eastern coast. They and the agrarians of the original southern colonies, particularly Virginia, dominated the country's politics, if not its social and financial life, through the first half of the nineteenth century.

✒

Curiously, despite the social role that religion played in planting and propagating the American aristocracy, religiosity has tended to have an inverse relationship with class. From the American Revolution onward, established upper-class Americans chose to worship at churches that were less fundamentalist in philosophy and more tolerant in practice, albeit often derided as rigid, miserly, and emotionless, or simply despised by more religious and recently arrived Americans.

Episcopalians claimed the highest social rank, although their political power ebbed and flowed, as in the early nineteenth century, when the rise of the seventh president, the populist Andrew Jackson, diminished their standing for a generation. Though a Democrat like the patrician Thomas Jefferson and his three successors, two from Virginia and one from Massachusetts, the Scots-Irish Jackson, who lived in Tennessee, was the first frontier president, elected by, and primarily representing the interests of, the poor but rising conservative WASP population of the young nation's agrarian interior.

As America developed, entry to the WASP patriciate grew easier. Merchants and professionals, soldiers, and other public officials were able to edge into the elite, and even industrial plutocrats, initially disdained as crass new-money arrivistes, would eventually be absorbed and accepted into the American aristocracy, though sometimes a conversion was deemed advisable. The financier J. P. Morgan, for instance, would convert from Congregationalist (now called the United Church of Christ) to Episcopalian in 1861.

And so conservative Protestants, even those disdained as "vulgar interlopers" in the early days of their accumulation of wealth, were eventually co-opted, refined, and incorporated, often through the intermarriage of new money with old. By the late nineteenth century, a relatively stable, homogeneous elite had emerged, blending America's original landed aristocracy with the powerhouses of the industrial plutocracy. For example, members of the Livingstons, a land-grant family and in many ways the ur-Americans, had married not just equivalent Beekmans, Jays, Bayards, and Van Rensselaers but also the nouveau riche Astors. Vanderbilts merged with the *Mayflower*-descended Whitneys and the Dutch-English Morris clans. Theirs was a very rich yet very small world—even as it inched open its doors.

Ostracism was as important as assimilation, however. While some new-money arrivistes were welcomed into the upper class—sometimes called the *bon ton*, or just the *ton*, a pretentious adaptation of the French phrase for well-mannered folk first used in Regency-era England—others, especially more recent immigrants, particularly Jews and Catholics from eastern and southern Europe and Ireland, were not. "Urban patriciates that maintain hegemony over a long period neutralize the challenge of new men by either co-option or effective exclusion," Frederic Cople Jaher wrote in his 1973 essay "Style and Status: High Society in Late Nineteenth Century New York."[16]

Eventually, though, the doors of elite society opened to almost everyone as WASP hegemony gave way, after World War II, to the world I grew up in, one characterized by an increasing, if highly imperfect, acceptance of American diversity. By 1960, the country had its first non-WASP president, the Roman Catholic John F. Kennedy. But though his election—thirty-two years after Al Smith, the first Catholic to run for that office, lost in a landslide to Herbert Hoover—appeared to some as the end of old-stock dominance, Kennedy had been raised to honor the ideals, manners, moral authority and standards (and, yes, sexual hypocrisy), sense of duty, and desire to lead that characterized the WASP oligarchs. Kennedy was ethnic, but also a symbol of how an inclusive aristocracy replenishes itself, absorbing and even embracing those willing to learn and adapt to its ways.

But it is no surprise that the demise of the WASP was first proposed at the moment of Kennedy's triumph. E. Digby Baltzell even predicted that their noblesse oblige would fall out of fashion. While WASPs would still have some social status, he worried that their inevitable loss of functional power to rising new economic elites was causing them to reject the rejuvenation of assimilation and instead retreat from a socially useful aristocracy into a closed caste defined solely by bloodlines.* That would leave upper-crust society adrift in a world where no one would have the same economic, political, and social power because, he wrote, rising new groups can never duplicate "accidents of ancestry."[17] Baltzell wondered if WASPs would lose their leadership or share it, and predicted they would land in between, retaining some privilege, as in fact they did.

In an update to *The Protestant Establishment* published in 1976, after the Black Power, women's liberation, and radical student movements, and after the debacles of the Vietnam War and Watergate caused a general loss of faith in American institutions, Baltzell would sound considerably bleaker. "What remains of the Protestant establishment has been watered down beyond recognition," he lamented. "No authority or conventions of decency exist. . . . When class authority declines, money talks, echoing in a moral vacuum." Money and the sort of superficial charisma that seduces the media had "steadily replaced class authority as the principal characteristic for leadership in our atomized society," Baltzell concluded.[18] His perspicacity has been repeatedly affirmed in the decades since. Donald Trump was Exhibit A of the phenomenon.

As Baltzell feared in 1976, the WASP elite promptly degenerated into what he had derided as a caste, a closed class that no longer sought out new blood or provided leadership; in the process, the vulnerability of the American establishment was exposed. Increasingly isolated by the flow of history and their own predilections, WASPs did become irrelevant, culturally, politically, and practically. If they didn't quite disappear from the American narrative, they were reduced to an aside, a footnote—albeit a vital one—to the central plot line. Trump's disdain for the WASP Bush dynasty was Exhibit B.

---

* "I personally think the key element is 'Anglo Saxon,' and an imagined connection to the early settlements in Massachusetts," said the late writer Michael M. Thomas, whose mother's family came to Plymouth in 1623 aboard the *Anne,* the second Pilgrim ship. "Another quality that sets us apart is a regard, tantamount to a fixation, with the past: our past. Where we came from, who our people were."

By the 1970s, it could be (and was) said that those traditionally on the lower rungs of society—Blacks, Hispanics, and even the disparate group collectively (if sometimes unfairly) disparaged as white trash and, later, deplorables—had more cultural clout than the fruit of the American aristocracy. Simultaneously, traditional notions of upward mobility were challenged by a revival of fundamentalist religions, Christian, Jewish, and Muslim, stressing differences, not similarities. Into the Reagan eighties, WASP forms might still be aped, but by the millennium, most Americans would simply ignore the source, if they recognized it at all.

And so it came to pass that the WASPs abdicated, retreated, found themselves priced out and bought out of their exclusive enclaves; their clubs and institutions made increasingly irrelevant; their once all-powerful culture more often regarded as an anachronism—and, many felt, deservedly so. And yet they remain a force in America's present as well as its past.

I seek to look back, not in anger, envy, or mourning, but with a fresh eye, curiosity, and some well-tempered admiration, at a handful of totemic WASP families who made America what it is, for both good and ill. The book introduces each family through an individual member who was a quintessential figure in his era; I say "his" because WASPs who were generally recognized as leaders well into the twentieth century were uniformly male, and like most other Americans, ruled by the ingrained sexism behind the cliché that a woman's place was in the home. This by no means suggests that male primacy was right or just, but merely recognizes what was. In each case, I place those individuals within a family context, with many women playing notable roles, and then step back to look at those families over the more than four hundred years of their life in America, digging up the roots of their family trees and following their branches as they spread and intertwined through marriage, interpersonal relationships and business mergers.

In the colonial era, the focus is on Governor William Bradford, leader of the Plymouth Colony. Gouverneur Morris, the New Yorker most responsible for the writing of the U.S. Constitution, and John Randolph, a plantation owner, slaveholder, and politician from

Virginia, represent the years just before and after the American Revolution. Lewis Cass, who governed the Michigan Territory, guided the Jackson administration policy known as Indian removal, and once ran for president, and Nicholas Biddle, the Philadelphia gentleman and polymath who ran the Bank of the United States, open a window on the young American nation at the start of the nineteenth century. Henry Sanford, a businessman from Connecticut who created America's first spy network as Abraham Lincoln's envoy to Belgium and then laid the groundwork for Florida's tourism and citrus industries, illuminates the Civil War era. George Peabody, who founded the firm that became today's JPMorgan Chase and is sometimes called the founder of modern philanthropy, and William Collins Whitney, a descendent of Governor Bradford, cabinet secretary, businessman, and member of the Four Hundred, along with a cast of similarly wealthy or well-born swells like Winthrop or Lewis Rutherfurd, dance the story through the Gilded Age. Fairfield Osborn, the railroad heir who ran the American Museum of Natural History for decades, reveals that players who emerged from the Progressive Era weren't necessarily forward-thinkers. And Michael Butler, the paper products and aviation heir who produced the Broadway hit musical *Hair* in the 1960s, shows how WASPs tried (and often failed) to adapt as the world changed around them at the end of the twentieth century. A final chapter focuses on members of most of their families in recent times, to demonstrate the wide range of contemporary WASP experience, from drug addiction to engagement in the most pressing challenges of the world today.

They, their antecedents, and their descendants are the protagonists in this crucial slice of the story of the creation of a nation and a national ethos, as well as the shame and stain left by the practice of slavery, the oppression of Native Americans, and systemic racism, intolerance, and misogyny. By looking at some key WASP figures, I hope to illuminate at least a few corners of their and America's transformations in the four hundred years since the *Mayflower*'s arrival.

Part One

FAITH

1609–1750
WILLIAM BRADFORD

1

William Bradford was long considered America's earliest tribal chief. The founder and governor of Plymouth, Massachusetts, the fourth permanent European settlement on the North American continent,* and the first chronicler of its history, he gave the name "Pilgrims" to the group of travelers who had instigated the 1620 transatlantic voyage of the square-rigged ninety-foot-long sailing ship called the *Mayflower*. It has captured American imaginations for centuries. Though the Pilgrims were free men and women, "a group of English emigrants more socially insignificant" than the *Mayflower* passengers "could hardly be imagined; time and sentiment alone have given them the luster they possess," the historian Dixon Wecter observed.[1]

Bradford led the first white Anglo-Saxon Protestants to take up significant residence on the North American continent. Still on the *Mayflower*, the free male passengers onboard (indentured servants, who had agreed to a term of unpaid labor in exchange for passage, food, clothes, and shelter, were not involved) drafted a legal statement, and the "noble document" they signed, known as the Mayflower Compact, became "one of the basic charters of American liberty," anticipating

---

* The first was St. Augustine, Florida, founded by Spain in 1565, followed by the English at Jamestown, Virginia, in 1607, and French Quebec in 1608. Though the Netherlands claimed the Hudson River Valley in 1609, on the arrival of explorer Henry Hudson, the Dutch didn't establish a successful settlement until 1624.

key elements of both the Declaration of Independence and the United States Constitution.[2]

In an 1802 speech commemorating the landing at Plymouth, the future sixth president, John Quincy Adams, would call the Mayflower Compact "the first example in modern times of a social compact or system of government instituted by voluntary agreement, conformably to the laws of nature, by men of equal rights, and about to establish their community in a new country."[3]

Prideful self-promotion factored into the persistent importance given to the Pilgrims, although they were neither the first American WASPs nor the founders of a particularly important community. There is argument whether the first Thanksgiving feast was actually held in Plymouth, but over the centuries, the legend of the holiday first proclaimed by George Washington in 1789, and legally sanctioned by Congress in 1870, has called the town its birthplace.

In 1894, American ancestor worship was given formal structure by the first Society of Mayflower Descendants, formed in New York by seven lineal descendants of *Mayflower* passengers. Three years later, a national descendants' society was born at a meeting at Pilgrim Hall in Plymouth, the headquarters of the Pilgrim Society, itself conjured up by the Commonwealth of Massachusetts on the two hundredth anniversary of the ship's arrival, "to perpetuate the memory of the virtues, the enterprize, and unparalleled sufferings" of Plymouth's original band of 102 colonists. Most, but not all, of them were religious dissenters and had sailed from Southampton, England, in September 1620.

One died at sea and four more between the *Mayflower*'s November 11 arrival in what would become Provincetown Harbor, off Cape Cod, and its final destination twenty-six miles southwest. One of those was William Bradford's wife, Dorothy, who is thought to have fallen into a depression and jumped overboard, perhaps because she and her husband had left their three-year-old son John behind, perhaps because Cape Cod looked frighteningly desolate and inhospitable. Either way, on December 7, her body was spotted floating beside the ship; she was dead at twenty-three.

Today, the Mayflower Society keeps its documentation confidential, but anyone searching for descendants of William Bradford (or his fellow passengers) will have an easy time finding lists of the most famous ones.* Bradford is said to be descended through his son with Dorothy, and through three more children with his second wife, Alice, to William Rehnquist, a chief justice of the Supreme Court; Senator Adlai Stevenson III; four state governors; and a wide range of notables including lexicographer Noah Webster, Civil War general George McClellan, the artists Frederick E. Church and Charles Dana Gibson; Kodak film inventor George Eastman, Dr. Benjamin Spock, chef Julia Child; novelists Ambrose Bierce and Thomas Pynchon, the former *New York Times* publisher Arthur Ochs "Pinch" Sulzberger Jr., *Playboy* founder Hugh Hefner, and the movie stars Sally Field, Clint Eastwood, John Lithgow, and Christopher Reeve.† Bradford's less notable descendants were considerably more numerous (a 1951 book covering only six generations lists 11,272 of them), and a few had an impact on contemporary America nearly as significant as, and perhaps more relevant to modern times, than the Pilgrim leader's.

His natural reticence would probably have kept William Bradford from expressing pride in the way his blood still flows through American veins. Certainly, he was proud of his and his fellow Pilgrims' American progress, but in the pages of *Of Plymouth Plantation 1620–1647*, Bradford's history of those times, he refers to himself rarely, and only in the third person. That said, he was, as the scholar Samuel Eliot Morison notes in his introduction to one version of that book, which he edited, "the man who made the major decisions [and] exercised more plenary authority than any governor of an English colony in his day, with the possible exception of Sir William Berkeley in Virginia."4

The Pilgrims' original destination wasn't Cape Cod or Plymouth but the same as that of the slaves who had preceded them: Virginia, or rather, the northern border of the Virginia Colony, which was set by England's King James I in the Charter of 1606 at latitude 41°N,

---

* For the sake of easier reading, distinctions will not always be made in this text between lineal (direct) descendants, collateral relations (side branches—sisters and brothers, aunts and uncles, nieces and nephews, etc.), and affinal relations (through marriage), although those connections will be spelled out when appropriate.
† A few of those claims are questionable, apparently.

which runs across the lower Hudson River.* The first Virginia settlement, Jamestown, where the colonists were employees of its owner-founders, the shareholders in a British joint stock trading concern called the Virginia Company of London, was a failure. Seventy of its original 108 settlers had died. In 1619, the first representative assembly in America convened there and those first slaves in English America arrived.

Portugal had been granted a monopoly on West African trade and the right to enslave sub-Saharan Africans by Pope Nicholas V in papal bulls issued in the 1450s, designed to "civilize" and Christianize them. Spain soon began shipping Africans to its colonies in the Americas, and other European powers—Denmark, England, France, and the Netherlands—began practicing race-based slavery and trading human chattel, too. Ultimately more than twelve million captives were forced into slavery.

Though they were not the first African slaves in America—that horrible distinction accrues to Africans brought to Florida by the Spanish in 1565—the first slaves in English America were captured in southwestern Africa, likely late in 1618, brought to the port city of Luanda, and packed into a Portuguese slave ship bound for Mexico before it was seized by two English pirate ships owned by Robert Rich, the Earl of Warwick, *White Lion* and *Treasurer*. In August 1619, the twenty or so "odd Negroes" were traded for food by the English pirates to Virginia's governor, George Yeardley, and a merchant, Abraham Piersey. And with that barbarous act, some of the first colonial WASPs committed America's original sin. Little is known about the individual victims, but a Virginia Company stockholder seems to have taken possession of two of them, known as Anthony and Isabela.[5]

Between 1619 and 1622, three thousand more of Jamestown's thirty-six hundred settlers perished, but the settlement's backers, aristocratic and wealthy Protestants from London, didn't give up. They restructured their investments to give patents, the right to occupy and cultivate large tracts of land, to groups of settlers whose title would

---

* That same line would later define the border between New York and New Jersey.

become permanent if they persevered. Both the backers and their settlers were products of the religious Reformation, which began when Martin Luther, a German professor, priest, and monk, and John Calvin, a French pastor in Geneva, objected to practices of the Roman Catholic Church in the early sixteenth century, and Henry VIII, the King of England, broke with Rome in 1527 and created the Protestant (aka Anglican) Church of England after the pope refused to annul his marriage to Catherine of Aragon so he could marry Anne Boleyn in the hope she would produce a male heir. In repudiating the papacy and establishing royal supremacy over the church, naming himself its supreme leader, he launched the English Reformation, but it was clearly not in the separatist mold of Luther and Calvin, who championed a priesthood of all believers. Henry cared about power, not moral principles or what Protestants saw as the corruption of the hierarchy of Catholic Rome.

Soon England's Parliament required conformity with this official church, and, inevitably, separatist congregations formed to protest the Protestants. After 1618, when the Thirty Years' War pitted German Protestants against the Hapsburgs of the Holy Roman Empire, and the Dutch against Roman Catholic Spain, the current English monarch, James I, realized that sending dissident Protestants across the Atlantic would not only lessen any impact of their Nonconformism but also give England a human bulwark in the new world against its rival Spain, which had established itself in the Canary Islands, Santo Domingo, Cuba, Mexico, Peru, and the Philippines. If the colonists made money for London capitalists in the process, all the better.

William Bradford would prove to be one of the most consequential of those Protestant dissidents, starting his life as a shepherd before leading a human flock on an extraordinary expedition. He was born in Yorkshire in northern England in 1590, the son of a farmer and his wife, a daughter of their village's shopkeeper. They were at first prosperous, but William's father died when he was one, and his mother followed him to an early grave; even before that, she sent the child to live with his grandfather and uncles. He had grown up sickly, but he could read and write, and the Bible became a source of comfort and guidance.[6]

A biographer suggests that through young Bradford's work as a shepherd, he met another boy who took him to All Saints Church in a village eight miles away, where the pastor was a Puritan, a Protestant who advocated reform of the Church of England, where the ceremonies, sacraments, and hierarchy too closely resembled Roman Catholic practices. Over his uncles' objections, Bradford became a follower.

In his teens, the intellectually curious Bradford found his beliefs evolving, and he migrated to another church whose pastor advocated separation from the Church of England—one of a growing number of secret congregations, modeled after those in the New Testament, that thought themselves uncorrupted and sought a direct connection to the Deity, unmediated by clergy.[7] The new church's foundational principle was that its members were all equals who chose to worship together under a minister also of their choice, an independent stance anathema to a monarch who doubled as head of his country's official religion. James I had ascended to the throne in 1603 on the death of his cousin Elizabeth I, who had sent separatists to the gallows, inspiring some to move to Holland seeking freedom to worship as they pleased. James I, a Scottish Presbyterian, was less draconian, but after he escaped death in the pro-Catholic Gunpowder Plot led by Guy Fawkes in November 1605, James I demanded conformity, too, forcing separatists out of the Church of England.

Bradford's new church group met in Scrooby, a small village closer to his home, and its pastor's assistant would become his spiritual mentor. William Brewster was twenty-five years Bradford's senior, a local postmaster from a well-connected family who would become the "elder," or spiritual leader, of the Plymouth colony. Brewster was worldly; he had worked for one of Elizabeth I's diplomats in London, and traveled to Holland when its Protestants were fighting Catholic Spain. But, disgusted with court life, he returned to his boyhood home, where his religious radicalism, fed by the Dutch passion for religious freedom, flowered and was shared with his young protégé. Brewster became William Bradford's tutor and surrogate father, giving him knowledge, context, and the sense of security he had been lacking most of his life. The church they shared gave Bradford a sense of direction that would guide the rest of his days and turn him from follower to leader.

When Brewster and four others were charged with disobedience by Church of England officials in 1607, the Scrooby congregants decided to flee to Holland, which they saw as a Protestant Jerusalem offering liberty and spiritual safety to religious immigrants. Its victory over Spain that year had set the stage for the Netherlands to emerge as Europe's newest commercial, cultural, and intellectual power; it became a haven for Nonconformists.

Getting there wasn't easy. A first attempt to escape England ended with the dissidents in chains. Bradford would later recall how the authorities "rifled and ransacked them, searching to their shirts for money, yea even the women further than became modesty," making them "a spectacle and wonder to the multitude which came flocking on all sides to behold them."[8] After a month in jail they were released, and the next year they began reaching Amsterdam in small groups. They stayed a year, worshipping with another group of English Protestants, but "flames of contention" erupted between them after the other group's elder was accused of inappropriate behavior with several women, some of them underage, and the Scrooby group "removed to Leyden, a fair and beautiful city" in southern Holland, birthplace of Rembrandt and home to the Netherlands' oldest university.[9]

By the time Bradford turned twenty-one, he had become a citizen of Leyden and a serge weaver, joined a guild, and become "an autodidact of great culture and vast reading," and, alongside Brewster, served as one of their congregation's leaders.[10] He had also received an inheritance from his parents' estate, sold their land in Yorkshire, bought a small house in Leyden, and married in 1613.[11] He had met his wife, Dorothy, when she was only ten, in Amsterdam, where her father was an elder of the church group he would soon abandon. When they married, she was sixteen, he twenty-three.

Though they broke British law by moving to Holland, the Scrooby crew managed to avoid further conflict until early 1619, when their spiritual leader Brewster's printing business, Choir Alley—established, like Bradford's serge-weaving operation, to make a living, but also to surreptitiously promote their religious beliefs by printing and shipping banned books to England—attracted unwanted attention. A Calvinist pamphlet attacking James's latest attempts to control the Scottish church had been smuggled into Scotland in French wine vats—and traced to its source. The king ordered his ambassador to make Brewster pay for this "atrocious and seditious libel," and the elder went into hiding.[12]

The Scrooby group didn't want to assimilate and become Dutch. Bradford later wrote of his concern with the permissiveness and dangerous licentiousness of the culture in Leyden. A truce between Spain and the Dutch that had held throughout their stay in Holland was also ending, and renewed conflict was an unappealing prospect. "In the agitation of their thoughts," Bradford recalled, they began to consider "removal to some other place," perhaps "those vast and unpeopled countries of America, which are fruitful and fit for habitation, being devoid of all civil inhabitants, where there are only savage and brutish men which range up and down, little otherwise than the wild beasts of the same." Despite "fears and doubts" about the many "unconceivable perils and dangers" of a lengthy journey across the Atlantic, the indigenous population among them, "it was answered, that all great and honorable actions are accompanied with great difficulties and must be both enterprised and overcome with answerable courages. It was granted the dangers were great, but not desperate. The difficulties were many, but not invincible."[13]

With courage and idealism more remarkable in those times than their fierce intolerance and prejudice, the dissidents considered and rejected moving to Guiana on South America's northern Atlantic coast and instead hoped "to live as a distinct body by themselves under the general Government of Virginia." They sent representatives to the London Virginia Company, the joint stock company that was one of about ten groups of English export merchants who were the venture capitalists of their day, created to exploit colonization. The Scrooby group hoped to negotiate a patent and passage and to convince "His Majesty that he would be pleased to grant them freedom of religion."[14]

The export merchants had their own priorities, including profit, colonization, and competition with Spain, as well as the propagation of their religious faith. The Crown was supportive. Ever since 1584, when Elizabeth I first thought about America, and 1588, when England defeated the Spanish Armada and became a sea power, it had seen the new world as a front for the advance of Protestantism, as well as fertile ground in which to cultivate English influence and wealth.

Virginia would eventually develop into a colony defined by an elite class of royalist settlers, members of the English aristocracy opposed to Puritanism and more interested in financial than spiritual growth. In the 1640s they would become known as Cavaliers, as they sided with the Royalists in the English Civil Wars. But earlier in the seventeenth century, "there was no breach as yet between the Non-Conformist and Conformist elements in the Church of England."[15] Settling American lands was in everyone's interests.

That spring of 1619, the Scrooby congregation had received a patent from the Virginia Company with the help of a friend of Brewster's father. Bradford sold his Leyden house. Simultaneously, the emigrants, immodestly calling themselves "Saints," got financing for their trip from a separate, smaller group of financiers, the London Merchant Adventurers, consisting of about seventy businessmen and promoters, white, Anglo-Saxon, and Protestant, of course, who had designs of their own—some religious, some less savory—on America. To make matters more confusing, a second Virginia Company, based in Plymouth, England, and created by James I at the same time as the London operation, was simultaneously being reorganized under an explorer, Sir Ferdinando Gorges, to create colonies and exploit fishing in the waters of what it called New England, a territory mostly north of, but also overlapping, the London Virginia Company's lands, which ended at the mouth of the Hudson River. But the rights to that northern land had not yet been established, so the plan was for Brewster, Bradford, and about fifty of their co-religionists to sail to the northernmost reaches of Virginia, where they could legally settle and govern themselves, far enough from the English at Jamestown to avoid persecution over their separatist beliefs, but close enough to Virginia to get support if needed. The legal paperwork from the Merchant Adventurers would follow. Thomas Weston, that group's organizer, appeared to want the option of playing the two Virginia Companies against each other. Bradford and Brewster, meanwhile, believed they had "a gentleman's agreement with Gorges" to eventually confirm their right to settle in New England.[16]

The Adventurers found the *Mayflower*, a cargo ship that had pre-viously plied the wine trade, and the self-anointed Saints prepared to emigrate in 1620.[17] "So they left that goodly & pleasant city, which had been their resting place near twelve years; but they knew they were pilgrims, and looked not much on those things, but lift up their eyes to the heavens, their dearest country, and quieted their spirits," the determined Bradford wrote.[18]

The *Mayflower* was waiting (with the fugitive Brewster hiding be-lowdecks) off Southampton, England, as the Saints sailed from the Netherlands on another boat, the *Speedwell*. Both craft would then head for America. More than half the passengers would be non-Saints, relatively secular colonists, including merchants, workers, and servants, recruited by the Merchant Adventurers to bulk up the number of settlers and better their chance of success; they were dubbed "Strangers." Miles Standish, a well-read soldier, was among them, hired to provide security in the new world.

The two ships departed that August, but off the coast of Devon, the *Speedwell* took on water, so they all returned to England and, leav-ing it and some of the passengers behind, the *Mayflower* set off again alone in September, stuffed with passengers, a third of them under age fifteen. If they had left England sooner, they likely would have called at Jamestown to ensure their initial Virginia Company patent was in order, but due to the delays and the approaching storm sea-son, they sailed north on a shorter route, heading straight for the mouth of the Hudson River. Had they managed to reach it, the Pil-grims might well have settled Manhattan.

The *Mayflower* spent sixty-four days under sail before the Truro highlands of Cape Cod rose from the sea. Equipped with a map of New England drawn in 1616 by the English soldier and explorer Cap-tain John Smith, the Pilgrim leadership realized they were north of the boundary of Virginia, making their patent invalid. But an attempt to sail down the coast was foiled by weather and abandoned, and the ship anchored in current-day Provincetown's harbor on November 11.[19]

Their legal status in doubt (while they were at sea the new Plym-outh Virginia enterprise had been established but wouldn't grant them a patent for a year), the free male passengers on board (four-teen of the men were indentured servants) drafted and signed their compact, which reflected their initial patent, in which the London Virginia Company had granted them self-government. The Pilgrims added some Dutch-inspired concepts, like the separation of church and state, and the accountability of a sovereign to the people. So they "anticipated the need to create a government based on civil consent rather than divine decree."[20] The compact was a covenant tying all together, "for none had the power to command them."[21]

All of these notions would be foundational to the American experiment. Still, Bradford would later write, "What could now sustain them but the spirit of God and His Grace?" Another, better-grounded answer to that question was one man, Brewster, who was named the community's elder, or senior officer of the church. At his side was Bradford, who inevitably rose in the Pilgrims' hierarchy through "character and leadership . . . authority and kindliness."[22]

At first the passengers stayed on board the ship in Provincetown harbor as scouts went ashore to look for Native Americans and building sites. Bradford stumbled, literally, into the first evidence of pre-existing civilization on American soil when his foot was caught in a rope noose. He called it a "very pretty device."[23] A first sighting of Natives, from the tribe called Wampanoags, followed; then a first attack (a barrage of arrows answered with flintlocks at a spot later named First Encounter Beach); the discovery of a freshwater spring and a cache of multicolored Indian corn; and as December's cold arrived, the first deaths.[24]

The need for dry, habitable land was urgent. So Bradford and others took a small open boat farther afield, bringing back more corn after gracelessly desecrating several Indian graves. Then they sailed into Plymouth harbor, across today's Cape Cod Bay, where brooks converged, and fields and cleared ground indicated habitation. They would learn that a few years earlier the native inhabitants had been wiped out by disease, likely caught from European traders who had been visiting for a century, though they never attempted settlement.[25] The Pilgrim advance guard rejoiced at finding "a place (as they supposed) fit for situation," Bradford reported. "At least it was the best they could find."[26]

On his return from this expedition to Plymouth, Bradford learned that his wife, Dorothy, had died five days earlier.[27] With no time for him to mourn, let alone solve the mystery of her death, the *Mayflower* sailed to Plymouth, first named New Plimouth by John Smith on his 1616 map of the coastline of what he called New England, and began slowly putting its passengers ashore. Even as more of them fell ill of scurvy and other ailments and died, many before ever setting foot on American soil, a common house was built; work had commenced on Christmas Day.

By January they were marking out home lots, and Bradford and Standish and a few others who remained healthy "fetched [the sick] wood, made them fires, dressed them meat, made their beds, washed their loathsome clothes, clothed and unclothed them . . . willingly and cheerfully . . . a rare example and worthy to be remembered," as Bradford would.[28]

The first few months were hard on him, too, and he collapsed; later he credited Standish and Brewster for the strength that helped all to pull through.[29] In March, the last colonists disembarked from the *Mayflower* (only three married couples had survived the ordeal intact) and began fishing and hunting game birds. Then the first Native American to make contact with them, Samoset, made a startling entrance into the colony.

"Hello, English," he is alleged to have said; he had learned their language from fishermen who sailed to his native Maine. He had been sent by the Wampanoag sachem, or chief, Massasoit, whom he was visiting, to assay the Pilgrims' intentions. Samoset was followed by Squanto, another English-speaking emissary of the Wampanoag. Squanto had been captured by an English explorer and sold into slavery in Spain, but was lucky enough to have been bought or taken by monks who gave him a Western and religious education. Freed— history does not record how—and just returned from England, he learned he had been saved from the disease that wiped out his people, the same ones who had cleared and cultivated the land that was slowly becoming the American Plymouth.

Massasoit himself followed, with sixty warriors and his son, and made a treaty of peace and mutual aid with John Carver, a church deacon and the first man to sign the compact (Bradford was the second), who had been elected the settlement's first governor. The Wampanoag chief was motivated by fear of another powerful and ag-

gressive Native American tribe, the Narragansett, who lived nearby
in what would become western Rhode Island, and thus wanted Plymouth's Englishmen as allies. When the sachem departed, Squanto
remained and became the Pilgrims' translator and advisor, most crucially teaching them how to plant and sow local crops. The seeds
they had brought from England wouldn't yield food in Plymouth's
sandy soil, and in abandoning the small and agile *Speedwell* they had
lost their ability to easily fish and trade with coastal Indians, which
they had hoped would be their primary sources of income. Squanto's aid "made the difference between living and starving."[30]

In April 1621, the *Mayflower* finally sailed back to England. Mere
days later, Governor Carver died, and Bradford replaced him in a position he would hold, with brief interruptions, for almost forty years.
His first challenge came from other quarrelsome Native Americans,
"allied to Massasoit but never any good friend to the English." When
he heard that they might have killed Squanto, Bradford showed that
though he was a man of religion, he was no pacifist, ordering Standish
to find out what had happened and, "if they found out Squanto was
killed, to cut off [their sachem] Corbitant's head, but not to hurt any
but those that had a hand in it."[31] Fortunately, Squanto was still alive.

"Erudite, sometimes sardonic," Bradford rose in influence, even
more so as their aging religious leader, Brewster, slowly declined.[32]
Plymouth rarely had a pastor. So, alongside Brewster, Standish, and
Edward Winslow, another of the original Leyden group who became
Plymouth's chief diplomat and sometimes spelled Bradford as
governor, he would run the colony, even though the few surviving
members of the original congregation were far outnumbered by
Strangers. "That he was Plymouth's greatest man there is no doubt,"
wrote his biographer, a descendant named Bradford Smith.[33]

Though "the government of Plymouth was a personal affair, and
the personality was William Bradford," he has been less well remembered than Brewster and the three protagonists of Henry Wadsworth
Longfellow's narrative poem about the Pilgrims, "The Courtship of
Miles Standish" (the others were the Stranger John Alden and Pris-
cilla Mullins, who married and were among Longfellow's ancestors).[34]
But Smith argues persuasively that the modest-to-a-fault Bradford
was the key to Plymouth's persistence. He was certainly singularly

influential in laying the foundations of American society, blending the best attributes of English and Dutch culture to make the Pilgrim settlement a radical experiment combining freedom of religion; strict separation of church, state, and commercial interests; government by and for the people; and an end to both feudal landholding and strict, brutal class distinctions. Middle-class, self-made, defiantly plain, and fiercely independent, Bradford, the Pilgrims, and the Strangers were the ur-Americans.

That fall, perhaps inspired by Leyden's annual day of thanks for the defeat of Spain, Bradford declared a holiday just after the harvest—and created the ur-American Thanksgiving celebration. He ordered hunters to kill ducks and geese to add to their "good store of wild turkeys," shellfish to be gathered from nearby flats at low tide, and eel from a brook, so that the Pilgrims could "rejoice together."[35] More than a hundred Native Americans joined them, contributing fresh-killed deer to the feast. Unfortunately, that early shared meal, later mythologized, would be the height of good relations between WASP settlers and Native Americans.

In November 1621, the rest of the Pilgrims arrived on the ship *Fortune* carrying the promised patent from Gorges and his Virginia Company, giving them permission to stay in the American Plymouth. Unfortunately, the terms of their arrangement with the Merchant Adventurers remained in force, to their economic detriment; contractually, the colony's wealth, including each settler's land and home, was held communally until the settlers' debts to the investors were repaid, and so for seven years they would be working for the community and its backers, not themselves. With thirty-five new residents disembarking from the *Fortune* (including Brewster's son and Philippe de la Noye, the first of Franklin Delano Roosevelt's ancestors in America), the still-tiny colony was full to bursting, even though only 56 of the original 102 *Mayflower* passengers had survived the first year in America.* The ship also carried a letter from the head of the Merchant Adventurers, "full of complaints and expostulations," Bradford would write, chief among them that the *Mayflower* had lingered too

---

* The colony grew, though suffrage didn't. Bradford believed women and children should be excluded from government, "as both reason and nature teacheth they should be."

long in Plymouth and returned to England without any valuable cargo.[36]

2

Debt was a blade at the Pilgrims' throats, and it began to cut when the cargo the *Fortune* carried back to England—animal skins, plus sassafras and oak clapboards used for making barrel staves, worth about £500—was seized by the French and lost.[37] The colony's backers' doubts festered as food grew scarce (ill-prepared to fish, the settlers were sometimes forced to live on nuts, clams, and mussels). The Narragansetts, perhaps perceiving weakness, threatened. They sent a snakeskin full of symbolic arrows to Plymouth, but Bradford remained resolute. He returned it full of gunpowder and shot and strengthened Plymouth's defenses just before *Discovery*, a mapping ship, arrived with goods they could trade to the Native Americans for food and beaver skins. Every now and then, fortune bent toward Bradford—who immediately launched a trading expedition.

As 1622 ended, Squanto fell ill and died, further disrupting relations with the Natives, which worsened the following spring when Massasoit learned of another plot against Plymouth involving several tribes and Standish staged a deadly raid, killing some of the plotters, including a sachem whose skull was mounted over their fort's roof. Though the brutal raid cemented Plymouth's alliance with Massasoit, it apparently didn't sit well with Bradford, who left it out of his history. In larger terms, it demonstrated that lines of division among and between settlers and Native Americans were permeable, not set, and the divide between enemies and allies wouldn't always be predictable. That set an opportunistic pattern for centuries to come.

The following spring, the Merchant Adventurer leader Thomas Weston appeared—in rags—in Plymouth after nearly dying aboard a fishing ship in a storm. Though Bradford was aware of quarrels between Weston and his partners, he "loaned" Weston some beaver skins to use as trade goods to finance the repair and provisioning of his ship—only to be repaid with betrayal; Weston had hatched a plan to create a competing community, and expected Plymouth to host its settlers on their arrival.[38]

Whether what followed was connected is unrecorded, but Bradford decided that the colonists needed the incentive of private property—land of their own to grow food for their families—and despite a drought that summer, a distribution of one-acre plots for private use led to Plymouth's first food surpluses, effectively strengthening its hand with the distant financiers.[39] Problems with the Merchant Adventurers continued, though, so beginning in 1626, the Pilgrims negotiated a buyout with a long payment schedule of their obligations to the financiers, and by 1627 the colony would start distributing its livestock and the rest of its land to its inhabitants. Simultaneously, a new focus on fur trading lifted its economy.

But before all that, the arrival of a hundred additional colonists on the *Anne* in summer 1623 was a personal bright spot for Bradford; among them was a widow from Leyden he asked to marry him. "Yet even as he offered [Alice Southworth] his arm to lead her up the hill, a twinge of shame struck him at the thought that the best he could offer her was a lobster (always indifferent fare to the Pilgrims) and a cup of fair spring water with never a morsel of bread."[40] He felt shame, perhaps, at the necessity of eating shellfish—deemed detestable in the Bible's Book of Leviticus—but it must have been mixed with pride, since at thirty-four he was the undisputed leader of Plymouth, an established and soon-to-be thriving town that had grown to thirty-two houses, 180 citizens, and about a hundred head of livestock (pigs, goats, and cattle). Ships carrying more colonists and trade goods kept arriving, and Plymouth's commercial activity expanded with the opening of a trading post in Maine in 1628.[41]

In the meantime, the Dutch had acquired Manhattan and founded New Amsterdam, and in 1627 Peter Minuit, the director-general of New Netherland, had written to Bradford and, noting "our common enemy, the Spaniard," offered to trade "any goods that come to our hands" for "any beaver, or otter, or such like commodities as may be usefull for us, for ready money." Bradford's positive reply noted that Plymouth might also sell the Dutch "tobacco, corne, or other things."[42] When trading began, the Dutch introduced Plymouth to wampum, the strung shell beads that Indians considered valuable currency, furthering the colony's ability to trade.

Miles Standish had been in England negotiating the deal freeing Plymouth from its financiers, and when he returned in 1626, he brought news that the father of Thomas Cushman, a young man Bradford had taken into his household five years earlier at age fourteen, had died. Feeling the loss acutely, Bradford insisted that his first son, John, still in Holland at age eleven, come to Plymouth and join a family that had grown with the addition of William Jr. and an infant daughter delivered by Alice. She sent for her two children as well. Though Alice's son Thomas Southworth, Thomas Cushman, and Bradford's namesake would all become leaders of Plymouth, John Bradford would never fit in. He married and moved away, part of a dispersal of the Pilgrims that would greatly trouble his father in years to come.

Equally discouraging was the behavior of Isaac Allerton, one of the original *Mayflower* passengers and husband of one of Brewster's daughters, who had also negotiated with the Merchant Adventurers. He had joined with Bradford, Standish, and a few others to form what they called the Undertakers, a monopoly designed to trade fur to pay off Plymouth's debt. But Allerton put his own interests in front of the colony's, costing his partners huge sums that, in 1648, would force them to sell land to make good. Allerton, meanwhile, had been relieved of his duties and left Plymouth. Bradford's disappointment was made clear in the colony records, where he noted bitterly, "Mr. Allerton doth wholly desert them having brought them into the briars, he leaves them to get out as they can."[43]

Allerton decamped for the Massachusetts Bay Colony, which had been established in 1626 in the area around present-day Salem. It grew quickly after the 1628 arrival of John Endecott, a signatory to a later land grant from the same British investors who established Plymouth. Settlers arrived in an armada of four ships in 1630, in the wake of Charles I's marriage to a Catholic Bourbon princess and a crackdown on Nonconformism that followed. Though also Puritans, the new colonists were more elite, socially and economically, and they spread to Boston (which, like Plymouth, was named for an English town), Charlestown, Newton, and eventually the Connecticut Valley. Also arriving in 1630 were John Winthrop, a future governor of the Massachusetts colony, and Roger Williams, who lived in Plymouth briefly and would break away to found the more tolerant Rhode Island in 1636.

Between 1629 and 1640, the years when Charles I ruled without a Parliament and his church viciously persecuted Puritans, eighty thousand English left their suddenly inhospitable country and more than twenty thousand of those, on dozens of ships, ended up in Massachusetts.[44] They sought, in Winthrop's oft-quoted words, "a City upon a Hill," a religion-based, spiritually sound society. Though guided by Scripture, the new colony was vastly different from Plymouth. Settlers in the Massachusetts Bay Colony were carefully vetted and were required to demonstrate their religious credentials. Only those who passed religious tests, demonstrating adherence to Calvinist doctrine and a spiritual conversion, and lived a godly life were allowed to ascend to secular and religious leadership positions.[45] Some potential settlers were even required to submit letters of recommendation.[46] Though those leaders generally came from the gentry, the Bay Colony's masses were neither rich nor poor, but "sturdy middle class." Only a quarter came as servants, compared to three-quarters of the Virginia colonists. Most Massachusetts settlers were from market or large towns in England, giving them some urban sophistication.[47]

The Massachusetts Bay Colony and Plymouth had other advantages over their predecessor in Jamestown, despite its head start. The hard life of New England "stimulated its inhabitants to high achievements."[48] And the cold climate of Massachusetts proved healthier than that of swampy tidewater Virginia—at least for northern Europeans. African slaves were less useful to colonists in the North, which limited the contentious, barbaric practice of slavery. But the arrival of enslaved Africans in Virginia in 1619 was not an isolated phenomenon. There slavery became an industry, with battalions of Africans forced into labor over the next two centuries in the ever-expanding agricultural operations of southern plantations. In the North, a shorter growing season and less fertile land encouraged small-scale agriculture rather than the sort of large-scale farming that made forced labor profitable. So, it was more common for slaves to be owned in small numbers, pressed into service on small farms or in households and the wide range of businesses that sprang up there, often acquiring skills that made them more valuable to slaveholders, who could be ministers, doctors, and political leaders as well as craftsmen, merchants, and other businessmen, slave traders among them. Even more than in the South, where what mattered most was the number of human beings held in bondage, northern slaves were status symbols, serving as displays of the wealth and entrepreneurial accomplishments of the heads of their households.

Slavery also crept more slowly into the North, where the culture of indentured servitude was entrenched early and deeply, offering a considerably less abhorrent alternative to trafficking in men, women, and children. But creep it did; slavery stained all the American colonies, their professed commitment to holiness and brotherly love notwithstanding. Connecticut, Massachusetts, and especially Rhode Island held large slave populations. In 1641, the Massachusetts Bay Colony passed legislation distinguishing slaves from indentured servants, whose superior status and rights became a matter of law. By the mid-eighteenth century, 30 percent of the population of some towns in Rhode Island were slaves of African descent.[49] Slaves also made up 10 percent of the population of Boston and more than 7 percent of New York's. Many Pennsylvania Quakers, whose sect considered slavery sinful, owned slaves nonetheless. Though anti-slavery movements sprang up in the North in the late eighteenth century, their accomplishments would be limited; so, while census data show few if any slaves living in Vermont, New Hampshire, Maine, and Massachusetts in the first decades of the nineteenth century, Pennsylvania and New York would be home to significant numbers into the 1830s, and well beyond that in Maryland, Delaware, and New Jersey. Rhode Island and Connecticut would not abolish slavery until 1843 and 1848, respectively.

Despite its constricted worldview, the larger and more populous Massachusetts steadily stole a march on Plymouth—and left a more lasting mark on American society, even as its religious purity was diluted over succeeding generations.* Before the Revolution, its Puritans would establish several colleges, including the predecessors of Harvard, Yale, and Dartmouth.† Though its economy was mostly based on farming, Massachusetts Bay also created the first American manufacturing, with its textile factories.[50]

The neighborhood grew crowded fast. The French had interests in North America dating back to 1534, when they began to explore and exploit the St. Lawrence and Hudson waterways, and the Dutch were up and down the Hudson. Maryland was created in 1634 as a sanctuary for Catholics. Four years later, New Sweden was formed in parts of today's New Jersey, Pennsylvania, and Delaware (in 1681, it would be granted to the Quaker leader William Penn). So even though the Pilgrims had been the first to arrive and succeed, and profited from the rush that followed, which caused prices for their corn and cattle to skyrocket, they remained comparatively small in number. And in 1633, a smallpox epidemic and a plague of locusts slowed what little momentum the colony had. Prosperity stayed just out of reach.

In 1637, Ferdinando Gorges was appointed governor-general of all New England, including Plymouth; Bradford's autonomy was only uneasily restored when Gorges's ship was damaged and failed to sail, and the accompanying losses left him dry-docked in England for several years. In 1639, Gorges seemed poised to recover when he won a royal charter granting him feudal power over a vast territory stretching from today's northern Massachusetts to southern Maine. But then the so-called Long Parliament was convened in London, and the Archbishop of Canterbury, an uncompromising anti-Calvinist, was arrested for treason, setting off the chain of events that led to the English Civil War, the execution of the king in 1649, the triumph of the Puritan general Oliver Cromwell in 1653, and the unexpected rise of Puritans to power in the church, all of which brought emigration

---

* The experience of personal conversion required for membership in some Puritan congregations grew less common over time, leading to the adoption of what was sometimes called the Half-Way Covenant, loosening entry requirements.

† Anglicans founded William & Mary in Virginia, and the predecessors of Columbia in New York and the University of Pennsylvania, and Presbyterians created the future Princeton.

to New England to a screeching halt. For the next fifteen years, smaller numbers of Royalists, not hordes of religious dissenters, fled England for Virginia, not New England.

With the price of their livestock plummeting due to decreased demand, Plymouth's broader citizenry challenged the monopoly of the Undertakers, who had saved the colony from death by debt. Early in 1639, Bradford unilaterally offered to give up their privileges and control of Plymouth's lands, effectively surrendering "a personal empire which Bradford might have claimed for himself and his heirs . . . It was not power or wealth he wants, but a way of life."[51] His dream of saving that way of life was doomed, however. In 1645, when Bradford opposed a petition demanding religious tolerance, reflecting the new attitude in England, the measure failed. Plymouth, once a leader, had become irrelevant in a Christian America newly dominated by English Presbyterians and Boston's Congregationalists.[52]

Plymouth's population stagnated and then began to decrease, the dispersal of its citizens—encouraged by their need for more arable land for farming and grazing—slowly sapping its strength. Original colonists (including Alden, Standish, and Jonathan Brewster) had begun moving across the Jones River north of town to Duxbury before Plymouth's first decade ended. Sometimes there were sudden population drops, as in 1643, when about a half dozen families decamped en masse for Cape Cod after a resolution to move the whole colony there failed. Bradford perceived rising secularization and a sharp decline in morals, too; cases involving drunkenness, extramarital fornication, and even one in which a Brewster servant was charged with buggery of "a mare, a cow, two goats, five sheep, two calves, and a turkey" came before Plymouth's court.[53]

As the numbers of secular colonists and malcontents grew, the Plymouth pantheon was decimated. Elder Brewster had lost his daughters, Fear and Patience, to smallpox a decade before he died in his late seventies in 1644. Edward Winslow never returned to Plymouth after a diplomatic assignment took him to Puritan London in 1646, and he went to work for Cromwell. Bradford, though he still resided in Plymouth, acquired a three-hundred-acre farm in Kingston, four miles north, and more property on Cape Cod and to the west in Bridgewater—more land than anyone else in Plymouth. In

Boston's first decade, meanwhile, its population had grown tenfold as its neighbor devolved into an isolated backwater. Plymouth built a new corn mill and tannery, but Massachusetts took over its trading post in Maine and its rights to extensive lands in Rhode Island. "It was not for want or necessity so much that they removed as for the enriching of themselves," the now-wealthy Bradford would grumble. "She that made many rich became herself poor."[54]

Bradford and Winthrop got along at first despite some fundamental differences. But when Indians in the Connecticut River valley, where Brewster's son Jonathan ran a trading post, started dying en masse from smallpox in 1634, settlers from the Bay Colony took advantage and began to pour in, threatening Plymouth's hegemony and income. "Today the fact that Plymouth pioneered the Connecticut country is all but forgotten," wrote Bradford Smith. "Thus ended the honeymoon between Plymouth and Boston."[55]

Beginning in 1636, the Bay Colony drove a wedge between Plymouth and its indigenous neighbors. Endecott, Boston's Standish, led an expedition against Block Island's Native Americans to avenge the death of a settler, infuriating the Pequots, who took their anger out on all the English—including the Pilgrims. After the Pequot War ended in 1638, Native prisoners were sent to the West Indies as slaves aboard the *Desire,* a ship built in Marblehead, Massachusetts, and on its return, its master, a William Peirce, brought back cotton, tobacco, and the first Africans to arrive in Salem. Sugar, produced in the Caribbean with slave labor, would be the source of almost half of the wealth of New England in years to come. The region's age of innocence was ending.

In 1643, a threat of war between the Mohican and Narragansett tribes put the settlers on edge and inspired a mutual defense pact and creation of a confederation called the United Colonies of New England—Massachusetts Bay, Connecticut, New Haven, and Plymouth. Standish led a band of Plymouth men against the Narragansetts. Five years later, Bradford went to Boston to join Winthrop in arbitrating a dispute between New Haven and the Dutch, who were stirring up the Native Americans, selling them arms, and making forays into English territory. But Bradford's public career was winding down. Plymouth's governor, who also served as a commissioner to the confederation, skipped an official trip to Connecticut due to his first illness since 1621. He also put aside the history he was writing, *Of Plymouth Plantation*, begun in 1630 and mostly finished by 1646, though he made additions and corrections through 1650, when he penned the words, "I am grown aged."[56] Tellingly, the book ends abruptly with an account of Winslow's 1646 departure for England, written four years later. Though Bradford's hand inscribed one last heading in 1650, "And Anno 1648," nothing follows.

Bradford remained Plymouth's leader and active in business, studied Hebrew, wrote poetry, took pride in the successes of his children with Alice and those they had raised, and likely was blessed to meet some of his grandchildren. Winslow died in 1655 and Standish in 1656. By then, Bradford was sometimes forced by failing health to abandon his duties, though his mind was clear on the morning in May 1657 when he asked to make a will. He died that same night and was buried on a hill overlooking the town he founded, as soldiers shot guns in his honor. He left the largest estate Plymouth had seen to that time to his children and his extended family, appointing Alice his executor.* She lived thirteen more years. Plymouth survived for another thirty-five before, inevitably, it (and the twenty-one nearby townships it had spawned) merged into Massachusetts Bay in 1691. "All those who can trace descent back to him would fill a large city," Bradford's biographer would conclude.[57] It would be a city considerably larger than Plymouth.

3

Two of Governor Bradford's children had no known offspring. Among the most notable descendants of William Jr., who served as Plymouth's deputy governor and treasurer and as a Bay Colony councilman, were a series of boys stretching into the twentieth century named Gamaliel (meaning "God is my reward" in Hebrew)—likely after one of St. Paul's teachers in the New Testament. Though some

---

* A daughter had by then moved to Boston, and two sons to neighboring Kingston. In the family's third American generation, a number of Bradfords would settle in Connecticut.

of them were engaged in the life of their country, none surpassed the first Bradford in America.

Gamaliel IV, born in Boston in 1795, was ready to apply to Harvard when he was just twelve, but his father, also Gamaliel, felt he was too young, and took him to Europe. He returned to enroll at Harvard at fifteen and went on to study medicine while volunteering in a poorhouse where he was exposed to typhus in the winter of 1818; for the rest of his life the disease compromised his health. After further studies at the University of Edinburgh, he began a medical practice in Boston in 1820, and married the daughter of a Revolutionary War officer.

In 1826, Gamaliel IV quit medicine and took over a South Boston brewery. Though he was a temperance advocate, beer and wine weren't considered as dangerous as hard liquor. He also wrote for journals in support of pacifism and other progressive causes, and as a critic of scientific quackery; he lectured against phrenology, the study of head shape as an indicator of character and intellectual ability. His intellectual credentials were established through a relationship with Ralph Waldo Emerson, one of the founders and leaders of the Transcendentalist movement, which flourished in the 1830s, promoting personal freedom and self-reliance. In 1818, Gamaliel's sister Sarah Alden Bradford had married one of Emerson's uncles. Emerson considered Gamaliel IV one of his great benefactors.

He returned to medicine in 1833 when he was appointed the superintendent of Massachusetts General Hospital. At the same time, he emerged as one of Boston's leading anti-slavery advocates. He had been present at the formation of the New England Anti-Slavery Society in 1832, though he didn't join, as he disagreed with its emphasis on immediate emancipation and intensely disliked its founder, William Lloyd Garrison, "repelled by [his] bellicose language and inflammatory tactics."[58]

But he was a factor among abolitionists, and in autumn 1835 he spoke out when Boston's political elite tried to silence them, writing a pamphlet that called slavery "a great moral and political evil" and insisting on the abolitionists' right to speak, write, and protest.[59] The next year he addressed a special committee of the state legislature that was considering a ban on abolitionists. "When the man of the South ventures to reach his odious cart-whip over Mason and Dixon's line, when he dares even to think of such an insult as shaking it over the head of a New England man—I can see immediately which side of the fence to claim enough for my walking on," he argued. "I for one am ready to tell him that there were other persons imported into America, in times past, than either black or white slaves—that there was such a vessel as the good ship *Mayflower*, and that her cargo is not yet all out of the market." Garrison's newspaper, the *Liberator*, called the speech "eloquent, thrilling, and impassioned."[60] Within a year, the same legislature would let the anti-slavery society use its premises for meetings.

There was one enemy Gamaliel Bradford's eloquence and strength couldn't vanquish, however. In 1832, he developed epilepsy, and six years later the severity and frequency of his fits led him to leave his work at the hospital for four recuperative months in the Mediterranean. Unfortunately, that failed to cure the disease, and in fall 1839, after years of increasingly severe attacks, he died at only forty-four.

His first son, born eight years earlier, the next Gamaliel Bradford, was a public figure, too, but more self-made celebrity than man of substance. After graduation from Harvard in 1849, Gamaliel V went to work for a cousin who owned a Boston bank and stock brokerage called Blake, Howe & Co. Made a partner, and by his own vague admission to the *Boston Daily Globe* "unable," for unspecified reasons, to serve in the military during the Civil War, he ran the firm's foreign exchange desk. "I should have enjoyed a great deal more personal comfort if I had been a soldier on the battlefield," he claimed dubiously decades later, when he first ran for office.

When the war ended, a department that had "made no money" during the conflict suddenly generated profit sufficient that Bradford was able to retire in 1868 and devote himself full-time to the study of government "and to use what knowledge I acquired toward the solution to some extent of the problems of politics," such as congressional procedure and civil service reform.[61] He spent a year in Washington, and for the next two and half decades he devoted himself to writing hundreds of letters to the editor and speaking to politicians and at his several clubs and historical societies about the importance of state government and the need to reform it. In 1884, he left the Republican Party after it nominated James G. Blaine, whom he thought corrupt, for president. Thirteen years later he announced a quixotic run for the Massachusetts statehouse. The *Christian Science Monitor* would describe his platform as "anti-imperialistic."[62]

During a second failed attempt to win office in 1901, the contempt for him was so palpable that the *New York Times* ran a column headlined "A Bay State Agitator." "He sometimes makes it hard to worship him duly," the uncredited author wrote. "If he were another and not GAMALIEL BRADFORD, he would be justly loathed for the pestilent way in which he is now going about the Old Commonwealth of Massachusetts brewing discontent and setting class against class; also, he would be ridiculed for his silliness and flouted for the miserable sterility of his ideas."[63] To give one example, he announced that instead of fighting the Civil War, the North should have simply bought *all* the South's slaves. The most impressive public post he ever held was as a member of the Wellesley, Massachusetts, school board.

A more favorable view of Bradford's career came from the Hartford *Courant* after he was killed at age eighty by a passing trolley car in Boston in 1911. "We can ill spare such men even in their old age," the paper said, "for they hold up the ideal in politics to a generation groveling in the gilded puddle of plutocracy and buying access or defeat at the polls by lump sums of $10,000 to half a million, which they have amassed by profligate legislation."[64]

While relatives would thrive in the gilded puddles of plutocracy, that fate eluded the last Gamaliel. Gamaliel VII was a suicide in 1910, and the circumstances, combined with his *Mayflower* ancestry, brought likely unwanted headlines around the country. He had graduated from Harvard in only three years and taken a job as a banker in Boston, but at age twenty-two he stood in a local railroad station and begged a woman twelve years his senior to break her engagement to another man and marry him. She refused, and Bradford stormed off and checked into a hotel in South Framingham, Massachusetts. A half-hour later, four shots rang out, and when hotel staff broke down the door, they found him unconscious and with a gunshot wound in his head, clutching a book of poems by Lord Byron. His first three shots had somehow missed, but he finally succeeded. Told what had happened, the woman fainted; when she recovered, she rushed to him at the hospital, where he died a few hours later without regaining consciousness.

His father wasn't surprised. Knowing of his son's obsession with the woman, he had removed the bullets from Gamaliel's revolver the night before, but Gamaliel bought a new gun the day of the fatal encounter. Compounding the tragedy, the woman who jilted him, a telegraph operator who married her fiancé six weeks after the suicide, died of heart failure just two years after that. The name Gamaliel Bradford appears to have died with Gamaliel VII and his father.[65]

Another of William Bradford Jr.'s children, Alice, known as Abee, died in 1744 at age eighty-two after two marriages and five children. Her second husband, Major James Fitch, a public official and town founder in Connecticut, helped set the boundaries between Connecticut, Massachusetts, and Rhode Island, and he served in King Philip's War, named for Massasoit's younger son. After Plymouth executed three of Philip's warriors in spring 1675 for the murder of a Harvard-educated Native American who had become a Puritan, English settlers and some Native American allies fought the Wampanoag and Narragansett over land and festering racial tensions. By the time Philip was shot, killed, drawn and quartered, and beheaded in August 1676, and his head put on display in Plymouth more than a year later, the future course of relations between the settlers and indigenous Americans had been set.*

As a result of King Philip's War, several English settlements in Rhode Island were eradicated and Plymouth lost 8 percent of its men; more than half of the Native American population of New England was killed, and many survivors were enslaved. Native resistance effectively ended after that, and the seizure of land by whites accelerated. Some of the Native Americans sided with the colonists, but conflicts continued and would eventually bleed into a series of wars for control of the American continent.†

---

* Philip's head remained atop a pole in Plymouth for a quarter century.
† Those wars pitted France first against England and then, after 1707 and the union of England and Scotland, Great Britain. What Americans think of as the French and Indian War was the continental American theater of the larger Seven Years' War of 1756–1764. It ended with a British

In the meantime, after King Philip's War Fitch had bought more than a thousand acres in northeastern Connecticut in two transactions in 1680 and 1684 from the sachem of the Mohegans and promoted the notion, unpopular among avaricious whites, that European royal charters conveyed the right to govern but not land rights, which he insisted could only be granted by Native Americans. That didn't sit well with two privileged grandsons of John Winthrop, the first governor of Massachusetts, who claimed some of Fitch's land.

Ten years after his 1687 marriage to Abee Bradford, Fitch moved their family to that land, inspiring the Winthrops to implant tenants and to seek confirmation of their charter from the latest British monarchs, William and Mary. Fitch was promptly stripped of his title as presiding officer of New London's court, deprived of some of his land, officially condemned, and forced to make a public apology to the Winthrops. But he was still rich enough to help endow Yale University with the gift of a 637-acre farm in 1701. He also gave Yale the glass and nails used in its first building, and is credited for his "critical role in the evolution of Connecticut society, from one stressing traditional Puritan values to one emphasizing more acquisitive and assertive Yankee ones."[66]

Four generations later, Abee's great-great-great-granddaughter Laurinda Collins, born in 1810, the daughter of a farmer and state legislator, would turbocharge her family's parallel transformation when she married into another large if less distinguished colonial family, the Whitneys; they, in turn, would help define American society from the Gilded Age through the end of the twentieth century, and, improbably, connect the Bradfords of the *Mayflower* to Andy Warhol and the Rolling Stones.

~

John Whitney had emigrated to Boston from England in 1635. Born in 1592 and baptized in St. Margaret's Church, Westminster, London, he was apprenticed to a tailor and cloth merchant at age fourteen

---

victory and the signing of the Treaty of Paris in 1763. At its conclusion, France ceded Canada to Great Britain and relinquished many of its other claims to American land, losing its dominant position on the continent and leaving Britain in control of the entire eastern seaboard.

and joined the Merchant Taylors' Company, one of London's great guilds, in 1614. After taking oaths of allegiance to Charles I and of conformity to the Church of England, he left London with his wife, five sons, and their extended family for Massachusetts aboard the *Elizabeth and Ann*. John immediately bought a sixteen-acre homestead in the five-year-old town of Watertown outside Boston, also known as the Saltonstall Plantation for one of the town's well-born founders, an original signatory of the Massachusetts Bay Colony charter. Whitney would accumulate 212 acres and a public profile, serving as constable, a selectman on Watertown's board, and its town clerk.

Among John's great-grandchildren was Josiah Whitney, who left land his father gave him in central Massachusetts to fight in a victorious battle against the French and their Native American allies at Lake George in 1755, and returned there in 1757 during the siege of Fort William Henry. In 1776, having allegedly taken part in the Boston Tea Party after conflict with the British erupted, he was named a lieutenant colonel commanding a battalion charged with defending Boston Harbor. Josiah Whitney fought at Concord, where the first shots were fired in the American Revolution, and then, following the British victory in the Battle of Long Island, their seizure of New York that September, and the retreat of the Continental Army, crossed the Delaware River with George Washington to capture Trenton and Princeton, New Jersey. After more battles, the defeat of the British at Yorktown in 1781, and their departure from Savannah, Georgia, and Charleston, South Carolina, in 1782, Whitney become a brigadier general of the state militia before resigning in 1783 to return home. He then served on the state delegation that ratified the U.S. Constitution. Arrested for treasonable complicity in Shays' Rebellion (against state taxes and the foreclosure of farms for unpaid debts) in 1787, he was released by a grand jury and promptly elected to the general court of Harvard, Massachusetts.

With his two wives, the fecund Whitney had twenty-five children, almost half of whom survived into adulthood. Among his grandchildren was Stephen Whitney, who married another *Mayflower* descendant and was one of the commissioners who supervised construction of the state lunatic asylum at Worcester. Their first son, James, born in 1811, would carry the Whitney name the furthest at the end of that century through his marriage to William Bradford's relative Laurinda Collins.

James Scollay Whitney had started working in his father's store as a boy, and at twenty-one he bought the business. Following the family's military tradition, he helped reorganize the state militia and at twenty-four was named a brigadier general, though his service was apparently confined to riding in parades. In 1838, he opened a factory making cotton bags. A Democrat in the age of the populist president Andrew Jackson, he opposed anti-slavery agitation, but he also opposed slavery.

Whitney held various public posts, including sheriff, and in 1854, during the presidency of the Democrat Franklin Pierce, was named superintendent of the U.S. Armory in Springfield, Massachusetts. The next president, James Buchanan, made him collector of the Port of Boston, ensuring that shippers and traders paid import duties, but within a year he was replaced when the Republican Abraham Lincoln became president. He then returned to business as president of a water company and a line of steamships plying the Boston–New York trade route. His last public post was as president of the Massachusetts Democrats' state convention in 1878. Shortly afterward he collapsed in a street car and died of heart disease. James and Laurinda Whitney's elder son, Henry, succeeded his father at the steamship company, and later helped organize a street rail line, coal, iron and steel, and gas companies. But despite his wealth and the power he accumulated in a rapidly industrializing nation, Henry would be surpassed by his younger sibling, William Collins Whitney, whom the *New York Times* would proclaim decades later, after his death, "one of the most remarkable men the country has ever produced."[67]

In 1860, when the Whitneys had moved to Boston, William was at Yale, where one of his classmates was Oliver Hazard Payne of Cleveland, Ohio, a child of pioneers from Connecticut. Payne's maternal grandfather, Nathan Perry, had risen from trading with Native Americans to become a merchant with a fancy home. Oliver's father, Henry Payne, a lawyer, had founded one railroad, bought into another, become a state senator, congressman, senator, and governor, and entertained notions of seeking the presidency. When Oliver left school to fight for the North in the Civil War, William Whitney stayed at

Yale, was tapped for the elite secret society Skull & Bones, was chosen to give the class oration when he graduated in 1863, and proceeded to Harvard Law School.[68] Moving to New York, he promptly won his first case, defending a former classmate, the publisher of a newspaper, from a libel charge over a bad review of a novel.

In 1868, Oliver Payne, recovered from wounds suffered at the 1863 Battle of Chickamauga and a businessman in iron and oil, came to New York, where his former roomate Whitney was a Wall Street lawyer—representing railroad investors and insurance and industrial companies—and sought him out with an enthusiasm not entirely justified by their prior acquaintance. He brought with him his sister Flora, at twenty-six already considered a spinster, and a bit too self-assured to be good marriage material in that chauvinistic era, and invited his college friend to the fashionable Fifth Avenue Hotel in hope of lighting a spark between them. Whitney didn't jump at the proffer, but Flora persevered, returning to New York ten months later, and they soon announced their betrothal.[69]

After Flora's other brother, Henry, bought them a house at 74 Park Avenue and refurbished it, too, William C. Whitney was torn between the two competing impulses that had traditionally motivated the American oligarchy and had come into sharp focus in the years immediately after the Civil War—the drive to do well, in order to accumulate money and power, and the desire to do good, and make the world a better place. Worried about his relative penury compared to his wife's family, Whitney decided he needed to make a fortune of his own, but when his early attempts at stock speculation failed, he turned to a very different source of potential power: reform politics.[70] After an 1869 election that saw Tammany Hall, New York's corrupt Democratic Party "machine" run by "Boss" William Tweed, take over the city, Whitney helped organize a competing club of young Democrats opposed to the corrupt politicians and caught the attention of Samuel J. Tilden, the party's state leader, who broke with Tweed and launched investigations that brought the Boss down.

Whitney proved better at politics than at stock-picking, but nonetheless lost his first and only race—for district attorney in 1872. He did, however, back Tilden for governor of New York, even inspecting polling places on election day and reporting irregularities. Elected and grateful to "boys" like Whitney who had helped him win, Tilden began promoting him.

His pecuniary fortunes, meanwhile, changed for the better. Flora and William's first child, Henry "Harry" Payne Whitney, was born in 1872, and Flora's father gave them a small fortune in gratitude for producing a grandchild. That same year, her brother Oliver sold his Cleveland oil company to Standard Oil and become an early associate of John D. Rockefeller. He would stay with the Whitneys when he came to New York, "dripping with money."[71] The Whitneys' daughter, Pauline, was born in 1874, just before a panic briefly wiped Whitney out, and he became distant, consumed with worry. But in 1875—thanks to a grateful (and, for the moment, honest) Tammany, and his political mentor, Tilden—he got a new job as corporation counsel for New York City, working for a merchant friend who had been elected the city's mayor. He was so unknown that the *Tribune* called him John Whitney, and so even-handed that he fired none of his Republican predecessor's appointments.

Among his cases were lawsuits related to the disgraced Tweed Ring. There were thirty-eight hundred such cases pending against the city, many of them stemming from fraudulent deals made by Tweed; the city's exposure was nearly $20 million. The most important was a suit against the city by the widow of the architect of the Tweed Courthouse in downtown Manhattan, infamous for cost overruns and kickbacks. Whitney limited the payments to the honest cost, not what Tweed's ring had paid (and skimmed), saving the city a huge sum. He also resolved a $2 million claim by the city's stationery suppliers; after he had them arrested for fraud, they settled for $50,000. He earned the nickname "Fool Killer."[72]

William C. Whitney kept his job through two subsequent mayors, learning, among other things, about urban rail lines—knowledge that would soon come in handy. Then came a chance conversation at the 1882 Democratic state nominating convention in Utica with the party's latest chairman. Again opposing Tammany, Whitney suggested that Tammany's candidate for governor, though he was leading, be replaced with "that man Cleveland," meaning Grover, the mayor of Buffalo, who at that point was in third place in the race. Not only that, "we'll elect him . . . President a little later," Whitney promised. Turning to a stout man nearby, the party chairman introduced Whitney to Cleveland.[73] A political alliance was sealed, and it would turn this descendant of farmers and of soldiers into the progenitor of a great fortune.

Twenty-two years later, the German sociologist Max Weber would publish his epochal work *The Protestant Ethic and the Spirit of Capitalism*, connecting "the spirit of modern economic life with the rational ethics of ascetic Protestantism."[74] Weber argued that the Protestant outlook was conducive to the development of worldly "business acumen," and that the fierce religiosity of preachers and settlers alike brought the spirit of capitalism and a "hard frugality" to the American colonies of New England, which proved to be fertile ground for the cultivation of "ruthless acquisition."[75] Doing business had become a quasi-religious calling for American WASPs, a duty and, to Weber, "the essence of moral conduct."[76] But in the quarter millennium since the founding of Plymouth, something had changed: "the religious roots died out slowly, giving way to utilitarian worldliness," with "the security of possession, the enjoyment of wealth . . . and the temptations of the flesh" eclipsing "the pursuit of a righteous life" and becoming the new WASP ethic.[77] William Collins Whitney became its personification.

Over the years, the sprawling Whitney clan would produce many notable Americans. Eli Whitney was the inventor of the cotton gin, the device that made slavery even more vital and profitable in the American South before the Civil War. Amos Whitney co-founded the machine-maker Pratt & Whitney. Mt. Whitney in California was named for Josiah Whitney, a geologist. Mary Watson Whitney was an astronomer and the head of the Vassar College Observatory. Several Whitneys became leaders of the Mormon Church. Willis Rodney Whitney founded General Electric's research laboratory. Charlotte Anita Whitney was a suffragist and American Communist organizer. And U.S. Army major general Courtney Whitney helped reorganize Japan after World War II. But William Collins Whitney towered over all of them, proudly perched atop a mountain of money.

Part Two

ENLIGHTENED SELF-INTEREST

1750–1789
GOUVERNEUR MORRIS

4

Three generations before Gouverneur Morris put quill to paper and wrote the first words of the United States Constitution, "We the People," the first member of his family in America, his great-uncle Colonel Lewis Morris, was thrown in prison at least three times for piracy, bribery, and failure to pay debts. So Gouverneur was more a product of buccaneers and brigands than of dour, sour Puritan preachers. A lawyer, statesman, entrepreneur, raconteur, diarist, and world-class womanizer, Gouverneur Morris was decidedly *not* a man of the people, or a politician. But he was a Founding Father, if a less well-known one, of a nation that would alternately honor and emulate, disdain and deny him: a native-born, natural aristocrat in a nation that has always affected to have none, licentious but not a libertine, publicly conservative but in private a man who cherished and took full advantage of his personal liberty.

As early as 1835, Alexis de Tocqueville observed the all-too-obvious reality of America's ruling class and defined it. "It is not by privilege alone, nor by birth, but by landed property handed down from generation to generation that an aristocracy is constituted," the French political historian wrote in his *Democracy in America*.[1] Despite his family's raffish origins, by the time Gouverneur was born in 1752, the Morrises fit that bill. And Gouverneur would grow to be entitled—believing himself to have been born privileged—as well as a beneficiary of entail, the English feudal law practice designed to protect landed aristocratic families by restricting the sale and inheritance of their land.

The Morris family first bought property on the American mainland in June 1668, three years after England took over the Dutch colony of New Netherland and renamed it and its port city New York. In the 1650s, the Dutch Republic (aka the Netherlands), just eight decades old, was enjoying its golden age as a colonial power and an international hub of finance and culture. But a growing rivalry with England threatened all that, and the outbreak of the first of four Anglo-Dutch wars, fought over the next 130 years, presaged that nation's decline. The first of those conflicts ended inconclusively in mutual exhaustion in 1654. Eleven years later, in a second series of clashes, the English took power in New York.

Shortly thereafter, Lewis Morris, then a wealthy plantation owner on the island of Barbados, and his younger brother Richard bought five hundred acres just across the Harlem River from Manhattan, at the southern tip of what is now called the Bronx, from a real estate speculator named Samuel Edsall. It was the first piece of Morrisania, a tract that would eventually quintuple in acreage, and of a family property empire that would also include a house in Manhattan and thousands more acres in the future Oyster Bay and Center Island on Long Island and along the Delaware River in New Jersey.[2] Morris and his descendants were among a handful of New York clans "steeped in antiquity," in the words of the social observer Cleveland Amory, but rooted in a feudalism unique to America. Mixing colonial English and Dutch blood and traditions, early settlers like the Morrises helped create "America's made-up Aristocracy."[3]

Despite their broad ambition, piety, culture, and erudition, the founders of New England weren't landholders on the scale of the families that laid the foundations on which New York's—and America's—highest echelon built its pride. Power and glory initially flowed from land, huge swaths of it, first granted to wealthy New Amsterdam colonizers by the Dutch West India Company in what were called patroonships.

A form of aristocratic social organization, patroonships—and, later, similar grants by the English crown called manors—were originally a creation of the Roman Empire, and evolved into an institution designed to consolidate control of land and the people who occupied it: peasants, farmers, and laborers, and their families. Rulers granted huge swaths of conquered land as a reward to a handful of favored, well-connected and strong subordinates to cement their control and encourage colonization, stable settlement, and economic development. Those who worked the land sacrificed their freedom and any rights to the meager plots of soil they labored on in exchange for the protection of the patroons or lords of the manor and continued access to that land so that they could work and feed themselves. Dutch patroonships in America came with sweeping political and economic privileges, including the explicit right to acquire slaves and exploit their labor. The practice was continued by England's royal families, who handed down their manorial grants, as well as the sort of patents given to organizations like the Virginia Company and the Pilgrims' Merchant Adventurers, which, though also designed to encourage colonization, were more commercial in intention, and had the added benefit of serving as a release valve for potentially disruptive religious fervor.

Rensselaerwyck, about 700,000 acres on the west bank of the Hudson River in upstate New York, was the first and most successful of the Dutch patroonships, established on land purchased but never even seen by its patroon, an Amsterdam merchant. Under the English, Robert Livingston, a Scot, was granted feudal rights to Livingston Manor, 160,000 acres on the Hudson's eastern shore, and Thomas Pell, a doctor, to the 50,000-acre Pelham Manor, by James II in 1686 and 1687. William and Mary, who merged England's Stuart dynasty with the royal House of Orange-Nassau, which had led the revolt against Spain that established the Dutch Republic, granted the 52,000-acre Philipsburg to Frederick Philipse in 1693, and in 1697, Cortlandt Manor (83,000 acres) to Stephanus Van Cortland, Scarsdale (6,000 acres) to Caleb Heathcote, and Morrisania to Richard and Lewis Morris. Notes Amory: "Of these Families the two which most resembled the landed gentry of England were the Livingstons and the Morrises."[4]

The Morrises of Morrisania didn't start out that grand—but their reinvention through pilferage, adventurism, intelligence, ambition, and the persecution of their fellow men made them exemplars of American WASPs in all their boundless complexity.

～～

Lewis and Richard Morris were born in Tintern, on the river Wye in Monmouthshire, Wales, early in the seventeenth century. As a young man, Lewis was an apprentice navigator for the Puritan-led Providence Island Company, which colonized and ran privateers in the Caribbean Sea. Government-sanctioned pirates, privateers were given letters of marque authorizing legalized theft and granting them a share of anything they stole.

Lewis had started out an indentured servant to the Earl of Warwick, who helped organize the 1609 Jamestown settlement and the Massachusetts Bay Colony. In 1628, Lewis headed to Providence Island, off the coast of Nicaragua, in a three-ship convoy captained by the same seaman/privateer who had brought the first slaves to North America nine years earlier. It sought to establish the island as a base for attacks on Spanish shipping. Their letters of marque gave the crew rights to four-fifths of whatever they seized.[5]

The primary restraint on cross-Atlantic trade was the ongoing conflict among Spain, the Dutch, and the British, and later the French. The Protestant powers used privateers to harass Catholic Spain and disrupt its triangular trade—the profitable shipping system that moved goods and slaves among Europe, Africa, the West Indies, and the Americas, where that system would ultimately be perfected by middlemen in New York and New England. The Spanish were already producing sugar in Hispaniola when the British crashed into the Caribbean, establishing tobacco and sugar plantations in Barbados around the same time the Massachusetts Bay Colony was born.

Britain also controlled Bermuda, where Morris's convoy stopped to recruit women to join the prospective colony, before reaching its destination at Christmas 1629. The ships then went off to trade with Native Americans while the settlers planted tobacco.[6] Though a peace with Spain was negotiated, piracy persisted: Spain sacked Tortuga

island, Charles I issued Warwick new letters of marque in 1635, and
Morris went back and forth to England and back to the skull and
crossbones. In 1637, he married a widow—nothing more about her
is known—and became the company's negotiator with the indigenous
Moskito Indians of Honduras. In 1639, the company sent Morris back
to the western Caribbean to search for a rumored silver deposit.[7]
After a stop in Barbados, his ship headed east and was captured by
North African Barbary pirates. The crew, enslaved in Algiers, was ran-
somed and returned to England in 1640.[8]

By the time a new privateering venture was readied, Lewis had
risen to sailing master, second-in-command of an armed armada of
seven ships that sailed back to Barbados. There were 1,100 men in
the fleet as it terrorized the Caribbean, capturing Spanish gold, looting, shooting, drinking, and wenching.[9] They took several ports of
Jamaica from the Spanish, later returned for ransom.

Morris was promoted to captain and given command of one of
the ships.[10] Dodging cannibals, who apparently ate one foraging
party, they next took a port in Colombia, sailed to Jamaica and Cuba
to rest and reprovision, then went to Mexico, where they took ancient
silver, before returning to Bermuda in fall 1644. The next spring,
the fleet returned to England, where a dispute with a powerful rival
would put Morris in debtor's prison. He was released after appealing to England's House of Lords—and soon his fortunes changed
considerably.[11]

Let in on the secret of a new process for refining sugar, Morris
devised a plan to make his fortune.[12] After seventeen years in Warwick's employ, Morris had become a principal in his company and
was wealthy enough to set himself up as a Barbados plantation owner
and shipping merchant.[13] Barbadian sugar was soon the best in the
world, and Morris not only farmed sugar cane and processed it,
he sold and shipped the sugar, too, on a fleet of ten vessels, which
made him richer—and, finally, respectable.[14] He'd even be elected
to the local assembly and by the late 1660s would join the Barbados
governing council.

But before that, Morris eluded his latest arrest warrant by escaping to England.[15] As Oliver Cromwell sought power in England,
Morris became a leader of his anti-Royalist faction, known as the

Roundheads, joined Cromwell's anti-Royalist Army of the Commonwealth, and was put in charge of a 1648 assault on Chepstow Castle, which dated back five hundred years to the time of William the Conqueror. The Morris family coat of arms, showing a castle in flames over a shield and the motto *Tandem vincitur* ("At length it is conquered"), honors both a familial reputation for obstinacy and his bravery and resourcefulness in that engagement. Charles I was so angry over that loss that he confiscated the Morris family's land in Wales before he was executed in 1649. His victorious opponents in Parliament named Morris, then in London studying law, an advisor to its Council of State, advising on how to conquer royalist colonies.[16]

A civil war erupted on Barbados between 1650 and 1652, pitting its ruling proponents of the crown against those like Morris who favored Cromwell and Parliament. And in 1651, when a fleet sailed to retake Barbados, Morris was aboard; he'd finally left England for good. Outnumbered, the fleet blockaded the island, and when reinforcements arrived, Morris led an invasion. His four hundred men defeated twelve hundred royalist troops in a raid but couldn't hold the island until Morris recruited even more men. Finally, the Barbadian governor surrendered, peace was negotiated, and all concerned went back to their estates as if nothing had happened. Cromwell subsequently made Morris a colonel, and until his death he would be known as Colonel Morris.[17]

Initially, his plantation workers had all been indentured servants, but after 1650, African slaves began arriving on Barbados in large numbers; most would die, worked to death, and were replaced. The cruelty of Barbadian plantation owners and the wealth their slaves generated made them "the richest men by far in any British colony in the Western Hemisphere."[18]

Slavery, the practice of owning other human beings, had existed since at least the Sumerian civilization of today's Iraq, thirty-five hundred years before Christ, and was later practiced across the Middle East, in China, India, and Africa, and among indigenous Americans. While it evolved into serfdom in Europe in the Middle Ages, religious wars pitting Christians against Arab Muslims over holy lands around the Mediterranean Sea saw both sides enslaving enemy prisoners.

Sugar, first refined in India and carried along trade routes east and west, was an accelerant of the slave trade. Used as medicine in the Middle East and as a luxury product in Egypt, it caught the attention of Venetian merchants, who brought it to Europe. There, during the Crusades, Christians developed a taste for the sweet stuff. The first plantations to mass-produce sugar for its many new markets were established in the Canary Islands in the 1100s, creating an international trade in the slaves who made up the required workforce. In the 1400s, Europeans exploring and exploiting West Africa, where North African Arabs and African chiefs had owned and dealt in slaves for centuries, saw the potential for profit in slave labor. By the 1500s, they had turned the Americas into a major market for human beings, who were bought and forced onto ships across the Atlantic and into work in mines and on coffee plantations in Portuguese Brazil and on sugar and tobacco plantations established by the Spanish, and later the English, Dutch, and French, in the Caribbean. Beginning in the next century, slaves also worked the cotton and tobacco plantations in the American South. Lewis Morris was a beneficiary of that barbarous trade.

Shortly after missionaries brought the new Quaker sect to Barbados in 1655, Morris joined and became a community leader.[19] Despite his faith, which had held from its seventeenth-century founding that all human beings were equal and owed the same respect, and the fact that he'd been enslaved himself by Barbary pirates, Morris not only was a major slaveholder but is said to have had sex with female slaves. He also encouraged his slaves' conversion to Christianity, part of a broader, if ultimately futile, Quaker effort to reconcile their religion with their profitable but inhumane practice of human bondage.[20]

Drawn back into military action in 1668, Morris was among those given permission by King Charles II—despite his Cromwellian past—to return to privateering against the French. That year he once again ended up imprisoned, this time for bribing local natives to help force French settlers off St. Lucia.[21]

Claiming his conversion to Quakerism as proof that he would never have done what he was accused of, Morris was released in 1670 and returned to Barbados.[22] By then, though, the Barbadian economy had weakened. The secret of sugar refining was out, and the locus of economic activity had moved to North America's colonies, where the British, flexing their muscles, had taken over New York and New Jersey in 1664. Morris appears to have quickly set his sights on this new frontier for reasons economic, political, and religious; plus, he had gotten in trouble with the authorities on Barbados and was fined after he claimed his Quaker convictions barred his paying tithes to the Anglican Church or contributing men or funds to the local militia when a slave and Indian revolt threatened plantation owners.[23]

As Lewis Morris's acreage on Barbados grew, he convinced his brother Richard to join him there. Richard married the daughter of another planter and started traveling to New York; by the late 1660s he had established a sugar trading business. In 1670, Richard moved his family north permanently after buying the first piece of the property that would become the manor of Morrisania, and ultimately the South Bronx, but was then wilderness far from the newly renamed British port of New York. There the English and the Dutch initially cohabited uneasily but ultimately gave birth to a new breed of American, urban cosmopolites like Gouverneur Morris, a product of the merger of the English Morrises with a French Huguenot family from Holland, as the two most powerful provinces of the Dutch Republic were known.

Lewis Morris already embodied the creative tensions that made New York. After the West India Company relinquished its monopoly on trade out of New Netherland in 1640, New Amsterdam had become a magnet for seekers of profitable opportunity, and an incubator for "an intensively active merchant class, people who wanted to buy, sell, grow, spend"—and exercise control over their community through self-government, an idea more often credited to their Calvinist counterparts in New England.[24] Nominally Calvinist, like its Massachusetts predecessors, New Amsterdam was differentiated by "a raggedness, a social looseness," that was thoroughly Dutch—and would add a vital libertarian dimension to the American enterprise.[25] Toleration of religious differences, but also of excesses like prostitution, deviance, and drunkenness, became a defining characteristic that survived not only the transition to British rule but American independence as well.

But most of all, like the city he lived in much of his life, Lewis Morris was defined by enlightened self-interest, which required liberty but demanded a certain caution in both its acquisition and its exercise. Wealth, New Yorkers understood, was the reward for striking a balance between individual desire and the common good.

5

The British explorer John Smith had given his countryman and colleague Henry Hudson maps of the North American coastline before Hudson headed to Amsterdam, commercial hub of the Dutch Republic, in autumn 1608. Seeking a sea route to Asia, Hudson sailed the next spring in the *Half Moon* and instead ended up exploring what would become New York's harbor and the river that fed it from the north, which would be given his name.

By 1624, ships were leaving Amsterdam carrying settlers, many of them from the Pilgrims' former home, Leyden, to strengthen Dutch claims to American lands. They spread out along the routes of the North (later Hudson), South (later Delaware) River, and Fresh (or Connecticut) Rivers—and in 1626, left their first settlement on what is now Governor's Island in New York Harbor and moved to nearby Manahatta, as the future Manhattan island was then called. It was purchased by their commander, Peter Minuit, for sixty guilders' worth of trade goods, famously valued by a nineteenth-century historian at \$24.[26] Minuit named the little village he founded New Amsterdam, "after its Dutch parent, some of whose culture and way of being—its openness and its swagger—[it] . . . would inherit."[27]

As New Amsterdam grew and some there prospered, it attracted others. In 1643, the creation of the United Colonies (Massachusetts Bay, Connecticut, New Haven, and Plymouth) seemed at least partly inspired by emigration from those intolerant colonies to Manhattan, where new arrivals could worship and behave as they wanted. The largest ethnic group in the earliest days of New York was the Dutch, a population large enough that it supported three Dutch Reformed churches. Over the decades before the American Revolution, they would be joined by Presbyterian, Anglican, French, Lutheran, and

Calvinist houses of worship, as well as Baptists, Quakers, and Jews who practiced their religion in small groups.*

In 1647, Petrus Stuyvesant—who had worked for the Dutch West India Company, formed to exploit Dutch claims to West Africa and the Americas in Brazil and Curacao, and lost a leg in a battle with the Spanish for control of Sint Maarten—arrived as the seventh (and, in the end, last) director-general of its New Netherland settlement. But two years later, as New Amsterdam was becoming the trading hub of America, its occupants began to agitate for the Dutch government to take over the colony from the company, which was considered undercapitalized, autocratic, and badly run.

To the north, John Endecott had replaced John Winthrop after the Bay Colony governor's death. Hoping to settle boundary disputes with the United Colonies, Stuyvesant arranged a parley with Endecott at a Dutch fort in Hartford in 1650. He surrendered territory already effectively controlled by New Haven and Connecticut, and in return the English agreed to set borders between them and the Dutch. But larger forces were in play: England was also expanding its maritime fleet, hoping to disrupt the Dutch trading monopoly, and in response, in 1652, the Dutch declared war on England.

The next winter, the Dutch government heard the pleas of the settlers and made New Amsterdam a thriving independent town; officially, the company and Stuyvesant remained in charge, but the citizens and businessmen of the colony took control. The British dispatched four frigates to Manhattan early in 1654, but they turned around after a surprising peace deal between the Dutch and the English was announced, ending the First Anglo-Dutch War.

John Winthrop's son, John, known as "the Younger," was then governor of Connecticut, which, like New Haven, was a thriving colony despite the fact that it had never been given official status by Britain. In 1661, he sailed to Europe to seek that sanction and inspired England's next colonial gambit by handing over a map of Manhattan's defenses. In return, he was promised control of not only Connecticut but New Haven and New Amsterdam, too.

---

* There was no Roman Catholic church in Manhattan until after the Revolution.

Envisioning a new war with the Dutch and the seizure of both its slave ports in West Africa and its New Amsterdam colony, intended to catapult Britain over the Dutch into the status of the world's greatest trading nation, the reigning English king, Charles II, gave his brother James, the Duke of York, control of all the British colonies in America. Over time, James would grant some of that land to friends and allies.

In March 1664, England sent four more gunships across the Atlantic to finally take Manhattan. When the ships arrived in New York Harbor, Stuyvesant wanted to defend New Amsterdam, but its leading citizens, already jaundiced toward the West India Company, were against it, and without a shot being fired, the orange, blue, and white flag over Fort Amsterdam was lowered and the Union Jack raised, and the settlement's name was changed to New York to honor its new overlord. Charles II also reneged on his promise of more land to Winthrop the Younger and instead negotiated a deal with Stuyvesant that promised "a guarantee of rights unparalleled in any English colony . . . The thinking was that the inhabitants of the island should be allowed to maintain their way of life for the very good reason that the place worked."[28]

The Second and Third Anglo-Dutch Wars followed, and in 1673, the Dutch retook Manhattan, only to return it in a peace deal fifteen months later. It is a tribute to what Peter Stuyvesant helped create that he ended his days on his eighty-acre New York farm, or bouwerie, and his family would remain prominent in the city for centuries. Stuyvesant was buried in 1672 in a vault under a chapel on his estate, now the site of St. Mark's Church in the Bowery, erected by a great-grandson.

What is now the Bronx, a borough of New York City, was originally the property of a Dutch farmer, Jonas Bronck, who bought it from local Native Americans and built a tobacco farm and stone house there. After Bronck died in 1643, the property passed through several hands before Richard and Lewis Morris acquired it and a two-story, nine-room house with a view from a promontory straight down the East River from that real estate speculator. They had already signed a written agreement providing that if either of them died, the other, or his survivors, would take precedence to inherit their shared property. Shortly after Richard and his wife, Sarah, moved to Bronck's 520 acres, they had a son they named Lewis, who would become the beneficiary of that agreement much sooner than expected.

In 1672, Richard and his wife died within a week of each other. The next year, after the Dutch briefly retook New York, Colonel Morris sailed from Barbados to fetch his brother's orphaned son, and discovered that Dutch officials had confiscated his share of the Morris land, livestock, and merchandise, claiming that, as an inhabitant of Barbados, he had no rights to it. They also refused his request for guardianship of young Lewis, who was placed with another relative.

Morris used British New Jersey as his base to fight for both guardianship of his nephew and the return of his property. He prevailed and in 1674 got back what was still known as Bronck's land. Disposing of his holdings in Barbados, he returned to America with his second wife, Mary, described as low-born, grasping, and perhaps a former household servant, just after the British defeated the Dutch and the Treaty of Westminster gave New York back to the crown. In 1676, when Morris helped New York's English governor, Edmund Andros, in a maneuver to divert customs duties on rum from New Jersey, a grateful Andros deeded him an additional 1,420 acres adjacent to Bronck's land, bordered by the Harlem River to the south and the East River to the southeast, adding meadows and timberland to his holdings. Charged by the Duke of York with conspiring with Morris over those customs duties, Andros was recalled to London, where, despite his troubles, he was soon rehabilitated and made a gentleman of Charles II's privy council.

Still in New Jersey, Morris diversified. Iron, like gold, was a medium for trade as well as good ballast for ships. Morris acquired thousands of acres containing iron deposits in New Jersey and established saw- and gristmills and an ironworks, naming the community Tinton after his family's confiscated property in Wales.[29] Work there was done by between forty and seventy slaves, many of them brought from Barbados, making Morris the largest slaveholder in New York and New Jersey. He built barracks for the captives at his ironworks, encouraged them to breed a self-reproducing labor force, and trusted a few of them enough to serve as his agents in business.[30]

In February 1682, leading Quaker William Penn and eleven partners, who already owned a half interest in West New Jersey, bought the colony's eastern half from Sir George Carteret, who'd been given it by his friend the Duke of York as a reward for his service during the English Civil War. The next year, Morris was named an official in its government, built a new home, and took part in the division of the colony into four counties, the appointment of its first sheriffs, and the reorganization of its courts; he was made chief justice. Quaker hypocrisy over slavery persisted: trading in slaves was prohibited, but owning them was not.[31]

Simultaneously, Morris, a major landowner in both colonies, also sat on the governing council of New York, which advanced democracy by establishing an elected assembly, setting up a court system, and passing a charter of liberties and privileges, though it was applicable only to white men and was ultimately vetoed by the king.[32] When the latest governor of New York started picking fresh fights with New Jersey over borders, trade, and taxes, Morris, who moved back and forth between the states, played a constructive role as mediator.

In 1688, Morris's nephew, then seventeen, disappeared. Accounts offer two reasons that are not mutually exclusive. Young Lewis was a willful, rebellious teenager who taunted the strict Quaker tutor hired to teach and rein him in.[33] And the colonel's wife, Mary, had tried to turn the older man against his ward to ensure he did not inherit her husband's fortune. Young Lewis ran away to Virginia and then Jamaica before he was found and returned on one of the colonel's ships just days before his guardian died in 1691. America might have been a very different place had this prodigal not returned.

Mary died a week after the colonel. The elder Morris's will, written a year earlier, was opened and found to be full of irregularities, erasures, and changes. But it said that due to young Lewis's "many and great miscarriages and disobedience" the colonel had changed his original intentions, and made Mary, not Lewis, his executor. He nonetheless left Lewis his New Jersey property, as well as most of the slaves there.* Bronck's land and his house in New York, where, the 1710 census showed, fourteen male and twelve female slaves were then in residence, were earmarked for Mary and her heirs.[34]

Showing off legal skills he seems to have gained through osmosis, young Lewis claimed the will had been altered by Mary and one of the colonel's servants to deprive him of his fortune. The changes were all in the servant's hand. And, in a circumstantial coup de grâce, Lewis produced evidence that the servant had purchased rights to a play about the theft of an estate. With Mary dead, the will was thrown out, and Lewis, as next of kin, became its administrator and inherited most of his uncle's property. That included human chattel.

⟍

The death of his uncle caused the second Lewis Morris to grow up suddenly. Late in 1691, he married the eldest daughter of the attorney general of New York, and at just twenty he was appointed a judge in New Jersey and shortly thereafter a member of the colony's governing council. An autodidact, he began amassing a huge library later said to be rivaled only by Harvard's.[35] In 1697, New York's governor, on behalf of King William III, made him a lord and Bronck's land his manor, naming it Morrisania. But Morris remained in New Jersey, continued his political career, and started a family there. His father-in-law took up residence at the manor, where he lived out his life.

Lewis's ambition made for a turbulent career. He was tossed off New Jersey's governing council in 1698, then pushed a 1702 effort to convince Queen Anne to take over East and West Jersey and merge them with New York, which failed when he asked her to make him governor of the enlarged province. After that he conspired to have a later governor removed, which inspired a petition to the queen calling him a man of "turbulent, factious, uneasy, disloyal principles."[36]

Perhaps Morris made too many enemies in New Jersey, because he moved to Morrisania. In 1703, he was named to New York's Governor's Council, traveling south to the city for meetings in a sloop

---

* He had, according to the City University of New York's Slavery Records Index, 66 negroes valued at £844.

he docked near his house.[37] By 1710, he was its leader, and in 1711, he was appointed to its supreme court and would shortly be made its chief justice, a job he held for two decades. In that office, in 1733, he ruled against William Cosby, then the British-appointed governor of both New York and New Jersey (East and West Jersey had been combined and annexed to New York as a single royal colony in 1702), in a suit seeking salary in arrears that had already been paid to his predecessor, and Morris was removed from the court by the governor. "I can neither rely upon his integrity nor depend upon his judgment," Cosby said. "He is a person not at all fitted to be trusted."[38] He also accused Morris of "intemperate drinking, in which he often spends whole nights."[39] In reply, Morris noted that "judges are no more infallible than their superiors are impeccable. But if judges are to be intimidated so as not to dare to give any opinion but what is pleasing to a governor, and agreeable to his private views, the people of this province . . . may possibly not think themselves so secure."[40]

Morris didn't stop with that. He ran for and won a seat in the provincial assembly—defeating a candidate backed by Cosby—and immediately he and two lawyer allies hired a printer, John Peter Zenger, to put out a newspaper (not coincidentally competing with another that supported Cosby) that, in its debut issue, branded the governor an election-rigging tyrant. Cosby ordered Zenger investigated for seditious libel, the intentional publication of unjustified, but not necessarily false, charges against a public figure.

The case that resulted would be the first to confirm a vital principle later enshrined in the First Amendment to the American Constitution: freedom of the press. When two successive grand juries failed to issue an indictment against Zenger, Cosby tried but failed to have the public hangman burn copies of the newspaper. Cosby then induced his attorney general to prosecute Zenger without an indictment, and had him arrested. Unable to afford the bail set by a judge who was Cosby's ally, Zenger stayed in jail as the court disqualified his lawyers, who were Morris's partners in the newspaper. Morris then hired a preeminent Philadelphia lawyer, Andrew Hamilton, to defend Zenger, and in his opening remarks the lawyer surprised all concerned by admitting that Zenger had published the statements in dispute, then reframing the matter.

"The question before the Court and you, Gentlemen of the jury, is not of small or private concern," he pleaded. "It is not the cause of one poor printer, nor of New York alone, which you are now trying. No! It may in its consequence affect every free man that lives under a British government on the main of America. It is the best cause. It is the cause of liberty."

Hamilton had admitted that Zenger had violated the letter of the law, but Zenger was set free in an early case of jury nullification. Years later, Morris's grandson Gouverneur would call the case "the germ of American freedom, the morning star of that liberty which subsequently revolutionized America!"[41] In years to come, it would be seen as a legal landmark, "upholding the right to publish the truth no matter what damage it might inflict on the government."[42]

In 1738, New York and New Jersey, after being ruled together for thirty-five years, were separated again and each was given its own royal governor; Lewis Morris, who'd advocated for the split, was named the royal governor of the latter at age sixty-six, and despite more controversy attributed to his imperious manner, his hectoring of the assembly, and his "inordinate vanity" and hunger for power, he would serve until his death in 1746.[43]

Lewis Morris had twelve children and left six daughters and two sons. The eldest, Lewis II (as he was the second Lewis in the nuclear family descended from Richard), born at Tinton, became second lord of Morrisania, where he kept forty-six slaves.[44] He held political and judicial office and was said to be "exceedingly unlike his father," as he had "less forensic ability, rarely indulged in offensive sarcasm and possessed great suavity of manner, genuine humor . . . and his pluck almost reached audacity."[45] He was also a notable eccentric who sometimes wore a hat made from the skin of a loon, complete with its feathers.

Lewis II married twice. His first wife had four children, including a son, Lewis III, who would become one of the fifty-six signers of America's Declaration of Independence, as well as a congressman, judge, and officer in the Revolutionary War against Britain. But long before that, in 1746, Lewis II remarried after fifteen years as a widower to Sarah Gouverneur (pronounced GOOV-noor). The Gouverneurs were Huguenots, French Protestants who had emigrated to

Holland in the late sixteenth century and to New Amsterdam in 1663.[46] Sarah was a cousin of Lewis II's first wife; he was already fifty-four when his and Sarah's only son, Gouverneur, was born in January 1752 and christened in the Anglican Trinity Church. Gouverneur's youngest half-brother was thirty-two years his senior, and the child was only six when his father, Lewis II, died in 1758 and Gouverneur inherited about £2,000, "a Negroe Boy called George," and some of his father's heirlooms.[47] His mother inherited a life interest in part of Morrisania; at her death it would pass to Lewis II's children and their offspring.*

Sarah, following Lewis II's instruction to give Gouverneur "the best Education that is to be had," sent him to a Huguenot country academy in New Rochelle,† where he studied her native French language.[48] "It was perhaps the French blood in his veins that gave him the alert vivacity and keen sense of humor that distinguished him from most of the Revolutionary statesmen who were his contemporaries," wrote future president Theodore Roosevelt in an 1898 biography of Morris.[49]

At nine, Gouverneur attended the Philadelphia Academy, founded by Benjamin Franklin, and then entered the Anglican King's College (the future Columbia University) at twelve, slightly younger than most of his classmates, who were generally upper-class adolescents. He was three years younger than another prodigy there who became a close friend and fellow Founding Father, John Jay, also from a wealthy Huguenot merchant family.‡

When Gouverneur was fourteen, he damaged all the flesh on his right arm and side when he spilled a kettle of boiling water on himself—reportedly while trying to leap over it. Saved from gangrene and amputation but scarred for life, he took a year off from college,

---

* Lewis III, who already owned and occupied the rest of the estate across a creek to the north and west, would be the third and last lord of the manor of Morrisania, as entail and primogeniture—the laws that passed property to firstborn sons—were abolished in New York before his death. But he was devoted to the estate, where he was born, and he constantly improved it through his life, though he was forced to abandon it during the American Revolution.

† The French school in New Rochelle was set up by the Livingstons, Van Rensselaers, and Van Nesses, all wealthy Francophiles, after the wars with the French ended in 1763.

‡ Jay would precede a Morris half-brother as chief justice of New York's Supreme Court.

yet wasn't slowed down; he graduated at sixteen with his class in 1768. He had shown aptitude in math (at eighteen he would publish essays about financial legislation, signed "An American," that showed a sophisticated grasp of economics). His thesis also revealed his urbanity, arguing that reason requires beauty to achieve civility.[50]

Gouverneur immediately apprenticed as a law clerk, and he joined the bar before he turned twenty in 1771. As a lawyer, he represented his own family and the similarly situated Livingstons. He wore "the height of fashion, with costly lace on his cuffs, was handsome and prepossessing. His brow was broad and white, eyes large and expressive, nose prominent, and his mouth rather large with full lips, while his hair was thick and curly, and he had a full chin and erect figure."[51]

Considering the idea of a long, pre-career trip to Europe, Morris thought it would "curb that vain self-sufficiency which arises from comparing ourselves with companions who are inferior to us."[52] Advised to remain in New York, he did and stood out from the colonial crowd, aided by his tall stature, good looks, name, wealth, wit, and the self-assurance that came from it all. And though he had vowed to "avoid those low pleasures that abound on this as well as on the other side of the Atlantic," he found them anyway, and was frequently up all night at balls, concerts, and assemblies, "all of us mad in the pursuit of pleasure."[53] He was as attractive to women as they were to him. "Tell the women they must all love me for I love them all," he wrote to his friend Robert R. Livingston.[54] "Gouverneur is daily employed in making Oblations to Venus," John Jay drily noted.[55]

6

The end of the French and Indian War reignited tensions between Great Britain and her American colonies, but young Morris seems to have paid little attention. "Politics I dislike and only look on with pity," he announced.[56] He was already developing a conservative political philosophy and dabbling in public finance, though, interests first revealed when he vocally opposed a bill in the New York Assembly that proposed paying war debts by printing money to delay an inevitable reckoning.

The lawyer he clerked for, a friend of three generations of Morrises, was more involved in politics, a partisan of the cautious, politically moderate Livingstons. Though they had always been royalists with an aristocratic mindset, their control of one of New York's manors eventually allied them with other landowners who had begun to worry about what they saw as the British Crown's blunders. So too Morris's legal mentor, who became a "prudent" opponent of the Sugar and Stamp Acts of 1764 and 1765, which imposed taxes on the colonies to pay for the Seven Years' War, the global counterpart of the American conflict. Those acts, which inspired the phrase "no taxation without representation," were signposts on the road to the American Revolution.[57]

Gouverneur was too aristocratic, hedonistic, and uncompromising to succeed in electoral office. Initially attracted to business, he became a real estate speculator with his mother's backing at twenty-one in 1773, buying wilderness land north of Albany, but he paid attention to current events and feared that increasing conflict with England might lead to the rule of the mob. His conservatism sprang from the soil of New York, a colony run by wealthy old landed families like his own, whose vast real estate holdings reflected their social position and political power. The Morrises, like the Livingstons, were original American aristocrats, of more recent vintage than their British equivalents, but just as proud and preeminent.

In April 1774, a ship arriving in New York Harbor was found to be carrying tea in violation of the Tea Act, passed the year before to favor an indebted British company. Anger that was already festering in Boston and Philadelphia came to New York when a mob tossed that cargo overboard in an act of defiance; around the same time Parliament closed Boston Harbor to trade in punishment for its earlier, similar "Tea Party." A radical band called the Sons of Liberty began agitating for an embargo on all English goods, alarming New York's merchant community, many of them moderates or Whigs, who remained allied with England. Though they had begun to harbor doubts about rule by an absolute monarch, they feared the radicals might provoke retaliation and cause chaos.

Morris, still apolitical, shared their concern, but he and his friends couldn't help being moved by the excitement of the times. In May 1774, he attended a protest meeting at Fraunces Tavern, and Jay and Livingston joined groups seeking to address the colonists' grievances. That spring, the Committee of Fifty-one was formed as a parallel government to the crown, and suggested to its Boston counterparts a gathering of all the colonies. The First Continental Congress opened in Philadelphia that September, and Jay and Livingston's brother Philip were delegates. Representatives from Virginia and Massachusetts wielded the cutting edge of American anger. Morris was still not committed, and his family was torn, too. Lewis III was sympathetic to the patriots, and relatives in the Caribbean sent cannons to help the cause, but like many New York Anglicans, Gouverneur's mother remained a royalist, Lewis III's son Staats had become a British officer, and several of the women in the family had loyalist husbands. "This struggle arrays brother against brother and introduces discord and strife into families, and mine is an instance," Gouverneur told Jay. "Family ties are ruptured as well as all the links which bind us to the mother country."[58]

As the embers of revolt smoldered and its heat spread through the colonies, future revolutionaries found each other. New York's vocal supporters of the Crown included Miles Cooper, the president of King's College, and a printer and newspaper publisher, James Rivington. Morris first noticed Alexander Hamilton, a young King's College student, when he helped Cooper flee an angry mob early in 1775. The same mob then turned on Rivington, inspiring Morris to write to friends in Philadelphia defending the printer from any sanction as a symbol of both a free press and the status quo.[59]

But soon Gouverneur and his half-brother Lewis got more involved with the patriots, and they were elected delegates to New York's first Provincial Convention, which met in May 1775, after the Battle of Lexington and Concord and the start of the military campaign for independence, to nominate delegates to a second Continental Congress. Jay, Livingston, and Lewis III would sign the Declaration of Independence, which marked the formal start of America's revolution against Britain.

Swept into action by the spirit of the times, the Morris brothers steadily grew more radical. Gouverneur was named to a committee charged with financing the war, and wrote its report, which recommended issuing national paper money rather than letting each colony print its own, beginning what would become a years-long, relentless campaign for a strong central government to unify the separate American colonies. His firm belief that America needed to be a single nation, not a loosely linked collection of separate states, propelled Morris into its leadership. By that summer, Congress (then in Philadelphia) would be printing money and raising an army.

In early 1776, Parliament banned trade with the thirteen colonies, and Congress responded by opening American ports to every nation except Great Britain. By then, Gouverneur Morris, Jay, and Livingston were fully invested. At New York's third Provisional Congress, convened in May, Morris declared "independence . . . absolutely necessary."[60] He opened the proceedings with a stirring oration. "Great Britain will not fail to bring us into a war with some of her neighbors, and then protect us as a lawyer defends a suit—the client paying for it," the young lawyer said. "I maintain there is no redress but by arms."[61] Along with Jay and Phillip Livingston, he joined a committee that had direct dealings with General George Washington, leading the Continental Army then preparing to defend New York. Similar in confidence and physique, Morris and Washington became fast friends that spring and summer.

But when Morris sought a commission in a New York battalion, he found his lack of military experience disqualifying, and his elitism reared its head in a letter to his brother complaining that "a herd of Mechanics are preferred before the best Families in the Colony."[62] He would never waver from his belief that the masses needed guidance from an educated elite. However, his instincts remained contradictory: he urged policies of terror and scorched earth against loyalists but had some sympathy for individual royalists, perhaps because among them were family members and the lawyer who had been his professional mentor. That June, Morris was named to a committee investigating a plot to foil the rebellion and perhaps even kidnap or kill Washington. Among those suspected in the plot was

Gouverneur's half-brother Richard, who swore allegiance to Congress to ensure his continued freedom.

By then, Gouverneur had blossomed into a powerful public speaker, extolling "the unconquerable spirit of freemen deeply interested in the preservation of a government which secures to them the blessings of liberty and exalts the dignity of mankind."[63] Lewis III was less eloquent but equally fierce when it came time to sign the Declaration of Independence in Philadelphia that summer. Though his younger brother Staats, the British officer, warned him in a letter "not to take so rash a step," Lewis barked, "Damn the consequences; give me the pen!"[64]

In late August, Washington and his army escaped to Manhattan after losing the Battle of Long Island and Brooklyn. But British general William Howe captured the city in September 1776, and it would remain in British hands until two years after another British general, Lord Cornwallis, surrendered to the Americans at Yorktown in 1781, marking the beginning of the end of the war. A month after taking Manhattan, Howe landed troops in the Bronx, hoping to trap Washington's retreating army. The Battle of Pell's Point on October 18, 1776, led to a rout that got worse ten days later at the Battle of White Plains, forcing Washington across the Hudson River into New Jersey and then Pennsylvania.

Morrisania was seized during that campaign, just after Lewis III buried many of his valuables and fled to Pennsylvania's Lebanon Valley, where he had relatives. His slaves were sent to New Jersey to farm produce for his family. Between British and American lines through much of the war, Morrisania was alternately raided by patriots and recaptured by loyalist cavalry—who broke into the family burial vault and scattered the bones they found, killed and ate livestock, cut down timber, and burned buildings.*

As Washington retreated, Gouverneur Morris briefly dropped from public view. When he returned to New York's Provincial Convention, on the run and meeting in upstate Fishkill, he explained that

---

* The family didn't return until the war's end. Though his retirement would be interrupted by service in the state legislature, Lewis III lived out his life and died at Morrisania in 1798.

his absence was due to "a series of Accidents too trifling for recital."[65] Friends who knew his proclivities assumed he had been with a woman. He followed the convention to Kingston, where, in quarters over the local jail, New York's state constitution was adopted in April 1777 after eight months' work, primarily performed by Morris, Jay, and Livingston. It cut ties to the Anglican Church and granted religious freedom subject only to the state's right to protect public safety.

Typically, in debates over the document, Morris sought to balance democracy with aristocracy, the risk of "the domination of a riotous mob" with the deceptive "despotism of the few."[66] He proposed that the right to vote should be limited by income and possession of property, but also that slavery should be abolished—eventually.* It wasn't, but Morris had made more effort than most to inch his country closer to an enlightened stance on human bondage. The fate of his inherited slave—the "Negroe boy called George"—is unrecorded.

Morris was elected a New York delegate to the Continental Congress that May, but when the British invaded from the north and took Fort Ticonderoga, the state's Council of Safety asked him to first investigate how the fort fell.[67]

The war's tide turned in October 1777, when a British army led by General John Burgoyne surrendered to his American counterpart, Horatio Gates. Five days later, Morris, then twenty-six, headed to Congress, but before he could get there (delayed, some gossiped, by another dalliance), it fled Philadelphia ahead of an advance by the British under General Howe and settled on the banks of the Susquehanna River. Almost simultaneously, on learning of Burgoyne's surrender, Louis XVI, king of France, told Benjamin Franklin, the American minister to Versailles, that he wanted to acknowledge American independence and make a treaty with the new nation—an alliance that would surely hasten American victory against Britain.[68]

---

* The first abolition laws were passed in Pennsylvania and Vermont (then a republic) in 1777. In 1781, New York's legislature agreed to compensate slaveholders who gave their human property to the military during the Revolution, and those slaves-turned-soldiers were promised freedom after the war. In 1782, Virginia allowed slave owners to free their slaves, and Massachusetts courts decreed slavery inconsistent with the state constitution. The slave trade wouldn't be banned in New York until 1785 (and emancipation didn't become the law there until 1799, and remained incomplete until 1827).

As that news sailed slowly across the Atlantic, in January 1778, Gouverneur Morris was assigned to a congressional committee assessing the state of the Continental Army, then in its winter encampment seventy-five miles east at Valley Forge. Guided by Washington, Morris drew up plans to eliminate waste and fraud and improve the organization and supply lines for the American force, which he described as "the skeleton of an army . . . in a naked, starving condition, out of health, out of spirits."[69] A lifelong intimacy with Washington resulted (he would later be trusted to commission a French watch for the president, purchase and ship him fittings and ornaments for his residence, and stand in as his body double when the president was sculpted by Jean-Antoine Houdon). At Valley Forge, Morris also met the Marquis de Lafayette, a foreign volunteer who would be tangled up with Morris for the rest of their lives.[70]

Morris next drew up a plan for Congress to address the underlying causes of the army's issues (the weakness of the government and its credit) and to overhaul the national financial system, suggesting taxes, tariffs, and the leveraging of American land to gain foreign loans. Significantly, he proposed a national executive, perhaps an individual, perhaps a small committee, to oversee national finance and the military. He also again advocated for replacing state-issued currency with a single federal currency, and that summer he brought his ideas to Congress.

Morris was a workhorse—he would sit on sixty-five committees in 1778 alone—and that "made him, in many respects, Congress's foreign secretary."[71] Thus he was central to the decision-making when, after America's victory at the Battle of Saratoga, Britain sent a peacemaking team to America, hoping to derail a French-American renewal of military operations aimed at independence with an offer to give up taxing the colonies. Morris smelled surrender and rejoiced that "a spark hath fallen upon the train which is to fire the world."

In response to the British commissioners, Morris both published essays and wrote directly to them: "When the king of Great Britain shall be seriously disposed to put an end to the cruel and unprovoked war, Congress will readily attend to such terms of peace, as may consist with the honor of independent nations."[72] He demanded a British withdrawal and acknowledgment of American independence, predicting that "the portals of the temple we have raised to freedom, shall be thrown wide, as an asylum to mankind. America shall receive to her bosom and comfort and cheer the oppressed, the miserable and the poor of every nation of every clime."[73] Despite his efforts in New York, slaves and indigenous peoples were still excepted.

In July, a squadron of French warships sailed into Delaware Bay and delivered France's first minister plenipotentiary to America, Conrad-Alexandre Gérard. Drafting instructions for his counterpart in Paris, Franklin, the first such dispatch ever sent by Congress to an American diplomat abroad, Morris wrote that America's goal was to be an independent nation stretching from Maine to Georgia and west to the Mississippi River, which would remain a Spanish waterway. Worried about the Native Americans who occupied the rest of the continent and the difficulties of navigating its great distances, he proposed that Spain could take Florida if it guaranteed Americans access to the river, and France could have Nova Scotia in exchange for fishing rights on the Grand Banks of Newfoundland.[74] By favoring restricting American growth to both the south and the west, he demonstrated an uncharacteristic shortsightedness. But his fear that settlers rushing into the continent's interior would inevitably ally with their southern counterparts and provoke another war with a European nation was equally prescient and misguided.[75] Eighty-two years later, in 1860, he would be proven right about the war, if wrong about the combatants.

Morris also set out America's financial situation to aid Franklin in making a case for aid and loans—the same case he had made when urging a national currency, debt, taxes and tariffs, and a national treasury. Relations with France revealed a split between the American North, where international trade, manufacturing and commerce, and a far more diverse population encouraged a broader perspective, and the southern states with their agrarian planter-slave economy and anti-urban, anti-business ideology.* Between the two camps were provocateurs, often operating out of self-interest, a preference for

---

* Virginia's Thomas Jefferson foreshadowed the current disdain for globalism when he noted, "The selfish spirit of commerce knows no country, and feels no passion or principle but that of gain," in a letter to Larkin Smith on April 15, 1809.

England or France, or simply a desire to make mischief. Morris hoped America could negotiate safe passage through its own competing sectional interests and show its gratitude for French military assistance without subordinating itself to the French throne.

Emerging political struggles would soon divide Americans into radical and conservative parties. Like Washington, Morris feared that eventuality. "Party," he predicted "is a word that can do no good, but which may produce much evil."[76] Northerners, who would later coalesce as Federalists, were accused of being sympathetic to their Anglican brethren, and Jay admitted as much to Morris: "The destruction of Old England would hurt me; I wish it well; it afforded my ancestors an asylum from persecution."[77]

Morris's Anglophile friends and relations and his political views dogged him, and his "realism," a biographer wrote, caused the New York legislature to replace him in Congress, after he privately disparaged the state's claim to the land that would become the state of Vermont, even as he publicly supported it.[78] By putting the national interest ahead of New York's, he had made himself admired but politically controversial. So late in 1779, at age twenty-seven, with war still raging, he decided to leave public life, settle in Philadelphia, make his fortune, and again indulge in social life.[79] "He ranked as a wit among men, as a beau among women," wrote Roosevelt, "sought for dances and dinners . . . a fine scholar and a polished gentleman; a capital story-teller [with] whimsical peculiarities."[80]

＿＿＿

Morris professed to be glad to leave the stage. "My restoration to the beau Monde is like a resurrection from the grave," he wrote Livingston, with patrician aplomb, in October 1779.[81] Seven months later, an accident slowed—but didn't stop—his return to society. Thrown from a phaeton drawn by two horses, Morris got his left leg caught in the spokes of one of its wheels, dislocated his ankle, and broke several bones, forcing a doctor to amputate the leg just below his knee, as it couldn't be repaired. His recuperation lasted half a year.

Though the loss of a limb was then more common than it is today, for most it would have been devastating, Yet in years to come, Morris would be stoic—and even humorous—about the accident.

"The leg is gone and there is an end of the matter," he wrote to Jay.[82] But he was responding to a 1780 letter from Jay that hinted at a different cause: rumors flew that he'd lost the leg escaping a husband who had discovered Morris in flagrante with his wife. Jay had joked to Morris "that a certain married woman after much use of your leg had occasioned your losing one."[83]

Morris dismissed that as "facetious. Let it pass." But he recovered at the home of a Maryland couple and grew curiously close to the wife, who was Morris's age and much younger than her husband. In years to come, that pattern of closeness to married women would repeat, often in overtly sexual ways.[84] The pegs and false legs Morris wore for the rest of his life never curbed his taste for vigorous activity, sexual and otherwise. He was the life of whatever party he attended. When the more puritanical Jay worried at another point about the luxuries of Philadelphia, Morris replied tartly, "The very definition of 'luxury' is as difficult as the suppression of it."[85]

～

In March 1781, the Articles of Confederation, a first attempt to forge an American government, were finally ratified by the states, spotlighting their ability to impede a central government. But a countermovement to strengthen it was beginning, and in Congress Morris had met the businessman who would help shape it—and become his partner and lifelong friend: Robert Morris, who was no relation. He allegedly had read and been impressed by Gouverneur's early essays on finance.

Born in England, Robert Morris had come to Maryland from London in 1747 as a teenager and worked with his father, exporting tobacco. Sent to Philadelphia for schooling, he went to work for a firm of shipping merchants and importers of British goods and was made a partner before he turned twenty-one. He engaged in privateering and speculation in government debt, and in the 1760s he opposed the Stamp Act. A decade later he declared himself a patriot, serving on a Philadelphia committee to procure ammunition and supplies for the Continental Army. He also functioned as the Continental Congress's banker, using both his personal funds and lines of credit to finance the armed struggle. Though controversial because he collected commissions, profited on his deals, and initially voted against the Declaration of Independence, which he considered premature, he was nonetheless another signer.

When, early in 1781, the businessman was named superintendent of finance in a governmental reorganization that also saw Livingston put in charge of foreign affairs, Gouverneur agreed to be his assistant—a position he would hold into 1785. They were aided by an infusion of funds from the French that ensured the continued service of American troops, then centered in Yorktown, Virginia.

Believing that the powers reserved to the states made the country's finances unsound—though Congress could ask the states for money, it lacked the power to collect it, damaging its credit at a time of rampant inflation—Morris and Morris proposed a Bank of North America and Congress approved it in May 1781, just before word reached Philadelphia of the surrender of the British at Yorktown.[86] Early the next year, the Morrises also proposed that American currency be based on a decimal system (i.e., easily understood units of ten) and that coins—cents, nickels, and dimes—be introduced to replace the foreign currency circulating in the country. Later, his fellow Founding Fathers Thomas Jefferson and Alexander Hamilton, fierce rivals whose ever-growing disagreements would inspire the emergence of America's first political parties, would both take up Morris's argument that money should be consistent, intelligible, and easily divisible.

In July 1782, the Morrises suggested issuing bonds paying 6 percent, backed by tariffs and taxes, to pay the army, establish national credit, and consolidate and lessen the national debt, rather than letting the often-quarrelsome states deal with it in their separate ways. They understood that those structures would help strengthen a central government that still didn't exist. Congress wouldn't pass the bill, rejecting the tariffs and taxes required to fund it, and Gouverneur Morris, criticized for alleged conflicts with creditors, was branded a monarchist.[87] But his work helped sustain the dream of a coherent nation. "This generation will die away and give place to a race of Americans," he would write to Jay in January 1784.[88]

The Morrises worked well together. Both were as cocksure as they were controversial. Before accepting his post, Robert Morris insisted on continuing his personal business while serving the public, and demanded complete authority over anyone who dealt with public funds. He even invested his private fortune in the fledgling republic, introducing both banknotes and what were called Morris notes. He and his friends who invested in the bank would profit handsomely, doing well while doing good.[89] Though Robert Morris had many enemies, including Thomas Paine, who accused him of fraud, and numerous others who were likely motivated by envy of one of the richest men in America, Hamilton approved of the appointment of the Morrises, "introducing order into our finances."[90]

The country was still nowhere near solvent; a single state—Virginia—could and did disrupt its ability to pay the army, which was wintering in Newburgh, New York, while awaiting a final peace treaty. Though the threat of a mutiny was in the air there, and the infant nation was on the brink of insolvency, the North and its advocates for a strong central government would continue to bicker with southern states' rights advocates for years.

Unable to shape events to their liking in the face of unyielding opposition to a strong central government, the Morrises retreated, giving up their public positions and returning to private business, together and separately, accumulating capital, supplying Virginia tobacco to the French government, and investing in land and ships.* Meantime, wealthy Philadelphians defended the Bank of North America against radical and rural populists. "Do these gentlemen believe that it will rain money, as it did manna of old?" Gouverneur Morris asked the Philadelphia Assembly in a pro-bank oration.[91]

Gouverneur had briefly returned to Morrisania—for the first time in seven years—in June 1783, though it was still behind British lines. Like his aging mother, it was in bad shape and would deteriorate further, but he catalogued the damage done ("Happily, the British had not touched the wine") and sent a bill to the British commander in New York, who passed it to Staats Morris in England

---

* Alexander Hamilton, James Madison, and Robert Livingston also left Pennsylvania at the war's end, the first retiring from Congress, the second returning home to Virginia, the last resigning as secretary of foreign affairs.

for payment. Gouverneur finally got less than twenty-five cents on the dollar.[92]

Gouverneur then watched as his half-brother Richard demanded an accounting of their late father's estate, questioning Sarah Morris's expenditures. In the midst of that inquisition, she died in 1786, and her life interest in the eastern portion of Morrisania passed to their brother Staats, by then a retired British general and member of Parliament.* Under their father's will, Staats was required to pay £2,000 each to Richard and Gouverneur, but he decided to sell instead, and when Richard declined to buy, Gouverneur, though he reportedly had no money to spare, arranged to take over the estate. He paid his half-siblings a quarter of the price from his own inheritance and the balance with the help of a loan from a Philadelphia merchant banker and speculator, William Constable. To close the deal, Gouverneur had to threaten to walk away from it.[93]

In 1787, the states defaulted on interest payments due to France, just as a new Philadelphia convention was called to revise the desperately flawed Articles of Confederation. The weak national government was broke and the states were barely better off. Washington, Hamilton, and Gouverneur Morris, who was appointed a delegate in absentia by the Philadelphia Assembly, were among those who wanted the convention to totally overhaul the governing charter. Meeting beforehand at Benjamin Franklin's house, several delegates, including Morris and Virginia's Washington and Governor Edmund Randolph, agreed to seek a truly national government.[94]

Though he missed the first month of meetings—having to deal with Morrisania and with attempts by Virginia tobacco growers to disrupt Robert Morris's deal with France—in July 1787, Gouverneur Morris took his seat at the convention, alongside Washington, Franklin, Hamilton, and James Madison, a wealthy Virginia planter, and by August was constantly engaged in debates over the powers and duties of Congress, the executive, and the judiciary; direct elections versus an electoral college that would give small states an advantage

---

* The western portion of the estate had already passed to Lewis III, and in 1789, he would propose it be made the new nation's permanent capital. Congress declined. At the time, 13 separate families of Morris relations, 103 free people, and 30 slaves, 17 of whom belonged to "the signer," lived within the broader Morrisania.

out of proportion to their population; whether property should be a requirement for enfranchisement; and whether to allow slave trading to continue in Georgia and the Carolinas, the only former colonies that still allowed the importation of human chattel from Africa. Morris wanted it made explicit which states insisted that the evil trade continue.[95] Later, he would argue against the "three-fifths rule," by which representation in the lower house of Congress, apportioned on the basis of population, would count slaves as fractional beings while denying them the vote, increasing the white South's political power. "Are they men?" Morris asked on August 8, 1787. "Then make them citizens and let them vote. Are they property? Why then is no other property included?" He railed against a system that gave states promoting "cruel bondage . . . more votes" than states that viewed "with a laudable horror so nefarious a practice."[96]

When South Carolina and Georgia refused to join the Union if the new Constitution banned slavery, they forced an agreement to allow it for twelve more years, later extended to twenty with the support of New England, where rum manufacturers profited from the triangular trade. Morris objected, which made him exceptional.* But he also demonstrated the WASP trait of accommodating necessity, and acceded to the rule being enacted. The net effect of those compromises would be to forge the Union by giving southern and rural states disproportionate and undemocratic power in Congress and in national elections into the twenty-first century.

The western territories were another matter of dispute. That year, the new Northwest Ordinance spelled out the means by which Ohio, Indiana, Illinois, Michigan, Wisconsin, and Minnesota would join the Union. Expansion still worried Morris, due to the unanswered question of where slavery would be allowed, and an ingrained doubt that vast territory would be conducive to republican government.[97]

The loquacious Morris spoke more than any other delegate to the Constitutional Convention, though not always wisely: On impeachment, he said, "[If the president] should be re-elected, that will

---

* There were almost seven hundred thousand slaves in America in 1790, representing about 18 percent of the total population. That number would grow, even after the international slave trade ended in 1808, to four million souls on the eve of the Civil War.

be sufficient proof of his innocence."[98] But he finally assented to the possibility of an impeachment, on three conditions: the executive was awarded the trade-off of veto power over legislation; impeachable offenses were limited to bribery, treachery, and incapacity; and the Senate was charged with conducting any trial, with removal requiring a two-thirds vote.

Morris was eloquent in his defense of propertied interests over populist democracy. James Madison considered him an instinctual master of checks and balances. Another Morris biographer observed that he "believed it was necessary to temper the influence of the popular will, to keep the executive independent of the legislature, and to assure the cooperation of the rich . . . a bald but realistic appraisal of men's motives."[99]

Proposing a limited voting franchise, he told the convention during the debates, "The people never act from reason alone. The rich will take advantage of their passions and make these the instruments for oppressing them." And: "Give the votes to people who have no property, and they will sell them to the rich."[100] He proposed a system of legislative checks and balances, with a house of Congress for the rich and another for the poor, saying, "One interest must be opposed to another interest."[101] He felt an aristocracy was unpleasant but inevitable, so it needed to be kept "as much as possible from doing mischief."[102] His common sense helped shape the Constitution into what Theodore Roosevelt called "a bundle of compromises" that not only won the support of the contentious delegates but stood for the next 235-plus years.[103]

Morris and his allies had favored proportional representation of the states by population in the future Congress. That would end up the case only in the House of Representatives. But they succeeded in their most important task: creating an American government. South and North even came together when Madison and Virginia governor Edmund Randolph supported the nationalist argument, a triumph of enlightened self-interest. That wouldn't be Morris's last entanglement with the wealthy and influential Randolphs, who were considered the foremost of eighteenth-century Virginia's First Families.

Though James Madison is sometimes called the Constitution's father, credited with creating its framework, Morris was its author. In

September, a five-man Committee of Style was named to write and arrange the draft proposals into a final document, and assigned the task to Morris, whose speeches to the convention had clearly shown him to be up to the task. He was done in four days.[104] "That instrument was written by the fingers that wrote this letter," he later stated.[105] As Madison wrote in a letter to the historian Jared Sparks in April 1831, "A better choice could not have been made."[106]

~

The Preamble was Morris's alone, aside from the words "We the People," which he seems to have adapted from the third paragraph of the Massachusetts constitution of 1780. The next four words, "of the United States," replaced the first draft's list of each state, making his "more perfect union" primary—a subtle point, but he was a subtle man.[107]

Morris felt the document was imperfect, but he was content and, his work finished, headed to Virginia to do tobacco business, stopping to visit the plantation of Thomas Mann Randolph, a direct descendent of both that family's American founder and of Pocahontas. There he met Randolph's children, including the youngest, Nancy, fourteen, who would reenter his life many years later. He also attended that state's constitutional ratifying convention in June 1788, reporting to Hamilton, in his typically droll and dismissive manner, "I feel faith as I lose confidence. Things will yet go right, but when and how I dare not predicate. So much for this dull subject."[108]

Morris thought business anything but dull. "I wish not to accumulate but to enjoy," he would write in a February 1789 letter to an American diplomat, William Carmichael.[109] He wouldn't get his wish exactly or immediately, but he would soon have firsthand experience of a second revolution, as well as the thrills of dangerous liaisons in a foreign land.

7

At the end of 1788, Robert Morris was in trouble, as tobacco shipments to France had lagged after he had accepted payment for them.

He sent Gouverneur there, simultaneously hoping to straighten out his tobacco business, sell the U.S. land they had acquired on speculation to Europeans, supply the French with American wheat, and try to buy the U.S. debt to France at a discount, seeking to leverage that into a role in European finance. Some have argued that Virginia's Jefferson, already upset with the Morrises over their tobacco dealings, actively opposed that venture, gravely wounding a bankrupt France, even though Jefferson was then minister plenipotentiary from the United States of America at the Court of Versailles. Still, George Washington, Benjamin Franklin, and France's minister to America, the Comte de Moustier, gave Morris letters of introduction.

On his arrival in Paris early in 1789, Morris lived at the Hotel Richelieu, near the Palais Royal, a real estate venture of the duc d'Orléans, King Louis XVI's cousin. He had remodeled Cardinal Richelieu's old palace into the eighteenth-century equivalent of a modern mall or promenade offering retail, restaurants, and vice of all sorts. Morris joined the Club Valois there, a gathering of reform-minded aristocrats headed by the duke, where he dined and indulged in gossip and political palaver.[110] As he made his rounds, visiting as many as eight new contacts a day, he expressed to some of them his doubt that France was ready for republican government, causing Madame de Lafayette to deride him as an aristocrat.[111] He thought the king "an honest and good man," yet also "small beer."[112] In his nuanced view, though reform was necessary and the reactionaries among the nobility were out of step, total freedom would be a mistake.[113] "I preach incessantly Respect for the Prince, Attention to the Rights of the Nobility, and Moderation not only in the Object but also in the Pursuit of it," he wrote in another letter to Carmichael.[114]

In the duc d'Orléans's circle, Madame de Chastellux, the Irish widow of a marquis Morris had met in Philadelphia, provided him with an entrée to Parisian society.[115] He was quickly educated on its morality, or the absence of it; at one of his first dinner parties, he watched as France's ambassador to Russia, a grandson of the duc d'Orléans, took his hostess into an adjoining room and bolted the door for "a convenient Time." Morris kept a detailed diary of his time in Paris but didn't always say outright what he meant to imply.[116]

At first he found Paris depressing and thought himself invisible, "alienated by the unfamiliar manners and handicapped by his as yet unrefined ability in French." He was also put off by the city's blatant immorality, writing in his diary that it was "perhaps as wicked a spot as exists. Incest, Murder, Bestiality, Fraud, Rapine, Oppression, Baseness, Cruelty; and yet this is the City which has stepped forward in the sacred Cause of Liberty."[117]

Another new friend was Adèle de Flathaut, the wife of the comte de Flathaut, the keeper of the king's gardens. The daughter of a mistress of Louis XV, she was a friend of the current king and a sexual mercenary who also held salons for the artistic, the scientific, and the political in her apartment at the Louvre, where her husband lived one floor beneath her.[118] She was in a relationship with Charles-Maurice de Talleyrand-Périgord, the Roman Catholic bishop of Autun, and he was the father of Adèle's illegitimate son. At twenty-eight, she was nine years younger than Gouverneur; her husband of ten years was sixty-three. She and Morris would become intimate after he, sensing interest, laid siege. "I cannot consent to be only a Friend . . . I know myself too well," he wrote her. "I know it to be wrong but I cannot help it."[119]

The women got him up to speed on the current political and economic climate: France was nearly bankrupt, so in June 1789, needing to introduce financial reforms and hoping to attract loans by raising taxes, the king had agreed to convene the Estates-General, a meeting of the country's three estates—the nobility, the clergy (Talleyrand was their deputy), and the people—for the first time in 150 years. Thus the French Revolution began. Morris expressed his concerns in a letter to Jay: "The sword has slipped out of the Monarch's hands without his perceiving a tittle of the matter."[120]

Morris covered the opening ceremonies at Versailles in his diary and wrote long letters to colleagues in America, including Washington and later Jefferson, who would shortly leave his post as minister to France after five years to return to America when Washington named him the first secretary of state. Morris worried about Jefferson's politics: "He, with all the leaders of liberty here, is desirous of annihilating distinctions of order. How far such views may be right

respecting mankind in general is, I think, extremely problemati-
cal."[121] Their differences would only grow.

Louis XVI had agreed to double the size of the Third Estate—
the people's delegation to the Estates-General—giving it effective
control of France. Morris thought the French wanted a constitution
like America's but lacked the knowledge or experienced citizenry to
make it work. "To fit people for a republic . . . a previous education
is necessary," he wrote. "In despotic governments the people, habituated to beholding everything bending beneath the weight of power,
never possess that power for a moment without abusing it. . . . In such
societies the patriot, the melancholy patriot, sides with the despot,
because anything is better than a wild and bloody confusion."[122] As
the citizens of the Third Estate tried to create a constitution anyway,
Louis pushed back.

Under Adèle's tutelage, Morris added subtlety and upper-class
slang to his schoolboy French and burrowed deeper into Paris society, despite disdaining it as feeble, inconstant, licentious, corrupt, and
the cause of the popular revolt. Yet he chose to make the most of his
close encounter with the French aristocracy, which quickly embraced
him. Aside from Adèle, he embraced the *salonistes* Germaine de Staël,
the daughter of Jacques Necker, the king's finance minister and another of Talleyrand's lovers, who suggested that they might become
intimates, and the duchess d'Orléans, who confided her need to be
loved. Morris told his diary in March 1789 that "the less I have the
honor of such good company, the better."[123] But they all stayed friends.

Though he worried that the French were building an "Edifice
of Freedom" on a foundation of shifting sand, on July 13, 1789, Morris put a green cockade on his hat—aligning him with the common
people—and wandered the streets, later writing to his friend Carmichael that he had taken in "a fine Display of human Nature. It claims
my Attention more than all the Palaces Paintings and Sculptures put
together."[124] The next day, the Bastille prison was stormed and fell,
and two of its officials were captured, their heads cut off and carried
"in triumph through the city," Morris noted. "Yesterday it was the fashion at Versailles not to believe that there were any disturbances at
Paris. I presume that this day's transactions will induce a conviction
that all is not perfectly quiet."[125]

A few days later, in the Palais Royal, he watched as the head of a minister to the king was carried off on a pike, its mouth stuffed with hay (because he was rumored to have suggested the hungry eat the stuff), and was also confronted with the sight of the man's son-in-law "cut to Pieces" on the spot, "the Populace carrying about mangled Fragments with a Savage Joy . . . Gracious God what a People!" he told his diary.[126]

On July 27, Morris consummated his affair with Adèle at the Louvre. "She says we must be chaste," he told his diary. "We chat and laugh but approach to a breach of her Order. . . . At last I confer the Joy repeatedly."[127] They had another dalliance a day later.[128] The affair continued, their lovemaking opportunistic, even in a convent, within earshot of Adèle's niece, and on a carriage ride in the Bois du Boulogne.[129] He described their amorous adventures in a sort of code to his diary: "We join in fervent Adoration to the Cyprian Queen, which with Energy repeated conveys to my kind Votary all of mortal Bliss which can be enjoyed." He added that "appearances are scrupulously observed," and immodestly claimed his appeal was "the combination of tenderness and respect with ardency and vigor [which] go far towards the female idea of perfection in a lover."[130]

If Morris felt himself in personal danger, he rarely admitted it. Nor did his dealings on behalf of Robert Morris greatly disturb him, though his partner was in a financial bind. Gouverneur Morris successfully negotiated payment of some of the money already due under a contract to deliver American tobacco, but his attempt to renew the contract faltered. Still, he kept his aplomb. "A man in Paris lives in a sort of whirlwind," Morris wrote a friend.[131]

His diaries present sharp portraits of those he met, as well as the tidbits of salacious gossip that fueled their world. At a dinner at the Orléans chateau at Raincy, "the conversation . . . varied between the vicious and the frivolous. There was much bantering, well-bred in manner and excessively under-bred in matter."[132] Talleyrand, whom Napoleon would later deride as a "silk stocking stuffed with filth," was, to Morris, "sly, cool, cunning, ambitious and malignant."[133] The king tortured cats, and sexual impropriety, hypocrisy and moral fecklessness were commonplace.[134] Cardinal de Rohan had been Adèle's sister's lover. Her trysts with Morris weren't out of the ordinary.

One day Adèle, concerned that France was going bankrupt after it cancelled pensions given to courtiers like her, announced she would leave Paris. She was ruined, she declared, though her considerable income had only been cut in half. "I try to console her, but it is impossible," Morris told his diary. "The stroke is severe; for, with youth, beauty, wit, and every loveliness, she must quit all she loves and pass her life with what she abhors."[135]

The National Assembly approved the Declaration of the Rights of Man and the Citizen in August, but Morris thought a constitution more important. He was also increasingly skeptical of Lafayette; the democracy-loving marquis wouldn't lead the revolution, though he declared its victory nigh. That October, the royal family was forced back to Paris from Versailles by a mob joined by the National Guard, ostensibly led by Lafayette, "the prisoner of his own troops." The same day, Adèle demanded Morris marry her. Morris declined, pointing out that he considered both her husband and her lover Talleyrand to be obstacles.[136]

Morris decided Lafayette was vain, a glory hound who lacked the ability to lead, preferring to follow the crowd.[137] "There is no drawing the sound of a trumpet from a whistle," he told his diary.[138] Morris often advised his French friends on financial matters and foreign policy, and urged Lafayette to rally the French people by focusing their attention on a common enemy and, perhaps, declaring war against Austria and Britain, a Machiavellian ploy to unite a weakened and divided France.

Early in 1790, simultaneous with the appointment of Washington's first cabinet, the new president asked Gouverneur Morris to speak informally to British officials about the unfulfilled terms of its peace deal with the United States. Washington hoped he could clear up issues like Britain's frontier forts on American land and compensation to Americans whose slaves had been liberated in the Revolution. America also wanted a new trade treaty and the appointment of a British minister to its government. Morris's talks in London with the still-hostile Britain, which felt no need to cater to its former colony, yielded nothing, and he returned to Paris empty-handed, explaining to Washington that patience was key: "A present bargain would be that of a young heir with an old usurer."[139] America could wait; it wouldn't be long before it would "astonish the world."[140]

WASP confidence was contagious, but Hamilton, desperate for a deal with the British, turned against Morris.[141] His attacks—disparaging Morris in secret back-channel negotiations with a British agent in America and then telling Washington a fabricated story about diplomatic indiscretions in Morris's dealings with London, among them unauthorized contacts with the French ambassador—would harm Morris's reputation. But even as the president took heed of his accusations, neither Hamilton's objections nor similar ones from James Monroe and others changed the president's positive feelings.[142]

On his return to Paris, Morris learned noble titles had been abolished, that Adèle had found a new lover, a British nobleman, and that Adèle's husband had lost not just his title but a third of his salary. Unsure of how she would support herself and her son, Adèle was flailing, desperately seeking a high-life preserver. Morris remained as besotted with Adèle as he was skeptical of both marriage and the leaders of France. "There is not a man among them fitted for the great tasks in which they are engaged, and greater tasks are perhaps impending," he told Washington.[143] When the king and Marie-Antoinette tried to leave Paris again in April 1791 to celebrate Holy Week at a royal chateau in Saint-Cloud, the royal carriage was blocked by a mob, and over Lafayette's objections, the couple was forced to remain in their palace at the Tuileries.

Back in London again for business in June, Morris heard that the royals had once more tried to flee, this time for the northern border, but were returned to Paris, forestalling a war with the queen's Austrian relatives. Morris was likely disappointed; he was still advocating that France go to war—almost any war, but best of all a war against Britain—believing it would be a safety valve for the popular fury against the nobility. This position directly opposed American policy, which sought to balance renewed ties to Britain with "gratitude and loyalty to France."

Despite that official neutral posture, and Morris's own conservatism, his instincts leaned toward realpolitik. "There was no word perhaps in the dictionary which would take the place of aristocrat as readily as *Anglais*," he half joked to Lafayette. "You want just now great men to pursue great measures."[144] He had still not lost the wit or positive outlook he displayed when he wrote to President Washington in November 1790 to enumerate the virtues of a French revolution: the end of class privilege and feudal tyranny, the redistribution of the wealth of the clergy, the likelihood of a new era of social justice and liberation. "From the chaos of opinion and the conflict of its jarring elements, a new order will at length arise," he predicted.[145]

But in that same letter, he also gave a somber assessment of the immediate situation in revolutionary France, where "Daws and Ravens and the Birds of Night now build their Nests in its Niches. The Sovereign humbled to the Level of a Beggar's Pity . . . One Thing only seems to be tolerably ascertained: that the glorious Opportunity is lost, and (for this Time at least) the Revolution has failed." Though he saw glimmers of hope, Morris predicted that things would get worse before they got better. "*Guerre*, Famine, *Peste*," he quipped grimly at a party, responding to a request for the horoscope of France.[146] In this he stood opposite Jefferson, whose view of the revolution was much less critical. Morris supported the king because there was no alternative; he despised the ancien régime but distrusted the republicans more.

On July 17, 1791, he and Adèle watched through Morris's telescope from the heights of Passy as fifty republican protesters were cut down on the Champs de Mars by Lafayette and his militia. A few days later, a Parisian friend proposed he become France's new minister of foreign affairs. Morris laughed him off.[147] Yet he continued to advise Louis, sending him letters, even drafting a speech for him accepting the French constitution despite what he described as its defects; in the letter, he pointed out that Louis was now "only a private individual" and "no longer your King." Louis accepted the constitution but not the speech, while privately acknowledging that Morris was correct in predicting that the constitution's flaws would soon be revealed.[148]

In February 1792, Morris learned Washington had named him the new American minister to France, after a heated battle in the Senate. His machinations for Robert Morris over America's debt to

France argued against his appointment to a diplomatic position, as did others who had hoped to profit from it. He was considered a monarchist and indiscreet, was both worldly and superior, and "displayed a singular indifference to currying public favor."[149]

In general, though, Morris's opinion of events in France coincided with Washington's, so the president prevailed, though he privately warned Morris against his characteristic "levity . . . imprudence . . . hauteur . . . sallies, which too often offend, and . . . ridicule," urging he operate with "caution and prudence." Morris responded, "I now promise you that circumspection of conduct which has hitherto I acknowledge formed no part of my character."[150]

He took up his new post in May, much to the distress of his enemies, including Hamilton, Jefferson, the chargé d'affaires in Paris who also wanted the ministry, and the radical pamphleteer Thomas Paine, who wrote in a 1795 letter to Washington, "Morris is so fond of profit and voluptuousness that he cares nothing about character."[151] France had just declared war on Austria, and the guillotine had been introduced, mechanizing what some considered justice and others revolutionary violence. Then Prussia declared war on France, and Morris, in an astonishing lapse of judgment for a foreign official, began plotting the king's latest escape attempt.

"We stand on a vast Volcano," he wrote to Jefferson in June after a proposal was made to the Assembly to "suspend" the king. "We feel it tremble and we hear it roar but how and when and where it will burst and who may be destroy'd by its Eruptions is beyond the Ken of mortal Foresight to discover."[152] A few days later, the republican rabble known as sansculottes occupied the Tuileries for hours, forcing the king to don a phrygian cap, a revolutionary symbol.[153]

Louis gave Morris the royal fortune of 750,000 livres for safekeeping—and, quite likely, to use for bribes to help him escape. The king sent the money in two batches, the first in July and the second on the last full day of his reign. The Tuileries was stormed and the monarchy overthrown on August 10, five days after Morris noted that the court had been up all night, "expecting to be murdered."[154] He'd made love to Adèle for the last time a night earlier. Six weeks before that, Morris had predicted the king's fall to Lafayette, down to the day. Lafayette would end up in prison, first in the Luxembourg Palace and later in Austria. Morris couldn't win his release, but he arranged payments and loans to help him and his family.

"Paris is in great Agitation," the new ambassador told his diary.[155] By September, the new National Convention had declared France a republic and taken dictatorial power. Mass arrests began and mobs emptied the prisons, killing inmates. More heads ended on pikes, including that of the duchess d'Orléans's sister-in-law, who was "beheaded and embowelled," Morris reported to Jefferson, with her "Head and Entrails . . . paraded . . . thro the Street and the body dragged after them."[156] The duchess herself was imprisoned. Louis XVI would be condemned and executed in January 1793.

A week after the king was beheaded, the republican National Convention declared war on England, Spain, and Holland. All took that as an opportunity to prey on American shipping. When the coastal city of Bordeaux rebelled and split from the Convention, ninety-two American ships were trapped in its harbor. Morris could do nothing, even as his enemies charged him with negligence.[157] "I fear it will end badly," he wrote Washington just before food riots broke out.[158]

That summer and fall saw the beginning of the Terror, or "uncheck'd murders," as Morris put it. In October, the constitution was suspended and Louis's widow Marie Antoinette was executed. Jefferson rejoiced. Morris thought her dignified.[159] Then, coldly, he bought some of her royal furniture at an auction of property from her private apartment at Versailles.

Chaos reigned. The U.S. government inexplicably stopped communicating with its ambassador for some nine months, leaving Morris to fend for himself as revolutionaries began attacking each other. The revolutionary leader Georges Danton was arrested and sent to the guillotine by his rival, Maximilien Robespierre. During Morris's tenure as envoy, France had eight different foreign affairs officers, of whom "six were condemned as traitors, one was murdered, one was guillotined, one was imprisoned, and one defected to the Austrians."[160] Each hated his predecessor and was hated by his successor. Understandably cautious, Morris stopped writing in his diary but remained in Paris when the rest of the diplomatic corps fled. "He was able to hold his own only by a mixture of tact and firmness," Roosevelt wrote.[161]

Morris wasn't tactful in private. "The voracity of the court, the haughtiness of the nobles, the sensuality of the church, have met their punishment in the road of their transgressions," he wrote a friend. "The oppressor has been squeezed by the hands of the oppressed; but there remains yet to be acted an awful scene in the great tragedy, played on the theater of the universe for the instruction of mankind."[162]

Morris's tenure in France took a turn as he faced the arrests of friends and Americans; the issuance of decrees that hurt America's tobacco business and trade with the French West Indies; the new government's demand for payment on America's debt; and more requests for sanctuary and passports from those desperate to escape, including William Constable and the countess d'Albani, widow of Charles Stuart, aka "Bonnie Prince Charlie," a pretender to the British throne. She begged Morris, to no avail, to help her arrange a British passport. He was in danger himself and started thinking about leaving France, having infuriated the Jacobins then in power by insisting on international rules and diplomatic immunity—as well as by sheltering their foes, whose names he understandably did not list in his otherwise name-dropping diary.[163] The French rebels found support from Jefferson and Monroe, who would write to a Richmond, Virginia, newspaper in October 1793 that Morris was "wedded to monarchy and opposed to the great principles of the French revolution."[164]

Well before that, Adèle and her son had turned up at Morris's door. He gave her shelter and money to buy forged passports and flee to London.* Within weeks, the militia attempted to search his premises despite diplomatic immunity. He got rid of them, but the revolutionaries would return, even once arresting him. The harassment continued into spring 1793, when he bought a large property down the Seine and began spending most of his time there, writing letters on behalf of American captains whose ships carrying British goods had been seized by French privateers.

That April, the latest French government—the leadership having changed frequently and violently—sent a new minister to the

---

* Adèle's husband would soon be beheaded. She supported herself in London by writing novels and making bonnets, and continued her relationship with the Earl of Wycombe.

United States, Edmond-Charles Genêt. By then, America's newborn politics had begun to splinter, with Jefferson's partisans (southern agrarian supporters of decentralized government, opponents of a strong national bank and admirers of France) calling themselves Republicans, in a nod to the Roman republic, and Hamilton's (business-minded urban northerners favoring centralized power, a strong national bank, and an alliance with Great Britain) taking the name Federalists, signifying their support of the Constitution. While the Republicans admired the ideals behind the French Revolution, Federalists opposed the violence that increasingly defined it.

The Republicans, who considered their opposition proponents of monarchy and aristocracy, and found ways to excuse the excesses of Genêt's government, were receptive to him, but when he challenged Washington, even Jefferson turned on him and asked that he be recalled. Though Genêt stayed in America rather than risk execution at the hands of the latest ruling revolutionaries, the recall request allowed the French to reciprocate and ask for Morris's recall. "The revolutionary authorities both feared and disliked Morris," Theodore Roosevelt would observe. "He could neither be flattered nor bullied, and he was known to disapprove of their excesses. They also took umbrage at his haughtiness"—though he stayed for months until a replacement arrived in August 1794. Four days before James Monroe took over, Robespierre fell and was executed. A few weeks later, Morris wrote to William Short, another American diplomat in Europe, "I rejoice that I am no longer in the pitiful situation which I have so long endured."[165]

8

Gouverneur was forty-two and wealthy enough to ship all his belongings home and embark on four years of wandering war-torn Europe, avoiding as best he could the fighting between France and its enemies, Austria and Prussia. He had a small fortune of gold in a trunk in the baggage wagon that followed his carriage as he and his entourage—coachmen, postillions, and valet—set off in October 1794.[166] Why he stayed away from home so long is unclear, though he claimed to a brother-in-law that he was avoiding being called back to public life, and concerned with settling personal matters regarding his property and reputation.[167] But he also remained in touch with Adèle, unable to cut ties completely.[168]

His first stop was Switzerland, where he met his friend the exiled Necker. He also predicted, rightly, in a letter to Washington, that a despot would replace the French revolutionaries; all he was missing was the name Napoleon Bonaparte.[169] He proceeded to Hamburg, where flare-ups of his chronic gout and a bout of venereal disease may explain the last line in his diary for 1794: "Another Year is added to the many which have been lost in the Abyss of eternal Damnation."[170] He rented a house in a Hamburg suburb where he rendezvoused with Adèle again in March 1795. She arrived with the latest duc d'Orléans, who at twenty-one was in line to inherit the French throne and had been traveling incognito for two years, since being charged with treason by the revolution. Morris rented them an apartment and gave the duke (and future king of France) funds to travel to the United States before himself proceeding to England. Closure with Adèle still proved elusive, despite the end of their love affair.

In London, Morris hobnobbed with Britain's political leaders, was presented to George III, whom he had fought in the American Revolution, and on a trip to Scotland saw a new canal and wrote, "My mind opens to a view for the interior of America which hitherto I had rather conjectured than seen"—the possibility of creating sea routes that would fire up economic growth was a notion he would act on years later.[171] Still in England in May 1796, he learned that Adèle was engaged to a Portuguese diplomat seven years his junior. He returned to Hamburg, waited weeks for her to admit it, and promptly set off traveling again—this time for eight months.

He passed through the aristocratic circles of Vienna, where he tried in vain to get Lafayette released from prison; had a ninety-minute fling with an Italian noblewoman ("at last she surrenders and is a very fine Woman indeed"); attended midnight Mass on Christmas Eve at St. Stephen's Cathedral, where he was shocked to realize the worshippers were more interested in assignations than in prayer; and caught sight of the richest noble in Europe, a Hungarian

Guard captain whose estate was mortgaged to creditors who had put him on an allowance, inspiring Morris to muse in his diary in January 1797, on "the history of the feudal system in its decline . . . The government rejoices at the consequent humiliation of a haughty nobility without consider[ing] . . . the power which is to spring up in its stead."[172]

In Leipzig, Morris appears to have taken another lover, the wife of a banker and diplomat, who made enough of an impression on him that he ripped out some of the pages in his diary. In Berlin, Morris met the king of Prussia, Frederick William II, and his mistress, who "lets me see that I am welcome to make my Approaches but one must not have too many Irons in the Fire at once." Fortunately, the banker's wife had followed him, though a bumpy carriage ride together led him to comment that "this Town is very badly pav'd."[173] Upon his return to Hamburg, Morris found his ardor for Adèle faded, and she returned to Paris with forged papers.

In October 1797, Austria released Lafayette from prison and into the custody of a Morris business associate, the American consul in Hamburg. Lafayette didn't know Morris had helped negotiate his release and refused his advice to move to America. Meanwhile, the French revolutionary army, led by Napoleon, who had taken command in spring 1796, was conquering Europe. Morris spent another nine months traveling in Germany, giving money and advice to French refugees, making clear he didn't expect repayment, and sharing his experience that bad fortune can teach valuable lessons. Finally, in fall 1798, he returned to America, attending New York's Trinity Church on the last Sunday of the year.[174]

His companions on the voyage home hint that his travels around central Europe hadn't been as aimless as they seemed. They were the wife and children of James LeRay, from a family of slave-trading merchants (his father was also a counselor to Louis XVI) who had demonstrated their wealth by buying the exquisite Château de Chaumont in France's Loire Valley. LeRay had learned English from American diplomats like Franklin, who occupied a cottage rent-free on his family's estate in Passy, near Versailles. LeRay had lived in America from 1785 to 1790, trying to collect debts owed to his father, whose business empire was failing, and became an American citizen in 1788.[175] The LeRay family's presence also hints at how Morris came by the trunk of gold he carried across Europe.

⟜

Coincident with Gouverneur Morris's appointment as minister to France, William Constable had joined him in Paris. The Irish-born and -educated Constable had settled first in Detroit, where he traded fur, moved to Philadelphia, where he met Gouverneur while serving as a procurement agent for the Continental Army and an aide-de-camp to Lafayette in the Revolution, and then moved to New York in 1784 and formed a partnership with Robert Morris and Gouverneur. Before its dissolution in 1791, William Constable & Co. outfitted the first American ship to trade tea, textiles, spices, and fur with China and India, and provisioned British troops in the West Indies.

In France, Constable and Morris tried to sell land they had purchased in speculative dealings separate from Robert Morris, primarily in northern and western New York.* Their most significant holdings were vast tracts north of today's Albany between the Mohawk and St. Lawrence Rivers, bought from an Irish speculator and acquaintance of Constable's who had acquired more than four million acres in the largest purchase of land ever made in New York's history.[176] Robert Morris had bought and sold millions of acres in upstate New York, too, including five hundred thousand acres he hoped to offer to Revolution veterans as homesteads.

Land looked like a dicey investment. The international economy was tottering after years of war among the European powers. Barbary pirates terrorized shipping. The American states couldn't agree on much besides their shared thirst for funds. Though the country had a plethora of land, its value was plummeting, and American currency was worth even less. So, Morris and Constable had a brainstorm to sell acreage to French nobles worried about their future in a revolution-ravaged country, and more broadly to the wealthy in war-torn Europe, offering them an American refuge and the partners stable foreign money.

---

* They would also invest in land in Ohio, Kentucky, Georgia, and Virginia.

Their efforts failed, and Constable was forced to return to New York in spring 1801, when the city's first major financial panic erupted and he spent time in debtor's prison. The crash was caused, in part, by speculation in government securities by the Irish speculator who had sold them the New York land and was seeking to lessen his obligations by transferring more to his major creditors, Constable and the Morrises among them. That didn't help Constable in the long term; his holdings were used to liquidate his debts, his company went bust, and he died in 1803.

Their need to sell their land holdings only increased, but fortunately, Constable and Morris knew LeRay through another of Gouverneur's mistresses. LeRay bought a share of their land, as did the painter Benjamin West; a band of capitalists in Antwerp, who hired Morris as their sales agent; and LeRay's brother-in-law, who took 210,000 acres for a colony of émigrés escaping the Terror (LeRay would eventually own that, too).

Morris sold off more acreage all through his time in Europe. Madame de Staël, who was a tenant of LeRay's at Chaumont, bought thirty-five thousand acres, and more went to David Parish, from a Scottish merchant banking family in Hamburg that was so close to Robert Morris it served as America's principal agent there during his years as superintendent of Finance.[177] Parish hoped to create a sheep farm, intrigued by Morris's promise he'd become a baron "not by conquest but by purchase."[178]

Robert Morris also suffered from speculation and the ebb and flow of events in a world in constant crisis, and not only because he had pledged the same collateral to secure several different loans. In 1794, he had formed both the Asylum Company, to develop a million acres in Pennsylvania, and the North American Land Company, in part to develop six thousand building lots in America's future capital on the banks of the Potomac River. Unfortunately, another partner in his multiple land transactions was "incompetent, crooked and vindictive," and banks he borrowed from, concerned that Morris and his partner were in over their heads, grew skeptical about their business prospects.[179]

Unable to sell shares in Europe, Robert Morris was devastated further when he lost a fortune in a London bank collapse. Then a land deal in Yazoo, Mississippi, in which he held a huge stake, fell apart amid charges of bribery and fraud. Back in Philadelphia, a personal real estate venture was in trouble as well. The financier had hired Charles L'Enfant, the planner of Washington, D.C., to build and furnish a massive home, but its cost rose as the house itself failed to, and "Morris's Folly," as it was known, became a money pit. By 1797, though he still owned $1 million in Pennsylvania land, creditors and process servers were circling him like vultures. He owed almost $3 million. As his sympathetic biographer William Graham Sumner wrote, "It is impossible to resist the conviction that his . . . errors and misfortunes must be attributed in a large degree to the bad habits and desperate measures to which he was habituated in the administration of a bankrupt treasury" during the Revolution.[180]

As he was thought to have "smuggled and speculated and, it was said, felt free to trade with the enemy during the Revolutionary War," few shed any tears when, in February 1798, he was threatened with arrest by a creditor and called the sheriff, consigning himself to debtor's prison, albeit in a private room in what he called the Hotel with Gated Doors.[181] President Washington dined with him in his cell.[182]

～

Gouverneur Morris prospered even as his partner failed. In 1800, Congress, inspired in part by Robert Morris's circumstances, passed the Bankruptcy Act, which allowed him to be released with the agreement of a majority of his creditors. "I now find myself a free citizen of the U.S. without a cent that I can call my own," the sixty-six-year-old financier said.[183] Gouverneur gave his former partner an annuity of $1,500, sufficient to live out his days in relative comfort when he was finally released.[184] He would die in 1806. He left Gouverneur a telescope he had bought from a Frenchman who escaped a slave revolt on Saint-Domingue (now Haiti).

Back home, Morrisania became Morris's first priority, and he spent the equivalent of more than $500,000 restoring the land and gardens and building a new, gambrel-roofed manor house. The floors of the large and lofty-ceilinged dining and drawing rooms were laid with wood Morris had shipped home from France. Morris especially loved his 130-foot-long terrace. "I go out from a side door and . . . enjoy one of the finest prospects while breathing the most salubrious air," he wrote to a friend.[185] But despite his desire to leave the public sphere, he was quickly dragged back into it. George Washington's death at the end of 1799 let the partisanship that had been bubbling for years rise to a full boil.

Five years earlier, John Jay had finally negotiated a treaty between Britain and America, which turbocharged the battle between Federalists like Morris, who favored a strong central government, and Jefferson's pro-French agrarian Republicans. Under Alexander Hamilton, the Federalists seemed to have the upper hand after electing John Adams, the first vice president, as George Washington's successor, but the Republicans were about to demonstrate an astonishing command of the politics of the moment.

Part Three

OPPRESSION

1773–1833
JOHN RANDOLPH OF ROANOKE

9

The year before George Washington died, a twenty-five-year-old Virginian possessed of epicene looks, a high-pitched voice, an undisciplined but acute intelligence, an explosive personality, a delicate constitution, and a troubled past was invited to run for Congress as a candidate of the newly christened Democratic-Republican Party. Thomas Jefferson's Republicans had embraced and added to their name a Federalist-coined epithet designed to tie them to the most excessive of France's revolutionaries. The candidate was also excessive, but as a reactionary, not a revolutionary. He was, in modern terms, an archetype of entrenched white privilege, an exemplar of WASP clannishness and elitism, a beneficiary of institutionalized racism in a society built on slavery.

Pale, spindly at six foot two, and beardless, the flaxen-haired, hazel-eyed John "Jack" Randolph already stood out in a crowd, and not just for his odd appearance. For 125 years, the Randolphs had dominated the so-called Old Dominion of Virginia from their family seat on Turkey Island, just above the junction of the James and Appomattox Rivers, thirty miles west of Jamestown.[1]

The first American Randolph was born in England in 1650. Colonel William Randolph emigrated to Virginia around 1674, married a well-to-do widow, savvily developed and worked royalist political connections, won perpetual land grants from several colonial governors, and became a merchant, tobacco planter, and co-owner of several ships. Before his death in 1711, Colonel Randolph of Turkey Island, as he was known, also served as a member of Virginia's Royal Council, speaker of the Virginia House of Burgesses, and the colony's attorney general, and was a founder of the College of William & Mary.

Over succeeding generations, despite their late arrival in the Old Dominion, the fecund Randolphs became a sprawling, powerful clan owning tens of thousands of acres of land on a dozen vast plantations worked by hundreds of slaves. They built mansions, wielded the power of political appointment, supplied credit to lesser planters, and were pillars of the Anglican Church, which became the dominant religion after the revocation of the Virginia Company's charter in 1627, when the territory became an Anglican crown colony.

Colonial Virginia was nothing like Puritan New England. In the mid-seventeenth century, under Sir William Berkeley, for thirty-five years its governor, the province banished Puritans and offered safe haven to British Royalists fleeing Oliver Cromwell. Berkeley diversified Virginia's economy, increased its population, and established a well-defined society.[2] Virginia's First Families, including the Randolphs, arrived in waves after Charles I's execution. Like Berkeley, these émigrés, known as Cavaliers, were typically younger sons barred under England's customs from inheriting lands or titles, hoping "to reconstruct from American materials a cultural system from which they had been excluded at home."[3]

In stark contrast to Plymouth, there was hardly any middle class in Berkeley's Virginia. The planter elite owned most of Virginia's land but in 1703 comprised only about 10 percent of its population. At the bottom of Virginia's pecking order, fully 75 percent of the colony's population were initially indentured servants, predominately white contract workers from England who made the preferred agrarian lifestyle of the First Families of Virginia, known as the FFVs, possible in their new land. In 1674, twenty-four-year-old William Randolph imported twelve servants, laying the basis of his family's wealth through what was called the headright system.

Established by the Virginia Company in 1618, that system allowed any settler in Virginia, or anyone who paid the cost to bring a
settler to Virginia, to receive fifty acres of land for each immigrant
(i.e., head) who settled in the colony. The system survived the dissolution of the Virginia Company and the establishment of the royal
colony. Randolph used headrights to build his land holdings, ultimately importing seventy-two whites and sixty-nine Blacks on his
own and another twenty-five whites with partners. Existing records
don't indicate how many immigrants, indentures, and slaves made
up those numbers, but the majority were likely not slaves but individuals in bonded servitude.[4]

Virginia's culture, like England's, was defined by class and its accompanying baggage of elitism and arrogance, deeply conservative
and resistant to new ideas. Hugh A. Garland, a biographer of John
Randolph who had been a Virginia lawyer and slaveholder himself,
observed that "under the title of gentlemen, with their broad domain
of virgin soil, and long retinue of servants, [they] lived in a style of
elegance and profusion, not inferior to the barons of England."[5]

But the numbers of willing emigrants dwindled as Virginia's
plantation system grew, and indentured workers were often discon-
tented and difficult to manage. So by the time Randolph arrived in
the colony, the desire for increased profits, which were needed to preserve the indolent Cavalier culture, had already led planter society
to embrace slave labor. Berkeley at first tried to enslave Native Americans. When that failed, he promoted African slavery to provide a
cheap, easily controlled workforce to till the fields and pay the bills.

The first Africans had arrived in Virginia in 1619, and in 1625
there were only twenty-three in the colony. Even in 1640, there were
more slaves in New York and New England than in Virginia. Forty
years later, though, Virginians owned more than twice the number
of slaves northerners did.[6] Slavery allowed elite Virginians to disdain
labor and mercantile trade and live as if they were still entitled Englishmen. But after the Seven Years' War ended in 1763, their lust
for material goods, slaves included, caused the competitive Virginia
gentry to borrow recklessly to keep up appearances, even when the
postwar colonial economy weakened. William Randolph didn't live to
see that, but he had stopped importing settlers by 1697, when he

owned sufficient land and slaves had become the bulk of the Virginia workforce. Aside from any he imported, Randolph also bought slaves from William Byrd I, another early settler, fur trader, and politician, and when Randolph died in 1711, he owned about seventy.[7]

Debt and slavery had by then recast plantation culture and created a thirst for self-government among the Cavaliers.[8] The elite of the Old Dominion felt they deserved dominion over themselves and others, and chafed at the restraints put on them by both their creditors and the Crown. Virginia planters claimed the right to deprive their slaves of liberty while demanding their own, and in the 1700s they evolved from Royalists into Whigs, supporting constitutional monarchy; finally, when they came to feel that Britain's governing elite had turned on them, they followed the lead of less privileged, more republican Virginians and embraced revolt in the 1770s. Through it all, the gentry remained steadfast, superior libertarians.[9]

The Randolphs had been staunch royalists until 1773, when Peyton Randolph, a grandson of William, sided with the Revolution and the next year assumed the presidency of the first Continental Congress. His nephew Edmund, who held various state offices in and after the war, was elected the first governor of Virginia after the adoption of the U.S. Constitution, and served as America's first attorney general and Thomas Jefferson's successor as secretary of state.* Jefferson's mother was a Randolph, too.

In 1775, Jack Randolph's father died, leaving his wife twenty-four slaves plus livestock and his three sons forty thousand acres divided among three plantations. Three years later, their mother was remarried to St. George Tucker, a Bermuda-born polymath and lawyer with

---

* Edmund Randolph would resign in a corruption scandal—accused of soliciting a bribe from the French—that marked a turning point for the family, and he died eighteen years later "a broken man, publicly disgraced, morally convicted, ruthlessly pursued by his debts and his poverty," a distant relative, Francis Biddle wrote in a family memoir. Randolph was a victim of the fight between Federalists and Jeffersonians over the Jay Treaty. Randolph opposed the Federalists, who wanted Washington to sign it, and when he didn't, the Federalists implicated Randolph in that decision. Charges against him were never proven, but he resigned as a matter of honor when Washington retreated and agreed to the treaty. Biddle judged Edmund Randolph "ambitious . . . naïve [and] wronged" by history.

the resources to sustain their privileged existence, as well as a deep commitment to the intellectual foundation of the revolt against England, which aspired to replace the tyranny of monarchy with a virtuous and rational republic.

The children grew up on a family plantation, Matoax, in a well-populated, upscale neighborhood on the Appomattox filled with "the residences of gentlemen of ample fortunes, liberal educations, polished manners, refined hospitality, and devoted patriotism."[10] But early in 1781, Jack, age seven and a half, his siblings, and their mother were forced to flee an invasion of British troops commanded by the recent defector Benedict Arnold when Tucker was elsewhere, fighting redcoats alongside Lafayette, and took refuge at Bizarre, a curiously named family property ninety miles upriver.

Land anchored the Randolphs' security, wealth, and position. Riding on another property at Roanoke a few months later, Jack's mother warned him to never sell it: "Keep your land and your land will keep you."[11] Attached to his Anglican mother, "as inseparable as her shadow," Jack took her words to heart.[12] But the well-educated Tucker had much to teach him as well. The war and the heady but challenging peace that followed meant the gentry would no longer be able to count on their land to sustain them and protect their status, but would need to achieve to keep their privileged place in the newborn American hierarchy. Land, important as it was, would no longer suffice to ensure the gentry's power.[13]

Young Jack loved to read, devouring *The Arabian Nights, Tales of the Genji,* Homer, Plutarch, Shakespeare, Hogarth, Cervantes, and Swift before turning eleven, and proved a solid student once the war ended and he was sent to school, where he abandoned Protestantism and, like many of the founding fathers, became a Deist. Steeped in the works of Voltaire, Rousseau, Hume, and Gibbon, Deists believed that reason, not divine revelation, established the fact of Creation without resort to superstition or religion. An early biographer says that at eighteen Jack first read the Irish Whig philosopher and member of Parliament Edmund Burke, who would become the father of modern conservatism, and that later Randolph's political views displayed Burke's influence, especially in a desire to preserve at all costs and support reform only in defense of "permanence against change."[14]

As hot-tempered as he was entitled, Jack Randolph was a product of his time and place. Of his Virginia peers, he said, "Better bred men were not to be found in the British dominions."[15] He was committed to live the life and uphold the standards of a gentleman, even in the new republic. A good if erratic student, at fourteen he had gone to Princeton, but he preferred New York and was carousing there with his middle brother, Theodorick (who had "a strong aversion to books and a decided taste for pleasure"), when they were summoned to their dying mother's bedside in 1788.[16] Only thirty-six, she had borne eight children in eighteen years.

That year, Jack and Theodorick entered Columbia College in New York, where their older brother, Richard, joined them as they celebrated the ratification of the Constitution and establishment of the American government, and Jack fell back into bad habits, encouraged by his self-indulgent, impractical, and equally entitled brothers—Richard was licentious, Theodorick a drunk—and gained a reputation for debauchery. Then they learned from Tucker that their late father had been so deep in debt to English creditors that their inheritance was needed to pay them. Suddenly threatened with poverty and the loss of his identity as a genteel Virginia planter, Jack lost interest in formal schooling and fell ill and depressed, conditions that would plague him for the rest of his life.

Politics diverted him. He saw, though he couldn't get close enough to hear, George Washington's 1789 inauguration at New York City's Federal Hall as first president of the United States. He attended sessions of the First Congress, which included several relatives, where he heard debates over the tensions between the states and the central government, and the rights of slaveholders. And he dined with congressmen, among them an uncle and Tucker's brother, and his cousins Jefferson and Edmund Randolph, some of whom believed their new government was actively oppressing the southern gentry. Jack would come to agree.

In 1790, at seventeen, Jack convinced Tucker to let him go to Philadelphia, which became the seat of the federal government late that year, to study law under his cousin Edmund. There he was riveted by a clash of views over the French Revolution expressed in pamphlets penned by Burke and Thomas Paine. They championed, respectively, a cautious conservatism and a radical defense of revolutionary leveling. Like the Federalist Gouverneur Morris, Randolph "could not fail to perceive that [the French people] were better fit ted to destroy tyrants than obey laws."[17]

Two years later, at nineteen, Jack returned to Virginia a changed man, ready to be a gentleman planter, even as his stepfather sold his own plantations and became a professor of law. Jack saw his future in the past. "His position in society, his large hereditary possessions, his pride of ancestry; his veneration for the commonwealth of Virginia, her ancient laws and institutions; his high estimation of the rights of property in the business of legislation—all conspired to shape his thoughts," wrote his biographer Garland.[18] But as self-sure as he had become, a series of unfortunate events would change the course of his life.

In the winter and spring of 1792–1793, scandal enveloped Bizarre. Self-indulgent and a supporter of the French Revolution, Richard Randolph had followed a family tradition and on Christmas Day 1789 married a cousin, Judith Randolph.[19] They had met the year before at the Virginia convention that ratified the U.S. Constitution. Richard, Judith's father, St. George Tucker, and Theodorick were all delegates, and Gouverneur Morris of New York was an observer. Judith, a dour and religious young woman, was seventeen and Richard only nineteen, so his family worried about his ability to provide.* Yet, after persuading his guardian to give him his inheritance—the farm at Bizarre—early, he began a new life as an overextended plantation owner.

In 1791, Judith and Richard had a son, St. George. Judith's seventeen-year-old sister Anne Cary Randolph, known as Nancy, had meantime joined their household after their mother died and their father remarried. Nancy's stepmother expected her to marry, too, but instead she fled to her sister's new home, where she attracted the attention of Theodorick, nineteen, who also lived there. Jack joined them all at Bizarre that summer, and found an odd menage: both Theodorick and Richard, whose wife was pregnant at the time, ap-

---

* Judith's brother, Thomas Mann Randolph Jr., was married to Thomas Jefferson's daughter Martha, whose father had grown up on a Randolph family plantation.

peared to be pursuing Nancy, who would later say that she had been in love with Theodorick and pursued him. Nonetheless, Jack claimed the household was "in perfect harmony" when he left in September.[20] The truth would prove to be anything but perfect or harmonious. Theodorick was near death from consumption, and though she kept it a secret, Nancy was pregnant. Then, on St. Valentine's Day 1792, Theodorick died.

That fall, Jack, Nancy, Richard, and Judith visited the plantation of some Randolph relations. All but Jack stayed for a troubled night, rent by screams and heavy footsteps on the staircase. Offering the excuse that Nancy had been ill, the visitors departed the next day, leaving Nancy's pillowcase stained with blood that also spattered the stairway. Soon, word spread from the house's slave quarters into the Randolph family's social circles that in the night Nancy had miscarried (or aborted, or, even worse, given birth to) a child whose lifeless body was later found by slaves on a pile of shingles on the property. Questions were asked sotto voce. Was Richard, with his reputation for irresponsible behavior, the father? Would the state dare indict such eminent citizens?

The events at Bizarre proved a turning point for Virginia's aristocracy, already in decline from the seventeenth century, when the elite's huge landholdings gave it total power over politics, the economy, and social life. Even in deep debt, they had continued to live and spend grandly, buying imported products as the price of their tobacco dropped, the soil wore out, and then shipping costs and duties rose precipitously after independence. Abandoned fields, ruined plantations, and great families in decline were just around the corner.

Along with their land and slaves (Richard still owned forty), the latest crop of Randolphs had inherited the habit of not repaying debts—at least until 1796, when the Supreme Court ruled against Virginia's planters, who had withheld repayment to creditors while seeking compensation for slaves lost to the British during the Revolution. But long before that, Virginia merchants had begun refusing Richard further credit. Late in 1790, attempting to economize, Richard had moved his family from Matoax to the smaller and less accessible Bizarre, which more than lived up to its name; it appeared grand but was decaying due to the family's financial condition, with the dining room windows stuffed with paper and rags in place of glass.[21]

The Randolph's "lessers," not bloodless Anglicans like the aristocrats but fervent, backwoods Protestants, had begun paying them less deference—and gossip became a weapon used against them by their supposed inferiors as well as envious, competitive peers. Martha Jefferson Randolph would observe that the affair opened their family to criticism from "inconsiderable people."[22] But more responsible members of their class also worried that Richard was a harbinger of its decline into irresponsibility and irrelevance.[23]

Richard, Judith, and Nancy left Bizarre for another visit with relations in January and learned that the women's brothers were spreading the story that Richard had seduced Nancy. By March, Richard was demanding satisfaction, but a duel—a common form of dispute resolution among military officers and patricians—was declined, so he turned to intrafamily legal action. Some relatives, including Nancy, gave him statements of support, but others insisted he had to protect her at all costs. After Nancy's father refused to sue one of his sons for slander, Richard wrote an open letter demanding a public inquiry; it appeared in the *Virginia Gazette* in April 1793, on the same day the newspaper reported that Louis XVI had gone to the guillotine. One chronicler of the Bizarre affair argued that Richard was trying to influence public opinion, but if so, he failed. He surrendered to the local sheriff, and a week later a court met to examine whether he should be charged with incest and the felonious murder of an infant.

His stepfather St. George Tucker, a legal eminence in Virginia, organized Richard's defense, assembling a remarkable legal team: the future Supreme Court chief justice John Marshall, a distant relative of Nancy's; Alexander Campbell, a relative of Tucker's, then the U.S. attorney for Virginia; and Patrick Henry, a lion of criminal law as well as a Revolutionary hero. Desirous of his oratorical skills, Tucker lured Henry out of semiretirement with the promise of a huge fee, which Henry earned with biting examinations of witnesses like the girls' aunt, who testified she had seen signs of Nancy's pregnancy. Henry accused her of spying on her niece. "Which eye did you peep with?" he demanded to peals of laughter in the courtroom. "Great God, deliver us from eavesdroppers!"[24]

Though the charges had originated with slaves, under Virginia law none were allowed to testify against a white man, so white witnesses repeated what the slaves had told them. Jack, who hadn't been present at the time of the events, also testified, repeating Theodorick's claim of an engagement to Nancy, and insisting that while he had lounged on a bed with both sisters, he never thought Nancy was pregnant, but if she had been, the father was Theodorick. The only change he had noticed in his sister-in-law thereafter was a slight improvement in her complexion.[25] Years later he would tell a different story, painting his cousin as a hussy, but for the moment the family's solidarity held.

Marshall delivered a brilliant summation, and Richard was declared not guilty and freed. But the impression lingered that a child had been born, dead or alive, and its body abandoned that night—a fact confirmed by Nancy years later. Jack's diary recorded their post-acquittal trip back to Bizarre in a blunt seven words: "The trial. Return. Quarrels of the women."[26] If Richard had hoped for absolution, he had clearly failed. Thomas Jefferson recorded his verdict: "I see guilt but in one person, and not in her [i.e. Nancy]." Martha Jefferson Randolph judged Richard "a vile seducer."[27]

Jack returned to Philadelphia, where his law studies again took a backseat to attending Congress by day and carousing at night. Patrick Henry was forced to go to court to collect his fee from Richard. Judith continued to defend her husband, but a changed attitude toward her sister indicated she had her doubts: Judith made Nancy's life miserable, treating her as a servant, refusing her wine or use of a horse or her harpsichord.

Meantime, Jack grew erratic. In early 1793, briefly studying at the College of William and Mary in Williamsburg, he wounded a fellow student in a duel over which syllable to stress in the word "omnipotent." But the antagonists ended up friends.[28] He left school for good and moved home in 1794, taking charge of his property at Roanoke, but staying miles to the north at Bizarre with Richard, his wife, and her sister. As the family's circle shrank with their fortunes, Richard cut off anyone who reminded him of his travails.

Jack's inheritance had become a burden, and he would complain of having "to grope my way without a clue through the labyrinth of my father's affairs." Claiming, too, that as he had become an *ami des noirs* (friend to Blacks) through his association with Quakers, he hated the inevitable quarrels with slaves and their overseers triggered by his need to make a profit from his land.[29] He took long night rides on his horse with loaded guns, and visited friends across the South, but his aimless existence caused him to despair. Late at night he paced his bedroom, exclaiming, "Macbeth hath murdered sleep!"[30]

At the time, Jack still claimed to be sympathetic to the French Revolution, calling it "the noblest cause in the world" in a 1793 letter to his stepfather, lauding its superficial resemblance to America's, and equating the financiers of the North with the French monarchy.[31] He cursed the Jay Treaty resolving America's open issues with the British, even as Washington pursued a policy of neutrality between England and France. "May he be damned if he signs Jay's Treaty," Randolph said in a sardonic toast to Washington at a 1795 dinner.[32] Already Randolph had to balance glaring inconsistencies "between his Anglican tastes and his Gallican policy . . . his aristocratic prejudices and his democratic theories, his deistical doctrines and his conservative temperament, his interests as a slave-owner and his theories as an *ami des noirs,* and finally in the entire delusion . . . that a Virginian aristocracy could maintain itself in alliance with a democratic polity."[33]

Richard Randolph died suddenly in 1796, and while Judith inherited the plantation and its dozens of slaves, Jack took over management of his brother's properties atop his own, and found himself saddled with even more debts, responsible for Judith and her two sons, St. George, a deaf-mute, and Tudor, who was consumptive.* Reflecting his own admiration for the French Revolution and their stepfather Tucker's republican belief that the plantation system was untenable and the gradual emancipation of slaves inevitable, Richard's will had freed his slaves and promised them land to live on, in what some saw as an attempt to balance his disgrace and others took to be a public rebuke of the slaveholding peers who had condemned him. But his lingering debts made it necessary for Jack

---

* By 1815, both of Richard's sons would die without issue. Jack Randolph's only survivors would be half-brothers, sons of St. George Tucker.

to keep them in bondage for years. Losing his older brother, even after his downfall, was a severe blow, made worse by Jack's fragile health. In desperation, he sold Matoax and moved its slaves to Bizarre—and within three years he managed to pay off the family's debts and began to increase his landholdings.

But his family life remained troubled. Judith told Jack that she believed Nancy had poisoned her husband. And while some were sure that the murderer was actually Judith, subsequent events indicate that, although they got along superficially, Jack began blaming Nancy for at least his brother's disgrace and their family's travails. And in winter 1798, when they visited St. George Tucker in Williamsburg, Judith and Nancy's estrangement burst into view when Nancy began to socialize again and Judith refused to join her, then cut off contact with Tucker. Though all their relationships would wax and wane, life at Bizarre was increasingly uncomfortable.

Jack still had a romantic life, but his only known relationship, with a younger Virginian woman, ended with a broken engagement in 1799, and his fiancée married one of Edmund Randolph's sons. Jack appears never to have loved anyone but himself again. Opinions differ on the cause of his stunted emotional development, but most attribute it to medical problems. Some date those to his bout with scarlet fever, but others have speculated that he suffered from syphilis, or perhaps from Klinefelter syndrome, a rare genetic condition caused by an extra X chromosome. Regardless, he was left beardless for life, with a soprano voice that never changed, impotent, and allegedly sterile.* Later in life, his medical complaints would include nausea, headaches, diarrhea, spasms, and lung, kidney, liver, and digestive ailments. "I can no longer do," he'd complain. "I can only suffer."[34] He took medicines and quack cures, graduating to laudanum,

---

* Francis West, a doctor who attended Randolph in the hours before his death in 1833, left behind a reminiscence (held in "Dr. Francis West's Reminiscences of the Last Moments of the Honorable John Randolph of Roanoke," John Randolph Papers, University of Virginia) that includes an account of a post-mortem "examination of his genital organs . . . The penis was small but well-formed; there was no hair upon the pubes; his scrotum was scarcely at all developed; in the right half of it a small body was found of the size of a small bean; in the left half there was no body at all, but on this side a similar body to the above, in both cases supposed to be his testicles, was discoverable at the exterior ring, not having descended into the scrotum. [Our] conclusion was that he must have been destitute of the powers of virility."

morphine, and opium. Some would later argue that the belligerence that characterized his personality developed in compensation for his underdeveloped masculine attributes. His drug intake surely didn't help matters.

Fortunately, he had already found an outlet in what would become his life's work: politics. In 1799, at twenty-six, while visiting friends in Georgia, he learned of the Yazoo land fraud—the corrupt bargain sale four years earlier by the state's legislature of twenty million acres (most of today's Mississippi) to four land companies in which the politicians had been given interests. Popular revulsion led to the election of a new legislature, which cancelled the sale. But the land had already been sold again and the purchasers refused to sell it back to the state. The dispute—which helped to bring down financier Robert Morris—would continue for years.

Meantime, the underlying fissures in American politics were exposed when Britain and revolutionary France both began to seize American ships in the 1790s, hindering trade—a situation exacerbated by subsequent wars pitting France against Austria, Prussia, England, and Holland. The Jay Treaty resolving America's issues with Britain had seemed to tilt America toward Britain and President John Adams pushed back against France. In 1797, he'd sent three diplomats to Paris in an attempt to repair relations, but they were promptly rebuffed when three French foreign affairs officials, referred to in diplomatic dispatches as X, Y, and Z, made a series of demands, including one for a large bribe to proceed with any negotiations. When the so-called XYZ affair was revealed, a diplomatic scandal ensued, amplifying Federalist acrimony toward France. The next year, Congress authorized a limited use of force against marauding French warships in American waters in what would come to be known as the Quasi War. Opposition from die-hard pro-French Republicans then incited Adams to impose four unfortunate laws collectively known as the Alien and Sedition Acts, aimed at outlawing their dissent. The two-party system, seeded by the long-standing economic arguments pitting Jefferson against Hamilton, sprouted from that series of events.

Jefferson, then Adams's vice president, and Madison, who had just left Congress but would shortly become Jefferson's secretary of state, responded with the Principles of '98, formalized in what are known as the Virginia and Kentucky Resolutions of that year, calling the Alien and Sedition Acts unconstitutional.* They proposed states' rights as a vital check on the federal government, holding that states could judge and refuse to enforce federal laws. Organizing their own political party, through which Jefferson would run to replace Adams in 1801, they may have intended only an immediate response to the Federalist president and his overreaching policies, not a statement of Republican philosophy. Jefferson, for instance, would soon support the Federalist Hamilton's notion of a strong central bank, which he had initially opposed as an expression of strong central government. However, to Jack Randolph, states' rights and strict constructionism, elitism and reaction, became articles of faith, Burkean bulwarks against the despotism of central government and the infringement of concentrated power on personal liberty. "The principle that a central government was a machine, established by the people of the States for certain purposes and no others," would later become not just a tentpole but the stiff spine of Slave Power.[35] That argument has, at various times, thrown a wrench into the works of American history.

In 1799, Randolph agreed to run for Congress—and quickly abandoned his family's flirtation with abolitionism to reassure proslavery voters. Patrick Henry was seeking a seat in the Virginia legislature in that same election, and Randolph made his first political speech when he followed the famous orator onstage at a debate, reportedly speaking for three hours. "Should the Federal government step beyond its province, and encroach on rights that have not been delegated," he warned, "it is the duty of the States to interpose."[36] Apparently he acquitted himself well, as at twenty-six he was elected to Congress. He looked so young at his swearing-in that he was asked his age. "Go ask my constituents," he snapped.[37]

A supporter of agricultural interests, traditional values, individual liberty (as opposed to Locke's natural rights), and states' rights, Jack was supported by Virginia's tight-knit ruling gentry, the only constituency he deemed worthy of suffrage. In his worldview, all

* The first, ghostwritten by Jefferson, became law in November, the second, penned by Madison, a few weeks later.

men were not created equal; white men with property, skills, and education were entitled to independence and freedom, and an aristocracy among them—Randolph's own caste—had a duty to lead. He was a man of the Constitution, that bundle of compromises, not Jefferson's ringing Declaration of Independence, and considered himself a practical man, not an idealistic proponent of abstract notions of what should be.

"I am an aristocrat," he said. "I love liberty, I hate equality."[38] In one of his first addresses to the House, Jack would denounce a petition from freed slaves for emancipation and the abolition of the international slave trade. "He defended slaveholders and slavery with legislative maneuvers, blunt political power and, if all else failed, inflammatory rhetoric. His stated political goals of frugality, antimilitarism, and a weak federal government emanated from his desire to protect Virginia, the South, and its slaveholders."[39] In his first terms, he also voted to eliminate taxes, reduce the national debt and the size of government, and in 1802, repeal the Federalists' court-packing Judiciary Act.

But, simultaneously champing at the bit of party discipline, he was an accident waiting to happen, even as he started his second term in 1801 and his party made him chairman of the Ways and Means Committee, generally considered a springboard to higher office. His glib tongue (he called the judiciary a "hospital for decayed politicians") and skill at overturning Federalist initiatives and turning the new President Jefferson's proposals into law had made him a leader despite his odd personality and glaring contradictions: his opposition to big government didn't stop him from voting to strengthen a federal fugitive slave law that year.[40]

In 1803, the man Henry Adams called an "aristocratic democrat," having proved to be a master of parliamentary procedures, became House majority leader for the Jeffersonian Democratic-Republicans.[41] But unlike Jefferson and many of those who voted for him, Randolph was no longer a supporter of the French Revolution, which had first disillusioned and then disgusted him when it gave way to Napoleon Bonaparte, who proclaimed himself First Consul of the French Republic in a coup d'état in November 1799. Neither was Randolph a fan of a monarchical presidency, and as the Jefferson administration matured, he came to think the president was a bit too enamored of executive power, particularly when he controlled it.

Various forces—both Federalist and on the frontier—were pushing America toward war with Europe's powers, whether seeking new territory and the right to navigate the Mississippi or siding with the British against Napoleon. In fall 1802, Spain's king Charles IV had transferred Louisiana to France and America's long-standing access to warehouses in New Orleans was revoked, closing the Mississippi to American shipping. In 1803, Monroe and Robert Livingston arranged the $15 million Louisiana Purchase and, with an assist in Congress from Randolph, Jefferson's popularity reached its apex. A perhaps unintended consequence of doubling the size of America was a dilution of the power of the original states and their citizens, drastically altering the nature of the Union. Jefferson admitted that the purchase was an extraconstitutional action, and Randolph, in what appeared an act of loyalty to his president and relative through marriage, raised no objections. It was his latest, but not last, inconsistency.

~

Jack Randolph made enemies with ease. Federalists naturally disliked him, but so did a Republican congressman from Virginia, John Eppes, another son-in-law of Jefferson. The president brushed off the feud, but Eppes would remain an irritant to Randolph, particularly after Jefferson's reelection, when their alliance began to erode. Randolph's protracted political descent arguably began in the run-up to the 1804 vote, with his call for an investigation of Supreme Court justice Samuel Chase, a signer of the Declaration but also an arrogant, violently political partisan whom the president thought seditious. Chase's highhanded actions on the bench led to an impeachment trial. But like his philosophical guide star Burke, who had tried to impeach Warren Hastings, the British colonial governor-general of India two decades earlier, Randolph's effort would end in an acquittal.

A year later Randolph publicly denounced the latest proposal to reverse the Yazoo land fraud, which he called a "monstrous sacrifice of the best interests of the nation on the altars of corruption"—the notion that Georgia sell the disputed land to the U.S. government

for $1.25 million and other properties, all to be used to make the Ya-
zoo victims whole.[42] Randolph led the charge in Congress against
the deal, calling it more federal interference with state sovereignty.
"Placing expediency above principle," he felt, "was the essence of
tyranny."[43] The dispute—which included a glass-throwing fight between Randolph and a fellow congressman—would continue for
years.

Seven days later, the impeachment of Samuel Chase began with
Randolph as chief prosecutor. Chase was acquitted when the Senate
failed to reach the required two-thirds vote on any of the articles of
impeachment, though the Republicans held sufficient seats to con-
vict. Randolph was blamed for the failure; his weak and disorganized
three-hour summation, roundly excoriated, marked a turning point
in his political career. The Chase affair ate away at his confidence in
both colleagues and himself. A fight with Jefferson over the president's request for a $2 million appropriation to buy West Florida
from Napoleon proved the last straw. In mental and physical distress,
Randolph resorted to opiates and, crushed, gave a speech in January 1805, condemning his Republican colleagues for their support
of a Yazoo settlement. He shortly thereafter turned against the Louisiana Purchase and Jefferson and Madison, too, feeling they had betrayed both the original states, their Virginia especially, and party
purity, in favor of big government, corruption, and fraud.

10

Nancy Randolph may have been a factor in Randolph's breakup with
Jefferson. The president had hosted her at his home, Monticello, on
several occasions, and Nancy's brother and Jefferson's son-in-law,
Thomas Mann Randolph Jr., became overtly antagonistic to Jack after
mid-1805, just as Nancy's tenure at Bizarre finally came to its inevitable end with Randolph, still smarting from his stinging defeats in
Washington, abruptly demanding that she leave. Since Jack's election
to Congress, Nancy had paid her rent by helping around the house,
leaving on trips as often as she could, and stoically enduring Judith's
sporadic taunts about Richard, as well as her own constant worries

about money. Now Jack had somehow decided that Nancy had cavorted with a slave, and she departed early in 1806, just after the
confrontation, likely glad to get away from a family she had already
decided was "ever ready to blow me into a whirlpool."[44]

Throwing off Judith's "tyrannic power" over her, Nancy left for
Richmond, where a number of relatives and friends lived, and
bounced between them, feeling poor and unwanted.[45] A brother-in-
law finally paid three months' rent on a room for her; she slept on a
blanket spread over sacks for four nights before fleeing to the home
of the owners of a local amusement park, inspiring the disdain of
the city's snootier residents. She and her slave housekeeper stayed
there for several months as gossip about her continued to circulate,
encouraged by Jack, who intimated she'd become a prostitute.

Nancy wasn't alone in finding Jack Randolph increasingly troublesome. Friends and some enemies had been amused when he
showed up in Congress in riding boots and spurs, his dogs trailing
him. "He could stand on the floor of the house two or three hours at
a time, day after day, and with violent gesticulation and piercing voice,
pour out a continuous stream of vituperation in well-chosen language
and with sparkling illustration."[46] But as time passed, Jack was increasingly seen as mad and bad, both fascinating and dangerous to know,
a target of both ridicule and cautious admiration. "Madman he may
have been," wrote Henry Adams, the grandson of the second president, "but his madness had a strong element of reason and truth."[47]

In 1805, Jefferson announced his intention to retire at the end
of his second term, making Madison, whom Randolph considered
"a Yazoo man, a colorless semi-federalist, an intriguer with northern
democrats and southern speculators," the leading candidate to succeed him.[48] Making matters worse, rumors circulated that Jefferson
wanted Randolph out as House leader. Then, at the start of the Ninth
Congress, Jefferson's allies snatched away Jack's chairmanship of
Ways and Means. A final breach became inevitable.

It came in January 1806, when Andrew Gregg, a Democratic-
Republican congressman, demanded an embargo against British
imports as punishment for its violations of American neutrality. Randolph saw this as a sign of a rush into a war that America couldn't win,
one that would threaten its liberty and prosperity, and so he sided

with the Federalists against Gregg. A month later, he broke from the Jeffersonians entirely, giving one of his most famous—and toxic—speeches in Congress, appointing himself founder of a third party, an anti-Madison, anti-Federalist opposition called the Old Republicans, also referred to as the quids or quiddists, a short form of *tertium quid*, "third something."

Then only thirty-three, Randolph turned himself into a spectacle, passing "hither and thither, uttering sense and nonsense, but always straining every nerve to throw contempt on Mr. Madison and his supporters," demonstrating "an astonishing genius for destroying his own influence and strengthening his opponents."[49] In 1806, he even came close to fighting a duel with Nancy's brother Thomas Mann Randolph Jr., husband of Martha Jefferson, after Randolph called Jack "bankrupt . . . as a popular statesman," but Randolph then apologized at the behest of his father-in-law. Nonetheless, the president's own final verdict on Jack Randolph in an 1806 letter to his son-in-law was devastating: "A single life, of no value to himself or others."[50]

Back at Bizarre that spring, Jack Randolph was "a ruined statesman, never again to represent authority in Congress or to hope for ideal purity in government."[51] His aristo-democratic model was irretrievably broken, as was his quixotic party. The Old Republicans were obsolete but not extinct as long as Randolph stood. His relationship with his stepfather also deteriorated—perhaps because Tucker sympathized with Nancy, who moved north in 1807 in an attempt to escape her awful predicament.

＊

Though left for dead politically, Randolph tenaciously clung to his public life. At the end of 1807, he lost another fight when Jefferson won passage of an Embargo Act, punishing both France and England for their depredations against American shipping. It and its successor, the Non-Intercourse Act, prohibiting trade, respectively, with Europe, and with Britain and France, gravely damaged New England exports and shipbuilding as well as southern farm prices. More portentously, Randolph denounced the passage of a bill banning the slave trade after 1808. Discarding his alleged affection for its victims, he presciently predicted that "if ever the time of disunion should arrive, the line of severance would be between the slave-holding and the non-slave-holding states."[52]

In the 1807–1808 presidential election, Randolph supported James Monroe (who was St. George Randolph's guardian and American minister in London at the time) against Madison, who won, despite Randolph's published opinion that he was "unfit to fill the office of President."[53] Utterly defeated, Randolph gave the impression he was having a nervous breakdown.[54] His health again declined and his opium and alcohol intake increased, but he couldn't stay away from Washington even as Madison made Monroe his secretary of state and Randolph and Monroe began to fight. Henry Adams later observed that Randolph's "spirit of pure venom . . . went far to sink his character."[55]

～

Randolph fought with his family, too. After years of arguments over finances, by 1810, he was so estranged from sister-in-law Judith that he and his slaves—one report says he then owned 150—moved to his property at Roanoke. He added a few more buildings to the secluded farm's single cabin, where he slept; he described Roanoke as being in a state of "savage solitude."[56] He adopted the name John Randolph of Roanoke (his visiting cards read simply "Randolph of Roanoke"), and his new name advertised his pride as much as his connection to his land. Adams saw him as beset by ancestral pressures, greed, and drink. There were also the opium and constant brooding over the loss of his idealized, vanishing world. Yet he remained a potent advocate of states' rights and individual liberty for white men.

Unbound by party constraints, Jack remained a force in Congress despite his personal troubles, thanks to his oratorical prowess and undimmed, if untethered, intellect. "Randolph stultified House members with wit, sarcasm, metaphors, and epithets," wrote a biographer.[57] When a fellow member countered with a taunt about his sexual potency, Randolph spat back, "You pride yourself upon an animal faculty in respect to which the negro is your equal and the jackass infinitely your superior."[58] He came close to a duel with a journalist who criticized his bringing his pack of dogs onto the House floor "in contempt of what in civil society is called gentlemanly good manners," and in 1811, when a fellow congressman called him a puppy during a debate, he beat the man with his cane.[59] Charged with breach of the peace, he paid a $20 fine and joked that his victim's wounds were "fixed at a very moderate estimate."[60] In that same session he almost fought a duel with John Eppes after calling him a liar on the floor, but this time mutual friends intervened.

Eppes bore a grudge and in 1813 would beat Jack to take his seat in Congress, less because of Jack's growing instability than because of his opposition to the War of 1812, which he deemed "a war not of defense but of conquest, of aggrandizement, of ambition."[61] He had found himself fighting a pro-war tide in Congress, led by Henry Clay of Kentucky and John Calhoun of South Carolina. Elected Speaker in an effort to control Randolph, Clay promptly ordered Jack's dogs removed from the House, and their colleagues, no longer cowed, approved.

In the same anti-war speech, Randolph had blamed Congress for an alliance between the British and Native Americans, quite accurately describing the latter, who had steadily lost control of their lands to white settlers, as "pent up by . . . treaties into nooks, straightened in their quarters by a blind cupidity seeking to extinguish their titles to immense wildernesses for which . . . we shall not have occasion for half a century to come."[62] But indigenous peoples weren't Randolph's abiding interest. He had presaged his future focus when he warned that, encouraged by northern manufacturers and expansionists (whom Randolph, the self-described *ami de noirs*, subtly conflated with abolitionists), the rush to war would encourage slave insurrection. Calhoun countered that war with Britain was necessary to defend American independence and honor.[63] Congress sided with Calhoun, and war was declared in June 1812. Randolph responded with a blunt warning to his friend John Taylor, another anti-war Republican: "The reign of horror has begun."[64]

In exile from politics in 1814, Randolph took a tour of eastern Virginia's Tidewater region, where he had grown up, and mourned "dismantled country-seats, ruined churches, fields forsaken," the "old gentry" gone, replaced by "the rich vulgar," as he wrote to Josiah Quincy that March.[65] Throwing off his Deism, he lamented how the

WASP traditions he worshipped—churches, the lands owned by par-
ishes known as glebes, schools, mansions, and the families who
occupied them—had fallen into "general ruin," the Episcopal denomination of his birth had been decimated by "sacrilegious violence" and the disdain of Jefferson and his ilk, and its churches had
been abandoned as middle-class and poor whites flocked to Methodist and Baptist congregations. He had even fallen out with his stepfather, writing to Tucker and blaming him for inspiring Jack's turns
away from the church as a younger man with his "sneer of skepticism"
and "infidel books."[66]

Black as his mood was, it would grow darker still. For Gouverneur Morris, that arch-Federalist, and quintessential New York sophis-
ticate, was about to marry into the Randolph family.

In 1800, Morris had been pulled from his pastoral retirement at Morrisania when he was appointed to fill out the term of a U.S. senator
from New York who had resigned. He moved to swampy, almost empty
Washington, which, he wryly noted, was "the very best city in the world
for a future residence."[67]

That fall's presidential election had ended with the defeat of
the incumbent, John Adams. But due to the prevailing voting laws,
Jefferson and his Democratic-Republican running mate, Aaron
Burr, were also running against each other and ended up tied in the
electoral college. So it was left to the House of Representatives to
determine which would be president and which the number two.
Many defeated Federalists felt that despite his party affiliation, Burr,
as a New Yorker, was more acceptable than Jefferson, whom they detested, ensuring a deadlock in the House. Morris, like Alexander
Hamilton, sided with Jefferson against Burr, earning Burr's enmity.

The protracted dispute was finally broken after thirty-five ballots and a whispered conversation between Jefferson and Morris outside the Senate chamber. President Jefferson henceforth maintained
that he had not agreed with compromises suggested by Morris that
might have gained him Federalist support, but the fact remains
that when Lewis Richard Morris, a nephew of Gouverneur's who
had represented Vermont as a Federalist in the House since 1796,

conveniently failed to show up for the final ballot, the state's other representative, a Democratic-Republican, cast Vermont's deciding vote for Jefferson.

Most Federalists were furious, but not Morris. "This farce of life contains nothing which should put us out of humor," Morris wrote to his Democratic friend Livingston, who had briefly been considered for the ballot line Burr eventually won.[68] Morris had concluded that parties were another vital aspect of the checks and balances needed in a republic. Party politics also saved him from living in Washington very long. Burr and the Democratic-Republicans soon got control of the New York legislature, and Morris, defeated for reelection to the Senate in fall 1802, returned to Morrisania, determined to remake it as a true home. Then, in 1804, Burr was kicked off Jefferson's reelection ticket. He subsequently ran for governor of New York, and Hamilton opposed him. When Burr lost, he challenged Hamilton to a duel on July 11 in Weehawken, New Jersey. Shot in the abdomen, Hamilton was rowed back across the Hudson River, where he was taken to a bedroom in a friend's home in what is now Greenwich Village. Despite their many differences, Morris raced to Hamilton's side and was with him when he died the next day. Though Morris declared himself "wholly unmanned by this day's spectacle," two days later he delivered Hamilton's eulogy at Trinity Church, and then organized a fund to support Hamilton's family.

Morris approved of Jefferson's Louisiana Purchase, which included land in what would become fifteen states west of the Mississippi River, notwithstanding his continuing doubts about westward expansion, the accompanying diminution of Federalist power, and the president's belief "in the wisdom of mobs."[69] He claimed he'd known all along that the United States would eventually have to absorb the rest of North America. But the West still vexed him, particularly after he contemplated Jefferson's likely reelection in 1804. He felt sure that Jefferson's efforts to reduce the size and revenues of the government would hinder development, commerce, and international trade.[70]

All of that was on his mind as he traveled around New York State, visiting land he had bought over the years—and returned to his notion of a great canal that would open the American interior by connecting New York City to the Great Lakes via the Hudson River. "The proudest empire in Europe is but a bauble, compared to what America will be, must be, in the course of two centuries; perhaps of one," he wrote.[71] In March 1807, he was also appointed to a three-man commission that planned the Manhattan street grid, producing a report "marked with his prose rhythms" that described twelve avenues and 155 streets that would define the island.[72]

Then, as so often before in his life, a woman entered the picture, only this time, perhaps inevitably for a man just past age fifty, she became his wife. After leaving Richmond at the end of 1807, Nancy Randolph, then thirty-three, had headed first to Newport, where wealthy southerners predominated in a seaport becoming a resort. Since she had family there, her story was well known, leaving her existence as tenuous as it had been in Richmond. So, calling herself Anne Cary Randolph, she left for New York and then Fairfield, Connecticut, and during those travels she encountered Morris, who "took an interest in her [and] paid for her lodgings" while she looked for a post as a paid companion to a female traveler to England.[73]

That fall, he came to her Greenwich Village boardinghouse and announced that he was looking for a "reduced gentlewoman" to manage the staff at Morrisania: his French chef and coachman quarreled with his Black household servants. Nodding to his reputation, he added that he had never approached either of his two prior housekeepers "with anything like desire."[74] A few months later, he offered her the job of running his household, assuring her he was unconcerned about her reputation.

Anne/Nancy came to Morrisania in April 1809, taking charge of a staff of as many as thirteen, including one slave and four emancipated Blacks. Anne had brought her own enslaved maid, Phebe, with her.[75] Morris had already expressed his affection for her, and that December he wrote to John Marshall, by then chief justice of the Supreme Court, wondering about Nancy's reputation. Marshall's reply was careful, but he pointed out that her sister Judith had continued to shelter Nancy for twelve years after the scandal. On Christmas Day, Morris invited guests to Morrisania and surprised them by marrying Anne Cary Morris, as she was henceforth called, cutting her ties to her past.* It would emerge that Morris's nieces and nephews, counting on a big inheritance from their unmarried uncle, weren't pleased.

⤙

The next year Morris was named chairman of a commission to study the feasibility of what became the Erie Canal. After a long trip with Anne to study the region and visit his remaining properties, Morris drafted technical instructions for the surveyors of the canal's route in 1811.[76] Approval by New York's legislature took time—construction of the canal wasn't begun until 1817 and only finished in 1825. The delay was partly caused by the war with England, which pitted Morris against Jefferson and his successor in the White House, Madison. Though Jefferson ended the trade embargo as he left office in March 1809, Britain began seizing American sailors and supporting Native American attacks on U.S. settlers, and the approach of war revived all of Morris's fears about America's future. As southern and western Democratic-Republicans pushed their agenda, Morris worried afresh that the frontier territories would gain control of the government.

Morris's opposition to what was called "Mr. Madison's War" traced back to his opposition to slavery, which he had called "a nefarious institution" during the 1786 debates on the Constitution, and to the three-fifths rule for voting that had given slave states an edge over the North, as he had predicted years earlier. Despite having established a federal government, a central bank, economic stability, and military and customs services, the Federalists had stumbled, and their decline accelerated after the death of Washington. Morris's contempt for the slaveholding Virginia politicians—who had taken power thanks to the three-fifths rule, which made their slaves as valuable in the electoral college as they were in the fields—was palpable in his remark that the war was about "strangling commerce, whipping Negroes, and bawling about the inborn inalienable rights of man."[77]

---

* Curiously, on the same day Gouverneur Morris and Anne married, Jack Randolph was at Bizarre, where he emancipated his brother's slaves as directed by his will (though he kept some of them as compensation for his payment of Richard's debts).

The likelihood of more slave states joining, he warned, spelled the end of the Union.

When Congress approved raising an army to fight the British, Morris seemed to lose his bearings, suggesting the northern states try to repeal the three-fifths rule and if they failed, secede from the Union he had helped create. "Commerce and domestic slavery are mortal foes; and, bound together, one must destroy the other," he wrote.[78] This spell of secession fever came around the time of a visit Morris and Anne made to Washington, where he lobbied for federal funding of the Erie Canal. During the visit, Anne met the Madisons, and the couple socialized in the capital, even having "an apparently cordial meeting with Jack Randolph," at Morris's insistence, that led Anne to tell St. George Tucker she felt "as if I had entered another world."[79]

As the war went on for three long years, Morris felt Madison pursued it with glaring ineptitude. "Reduced to its simplest elements," he wrote, the conflict posed one key question: "Shall the citizens of New York be the slaves or masters of Virginia?"[80]

⟍⟋

Family was a happier matter for Morris—for the moment. His love for Anne was profound, even before 1813, when he was sixty-one and she, at age thirty-nine, gave him a son, Gouverneur II. Jack Randolph sent a note of congratulations. But then he intruded on their happiness in the ugliest way. In summer 1814, British troops invaded Washington and burned the U.S. Capitol. Private shocks followed that public one. Richard and Judith Randolph's son Tudor, who was eighteen years old, fell ill, and Morris suggested Anne invite him to Morrisania to recover. That fall, Tudor's mother, whose house at Bizarre had just burned down, and who at forty-two was herself in failing health, followed, as did Tudor's uncle Jack, who had rediscovered his optimism after Napoleon abdicated his throne that spring.

On his trip north, rushing to catch a stagecoach, Jack fell on some stairs, injuring his shoulder, elbow, and ankle. He continued nonetheless, passing through war-ravaged Washington, arriving at Morrisania in October. Anne greeted him warmly. Though Jack, the slave-owning agrarian Cavalier, and Morris, the freethinking, urbane Federalist, could not have been more different politically, they were now family and also shared a distaste for Madison's war. But Tudor allegedly confided to Jack that his aunt Anne was having sex outside her marriage, and before heading back to Manhattan, Jack pulled her close and whispered a vague but disturbing threat: "Remember the past."

Jack's bad luck continued; his coach to New York hit some rocks and toppled over, exacerbating his injuries, which he chronicled in an October 24 note to a Randolph relative that ended, "I am a cripple for life."[81] He recuperated in a Greenwich Village inn, where he started taking opium again and was visited by David Ogden, a nephew of Morris's, who shared Jack's hatred of Anne, whose existence threatened Ogden's inheritance. Ogden filled Jack's ears with more tales of her lewdness, told Jack that Morris had asked John Marshall's opinion before marrying, and that she had cited Jack in defending her chastity and named him as a onetime hopeful for her hand. He also intimated that Gouverneur II was the offspring of an affair with a servant.

Jack sought but failed to get another meeting with Morris, and then penned a letter to Anne, hoping, he scribbled, "to rouse some dormant spark of virtue."[82] His vitriol toward her, and his personal and family frustrations, came to a boil as they poured onto the page. But he sent it in care of Gouverneur, ensuring that he would read it. Jack denied he had proposed to her, or that Marshall knew much about her, and gave his own account of the events the night her child was delivered, claiming she had tricked Theodorick into impregnating her and then seduced Richard Randolph into hiding the tiny corpse to protect her, to the detriment of his marriage and reputation. Jack implied she had killed the baby, that the whole family was guilty of a perjurious cover-up, and that later, after she poisoned Richard, he had evicted her from Bizarre when she indulged in "intimacy with one of the slaves," smearing her anew. He closed with a Gothic flourish, calling her "a vampyre that, after sucking the best blood of my race, had flitted off to the north and struck her harpy fangs into an infirm old man."[83]

Morris held on to the letter for weeks before sharing it with his wife, who insisted not only on replying but copying her reply—likely drafted by Morris—to a half dozen of Jack's political enemies in Virginia.[84] Admitting that she had given birth in 1792 to a stillborn baby (she said it was fathered by her fiancé, Theodorick), the letter accused Jack of a malicious "attempt to blacken my character and destroy [my husband's] peace of mind," and referred to Shakespeare's words, "It is a tale told by an idiot, full of sound and fury, signifying nothing."[85] She signed the letter Anne C. Morris.[86]

While her blatant attempt to harm Jack politically failed, he couldn't fail to see she had come out on top. Randolph and Morris had many similarities: opposition to the war; their aristocratic lifestyle, and their idiosyncratic natures. But the resemblance ended there. Morris was wealthy, secure and, finally, settled. Jack, in comparison, was stretched thin, unmarried, unloved, unhappy, and quite likely an opium addict.[87] Conflict may have been their inevitable destiny.

On Christmas Eve 1814, the War of 1812 effectively ended after Madison sent negotiators to parley with the British in Belgium, leading to the Treaty of Ghent. But before the news could cross the Atlantic, and the treaty could be ratified, General Andrew Jackson defeated the enemy at the Battle of New Orleans. The America that emerged, in debt, its economy in shambles, but possessed of a great military machine and savoring the taste of victory, was a vastly different country. Though talk of secession was now more heard in New England than the South, Morris regained his sangfroid and conceded error in the Federalist position. "Let us forget party and think of our country," he wrote to his allies.[88] At least his canal could help bind its wounds.

The end of the war also spelled the end of the Federalist Party; divided and elitist in an ever more populist nation, it had grown consistently weaker after Washington's retirement and the Louisiana Purchase. Conservatives would have to wait until the 1830s to have a party of comparable strength, the Whigs.

By 1816, Morris, still suffering from gout and now sixty-four, was also in steep decline. Though he and Anne were invited to Monticello to visit that fall, they were unable to travel. Instead, Gouverneur stopped writing in his diary and made a new will, giving Anne a life interest in his share of Morrisania and making her his co-executor, with his son, then about three years old, as his principal heir.* He died on November 6, shortly after he tried but failed to open a narrowing of his urinary tract with a piece of whalebone, apparently in the same room in which he had been born, and developed a fatal infection.[89]

Though he left most of his estate to his son, Gouverneur's will made it clear he had total confidence in his wife, to whom he also left $2,600 a year; he even gave her sole discretion to choose his heirs if Gouverno, as their child was called, predeceased her, and bequeathed her an additional $600 a year in the event she remarried—a remarkable endorsement of that notion. Anne took her role quite seriously and soon discovered that the same nephew, David Ogden, who had inspired Jack Randolph's final assault on her, had defrauded Gouverneur out of more than $100,000, used his name to take out loans, and cost the estate even more by the time the damage was repaired. The next year, she gave up her annual payments, mortgaged most of Morrisania, and sold property to clear up those debts. By 1818, her staff had shrunk from thirteen to one eleven-year-old indentured girl.

Ogden continued trying to gain an inheritance, scheming to disinherit Gouverneur II, and spreading vile rumors about Anne. "Everything low and mean—everything indecent—has been put into the mouth of every Servant in New York," Anne wrote to a lawyer.[90] Among those who turned on her was Ogden's mother, Morris's sister Euphemia, whose husband, a Morris cousin, had invested in Gouverneur's land deals; they had twelve children and were in financial straits. It all left Anne feeling that New Yorkers were "mercenary, deceitful, and corrupt," and nostalgic for the lost Virginia that had so long haunted Jack Randolph.[91]

---

* By then, vast swaths of the original estate, mostly to the north and east, had passed to various Morris relations, but Anne and Gouverneur II would retain control of the mansion and southernmost portion of "Old Morrisania."

Through the early 1820s, Anne cared for her child and worked to restore Morrisania's farm, in order to pass it to him debt-free. She continued to correspond with her old Virginia circle, including St. George Tucker and Martha Jefferson Randolph, compiled a family genealogy, and sorted her husband's papers. Handwritten notations reveal her feelings about her sister-in-law Euphemia, who often asked for financial help: "Precious Sister and Friend she wanted to shew her love by using his money."[92] By 1824, Ogden's influence had faded, Anne's relations with most of the Morrises had improved, and her good life at Morrisania was mostly restored.

11

Back in Virginia, Jack Randolph of Roanoke remained unhappy and dissatisfied, even though he had been returned to Congress in 1815, riding a wave of Virginian chauvinism and disdain toward New England and its latest attempt to diminish Slave Power—a renewed demand to repeal the three-fifths rule. He wrote his friend Francis Scott Key, who had just finished a poem called "The Star-Spangled Banner," saying that his reelection gave him no pleasure. The Democratic-Republican Party remained in power but was evolving away from its original principles and its commitment to the Anglo-Saxon founders of Virginia's dying planter culture. In distress, Randolph renewed his ties to the Episcopal Church and rediscovered a little of his youthful anti-slavery fervor and his contradictory instincts, suddenly declaring that while "he would never weaken the form of the contract between the owner and his slave," he favored banning the sale of slaves in Washington, D.C. As it was controlled by the federal government, this stance did not conflict with his unwavering support of states' rights.[93]

After his sister Judith and nephew Tudor died within a few months of each other, also in 1815, the complexities of Jack's personality—his need to act out and dominate to establish his masculinity; his assumption of intellectual and social superiority; the contradictions between his self-interest, his political loyalties, and a "familial notion of moral culpability" concerning their inherited slaves; and his nostalgic mourning for the vanishing South of his youth—seemed to metastasize into "an unwavering, unprincipled, and often irrational devotion to obstruction in governance."[94]

He turned his attention to fighting the nationalism that flourished in the postwar Era of Good Feeling. Accelerated by Napoleon's defeat at Waterloo and the resumption of trade with Great Britain, it brought on expansion and calls for new taxes to pay for it. Jack considered such extravagance, the military required to protect it, and the taxes and tariffs needed to pay for it anathema. He felt the same about the nationalist Calhoun's bill, introduced in January 1816, to incorporate the Second Bank of the United States. The charter for the first national bank had been allowed to expire in 1811 after the Senate failed to renew it. Madison, who'd called the first bank unconstitutional and allowed it to die, nonetheless issued the charter for the second. Jack insisted to Congress that the restoration of a central bank—a hated symbol of Federalism—was "unconstitutional, inexpedient and dangerous."[95] It all made him ill-tempered and drove him back to opium, drinking, and despair. "I am the last of my family," he told his diary the next year, "and I am content that in my person it should become extinct."[96] But he would defend his greater family, Virginia's gentry, despite its obvious failings and decline, until the day he died.

Jack Randolph's early opposition to slavery was likely a brief, youthful flirtation, like his enthusiasm for the French Revolution. While he often spoke against the slave trade, which he called "this infernal traffic," never bought or sold human beings himself, and reportedly always treated his inherited slaves humanely, he nonetheless willingly owned other human beings and felt "the necessity of keeping them in a proper awe."[97] For most of his public life, Randolph championed what came to be called Slave Power, redirecting the doctrines of states' rights and strict constitutional constructionism into weapons defending it. The slave states were his audience and would adopt his positions. Randolph became one of the foremost defenders of slaveholders throughout the South, even supporting otherwise detestable federal power when it upheld the rights of slave owners. He told the son of a friend that whenever "two distinct races have occupied the [same] soil," they would divide into "master and slave."[98] He considered the continued oppression of enslaved Africans a matter of life and death for his fellow southern planters, at least so long as it remained profitable.[99]

The founders didn't go that far, but they had made huge concessions to ensure the approval of the Constitution by the slaveholders of the South, starting with its never mentioning the practice of slavery. In addition to the three-fifths rule, the document required that runaway slaves be returned to their owners, enshrined the electoral college as a pro-slavery mechanism, prohibited Congress from outlawing the Atlantic slave trade for two decades, and gave the government the power to suppress slave rebellions. Though the delegates to the Constitutional Convention (almost half of whom owned slaves) felt, with some justification, that they had crafted a deliberately ambiguous document in order to win agreement, their Constitution both acknowledged and approved of the continuation of human bondage.*

Perhaps in part because it was so protected, Randolph felt he could oppose the slave trade. He sporadically supported manumission and the resettlement of freed slaves as well. As a young man, he had fallen under the influence of a British abolitionist who decried their loss of the liberty Randolph put above all other human rights. Into the 1820s, when politicians from lower southern states more dependent on slaves began to outflank him and promoted slavery as a positive good rather than a necessary evil, he supported creating a refuge in Africa for freed slaves. But he eventually admitted in a mid-decade congressional debate that "pleasure, or business," argued for his submission to his slaveholding fate and called his opposition to slavery a "madness" that "I worked myself out of."[100] In effect, he considered slavery an unpleasantness better ignored than used to challenge originalism.

Randolph often justified his hypocrisy with his fear of slave revolts. In 1791, a cousin had heard gleeful slaves extolling the slave rebellion on the French island of Saint-Domingue, and Randolph

---

* In our time, and despite some evolution, the doctrine of original intent so beloved by conservatives remains, for some a potent justification for inequality.

attended the trial of the leaders of Gabriel's Insurrection in summer 1800, when nine hundred armed slaves planned a march on Richmond. That September, he wrote to an ally in Congress, Joseph Hopper Nicholson, that he feared they would "deluge the Southern country with blood."[101] He was acutely aware that Blacks had a clear sense of their rights, were contemptuous of danger, and thirsted for revenge, and he feared a demand for their emancipation and a quest for retribution; the first was a moral inevitability, the second a "great and serious" evil that filled him with dread.[102] That may explain his, and at least some other slaveholders', claims to humane behavior, treating their "property" with affection but also firm discipline, keeping them healthy so that, as he would write to a friend in 1818, he could "extort from the laboring portion of my slaves as much profit as will support them and their families in sickness and in health."[103] Presumably he knew that his slaves supported his lifestyle, too.

In 1802, Randolph opposed a petition from the people of Ohio, then a territory, to suspend a federal prohibition on slavery there, and in 1804, he also opposed South Carolina's reopening of the slave trade, again warning in a letter to a Virginia congressman of the "dreadful retribution which this horrid thirst for African blood . . . may bring upon us."[104] He would sporadically call for gradual emancipation and improving the plight of slaves, but at least once admitted to a fellow Virginia politician that those were unlikely unless the very uprisings he feared, "the blaze of their houses and the shrieks of their wives and children," countered "the stupidity and the apathy" of Virginia's Assembly.[105]

And yet in 1807, when a bill to prohibit the importation of slaves was proposed in Congress, Randolph opposed it on the principle of property rights, as allowing the federal government to halt the foreign trade implied that it could regulate the movement of slaves between states, as well, potentially preventing an owner from exercising "the Constitutional use of his property." A battle line was drawn there, and inexorably, Randolph's position hardened. Federal interference with slavery was anathema, he rationalized in a speech to the Ninth Congress, and slave ownership "was a thing with which [slaveholders] had no more to do than with their own procreation."[106] He couldn't help that he owned slaves, nor could he help them beyond treating them with firm kindness. "Teaching them that they are equal to their masters," he told his fellow lawmakers, was equivalent to "advising them to cut their throats."[107] Briefly, in 1816, he joined a number of other prominent men to create the American Colonization Society, which advocated sending free Blacks, whom it blamed for stirring up slaves, back to Africa, but as so often in the past, he quickly abandoned that cause.

In 1817, Randolph, only forty-four, decided not to seek reelection, and again retreated to Roanoke, where he lived in seclusion, drinking and taking laudanum. For the next three years, his behavior would swerve erratically from normal to threatening, even as he rejoined Congress in 1819 and returned to battle in 1820, fighting a proposal prohibiting slavery in the Missouri territory.[108] "The Yankees have almost reconciled me to negro slavery," he wrote in a letter that February.[109] He opposed Henry Clay's Missouri Compromise, too, which proposed to admit Missouri to the Union as a slave state, balanced by a new free state in Maine.

Randolph argued that the deal gave the central government an unacceptable power to impose conditions on the South. In the heated debates that followed, Clay worried that Randolph and the other southerners in opposition were "shaking the Union."[110] Only when he decoupled his proposals, separating the compromise into three bills, was Clay able to move it through the House. Though his lungs were giving out and he suffered from constant diarrhea, Randolph summoned the energy to dub northerners who supported the bills "doughfaces." Secretary of State John Quincy Adams confided to his diary that one of Randolph's speeches, "as usual, had neither beginning, middle nor end. Egotism, Virginia Aristocracy, slave-scourging liberty, religion, literature, science, wit fancy, generous feeling, and malignant passions constitute a chaos in his mind, from which nothing orderly can flow."[111]

By 1820, the American center of gravity was moving west, and after that year's census, Randolph opposed an 1822 plan to alter the population ratio that determined the size of each state's congressional delegation and thereby the size of the House of Representatives.

Though the plan's model had been developed by his fellow Virginian Jefferson, Randolph feared that the ability to represent the common interest of constituents would inevitably be lost as the country grew. But again, he was on the losing side of history. A month after that apportionment bill passed, he left for a trip to England, where he spoke against the Atlantic slave trade, and stayed through much of 1822.

After joining Madison's cabinet, James Monroe had become a proponent of all the policies Randolph despised, but when Monroe eventually succeeded Madison as president, Randolph wouldn't oppose him in any sustained way for many years, despite the fifth president's support for internal improvements and tariff increases. He directed his wrath at Clay and Calhoun instead, and admitted to his error in supporting the Louisiana Purchase. "No Government, extending from the Atlantic to the Pacific, can be fit to govern me or those whom I represent," Randolph said on the floor of the House.[112] Expansion no more equated with progress than change did with reform. But Clay's American System, a series of proposals designed to support economic progress, demanded new infrastructure. In an 1824 speech against internal improvements proposed by Calhoun, Randolph argued that if Congress could do whatever it proposed, it could also "emancipate every slave in the United States."

Calling Randolph "wicked and mischievous beyond all precedent even in his mischievous career," Henry Adams labeled this argument as "a deliberate, cold-blooded attempt to pervert the old and honorable principle of states' rights into a mere tool for the protection of negro slavery, which Randolph professed to think the worst of all earthly misfortunes."[113] Clay won that fight, then sought new tariffs—and won again. Though Randolph was a loser in Washington, Virginians approved. Even his detractor Adams would later call his speeches against Clay quite clever, and from retirement in Monticello, the slave owner Jefferson also praised him. A cowardly, cynical, self-serving consensus emerged among mainstream northern politicians that it would be better to let time, nature, and economics nudge slavery to its inevitable end, as abrupt emancipation forced upon the South would be an invitation to disaster. Slavery was a curse—but one that slave owners had to bear. Only time would heal the wounds it had inflicted.

When Congress adjourned again, Randolph headed back to England, and then the continent, avoiding most of the 1824 presidential campaign, which pitted Clay and, briefly, Calhoun against John Quincy Adams and others, among them Andrew Jackson, the hero of the War of 1812, who won the popular contest but received insufficient votes in the electoral college, leaving Clay the election's kingmaker. Randolph was back for the decisive congressional vote in which Clay supported Adams, who made Clay his secretary of state in return. Randolph vowed to bring down this latest Adams, as he had helped bring down John Adams when he campaigned for Jefferson in the 1800 election.

After yet another trip to Europe, Randolph was reelected to the House, but at the end of 1825, Virginia's legislature appointed him to the Senate. There he sparred afresh with Calhoun, newly elected as Adams's vice president and thus presiding officer of the body. Randolph immediately mocked him, referring to him on the floor as a "would-be President of the United States, which God in His infinite mercy avert."[114] Once again he made a spectacle of himself, speaking for hours at a time, and once, reportedly, undressing on the Senate floor.

Following the second Adams presidency, America's political parties evolved again, with the Democratic-Republicans splitting into pro- and anti-Jackson factions. The former took the name Democrats, while the former Federalists became first National Republicans, and later, Whigs, led by Henry Clay. Randolph, his star again ascendent as a freshly minted senator, found himself allied with the Democrats, led by Jackson, New York's foremost political operator Martin Van Buren, and others, his recent target Calhoun among them. For his part, Calhoun not only ignored Randolph's attacks but assiduously sought his support.

Amid Randolph's often eccentric perorations, he was still capable of giving glimpses of a coherent philosophy, usually traceable back to Edmund Burke. "Principles, pushed to their extreme consequences, that all men are born free and equal, I can never assent to, for the best of reasons, because it is not true," he said in spring

1826, commenting on the Declaration of Independence before Congress. "If there is an animal on earth to which it does not apply— that is not born free—it is man. He is born in a state of the most abject want, and a state of perfect helplessness and ignorance."[115]

Randolph tried to mend his relationships with Jefferson and Calhoun. Yet a few weeks later, "intoxicated by the sense of old power returning to his grasp," Randolph gave a speech in which he called Clay "this being, so brilliant yet so corrupt, which like a rotten mackerel by moonlight, shined and stunk."[116] Clay demanded satisfaction in a duel, which took place in April 1826 in Virginia at Randolph's insistence; he appeared to think he was going to die, and chose to do so on his home soil. Both men shot wide; Clay shot again, piercing Randolph's cloak. No harm was done and they shook hands afterward. Randolph returned to Europe for a few months. On his return, he was defeated by future president John Tyler in a bid to return to the Senate, but three months later was reelected to the House. There, even as his health continued to deteriorate and he was often high on opium, he again became the champion of Slave Power, or as Henry Adams put it, "a worse man than in his youth, but a better rhetorician."[117]

In 1828, Randolph supported Andrew Jackson for the presidency; otherwise his last term in Congress was quiet, and, pleading "ill health," he retired at the end of it in 1829. Then, alongside Madison and Monroe, he served as a delegate to a Virginia Constitutional Convention, where he draped his hat and arm in black crepe, in mourning for the power of his planter class, which was threatened with dilution through a proposed change to population-based apportionment and expanded suffrage (albeit still limiting the vote to free white men). Along with Chief Justice Marshall, Randolph eloquently opposed these measures, which were championed by inhabitants of the western end of the state—"a Government of numbers in opposition to property was Jacobinism, rank Jacobinism," he said—and prevailed.[118] Voters in Virginia's east retained their electoral advantage.

A year later, the newly elected President Andrew Jackson made Randolph minister to Russia. Sailing in 1830, he spent ten days in St. Petersburg before illness forced him to abandon his post, then almost a year in England before returning home, where he occasionally lost his senses entirely. Taken in by Marshall, he recovered sufficiently to return to his eight-thousand-plus acres at Roanoke, but he continued abusing opium and alcohol, and sometimes his slaves, even having his cook whipped when a dessert she made displeased him.[119] He continued to defend Slave Power, too, as in 1832, when he wrote to Jackson, "Nations, like men, can be governed only by *Interest;* and the Slave Interest has the knife at its throat in the hands of Fanatics and rogues and Fools and we *must* and *shall* and *will* defend ourselves."[120] Despite his public stance, his latest will ordered that many of his slaves be sold. At that point he was said to own 383 human beings, all of them either inherited or born on his lands.[121]

By February 1833, Randolph was denouncing Jackson at the end of a crisis that pitted the nationalist president against the state of South Carolina, which sought to uphold its claimed right to nullify federal laws like tariffs within its boundaries. Jackson's ultimate threat to use force against South Carolina infuriated Randolph.[122] Then in May, after changing his will to again order that his slaves be freed and land and other assets be sold to settle them on property of their own in the free state of Ohio, a promise he had previously made and reversed, he died just short of his sixtieth birthday on May 24, 1833, in a Philadelphia hotel, en route to England, where he hoped to visit his nephew Tudor's grave.

"I have been sick all my life," he told Dr. Francis West, who spent Randolph's last hours with him. True to form, the emaciated Randolph barely slept, but lay in bed, alternately cracking a coach whip and counting the $2,000 in bank notes he was carrying, his mental clarity coming and going. Conflicting versions of his last moments exist. According to West, "his departure out of life was so easy as scarcely to be accurately recognized." But in a more satisfying, if apocryphal, account, his last word was said to be a shriek: "Remorse!"

What did Randolph of Roanoke regret? Certainly not his own contradictions, even if he had been willing to admit to them. As Ralph Waldo Emerson wrote in his essay on self-reliance just eight years after Randolph's death, "A great person does not have to think consistently from one day to the next."

Randolph's unyielding defense of individual liberty, states' rights, and the status quo is hard to square with his insistence that his attitude toward slaves—both his own and those held captive by others—was essentially benign. It somehow seems an apt, if not just, reflection of his tortured legacy that while all his slaves (aside from an unknown number whom he'd give to a brother) were freed after his death per the instructions in one of his three conflicting wills, his last wish would prove troublesome to enforce. The 383 slaves remained in bondage until 1846, when their manumission was finally upheld in court. But then, forced by a white mob off the Ohio land Randolph had directed his estate to buy for them, the freed slaves dispersed and were never able to recover their inheritance, despite more than seventy years of litigation; their lawsuit was finally dismissed due to the statute of limitations.

Randolph's own lands, on the other hand, were either bequeathed to relatives or sold by his executors: William Leigh, a Virginia judge; the state's Episcopal bishop, William Meade; and Randolph's close friend Francis Scott Key, who, with Meade, was one of the founders of the American Colonization Society. Its adherents sought—for various motives ranging from support of slavery to a desire to abolish it—to send freed American slaves to Africa.

Whether Jack Randolph was merely an entitled WASP prince reeking of arrogance and self-satisfaction (a relative referred to him as a "pampered child of fortune"), a landed elitist misanthrope, or sporadically insane, he was proudly unyielding in his commitment to agrarian individualism and the wealthy, white, male-dominated social order and class structure he revered. Profoundly conservative and anti-democratic, he was a product and potent symbol of its power and privilege.

Neither Randolph's lack of self-restraint nor his wit and rhetorical dexterity were notable WASP traits. But they contributed to the staying power that, in the mid-twentieth century, saw him resurrected as the godfather of American conservatism by the political theorist Russell Kirk, who deemed him America's Edmund Burke, its original defender of WASP tradition and sworn enemy of tyranny. Thus, echoes of Randolph are still heard across the land, from the halls of the patriciate to the shores of populism.

Part Four

ACQUISITION

1790–1866

LEWIS CASS AND NICHOLAS BIDDLE

12

Randolph of Roanoke fought the imposition of a national American identity with the same single-minded fervency Gouverneur Morris brought to insisting upon it. Different as they were, each helped define it, and as early nineteenth-century America broke free of its coastal confinement and began its inexorable expansion across the continent, Lewis Cass and Nicholas Biddle, polar opposites born within four years of each other, also became defining figures. Each in his own way, Biddle and Cass were instrumental in defining that new nation and setting its course. Having secured the freedom first sought by William Bradford and America's original WASP settlers, and the sovereignty for which their descendants fought the American Revolution, the Quasi War, and the War of 1812, Cass and Biddle represented the next stage of America's development, as it began to accumulate wealth and extend its reach westward to grasp its continental destiny.

But, as remains true today, wealth was hardly distributed equally. In Brooklyn, New York, one of the new nation's wealthiest cities in 1810, for example, the top 1 percent of taxpayers owned over 40 percent of the city's assets, the richest 10 percent owned 80 percent, and those in the bottom two-thirds of the population owned less than 1 percent. Great fortunes were being made "not by upstarts but by men whose parents and grandparents had already accumulated sizeable estates," according to a 1977 academic study. "Winning the race for material success," it continued, depended on "inherited wealth and standing," typically determined by religion and race. WASPs remained America's winners well into the twentieth century.[1]

But as Randolph and Morris demonstrated, WASP America was hardly a monolith. In the age of Andrew Jackson, Cass was one of the latest president's Jeffersonian allies, while Biddle was a mortal enemy (despite voting for Jackson). The former would eventually run for president himself and, though he lost, die of old age, fulfilled. The latter would dream of the presidency, too, but die young and in disgrace, his abundant ambition not just thwarted but ground to dust.

Yet Cass, slightly older, who was born into a yeoman family but died rich, would be mostly forgotten by history, despite the central role he played in one of America's most disgraceful and brutal episodes, the near-genocidal destruction of the society of Native Americans. And Biddle, who was born into wealth and privilege but lost almost all, would be long if inaccurately remembered as an enemy of democracy and the people, despite his stewardship of an institution, America's central bank, now recognized as vital to its best interests.

～

Lewis Cass was born in Exeter, New Hampshire, in October 1782. His parents traced their American family to a Puritan indentured servant who arrived in the state about 1640 and became an innkeeper and landowner.[2] When the former servant died forty years later, he was the largest property-holder in his small coastal town. But despite his solid Yankee origins, as an adult Lewis Cass was famous as a frontier politician.* Whether consciously or simply in a reflection of his times, he reinvented himself, as his country did in the early nineteenth century, assimilating into the rising, rougher-hewn ruling class of the Andrew Jackson era.

---

* Cass was another WASP who was more Deist than Protestant, though his wife was Presbyterian. He later played a role in attracting the first resident Protestant minister in Detroit and in building a church for his wife's denomination.

The first American Cass, named John, began a family tradition of public service when he was named a selectman, a member of his town's local government. The Casses were typical Anglo-Saxon Protestant Yankees, worshipping a God "under whose guidance they would 'get on' . . . ready to make anyone's business their own, but fiercely resentful of any intrusion into their own private affairs."[3]

A Cass fought Native Americans as a militia commander in and after King Philip's War in the later seventeenth century, and Lewis Cass's father, Jonathan, served in the Revolution, rising from private to captain, taking part in several key battles, and spending the winter of 1777 at Valley Forge. In 1786, Jonathan Cass took up a sword to protect the head of New Hampshire's legislature from an armed mob during Shays' Rebellion. Two years later, Lewis's mother, the daughter of an affluent West Indies merchant, took him to see the bonfires lit to celebrate New Hampshire's vote to ratify the Constitution. "I saw the Constitution born," he would later say.[4] A year after that, when the newly inaugurated President Washington came to Exeter, Jonathan Cass was part of his escort, and introduced his son to the great General.

In 1791, back in the army as a major, Jonathan Cass served in the Northwest Territory, one of two frontier regions added to the United States by the Treaty of Paris that formalized the end of the Revolution. The territory, created by congressional ordinance in 1787, included all or part of today's Ohio, Indiana, Illinois, Michigan, Wisconsin, and Minnesota. By banning slavery there, it made the Ohio River the border between free and slave states, extending the Mason-Dixon line of the 1760s—originally created to end border disputes among Pennsylvania, Delaware, Maryland, and West Virginia—to the west.

Major Cass built military posts and, following family tradition, helped conquer and pacify the region's Native Americans, who were backed by British allies. After winning the Battle of Fallen Timbers in today's Ohio in 1794, and signing a treaty with the local Native Americans in 1795, the army began preparing the land for settlement. Major Cass was granted about four thousand acres of military bounty land—a reward for service—outside today's Zanesville, Ohio. Meantime, his elder son studied at Phillips Exeter Academy before the family reunited in 1799 in Wilmington, Delaware, where the major served as an army recruiter and Lewis, at only seventeen years of age, briefly taught school and had his first encounters with slavery.

Though Delaware had prohibited the importation of African slaves in 1776, slavery was still allowed in the original thirteen colonies; the next year, Vermont would be the first to abolish slavery and enfranchise all adult males. Elsewhere, it was often excused by whites as a benign bond of mutual benefit, with slaveholders caring for and uplifting their captives. Like many other northerners, Cass disdained the practice of human bondage, but he could only "pray for its abolition," as he put it in an 1842 pamphlet, "where this can be effected justly and peaceably, and safely for both parties."[5]

The Casses moved to Ohio in 1800, and Lewis studied law under a justice in the local supreme court and joined the local bar. Zanesville was his base as he "rode the circuit," traveling to courts across hundreds of miles of territory with other lawyers and judges, building a public profile. Thickset and strong, with rough features, a dour aspect, and a large mole on one cheek, he wasn't attractive but had charisma that attracted others.

Though his father was a Federalist, when he began flirting with politics Lewis stood with the Jeffersonians, and was elected a local prosecutor in 1804 and to the Ohio state legislature in 1806 at age twenty-four. He married just before winning the election, and caught the attention of Jefferson himself late that year when he served on a committee investigating Aaron Burr's alleged plot to conquer Mexico, split the Union, and rule as emperor of the west.* Cass drafted a plan to stop a flotilla of Burr's allies heading west from Ohio, and a grateful president appointed him U.S. marshal for the state. He was also made a brigadier general in Ohio's militia, which faced both the British, who were still hoping to rebuild their fur trade and perhaps regain American lands in northern Michigan, and their Native

---

* In 1807, Jack Randolph served as grand jury foreman in a historic case against Aaron Burr set off by that plot. The former vice president and Gen. James Wilkinson, a controversial army officer and veteran of the Revolution who had secretly been on the Spanish government's payroll, were said to have plotted to invade Spanish territory in Louisiana and Mexico and proclaim Burr the emperor of the American Southwest. Charged with insurrection, Burr surrendered and was brought to Virginia for trial, but was acquitted that fall. When Wilkinson later challenged Jack Randolph to a duel, he replied, "I cannot descend to your level."

American allies, the western nations. They considered the Americans occupiers and had allied through the efforts of Tecumseh, chief of the Shawnee nation, and his brother, known as The Prophet. The British paid them bounties for American scalps. Even as American settlements spread, their inhabitants were uneasy.[6]

The United States paid lip service to Native Americans' rights to their lands. Statutes passed by Congress, primarily in the 1790s and known collectively as the Non-Intercourse Act, prohibited the purchase of American Indian property without federal approval, but while they erected a façade of legal protections for Native Americans, they had little real-world impact. Warfare against Native Americans began again under President Washington and would continue for a century. It is likely no coincidence that Washington's 1799 will reveals him to be "probably America's second-richest man at that time," owning real estate across Virginia and in Maryland, Pennsylvania, New York, Kentucky, and Washington, D.C., valued at over $500,000, the equivalent of $12 million in 2022.[7] But endless conflict with the original occupants of that land was only formalized as policy after the Louisiana Purchase, when Thomas Jefferson rethought a comparatively benign, if condescending, policy of "civilizing" American Indians by teaching them to change their nomadic ways.

Jefferson briefly sought a constitutional amendment authorizing a swap of Native American land for "indigenous homelands east of the Mississippi."[8] Instead, under Jackson, a Permanent Indian Frontier along the river was created, defended by forts strung between Minnesota and Louisiana, and a concerted effort began in the 1830s to force every original American from the land east of the Mississippi along what would become known as the Trail of Tears; Indian removal would have sufficient momentum to survive a financial panic in 1837 and the Civil War. But whites and Native Americans continued to compete, as did Eastern indigenous people with the Great Plains nations who were forced to share land with them. The argument, both cynical and utopian, that Native Americans were not being banished but rather were being offered the chance to have better lives in their own colonies had long since given way to a harsher reality, albeit one camouflaged as well-intentioned humanitarianism. The new policy would inevitably result in the near-extermination of the indigenous American population by the end of the nineteenth century. One of its prime proponents would be Lewis Cass.

13

A better life in a place they could call their own. That was also a tempting prospect for "the second son of an illiterate farmer in rural England," Nicholas Biddle's great-great-grandfather William Biddle.[9] He grew up in a large Anglican family in Worcestershire, learned to read with the Bible, and, as an apprentice shoemaker, met some of the first Quakers, another dissenting Protestant sect, when he went to London at sixteen in 1650, four years after the movement was founded. Like the Puritans, Quakers were persecuted after 1660, when Charles II took the throne, and Biddle, who joined the new sect, briefly went to prison as the Quakers began considering a move to the New World, where co-religionists like Lewis Morris had started settling in the West Indies and up and down the American coast. In 1665, Biddle married Sarah Kempe, a well-off widow.

The Quaker leader George Fox visited America in 1671 and became an advocate of colonization. After the Dutch and English signed the Treaty of Westminster in 1673, putting what became New York and New Jersey under England's rule, Quakers bought a large tract of land in New Jersey inhabited only by Native Americans. A year later, West New Jersey was sold to two London Quakers, and in 1676, William Biddle bought about 15,000 of their acres, a stake he increased over time, though he and Sarah didn't move there immediately, even as persecution increased.[10] He and his fellow "proprietors"—as the Quaker landholders were called—had the choice of being either distant landlords or colonists themselves.

The migration of the Quakers to America had begun in 1675 with a first ship to West New Jersey, and built slowly. In August 1681, the Biddles, two children, and a servant boarded the *Thomas and Anne* for the trip. It stopped in Barbados for supplies, and there the Biddles acquired three slaves; settlers were required to have a servant for each hundred acres they claimed.[11] Where Puritans favored liberty for a chosen elite, and Virginia's Cavaliers liberty for themselves as natural rulers, Quakers promoted liberty for all, regardless of their religion, a notion they inscribed on what became the Liberty Bell.[12] Yet many Quakers, including Lewis Morris and William Penn, a friend of Fox's and soon to be the founder of Pennsylvania, owned slaves, until an anti-slavery movement took hold among Quakers in the late seventeenth century and the practice declined throughout the eighteenth century. In 1775, one of the Pennsylvania Convention's first acts was to ban the importation of slaves, setting in motion the all-too-slow abolition of slavery in the state.

Charles II had granted Pennsylvania to William Penn in 1681 in payment of a debt he owed to Penn's father, an admiral in his navy. The next year, twenty-three ships sailed into Delaware Bay carrying Penn and his first colonists. The province called East Jersey was purchased in 1682 by another group of Quakers that also included Penn. Ninety more ships arrived by 1685; meanwhile, as its adherents became more settled and successful, Quakerism began to evolve from a radical, evangelistic sect into an enlightened, moderate one. The Quakers were more tolerant than many Protestants—and the Delaware Valley, where they settled, was pluralistic, like New Amsterdam. But slavery was permitted and by 1726, 8 percent of the population would be held in bondage.[13]

The Biddles settled in Burlington County, across the Delaware River from Philadelphia. It became the hub of the valley, run by a tight-knit group of interrelated families.[14] Though Penn had been a royal courtier, they were mostly of humble origins, but many invested in land (Penn capitalized the colony by selling large tracts that were then subdivided and sold to settlers) and grew wealthy, the Biddles prominent among them.

After their arrival in October 1681, William Biddle personally claimed 135 acres on the east bank of the Delaware River and a 278-acre island in the river, where they grew hay and grazed livestock.[15] Eventually, their personal homestead grew to 500 acres opposite the island with a huge meadow, woods, and flat land suitable for farming, and they chose a bluff over the river as the site for a home. There was a spot suitable for docking boats and a stream on which a mill and dam could be built, creating a pond for fish and fowl and providing ice in winter.[16] They built a house on the bluff in 1684 that they called Mount Hope, and a log cabin for their two remaining slaves.

Buying and selling more land, and farming their own, the Biddles became one of the wealthiest families in their community, and William naturally took public office. Once, faced with a defendant who lied in court, he was part of a panel that sentenced the offender to thirty lashes. Quaker tolerance notwithstanding, they didn't countenance threats to civil order. Whipping was also permitted for whores and adulterers, though the guilty could pay to avoid the lash.[17] Harsher penalties were meted out for burglary: a second offense required that the letter *T* (for "thief") be burned into the defendant's forehead, and a third brought a year at hard labor plus thirty-nine lashes a month.

But times were good for the law-abiding Biddles. William and Sarah's real estate speculation had added thousands more acres to their holdings, from which they stood to profit enormously.[18] By 1697, William was president of the Council of Proprietors of West Jersey, a post he would hold until 1706, when Lewis Morris followed him in the job. He and Sarah regularly visited the growing city of Philadelphia for Quaker business and worship meetings and, in 1701, bought their own city house there.

West Jersey's self-government ended the next spring when East and West Jersey were combined into one by the crown after the ascension of Queen Mary's sister Anne to the English throne. By then, William had spent twenty-one years in public service and was nearing age seventy. Though the latest governor did not name William to his council, he was made a justice and, in late 1703, a member of the General Assembly of New Jersey. He also remained on the Council of Proprietors, serving under Morris, until 1709, when Sarah died. But when administrators working for Queen Anne, who'd been raised a Protestant at the insistence of her uncle Charles II, demanded oaths that Quakers refused to swear in order to hold office, William was removed from his positions. New property ownership requirements also limited Quaker participation in the colony, new laws instituting harsh treatment of slaves were passed, a militia was created and service in it made compulsory, and both written verification and a payment were required for pacifist Quakers to be exempted.

When William Biddle died in November 1711, he had a large brood
of grandchildren who inherited Mount Hope, his other acreage, and
his fortune. The challenges they faced notwithstanding, the third
generation of American Biddles were well positioned to face the
future. Like their fellow WASP settlers throughout the American
colonies, they had established their communities and themselves,
and though they remained subjects of the British Crown, they were
poised to consolidate their gains and plot out their futures. Though
it didn't seem likely at the time, that process would result in the
ideological and political evolution that culminated in the War for
Independence.

That process was not inevitable, but it was inexorable, as families like the Biddles emerged from insular religious communities, accumulated wealth, power, and self-assurance, and joined an
embryonic American elite that would, in the next few decades, come
to believe that its separation from England wasn't only physical but
political and philosophical as well. America's WASPs had begun to
see themselves as separate from and equal to their western European
counterparts. There would be no holding them back.

Today, a family member estimates there are about 8,000 Biddles in
America. History has remembered those descended from William
and Sarah's oldest and youngest grandsons, brothers named William
Biddle III and John Biddle. Neither was particularly distinguished:
John ran a tavern and inn, and later a dry-goods store. William III, a
ne'er-do-well and bankrupt, never recovered and left little mark beyond his nine children.[19]

While some New Jersey Biddles remained Quakers, William III
was the first to drift away. His children from his first wife were baptized at Christ Church in Philadelphia, and he married his second,
an Anglican, there in 1730. In joining the Church of England, he was
one of many American Protestants of all other sects, including the
Penns, who would become Anglicans and later in the eighteenth and
early nineteenth centuries Episcopalians, a process supercharged by

the Revolution. E. Digby Baltzell would later quote Ralph Waldo Emerson's observation that "no dissenter rides in his coach for three generations; he invariably falls into the Establishment."[20] Protestant sects in America, Baltzell continued, tended to divide along class lines. Where Quakers led simpler lives, the educated, cultivated elite, who often revered British restraint, dignity, and good taste, if not their colonial policies, flocked to the more socially respectable Anglican and Presbyterian Churches.

The various Protestant sects in colonial America—primarily Anglicans, Quakers, and Congregationalists, and after the Great Awakening of midcentury evangelical Presbyterians, Baptists, and Methodists—often had different geographic origins, and all parted ways from some Roman Catholic beliefs and practices, like fidelity to the pope and the ordination of priests. They shared a belief in the Trinity, in Christ's redemptive death, in his status as both God and human, and in rejecting the authority and mediation of clergy as intermediary between believers and the deity. But their doctrinal differences over matters like interpretation of scripture, the route to salvation, the distinction between mortal and venial sin, the need for baptism, the training and ordination of clergy, and the role of church leaders grew less important over time.

A formal link between church and state existed in colonial New England (apart from Rhode Island), where Congregationalism was institutionalized, and the South, where the American Anglican Church, a child of the Church of England, was born in Jamestown, Virginia, in 1607, was formalized in 1619 by the colony's elected assembly, the House of Burgesses, and remained dominant until after the Revolution. Despite their different beliefs, both New England and Virginia passed laws that worked to the disadvantage of other sects and even criminalized so-called heresy. Such was not the case in Pennsylvania and New Jersey, where Quakers and Anglicans kept an uneasy religious balance, and New York, where the Dutch Reformed Church retained its early foothold. The competition among Protestant sects there bred diversity and tolerance.

The American Revolution ended Anglican dominance—with the Americans having overthrown the British king, there remained no argument to keep his religion, but like Henry VIII, the Church of England's American followers held on to their doctrine, even as they seized control of their denomination. The American Anglican Church was formally disestablished as the official religion of Virginia in 1786, when the Act Establishing Religious Freedom, written by Thomas Jefferson in 1777, was finally passed into law, with an assist from James Madison, whose *Memorial and Remonstrance Against Religious Assessments*, offered to the Virginia General Assembly in 1785, proposed complete religious freedom and the separation of government and religion.

All that notwithstanding, "the original colonies did not exude universal piety," according to a statistical study conducted in 1988. "In colonial America, no more than ten to twenty percent of the population actually belonged to a church congregation." In 1776, almost 21 percent of those churches were Congregationalist, just over 18 percent were Presbyterian, Baptists and Episcopalians represented 15 percent each, and 9.6 percent of the total were Quaker. Though German Protestant sects would see explosive growth in the immediate future, at the time they represented only 2 percent of churches, slightly more than Roman Catholics, who were mostly centered in Maryland, founded as a haven for them. The five extant synagogues in America represented a mere 0.2 percent of congregations.

New England was primarily Congregationalist, reflecting its British roots, with Baptists, many of them concentrated in Rhode Island, in second place. Baptists dominated the middle colonies, where the Episcopal and Quaker denominations were also quite strong. Baptists showed the most strength in the South. Despite their strength in Pennsylvania, Quakers were outnumbered there by the various German Protestant denominations. By 1850, Methodists would dominate the American Protestant landscape, with almost 35 percent of all churches. Baptists took second place with just over 25 percent, Presbyterians represented almost 13 percent. Despite their continued cultural strength, Episcopalians represented only 3.8 percent of American religious venues, though they still topped Roman Catholics at 3.2 percent and Jews, whose thirty-six American synagogues had dropped to only 0.01 percent of the total.[21]

⌁

The Episcopal Church, the successor to the American Anglican Church, was so named because it replaced governance by the British Crown with bishops, the first of whom, Samuel Seabury, was consecrated and ordained in 1784 in Scotland's Episcopal Church, which did not require an oath of allegiance to the English Crown. It became the de facto national religion after its founding as a unified national church with a constitution and set of canon laws in 1789 at Philadelphia's Christ Church (and remained so into the twentieth century, even as other religions grew and surpassed it). Confirming WASP dominance, George Washington, his vice president John Adams, most of his cabinet, and many congressmen worshipped at the Anglican-turned-Episcopal St. Paul's Chapel of Trinity Church in New York, when that city was the first national capital, from the time of the Articles of Confederation through the ratification of the U.S. Constitution in 1788 and until the seat of government moved to Philadelphia in 1791.

When the Revolution broke out, two of John Biddle's children, Clement and Owen, were "read out" of the pacifist Quakers after they organized volunteer militia units they called the Quaker Blues.[22] Clement, made an officer, fought in the Battles of Trenton, Princeton, Brandywine, Germantown, and Monmouth, was named commissary general of forage at Valley Forge, likely working with Gouverneur Morris, and would later serve as quartermaster general during George Washington's presidency. Fighting Quakers like Clement and Owen Biddle were the forefathers of Philadelphia's Episcopal elite. Nine of Clement's thirteen children married into other prominent Philadelphia families, keeping the family atop the city's social hierarchy for another century. Its original Quaker settlers—many of them grown wealthy—would mostly convert, abandoning "plain living and high thinking" in favor of "the more worldly social life" of Anglicans.[23]

In the Revolution, the Quakers lost not only numbers but political power in both the city and state due to the sect's pacifism, which conflicted with both the rising independent spirit in America and the traditional desire of aristocrats for military glory. Graves in Christ Church's yard attest to its rising status: they include Benjamin Franklin, four more signers of the Declaration, and James Biddle.

Born in the Northern Liberties neighborhood of Philadelphia in 1786, the year Sarah Gouverneur Morris died, Nicholas Biddle, a brother of James, was a child prodigy, and at birth a member of the city's elite. His uncles included a judge, a doctor, a speaker of the Pennsylvania Assembly, and a delegate to the first and second Continental Congresses. Nicholas's father, Charles, a seaman, survived adventures from shipwrecks to plague to capture at sea by the British to become a merchant and banker and, in 1785, vice president of the Supreme Executive Council of Pennsylvania under Benjamin Franklin.[24]

Precocious and bookish, Nicholas was a voracious reader who often recited verses to entertain visitors, and was himself entertained by listening to his father's conversations.[25] He sought to go to college when he was only ten, but his parents refused. Not until 1799, five months after his thirteenth birthday, did they let him enter Princeton's College of New Jersey as a sophomore. After a rough start due to his age, he won election to a literary and debating society, becoming president of the group, where his classical nickname was Grammaticus, or one who knows his letters.[26] He displayed his joie de vivre in papers like "The Evils of Intemperance and the Joys of Drinking Wine."[27]

Determined and impatient, he quickly matured and was known for his spirit as well as his chiseled features and long chestnut hair. He had a high forehead and round chin, and contemporaries said his eyes were chestnut or blue or gray beneath brows signaling active intelligence. He remained boyish and quite handsome, if stocky and at five foot seven not very tall, into adulthood, when he would be called the most noble, polished, and refined citizen of Philadelphia, then the heart of the American experiment.[28]

Biddle graduated from Princeton at fifteen in 1801, younger than anyone before him. As one of two students sharing first honors that year, he delivered the valedictory address, telling his fellow graduates, "With your superior advantages of improvement, doubt not you will one day be the statesmen and legislators of the country."[29] The experience left him with the conviction that rhetoric was a magic wand. "I believe the turn of my mind, or what may properly be called my genius, has at length decided itself," he would later write a brother, "to govern men, and particularly by means of eloquence."[30]

After three years studying law in Philadelphia under a prominent member of his hometown bar, while enjoying the races, dances, and theater in sophisticated society, he worried that he would die "like a mushroom on the soil which had seen me grow."[31] Fortunately for him, Biddle, then only eighteen, was offered an escape, a chance to go to Paris as the unpaid secretary of President Jefferson's minister to France, his father's friend General John Armstrong.

Then Charles Biddle had second thoughts. An older son, Edward, a naval midshipman, had just died at sea, and Nicholas's younger brother James, fighting in the undeclared Quasi War between France and America, had been captured and taken prisoner in Tripoli. But Charles finally relented, and at the end of July 1804 Nicholas left for France. Though he was a young Federalist, he didn't hesitate to work for a Republican. The Biddles had friends across the political spectrum; indeed, three weeks before his son's departure, Charles had given Aaron Burr shelter at the family home on Chestnut Street, thirteen days after his duel with Hamilton, and Burr stayed there for two and a half weeks, during which an arrest warrant was issued for him. Burr finally fled for an island off Georgia, convinced the charges would be dropped. Subsequently Jefferson would invite Burr to dine at the White House.[32]

That duel gave eighteen-year-old Nicholas pause as he was preparing to sail for France. He had been considering a career in politics, but this close encounter with its dangers led him to reconsider.[33] America's first political parties and the Burr-Hamilton feud were rooted in the same soil. Young Biddle had already claimed a place among his city's rising elite, and he mightily impressed Burr, who praised him as "a very extraordinary youth."[34] He wouldn't need to run for office to be visible. But before making that decision, living in Paris and traveling through Europe on a small allowance from his family, he would learn more about himself, kiss a Swiss girl, get drunk in France, and carve his name into a staircase of the royal château at Blois.

In Paris in November 1804, Biddle helped untangle the financial knots of the Louisiana Purchase, learned all about American trade with France, and personally negotiated the French government's and American merchants' claims against each other. Working with the merchant banking firms that underwrote the Purchase, Barings of London and Hopes of Amsterdam, he got a crash course in international finance—and, without knowing it yet, found his vocation.

Shortly after his arrival, Biddle saw Napoleon crown himself as emperor of France, and told his diary he was mightily impressed with "the hero whose name has sounded in every quarter of the globe & who has rivaled if not excelled all that antiquity can produce of hardy valor and successful enterprise."[35] Before he left Europe in 1807, he had also witnessed Napoleon's wars of conquest against Austria, Prussia, and Russia, and he'd seen how Thomas Jefferson's pro-French policies negatively impacted America's standing in royalist Europe, reinforcing Biddle's Federalist leanings.* Because he was young, and also vain, he adopted a serious demeanor and sometimes added years to his age so that he would be treated as the educated man he saw in the mirror.[36]

His job was not all-consuming, though, and in summer 1805, he traveled around Europe, seeking firsthand exposure to classical history and culture, an understanding of the Continent's advances in science and agriculture, and the sort of experience only a wealthy young man could then afford and a future American eminence would surely require.

He toured in the uniform of a colonel of the New Jersey militia, which he designed himself, in part to indicate his station.[37] He returned to Paris to arrange for the manufacture of plaster casts of antique statues in the Louvre for the Pennsylvania Academy of the Arts with the aid of Jean-Antoine Houdon, the sculptor who had

---

* Though Biddle would later come to think Napoleon a tyrant, he nonetheless read extensively on him and collected memorabilia, as well as paintings of him and the bed of his elder brother Joseph. Joseph escaped Europe after Waterloo and settled in New Jersey, where he became friends with Biddle.

used Gouverneur Morris as a model for George Washington. After preparing with language tutors, he embarked again, this time to the west and south of France and then on to Italy, with a servant and books by the likes of Rousseau and Cicero as his guides. Heading next to Turkish-ruled Greece, traveling with the U.S. consul to Palermo on a ship from Naples to Sicily, he befriended a Greek priest and "did a very foolish thing," he told his journal, by expressing skepticism of religious belief. "He related a miracle worked by a Patriarch of Constantinople who in an instant lighted with a touch of his beard a room full of lamps which Satan had extinguished," Biddle recounted. "I could not resist a loud & strong expression of my incredulity. I perceived he will never forgive me."[38] Indeed, Biddle was soon put ashore by the Greek ship's captain.

Biddle made his way to Malta, where the frigate *Constitution* was in port, its crew full of friends of his brother James, who had just been released in Tripoli. Eventually Nicholas made it to Greece, where he spent weeks viewing antiquities and archaeological wonders, despairing over both their condition and their ongoing looting by Lord Elgin, an Englishman who was taking sculptures from the Parthenon in Athens, an act Biddle considered robbery.[39] His visit made him only the second American tourist to stay in Greece.*

In summer 1806, after visits to Trieste, Venice, and Vienna, Biddle returned to France, full of new enthusiasm for classical design—as well as a renewed desire to become a better citizen and leader, devoted, he wrote a friend, "to the world and politics and building a sort of a name as a statesman."[40] Though he found its people crude, an idealized Greece would inspire him for the rest of his life.

Concluding his work in Paris, he again found time to indulge in social life, crossing paths with Gouverneur Morris's friends Germaine de Staël and Lafayette, before he finally quit his job early in 1807. He then briefly worked as secretary to James Monroe, the American minister in London, until leaving for Washington, where he delivered letters from Monroe to Jefferson and his secretary of state, Madison, and then returned home. Biddle's experiences in

---

* The first, an antiquities enthusiast and aspiring diplomat, Joseph Allen Smith, spent fourteen years in Europe, beginning in 1793.

Europe had convinced him of America's promise and superiority. When his family first came to the New World in 1681, they bet their lives on America. A century and a quarter later, Biddle was about to turn their winnings so far into a windfall for both himself and his young country.

On his return from Europe in 1807, a new war against Britain was in the air, and the Republican Party was in turmoil. Jack Randolph's quids supported Monroe over Madison as Jefferson's successor in the White House, so Biddle wrote to his former boss in London, encouraging him to come home and pursue his destiny. In the meantime, Nicholas found himself back in the law, representing, among others, the American consuls he had met in London and Paris. Other legal work followed, in partnership with a brother, William, before some old friends who were involved with a literary journal called *Port Folio*, run by a mutual mentor, asked Nicholas to help save it from collapse. Biddle and a few others sought to reinvent it.[41] He reviewed books, translated poetry, and wrote features (sometimes under the pseudonym Oliver Oldschool)—and again considered abandoning the law.[42] His literary bent was obvious: even before his years in Europe, he had begun building what would become one of the best private libraries in America. In 1803, a family friend gave him a ninety-two-volume set of the writings of Voltaire, and a fifty-eight-volume set of the *Histoire naturelle* by Georges-Louis Leclerc, comte de Buffon, a mid-eighteenth-century study of the animal and mineral kingdoms that greatly influenced later naturalists. Biddle later added travel journals, biographies, and literary publications to his collection.*

14

Though he, too, was considered a literary man, Lewis Cass lived in and wrote about a very different country. In 1811, the governor of

---

* Biddle's books remain in the library of the Biddle family seat, Andalusia, in Pennsylvania, alongside others collected by later family members. There are about three thousand books in the collection.

Indiana, William Henry Harrison, defeated the Shawnee at Tippeca-
noe, forcing the tribal leader Tecumseh to reinforce his alliance with
the British, who gave him refuge. Cass closed his law office to lead
militia troops to Dayton, where they were gathering in anticipation of
a new war with Britain. Decked out with his father's sword and "the
highest plume of any officer in the Army" on his hat, Cass commanded
a regiment.[43]

He was ready, perhaps even eager, for war. But he was unsure of
his commander, Michigan's governor William Hull, a veteran of the
Revolution who was generally hesitant, particularly about their first
mission, an invasion of Canadian territory across the Detroit River.
In Congress, Speaker Henry Clay had advocated seizing Canada. Cass
led an unopposed landing party, becoming the first American soldier
on British territory, and in his first engagement took a bridge leading to a British fort. He later claimed authorship of a warning issued
under Hull's name that threatened any Native Americans fighting for
the British with "indiscriminate . . . destruction."[44]

But Hull's soldiers were badly trained and ill-equipped, and the
governor doubted his officers. Despite Cass's success, Hull remained
indecisive, so he quickly retreated from Canada, and though he survived a plot against his command, he soon surrendered the fort at
Detroit without a single shot fired, was taken prisoner along with
other regular army troops, and lost a swath of territory to the British. Cass was said to have broken his father's sword in half to prevent
its surrender, or else to have done so out of frustration with his commander. Released because he was a militia leader and not in the army,
he went to Washington to blame Hull for the debacle.*

Cass won a regular army commission after testifying in Hull's
court-martial (found guilty of cowardice, unbecoming conduct, and
neglect of duty, Hull was eventually pardoned by President Madison).
Cass next served under Harrison, fighting Tecumseh's federation and
the British at the Battle of Thames. Cass identified Tecumseh's body
after he died in the battle, which secured American sovereignty over
the Northwest. During the engagement, Cass received Commander

---

* En route, he contracted an illness that caused his hair to fall out and necessitated his wearing a wig for the rest of his life.

Oliver Hazard Perry's famous note to Harrison reporting his defeat of British ships and the taking of Lake Erie, which read, "We have met the enemy and they are ours."

Cass's reward for his service under Harrison was two titles, both confirmed by Madison: governor of the new Michigan Territory and superintendent of the War Department's Office of Indian Affairs, with broad power supervising Indian agencies in today's Michigan, Ohio, Indiana, and Illinois. Ironically, as governor, he succeeded Hull.

Cass would prove to be a consummate politician. And his supervision of Michigan's thirty thousand Native Americans, many of whom remained allied to (and their chiefs paid by) the British, would eventually propel him into national prominence. Unlike the slaves he had encountered in Wilmington, the Native Americans offered few economic benefits to the white newcomers; Cass felt they were simply dangerous savages, marauders, and now and then cold-blooded murderers.[45]

The relocation of eastern tribal nations had begun under the British in the late seventeenth century and accelerated in the 1780s when, for instance, hundreds of Delawares, seen as defeated allies of the British and harassed by WASP-led American militias, relocated to Spanish Louisiana. The Louisiana Purchase uprooted them again and forced them farther west. In the two decades before 1820, indigenous people lost 600,000 square miles of land. Andrew Jackson used threats and bribes to move thousands of Cherokee from Tennessee in 1817.[46] That same year, Jackson invaded but failed to remove Florida's Seminole nation. Tens of thousands of members of a half dozen southeastern nations—many of them prosperous slaveholders like their white neighbors—refused to budge; two Cherokee leaders described federal policy as a "burlesque."[47] But it's generally agreed that the nations had been substantially weakened by European diseases, by land cessions, and by war against both whites and other indigenous peoples; though estimates of the pre-1492 native population vary widely, by 1800, only about 600,000 indigenous people remained on the continent.

Almost immediately Cass started negotiating the first of eighteen treaties, sometimes procuring federal funds to buy Native

Americans gifts to pacify them, but fighting when necessary, as in fall 1814, when he led troops that attacked a band of Chippewas who had killed a Detroit settler and kidnapped his son, and brought back several Native American scalps and a number of hostages who were then exchanged for the child.[48]

Cass's first priority was to tame the wilderness and make Michigan ready for statehood. That was deemed to require a shift in American policy away from seeking to assimilate Native Americans. Instead, it would work to remove them, attracting more settlers (the four thousand whites in the territory, most of them French, were far outnumbered by the forty thousand Native Americans) by gaining control of more land and creating the infrastructure of a modern civilization. Early steps included a road from Ohio to Detroit and making available public land for sale and military bounties. In 1818, the first steamboat crossed Lake Erie from Buffalo, opening a water highway to the West, and by 1821, the Detroit land office had sold 2.5 million acres.[49] By 1830, the white population of Michigan was thirty thousand, 140,000 square miles of Native American lands had been ceded, stagecoaches ran regularly from Detroit further west, new towns were established, land prices rose, and business boomed.[50]

Both the American Indians and their British allies in Canada remained active threats. Among the indigenous leaders Cass now dealt with was The Prophet, brother of Tecumseh, but Cass's gestures of friendship and attempts to remove the Shawnee to the west or onto reservations were rebuffed. Cass managed to make some deals, though; in 1819, he traded annuity payments, cattle, and farm equipment to the Chippewas for six million acres of timberland in Michigan. He also tried to limit sales of alcohol to Native Americans but allowed fur traders to continue those sales so as to remain competitive with their British competitors, who were generous with gifts.

Cass also had a close relationship with the monopolistic American Fur Company and its founder John Jacob Astor, a German butcher's son who had landed in New York at twenty-one in 1784, joining an older brother who made musical instruments, and another, also a butcher. John first worked in a bakery and then a fur store, where he beat pelts to keep moths away, eventually becoming a fur trader. The U.S. War Department and Cass considered support of Astor to be beneficial and integral to the struggle against the detested British, particularly around the newly acquired Great Lakes and near the mouth of Oregon's Columbia River where, in 1809, Astor established a permanent settlement to grow his business in a region previously controlled by British Canadian traders.

In fall 1819, Michigan's frontiers were mostly calm when Cass proposed an expedition to secure America's hold on what was then the far Northwest, stretching from the Ohio River to the Mississippi south of Lake Superior. He also hoped to make more agreements with Native American leaders, expand the fur trade, and seek more natural resources for exploitation. Monroe's eloquent, ambitious, egotistical secretary of war, the former congressman John Calhoun, agreed, and huge canoes were ordered to carry the party, which would include twenty-two soldiers, an engineer, a mineralogist, a doctor, an interpreter, and ten Ottawa, Chippewa, and Shawnee, who served as crew and hunters. The journey was more than paid for by the discovery of huge copper deposits along the way.

The expedition also continued Cass's devoted quest for expertise in Native American affairs. At Sault Ste. Marie, where he hoped to negotiate land cessions and gain the use of a former French fort from the Chippewa, he instead found Native Americans wearing British medals, carrying British arms, raising a British flag, and donning war paint. Sassabah, an extremist who had fought with Tecumseh, threatened Cass with death if he didn't leave Sault Ste. Marie immediately. Undaunted, Cass pulled down the Union Jack and carried it back to his camp, winning a small tract of land for an American fort from the suddenly more cooperative Indians. At a later stop in Prairie du Chien, he learned of lingering disputes among the Wisconsin bands of Sioux, Fox, Chippewa, Potawatomi, Winnebago, and Menominee, information that would prove quite useful.[51]

In 1821, Cass attended a treaty council in Chicago, hoping to take over all of southern Michigan from its Native American inhabitants, and addressed three thousand Chippewa, Potawatomi, and Ottawa, arguing that with fur and game depleted, and the Great Father in Washington offering gifts and annuities, they should take a deal. Tribal differences were overcome and five million acres were traded away for about $175,000 (or about $4.4 million today), eked out over two decades.[52] In response to troubles between the local nations after 1825, Cass was one of the commissioners who negotiated tribal boundaries for half a dozen of them.

Meanwhile, in the Southeast, where indigenous nations owned tens of millions of acres of land, white citizens, coveting it, began agitating for their removal, fearing that the federal government might attempt to sidestep the state of Georgia and give the Native Americans citizenship and equal rights. While their numbers had diminished elsewhere, in Georgia the population of Creek and Cherokee surpassed ten thousand souls who owned about a quarter of the state.[53] In 1821, Georgia's governor vowed to replace red men with whites.[54] The next governor went even further, signing a treaty with a Creek leader of dubious ethics, ceding all the Creek nation's land, and picking a fight with the new president, John Quincy Adams, who refused to recognize the deal. When it was renegotiated on terms slightly more favorable to the Creek, other nations in Georgia and Mississippi were inspired to take a harder line against the white usurpers.

The difficulty of moving a mass of people—some sixty thousand Native Americans in the South alone—was immense. Unlike slaves, Native Americans weren't profitable to anyone, so the cost of their relocation would be borne by government, not plantation owners. But after the Atlantic slave trade ended in 1808, domestic slavers had developed a robust business in moving their human goods. In the 1820s, nearly a hundred thousand Blacks were trafficked into the Deep South plantation belt, so clearly a forced migration could be accomplished. And many southerners would brook no interference from the hypocritical North, where, they argued, the indigenous population had been mostly exterminated and was otherwise the subject of harsh mistreatment and legal discrimination. But they hoped the federal government would make Native American expulsion a reality. When Jackson won election as president in 1828, they got the man they needed, and the next year Jackson made the South's wish official U.S. policy, though he sugar-coated expulsion as a strictly voluntary affair.

Cass had meanwhile written a series of articles for a prestigious journal, presenting himself as an authority on and supportive friend of Native Americans, and initially advocated leaving them alone rather than running the risk of "increasing their misery." But between 1825 and 1830, he did an about-face and effectively became a government spokesman advocating removal, even publishing an essay, "Removal of the Indians," a few months before the policy was made official, that a modern critic describes as "a morass of distortion and empty speculation."[55] Taken together, Cass's essays were trial balloons for federal policies and set the stage for what became bluntly known as Indian removal. They blamed the destruction of Native American "culture and habitats" and declining population on "their mode of life, their stubborn adherence to superstitious beliefs, and their passionate savage nature," rather than the true cause, rapacious colonization by Europeans.[56]

"The range of thought of our Indian neighbors is extremely limited," Cass wrote in a paragraph reeking of condescension and racism in 1825. "Of abstract ideas they are almost wholly destitute. They have no sciences and their religious notions are confused and circumscribed. They have but little property, less law, and no public offences. They soon forget the past, improvidently disregard the future and waste their thoughts, when they do think, upon the present."[57]

Cass's and Jackson's most significant opponent was Jeremiah Evarts, a Yale-educated reformer who started a public anti-removal movement, including a women's campaign to petition Congress that led the *New England Review* to quote John Randolph's comment that he liked to see women anywhere except in the legislature.[58] Southerners generally supported expulsion, largely to take land for more cotton plantations, which meant more slaves. Northerners, even some who favored shipping slaves back to Africa, more frequently objected. As so often in American history, the South, bolstered by the three-fifths rule, prevailed in Congress. But the act it passed authorizing the land exchanges left the logistical problem of moving tens of thousands of people unaddressed. Jackson thought he could drive the Native American population west through sheer force of will, but he underestimated their resistance.[59]

Georgia and Mississippi passed laws designed to aid the expulsion drive, and some nations yielded, but others (including the so-called Civilized Tribes—the Chickasaw, Choctaw, Seminole, Cherokee, and Creek) pushed back and made demands for educational support, statehood, and representation in Congress. Only minor concessions were made. A similar process was playing out in Ohio, where smaller Native American communities had even less leverage and ceded their land into the 1830s. In New York, near the head of the Erie Canal, 2,300 Seneca refused to emigrate. But like America's Blacks, Native Americans were hugely disadvantaged by a legal system they didn't always understand and which was rigged against them; neither group was allowed to testify in court against whites.[60] Native people were considered dependents, not equals, under the law.

Slavery was prohibited in the Michigan territory, and only a handful of slaves, owned by British and French settlers and grandfathered by treaties, and a few hundred free Blacks lived there. Cass himself had briefly owned one slave and felt the practice, which he once described as "this species of property," was both legal and acceptable.[61] Slavery "excited too much sensation" by setting slave and free regions against each other, he said in a tribute to Edward Everett, a lecturer who took a moderate, conciliatory stand on the subject.[62]

American Indian issues were more important than slavery to him and to his territory, and he felt that, ideally, Native Americans would assimilate into white America by learning to farm, but he simultaneously thought them "barbarous and impetuous children who needed to be treated with paternal care."[63] In an 1827 essay, Cass wrote that they were "so capricious in their tempers, so irresolute in their decisions," and "habitually improvident," living a life of "listless indolence" alternating with "vigorous exertion to provide for [their] animal wants or gratify [their] baleful passions . . . We must think for them."[64] Though he gave lip service to "the great moral debt" whites "owe to this unhappy race," his ethnocentric superiority was all too typical.[65] "The Indian was the one who had to give ground."[66]

~

Frontier exploration also played a vital role in Nicholas Biddle's life, though he experienced it at a distance. In February 1810, he was asked to edit the journals of Meriwether Lewis and William Clark, telling the story of their recent twenty-eight-month scientific expedition, the first to explore the American West.*

Biddle dithered for a month, then accepted what turned out to be an arduous job; the raw material consisted of a million words. But by the end of the summer he had accomplished enough that he agreed to also run as a Federalist for the Pennsylvania state assembly; his father was a candidate for the state senate in the same election, and that fall both won. Nicholas, then twenty-four, simultaneously met and fell for a girl, Jane Craig, seventeen, whose mother, Peggy, was the widow of John Craig, a wealthy shipping merchant of Scottish descent. Before he died in 1807, Craig partnered with several businessmen to import foreign goods into the United States and had extensive business dealings with Spain and its Mexican colony. That put him in the center of the great international economic conflict of an era that began with constant wars in Europe, followed by the American and French Revolutions. Constantly shifting alliances, Spain's weakening international position, the slave revolt against France on Saint-Domingue led by Toussaint L'Ouverture, the death of Napoleon's dream of an American empire, the Louisiana Purchase, the policy of discouraging American shippers from trading with either Britain or France, and British warships, privateers, and pirates all preying on Spanish shipping combined to make Spanish silver mined in Mexico a bounty hunted by many.

American bankers and British pirates both served as distributors of Spanish-American gold and silver.[67] While the Spanish Bourbon kings had briefly backed England against revolutionary France, they switched to a neutral role until English piracy gave them common cause with Napoleonic France, to which they promised Mexican silver in 1803—if they could get it past the British fleet. Spain was short of money, but so were the French and the British, and America had bought Louisiana with borrowed money piled atop its war debts. Into the breach stepped the first merchant bankers, hoping to profit from

---

* Lewis was originally going to write the book, but he committed suicide. Clark's first choice as ghostwriter was Thomas Jefferson, who had commissioned the expedition, but after the ex-president, then sixty-five, declined, Biddle, who was only twenty-four, accepted, and undertook the job without pay.

all concerned. A financier, Gabriel-Julien Ouvrard, concocted an extraordinarily complex scheme in which Mexican silver would pay the 70 million pesos Spain promised to Napoleon. The Barings and Hope merchant houses were to advance the funds against Spanish IOUs they would then sell to equivalent Dutch financiers—and neutral American ships would carry the silver at the center of the swirling scheme, while the British, French, and Spaniards looked the other way. All would profit and the bankers would earn big fees from this international stew.

During the Napoleonic Wars, the trade of European notes backed by Mexican silver for commodities like cotton, rice, and tobacco made many rich. Several Baring brothers married daughters of William Bingham, the richest man in Philadelphia, who connected them to John Craig, who had trading rights in Veracruz courtesy of the British Crown. Talleyrand enlisted the Parish family, Scotsmen who'd invested in Gouverneur Morris's upstate New York land, and they all signed on to the silver scheme, in which Mexico received European goods, Europe got American commodities, and America and France got Mexican silver. Alexander Hamilton's central Bank of the United States, established in 1791, got so much silver, it mitigated Jefferson's restrictions on trade with Europe.[68]

John Craig had acquired a farm outside Philadelphia in 1795. It got its name, Andalusia, in 1801, possibly honoring Don Francisco Caballero Sarmiento, Craig's Spanish partner and in-law, who had a summer house nearby. Craig died in 1807 and was buried in St. Peter's. With her substantial inheritance, partly proceeds from the silver scheme, his widow, Peggy, from a Tobago sugar plantation family, became one of the wealthiest women in America, and was turning their house, designed by Benjamin H. Latrobe but unfinished when John Craig died, into a mansion as Nicholas Biddle entered their lives.

Biddle had begun to establish his authority in matters financial when he used his position in the state legislature to defend Hamilton's central bank.[69] Hamilton sought to increase the capital available to business and facilitate its use, but the bank quickly became a political football, opposed by many Republicans who feared unsafe paper currency, thought it unconstitutional (as it wasn't mentioned in the Constitution), and worried that it favored wealthy financiers and foreign shareholders over American farmers. They preferred currency of silver or gold, known as specie, and smaller, local banks. Their anti-bank faction was also at odds with enemies within their Republican Party who supported the Federalist-nurtured national bank. When the Pennsylvania Assembly met late in 1810 to vote on rechartering the bank, Biddle gave a passionate three-hour speech defending it. Nonetheless, in 1811, the bank's twenty-year charter was allowed to expire by Congress.

His term in the Pennsylvania house over, Biddle returned to Lewis and Clark's journals and to Jane Craig, whom he asked to marry him early that year. Peggy Craig blessed the marriage.[70] Their combined wealth would allow Biddle to give up the law, manage the Craig properties and Mrs. Craig's affairs, and engage in philanthropy and culture. First, though, working seven-hour days for seven months, he finished the Lewis and Clark journals. They would be published—without his name on them—to great acclaim. Biddle's edit, which took the form of a you-are-there account, turned the two-volume work into an epic of nationalism that glamorized the West, portrayed the explorers as classical heroes, "downplayed confusion, doubt, dismay and human foibles," eliminated some of the more distasteful passages (including references to venereal disease and Native Americans offering their wives for sex to expedition members), and encouraged further exploration and America's transcontinental ambitions—the last a goal Biddle would never abandon.[71]

Biddle's next big speech was given on the Fourth of July in 1811 to the state's Society of the Cincinnati, a hereditary club for Revolutionary War officers. He spoke in favor of a monument to George Washington, reminding listeners that national unity should come before personal rivalry. His quiet hope was that his friend James Monroe, just appointed secretary of state, would hear of the speech and help him get a job in Washington.[72] No offer came, so Biddle focused on *Port Folio* and weekend visits to the Craigs at Andalusia before the October wedding. A honeymoon followed in Baltimore and Washington, where the Monroes took the Biddles to the White House to meet President and Mrs. Madison. Returning to Philadelphia, they moved into a double townhouse shared with Jane's mother, and

Biddle accepted a position as assistant editor of the journal. When its founder died just as their first collaborative issue was published, Biddle took over and revamped it to promote patriotism (war with Britain still loomed), add sections on the fine arts, and encourage a shift in the prevailing architectural style from British-influenced Regency to Greek neoclassical, reflecting the influence of his travels. Their wealth also allowed the Biddles to entertain and Nicholas to continue his study of "jurisprudence and politics."[73]

The Biddle family was deeply involved in the War of 1812. James, who remained in the navy after his imprisonment and release in Tripoli, was second-in-command of the frigate *Wasp* in Delaware Bay, and captain of the sloop *Hornet*, which sank the British *Penguin* in a brief battle in March 1815 that saw him shot through the chin. Then he sailed the world, preceding Matthew Perry to Asia and negotiating the first treaty between the United States and China. Nicholas avoided service after he hurt his leg climbing out of a carriage; he spent more than a year recovering, editing his magazine, running Andalusia for his mother-in-law, playing gentleman farmer, and watching with alarm as ten dozen new state banks were chartered and issued paper notes, many unredeemable for specie. They lent far more money than they actually controlled, and Biddle feared that the currency chaos set off when the issuing banks inevitably proved unable to make good on their paper could threaten the government's financial viability.

In editorials in *Port Folio*, Biddle inveighed against New England merchants whose trade, legal and not, with Europe, drained America's precious metal reserves. That put Biddle on the front line of the first skirmishes in the centuries-long conflict between capital and the American masses. Would they or money rule the new nation? That conflict had broken into the open with the formation of the Federalist and Republican Parties, which reflected the contradictions of the American enterprise. European colonization of America was a commercial venture. The boycotts of British commerce that set off the American Revolution were a democratic revolt against British capital. Alexander Hamilton had first joined that revolt in a mob fighting the British in New York—a mostly royalist, mostly commercially oriented city—and became one of Washington's top aides. At Valley

Forge he almost certainly told Gouverneur Morris of Washington's frustrations over the failure of Congress to provision American troops. The concept of federalism had grown out of that frustration, as the me-first sovereign states, barely united under the Articles of Confederation, proved they weren't up to the task.

At the time, accumulated capital, held as specie or hard money, determined national wealth. Lacking a currency of their own, Americans variously traded with British gold and silver coins, which were often counterfeits or else adulterated with less valuable metals, or Spanish silver from mines in Mexico and Peru, supplemented by wampum, and bartered products like tobacco and sugar as well as rights to land. When trade was strangled by the Revolution, cutting off American access to specie, the states and the Continental Congress issued paper notes of dubious value. The alliance with France gave America access to French livres backed by gold in the Bourbon regime's vaults, but they were mostly traded for war supplies in Europe—and were devalued when Louis XVI's generosity to America caused the livre's value to sink, accelerating the French Revolution.

Hamilton's experience with the Continental Army convinced him that control of currency and banks had to be taken away from the states and centralized, and that Congress should collect taxes and duties. He became an advocate of a national bank, but between the 1783 Treaty of Paris and the Constitutional Convention of 1787, little changed. American merchants, who held and loaned capital, advocated a strong, carefully managed currency. Farmers, often in debt, preferred weak paper money and high prices to help them borrow and repay their loans.

The new Constitution, ratified by the states in 1788 and put into effect the next spring, gave the government complete control of the economy and currency, as Hamilton and Gouverneur Morris had hoped. Soon after Washington was elected president, Hamilton proposed to let the government accrue debt and print money. That was designed to absolve the states of the need to pay back debts from the Revolution by having the central government assume them, paving the way for robust foreign trade.

But sectionalism hadn't gone away. Rural citizens resented northern urban capitalists, and New England states (encouraged by the aging, angry Morris) had even considered secession. After a secret deal was struck—the approval of most of Hamilton's plan in exchange for moving the nation's capital south from New York to just across the Potomac River from Virginia—Jefferson, then secretary of state, acquiesced. Hamilton next proposed a national bank to keep politics out of national financial management. Madison agreed with Jack Randolph's position that the idea was unconstitutional and argued that in the absence of a specific grant to the central government of the power to charter a bank, that power was implicitly reserved for the states. Jefferson agreed, but Washington sided with Hamilton, and many congressmen saw that a central bank might be personally advantageous. Thirty of them became shareholders when the first Bank of the United States received its twenty-year charter from the Senate in January 1791.

Biddle was still in the Pennsylvania legislature in 1811 when it became clear that the bank's charter would not be renewed. He thought the "dissolution of the Bank [was] especially inopportune," as it represented "the main artery of all [America's] resources" as well as a pipeline through which Spanish-American gold and silver flowed to the rest of the world.[74] But since Madison, by then president, disagreed, when war with Britain finally, inevitably broke out in 1812, the government's resources were stretched thin. Madison printed money, interest rates rose alongside American casualties, confidence fell, and then the British burned the White House and Capitol. As the country's debt grew and the value of its currency shrank, even the Federalists were no longer uniformly supportive of the central bank concept; many had made their peace with—and profited from— the state banks that filled the vacuum.

Meantime, Nicholas and Jane had a son, Nicholas Craig Biddle, in 1813, and Peggy Craig died in 1814. Then the infant died, too, within a month of his grandmother. Jane was devastated, so Nicholas quit the magazine and took her traveling through that summer, rushing home after the British captured Washington. By the time they reached Philadelphia, the war had turned in America's favor, and Biddle, who had won a seat in the state senate in 1813, met in Washington with Monroe, then the secretary of war. Monroe couldn't give Biddle what he really wanted, an important job, but he did share some encouraging news: the administration had seen the light and wanted a new national bank to solve America's financial woes.[75] In early 1815, American politics realigned, as the Federalist Party collapsed amid charges its anti-war position had bordered on treason. Biddle, following principles over party, moved toward the Pennsylvania Republicans, who chose to champion federalism and the centralized improvement of infrastructure like roads and canals. At President Madison's instigation, and over the objection of old-school agrarians like Jack Randolph's quids, the Second Bank of the United States was chartered in 1816 as both a quasi-central bank and a development bank to fund infrastructure projects. An unqualified, unsuccessful businessman was put in charge, though, and as a result, Biddle refused a request by the private stockholders to sit on its board of twenty-five (five of them, appointed by Madison, represented the government). He still hoped Monroe, who was elected president at year's end, would give him a foreign ministry, but in vain.

Increasingly frustrated by the rising tide of populism, which favored the poor over his propertied elite, Biddle left the state legislature again in 1817. A year later, the mismanagement of the new bank set the stage for a financial crisis later known as the Panic of 1819, and created a job opening when Monroe decided to remove the Second Bank's head and asked Biddle to serve as one of the government's directors, a job for which he was well prepared through both education and inclination. The bank would rule his life for the next twenty years.

15

Nicholas Biddle came to an institution in distress, opposed by the state banks it again threatened to supplant, by speculators who feared their activities might be curbed, by debtors distressed at the thought it might strengthen American currency, making it harder to repay loans, and by New York bankers who resented Philadelphia's dominance. Republicans remained skeptical of the bank, too. And some of its directors had engaged in speculation and fraud, harming its reputation further.

Biddle found the challenge of reforming the bank irresistible. America's landmass and farm economy had doubled in twenty-five years, and while European conflicts and British blockades had hindered trade, they encouraged the development of American manufacturing. But prices were unstable, careful business planning was disrupted, and the first forced removals of Native Americans from land east of the Mississippi had combined with loose money printed by state banks in preceding years to fuel a speculative bubble in property. So just as Biddle joined the bank, it was tightening credit. State banks called in loans, land prices fell sharply, and the economy screeched to a halt. To cite but one example, sales of public lands cratered in the Panic of 1819, from $13.6 million in 1818 to $1.3 million in 1821, when the depression slowly began to lift.

The new bank president, Langdon Cheves of Charleston, a former Speaker of the House of Representatives, proved unwilling to take the steps Biddle thought necessary to save both the economy and the bank—allowing its southern and western branches to resume normal operations such as the issuance of notes. In 1821, Biddle's frustration boiled over, and he decided to leave the board. Unfortunately, with Pennsylvanians already serving as ministers to Paris and London, Monroe was reluctant to give another a foreign post, and suggestions that Biddle run for governor or a seat in Congress didn't pan out. His malaise worsened when first his father and then his second son fell ill and died even as the national bank's restrictive credit policies threatened to extend the economic crisis.

In 1814, Biddle had bought Andalusia from John Craig's estate for $17,000 and added a two-story playhouse for billiards and card games. But the house would prove too small for a family that had grown to include six children as well as a cook, maids and nurses, a seamstress, two waitresses, and a coachman.* Despite long country

---

* In 1835, Biddle would add fourteen acres to the property, and in 1838, another fifty-three acres, which he later gave to a son on his marriage. A cottage was added that same year. Biddle took Andalusia's farming business seriously, studying irrigation, crop rotation, and fertilizer, speaking on those subjects, and serving as president of the Agricultural Society. Seven full-time farm workers and added help in summer tended to the farm, where he grew a wide range of fruits and vegetables. He also had an interest in breeding thoroughbred horses, which a Craig brother-in-law raced. And he kept a herd of Guernsey cattle, which remained on the property until 1951.

stays, the Biddles remained leading members of Philadelphia society, which thought that "the world, the whole world, and all the world, live in an extremely small compass," Nicholas wrote in an unfinished novel.[76] They felt at once a part of it and apart from it. "Distinctions in society, you must have, because wealth, beauty, notoriety, family connections create them; different circles in society you must have because no individual can be acquainted with everybody," he wrote. "But it is against the absurd pretension of being the first society, against the exclusion from your circle of persons fitted to adorn it because the pursuits of their fathers and brothers is not what is absurdly called genteel, it is against this that I must protest."[77]

Biddle was still very much an elitist, but his circle included scientists, artists, and even actors, and he attended a weekly gathering of intellectuals where the subject of politics was banned, but literature, religion, science, and philosophy were on the agenda.* A local diarist and librarian, John Jay Smith, remarked, "Coruscations of wit, and bright sallies abounding with anecdote and information were continually occurring to enliven [Biddle's] festive gatherings; never did I leave his society without admiration of his talents and superior social powers."[78] Biddle was, in short, a celebrity, "followed, praised, worshipped . . . Wherever he appeared there was a sensation and a crowd immediately formed around him. His manner was gracious, smiling, easy, gentlemanlike, a little condescending & exhibited supreme self-satisfaction and elation. His conversation was ready, fluent, elegant & witty. His language was always choice."[79]

But despite his wealth, social fame, and wide circle of friends, Biddle wanted more—and got it. Cheves, the president of the Bank of the United States, announced his resignation in summer 1822; Jane's uncle, who had become Nicholas's surrogate father, nominated him as a replacement. That November, he won the job and control of the bank's $53 million in resources and eighteen branches, which made it America's largest corporation—over the objections of the incumbent and, among others, Lewis Cass's friend John Jacob Astor, who thought Biddle too cultured and intellectual.[80]

* Biddle was also a member of the American Philosophical Society, the Academy of the Fine Arts, a founder of the Historical Society, and a trustee of the University of Pennsylvania.

His response showed both that culture and intellect and a sense of humor. He wrote,

> *I prefer my last letters from Barings or Hope*
> *To the finest epistles of Pliny or Pope.*

Biddle still hoped for a more important post, but he threw himself into the job, working with Monroe and his treasury secretary to revamp the bank's board and supervising the construction of a new Greek Revival headquarters, which had been commissioned before he became a director but reflected his neoclassical aesthetic that viewed public buildings as reflections of the ideals of both their builders and the nation.* Biddle took control of the exchange of banknotes across the young country, ensuring that distant western banks weren't disfavored over stronger ones in the East (infuriating not only state banks but also currency traders, who profited from discrepancies). When conditions (such as a trade imbalance that drew specie from the country, or crop failures that slowed the movement of money) warranted, the bank had discretionary power to "mitigate the drift of money to and from the economy, from region to region within it, and from bank to bank" if individual banks were "irresponsible, and precarious."[81]

After the War of 1812, Andrew Jackson, a champion of state banks and then a senator from Tennessee, gained a national following with his rough-hewn version of Jefferson's liberal democratic politics and overt hatred of both imperial Britain and privileged American aristocrats like Biddle. A Nashville lawyer, cotton magnate, and slaveholder, Jackson had been Tennessee's first congressman before his elevation to the Senate. Aiming higher, in 1824, he won the popular vote but lost the presidency in the electoral college to John Quincy Adams.

The Bank of the United States was especially disliked in Jackson's South and the West, considered both unrepublican and unaccountable and blamed for tight credit and the depressed economy. Biddle

---

* Biddle later remodeled both Girard College, where he was chair of the buildings committee, and Andalusia, to reflect his taste for classical design.

thus ordered his branches there to issue more currency, and increased loans "had an almost magical effect upon the national economy . . . the volume of business activity expanded, and profits increased."[82] He also restricted dividends on bank stock, annoying laissez-faire capitalists and speculators, including a New York banker who tried to take over the bank but ended up arrested for fraud. Though acquitted, he went bankrupt.

Biddle expanded the national bank's overseas operations, too, but that created new vulnerabilities: speculation in cotton in England caused a market frenzy, which he calmed by again restricting lending. When the Bank of England followed his lead, though, it caused a panic. Biddle ensured that wouldn't spread to the United States by gradually increasing lending again. The power to tighten and loosen credit and control the money supply was the bank's economic superpower. Steadiness, however, was anathema to speculators, lenders, and brokers, who all profited from fluctuating prices. Alexander Brown, America's first investment banker and a foreign exchange trader, "thought it impertinent of Biddle to interfere."[83]

Though he was making some capitalists into enemies atop those who simply hated the bank, it prospered, and its reputation was restored enough that by 1828, assuming its charter would be renewed, he considered resigning. Jane hoped for a return to a quiet life at Andalusia. Her interests tended toward the Episcopal Church, not playing society hostess. But play the part she did. The Biddles generally moved from town to country seasonally, bringing her piano back and forth. They hosted a ball every winter, and Jane gave regular musicales.

John Jay Smith wrote in his diary: "His house was the resort of the intellect of the country. John Quincy Adams, Webster, and the great politicians of the nation were entertained at his dinner."[84] Their guests also included businessmen like Vincent LeRay, a son of Gouverneur Morris's sometime partner in real estate, and the former king of Spain, Napoleon's older brother, who lived in exile nearby.

Biddle was vain enough to savor his success and stature as the city's most prominent citizen and, increasingly, a national leader. So without some new challenge, the argument against quitting the bank was strong. And there was a big job still to do—creating a national transportation network of roads, waterways, and, following the 1827 chartering of the Baltimore & Ohio, America's first railroad, train lines—and the bank had both the funds to make that happen and a need to put its money to work in ways that wouldn't encourage speculation and more financial problems.

In 1827, Biddle gave a speech to the American Philosophical Society eulogizing Thomas Jefferson, its former president, who had died the year before. He used it to set out, at age forty-one, his guiding principles—"a perpetual devotion, not to his own purposes, but to the pure and noble cause of public freedom. . . . the establishment of free principles, free institutions, freedom in all its varieties of untrammeled thought and independent action . . . to the improvement and happiness of his fellow men."[85]

Biddle's youthful Federalism had been tempered and he had come to see Jefferson as the sort of philosopher-statesman devoted to freedom that he, too, aspired to be. Little did he know that his country was about to elect a man who would turn Jeffersonian politics into a weapon against his bank. In 1824, Biddle had voted for Jackson for president. Accused of preferring John Quincy Adams, whom Jackson again opposed four years later, Biddle would write, "Money is neither Whig nor Tory, and we say with equal truth that the Bank is neither a Jackson nor an Adams man, it is only a bank."[86] But unfortunately for Biddle, Jackson, a land speculator, had experienced personal losses when he sold on credit and ended up mired in debt, and felt no affection for banks or bankers.

~

In the 1828 race, Adams lost to Jackson, the visually arresting symbol of direct democracy and the populism that grew as new states entered the union and ended traditions like enfranchisement based on property ownership.[87] Jackson's win with 56 percent of the popular vote was a repudiation of the rule of the high Protestant elite, and the triumph of his new Democratic Party reflected the rise of a new majority, the agrarian everyman, the common folk of the fields and mountains.[88] Though they, too, were largely WASPs, they bore no resemblance to Joe Alsop's elegant Ascendancy. Margaret Bayard Smith, whose father had been at Valley Forge with George Washington, wrote of Jackson's inauguration, "The Majesty of the People had disappeared. A rabble, a mob of boys, negroes, women, children, scrambling, fighting, romping..."[89] The old Jeffersonian elite watched, aghast. The ultimate elitist, John Randolph, declared in an 1829 letter to John Brockenbrough, the president of Richmond's Bank of Virginia, that their country was "ruined past redemption."[90] The old ruling class was also being challenged by a Protestant religious revival led by the more recent, less sophisticated folk, mostly from northern England—a quarter million of them arrived in the lead-up to the Revolution from 1718 to 1775—who had migrated to a secularized America and were rapidly settling the frontier.[91] Mostly of humble origins, they came seeking a better life rather than religious freedom, and had a businesslike approach to it, stressing "hard work and worldly asceticism."[92] On arrival, they tended to move west into the interior in Pennsylvania, Maryland, Virginia, the Carolinas, Tennessee, and Kentucky, and eventually spread out from Appalachia, sometimes squatting on land they didn't own. Though he was from the opposite end of the economic spectrum, Jackson, the grandson of a well-to-do merchant in Ulster, Northern Ireland, and related by marriage to the prominent Polk clan, would emerge as their first leader. His wife, Rachel, was also from a prominent family; though "barely literate," she was a grandniece of a Presbyterian president of Princeton.[93]

Jackson's constituents were not the sophisticates of New York, Boston, Philadelphia, or Tidewater Virginia. They were the original rednecks, often angry, xenophobic, and hostile to strangers, "without regard to race, religion or nationality."[94] An Anglican missionary described them as content with their "low, lazy, sluttish, heathenish, hellish" lives. They, in turn, denigrated organized religion and spartan churches, preferring intense outdoor mass meetings.[95] They sought freedom, not strong government; they believed in an eye for an eye and a politics based in personal loyalty.[96]

The Whiskey Rebellion in the early 1790s in western Pennsylvania—when whiskey distillers and drinkers took up arms against America's first federal excise tax—had demonstrated the stubborn frontier resistance to central government. A year later the backwoods allied with Jefferson's Democratic-Republicans in opposing Jay's treaty with Britain. When the Federalist Adams enacted laws expanding government, his high-handed superiority inspired resentment. In

1800, that fueled the Jeffersonian ascension that would dominate politics for a quarter century.[97] As Gouverneur Morris had feared, the Louisiana Purchase and annexation of West Florida in 1810 expanded the backcountry, shifting political power south and west, where the War of 1812 found greater support than it did in the mercantile Northeast.[98]

With the Federalists' collapse, personality gained the political upper hand. Opposition to John Quincy Adams invigorated the new coalition, and power flowed to Jackson. To his supporters, he was symbolic of the simultaneous advance of evangelical Christianity, democracy, and technological progress, moving liberty ever westward, a doctrine that would later be formalized as Manifest Destiny, a term that would be coined in 1845 by a Jacksonian journalist.[99] In his first annual message to the country in 1829, Jackson promised to veto the recharter of the Second Bank of the United States. Biddle was unconcerned, sure he would see the light, as previous presidents and treasury secretaries had, and confident that the many bank supporters around Jackson would be convincing, even as the president was usually silent on the subject.

Soon enough, however, Jackson supporters allied with anti-bank businessmen (many of them from New York, where Jackson's secretary of state, Martin Van Buren, had been a U.S. senator and governor) began making trouble by claiming the bank played political favorites, refusing loans to Jackson supporters when its real sin was its failure to submit to the political demands of Jacksonians. Biddle's insistence that it remain nonpartisan seemed purely partisan to the Jacksonians, and his attempts to refute charges the bank was corrupt didn't change minds. By 1829, it was clear that Jackson had no intention of rechartering the bank when its authorization expired in 1836. So Biddle began circulating reports on its efficacy, even paying newspaper editors to insert them in their papers and print and distribute them on the bank's behalf. A little arrogantly, he felt sure that the public would side with the bank if they only understood its value.[100]

Guided by Henry Clay, who planned to run against Jackson in 1832, Biddle initially resisted seeking a preemptive recharter for the bank. Clay assured Biddle that even if Jackson won again, he wouldn't shut it down. But neither did Clay want to run with the bank as a millstone around his neck.

In the meantime, Jackson was preparing an alternative proposal to take away the bank's independence, its ability to make loans and buy property, and put its operations under the Treasury, over the objections of many of his advisors. Jackson supporters like Missouri senator Thomas Hart Benton argued that the bank was a tool for "great capitalists" against "the needy and unfortunate."[101] In response to such demagoguery, Biddle insisted that high-minded discourse would win the day, but he also continued to pay—some would say bribe—newspaper editors. He paid politicians, too. Massachusetts's debt-ridden senator Daniel Webster was prominent on his payroll. Biddle also punished his opponents by tightening credit, taking the offensive to protect the bank. If he thought that would frighten Jackson, Biddle was sadly mistaken.

Andrew Jackson was fighting a multi-front political war. In spring 1831, he reorganized his cabinet. The faction led by John Calhoun, who had been elected John Quincy Adams's vice president and then Jackson's, was purged, though Calhoun himself stayed on even after he became an outspoken advocate of strict construction of the Constitution in the service of the right of states to nullify central-government-imposed tariffs. Some even advocated secession. The dispute was a fig leaf, though, covering the South's rising concern about slavery's future.

Calhoun was already on Jackson's bad side after an intracabinet dispute over an adultery scandal involving the wife of his secretary of war, John Eaton, whom the president defended. Eaton and Secretary of State Van Buren both resigned to facilitate a cabinet reshuffle. As the most prominent Democrat in the Northwest, Lewis Cass was an obvious choice for war secretary; Monroe had considered him for the same post, Van Buren supported him, and with Cass in the cabinet, Michigan was more likely to vote Democratic in the next election. Jackson was unaware of his relationship to Calhoun, who would himself resign at the end of 1832 just after South Carolina passed a nullification ordinance but then immediately return to Washington as a South Carolina senator. When that state began to raise an army to resist the federal government, Cass, who had taken over the War Department that summer, suggested Virginia intervene and urge the federal tariffs be eased. South Carolina backed down and Cass was a hero, but the real issue wasn't tariffs, it was the future of slavery, and that remained unresolved thanks to a fear of losing votes that paralyzed politicians on both sides of the issue.

John Biddle, brother of Nicholas and the congressional representative of the Michigan territory, had hosted a goodbye dinner for Cass in Detroit. Cass's new home, Washington, was presiding over the explosive growth of the still-new nation; his old one, Michigan, would achieve statehood six years later. Population and immigration were both increasing nationwide, business was booming, and industry and capital were expanding and spreading thanks to new transportation networks—new canals, railroads, and roads like those Cass had laid in the Northwest. The ruling Democrats saw themselves as egalitarians despite their biases against Blacks, indigenous peoples, and women.

Cass not only had power but could dispense patronage, which made him a man to know. He sought to reorganize the government's approach to Native Americans, using the war department's seven-year-old Office of Indian Affairs to execute Jackson's policy of pacifying Native Americans and relocating them, if at all possible, beyond the frontier of the Mississippi. That caused his first crisis in office, after a deadly intertribal conflict broke out in 1832 and a Sauk chief named Black Hawk reneged on a plan to move Sauk and Fox people from their homes near the junction of the Wisconsin and Mississippi Rivers to allow white settlers access to the region's lead resources. Militia troops ordered in by Jackson (including a young Abraham Lincoln) were ambushed by Black Hawk, and the war that bore his name ensued. Finally, soldiers crushed the rebellious band, leaving less than a hundred braves alive, and Black Hawk and others were held as hostages. More land cessions followed.[102] The aim, Cass admitted, was to eliminate Native American land ownership.[103]

An unintended consequence of the conflict was a rift between Cass and Zachary Taylor, a general and future president, after Taylor was sued for carrying out Cass's order to remove white squatters and miners from Native American land and Cass refused to say the general was only following orders.

Though it was the only case of American Indian removal in which Cass was in direct command, the Black Hawk War was of a piece with Jackson's general policy of using the military to get Native Americans off land coveted by white settlers. The focus of the policy was in the Southeast, where the large Cherokee nation and smaller nations had been guaranteed their lands between the Appalachian Mountains and the Mississippi River by the British in 1763, when George III's government drew a line along the Eastern Continental Divide and prohibited Anglo-American colonists from settling on western lands won from the French following the French and Indian War. That British proclamation helped set the stage for the colonists' revolt against the British even as some settlers and land speculators ignored it. Still, the Native Americans held on until 1829, when a gold rush in Georgia dialed up the pressure and Jackson, a speculator himself, sided with states' rights advocates against federal protection of indigenous peoples.

The desire to be rid of the indigenous nations had grown in Georgia ever since the state relinquished its claims on land to the west (during the Yazoo affair) in exchange for money and a federal vow to remove the Creek from the state. Two decades later, the Creek lands had been distributed in lotteries and Cherokee lands were in play. But the Cherokee had embraced the civilizing notion and were notably successful at farming; as their and other nations' land was nibbled away in treaties, sometimes secured with threats and bribes, they used the legal system to resist removal, even winning a Supreme Court judgment in March 1831 that they constituted a sovereign nation.

But after Jackson's election, the new president took Georgia's side, warning the nations that if they didn't sell and move, they would lose their federal protection and be subject to Georgia's laws. Jackson's Indian Removal Act passed in 1830, despite considerable opposition in the North, and he began applying pressure both subtle and overt to pry the Native Americans from the Southeast and send them to today's Oklahoma. Local citizens didn't bother with subtlety;

they imprisoned and tortured Indians, and burned and booby-trapped their homes. When the Supreme Court ruled that federal law, not state law, governed the relationship, all concerned just ignored that ruling, which is also how Jackson dealt with inconvenient treaties. Promised protections proved to be fiction. Even when reduced to destitution and starvation, Cass and Jackson felt that the Indians "had only themselves to blame," as Cass wrote to R. J. Meigs III, a Tennessee lawyer and politician, in October 1834.[104]

Lewis Cass supported Jackson's blatantly racist policy even before taking his cabinet post, contending that the only way to deal with barbarians was to get them out of the way of whites.[105] And anyway, the land west of the big river was, Cass assured the Creek leaders in a January 1832 letter, "fine country."[106] In fact, the War Department's maps were incomplete and inaccurate. And Native American leaders who visited the proffered land petitioned Jackson in 1835 to say they found it "good for nothing" and "too poor for snakes to live upon."[107] The proximity of other nations also increased the chances of intertribal conflict.

The first southeastern nation to agree to removal was Mississippi's Choctaw, but many of its members refused to go, perhaps wisely, as conditions on the march were deplorable and those on the trek in winter 1831 got little or no compensation for what they left behind, leading Cass to decide that better planning was required. He issued a new batch of regulations and guidelines and created a bureaucracy of removal agents while declaring that the government would have no liability in case of accidents along the way.[108] But the apparatus he constructed was ill-conceived and impractical.[109] Cass also farmed out provisioning of food and blankets to private contractors who would value profit over the quality of supplies for the dispossessed. Outsourcing was "more economical," Cass told the Creeks, assuring them that what was "better for the government [couldn't] be worse for you."[110] But relocation on the cheap would prove disastrous.

The Chickasaw and Creek peoples agreed to removal, though delays and conflicts kept them in place for years. Factions of the Seminole and Cherokee agreed to leave, but others protested. Meantime, cholera came to North America in 1832, spreading from the troops mopping up the Sauk War and killing many of the remaining members of that nation as it spread south along the Mississippi. That fall, the Choctaws were herded together for deportation, creating breeding grounds for disease at their encampments in Memphis and Vicksburg, where they met steamboats or, for those who refused to board, marched along oft-flooded roads. When survivors finally reached their destination in Indian Territory, provisions ran low, it was too late to plant crops, and more flooding destroyed homes and what fields were planted. A similar fate met Shawnee, Odawa, and Seneca dispossessed in Ohio. More than a fifth of them died en route west on what came to be known as the Trail of Tears.

After Jackson's second inaugural in March 1833, Lewis Cass joined him on a victory tour of the Northeast. In New York, 200,000 people turned out to greet them. Jackson and Cass were heroes there; the city's speculators profited from both the slave economy and the millions of acres taken from indigenous peoples, which were inextricably linked, since coastal land had been worn out and the introduction of industrial slavery to the highly fertile tribal properties in the Southeast increased cotton exports. None of that bothered Cass, but he was mortified when a causeway collapsed at an event and he was dumped into the Hudson River, surfacing without his wig.

On the other hand, Cass opposed Jackson's campaign against Nicholas Biddle's Bank of the United States, which he quietly supported as a public good, even overturning the politically motivated removal of military pension funds from its New York branch that had been undertaken by his predecessor at the War Department. When Jackson's treasury secretary balked at Cass's move, the president demanded unity, and Cass considered resigning. But Jackson asked him to stay, assuring Cass he would make clear the withdrawals were his decision alone.

Thus, Lewis Cass was still in place when the Seminole of Florida, led by a warrior named Osceola and allied with runaway slaves and free Blacks, went to war against white settlers in late 1835, refusing to move west as they had promised after previous hostilities. Osceola led a raid on Fort King, massacring the troops there. General Winfield Scott, put in charge and given wide latitude in how to proceed, launched the Second Seminole War, which would last seven years. Ultimately, the deportation of fewer than four thousand Native Americans cost about $35 million, and Cass's belief that force would convince the Seminole to stop their fight and leave proved wildly optimistic.[111] Cass resigned shortly after that second war began but was damaged by it, attacked for being unprepared and irresolute, and Jackson even called him "an old woman" in speaking to Amos Adams Lawrence, a Massachusetts businessman who reported the remark in a letter to his father in January 1836.[112]

By that fall, forty-five thousand American Indians had been forcibly relocated, and many more had died, but Cass continued to defend his thoroughly discredited policy. In truth, the policy of Indian removal had started a race war that would continue for decades. Just two years later, the U.S. military began forcing the Cherokee from their lands, first into ill-equipped internment camps, and then on brutal trips over land and water to Indian Territory, where they weren't always welcomed by the Native inhabitants of the plains. It's estimated that only about a quarter of the fifteen thousand Cherokees who set out on that journey survived. By the mid-1840s, eighty thousand souls had been moved across the Mississippi, allegedly to lands they would hold forever, at a cost of $75 million, which would be more than repaid through the sale of their emptied, expropriated land. *[113]

16

As early as 1831, New York was rising, and its rival, Philadelphia, falling in influence. For more than half a century, Philadelphia had been America's premier city and, with eighty thousand inhabitants in 1830, the largest.[114] It was also the center of America's Enlightenment culture, boasting leaders in art, medicine, and science. But New York's harbor and the opening of the Erie Canal in 1825 were making Wall Street the nation's new financial center, and Martin Van Buren, the former governor turned vice president, hoped to follow Jackson into

* Equivalent to $1 trillion today.

the White House. Philadelphia retained its centrality in publishing, banking, and the arts in part thanks to Nicholas Biddle, a leader in all three fields, who had carefully promoted his own image, commissioning multiple portraits and statues of himself, including seven miniatures, a drawing and a silhouette, five marble busts, and eight oil paintings.* Several were engraved for wide distribution. But pictures couldn't relieve the pressure of Jackson's hatred and New York's envy of his central bank's centrality.

The argument over whether to seek a recharter for the bank continued into the election of 1832. The anti-bank factions were quite willing to indulge in lies and fear-mongering to get their way. Biddle suggested a compromise, allowing Jackson to modify the charter to his satisfaction, though satisfying competing interests would be a challenge. Some opponents wanted it moved to New York, others wanted the Treasury put in charge, and a third group would only be satisfied with the return of gold currency.

Biddle's critics admired him even as they faulted his performance. On his deathbed, despite his long-standing opposition to the bank, Jack Randolph even handed the $2,000 he was carrying to Biddle for safekeeping.[115] Yet his management of the bank was disdained as clumsy by the more practical denizens of Wall Street. Biddle was too romantic, irreverent, erudite, and inexperienced, too reasonable, straightforward, naive, and trusting—that is, impractical. He "had the untempered intellectual's preference for what ought to be over what is. For the world of affairs, he was too naive and his air was too gay."[116] It all led Biddle to a fate straight out of Greek tragedy.

Suddenly sure that if Jackson was reelected he would veto a recharter, Biddle changed course and decided to ask for the new charter before the election after all. The motion narrowly passed Congress amid unproven claims that Biddle had paid for the winning votes. Biddle himself wasn't above making unproven claims, even once suggesting that the president wanted to control the bank as a patronage machine for his supporters, which infuriated Jackson, who vetoed

---

* Pennsylvania's Academy of the Fine Arts also made the city a center of portraiture. Thomas Sully's work in that field was significant, and in July 1826, after completing portraits of Lafayette and Napoleon, he began a portrait of Biddle. It and his famous—and rather similar—portrait of Lord Byron were both completed in 1828.

the bill and vowed to destroy the bank. The long-cold Bank War heated up.

On the Senate floor, Daniel Webster declared that the veto "manifestly seeks to inflame the poor against the rich."[117] One New England newspaper called it a "deranging, radical, law-upsetting document." It certainly upset the economy: the bank's stock plunged and business was paralyzed, leading Biddle to believe Jackson's electoral defeat was inevitable. Professing himself delighted, he wrote to Henry Clay that the president had shown "all the fury of a chained panther biting the bars of his cage. It is really a manifesto of anarchy."[118] And he began to openly support Henry Clay against Jackson and Van Buren in the presidential race, giving Clay money and publishing a pseudonymous attack on Jackson.[119] The bank itself stayed out of the race, though its existence remained a central issue. To Biddle supporters, Jackson was King Andrew. To Jacksonians, the bank was a tool of the privileged elite. In this latest fight of the people versus monarchy, King Andrew won in a landslide.

Desperately Biddle tried to keep the bank and commerce going, even as Europe suffered upheaval and prices for American farm products plunged. Then Jackson announced that government money would be withdrawn from the bank in September 1833, causing Biddle to halt lending, convincing the president and his allies that it was insolvent. Democratic newspapers encouraged runs on its branches. "The bank is too strong to have its credit shaken by such a combination," Biddle reassured a member of Congress.[120]

In a December 1832 letter Jackson asked Tennessee congressman James K. Polk to open an investigation of the bank, calling it a "hydra of corruption" that was "only scotched, not dead."[121] When Congress demurred, he persevered. Forewarned, Biddle bribed wavering Jackson supporters with profitable positions at the bank while continuing to choke the free flow of money, causing panic. Banks closed under the strain. "The Bank of the United States shall not break," Biddle vowed. "The worthy president thinks that because he has scalped Indians and imprisoned judges, he is to have his way with the Bank. He is mistaken." But right though he was about the bank's utility, it was Biddle who was mistaken.

"The Bank is trying to kill me, but I will kill it," Jackson promised Van Buren, comparing it to the biblical "golden calf" and calling it "a destroying monster." Only borrowers, lenders, and gamblers would be hurt if he succeeded, he thundered—wrongly. "The government will not bow to this monster," he berated a petitioner carrying six thousand signatures begging for relief. "Go to Nicholas Biddle . . . Biddle has all the money!" he ranted. Then he asked an aide, "Didn't I manage them well?"[122]

In the same cabinet reshuffle that made Lewis Cass secretary of war, a new head of the Treasury, William Duane, had taken office on June 1, 1833, committed to leaving its deposits in the bank, but that very night Duane learned Jackson was preparing his executive order to transfer all federal funds to state banks. When he protested, Jackson complimented his frankness but refused to reconsider. Within the bank, the private and government-appointed directors clashed, as the latter began questioning Biddle's conduct. After a Jacksonian newspaper announced that on October 1 the government would stop making deposits in the bank, the treasury secretary objected again, refused to resign, and Jackson, albeit reluctantly, fired him.[123] After his replacement, Roger Taney, abruptly withdrew more than $2 million in government funds, Biddle announced that the bank would henceforth prioritize the interests of its stockholders, *not* the government, and kept the squeeze on lending.

The Treasury's attacks on the bank and Biddle's countermoves continued into 1834, as Biddle's stranglehold on lending caused businesses to fail around the country. Many blamed the bank, but others accepted Biddle's defenses.* Petitions supporting him and demanding the government deposits be returned to the bank were rejected. Runs started on New York banks after Biddle refused to aid them, seeking to expose the new setup's weakness, but eventually he relented, still hoping, against all evidence, that Jackson would step back from the brink.

---

* A hundred and sixty-nine years later, the left-center historian Sean Wilentz would describe the "devious," "autocratic" Biddle descending "into megalomaniac fantasy" as he fought the president.

In anticipation of the next presidential election two years hence (Van Buren was expected to run), the former National Republicans and other Jackson opponents formed the Whig Party, a tenuous coalition organized around antipathy toward the president. Despite its fractiousness, Biddle hoped it would stay together and help the bank get rechartered or reborn after Jackson's departure. But he was worn out from the years of fighting and finally gave in to his wife's desire to take his first break in fourteen years, a summer 1834 trip to Newport and Niagara Falls.

With voters believing the bank was backing the Whigs, the Democrats won the midterm election, foreclosing the possibility of a rechartering. Emboldened, Jackson redoubled his efforts to hinder the bank's operations with public criticism and support for the return of gold money. Like the Whigs, Biddle came out of the election on the losing side. Though his mistakes were stylistic and not corrupt, as a Senate investigation would eventually reveal, all that was left for Biddle to do on his return was plan his beloved bank's liquidation, a process he set in motion in March 1835. That revived the false charges of insolvency, and many of the bank's enemies lost money by betting against it in its final months.* The bank was financially healthy even in its dying days.

Finally, Biddle was blamed by the public, which believed the president's claim that capitalists manipulated money solely for their own advantage, and he was abandoned by his political supporters. His detractors in Philadelphia even forced Biddle to hire armed guards to protect him, his family, and their city home.[124] Daniel Webster demanded that Biddle burn their correspondence. In 1836, Van Buren won the presidency and the bank's charter expired.

Still, Biddle fought, asking Pennsylvania to give the bank a state charter. It cost the bank a $2 million payment to the state and an agreement to loan another $6 million toward its infrastructure development

---

* Ironically, in December, when a fire devasted New York, and its financial industry in particular, the bank pledged $2 million to insurance companies, something it alone had the power and solvency to accomplish. Most were grateful; Jackson wasn't.

to effectively turn the federally chartered Second Bank of the United States into the state-chartered United States Bank. Charges that it paid bribes for the approval weren't proved. And Biddle had a weapon to counter any further demands from Pennsylvania: a threat to move the "new" bank to another state. He quietly hoped to continue to provide a national currency and regulate exchange without federal sanction. But he didn't help his cause when he gave a commencement address at Princeton that fall and attacked political pandering by "mere demagogues wandering about the political common without a principle or a dollar."

America's economy continued to suffer, and finally so did Biddle's shrunken bank. As federal money accumulated in state banks, they issued their own paper money, and the abundance of banknotes caused prices and sales of public lands to soar. Trying to pop that real estate bubble just before leaving office, Jackson had ordered land offices to accept only specie for government land, not the questionable state-issued banknotes his policies encouraged, but his "cure" worsened the economy's disease, causing hard money to collect in the West, away from where it was needed most, at the same time that the Bank of England was tightening credit for its own reasons. Interest rates soared, commerce ground to a near-stop, specie payments were again suspended, prices fell, merchant firms in the South collapsed and were followed by banks in the Northeast, and the Panic of 1837 was on.

Predictably, Biddle argued in open letters to John Quincy Adams and a petition to Congress that Van Buren should recharter the national bank, pointing to two lessons the nation needed to take from the crisis: "The first is that we can have no financial prosperity while the public revenue is separated from the business of the country and committed to rash and ignorant politicians with no guides but their own passions and interests." The second was "to distrust all demagogues of all parties who profess exclusive love for what they call the people." Ruptures in the bonds of mutual dependence of all classes, making "the laborer regard his employers as an enemy, and to array the poor against the rich," he continued, had brought the country to a point "where every step tends inevitably to make the rich richer and the poor poorer."[125]

The frozen economy supported his argument. Americans couldn't pay their debts in Europe, nor could America pay its national debt, and the only solution was to unfreeze international commerce and raise both the volume of American goods sold in Europe and the prices they commanded. But it was illegal for the new bank to support the markets on its own account, so Biddle formed an independent merchant operation and sent agents to America's ports to buy and ship cotton and produce to England and France, halting further price declines.

Specie redemptions wouldn't fully resume for years. But through 1839, Biddle worked to contain the damage and enhance America's reputation and credit, including the repayment of its national debt. It was the very definition of a thankless job, and Biddle's health suffered. Still, at fifty-two, he remained as ambitious as he was conflicted. He dreamed of quitting, but also of running for president. Diminished but still arrogant, he sniffed in a letter to the bank's European correspondents at Barings, Hope, and another bank that Jackson's and Van Buren's supporters, "the less intelligent part of our population," were hurt worst by the Bank War.[126] Comments like that did not further his ambition. A capitalist-friendly Whig would in fact be the next occupant of the White House, but it was William Henry Harrison, a former general like Jackson, not Biddle.

On his fifty-third birthday in January 1839, Nicholas Biddle proudly reminded his journal that he had sworn to beat Jackson and the Democrats. His account books backed up his confidence. His 1837 speculations in cotton and produce, financed from his personal funds, had produced a $1.4 million profit. He gave $600,000 of that sum to the bank and $200,000 to each of the two employees who ran the operation, and kept $400,000 himself. The distribution was made just after he resigned as president of Pennsylvania's United States Bank in March, still hoping the Whigs might nominate him to run for president. He bought himself a new mansion on Philadelphia's Chestnut Street for $50,000—but never moved in. Within six months the bank, his reputation, and his fortune would be gone.[127]

As state banks took over without the superego of the Bank of the United States to guide and constrain them, another panic ensued.[128] At the end of the year, the world plunged into a depression—and what was left of Biddle's reputation sank with it. He is said to have stepped back into the fray, albeit informally, working quietly behind the scenes to save the bank's reputation, and protect its bottom line. Despite his efforts, he and the bank were blamed.[129] Indeed, many held him personally responsible for the damage done to the American economy in the five-year-long depression that began in 1839.[130]

Those years saw public economic dissatisfaction peak, but the threatening atmosphere had been incubating for a decade and would persist. Riots, some of them targeting banks, were a regular feature of New York life in the 1830s and 1840s. Anti-banker riots also hit Boston, Baltimore, and Philadelphia. From the point of view of the targets of those disturbances, America was in chaos, with 99 percent of the population raging at the wealthy, seeking to swarm their cloistered world as the revelers at Andrew Jackson's inaugural party had swarmed the White House.[131]

In the end, the simplistic argument for "hard money" won the day; paper money, credit, and big banks lost, as politicians like Van Buren made them scapegoats. But the public rejected Van Buren in the 1840 election, putting Harrison, a rich man the Whigs hoped would appeal to the multitude, in the White House after a campaign in which he avoided the topic of the bank as much as possible. Then Harrison died at sixty-eight of a cold that turned into pneumonia, thirty-one days after his inauguration, and John Tyler, a longtime bank opponent descended from a blacksmith, and another Democrat, became president. After Tyler twice vetoed corrective banking legislation, most of his cabinet resigned.

In Philadelphia, instead of mounting a fresh defense or merely expressing a positive outlook, some of the directors of the Bank of the United States banded together in opposition to Biddle. In June 1840, the officers closest to Biddle resigned abruptly and stories began circulating that they had borrowed from the bank and were involved in speculation, fraud, and embezzlement. Biddle, unaware of any of this, considered himself responsible nonetheless. New directors, who had no love for Biddle, came after him for losses incurred in his attempts to stabilize the economy, arguing that his actions to support the American economy had actually hurt the bank.[132] And they blamed Biddle and his team for making their successors "dupes of a shrewd and self-interested conspiracy."[133] When the bank's financial statements were published early in 1841, showing $17 million in losses from operations, loans, and investments, it clearly couldn't survive, and panicked withdrawals followed. Investigations blamed Biddle's regime. That September, when the United States Bank finally collapsed for good, Biddle's public life ended.

The bank might actually have survived under better management, but that possibility didn't mitigate the public's rancor toward Biddle, who had remained its public face even after he left. He and several other bank officers were indicted for fraud and theft in December 1841, and Biddle was arrested on January 6, 1842, charged with conspiracy to defraud the bank and its shareholders of $396,000 "applied to unlawful purposes and to promote Mr. Biddle's own private views"; he was released on $10,000 bail.[134] Though the charges were dropped for lack of probable cause, he was finished. "He has no longer money for bribery and corruption," a North Carolina newspaper crowed, "and this talisman lost, the sceptre of power has departed from him. . . . [He is] now branded as a thief and swindler, abandoned and despised by all—defended by none."

His wife's fortune kept Biddle afloat. That fall, Jane Biddle headed off the seizure and forced sale of Andalusia by the sheriff of Bucks County by bidding $8,000 to pay off a loan John Craig's estate had made to Nicholas with the $200,000 property as collateral. The Biddles moved to the country full-time. By summer 1843, sickly and suffering, Biddle was on his deathbed with a heart condition and was taking digitalis four times a day. He recovered enough to briefly involve himself in Whig plans for the 1844 election. But on February 27, 1844, he died of bronchitis, a broken man, one year before Jackson followed him to the grave.

⌁

Arguments over Nicholas Biddle's legacy began with his downfall and have continued ever since. In his memoirs, John Quincy Adams recalled a dinner at Andalusia late in 1840. "Biddle broods with smiling face and stifled groans over the wreck of splendid blasted expectations and ruined hopes," he wrote. "A fair mind, a brilliant genius, a generous temper, and honest heart, waylaid and led astray by prosperity, suffering the penalty of scarcely voluntary error—'tis piteous to behold."[135] The diarist Philip Hone said he had been "indicted for high crimes and vulgar misdemeanors by a secret conclave of greasy householders" who had previously considered him the high priest of the Bank's Temple of Mammon.[136] William Cullen Bryant, a newspaper editor and Biddle antagonist, noted his death "at his country seat, where he had passed the last of his days in elegant retirement, which, if justice had taken place, would have been spent in the penitentiary."[137] Undeniably, overseeing the failure of the bank is Biddle's main contribution to economic history. Yet even his adversary Martin Van Buren had to admit, in his autobiography, that Biddle's "private and personal character has never, to my knowledge, been successfully impeached."[138]

Biddle's last days were witnessed by the diarist John Jay Smith, who wrote:

When the bank failed, and he was disgraced in public estimation, his heart was broken. The flatterers who had over-praised him now pursued him with vituperation to his solitude at Andalusia, his wife's country-seat on the Delaware. He had at first been overpraised, and now he was over-abused. Power such as he attained was a dangerous possession. I am not prepared to say he did not commit errors, though I am free to add my belief that the errors were caused by bad advisers, or the result of Jackson's hostility to the bank. . . .

There was something extremely touching in this loss of public confidence, and the consequent heart-broken death of Mr. Biddle. I was among the few who followed the remains from the house of his brother-in-law, Francis Hopkinson, in Chestnut Street, whither the body had been brought for interment in Christ Church ground. . . . The followers of that solemn cortege must have had, with myself, many striking reflections on the vanity of human ambition and the darkening of the brightest dreams of public adulation.[139]

Biddle was even implicated in the disappearance of America's aristocracy, as Philadelphia's upper class began to "privatize . . . withdraw[ing] from the world of public service into the counting house and factory . . . a money-insulated world of the great houses, private schools, and fashionable churches surrounding [Rittenhouse] Square."[140] In that, Philadelphia may have led the nation, but the transformation of America's WASP oligarchy from genteel aristocracy to hard-knuckled plutocracy had its roots in Andrew Jackson's victory over Nicholas Biddle. No longer would effete easterners, or even overly refined Virginians, presume to rule the country they'd done so much to invent. If they wanted power, they'd have to fight for it. The sharp elbow would henceforth be as valuable as the noble gesture. It was another triumph of rough-hewn America over its more genteel antecedents in Europe. America's upper class had found a new distinguishing characteristic.

17

Lewis Cass chose the winning side of the bank battle. With Jackson's presidency ending in 1836 and Van Buren's election foretold, Jackson rewarded Cass with the job of minister to France—a perfect spot for an avowed Anglophobe. Cass, his family, and his secretary Henry Ledyard, a Livingston descendent and lawyer, left for Europe in fall 1836, remaining through one-term president Van Buren's time in office and into the reigns of the Whigs Harrison and Tyler.

But despite his distance from Washington, Cass couldn't avoid the issue of slavery. In 1841, Britain, which had banned the practice in 1834, called a conference of five European powers to make a treaty allowing each to halt ships of the others on suspicion of carrying slaves. Cass warned it would lead to another war with England. France refused to ratify the treaty. But when Daniel Webster, Tyler's first secretary of state, negotiated a separate deal with England, promising cooperation in suppressing the slave trade without barring British searches of American ships, Cass, humiliated and enraged, resigned and headed home, setting off a war of words that increased his popularity with both southerners and northern Democrats, who would henceforth form the base of his support. While neither party wanted to talk about slavery, Democrats were willing to accommodate it. Van Buren's presidency had been damaged by the Seminole War and the Panic of 1837. From Paris, Cass had watched as the Democrats squabbled in the wake of his defeat by Harrison, and Calhoun and Van Buren positioned themselves to run again in 1844. Cass was touted as a compromise candidate, despite his lack of experience. Attempting to appeal to southerners, he openly opposed the abolition of slavery in a campaign letter as "not only unconstitutional, but fraught with dangerous consequences."[141]

When President Tyler agreed to annex Texas, his third secretary of state, Calhoun, declared that if it was not annexed as a pro-slavery state, the South would secede. Cass seized on the issue, warning that racial warfare—with the British allying with Blacks instead of Native Americans—might ensue. He succeeded in damaging Van Buren but didn't win the nomination. Instead, James K. Polk, a dark horse quietly groomed by Andrew Jackson, emerged triumphant from the Democratic convention—and beat Whig Henry Clay for the presidency.

In February 1845, the Michigan state legislature named Cass a senator. Still eyeing the White House, he became the body's most ardent proponent of expansionism and threw himself into a dispute with Great Britain over competing claims to the Oregon Territory, which encompassed today's states of Oregon, Washington, and Idaho, parts of Wyoming and Montana, and most of British Columbia. This time he encouraged war with the English, in a stultifying three-hour address to the Senate that was nonetheless deemed one of his finest speeches, advocating a strong stand against the British Crown.[142] Polk negotiated a compromise, and though Cass opposed it, he accepted defeat.

⌒

A year later, in May 1846, the United States went to war with Mexico, a conflict set off by America's annexation of Texas, a fight Cass supported not so much because he favored expansion but to keep Britain, which also had designs on the West Coast of the American continent, out of the Southwest. If America won more territory, so much the better. Cass allied with Polk in hopes of gaining New Mexico and what was called Alta or Upper California, including today's California, Nevada, Utah, and parts of Arizona, Wyoming, Colorado and New Mexico.

Mexico had outlawed slavery in 1829, setting off a civil war with Anglo slaveholders in its province of Tejas. In 1836, they had declared independence as the Republic of Texas. In the meantime, Congress was faced with a proposal to ban slavery from any territory taken from America's southern neighbor. The ban, named the Wilmot Proviso for the anti-slavery Pennsylvania congressman who proposed it, further confused a situation that already pitted expansionists against nativists and anti-slavery advocates. Cass, whose lodestar was expediency, was committed to the "unlimited power of expansion" as America's "safety valve," he told the Senate.[143] Unlike many of his fellow northerners, he was against abolition and was willing to annex territory where slavery was permitted. However nefarious the practice was, to Cass it was merely an annoyance, as it set free and slave regions against each other.

The 1848 Treaty of Guadalupe Hidalgo made Texas and Alta California American in exchange for a payment of $15 million to the impecunious Mexican government. Meantime, Cass had set out his position about the expansion of slavery in December 1847 in a public letter that would help him win the Democrats' presidential nomination the following spring. It was a clever bit of political tap dancing that claimed only residents of a territory had the right to "regulate their internal concerns," a notion that would come to be known as popular sovereignty and would eventually be adopted and made famous by Congressman Stephen Douglas in 1858 debates with an Illinois senatorial candidate, Abraham Lincoln. It took the position that slavery was a purely local concern in which the federal government had no power to interfere, and it implicitly granted whites the power to govern themselves while denying that to Blacks.

Cass's focus was on keeping the Union intact—no matter the human cost. That meant finding a middle ground between Wilmot's proscription of slavery in the former Mexican lands and Calhoun's position that any American should be entitled to bring his property (including slaves) into any American territory. Popular sovereignty offered a negotiable passage between these almost irreconcilable positions. At the Democrats' convention that May, Cass was nominated for president. But his nuanced position on slavery angered both its advocates and northern fans of the Wilmot Proviso. Some dissident anti-slavery factions formed a new Liberal or Free Soil Party, nominating Van Buren—which, due to his strength in New York, threatened Cass's chances. But Zachary Taylor, the Whig nominee, a slaveholder and avowed enemy of Cass from the Black Hawk War, had similar issues; his party split, too, with a group called Conscience Whigs opposing Taylor. Cass doubled down on expansion, calling for an American takeover not only of Mexico but also of Cuba and islands in both the Atlantic and the Pacific—a position the Whigs attacked, as they did Cass's war record. All concerned continued avoiding the divisive topic of slavery as much as possible.

Taylor, who boasted he had never voted and who had virtually no political record, won—and Cass reclaimed his Senate seat, but with orders from the Michigan state legislature to support free soil via the Wilmot Proviso. He decided to take his seat but resign if forced to betray his beliefs. Then he argued for continued waffling on slavery, saying "a spirit of compromise was necessary to create this confederation and it is equally necessary to preserve it."[144] His fence-straddling was fast becoming a painful posture.

⟶

Cass was correct that the Union was in danger, but ten years would pass before the spirit of compromise would be seen as appeasement and finally discarded. Forcefully repeating his arguments for popular sovereignty, he even pushed back against the Quakers when the sect pressed for the breakup of the Union.[145] In his last remarks to the Senate, Calhoun, dying of tuberculosis, warned that the fight over what he termed the "peculiar institution" threatened the entire American enterprise, and he insisted that the North must yield and allow slaveowners to bring their "property" into the western territories. Soon afterward Cass served as one of Calhoun's pallbearers (along with Clay and Daniel Webster). And shortly thereafter Michigan legislators withdrew their demand that he vote against his conscience.

The middle ground between the extremes of abolition and secession seemed to Cass like the only place to be, but it would soon prove to be a lonely place indeed, and Cass would edge ever closer to the South.

But for the moment, pressing his fellow senators to keep compromising, Cass fought for a package of bills devised by Clay and the young Democrat of Illinois, Stephen Douglas, recently risen to the Senate, that became known as the Compromise of 1850, admitting California as a free state; establishing a New Mexico territory (where slavery was rare due to Mexico's opposition) and a Utah territory in which popular sovereignty regarding slavery was instituted; prohibiting the slave trade in Washington, D.C.; and passing a fugitive slave law southerners demanded. A gratified Cass (who abstained from voting for the last because it failed to provide for a jury trial for accused slaves) hoped that the question was finally settled, but in fact a reckoning had merely been delayed. Efforts to overturn and maneuver around the Fugitive Slave Act led Cass to lament that northerners couldn't leave well enough alone. Slavery might be a "great social and political evil," he told the Michigan Democratic convention in summer 1854, but it was the South's problem.[146] The northern economy was doing well; business was booming; railroads were speeding commerce and settlement; immigrants were expanding the population. Many credited Cass and the compromise for creating what seemed, albeit temporarily, a "second 'era of good feeling.'"[147]

Cass still harbored presidential ambitions. After Zachary Taylor's sudden death and replacement by his vice president, the former upstate New York congressman Millard Fillmore, in July 1850, a year into their term, Cass was considered a front-runner, alongside James Buchanan, a Jacksonian lawyer, politician, and diplomat, and Douglas, who was a fellow expansionist but was only thirty-eight in 1852. But Cass, still a fence-sitter, was rejected by more vocal slavery advocates, and after multiple ballots, the Democratic convention turned to another dark horse, Franklin Pierce.

Pierce took the White House and appointed several Cass associates to his cabinet in a nod to the Michigan senator. Cass's influence could also be seen in the Kansas-Nebraska Act of 1854, drafted by Douglas, still eyeing the presidency, which allowed popular sovereignty in the two newest states. But while Nebraska was expected to be free, the open question of slavery in Kansas created a rush of activists into the territory, provoking a violent uprising that would destroy the fragile Whig coalition.

Moderation proved to be Cass's Achilles heel; his inability to see that slavery was a moral disgrace, his fatal flaw. That "last compromise" in the plains states lit the fuse that would ignite the Civil War by insisting, as Cass did, that Congress had no right to intervene, even in a practice that was increasingly seen as immoral, if not strictly unconstitutional.[148] A wound that had festered since Gouverneur Morris was forced to accept the "nefarious practice" at the Constitutional Convention, if not since 1619, was about to threaten the life of the nation.

As Cass held tight to his compromise position, opinions on both sides of the slavery argument hardened and Democrats rallied around support of slavery. Prior to the 1854 midterm elections, anti-slavery former Whigs in the former Northwest Territory—Cass country—joined with Democratic deserters and the fierce slavery opponents of the brief-lived Free Soil Party to create a new Republican Party in time for the midterm elections. Two years later, demonstrating national ambitions, it nominated the explorer and military man John C. Frémont to run for president. Cass, aging and in physical decline, took himself out of the running for the Democrats' nod, though his name was thrown into the fray anyway. Cass threw his support to James Buchanan, who won the nomination and ran against both Frémont and Fillmore, the latter the candidate of a southern-dominated nationalistic breakaway party called the American Party but commonly known as the Know-Nothings. The remnants of the Whigs also endorsed Fillmore for its last-gasp election.

Buchanan won the White House, and though the Democrats lost control of Cass's Michigan, spelling the end of his tenure in the Senate, the president appointed him secretary of state as an elder statesman and tenuous symbol of party unity.[149] Cass was worn out, but Buchanan expected to run his own foreign policy. And the president and Cass were aligned on the subject of slavery. Buchanan supported a pro-slavery Constitution in Kansas, several other cabinet members were sympathetic to the South, and after the Supreme

Court supported his narrow view of the Constitution on slavery in its 1857 *Dred Scott* decision, Cass moved even closer to the southern side of the argument in remarks quoted at the time in the *Congressional Record*, calling slavery "a constitutional and practical question," not a moral one. Blacks were "inferior" he declared, and "I would not emancipate the slaves were it in my power."[150]

But the Republicans were ascendent, and in the wake of the Kansas troubles and the Panic of 1857 the Democrats lost twenty-two congressional seats in the next midterm election. The rifts in the party were becoming chasms. By the time of John Brown's 1859 raid on the Union arsenal at Harpers Ferry, Virginia, Cass expected the worst—and got it. Stephen Douglas was chosen to run for president by the Democrats' northern faction, and the current vice president, John Breckenridge, was selected by the southerners and supported by Buchanan and Cass, who abandoned popular sovereignty, which had practically banned slavery in the West, in a vain effort to restore party unity. A fourth candidate, Tennessee's John Bell, also sought to protect slavery but wanted to prevent its spread. The Republican nominee, Abraham Lincoln, won the presidency when he held on to the North while the South splintered like the Democrats. Before Lincoln took office, Cass resigned his cabinet post to protest one of Buchanan's last acts, refusing to reinforce federal outposts in the South when, led by South Carolina, its states began to secede. Cass's public life ended just before Confederate guns opened fire on Fort Sumter.

Cass's wife had died years earlier, but their children were all doing well. Lewis Jr. served as his father's secretary and political advisor. His daughter Matilda had married Cass's first secretary, Henry Ledyard, who managed her father's real estate, served as mayor of Detroit, and in the state senate, and ended his career working for Cass again as an assistant secretary of state. Among their children was Lewis Cass Ledyard, born in Detroit in 1851, who would become the best-known lawyer of his time, representing railroad, steel, tobacco, and oil companies, as well as the Gilded Age financier J. Pierpont Morgan.

Cass didn't live to see his grandson join the elite, but he supported and survived the Civil War, albeit regretting both his enabling of the South and the North's raising "that abominable Negro question." Cass saw the states reunited before he died at eighty-three in spring 1866, twenty-two years after the reviled Nicholas Biddle. Cass was treated much better in death than Biddle had been. In his official death announcement William Seward, the latest secretary of state, praised Cass's "exalted patriotism at a recent period of political disorder."[151] Added the *Boston Post,* "America has produced few statesmen whose records were so stainless."[152]

But the policy of removal that Cass had nurtured left a terrible stain by presenting Native Americans with starkly unfortunate choices: accept white domination, fight efforts to herd them into ever smaller territories, or die of starvation if not war. Not even the Civil War reduced the pressure on the nations, and afterward it increased exponentially, as whites, freed from the burden of war, returned to expanding their nation, often at the expense of the Indians.

Some indigenous people did fight, turning skills learned in combat against each other toward battling the invaders in what would be known as the Indian Wars. Briefly, they had the advantage of fighting a downsized army after the Civil War, but "the whites were many, the Indians few . . . the buffalo were vanishing and settlers were overrunning the plains," threatening the existence of the Cheyenne, Comanche, and Kiowa.[153] Skirmishes among them, and bursts of violence against whites, panicked settlers and invited military intervention. "The more I see of these Indians, the more I become convinced that they all have to be killed or be maintained as a species of paupers," General William T. Sherman wrote to his brother in September 1868. "Their attempts at civilization are simply ridiculous."[154] Whites were killed, too, among them a grandson of Alexander Hamilton serving under the colorful cavalry officer George Armstrong Custer in the 1868 Battle of Washita.

By the end of the 1860s, American Indian policy would be in disarray as an impeached, disgraced President Andrew Johnson left the White House, replaced by the former general Ulysses S. Grant in 1869. Grant took office as a reformer; he even appointed a Seneca Iroquois sachem as commissioner of Indian affairs. The new commissioner's first significant act was to end the charade of treating Native American groups as sovereign nations. That sent them from the pan into the fire as "legal wards of the government."[155]

In the early 1870s, buffalo hide hunters swarmed the plains, killing off herds despite American Indian hunting rights, while horse thieves deprived the Native American population of its wealth and liquor eroded what remained of its self-respect. Mid-decade, weather and greed provoked a revolt on the southern plains that inspired another army offensive. Victory led to the confiscation of weapons and the sale of Native American war ponies. Settlers moved in and the surviving Indians settled on reservations known as agencies. More massacres of Native peoples followed. To the north, though, hostile bands remained at large, including a small number of Hunkpapa of the Lakota tribe led by a holy man, Sitting Bull.

When railroads began crossing the northern plains, General Sherman wrote to his colleague General Philip H. Sheridan that it could be the "final solution" to "the Indian problem."[156] And reports of precious metals—and potential riches—threatened to bring more whites into sacred Native American lands in the Black Hills. As the end of Grant's presidency approached, he determined to violate treaties and morality and allow white miners to invade Lakota lands. The Natives—or, at least, the thousands who had gathered around Sitting Bull on the banks of the Little Bighorn River—were unwilling to give up without a fight. Their 1876 massacre of Custer and his troops was the beginning of the end of the Indian Wars, finally inspiring the whites to seek decisive victory. More campaigns against nations in the Northwest (notably the Nez Perce in Oregon), the Utes of Colorado, and varied southwestern Apache tribes let whites finally take the entire continent, confining Native Americans to tiny reservations. The 1870s "closed with ironfisted intolerance of tribes that did not unconditionally indulge the United States' limitless appetite for land and confine themselves to the limits of their reservations."[157] Though Geronimo would continue the fight, his was a rear-guard action. And the Dawes Act of 1887, which broke up tribal domains and distributed the land to individuals in an effort to both assimilate Natives and eliminate tribal cohesion, made legal and final the theft of American Indian land.[158]

Twenty-one years after Lewis Cass's death, his tainted legacy was secure. Like Nicholas Biddle, he demonstrated how America's founding WASPs had navigated the rough seas of settling and founding a new nation and then, while still, inevitably, arguing among themselves, began moving on to fulfilling their—sometimes deeply flawed—individual ambitions. Both Biddle and Cass accomplished that through public service. More secure in their national identity, the next generation of American WASPs, who would still represent a majority of America's population—about 55 percent in 1900—would begin to prioritize personal agendas. But they would also be burdened by the weight of the disgraceful legacy of Native American removal and slavery, policies supported by many of their predecessors, and tolerated by even more, to their continuing shame.

Part Five

OPPORTUNISM

1846–1872
HENRY SHELTON SANFORD

18

Henry Shelton Sanford got precious little respect. Though his family had come to New England under the aegis of John Winthrop in 1631, and seven generations later he was the heir to a manufacturing fortune, his American ascent was punctuated by the sneers of many, who variously derided him as officious, insolent, ill-mannered, pompous, a plunger, and a business failure. He was much like his WASP cohort in the mid-nineteenth century, "forceful and energetic, intelligent and learned, cultured and charming," according to a sympathetic biographer, but "also ruthlessly ambitious, exceedingly vain, naively optimistic, frequently overzealous, and consistently undisciplined."[1]

Still, though mostly neglected by history, Sanford made his mark, for good and for ill. He embodied the words of New York congressman George Washington Plunkitt, who was born the year Sanford turned twenty-one: "I seen my opportunities, and I took 'em." Sanford didn't embody the best of America's WASPs, but the ruthless opportunism that arose among them after the Civil War is a significant part of their storyline. And it produced both bad and good.

As Abraham Lincoln's minister to Belgium in the 1860s, Sanford established America's first international espionage network in western Europe. But after the Civil War, as he tried to get even richer using connections made as a diplomat, he played an ignoble role aiding and abetting what was arguably the worst excess of European colonialism. Promoting the Belgian king Leopold II's scheme to rape and plunder his personally "owned" colony, the Congo, Sanford failed miserably in his personal attempts to get rich by exploiting its natural resources. Back at home during Reconstruction, he lost more money investing in sugar and cotton plantations. He also failed personally as a proponent of railroads, tourism, and citrus cultivation in northern Florida, but in the process he played a vital part in creating those three industries, which enriched others who came later and were more attentive and fortunate than he. Sanford, "a great man who doesn't get anywhere near the credit he deserves," can perhaps be called the original Florida Man.[2]

In both his accomplishments and his failures, Sanford reflects the experience of America's founding families as they faced challenges to their long-held status and sought to seize fresh opportunity in the late nineteenth century. Despite the rising political clout of less-tenured but more numerous Americans, those old families retained their influence. They still led the country as it experienced geometric growth in size, economic power, and social influence and edged into international leadership, reaching out across continents and oceans, flexing its muscles in Central and South America, Asia, and Africa as well as in its Protestant European crucible. Like Sanford, America on the verge of empire was perhaps most deficient in its capacity for self-examination, too busy growing to spare a moment to reflect on how it had gone so far.

⟍⟋

The Jacksonians had not triumphed without pushback. President Jackson's battle with Nicholas Biddle upset Philadelphia's gentry as well as many of their privileged brethren beyond the City of Brotherly Love, and his treatment of Indians, though no more than an extension of policies in place since George Washington, inspired widespread moral outrage. The American Whig Party, formed to counter Jackson's conservative WASP influence and represent urbanites, the educated, the accomplished, the forward-thinking, saw an advantage in scattering dirt over its own patrician roots. Its first president, William Henry Harrison, won by stressing his backcountry residence, not his Virginian Cavalier blood. The same was true of another successor, Zachary Taylor, though in between Appalachia's James K. Polk, a Methodist, won the White House. Taylor's successor was a Jacksonian Democrat, but also a reversal: New Englander Franklin Pierce was Episcopalian and a sixth-generation American.

Meantime, in the North, reformists had emerged among descendants of Puritans and Quakers and renewed their political power through abolitionism, the desire to rid America of the blight of slavery. Conflicts over slavery would bring about another political realignment in 1860, when the Democratic Party split in half, North versus South, and the six-year-old Republican Party, formed not to abolish slavery but to stymie its expansion, put Abraham Lincoln, effectively a Deist, in the White House.

By the mid-nineteenth century, the landed WASP aristocracy of the colonial era no longer held an iron grip on America's wealth. Though in the South the rich remained the same property- and slaveholders, in the North bankers, shippers, merchants, and real estate speculators like Lewis Cass's friend John Jacob Astor were emerging as the new rich. And after the Civil War, on the threshold of the Gilded Age, the North was ascendant, as was an incestuous new meritocracy. The Sanfords, who started out in America as yeoman farmers, would eventually rise to the middle of the top tier of that ever-evolving upper class.

⟜

Thomas Sanford, born in 1600 in England, sailed for America in 1631 as an indentured servant, somehow acquired land in Dorchester, Massachusetts, and was made a freeman in 1637. He later moved to Milford, Connecticut, which he helped establish, winning political connections along the way. By the time a grandson, Ezekiel Jr., died in 1728, he had a large estate and eight children. One of them, Ephraim, settled in a Redding, Connecticut, neighborhood later called Sanfordtown, and appears to have owned much of it. One of his great-grandsons, John Sanford, was born there in 1803.

It's said that at eighteen John decided to walk west, though he may have taken one of the half dozen stage lines that ran between Boston and Albany. In 1821, he arrived in Amsterdam, New York, thirty-two miles west of Albany, and got a job as a schoolteacher. First settled in 1738 by an Irish Catholic convert to Protestantism who later built a baronial home there, Amsterdam became a British stronghold (and that house a fort), and after the Revolution it developed industry powered by Chuctanunda Creek; by 1816, the town had seventeen mills. John married a local girl and moved often, but was back in Amsterdam in time for their sixth and last child's birth in 1836. By then, Gouverneur Morris's Erie Canal, which followed the route of the Mohawk River through Amsterdam, had put the town on the map of American commerce. John, a partner in a carpet company, also served a term in Congress.

In Connecticut, John's brother Nehemiah married Nancy Shelton, who was descended from the first royal governor of Connecticut. Their first child was Henry, the future minister to Belgium, born in 1823. Theirs was an upwardly mobile clan. Nehemiah, self-made and driven, an upper-middle-class merchant, and by the 1830s a state senator, bought land in Michigan, and in 1836 he organized the Shelton Tack Company with a brother-in-law before dying in 1841, leaving Henry $100,000.

Henry Shelton Sanford, lonesome, bookish, and entranced by tales of knights and maidens, was educated in the classics by private tutors, then attended Episcopal Academy in Philadelphia, and was introduced to his family's business interests at age fourteen on a trip to inspect his father's Michigan property. He followed an already well-worn WASP path to the future Trinity College but dropped out in 1840 after asthma affected his eyesight. When his father died, his health was precarious but his pockets were full, and his good fortune helped him come into his own.

In his twenties, he went back and forth to Europe, an aimless pleasure-seeker.[3] But he also learned several languages, developed sophisticated European tastes, put on weight, and began to blossom. At six foot one with chestnut hair, a high forehead, arched brows, prominent cheekbones, and a long nose, Henry became a ladies' man, considered "fast" by his European friends. His mother worried, warning him to "shun vice and disappation" that would ruin his body and soul. She disdained his attraction to "court society and nobility" and his avid pursuit of pleasure and urged him to be disciplined, marry, and move home. She even chose a prospective wife for him. A year later, in 1846, he dutifully proposed to his intended, but two years on, he broke it off.[4] Despite recurrent asthma attacks, he went to Michigan again, and then farther west to kill buffalo for sport.

After breaking his engagement, Henry finally found ambition, if not focus, and briefly worked at the tack factory with his uncle, who was overbearing, risk-averse, and unwilling to play fast and loose, as Henry preferred. By the end of 1847, he had sold out his share to his uncle. Henry also gave him power of attorney and control of his investments, then worth some $50,000, which his uncle put in bank and rail stocks. Fretting that his life hadn't been well spent, Henry admitted his impulsivity and concluded that he didn't have the self-esteem to succeed in business, so he sailed again to Europe, determined to study and find a way to "do something useful for my country."[5]

In Paris, he was soon invited by the U.S. minister to Russia, a family friend, to join an American delegation to the Russian court at St. Petersburg as a temporary attaché. He didn't care for the country, but politics and diplomacy intrigued him, as did proximity to power, and he next moved to Berlin as acting secretary to its American minister. Deciding on a career in the foreign service, he won a post as acting secretary of the American legation at Frankfurt, Germany. Though he lacked a bachelor's degree, he somehow managed to earn a doctorate of law, cum laude, after a mere eight months at the University of Heidelberg.

His mother still disapproved, warning him he was "castle Building," aiming too high for an uncertain target, though really she wanted him to come home and be near her.[6] Henry, briefly back in America, wasn't interested in a respectable Connecticut trajectory, however; he aspired to live like a European aristocrat, so he sought the post of secretary to the American minister in Paris. Rebuffed, he retrenched and began building alliances with prominent Whigs, beginning with his two Shelton uncles, who got Connecticut's political establishment behind him, as well as New York's Thurlow Weed, publisher of Albany's leading Whig newspaper; Weed's political protégé William Seward, an anti-slavery advocate who had been New York's governor and would soon be a senator; Millard Fillmore, then a Buffalo lawyer and former congressman; and the powerful New York businessman Moses Taylor, an Astor associate who shortly became president of the predecessor to today's Citibank. Henry Sanford was twenty-six when their concerted string-pulling won him his dream job, an appointment by the new president, Zachary Taylor, to serve as secretary to the head of the American legation in Paris, William C. Rives.

Henry's new job was mostly bureaucratic but also expensive, as he had to employ his own assistant, leaving him $5,000 in debt by 1854. He had assumed the burden of an expensive lifestyle as a leading member of the American expatriate community (and, after a promotion, the American chargé d'affaires): he was expected to escort visitors, and he also chose to keep a house big enough to host, as he did, a ball for 250 guests, as well as a carriage with four horses. A fellow diplomat warned that his lifestyle might forestall advancement, and his relatives were appalled at his extravagance, especially his mother, who was "grieved and pained" over his lust for status. She worried he had "cracked."[7]

But Henry went well beyond the call of duty between 1848 and 1853, producing papers on European penal codes and administrative changes in France. They were solid if not exceptional, rather like their author. When Franklin Pierce won the presidency in 1852 and Rives resigned, Sanford stayed on and hailed the latest secretary of state's decision to stop requiring diplomats to wear elaborate uniforms at European courts, instead encouraging them to don dress that reflected republican simplicity. Sanford chose a black coat and white tie, was relieved when Napoleon III seemed to approve, and won the nickname "Black Crow," reflecting the way he still managed to stand out from the crowd. But in a letter to Pierce in 1853, an American visiting Paris described Sanford as an un-American "toady to aristocracy."[8]

Early in 1854, his sartorial choice cost him his job when the new American minister to France insisted that he revert to traditional court attire. Sanford resigned, expecting that his stand would enhance his reputation with the state department; instead, the minister, infuriated, called Sanford conceited.

When Henry's uncle John left Congress in spring 1843, he recommitted to his carpet business and summoned his son Stephen, who had been studying at West Point, home to help. A move into inexpensive carpets encouraged by Stephen helped the firm prosper, and soon John was writing to his nephew in Europe to say the business was going so well that he was contemplating retirement at age fifty. But in 1849, when their mill burned down, the elder Sanford sold out to his partners and opened a new carpet firm, John Sanford & Son.

Four years later, when the company's new mill burned down, John retired, selling his share of the business to Stephen. But he wasn't done yet. Aware the Chuctanunda Creek was drying up, he and partners bought land outside town and created a reservoir, now Galway Lake, two years before he died in 1857, ensuring Stephen a water supply. The entrepreneurial Stephen, then thirty-one, added a yarn-spinning business and a knitwear factory, where during the Civil War he made blankets for the Union Army. His carpet business suffered but survived, and his growing family—he had four sons—continued to prosper.

Henry, meanwhile, quickly picked his next fight with the nation of Venezuela over an uninhabited private island, Aves, where another uncle had a business digging and shipping guano for fertilizer. Henry became his legal advocate for a 5 percent commission, eventually taking title to his claim, which was disputed by competitors. That inspired Henry to study the narrow subject of sovereignty over derelict islands, as well as the broader one of inter-American trade. After the Monroe Doctrine had claimed the Western Hemisphere as America's exclusive sphere of influence, businessmen like Sanford became stalking horses of a nascent American imperialism, soon to blossom. He instinctually saw the less developed world as a resource American business could exploit.[9]

Sanford's attitude toward the Venezuelans was condescending—he called them "pigmies" and urged America to use force to defend his guano claim.[10] The ineffectual fifteenth president, Democrat James Buchanan, seeking respite from arguments over slavery, hoped to divert attention with foreign aggression, and in fall 1857, at Sanford's urging, Buchanan's secretary of state, Lewis Cass, ordered his minister in Caracas to threaten to break off diplomatic relations.[11] The episode demonstrated Henry's focus, energy, all-American arrogance, and taste for political intrigue.* Between 1857 and 1860, he took assignments in Central America from both the government and railroads, and sought a diplomatic posting in South America, but his familial and fraternal ties to the Whigs, then becoming Republicans, made that unlikely under a Democratic president.

＿＿＿＿

While working in the Caribbean, Sanford commissioned a study of conditions of freed slaves there that was never completed.[12] That led Henry, thirty-seven in 1860 and seeking his next job, to Springfield, Illinois, to meet President-elect Lincoln. He urged Lincoln to make concessions to the slave states, reflecting the position of his business allies in New York, but also that the Union start growing cotton in Central America to put economic pressure on the South. Sanford came away from the meeting thinking that, as he put it in a letter to his former boss in Paris, William Rives, the "nigger question" would be resolved short of war.† Then Sanford moved to Washington, to continue his campaign for a new diplomatic post, wining, dining, and lobbying Republicans and capitalists on a daily basis, "in quiet costly English style," according to a future Lincoln cabinet official.[13]

South Carolina, which had started the nullification movement, led the South again in seceding from the United States that December.‡ When President Buchanan refused to hand over American forts, secessionists seized them. Lincoln took office in March and installed Sanford's ally William Seward as his secretary of state. With Democrats still occupying several European missions and the South sending its own diplomats there, Sanford sought to leverage his prior experience

---

* A revolution in Venezuela in 1858 made a solution possible and a settlement agreement was reached. But by 1863, less than half of the $130,000 total had been paid. It eventually took ten years (and another revolution) before the debt was finally settled, with Sanford taking a $20,000 loss. It wasn't until the 1890s that he was made whole through diplomatic channels.

† Rives had gone on to serve as a senator from Virginia and would shortly join the Confederate Congress.

‡ Mississippi, Florida, Alabama, Georgia, Louisiana, and Texas followed, forming the Confederate States of America in February 1861. Virginia, Arkansas, Tennessee, and North Carolina joined the Confederacy after war broke out. Though they allowed slavery, Delaware, Kentucky, Maryland, and Missouri remained in the Union, as did the western counties of Virginia, which became a separate state in 1863.

in France into a new diplomatic post, hoping to run the ministry in the relatively new, neighboring kingdom of Belgium.

Hailed as a model for a more professional diplomatic corps, Sanford was promptly nominated as minister to Belgium by Lincoln, and that April, three days after the first shots of the Civil War were fired at Fort Sumter, South Carolina, he arrived in Paris, where he worked briefly before heading to Brussels, the Belgian capital. Charged by Secretary of State Seward with countering the Confederate States of America in Europe, Sanford asked the French to spurn southern envoys and bar Confederate ships from the country's ports. Napoleon III's France, a major market for southern cotton, was less than cooperative, remaining officially neutral through the war, despite Sanford's protests, and though his short-term assignment in Paris had ended, he would continue to meddle there after he settled in the relative backwater of Brussels.

American arms manufacturing was insufficient to meet the needs of the Union's military, so he began arranging arms purchases and spreading pro-Union propaganda, backed by $1 million provided by Seward, who started calling him the U.S. minister to all of Europe.[14] "I am in my element!" exulted Sanford as he embarked on his greatest lifetime accomplishment, the creation of America's first overseas spy network to watch and foil the Confederacy as it sought to buy arms and supplies. "How it will be done," he wrote to Seward, "whether through a pretty mistress, or an intelligent servant, or a spying landlord, is nobody's business."[15] Within a few months, he recruited consuls and fellow ministers, private detectives and informers to join his surveillance team, keeping tabs on shipbuilding, factories, textile mills, ports, telegraph offices, and postal services across Europe.[16]

Since the South was doing most of its buying in England, he created a network there, too, identifying and monitoring Confederate agents and firms selling arms to the rebels. He even contemplated delaying shipments with lawsuits and seizing and sabotaging ships aiming to run the Union blockade of the South. "Accidents are so numerous in the [English] channel, you know," he wrote with joyous malice to Seward in October 1861. When he later proposed to purchase a European newspaper to be America's voice, Seward was skeptical. Instead, Sanford sought public support from journalists and editors, and like Nicholas Biddle before him, he wasn't averse to paying for it. He focused on France because, as he would write in a fall 1862 dispatch to Seward, he thought the British "bitterly Southern" in their sentiments.[17]

Outraged over Sanford's incursions on his diplomatic turf, the American minister to England, Charles Francis Adams, a son of John Quincy's, objected and demanded Seward stop Sanford. "I imagine [Sanford] will never forgive me," Adams told his diary. When Seward asked Sanford to limit himself to the Continent, Sanford ignored him—and proceeded to buy up all the available saltpeter, a vital ingredient of gunpowder.[18] When government funds weren't available to pay for operations, he used his own money.

He loved his job but made mistakes, too. After the Confederate victory at the Battle of Bull Run, Lincoln and Seward sent Sanford to offer the Italian general Giuseppe Garibaldi a command in the Union Army. Misunderstandings led Garibaldi to think he had been offered the post of Union commander-in-chief and he demanded that title and the right to free slaves at his discretion; Sanford had to tell him that was impossible. The story leaked and was portrayed as an act of desperation by Lincoln.

Sanford was also tarnished by his fearsome ambition and inability to get along with others. Gideon Welles, the secretary of the navy, judged him "fond of notoriety . . . pomp and power" and, though not "mischievously inclined," overly determined "to be consequential."[19] But consequential he was, proving himself one of the Union's most adept operators in Europe.[20]

Despite his occasional overreach and the opposition of Lincoln's War Department, which seemed both incompetent and intent on fostering competition that raised prices of military supplies, his canny arms purchases proved invaluable to the Union. Eventually Seward gave Sanford sole authority to buy weapons in Europe. He repaid that trust with clever manipulations of the market, saving the government huge sums. He sometimes bought second-rate guns, but that had the advantage of denying them to the South. In a letter to his mother, Sanford noted that he could have made a fortune in these deals "were I not a Gov't officer."[21] He was sneaky, not corrupt. Regardless, his many detractors accused him of profiteering.

Through it all, Sanford dreamed of a return to Paris to run the French ministry. He disparaged America's minister to France, William L. Dayton, who couldn't speak French.[22] In six months he visited Paris sixteen times, but, pointing toward his future, he also grew close to Belgium's royal family, headed by King Leopold I. The British-born son of Germany's duke of Saxe-Coburg-Saalfeld, Leopold was related to most of Europe's ruling houses; he was named the first king of Belgium in 1831 after that country won independence from Holland. Leopold's wife, Louise Marie, was a daughter of Louis-Philippe, the young Bourbon protected by Gouverneur Morris, who became the last king of France after the restoration of the dynasty in 1815. Sanford put this proximity to royalty to immediate use, asking that Leopold urge his niece Queen Victoria to prevent Confederate warships built in England from going to sea.

His relationship with Leopold proved crucial, as he was able to counter the king's concerns that the United States was too republican and commercially competitive with Europe. When the clothes-conscious Sanford realized he would make a better impression dressing up for the king after their first audience in 1861, he even made a donation to a Minnesota militia and received a commission as a major general, allowing him to wear a uniform again. He continued to do so until 1867, when his government banned the practice, though he continued to style himself as General Sanford. Leopold was by then enough of a friend to disregard the sartorial snub of civilian dress. He understood that America, after winning its Civil War, was becoming a great power.

～

Sanford spent eight years in Brussels serving Lincoln and then his successor, Andrew Johnson. Midway through the Civil War, Sanford met and married Gertrude de Puy, a Pennsylvanian of French descent living with an ailing aunt in Paris. Their 1864 wedding was the talk of the American expat community. Sanford was forty-three and she was in her mid-twenties, blond, blue-eyed, buxom, and attractive. He gave her two horses and a carriage and took her off on a Spanish honeymoon. The first of their seven children to survive, Henry Jr., known as Harry, was born just after the Civil War ended in 1865.

It was a love match as well as a comfortable one. They shared both the Brussels legation and a turreted, three-story château called Gingelom, surrounded by gardens and run by a staff of eight including "a chef, butler, coach, maids, gardeners and tutors."[23] Sanford's lifestyle was the most sumptuous of any American minister's in Europe, inspiring one of his secretaries to warn him that his conspicuous spending was off-putting to others.[24]

Aside from his stock investments, Sanford, like his father before him, speculated in western land, and earned $25,000 a year atop his $7,500 minister's salary. He would have made more if not for losses in unprofitable mining ventures and investments in a still that its inventor claimed would make rotgut whiskey into higher-shelf stuff, a wool spinner, and a device that lubricated railroad-car axles with water, all failures. Still, his wealth and spending bought the couple entrée into European society and its balls, resorts, and court life; they were received by Napoleon III and Queen Victoria. "I shall probably never again spend money as I have in the past few years," Sanford wrote to his ever-critical mother. "I see no object in not spending half my income or the whole of it if I found pleasure in it. The position is an exceptionable one. Youth does not last forever."[25]

His position may have been exceptional, but his pushiness, pride, and image problems contributed to his failure to win a promotion to envoy extraordinary or minister plenipotentiary, or a transfer to the more prestigious ministry in Paris, desires that reflected his lust for status. These machinations led to more bad press, his enemies maligned him, and his political positions—including support of President Johnson, advocacy of leniency for the South, and a perceived hostility toward Black Americans—made him increasingly unsympathetic. That last charge likely stemmed from his postwar activities, as he looked to the beaten Confederacy as a new source of income.

⟋

Abraham Lincoln had signed the Emancipation Proclamation on New Year's Day 1863, freeing all slaves then living in Confederate-controlled territory—some three million people. The Civil War had already disrupted the Slave Power economy, with Blacks revolting against their owners and overseers, fleeing for the Union lines, and being liberated in Union-occupied territories. In border states, some slaves enlisted to gain their freedom. Business in the fertile plantation belt that ran from the Carolinas to Texas was slowly strangled even as the war accelerated industrialization in the North.

Just as John Randolph feared, the imminent end of slavery gave the federal government vast new powers and imbued it with moral purpose, driven by the reformers and Republicans who embraced—whether quickly or reluctantly—the cause of abolition. But the postwar economy also fed dreams of a new South, with labor and enterprise, funded by northern capital, working in tandem to rebuild the region. Though he remained a diplomat until 1869 and stayed in Europe even longer, Henry Sanford caught wind of the scent of opportunity.

Lincoln's first Reconstruction plan, announced in 1864, laid out a fairly lenient pathway for southerners back into the Union. But the Confederacy's social structure had been destroyed and had to be rebuilt from the ground up. "Between the planters' need for a disciplined labor force and the freedmen's quest for autonomy, conflict was inevitable."[26]

In January 1865, the Thirteenth Amendment abolished slavery altogether, and some declared abolition a fait accompli, but the American Anti-Slavery Society persisted for five more years, seeking to give Black men full rights of citizenship, including the vote, equal education, and the ability to hold office and serve on juries. A radical faction of Republicans believed that the national government needed to do even more, but Lincoln stymied those efforts just before his 1865 assassination when he refused to sign the Wade-Davis Bill, which required that half the white men in each southern state swear loyalty to the Union, and also gave Black men suffrage. Lincoln felt the act's terms were too inflexible and his successor, Andrew Johnson, a pro–Civil War Tennessee Democrat who was born dirt-poor in North Carolina, thought the Thirteenth Amendment was enough, as planters and white privilege should be protected and the freedom of Blacks should be limited. Johnson pardoned or gave amnesty to most rebels and also reversed a brief-lived policy of redistributing confiscated and abandoned land to Blacks; many former slaves were evicted or forced to return the forty-acre plots they had been given. The issue of reparations for slavery has been an open question ever since.

In 1866, the radical Republicans, still advocating equality and suffrage for Blacks, swept congressional elections despite opposition from southern whites and northern businessmen whose profits depended upon southern cotton. Two more constitutional amendments were enacted—the Fourteenth, before the election, granting citizenship to ex-slaves, and the Fifteenth, just after, granting suffrage to all men born in the country, regardless of their race "or previous condition of servitude." And the Reconstruction Acts of 1867 and 1868 raised the bar for states seeking readmission to the Union: they would need new constitutions that included universal male suffrage and were required to ratify the Fourteenth Amendment. The three-fifths rule had finally been eliminated, though the Senate and electoral college still tilted toward southern and rural states, as they do to this day. As free men, former slaves would be able to speak for themselves, be counted in full, and run for office—at least briefly. But women of all races, who had been an engine of abolitionism, were left to fend for themselves. Important as those amendments were for civil rights, they also gave momentum to the feminist movement, born at the Seneca Falls Convention of 1848.

The House impeached Johnson early in 1868, ostensibly for removing Lincoln's secretary of war, but really for incompetence and opposition to the agenda of radical Republicans. He was narrowly acquitted by the Senate but hobbled, particularly after the Civil War hero Ulysses Grant resigned as commander of the U.S. Army and the Republicans nominated him to run for president. Johnson didn't seek renomination, and Grant, promising stability and with solid northern backing, defeated a colorless Democrat, Horatio Seymour. His election ended Sanford's career in diplomacy, but he had already launched his next act—in the beaten-down South.

19

Henry Sanford dipped his oar into business again at the start of Reconstruction. Sanford wasn't a carpetbagger, one of the northerners who moved south to run for office representing newly enfranchised Blacks. Indeed, he left neither Brussels nor his ministerial position, but he did get involved in politics as a conservative white Republican committed to economic expansion for personal profit, and he was willing to go easy on the South and avoid the subject of race when possible.

South Carolina's Sea Islands had already joined the new economy. After they were occupied by the North in 1861, whites had fled, and ten thousand slaves had sacked the cotton plantations and taken up subsistence farming. A few years later, the Treasury auctioned off some of the land for nonpayment of taxes—and military and government officers joined speculators in snapping it up, hoping to revive the plantation system with paid, as opposed to slave, labor. In 1867, a former Buchanan administration assistant secretary of state petitioned the government for the return of his family's cotton plantation on Barnwell Island, and Sanford, who was still in Belgium but had known him before the war, agreed to rent it in absentia and employ the twenty-seven former slaves who remained.

What followed was sadly typical. Like many Sea Island Blacks, those freedmen were reluctant to accept low contract wages. Such labor issues were common throughout the South and got worse in the near term because freed slaves were insisting on decent work hours and Black women and children could no longer be forced into labor.[27] Dire losses were commonplace. Sanford wasn't spared. Cotton prices sank, costs rose, and then an insect invasion left him in the red. As an absentee landlord, he also alienated his plantation manager. Discouraged, he broke his lease in 1869.

Sanford's friends were no longer influential enough to aid his diplomatic career after President Grant decided to replace him that year. Grant offered him the job of minister to Spain, but newspapers called him unqualified in any field besides fashion (he was "the poet of clothes" in his stovepipe hat over luxuriant facial hair, chain-draped waistcoat, pince-nez glasses, and gold-topped cane) and the Senate wouldn't confirm him, so he resigned in May 1869, blaming the "malicious and envious."[28] Though he remained in Brussels as a private citizen, likely at Gertrude's demand, in 1869, at forty-six years old Sanford and a brother-in-law took another plunge in the South, this time buying Oakley, a Louisiana sugar plantation. Years earlier, Sanford had acquired exclusive American rights to a new British sugar refining process and sold them to American refiners, that brother-in-law among them. Fifteen years later, with Cuba fighting Spain for independence, disrupting its sugar trade, they were sure Louisiana sugar would be sweet. But an uncle warned, "No man can manage a plantation in Louisiana" plus "other remotely situated points of business without being ruined. It is simply a question of time."[29]

Sanford didn't listen. The duo expanded quickly, buying adjacent plantations and investing in a sugar refinery. But labor remained an issue, and the refinery went bust, leaving his partner bankrupt and the Louisiana operation Sanford's alone. By 1875, he had lost nearly $100,000 due to rising costs, falling prices, bad crops, and flooding. Three years later it remained "a financial albatross."[30] Finally, in 1886, he gave up and parceled the land out to sharecroppers before selling it all in 1889 for a mere $20,000, less than he had paid for Oakley alone.

⟳

Sugar wasn't Sanford's only get-richer-quick scheme. Attracted by wild claims of the profitability of orange groves, he returned to America in 1870, still seeking to leverage his inheritance into greater wealth. Traveling by steamer, he visited the underdeveloped region of north-central Florida, where he shot alligators and admired the semitropical landscapes. At the southernmost navigable spot on the St. John's River, just north of today's Orlando, he bought more than twelve thousand acres fronting on a lake from a former Confederate general, intending to develop some of it, sell the rest, and make it a magnet drawing business investment and tourists to Florida. He founded the town of Sanford, the first liquor-free town in the state in 1872, as "the Gate City to South Florida," laying out streets and building a slaughterhouse, sawmill, general store, and wharf. That same naysaying uncle presciently predicted that "in a few years you will be comparatively a poor man."[31]

To prove him wrong and, perhaps, gain an edge, Sanford tried to elbow his way into Reconstruction-era Florida politics, seeking a Senate seat in 1871, in 1873, and again in 1875, but he was stymied by the contradictions of his situation: he was a Republican and Union man in a Democratic town full of Confederate veterans. While radical Republicans ran Congress, he was a moderate, nonpartisan champion of "property and intelligence," and though he presented himself as a champion of the "better element who pay taxes and have influence among white men," he tried to avoid talk of race, assuming Blacks would naturally support a Republican.[32] By simply ignoring them, Sanford hoped to forge a conservative coalition as a compromise candidate standing against violent partisans, former Confederates who identified as Democrats, and "irresponsible political adventurers who call themselves Republicans and who have done much to injure that fine name," as he put it in a letter to Florida governor George Franklin Drew.[33] But his lobbying trips to the state capital, Tallahassee, were no more successful than his plantations.

In the midst of this political fling, Sanford's fortune, worth $900,000 in 1872, took a serious hit when the worst financial crisis in decades arrived in 1873, setting off a hundred bank failures and the collapse of twenty thousand businesses. By the end of the decade, Sanford would face ruin, too.[34]

A terrible manager, Sanford refused to personally run his sprawling Florida operations, returning to Brussels, where his wife and children were, and depending again on overly optimistic, ill-equipped employees. Even when he visited, he was a negative presence, offending southern sensibilities. "Man is vile enough anyway, as you go South," he wrote to Thurlow Weed, "but 'reconstruct' him with the negro and carpetbaggers & the result is villainous!"[35] Sanford also alienated his few competent employees, and fared no better with local white workers and then imported Black ones, who raised the ire of—and inspired violence by—those they replaced. Finally, he imported Swedes as contract laborers, but they, too, were dissatisfied, and complained they had been lied to and ill-treated. Ultimately, Sanford settled on a mixed workforce, but labor problems were continual.

In 1876, the Sanford House Hotel opened, and immediately added to his losses. Designed to attract tourists and investors, it failed, and his real estate venture languished. While his experiments with citrus varieties were successful, that wasn't sufficient to cover his losses. Ill-timed railroad investments made matters worse, and in 1876, increasingly desperate for money to support his lavish lifestyle in Belgium, he sought investor-partners who would relieve his burden, while simultaneously hedging his bets by yet again seeking a diplomatic post.

Seeing a glimmer of hope in Grant's 1877 departure from the White House, Sanford temporarily relocated to a hotel in Washington, reprising the lavish entertainments that had won him his post in Brussels. After he roped off a section of a dining room for one of his "lobbying through the stomach" events, he won a new nickname: "Blue Ribbon Sanford."[36] Grant's Republican successor, Rutherford Hayes, nominated him to return to Belgium, but resistance persisted, and finally Hayes looked elsewhere.*

"I am not prospering nay more losing ground while time & precious years slip away," Sanford lamented to Gertrude in 1878. "Strain & pressure," he admitted, were his only takeaway from ten years in business.[37] Irritable and ill, he was homesick, finding the European high life he had pursued so avidly trivial and unsatisfying. Yet they stayed on in their château with seven servants, carriages, and tutors, and sent Henry Jr. to Eton. Though Gertrude's chef was dismissed and her entertainment budget slashed, she was in no mood to return to America, where she'd been born before spending most of her life in Europe, writing, "I detest Florida in particular & America has offered to me on my different visits a cup of mingled disagreeabilities."[38] And she pushed back against Sanford's pleas for economy. "I cannot understand the necessity of making the daily life joyless for the sake of some future good we may never attain." He responded, "I need in this time of worry & distress of mind . . . words of cheer—not of complaint."[39]

---

* Hayes's successor, James Garfield, would subsequently seek to help Sanford, and offered him the Italian embassy, but when he was assassinated, his successor, Chester Arthur, withdrew the offer after his 1881 election.

In 1880, Sanford organized the Florida Land and Colonization Company with investors, including a Scottish industrialist he had met through King Leopold, and attracted ex-president Grant and his wife to the groundbreaking of a new railroad in which he invested, running from Sanford to the Gulf of Mexico. That turned out to be the high point of his Florida adventure. Eight years later, the first luxury train in the United States would carry invited guests to the opening of the Hotel Ponce de León in St. Augustine, Florida, which immediately became the country's premier winter resort. But it belonged to Standard Oil co-founder Henry Flagler, the first of nine hotels he would build on the state's east coast, all connected by *his* railroads. Ever since, Flagler has been credited with launching Florida's hospitality and real estate industries.

In between, Henry Plant bought a Georgia railroad and added a South Florida line to his system. In 1887, Plant opened a hotel in Sanford itself, and eventually his rail system would cover most of central and western Florida—and connect it to New York. Plant and Flagler would join forces, too, and be credited with the "invention" of modern Florida, but as the former president of the South Florida rail line, J. E. Ingraham, once wrote, "General Sanford's work was the beginning of an interest in Florida by men of vision, enterprise and means. . . . He always contended that Florida was really so close to New York that it should be considered at the entrance of New York harbor."[40]

Mired in disagreements and litigation with his cautious new partners, Sanford won some financial concessions in return for a promise to stay away from Florida, but their company ground to a standstill. Freezes, fires, and a yellow fever outbreak made the business outlook worse and an 1883 visit by then-president Chester Arthur, who spent three days in Sanford, made a splash but no significant difference. Sanford's uncle's prediction finally proved correct: Henry was deep in debt, despite his promise to Gertrude that Florida would provide for their future. Finally, in July 1884, he returned to Brussels for good, "exhausted physically, emotionally, and financially."[41] Though Sanford, Florida, did become a functioning town and the hub of six rail lines, by 1888 he was forced to mortgage his remaining share of the property, which his widow would sell for a pittance after his death. But for the moment, though he was down, he still had cards to play.

Ever since Leopold I's death in 1865, Henry had cultivated his heir, Leopold II, the amoral, watchful son of his parents' loveless arranged marriage. Leopold II had made a dynastic marriage himself, at eighteen, to an archduchess of the Hapsburgs, rulers of the Austro-Hungarian Empire. Ambitious and restless, he was obsessed with the idea of empire. Belgium, the tiny constitutional monarchy he inherited, didn't have one, and his wife was a reminder that the older, more powerful countries around him did. Sanford's courtship of Leopold II—he even named his youngest son Leopold—was his only success in later life, though it, too, led to business failure. But the attraction was mutual. With flattery and attentiveness, Leopold drew the equally frustrated and financially desperate Sanford into an ambitious—and ultimately appalling—imperial scheme. "Everyone loves and appreciates you," an aide to the king wrote Sanford after his latest failure to win a ministerial post.[42] Leopold II would soon find a way to use him.

In the fifteenth century, the Portuguese initiated European exploration and exploitation of Africa, seeking wealth, the source of the Nile, or a passage to India, all seasoned with adventure and glory. In 1482, one of their sea captains was astonished to find on the West African coast the mouth of a river "larger than any a European had ever seen."[43] It ran through a realm of three hundred square miles, which was home to more than two million souls. The Kingdom of the Kongo, like much of Africa, practiced slavery, and the European trade in human beings that sprang into being made Kongo's rulers rich and increasingly corrupt. In 1665, Kongo's last king lost a battle with Portugal, and over the next two centuries the territory, riven by warring factions—hundreds of languages besides the predominant one, KiKongo, were spoken there—became a de facto colony. But white men still knew little about its interior or the river whose name the Portuguese rendered as Congo.

Two hundred years later, European exploration of Africa's interior—still controlled by local rulers—was inspired by both a desire for glory and a hunger for wealth, not in slaves but in gold, diamonds, copper, and ivory. Leopold II had studied British and Dutch colonies, where forced labor sent huge profits from coffee, sugar, indigo, and tobacco back to London and Holland, and he wanted his share. He also saw how rapacious behavior was justified: These "savage" lands were in dire need of civilization, Christianity, education—and in Africa of liberation from the supposedly Arab slave trade, never mind that it was run by Europeans with the full complicity of Africans and that the imposition of profitable "free" trade would nonetheless encourage and even require forced labor.

Since the new king's dreams of empire were limited by Belgium's legislature and its lack of a military, he decided to buy a colony himself, and to cloak his effort in altruism. In 1876, he announced his sponsorship of a scientific conference on Africa for geographers, explorers, business and military figures, and humanitarians. This eminent gathering established an organization, the Association Internationale Africaine, ostensibly to make a high-minded study of Africa, with Leopold II in charge; it was actually a private holding company camouflaged as a philanthropic entity to cloak his commercial ambitions. Leopold sought American backing, banking on that country's hunger for new markets for a growing surplus of farm and factory products, its missionary and expansionist zeal, its fascination with Africa, and the back-to-Africa movement then in vogue as a way to rid the North American continent of freed slaves by sending them "home." Sanford agreed that Africa could be "Canaan for our modern Israelites."[44]

In Africa, arrogant, self-satisfied whites believed, the ex-slaves' American experience of Christian civilization would inspire them to lift up a continent presumed to be benighted. "Contact with the white races and lately emancipation, education, and equality of political rights have made them by far superiors of the parent race and will tend to excite a spirit of enterprise, ambitions and desires for which central Africa opens a wide, peculiarly appropriate field," Sanford wrote in 1877 to John Latrobe, the association's American president.[45]

As a proponent of "civilizing" undeveloped countries and ending the African slave trade, Sanford, though he knew little to nothing about the continent, was a natural choice to serve as an American delegate at another conference conceived by Leopold after the king heard that the explorer Henry Morton Stanley was returning from a newspaper-sponsored trip to map the terra incognita of Central Africa. Stanley's discoveries along the mostly navigable Congo River had focused Leopold's attention on exploiting that previously unmapped region, and in 1878, Leopold charged Sanford with recruiting Stanley to help develop the Congo. Stanley was reluctant, but Sanford and Leopold doggedly pursued him, and when the English backers whom Stanley preferred to deal with declined to fund him further, the explorer began to look more favorably upon Belgium's king. By year's end, he agreed to a five-year deal to return to Congo.

Sanford turned to promoting the king's scheme to create a huge Central African nation, a wholly owned private country that was camouflaged and sold as a boon to free trade and humanitarianism, benefitting not just Black Africa and white America but America's Blacks as well. With his infinite capacity for self-regard, Sanford surely felt he was being high-minded rather than greedy and ingenuous.

In a further attempt to hide his intentions and please Stanley, Leopold set up a shadowy second group—the Committee for Studies of the Upper Congo—with backing from British, Belgian, and Dutch capitalists, though he personally controlled it. As Stanley sailed to the Congo in 1879 to study its trade and transportation prospects, that committee collapsed and secretly, at Sanford's urging, Leopold bought out its shareholders, but he didn't let Stanley know that because, "as a smokescreen, it was still useful."[46] The world at large needed to think Leopold's intentions were scientific and humanitarian. Finally, in 1882, Leopold would create a third African entity with a name designed to confuse: the International Association of the Congo. Sanford reportedly thought he controlled it, and he promoted it as a high-minded commercial venture that would benefit civilization.[47] But if he was really in the dark about the shell game Leopold was playing, it was likely willful blindness.

Between 1879 and 1884, the equally ambitious and even more naive Stanley negotiated four hundred treaties with local chiefs on behalf of Leopold's second group, unaware that the king had disbanded it. But the net effect of his operation was the sale of land and sovereignty over it—in effect, control of the Congo—to the

conniving Belgian king. Stanley cut trails, built roads, set up a network of base stations along the river, and named hills, towns, and
bodies of water for Leopold, all while playing geopolitical chess
against European rivals also eyeing the Congo basin (the British,
French, and Portuguese had launched similar efforts). Meanwhile,
Leopold had Sanford lead a parallel campaign of persuasion and,
ultimately, deception in order to gain international recognition of
the sovereignty of his latest front organization over the Congo, despite its being a private enterprise.

President Arthur's 1883 visit to Sanford's Florida orange groves
gave Leopold a connection to the White House. Though Sanford
stayed in Belgium, he kept up a lively correspondence with the president and at the end of that year sailed to New York and took an overnight train to Washington, charged with winning the president's
formal approval of Leopold's claim to own Congo, carrying an example of the king's treaties with its chiefs, altered to remove clauses
granting trade monopolies to Leopold.[48]

With a fervor that can most generously be described as blind or
amoral, Sanford lobbied the American government and prominent
citizens in business and science for everything from recognition to
the appointment of naval officers to command some of the twenty-
two trading stations Stanley had established along the river. Sanford
augmented his usual wining and dining with gift boxes of Florida
citrus.

President Arthur's administration seemed amenable to recognition, even incorporating language drafted by Sanford into a presidential address to Congress and sending a navy ship to the mouth of
the river, challenging Portugal's claim to the artery. Thanks to Sanford, Belgium's allegedly international effort was deemed more trust-
worthy and less greedy than that of Leopold's European rivals.

A former Confederate general, white supremacist Alabama
senator, and fervent back-to-Africa advocate, John Taylor Morgan, became a key ally, sponsoring a resolution in support of Leopold's claim.
Then the king's propaganda, conveyed by Sanford to politicians,
powerful businessmen, and President Arthur's secretary of state,
turned the tide. In April 1884, the U.S. government was the first

power to recognize the flag adopted by Leopold's dubious group as that "of a friendly Government," a huge step toward legitimizing the king's actions.[49] Other countries followed. Promising free trade for American interests, Sanford had proven that an individual in business could turn the American ship of state in his chosen direction. It was "the most sophisticated piece of Washington lobbying on behalf of a foreign ruler in the nineteenth century. Leopold . . . owed this great coup to Sanford."[50] Whether Sanford knew what Leopold was really up to remains a matter of dispute. Whether he had done anything admirable does not.

At a dinner with Gertrude, who was said to be the most beautiful woman at the Belgian court, Leopold flattered her about her husband. An international conference on European colonization and trade in Africa followed, hosted in Berlin by the German chancellor Otto von Bismarck, and the State Department asked Sanford to join the American delegation. He saw the Congo as his financial salvation. "If I can get a good hold there, it will fix me in regard to the future," he wrote to Gertrude in summer 1884, just before the conference— and just after giving up on Florida. "There is just the sort of work I would like, with both reputation & money to gain & the satisfaction of doing good."[51]

Though the United States never ratified the decisions of the Berlin West Africa Conference, it gave Leopold all he wanted: recognition, a right of way for a railroad, and access to the Atlantic Ocean. But early in 1885, familiar allegations of self-dealing by Sanford resurfaced, including suspicion of an under-the-table deal between him and Leopold. Sanford hoped the Belgian would make him a top official of the newly christened Congo Free State, but Leopold named himself its king-sovereign and appointed only Belgians beneath him. As consolation, he granted Sanford permission to create a company to gather ivory, develop trade, and advance scientific knowledge along the upper Congo.

Six months later, the Sanford Exploring Expedition was established with its namesake as a major shareholder and one of two top executives, and it launched the first two commercial steamboats, *Florida* and *New York*, on the river. Leopold promised the use of river stations and porters at cost but promptly reneged, the first of many ways he hurt Sanford. So did perpetual problems like Sanford's inability to hire capable managers and his disputes with administrators and investors, such as one he called a "horrid Jew" who wanted to "gobble" up the company in an 1888 letter to his wife.[52] Finally, abandoned by Leopold, Sanford lost control, and at the end of 1888, a Belgian firm took over. Over the next two and a half years, his fortune mostly gone, Sanford stayed afloat by selling his shares; after he died, his creditors would seize what remained.

In 1889, Sanford got his last official appointment—and, finally, the long-sought title of plenipotentiary and envoy extraordinary— to an anti-slavery conference in Brussels, which began as an attempt to push back against European colonialism, the Arab slave trade, and liquor distribution in the Congo and elsewhere in Africa, but degenerated into a squabble over business and land. When Leopold used the conference to push for import duties in the Congo, Sanford felt betrayed, and when he then learned that the Congo was engaged in slave trading and it became clear that he had been thoroughly deceived by Leopold, he bitterly opposed giving in to the king, but ultimately failed to protect America's right to free trade.[53]

His split with Leopold was fortunate for Sanford, as the king's regime would become internationally notorious for its brutal treatment of the Congolese, a two-decade campaign of land seizure, forced labor, and terror most garishly symbolized by chopped-off hands. It would leave some ten million dead (more than half the population) and lead to the 1908 dissolution of the Congo Free State and its reinvention as Belgian Congo, a colony controlled by the Belgian parliament.*

Leopold's atrocities led Mark Twain to suggest on the king's death in 1909 that a suitable memorial would consist of "forty grand avenues . . . thirty-five miles long, and each fenced on both sides by skull-less skeletons . . . festooned together in line by short chains stretching from wrist to wrist," leading to a replica of the Great Pyramid of Cheops made of those skeletons' fifteen million skulls and

---

* Though Leopold forced the government to buy Congo from him, he had little time to enjoy the windfall; he died the next year and was succeeded by a nephew.

topped by Leopold's body, stuffed, "robed and crowned," waving "a butcher knife and pendant handcuffs."[54]

⌐

Despite annual trips to take the allegedly curative waters in Hamburg, Sanford had suffered from insomnia and gout since the mid-1880s. Unable to relax, and plagued by debt and his shrinking net worth, he was living on borrowed money, selling art and furniture. In 1888, the Sanfords had traded down to a smaller château, but even though he owed his creditors enormous sums, the Sanfords still employed more than half a dozen servants and Gertrude remained unsympathetic. She described another attempt by her husband to return to America as trading "plum cake" for "corn bread" and demanded that her husband "keep 'in the swim.'" Florida, she concluded in a letter to Henry, was "a vampire that . . . sucked the repose & the beauty & the dignity & cheerfulness out of our lives."[55] Neglected and lonely, she thought Sanford cruel for sharing his problems.

Henry Jr. made matters worse. At Harvard in 1884, he skipped classes, overspent his allowance on cigars and wine, was put on probation, and fell into debt. Though he edited a school magazine and showed promise as a writer, he was expelled from an exclusive club and denied graduation with his class in Sanford's *annus horribilis* of 1888. He refused his father's suggestion that he go to law school, and when he asked to pursue writing, Sanford insisted he go to Florida instead, to manage an orange grove, and repay his father, who had covered his debts. He was installed in a cottage and worked under Frederic Rand, a banker and organizer of the South Florida Railroad.

Rand found Harry's work lacking and his late-night partying in the office annoying. "His foreign manners and . . . absurd dress caused much ridicule," according to a contemporary. "He usually wore a loud checked black and white suit, carried a cane and affected a monocle." After two years in Florida, Henry Jr. ran for mayor of Sanford and lost. Though his father lauded his effort, he and his son stopped speaking, even as Sanford spent that winter of 1890–1891 confined in a lodge at that same Florida grove. His son left for New York, where he hoped to work as a writer.

In May 1891, still seeking mineral-filled waters to give him relief from his many ills, Sanford went to the aptly named Healing
Springs, Virginia, but instead of getting better, he died there shortly
before his sixty-eighth birthday. Harry followed him to the grave a
few short months later, dying of tuberculosis at age twenty-six.
Gertrude Sanford would live on until 1902, when she died in
Connecticut.

A year after Henry Sanford died, his daughter, Ethel, would
marry her second cousin John, a son of Stephen Sanford of Amsterdam, New York, and their offspring carried the Sanford name into
the next century. Several would make auspicious marriages. One
would become a spy, another a polo player, a third a social butterfly,
fluttering, fluttering, but never finding a place to land.

Their inheritance can be best characterized as an absence of
lasting achievement. But in that, they were like Henry Shelton Sanford, "a terrible judge of character [who] had a penchant for rash
actions, invariably committed without the benefit of prior research.
Like many of his Gilded Age contemporaries, he was inordinately
optimistic . . . and all too inclined to grasp at each new 'main chance.'
Proud, vain and stubborn . . . acutely embarrassed by his business failures and chronic debts . . . [he] aggravated his naturally nervous
disposition. He was unable either to admit or to reconcile himself to
the fact that he would never reach the first rank."[56]

"Let us not be desirous of vainglory," the Bible warns in Gala-
tians 5:26, a proscription that was surely taken to heart on Plymouth
Plantation. But in the two and a half centuries between William Bradford's stand against tyranny in Plymouth and Henry Shelton Sanford's myopic and opportunistic collaboration with a tyrant in the
Congo, that trait had slid from the edges to the center of the American WASP Garden of Eden. Far from being anomalous, Sanford was
an early and wildly flawed example of a new breed of WASP who consistently equated self-interest with the national interest, often losing
sight of the latter in their blind lust for the former. Not yet dominant,
their vanity was no longer a recessive trait. But neither did it inspire
repentance or contrition.

Part Six

EXCLUSION

1869–1900

THE PEABODYS AND THE 400

20

Like Henry Sanford, George Peabody was a descendent of a religious dissenter and early New England colonist. But reversing Sanford's voyage from good fortune into debt, Peabody started with almost nothing, launched himself into the financial stratosphere with a single-minded devotion to making money, and then, having achieved great wealth, gave it all away. In between, like Sanford, he was a pioneer of the awful yet awesome self-absorption that would, within a century, be seen as a defining trait of the American WASP. But George Peabody demonstrated a larger truth: while a flaw can seem universal, individuals can and do rise above it, playing the part of exceptions to the rule.

The first American member of George Peabody's family, spelling his surname either Paybody, Peboddy, or Pabodie, had come from Hertfordshire, England, in 1634, shortly after the Sanfords. In the Peabodys' sixth American generation, George, dirt poor, started his career as an apprentice shopkeeper in 1806 at age eleven. Yet he would eventually compete with merchant banking legends like Barings and Hope, become the most important American in London, give J. Pierpont Morgan his start in finance, and be honored as an early icon of American philanthropy.

When Peabody died at seventy-four in 1869, Britain's Queen Victoria would offer him a grave in Westminster Abbey, beside kings

and queens of England and the likes of Geoffrey Chaucer, Isaac Newton, and John Milton. But on his deathbed, Peabody insisted he be
buried in his hometown, Danvers, Massachusetts. He returned to the
country that let him remake himself as a patrician after leaving it
behind some three decades earlier. That was at the start of the Industrial Revolution he ultimately played a huge role in financing.
With the country on the cusp of momentous change, self-made men
like Peabody were able to forge symbiotic relationships with their presumed superiors, the white Christians from "better" families who
had leading roles in creating the still-young nation and gave select
newcomers a hand in climbing its socioeconomic ladder. Then the
fresh arrivals pulled that ladder up, locked the door, and hung a sign
reading "WASPs Only."

Post–Civil War America, what Mark Twain called the Gilded Age and
Gore Vidal described as "this vigorous, ugly, turbulent realm devoted
to moneymaking by any means," was an offspring of Jamestown, Plymouth, New Amsterdam, Boston, and Philadelphia, a striving but narrow world, with its upper reaches open only to a few.[1] Becoming one
of them, Peabody was fortunate, even if at first without a fortune.

In early seventeenth-century England, the Peabodys were Protestants, owned land, and held public office, but were hardly members of
the elite.[2] After Charles I dissolved Parliament, and at the same time
chartered the Massachusetts colony, thousands, including John Peabody and his sons William and Francis, decided to leave.[3] In 1634, they
settled in towns ringing Boston. By their third generation in America,
fourteen Peabody men carried the name into the future.[4]

Several Peabodys fought in the Revolution. The first to distinguish himself in business, Joseph, started as a sailor in 1777, when
he joined the crew of a Salem-based privateer as an apprentice seaman, moving from ship to ship and seeing the world, before becoming a maritime businessman.[5] With partners, he bought more ships
and went into the Far East spice trade—and also trafficked opium to
China. By 1817, he was the wealthiest merchant in America, so important that President James Monroe would journey to Salem, Massachusetts, just to meet him.[6]

William Bradford, Mayflower passenger and Governor of the Plymouth Colony, left the colony's largest estate behind.

Massasoit, sachem of the Wampanoag, made a treaty of peace and mutual aid with the leaders of the Plymouth Colony.

Though signed only by the free male passengers onboard the ship, the Mayflower Compact, establishing Plymouth's legal status, was a foundational document of the American experiment.

Gouverneur Morris, a reluctant revolutionary, lascivious libertine, and the least-known Founding Father, was the primary author of the U.S. Constitution before becoming the new nation's ambassador to France.

The Continental Congress first met in fall 1774. Its leaders included (left to right) John Adams, Gouverneur Morris, Alexander Hamilton, and Thomas Jefferson, here painted by Augustus Tholey.

John "Jack" Randolph of Roanoke, from one of Virginia's fabled First Families, owned as many as 150 slaves, and was an androgynous, drug-addicted congressman who would later be proclaimed a father of American conservatism.

Born into Virginia's elite, Anne Cary "Nancy" Randolph was tarred by scandal as a young woman, but regained her status and wealth when she married Gouverneur Morris.

Hero of the War of 1812, Andrew Jackson was elected president in 1828. An agrarian Democrat like Thomas Jefferson, he became the first great champion of the WASPs of the South and West.

An erudite, handsome, highly social eminence, Nicholas Biddle headed the Second Bank of the United States, but ran afoul of the anti-elitist President Jackson.

Beginning in the 1830s, America's indigenous peoples were forced from their land and driven west of the Mississippi River along what was known as the Trail of Tears. Lewis Cass was the intellectual author of Andrew Jackson's policy of "Indian removal."

Lewis Cass, the longtime governor of the Michigan Territory, ran for President in 1848 as a Democrat.

Henry Shelton Sanford created America's first overseas espionage network during the Civil War, and pioneered Florida's tourism and citrus industries.

Born poor, George Peabody became a key American banker in London, gave J.P. Morgan his start in business, and was the father of American philanthropy.

Junius Spencer Morgan, from a Hartford trading family, partnered with George Peabody arranging credit for American farms and businesses, though he found the older man mean-spirited.

J. Pierpont Morgan—son of Junius, a convert to the Episcopal Church, protégé of Anthony J. Drexel, and a financial backer of Endicott Peabody's Groton School—was the preeminent financier of the Gilded Age.

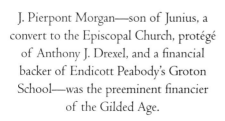

Elizabeth Palmer Peabody was a teacher, writer, publisher, intellectual, and saloniste whose West Street Bookstore in Boston was a home to the Transcendentalist movement. Her sisters Mary and Sophia married, respectively, Horace Mann the educator and novelist Nathaniel Hawthorne.

Great grandson of a shipping magnate and opium trafficker, Endicott Peabody was an Anglophile inspired by English public schools to found Groton, in order to instill self-discipline in the children of America's upper class.

The 1899 football team at Groton School included the future president Franklin Delano Roosevelt (second from left in the front row, in a white turtleneck).

August Belmont was an American agent of Germany's Rothschilds, financial rivals of J.P. Morgan. His Jewish roots made the Episcopalian convert suspect to WASPs, but they found him useful. Edith Wharton based the amoral Julius Beaufort in *The Age of Innocence* on him.

After Mrs. Astor made him an ally, Ward McAllister, from a prominent Savannah, Georgia, family, became the arbiter of American society, creating a group called the Patriarchs that conferred acceptance, even on the likes of August Belmont.

Caroline Schermerhorn, from a Knickerbocker family, married an Astor and became *the* Mrs. Astor, known to all concerned as the undisputed leader of American society.

An invitation to the 1896 Patriarchs' Ball from a Livingston to a de Peyster.

In 1888, at the peak of his influence, McAllister declared, "Why, there are only about four hundred in fashionable society." His downfall followed, and he became an object of derision.

One of the original Patriarchs, Lewis Morris Rutherfurd was a pioneer of astronomical photography and stellar spectroscopy.

William Collins Whitney, a lineal relation of Plymouth Governor Bradford, was the source of one of America's greatest inherited family fortunes of the twentieth century.

Alva Vanderbilt engineered her daughter Consuelo Vanderbilt's unhappy marriage to England's Duke of Marlborough, though Consuelo loved Lewis Morris Rutherfurd's handsome son Winthrop.

The sculptor and founder of New York's Whitney Museum, Gertrude Vanderbilt Whitney lived a liberated bohemian life in Greenwich Village and on Long Island.

The youngest son of Lewis Morris Rutherfurd, Winthrop lost the hand of Consuelo Vanderbilt, but won that of future president Franklin Roosevelt's mistress, Lucy Mercer.

In 1877, freshly graduated from Princeton, young Fairfield Osborn (shown holding a rifle), collected fossils in the Western U.S. as a member of a Princeton Scientific Expedition.

Henry Fairfield Osborn (shown with his wife LouLou, a relative of the Belmonts) was J.P. Morgan's nephew. An eminent paleontologist, he headed the American Museum of Natural History for decades, made it a world-class institution, but destroyed his own reputation by championing eugenics, the pseudo-science of WASP supremacy.

Osborn's close friend, Madison Grant, was a virulent white supremacist, a co-founder with Osborn of the Bronx Zoo, and a writer much admired by the Nazi leader Adolf Hitler.

Michael Butler (right), the bisexual heir to the Butler Paper and Butler Aviation fortunes, met Rock Hudson at the Venice Film Festival in 1960 and the pair had an intense but short-lived romance.

Michael Butler married and divorced three times before producing the Broadway phenomenon, *Hair*, but followed that undeniable accomplishment with decades of abortive schemes that led to his ignominious bankruptcy.

Michael, Jorie and Frank Butler with their father, Paul. After Paul died, the siblings fought for years over their inheritance, and legal fees ultimately drained his estate.

Though he was crippled in a childhood accident, Michael Butler
learned the family's favorite sport, polo. He's shown playing a
chukka in Santa Barbara, location of one of his many homes.

The cast of *Hair*. "I believed," Butler said, "that *Hair* was a gift
from God."

Gertrude Sanford, painted as a flapper by Sir William Orpen, circa 1920.

Gertrude Sanford Legendre and Bokara "Bobo" Legendre at a New Year's Eve, 1955, costume party. Gertrude hunted big game and was held as a prisoner of the Nazis in World War II. Bobo lived in her shadow until her death.

Whitney Tower Jr. and Mick Jagger at Whitney Park, William C. Whitney's camp in the Adirondack Mountains. "Mick wanted to befriend the A-list," Tower says. "He was very much socially minded.

Sisters Penelope Tree and Frankie FitzGerald, daughters of
Marietta Tree, the twice-married New York socialite, United
Nations official, and lover of Adlai Stevenson.

Mary Peabody, Frankie FitzGerald's and Penelope Tree's maternal
grandmother, was arrested at a 1964 civil rights sit-in in Florida.
Florida's governor called his Massachusetts counterpart, Mary's
son, Endicott ("Chub"), to say, "I got your mom in the slammer."

Nicholas Biddle and his father Ambassador Anthony Joseph Drexel Biddle, shortly after World War II ended.

Anthony Joseph Drexel Biddle is sworn in as the U.S. Minister to Norway, July 23, 1935.

George Biddle in 2018, showing a nursery school he helped build to Chief Theresa Kachindamoto, the only female paramount chief in Malawi and a partner of World Connect, where Biddle worked.

Liz Bonsal (right), a descendant of Gouverneur Morris, and Tracy Toscano (left), are married by Liz's mother, Elizabeth Lord Bonsal, in 2016. A Justice of the Peace in Greenwich, Connecticut, Bonsal married more same-sex couples than anyone else in her state.

George Peabody didn't share in that wealth. His father, Thomas, a fifth-generation Peabody raised on a family farm and a farmer himself, had eight children who survived childhood. The third was George, born in 1795, in a town between Salem and Boston. At eleven, apprenticed to a general storekeeper, he learned arithmetic and became the store's accountant.[7] At fifteen he spent a year on his maternal grandfather's Vermont farm, where an uncle, a China ship's officer, taught him how international trade was financed.[8]

A cascade of calamity ensued at home. George's father died in 1811 and two weeks later a brother's shop, where the teen had started working, burned down, as did another uncle's general store. Bankrupt, the uncle decided to rebuild his life as a shopkeeper selling dry goods in Washington, D.C., and George agreed to join him—and lend his name to the enterprise to avoid the taint of insolvency. A solvent friend gave them letters of credit, which they used to buy merchandise in Boston before sailing south to set up shop. After a brief stint in the artillery in the War of 1812, George returned, but fearing his uncle's profligacy, and the debt that accompanied it, he resigned in 1814 to start a new dry-goods firm with an older partner, who financed the venture while George, six foot one with a low forehead, dark brown hair, a round face, light blue eyes, large nose, small mouth and pointed chin, became its head of sales.[9] He also functioned as a shipping agent for the farmers and businessmen he encountered as Riggs and Peabody expanded to Philadelphia and New York.[10] Riggs retired in 1829 and the business was renamed, with Peabody, thirty-four, getting top billing. He had already made his first trip to England, selling cotton and buying machinery, and began selling the state of Maryland's bonds there, too.

London was the center of world finance, and at its summit were Barings, founded by a German Lutheran, and the German Jewish Rothschild bank. Both bankrolled American businesses. Barings had long been in America, having financed, among other things, the Louisiana Purchase.

In 1835, envious over the success of New York's Erie Canal, Maryland sold new bonds to finance a similar canal and a railroad. Selling a majority of those convinced Peabody that he could nibble away at Barings' and Rothschild's business if he set up shop in London. His intention was to become the go-between for British bankers and

American business by undercutting the interest rate on American loans to ensure his primacy.[11] To do so he needed to overcome a lingering British prejudice against Americans.

After cultivating relationships with purveyors of everything from simple pins and diapers to fine silks and merinos across western Europe, Peabody began separating himself from Peabody Riggs and moved to London permanently early in 1837, but not before making his first public-spirited gesture in his hometown, Danvers, writing a check to partly pay for a monument to commemorate the Battle of Lexington.

In a decade of financial exuberance, those Maryland bonds, like other American debt instruments, proved too popular; money flowed west across the Atlantic, as the international economy was plagued by inflation, causing the Bank of England to restrict the flow of specie overseas and severely tighten credit. That fueled the depression that began with the Panic of 1837, and in the 1840s, Maryland was one of several American states that stopped paying down debt, staining Peabody's reputation in London; at his nadir, he was blackballed by the exclusive Reform Club.[12]

To help bail Maryland out, Peabody gave a dinner in London for a dozen leading merchant bankers, and emerged with $8 million in credit for the state; he would later return his fee of $60,000 for services rendered.[13] Maryland eventually repaid its obligations, and that made Peabody rich, as he had bought and held the depreciated bonds himself when others thought them worthless—for as long as a decade—until interest payments resumed, making him a much-desired fortune. In the process, Peabody restored that tarnished reputation, even adding to its luster as he ensured the future of George Peabody & Co.[14]

In 1839, Peabody retired from Peabody Riggs, and over the years that followed, his deal-making spanned the globe and helped turn America into an industrial power. Among his many contributions was the purchase from England of most of the steel tracks on which America's early railroads traveled.[15] After twenty years of tight-fisted workaholism, Peabody developed a reputation for probity, reliability, and discretion equal to his European competitors at Rothschild and Barings. By 1854, he would be worth almost $4 million (about $125 million in today's currency) and had vanquished the European skepticism over the trustworthiness of American enterprise that had spiked up due to the 1837 panic.

Under the Franklin Pierce administration in the mid-1850s, Peabody became America's de facto social ambassador in London, someone visiting Americans of substance needed to meet. Pierce's American minister to Britain, the future Democratic president James Buchanan, then just a failed candidate for that job and happy to be far away from domestic disputes over slavery, was disinclined to adopt European extravagance. Peabody was known for his frugality, and some thought he "had positively no gift, except that of making money."[16] But even though he lived modestly, eating a homemade lunch at his desk most days and taking public transportation around London, he entertained lavishly and cleverly, surrounding his guests with American furniture and books while adopting English mannerisms so well that he managed to be seen as a gentleman by London's snobbish aristocrats. It was a delicate balancing act that he usually carried off with aplomb, a notable exception being a trying 1853 visit to London by the coarse transportation tycoon Commodore Cornelius Vanderbilt, then the wealthiest man in America, and as easy to dislike as John Jacob Astor had been earlier.

In 1851, Peabody had given a Fourth of July party, induced the Duke of Wellington to be the guest of honor, and subsidized an American exhibit at the massive International Exposition at the Crystal Palace after Congress refused, introducing American innovations like Cyrus McCormick's reaper and Colt revolvers to the English. These gestures so thoroughly improved English attitudes toward Americans that Congress eventually repaid him.

At fifty-six, Peabody decided he needed a successor, and took the advice of a Boston merchant colleague who suggested Peabody meet one of his partners, Junius Spencer Morgan, the son of a trader from Hartford. Finding Morgan sturdy and responsible, Peabody offered the younger man a ten-year partnership that would culminate in Peabody's turning over the business, its name, and perhaps his capital. Morgan declined at first but a year later, after reviewing the operation's books, accepted in fall 1854, and began arranging credit for American farms and businesses, trading currency, and placing European investment in America. The newly formed Peabody, Morgan & Co. issued securities to finance American industry and railroads, a business that continued to grow until the Civil War.

The relationship was not a warm one, even as the new partner slowly took over the business. "Morgan found Peabody petty and vindictive . . . a prototypical heartless banker, a one-dimensional hoarder."[17] Yet, freed from some of his responsibilities, Peabody seems to have reached a similar conclusion, as he abruptly began giving away the huge fortune he had accumulated. Whether the purge of wealth that followed had always been his plan, was a reflection of his native talent at public relations, or was inspired by repentance or contrition is unknowable. But it was as remarkable as his rise in business had been, and equally successful in transforming his image from one defined by greed to one best remembered for good works.

In 1856, George went home for a visit and was feted wherever he went, including the Peabody Institute in Danvers, a library built with his gifts, which would eventually total $1.5 million in order to, as he later said in an 1866 speech there, promote knowledge and morality. But back in London, financial trouble loomed, as the international economy stumbled again while America's was running too hot, and railroad stocks—mostly issued by Peabody, Morgan—tumbled. When his British counterparts offered to bail him out on condition he close his bank, Peabody won a loan from the Bank of England instead, bought in stocks, and forestalled the crisis.[18]

Not even that brush with financial ruin could knock him off his new trajectory. In 1857, he established another Peabody Institute in Baltimore, this one conceived as an intellectual and arts center for artists, teachers, and scholars, the first in an American city. In 1862, he set up a fund to build housing for the teeming masses of Victorian London. Its first homes for artisans and the laboring poor—sixty-six low-income families—opened in 1864 and included running water, shop spaces, and laundries.[19] Peabody Square, as it was called, was a philanthropic and architectural groundbreaker.*

In 1859, suffering from gout and rheumatism at age sixty-three, Peabody wanted to retire, but decided he couldn't until after the oncoming Civil War. Though Peabody supported the North, he cared more for his new career in philanthropy than taking sides in the war between the states.

Peabody finally retired in 1864 but broke his promises to Junius Morgan, taking both his name and his money away from the company. "Perhaps in his sanctity he wanted to erase his name from the financial map and enshrine it in the world of good works," suggests the firm historian. Junius's grandson, Jack Morgan, begged to differ, calling his demand that its name be changed the elder Morgan's "bitterest disappointment."[20] Thus J. S. Morgan and Co. was born.

In 1866, Peabody returned to the United States for good, carrying a gift from Queen Victoria, a $70,000 miniature portrait of the monarch.[21] He continued to give away money, building churches, libraries, and museums at both Harvard and Yale, and another in Salem.[22] Peabody's philanthropic gifts between 1852 and 1867 totaled some $8 million, ending with $2 million to set up the Peabody Education Fund to educate the children of the defeated South, earning him a medal from Congress. The town of South Danvers renamed itself Peabody in his honor.

Still suffering from rheumatism, Peabody went to White Sulphur Springs, West Virginia, in summer 1869, where he met the defeated Confederate commander Robert E. Lee and gave a gift to the future Washington and Lee College, which Lee ran, wrote a will leaving six-figure sums to many relatives, and then sailed for London, intending to winter in the south of France, but died before getting there.[23] The Queen, the Prince of Wales, and Prime Minister William Gladstone attended his funeral at Westminster Abbey, where his body lay in state another month before it was returned for burial aboard a

* Still in operation, the greatly expanded Peabody Estate today has sixty-six thousand homes, and offers care, support, and community services to thousands.

British warship, HMS *Monarch*. A statue of Peabody was erected in London's City financial district. Similar tributes followed in America. Thanks to his remarkable midcentury volte-face, Peabody's name would live on long after his death.

⟩⟩⟩

George Peabody's humanitarianism was a late-blooming phenomenon. But others in his sprawling family balanced his lifelong urge to accumulate with an equal dedication to education and social reform so fierce it would be a Peabody inheritance into the twenty-first century. As George was making his fortune, three Peabody sisters who were, like George, members of their family's sixth American generation, forged equally remarkable lives. Elizabeth Palmer Peabody, Mary Tyler Peabody, and Sophia Amelia Peabody were daughters of Nathaniel, a Salem dentist. Beginning in 1808, their mother, Eliza Palmer Peabody, operated a school for young women, and by age sixteen Elizabeth, also known as Lizzie, was running it. At eighteen she decided to go to Boston and start her own school while also studying Greek under Ralph Waldo Emerson, then nineteen. Though her first attempt at pedagogy was unsuccessful, she returned to Brookline, near Boston, after a brief stint as a governess in Maine—where a beau committed suicide when she said she wouldn't marry him if they had to stay in Maine—and she and Mary tried teaching again.[24]

Lizzie's second school also failed, but she forged friendships with educators, artists, and preachers, and began to develop a reputation as an intellectual before starting a third school in 1833. Meanwhile, Mary had met Horace Mann, a state legislator, founder of an asylum, and, late in life, an educational reformer. And Sophia, unstable and an invalid, fell for the then-obscure writer Nathaniel Hawthorne, who had a relative in Lizzie's first school.[25] Lizzie introduced them after she bought a house in Boston and, in 1840, went to work for Bronson Alcott, a liberal pedagogue and communitarian.[26] When a school he started failed, Lizzie, who had been writing books for youngsters, opened a bookshop and meeting place, which she ran from a rocking chair in its window, attracting Boston's intellectuals.

Elizabeth Palmer Peabody's West Street Bookstore became a home for the Transcendentalist movement, a philosophical outgrowth of the Unitarian religion. Ralph Waldo Emerson's father was a Unitarian minister, and after divinity school his son, too, briefly joined the clergy. Many Boston Puritans had found themselves attracted to Unitarianism's core belief in God as a single entity rather than a trinity, its rejection of stern dogma and a chosen few, and its embrace of the individual as a repository of universal morality and ethics. If God was in everyone, then the fearsome church of the Puritans and Calvinists could be left behind without a backward glance, a relic of harsher times.

Unitarianism was first practiced in Boston following the Revolution, after Anglican priests and lay leaders abandoned King's Chapel, the English religion's oldest New England congregation, many of them returning to England. It flourished anew after King's Chapel became the first American Unitarian church in 1787, preaching a gospel well suited to a young, strong, ambitious new nation. Eighteen years later, Harvard Divinity School began teaching Unitarian theology, ending the dominance of traditional Calvinist thinking. Transcendentalism, the associated school of philosophy, taught self-reliance, independence, the essential goodness of humankind, and the divinity of nature and of everyday experience.

The three Peabody sisters, like their distant relative George, were not born into wealth, but had the advantage of education and secular sophistication, thanks to their schoolteacher mother, who raised them to be independent achievers. So, just as George achieved wealth and prominence in finance, Sophia, an artist, Mary, an educator, and Lizzie, a writer, editor, publisher, bookstore owner, and *saloniste,* became important figures among Boston's intellectual elite at a moment when the newly independent America and its emboldened citizens were engaged in a frenzy of self-invention, defining themselves both for themselves and for the world.

Transcendentalism can be seen as the northeastern counterpart of the Second Great Awakening, the religious revival that began in Kentucky and Tennessee in the late eighteenth century and lasted well into the nineteenth, spreading out from the Jacksonian Midwest to the east through a western New York transformed by the Erie Canal. Protestant revivalism spread rapidly. By 1844, its most populous sect in America was the Methodist Church, followed by the Baptists and offshoots and alternative religions ranging from Mormonism to spiritualism and faith healing.[27]

The revivalists' signature was hellfire-and-damnation preaching by circuit-riding religious figures who spoke at frontier camp meetings. They provided both spiritual sustenance and entertainment to settlers who often lived great distances from others and found comfort and companionship in the frenzied religious gatherings. Asking adherents to turn away from their sinful pasts, seize control of their own salvation, and be born again as righteous servants of Christ, it offered an appealing alternative to northeastern Calvinism and its strict doctrine of predestination for the chosen. The notion of personal salvation reflected the rugged individualism of the frontier and offered solace to a population rocked by turbulent changes in economic and social status and desperate for stability and dignity. They were whipsawed by conflicts over currency and slavery, westward expansion, regional rivalries, and the fate of Native Americans. All of it was covered, chaotically, by a hyperpartisan press, which amplified the anxiety of a young nation and a fledgling government suffering from extreme growing pains and led by a president, Andrew Jackson, who embraced disruption.

Transcendentalism traded the Second Great Awakening's religious dimension for a secular, yet still spiritual, moral one. It preached high thoughts, simple lives, and universal education as the means to build character. It sought to replace European thought with the individualism and egalitarian ideas behind the American experiment, making it a crucible for abolitionism and feminism. But it also saw Jacksonian radical democracy as a threat and was a reaction to its excesses, its instability, its anti-intellectualism, and the materialism, rawboned capitalism, and greed that were the glue binding northern businessmen to southern slave owners, perpetuating slavery. Despite their focus on the individual and nonconformism, Transcendentalists wanted to make the world a better place. Reform required concerted action, which argued for a strong, enlightened Union, or at least, moral individuals taking a collective stand against injustice. Hawthorne, for one, embraced a realism that left his friends thinking him pessimistic and Hawthorne thinking they were naive.

As the West Street Bookstore flourished, Lizzie, who became a Transcendentalist, joining Emerson, Thoreau, and Alcott, went into publishing—starting with an abolitionist tract benefitting an antislavery group. Soon she would release three of Hawthorne's early books and a journal that included Henry David Thoreau's seminal essay "Civil Disobedience." She also supported nascent feminists and wrote for Alcott's latest venture, a magazine called *Dial* (later edited by Emerson). She became its publisher in 1841, the same year Hawthorne lived at Brook Farm, a utopian experimental commune, planned and partly financed in Peabody's bookshop, that attracted leading Transcendentalists.

Hawthorne wasn't a believer, though; he had moved there to save money so he could marry Sophia Peabody. Wed in 1842, they moved to Concord, where Thoreau was their gardener. Sophia and Hawthorne would later move to Europe and raise a family. Mary married Horace Mann in 1843 and went to Europe on a double honeymoon with Julia Ward, the suffragist daughter of a banker, and Samuel Gridley Howe, a doctor and an advocate for the blind. Both were dedicated abolitionists, and Julia would later compose "The Battle Hymn of the Republic."*

Lizzie Peabody suspended *Dial* in 1844, closed the bookstore in 1852, and returned to teaching and selling educational tools. She founded the first free English-language kindergarten in America in 1860, and only slowed down after she had a stroke at seventy-three in 1877.[28] But six years later she met Princess Winnemucca, a Paiute Indian, and they jointly promoted the cause of Native Americans and helped educate their children. She continued to write, lecture, and support women's suffrage, was caricatured in Henry James's *The Bostonians,* and stayed active until she died just short of age ninety.[29]

---

* Ephraim Peabody, born in 1807, was the most outspoken Peabody abolitionist, a farm boy, graduate of Bowdoin in Maine, and Congregationalist minister in New Bedford. In 1846, he moved to Boston's King's Chapel, and gave his cousin Anthony Preston Peabody, editor of *North American Review,* an article on the evils of slavery and how to remedy them. Published in autumn 1851, it proposed moving a hundred thousand slaves per year for a decade to a place where they might be colonists and prosper. He died in 1856, before the start of the Civil War, so he experienced neither the next chapter in slavery nor the disappointments that followed.

21

For the Peabodys, doing well and doing good were usually kept separate, but they merged in the person of Endicott Peabody, born in
1857. He was a great-grandson of the shipping magnate Joseph and
a grandson of Francis, an inventor who inherited a fortune and then
built another of his own, which bought him an estate near Salem and
a red-brick house in town. Endicott's father, Samuel, had spent a year
at Harvard, then joined the family firm and sailed on a Peabody ship
to the Far East. He married Marianne Cabot Lee, a descendent of
the seventeenth-century Massachusetts Bay Colony governor John Endecott and daughter of a founder of the Boston brokerage Lee Higginson.* Their third child, Endicott, born Unitarian, came to embody
the Puritan values of thrift and hard work as well as the reverence for
culture and education that defined what Oliver Wendall Holmes Sr.
in 1860 called Boston's Brahmin caste, the city's traditional upper
class.†

After George Peabody's death, Junius Morgan offered Samuel
Peabody a partnership, and the family moved to London.[30] Endicott
was put in boarding school, where he shot himself in the hand while
playing with dueling pistols.[31] But he was more athlete than klutz and
went on to Cambridge, where he rowed and played cricket, and converted from Unitarianism to the Church of England.[32] In 1878, his
father decided to retire and go home, and Endicott, abandoning the
idea of studying law, went to work for Lee Higginson and became
"quite the young man of Boston society." But, encouraged by the rector of Boston's Trinity Church to follow his religious inclinations, he
turned to the ministry at age twenty-four in 1881, entering the Episcopal Theological Seminary in Cambridge, where he proved to be a
natural.[33]

---

* According to research by William T. Endicott, Joseph Peabody employed a number of mem-
bers of the Endecott/Endicott family, and in the nineteenth century several marriages linked
the two families.
† Aside from their multiple Boston Brahmin connections, the Peabodys were also related to
New York's Roosevelts through Alice Hathaway Lee, Theodore Roosevelt's first wife, whom
Endicott's granddaughter Marietta Tree once described as a "vague cousin."

A few months into his studies, and at the start of his courtship of a first cousin, Frances, the tall, blue-eyed, big-shouldered "Cotty" was offered a ministry in Tombstone, Arizona, and in January 1882 left for the frontier town just after the famous shootout at the O.K. Corral. He stayed only a few months, but even so, he was a success, holding services, teaching Sunday school, starting a baseball team, and raising the money to build a church. He was homesick, though, wanted to return to his seminary education, and was in love. Over his father's objection, he pursued Fannie, as she was known, as he did an urge to enter the field of education after visiting a religious Massachusetts boarding school called St. Mark's. Since he wasn't ordained, he couldn't pursue the notion of becoming its headmaster, so like Lizzie Peabody before him, he envisioned a school of his own.

America's first boarding school, the Governor Dummer Academy, was founded in 1763 and was named for its benefactor, a former colonial governor of Massachusetts, who funded its establishment in his will. Two Dummer alumni, Samuel Phillips Jr. and Eliphalet Pearson, went on to, respectively, found Phillips Academy in Andover, Massachusetts, in 1778, and serve as its first headmaster. Phillips's uncle John and his wife, Elizabeth, started the competing Phillips Exeter Academy in New Hampshire in 1781. All three schools stressed moral education with a Congregationalist bent, but also laid the foundation for an exclusive patriciate. Deerfield Academy and Milton Academy followed in 1797 and 1798, also in Massachusetts, and Lawrenceville, a Presbyterian boarding school, was created in New Jersey in 1810. Other, similar schools followed, including the all-girls Emma Willard in New York in 1814 and Connecticut's Miss Porter's School in 1843. Then, before and after the Civil War, a wave of newer private schools, many of them affiliated with the Episcopal Church, became, in Digby Baltzell's words, "a vital factor in the creation of a national upper class, with more or less homogenous values and behavior patterns," including St. Paul's in New Hampshire in 1856, the nondenominational Northfield Seminary for Young Ladies in 1879 and Mount Hermon in 1881 (which merged in 1971), Taft and Choate in 1890, and Hotchkiss in 1891.[34] Whether it was intentional or not, these schools reinforced the notion of an "associational aristocracy," an invisible barrier against incursions on WASP dominance.[35]

Rather than exclusion, the Anglophile Endicott Peabody was inspired by both English public schools, designed to educate future leaders, and a Swiss boarding school that captured the attention of scholars associated with the Anthology Society, a short-lived intellectual club begun in 1804 by Ralph Waldo Emerson's minister father. Admiring the European notion that to develop intellect and leadership skills children should be protected, carefully guided, and challenged mentally and physically, those scholars brought the idea to America, opening the Round Hill School in Northampton, Massachusetts, in 1823. In place of the harsh practices of England's public schools, where flogging and fagging—forcing young boys to serve older ones—were common, they introduced a system that put adults in close contact with students.

Their constituency was what Thomas Jefferson famously described as America's "artificial aristocracy, founded on wealth and birth."[36] Round Hill closed after eleven years, but during that time, an Episcopalian minister founded the similar Flushing Institute in Queens, New York, which "emphasized the development of Christian character" and required regular chapel attendance.[37] St. Paul's, another church-affiliated school, was started in 1855 by a wealthy Round Hill graduate at his family's summer estate in New Hampshire, with a young clergyman and graduate of Flushing as its headmaster. Ten years later, a St. Paul's father founded St. Mark's in Massachusetts with the Latin slogan *Age quod agis*, which it translated as "Do what you do best." In 1883, that founder sent Endicott Peabody down his new path.

Peabody was a man on a mission—to be a teacher of both secular and religious gospel. And he decided to start a school of his own on land in Groton, Massachusetts, offered to him by his devout Episcopalian sister Caroline's husband, a wealthy farmer and livestock breeder. They induced Frederick Law Olmsted, the eminent landscape architect, to design it. Thanks to his Brahmin family background, financial connections, and forceful nature, Peabody was able to raise a lot of money quickly ($4,000 alone from J. Pierpont Morgan, who joined Groton's board of trustees).[38] Groton opened in October 1884 with the former dean of the Episcopal Theological School as its president, dedicated to forming "manly Christian character, having regard to moral and physical as well as intellectual development."[39]

Peabody's pointed educational philosophy indicated an awareness that its natural constituency, children of the upper class, needed to be weaned from the advantages and indulgences that came to them at birth and reminded of the strict Puritan verities of religiosity, frugality, and self-discipline that were the historical foundations of their parents' privileged lives.[40] Peabody's primary intention was not the protection and propagation of an American aristocracy through the indoctrination of its offspring, but that's what his backers wanted, and as a defector from an investment bank, he knew enough to leverage their ambitions for his own purposes. Ironically, Peabody immediately emerged as the educational opposite of his relative's husband Horace Mann. In the pitched battle that followed, Peabody was a Christian soldier defending private education for the children of privilege.[41] In 1886, he married his cousin, and together they ran Groton for more than half a century. He retired in 1939, though he stayed close and kept tabs on students like Franklin Roosevelt, Francis Biddle, and Averill Harriman. Through men like those, Peabody ensured that his influence and devotion to muscular Christian values and American democracy would be passed down and honored long after he was gone.

～

Another nineteenth-century Peabody combined business acumen with an abiding philanthropic streak. George Foster Peabody was born in 1852 to a successful Ohio storekeeper reduced to poverty by the Civil War. The family moved to Brooklyn, New York, where George, like his distant cousin with the same first name, took a job with a dry-goods wholesaler at age fourteen. At a nearby Dutch Reformed church he met Spencer Trask, an investment banker, who befriended him and fifteen years later made him a partner in his firm. In the 1880s, George joined an Episcopal church, bought a seat on the New York Stock Exchange, and became an expert in rail bonds, promoting Mexican lines in partnership with a former Civil War general who had built the town of Colorado Springs and supported freed slaves. They made a fortune together before the turn of the century, and then Peabody made another investment in Edison Electric, which brought him into the orbit of Junius Morgan's son John Pierpont Morgan, known as Pierpont and educated in Switzerland and Germany in preparation for a career in international banking. He was a fresh-faced Wall Street twenty-year-old until the Panic of 1857 chastened one and all, and he and his father lost a fortune when their investment in the first transatlantic communications cable cratered after the cable snapped in 1858.

America's first Morgan, Miles, arrived in Massachusetts in 1636, farmed, fought Indians, and accumulated land; Joseph Morgan fought in the Revolution and moved to Hartford, where he prospered in business, opened a coffeehouse, invested in boats and canals, and helped found Aetna, the insurance company, in 1819. Joseph bought his son Junius a share in a dry-goods company just before Junius married Juliet Pierpont, whose family traced back to the Norman Conquest. Juliet's father was a Congregational minister who became an abolitionist and a Unitarian, questioning both the Holy Trinity and the property rights of slaveholders.

A decade later, Junius moved to Boston and bought into the international trading firm that led to his partnership with George Peabody. Junius groomed his son Pierpont, born in 1837, to be his partner and successor. The younger Morgan fell madly in love with Amelia Sturges, a sickly girl who would die of tuberculosis on their 1861 honeymoon. Then, after making a few rash financial bets, Pierpont settled down and opened the first of several J. P. Morgan companies in New York, where he worked as his father's agent and local eyes and ears for the next three decades.

That year, too, Pierpont joined the Episcopal Church, converted by the rector of St. George's Church; Morgan would soon finance its move to fashionable Stuyvesant Square and eventually became senior warden, its most powerful layman. It was a mutually beneficial relationship. Morgan had collected the autographs of Episcopal bishops, among other eminences, as a boy, and would serve on the boards of several Episcopal institutions, becoming a key point of connection between the Episcopal Church and the American oligarchy. Years later he would threaten to resign from St. George's when a worker was appointed to its parish board, remarking, "I want it to remain a body of gentlemen whom I can ask to meet me in my study."[42] At the end of the Civil War, Pierpont was married again, to the daughter of the warden of St. George's. His faith would prove to be livelier than his second marriage, which produced four children but lacked the passion and commitment of his brief first love.

All along, the Morgan interests grew in size and influence. In 1869—the year George Peabody died—Pierpont helped the owner of a small railroad fight off corporate raider Jay Gould and his partner Jim Fisk. When the dust settled, Morgan was on the railroad's board of directors, a pattern that would become his modus operandi. The next year, the Morgans elbowed into the ranks of Barings and Rothschild as European state financiers when their bank floated loans for France after Prussia brought down Napoleon III. When the latest French government fell a year later, so did its bonds, but like Peabody's bet on Maryland, they later made millions for Morgan, who bought them in and held them until they recovered their value.[43]

The same year those bonds cratered, thirty-four-year-old Pierpont's partner retired and he became the protégé of Anthony J. Drexel, a Philadelphia banker who had recently proposed a closer affiliation with Junius Morgan, who already represented Drexel in London. The Drexel bank's ties to the American government were exceeded only by Jay Cooke's. Drexel and Cooke, a former bank clerk who was less experienced at finance but politically connected and a pioneering bond salesman, were simultaneously partners and rivals.

Morgan, Peabody had traded U.S. bonds issued by the bankers the government sought out to finance the Civil War, particularly Drexel and Cooke, and the first of a new group of German Jewish bankers on Wall Street like J. & W. Seligman & Co., who placed their bonds with Union sympathizers in Europe. After working together to finance the Union, Drexel and Morgan then competed with Cooke to expand the vital-to-all public-private financial partnership, but with an edge: American bankers who could tap European markets could earn more than profits, finding themselves with influence over monetary policy.[44] So, after Junius suggested Drexel make Pierpont a partner at both Drexel & Co. and at an affiliated firm in France, Pierpont was also installed as manager of a reorganized Drexel Morgan & Co. in New York. Under Drexel's tutelage, J. P. Morgan would emerge as the principal financier of American railroads, the human hub of the Industrial Revolution.

Morgan embodied WASP dominance in banking, even as Jewish competitors began a slow but steady rise. The Seligmans, who'd first gone into business as New York storekeepers in 1846, founded an investment bank in 1864, and a decade later would partner with Morgan and the Rothschilds to sell United States bonds. Kuhn Loeb was founded by merchants from Ohio in 1867 and began financing railroads a decade later. The Lehman brothers, who got their start in 1850 in New Orleans retail, wouldn't enter investment banking until 1899. The precursor to Goldman Sachs began financing small businesses in 1869. With their initial focus on high-risk ventures like commodities and the issuance of speculative commercial debt, they were the future, but through the next century, high-level banking would remain a WASP specialty. As late as 1986, the *New York Times* would report, "White Anglo-Saxon Protestants still dominate top management at the nation's dozen or so largest commercial banks," though "it is no longer their exclusive preserve."[45]

⌐

The Drexels were descendants of Francis M. Drexel, an Austrian who fled the Napoleonic Wars to be an itinerant portrait painter in Europe, and then opened an art studio in Pennsylvania in 1817. At forty-six, in the wake of the Panic of 1837, Drexel discovered an unsuspected flair for speculating in state-bank notes, known as "wildcat" currency. Drexel used his contacts to redeem the notes at advantageous rates, profiting from the collapse of Nicholas Biddle's Bank of the United States.*

When Francis Drexel founded Drexel & Co. in 1838, his expertise helped to stabilize the currency market, and he soon became a

---

* While the first U.S. coins had been struck in the 1790s, paper bills remained the province of private banks until 1861, when the federal government introduced so-called greenbacks to finance the Civil War; a national currency was formalized by Congress in 1863.

financier to governments and business, taking deposits, lending money, and buying and trading bonds. Railroads were his lucrative specialty. By 1846, Drexel was so powerful and respected that the federal government charged Drexel & Co. with the issuance of $49 million in Mexican War bonds. The next year, he made his elder sons Francis Anthony and Anthony Joseph partners and went back on the road, lured by the California Gold Rush of 1849, which fueled the bank's growth into the 1850s. The founder died back home in Pennsylvania in 1863 after he accidentally stepped off a moving train and was run over.[46] By then, Anthony had moved the company into international government and corporate finance through Junius Morgan. Drexel's position was only enhanced when Anthony spurned Ulysses Grant's invitation to be secretary of the Treasury.

In 1879, cabinet members, elected officials, judges, and railroad owners joined Morgan and Anthony Drexel when the latter feted Grant at a party for a thousand guests, including any number of Biddles. The Biddles and Drexels—one family old and esteemed, the other younger and richer—had joined forces seven years earlier, when Edward Biddle, educated in Germany, France, and Switzerland, and a Drexel & Co. employee, married the boss's daughter Emily. The alliance of the Drexels and Biddles ensured the continuing dominance of the latter clan over Philadelphia's social life.

An even more powerful alliance, Drexel Morgan went head-to-head with Jay Cooke over a refinancing of America's debt in 1873. Cooke's reputation had suffered from an earlier promotion of bonds for the Northern Pacific Railroad, an effort notable for Cooke's aggressive chicanery.[47] Cooke then joined forces with two Jewish banks, including Rothschild, to fight for the refinance job, but ended up sharing it with Morgan and partners including Barings. Then, Cooke's bank failed in the financial panic of 1873, which took down countless American companies and Wall Street firms.

Drexel Morgan didn't just survive; it would rule American finance for decades to come, enhancing its reputation for probity by focusing on the efficient operation of the railroads that, despite huge losses in the panic, remained the engines of American growth. Pierpont proved to be the man for that job. He would soon team up with Rothschild to clear America's remaining Civil War debts, saving the government tens of millions of dollars in interest, even though Pierpont found the Jewish bank and its American agent, August Belmont, arrogant and hard to stomach.[48]

22

Sometimes said to be a bastard Rothschild, August Belmont was born in Germany in either 1813 or 1816 with the last name Schönberg which, like the French name he later assumed, means "beautiful mountain." His father, a businessman lawyer, was president of their local synagogue. After his mother died young, August went to live in Frankfurt with his father's mother, whose second husband had connections to the German branch of the Rothschilds. When Belmont's family had money trouble, the bank took him on as a fourteen-year-old apprentice, sweeping floors and polishing furniture, and he quickly rose in the ranks, becoming secretary to a partner and then, in his twenties, sailing west to represent the Rothschild bank in Cuba.

Arriving first in New York in 1837, Belmont learned that the agency representing the Rothschilds there had gone bankrupt in the panic; he audaciously opened an eponymous banking firm and, acting as an agent for the Rothschilds, started investing in tobacco, cotton, and price-battered securities, proving his judgment, initiative, and value to his sponsors. Within a decade, Belmont, alongside Drexel, would be underwriting loans to finance America's war with Mexico.[49] By 1845, one of the first American "rich" lists would estimate the thirtysomething Belmont's wealth at $100,000.[50]

Cleveland Amory would later observe that due to Belmont's "constant associations with non-Jews, and the adaptability of Nature which has given the Belmonts scarcely any Semitic cast of feature except in their patriarchal age, a complete break with [his] Old World background has been successfully effected. In social acceptance, no later Jewish Family can compare with them."[51] Jews, like women and Roman Catholics, remained second-class citizens. Belmont wasn't accepted as a WASP but proved useful nonetheless.

A shrewd social climber, Belmont became a naturalized American, served as consul general to Austria from 1844 to 1850, and in

1849 converted to the Episcopal Church when he married Caroline Perry, daughter of the naval commander Matthew Perry, hero of multiple wars, who would shortly gain more renown as a practitioner of gunboat diplomacy when he opened Japan to American commerce. Conversion to the Episcopal faith was considered a sure step toward acceptance on a higher social plane. According to the 1860 census, 32 percent of Americans who belonged to religious congregations worshipped as Methodist then, 19 percent as Baptists, and only 14 percent as members of mainstream Protestant churches. After the Civil War, Episcopal churches experienced a minor surge thanks in part to the example set by the new plutocrats. One statistical study estimates that the 172,000 practicing Episcopalians in 1850 more than tripled by 1890, when the industrialists Henry Clay Frick and Jay Cooke followed Belmont and J. P. Morgan's lead and joined that tasteful, simple, liberal religion.[52] William A. Rockefeller and many others followed. Between 1866 and 1900, the American Episcopal Church grew from 160,000 communicants to 720,000.[53] Their small numbers didn't diminish Episcopalian power. "Never forget that in the life to come the Presbyterians will not be on the same plane as the Episcopalians," Henry Coit, first rector of St. Paul's School, once told a student's parent.[54]

August Belmont was named minister to the Netherlands from 1853 to 1857, and on his return he got deep into politics. Though he supported Stephen Douglas, who made him chairman of the Democratic National Committee for a dozen years beginning in 1860, Belmont worked as a banker and advocate for the Union in the Civil War, despite the Rothschilds' decision to deny loans to Lincoln's government.

Like the other Jewish bankers whom WASPs would use but never allow in their clubs, Belmont would remain slightly suspect, even as he made opportunistic alliances with the likes of J. P. Morgan. Belmont also opposed reformers who set out to dismantle Tammany Hall, New York City's Democratic political organization, almost a century old and run by the Tweed Ring, the notoriously corrupt political machine. Belmont sheltered "Boss" Tweed from criticism on behalf of the Rothschilds, who underwrote the city's debt, even though Tweed had tried to eject Belmont from the Democratic

National Committee. After Tweed was driven from power in 1871, Belmont was made a sachem, or leader, of Tammany. These political maneuvers and associations ensured that his social position remained tenuous, which may explain why he is thought to have been the model for Julius Beaufort, the mysterious, amoral, and finally disgraced banker character in Edith Wharton's *The Age of Innocence.*

At the end of the 1870s, Junius Morgan began to step back and let his son emerge as their bank's leader; Junius would die in 1890. Even before that, the 1877 death of Cornelius Vanderbilt vaulted Pierpont to the pinnacle of American finance. The Vanderbilt saga illustrates how social distinctions in Gilded Age America could be both fine and coarse. Five generations of American Vanderbilts had preceded the Commodore. Jan Aertsen of De Bildt, Holland, arrived in New Amsterdam just sixteen years after the first American Morgan, and renamed himself Vanderbilt. Cornelius was born on Staten Island ten years after the Astors came to America. He bought his first boat at sixteen in 1807, three years after the introduction of the steamboat. In 1828, he started a shipping line, and in 1857, he began to buy railroads. A decade later he won control of the New York Central, combining ten smaller lines connecting the East Coast to the Great Lakes, and in 1869, he built New York's first Grand Central Terminal. Constantly expanding his rail holdings, by 1873 he would own trunk lines and branches running 4,500 miles and be able to carry passengers from New York to Chicago.

The commodore died in 1877 at eighty-six, leaving about $100 million. Most of his New York Central stock went to his uninspiring eldest son, William Henry, whom the commodore had once banished to the family farm on Staten Island after a nervous breakdown but later took into the business. After his father's death, political pressure over the revelation of secret deals made by the New York Central that benefitted oil refiners induced William H. to sell much of his stake in the line, and he chose Pierpont Morgan to do it, hoping he would manage the job without damage to the company's share price. Morgan did, earning a huge commission and a seat on the line's board, representing some of the foreign investors who had bought shares.

Morgan followed his decade of railroad consolidation by arranging the mergers that created General Electric in 1892 (where George Foster Peabody was a director) and U.S. Steel in 1901. The next year, he managed the mergers that gave birth to International Harvester. He also oversaw the financing of the Panama Canal and bailed out the U.S. government and the banking system in the Panics of 1893 and 1907 before stepping back to concentrate on art collecting and philanthropy until his death in 1913. But even as he had made the Vanderbilts' wealth liquid, the righteous and discreet Morgan gave the impression that he disdained them as show-offy nouveaux riches. So even as the Vanderbilts and the rest of fashionable society moved steadily uptown, Morgan, the king of finance, remained in a grand but stuffy brownstone in Manhattan's Murray Hill. Pierpont had moved there in 1879 from a rented house next door to the mansion of William Henry Vanderbilt, so he knew the family up close. And his disapproval was widely shared.

The commodore's death set off a building spree by his heirs. William Henry, a church-goer and really more a Victorian accountant than a swell, invested his windfall in government bonds and by 1883 was worth $194 million, having doubled his inheritance and become the latest richest man in the world.[55] To celebrate, he built his immediate family a double brownstone on the west side of Fifth Avenue between 51st and 52nd Streets, completed in 1881. Famous for saying "The public be damned" in 1882—he was vilified, though the remark was taken out of context—William Henry retired in 1883 and died at sixty-four in 1885, splitting his fortune among his six surviving children, though two, Cornelius II and William Kissam, controlled trusts that held its bulk and they followed their father to the short stretch of Fifth Avenue that became known as Vanderbilt Row.

That triple thrust uptown proved decisive in a social cold war then simmering with the Astors, who had already tussled with the Vanderbilts in business; John Jacob III was a major investor in the New York Central. The Astors had been similarly disdained by New

York's WASP elite for generations, despite their ever-increasing real estate wealth. But after raising her children with William Backhouse Jr., another grandson of John Jacob Astor Sr., Lina Astor would lift her new family from the plutocracy into the aristocracy—and, finally, pull the Vanderbilts up alongside her.

23

Tracking social status was a New York preoccupation almost as old as the country. Mrs. John Jay, the former Sarah van Brughe Livingston, arguably invented America's A-list when she committed to writing a list of the guests she invited to her thirty-seven dinner parties in the winter of 1787–1788, the year before the federal government left New York for Washington, when her husband was George Washington's secretary for foreign affairs. Lewis and Gouverneur Morris were both on that list.[56]

From before the Civil War until his 1880 death, the sexton of Grace Church, one Isaac Hull Brown, closely studied his fashionable Episcopal congregation's parishioners in order to rank and seat them according to their social position at services.[57] When Lina Astor set out to conquer society in 1873, she formed an alliance with the next in the line of Manhattan's society list-keepers, who would help her mix a cocktail of old and new money, nobs and swells, rejecting only politicians, tradesmen, nonwhites, Jews, Catholics, and the culturati.[58]

That latest arbiter, Ward McAllister, was an offspring of a prominent Savannah, Georgia family. Related to a Revolutionary War hero, a chief justice of Georgia, and an American agent of Baring Brothers, he was also a cousin of the abolitionist and suffragist Julia Ward Howe, the composer of "The Battle Hymn of the Republic," who with her new husband had accompanied Mary Peabody and Horace Mann on their honeymoon.[59] Ward's mother, Louisa, was Julia's sister. Their brother, Samuel Cutler Ward, who was married to John Jacob Astor's daughter Emily, had introduced Louisa to her husband, a lawyer from Savannah, where Ward was born in 1827. At twenty-one, also under Samuel Ward's wing, Ward McAllister came to New

York, where, in 1849, he attended his first balls and saw his future dancing before him.[60] As Cleveland Amory would later write, "To Ward McAllister descended the honor of leading [America's elite] out of the wilderness of just plain wealth into the promised land of highly decorated Society."[61]

Back in Savannah, young McAllister studied law until his lawyer brother's tales of Gold Rush San Francisco lured him there in 1850. Wining and dining his brother's legal clients for two years, McAllister made both money and a good impression. But his future lay in the East, where he courted the daughter of a Georgia millionaire living in New Jersey, whose wealth bought the newlyweds a farm on Narragansett Bay in Newport, Rhode Island. Though she had several children and bankrolled her husband, Sarah McAllister played no role in his very public future, instead becoming a recluse. So on several solo trips to Europe, McAllister was able to obsess over the lifestyle of royals and their courts while he lived for two winters "with a luxury I have never since enjoyed" in southwest France as the guest of an American friend. There and in Baden-Baden, where he spent two summers observing the future emperor of Germany, "the desire to entertain took possession of me."[62]

Returning to New York in January 1859, he hosted a dinner for Commodore Vanderbilt, who praised a menu that included oysters, lobster, filet mignon, quail, lamb, duck, and five desserts, and encouraged him to "go on giving such dinners."[63] Then he returned to Savannah and did the same for two visiting British aristocrats before heading north again. In Newport, southern families had established a beachhead among New Englanders whose commercial ties to the South were strong, and arguments about abolition and secession could be avoided. There, in the 1860s, Ward McAllister found his métier, while bridging the gap between northerners and southerners.[64] The wealthy demanded sophisticated private entertainments and, determined to use his newfound connoisseurship to gain entry to American society, he gave them lavish picnics that showed off all he had learned.[65] He also promoted local women as social royalty by assigning them the job of escorting honored guests into meals at his farm. One was August Belmont's wife Caroline, known as "Tiny," whose husband had hired New York's first private French chef when he returned from the Hague in 1857. The Belmonts were experts at "competitive display," "the most prominent leaders of the older set," entertaining "everyone who was really worth knowing."[66]

McAllister understood that while the Belmonts were adored in Newport, which was Tiny's father's hometown, they had less-sure footing in New York. He also was aware that new money earned in and around the Civil War and the Industrial Revolution was challenging the established hierarchy, the quiet old WASP families, and their treasured verities of discretion, conformity, and public modesty. Belmont made it plain that America's new industrial royalty would outspend and outshine those who had come before them, buying houses, friends, and position. "In the socially-insecure times in which he lived he was soon taken extremely seriously by people who should have known better," wrote Cleveland Amory years later.

McAllister's genius was in shoring up the old hierarchy—paying devoted attention to the old Knickerbocker elite—while helping Belmont and other parvenus navigate the patrician transition. That balancing act helped create a stronger, more resilient social hierarchy through the careful crossbreeding of old and new money. Then he raised the stakes, Amory wrote, and allied with Mrs. William Backhouse Astor, who arrived in Newport just as Tiny Belmont abandoned society after the sudden death of her nineteen-year-old daughter. Lina Astor couldn't just waltz into town and take over, due to the competing presence of her richer sister-in-law, Mrs. William Waldorf Astor. But with McAllister's guidance, Lina bested her rival, who shortly left the resort—and the country, moving to England.[67]

Under the wing of Lina, who promptly seized the title of *the* Mrs. Astor, McAllister's dreams came true; he was New York's, and thus America's, new arbiter of who mattered and who didn't. And that role carried clout in a world newly connected by railroad tracks and telegraph wires, which accelerated communication and connected disparate populations into a national audience for increasingly influential newspapers and magazines.

Ralph Waldo Emerson, in his 1860 essay "Representative Men," chose Napoleon Bonaparte as a somewhat ironic embodiment of democracy in the Jacksonian Age, writing, "such a man was wanted, and such a man was born." Napoleon shared with America's upwardly mobile masses "their virtues and their vices; above all, he had their spirit or aim. To be the rich man, is the end."[68] Whether or not he read Emerson, McAllister understood that point in his bones, and he helped create a new class of celebrities, who became willing, even eager, performers on the American stage. Desperate for admiration as confirmation of their achievements and acquisitions, but cosseted by their wealth, New York's social eminences evolved into a new sort of celebrity perfectly attuned to their times. Their "ostentatious reticence"—they were on display yet just out of reach, visible yet untouchable—made them irresistible role models for the striving hoi polloi.[69]

The Civil War had nudged the WASP elite into this new role, and even as they accepted it, seemingly inviting scrutiny, they also pushed back. As industrial fortunes rose and new, non-WASP immigrants flooded America, the patrician class founded and supported exclusive institutions—from northeastern boarding schools like St. Paul's and Groton to New York's Metropolitan Museum of Art (1870) and Metropolitan Opera (1883)—that simultaneously celebrated their accomplishments, demonstrated to disdainful Europeans that cultural sophistication could be acquired, created barriers to newcomers, and also allowed a carefully edited few into their sanctums. Thus, the Belmonts and Vanderbilts gained status while those the poet Emma Lazarus described as the huddled masses in her 1883 poem inscribed on the Statue of Liberty were kept at bay.

In the three decades before 1900, the new industrial plutocracy would usurp the Northeast's original Anglo-Dutch Knickerbocker elite, ending the dominance of old families and eroding their traditions and prerogatives. The newcomers would encourage conspicuous consumption, publicity over discretion, and the emergence of cliques vying for social status, and balanced lineage with lucre as the primary determinants of position. Before the Civil War, a smaller American establishment had given lip service to its openness to a wider range of white male aspirants. But under increasing pressure in the Gilded Age, lines were drawn and new gates were erected to specifically bar non-WASPs and questionable members of the clan from its upper echelon.

Exclusionary resorts grew in renown, among them New Jersey's Long Branch (first popularized in the 1839s) and Cape May (visited by Henry Clay in 1847), the Berkshires in Massachusetts (which attracted Henry Melville in 1850), Saratoga Springs, New York, where thoroughbreds first raced in 1863, and Maine's Bar Harbor, where the first summer "cottage" was erected in 1868, and Northeast Harbor, where eight hotels were built beginning in 1880. Tuxedo Park opened in 1885 as a gated private community for New York's plutocracy. The first modern golf and hunting clubs were the St. Andrews Club in Yonkers and the Meadowbrook Hunt Club on Long Island, both opened in 1888, following the Country Club in Brookline, Massachusetts, which had debuted in 1882 for equestrians and added golf in 1893, after Florence Boit, whose uncle lived nearby, brought golf clubs home from a winter trip to France and one of their neighbors, a member, asked the club to lay out a course.[70] Nonetheless, women would only be admitted to the Country Club on the arm of men and were barred from voting membership until 1989. Catholics, Jews, and Blacks were, of course, unwelcome at the Country Club for decades, too.[71]

White Protestants still topped the heap and still wanted others to know it, but secular institutions replaced overtly religious ones as lineage became more important than piety. Ancestor worship had first come to America with the St. Andrews Society in 1756, the German Society in 1784, St. George's Society in 1786, St. Patrick's Society in 1789, and the Society of the Cincinnati in 1795. The New-York Historical Society was formed in 1804. Then, in the dozen years after 1885, there was a fresh rush to exclude: the Holland Society, Daughters of the Cincinnati, Sons of the Revolution, Daughters of the American Revolution, Colonial Dames, Colonial Order of the Acorn, Society of Mayflower Descendants, Baronial Order of Runnymede, Aryan Order of St. George of the Holy Roman Empire in the Colonies of America, and New York Society of the Order of the Founders and Patriots of America were all formed to honor heredity over wealth or merit.[72] No longer, all these new institutions implied, could all forms of status simply be absorbed.

Ward McAllister's tangible contribution to Gilded Age sorting was a group he called the Patriarchs, formed in 1872 to do no less than define New York City's society and guide its evolution. Today, the Patriarchs are less well known than the Four Hundred, another McAllister creation, referring to the four hundred souls he once said comprised society, but the former gave birth to the latter. Launched just after the downfall of the Tweed Ring (Tweed himself would go to jail for larceny and forgery in 1873), the Patriarchs and an adjunct for youngsters, the Family Circle Dancing Class, also addressed what some considered the Belmont problem—how to rank arrivistes and decide whom to assimilate and whom to exclude.

McAllister's Patriarchs appeared regressive but were actually a clever means to manage New York's evolving upper class. August Belmont was the exception who proved the rule. After a brief wait, he not only would be included but also would open the winter 1880 Patriarchs' Ball. In the progression to the first traditional quadrille that was described by the *New York Times* as including "only the original members of the society," Belmont appeared just after McAllister and Mrs. Astor, paired with a descendant of Peter Stuyvesant.[73]

Some applauded McAllister's feat. Frederick Townsend Martin, a writer, lawyer, and society figure, first met "the great social leader and the Beau Brummel of his day" at an upstate New York spa. In a memoir decades later, he noted that McAllister's father had been a prominent officer in the Georgia Hussars, a "crack regiment of the South," owned a famous wine cellar, and lavishly entertained "the wits and beauties of the day." The well-mannered McAllister, "a handsome double of Napoleon III," Martin continued, followed in his father's footsteps.[74] He "was always progressive, feverish and restless," and stood tall in Newport, then "a place where one went to meet friends, not to make them," before it became one where "wealth seems to be the Golden Key which unlocks most doors . . . But it is an age of change, and Newport has shared the universal fate."[75]

In his symbiotic relationship with Lina Astor, McAllister was the agent of that change. Consisting of twenty-five gentlemen from revered families—the Astors, of course, but mostly old Knickerbocker names like Livingston, Schermerhorn, and van Rensselaer—the Patriarchs defined American society by first formalizing their place atop it with "a list of men, drawn not from the 'fast set' around Belmont," wrote historian Eric Homberger, "but from the 'quiet representative men of this city.'"[76]

For the first seven years of the group's existence, the dinner dances they called balls were held in private homes, including Mrs. Astor's, but by 1879, larger parties had moved to public places, particularly Delmonico's, America's first fine-dining restaurant, which had opened in 1837. There, immediately after the Civil War, McAllister briefly hosted a series of debutante cotillion suppers. After their move to that public place, the Patriarchs' dinners (and the guests who attended) began to attract regular attention. In January 1880, the *New York Times* noted that invitations "are just now rather eagerly sought in uptown circles."[77] After the first ball of 1881, the *Times* added that "these parties were always exceedingly select," but as they had grown in popularity, they grew in size, as did the Patriarchs; eventually there were fifty of them.[78]

"The object we had in view was to make these balls thoroughly representative," McAllister would later write, "to embrace the old colonial New Yorkers; our adopted citizens, and men whose ability and integrity had won the esteem of the community, who formed an important element in society. We wanted the money power, but not in any way to be controlled by it."[79] Rather, the Patriarchs would teach wealthy aspirants what it took to join them. Though the Vanderbilts were at first excluded, the "measured rebuke . . . was not sustainable. . . . a symbolic gesture. The *idea* of exclusivity was the point of the Patriarchs, not its practical application."[80]

William H. Vanderbilt was among the guests at an 1882 Family Circle Dancing Club ball, and the following year members of another oft-derided industrial family, the Harrimans, appeared on the guest list, which numbered 225. It was said that 150 other aspirants were refused entry and didn't get to dance to the two bands that played for the couture-clad, diamond-draped elect, or taste the latest dish served to McAllister's guests, truffled turkey, described as "a Parisian luxury."

History has not looked kindly on Ward McAllister. He liked being known as "the Autocrat of Drawing Rooms," but one social historian suggested he was really "the glorified butler of the Four Hundred rather than its master," and described him as "a slightly adipose Petronius Arbiter reveling in the new elegance."[81] Paunchy, with "a weedy little Van Dyke," thinning hair, and expensive clothes but little style, he made up for his failings with determination and knowledge of the minutiae of family trees and social life. More recent accounts have dismissed McAllister as "an epicene fop" and Lina Astor as "an overweening old biddy."[82] McAllister had a higher opinion of her, deeming her his Mystic Rose.

McAllister's innovations, too, have been disdained. "Entertaining in public restaurants or dancing in their 'private rooms' was not a mere whim, but a serious early symptom of the restlessness, disintegration and informality of present Society. . . . Society had tired of its own game," Dixon Wecter, an Oxford-educated historian at the University of California at Berkeley, wrote half a century later.[83]

William Kissam Vanderbilt, known as Willie, and his wife, Alva, were first invited to a Patriarchs' Ball on January 15, 1883. "People seem to be going quite wild and inviting all sorts of people to their receptions," the Mystic Rose had earlier sniffed, refusing to meet them. "I don't know what has happened to our tastes."[84] So Alva challenged Lina Astor with a costume ball of her own to show off the new Richard Morris Hunt–designed palace her husband had commissioned at Fifth Avenue and 57th Street. When Alva learned that Lina's daughter hoped to attend, she let it be known that as she had never been properly introduced to the young lady's mother, that was quite impossible. Consequently, Mrs. Astor made a formal visit, dropping her calling card chez Vanderbilt; the gesture worked and the Vanderbilts finally gained access to the inner sanctum. Five weeks after Alva's party, William H. Vanderbilt retired, handing the family business to sons Willie and Cornelius II, and in 1884, Willie and Alva would be invited to their first ball at the Astor home.[85]

Ward McAllister's reign ended with the decade. In 1888, he hit the peak of his fame when he coined the term "the Four Hundred," telling the *New York Tribune*, "Why, there are only about four hundred [people] in fashionable New York society." The coinage caught on; in an item from Newport that summer, the *Times* even referred to "McAllister's 400"—but he would come to regret his raised profile. The next year, he resigned from a committee planning a ball for the centennial of Washington's first inauguration after an argument with several Patriarchs. When McAllister sniped that they didn't know what they were doing, Stuyvesant Fish called him an aging demagogue and dismissed him as "a caterer [and] discharged servant."[86] Damaged, he then finished himself off with a slight memoir he published in 1890, *Society as I Have Found It*, which ended by describing that year's New Year's Ball for eleven hundred at the Metropolitan Opera, which he had organized. After he dismissed the Four Hundred as "nonsensical," since he had just demonstrated he could single-handedly "enlarge the circle of society," he became a laughingstock, seen as more pompous than profound. The following winter, a Patriarchs' Ball was again limited to four hundred at Delmonico's.

Yet McAllister kept grasping at publicity, and on February 16, 1892, he gave his invitation list for Mrs. Astor's annual ball to the *Times* after another newspaper, the *New York World,* printed a partial guest list of about 150 names. Defensive and flustered, McAllister spluttered to the *Times* that the *World*'s list was "incomplete . . . unauthorized . . . [an] injustice . . . absurd . . . senseless . . . the invitations, don't you see, are issued to different ladies and gentlemen each time, do you understand? So at each dinner dance are only 150 people of the highest set, don't you know? So during the season, you see, 400 different invitations are issued. Wait a minute," he concluded, "and I will give you a correct list, don't you know, of the people who form what is known as The Four Hundred. Do you understand it will be authorized, reliable and, don't you know, the only correct list?" Though the story was headlined "The Only Four Hundred," people counted, and the list contained only 273 names.[87] Meanwhile, that year there were 4,047 millionaires in America.

~

Ward McAllister died suddenly at age sixty-eight late in January 1895. Cornelius Vanderbilt II served as a pallbearer, but Mrs. Astor pointedly gave a party the night before his funeral.[88] "The Patriarchs ignored him as a dead lion," wrote Frederick Townsend Martin, "and it was difficult to realize how little his memory seemed to be appreciated. There was but a handful of Society people present at the [funeral] service [though] the general public had crowded in out of curiosity. . . . As I left the church I was struck anew by life's ironies, and how a malicious Fate seems to derive pleasure in rending the mantle of our self-esteem."[89] Two years later, the Patriarchs disbanded. In 1906, Lina Astor had a nervous breakdown and at seventy-six departed the social scene, dying in 1908. The two children of Ward McAllister, that great champion of lineage, would die without issue. But McAllister had succeeded, perhaps beyond his wildest dreams. An American WASP aristocracy had been formalized, as had the means by which it would accept, even embrace, new members. Indeed, despite its many continuing exclusions, that process of expansion had progressed so far that a backlash had already set in.

A populist political movement began in 1891 after midwestern farmers banded together and formed the People's Party to demand regulation of commerce and an end to the monopolies that had enriched so many of the haves.[90] In the Panic of 1893, the bankruptcy of the Philadelphia & Reading Rail Road had triggered another depression and the collapse of eight thousand businesses, among them 156 rail lines and 400 banks. Twenty percent of Americans lost their jobs while the Patriarchs partied on.[91] A Nebraska congressman, William Jennings Bryan, began tub-thumping against eastern business interests and for an income tax, and the Democrats nominated him to run for president in 1896 against Republican William McKinley. Businessmen donated heavily to the latter, whose campaign raised more than $3.5 million en route to victory. But the Progressive Era followed, bringing calls for reform, and a new Social Gospel preached by religious leaders, encouraging followers to fight for the underprivileged in sermons that echoed the Republicans' success at abolishing slavery. Progressivism, like abolitionism and the women's suffrage movement before it, owed a great debt to Protestantism.[92]

In 1897, Theodore Roosevelt, a former New York police commissioner who had been a regular at McAllister's balls, went to Washington as McKinley's assistant secretary of the navy. Like many WASPs in that era, who followed a well-worn path into respectable, gentlemanly professions like brokerage and banking, he had studied law at Columbia after graduating from Harvard, but, disinclined toward commercial activity, he set his course toward politics. His rapid rise catapulted the WASP elite back into the highest level of government. In 1898, T.R., as he was known, was elected New York governor, and then, in 1901, vice president under McKinley. When the president was assassinated that September, Roosevelt became, at forty-two, the youngest-ever occupant of the office—and then won his own term in 1904.

Wrapping himself in the progressive agenda—he opposed trusts like U.S. Steel and Standard Oil, demanded the railroads be regulated, and fought for controls over food and drugs—Roosevelt was buoyed by public disgust with the excesses of the Gilded Age. The populist energy that bubbled up from the masses made him a model for many of his ilk who followed his path. Blessed with inherited, private incomes, WASPs like Henry Stimson, Averill Harriman, Dean Acheson, McGeorge Bundy, John V. Lindsay, Nelson Rockefeller, and John Kerry would enter into public service and create a counternarrative showing that the patriciate didn't have to be insular, superior, lazy, greedy, or uniformly reactionary.

Though he was surely a product of his times, and a century later would be disdained by the latest iteration of progressives as a political dinosaur, Roosevelt was vocal in his scorn for "lives which vary from rotten frivolity to rotten vice."[93] And he epitomized the notion that, once a family's fortune was made, descendants should serve, whether through politics or philanthropy. This became the primary justification for America's aristocracy in the twentieth century, deploying its inherited economic and political power and moral and social authority as a potent weapon for good in the world. "In order to survive, America's aristocracy had to justify itself."[94]

Part Seven

ENTITLEMENT

1873–1900

THE RUTHERFURDS AND THE WHITNEYS

24

Among the original Patriarchs was Lewis Morris Rutherfurd, the product of a marital merger of two of America's great colonial families. A great-great-grandson of Declaration of Independence signer Lewis Morris, born into privilege in 1820, Rutherfurd graduated from Williams College at age eighteen, studied law under William H. Seward, the future secretary of state, and practiced law with John Jay's son and Hamilton Fish, another future governor and secretary of state. In 1841, he married a twenty-one-year-old Knickerbocker heiress, Margaret Stuyvesant Chanler; the union allowed Lewis to stop practicing law and spend seven years in Italy, France, and Germany pursuing science, which he had studied at Williams. He worked with prisms that separated light into its spectral components: visible, infrared, ultraviolet.

On returning to New York and moving his family into a cottage in Newport and a four-story brick mansion at Second Avenue and 11th Street built by his wife's relation Peter Gerard Stuyvesant, a wealthy landowner and real estate developer, Lewis Rutherfurd switched his focus to astronomy and built an observatory in their yard, installing the best telescopes available and devising instruments that could photograph the heavens. He became a pioneer of astronomical photography and stellar spectroscopy, examining the light spectrums emitted by stars, moons, and planets, and set up Columbia

University's Department of Astronomy after joining the university's board in 1858. He is said to have inspired the unpopular eccentric Emerson Sillerton in Edith Wharton's *The Age of Innocence*, "who filled the house with long-haired men and short-haired women, and, when he travelled, took [his wife] to explore tombs in Yucatan instead of going to Paris or Italy. But there they were, set in their ways, and apparently unaware that they were different from other people."

Though other astronomers would ignore him or dismiss him as a dilettante, Rutherfurd's photographs of celestial bodies would ultimately gain international accolades. And though the Morris name would survive well into the twentieth century and Morris descendants would still be making a mark on the twenty-first, thanks to Lewis's offspring the Rutherfurds shined brightest in the Gilded Age. But their blended family's trajectory flipped George Peabody's journey from wealth to public service on its head.

By the time Lewis Morris Rutherfurd's children met the Gilded Age, the family symbolized entitlement, narcissism, exhibitionism, and self-absorption. Their great style and the wealth that paid for it camouflaged their unfortunate significance for the larger WASP elite, because even as this subset of a subset marked a downward turn in their cohort's cultural significance, they attracted ever-increasing attention. An audience for their antics coalesced as men like McAllister marketed them and newspapers from the *New York Times* to the yellow journalism outlets of Joseph Pulitzer and William Randolph Hearst covered them, creating a new industry best described as organized social voyeurism. Their private schools and clubs fenced them off from the public but perversely made them stand out even more. Louis Keller, a publisher who had run *Town Topics*, a society magazine that debuted in 1879, went on to found *The Social Register*, a directory of society first published in 1886. The first was a notorious scandal sheet, the second an exclusive phone book, but together they functioned as scorecards tracking the players and their games, and were eagerly studied both by the insiders and by the uninvited. And, inevitably, doing nothing beautifully, or at least garishly, replaced doing good as the newly anointed in-crowd's reason for being. Finally, their celebrity, constantly reinforced through display in the glare of public attention, saved them from utter irrelevance.

Descendants of Lewis Morris served in the Revolution and the Civil War, but many later Morrises made not war but love—specializing in auspicious marriages. The most auspicious of all was that of Lewis's tenth child, Helena, who married the largest landholder in New Jersey, Senator John Rutherfurd. He came from a powerful Scottish clan that owned castles and vast lands. In the seventeenth century a Rutherford (the name has been spelled both ways) fought for Charles I in the English Civil War, and in 1671, Charles II gave another Rutherfurd feudal rights over more land. Senator Rutherfurd's grandfather was even knighted by Britain's Queen Anne.

In the interceding generation, Walter Rutherfurd joined the British navy as a teenager and sailed for America in 1756 to fight in the French and Indian War. In 1758, a few months after the Battle of Ticonderoga (in which he fought and a brother, John, a major, died), Walter married a widow, Catherine Alexander Parker, descended from a twelfth-century Scots warlord. They were often separated after their marriage; he felt duty-bound to return to his regiment in upstate New York. In 1760, he was stationed in Montreal when his first child, John, was born. Two children later, Walter retired and returned to his family, eventually building a Manhattan home opposite the new St. Paul's Church on Vesey Street. Catherine was independently wealthy; she owned land, and Walter, in 1775, had been given a patent on five thousand acres in upstate New York in recognition of his military service. He also invested wisely and owned a trading post on Lake Huron near Detroit.

Though he was sympathetic to the cause of the rebellious Americans, Walter couldn't bring himself to fight the British, so he contrived to retire to an estate in New Jersey in close proximity to Pennsylvania's Lebanon Valley, where several relatives lived. Lewis Morris fled there when Morrisania was taken by the British. Hauled before a revolutionary council headed by a Livingston in 1777, Rutherfurd was accused of siding with Britain and asked to take an oath of allegiance; when he refused, he was put in jail, but he was eventually exchanged for two patriot prisoners.

His dual loyalties notwithstanding, Walter Rutherfurd would correspond with Gouverneur Morris in Philadelphia after the approval of the Constitution, dine with Alexander Hamilton, Aaron Burr, and the governor and mayor of New York, and sit with President Washington (who "seemed to remember me") at Robert Livingston's table celebrating his inauguration.[1] In 1790, Walter's son John was elected senator from New Jersey. "Innumerable are the congratulations," Walter wrote to him. "I didn't know we had so many friends."[2]

Before he won his Senate seat, John married Helena Morris at his father's house in Hunterdon, New Jersey, and entered the law office of Richard Stockton, another signer. The couple lived on New York's Wall Street, and John managed Trinity Church's real estate while practicing law as well. He and Helena also owned a New Jersey farm, Tranquility, where they moved full-time in 1787. Rutherfurd quit the Senate in 1798, and in 1807 he joined Gouverneur Morris and another commissioner to create the street-grid plan for Manhattan above 14th Street. Walter had died in 1804, but the Morris and Rutherfurd families grew even closer around 1810, when Sabina Morris, a daughter of Lewis Morris IV, married Robert Walter Rutherfurd, the only son among the senator's five children, who sat in New Jersey's Assembly. He and Sabina had five children. Among them was Lewis Morris Rutherfurd.

By its third generation in America, New Amsterdam governor Petrus Stuyvesant's family had also demonstrated a knack for world-wise marriage. But only a great-grandson, also a Petrus, born in 1727, would carry their name into the future. His youngest child, born when he was fifty, was Peter Gerard Stuyvesant, a lawyer and founder of the New-York Historical Society, whose second wife was another Helena Rutherfurd, one of the senator's daughters.

Peter Gerard and Helena were childless, but his eldest sister Judith had married Rev. John White Chanler, a great-grandson of Massachusetts governor John Winthrop, and as noted, their daughter,

Margaret, married Helena's uncle, Lewis Morris Rutherfurd, in 1841. The next year, Margaret and Lewis's eldest son was born, and they named him Stuyvesant Rutherfurd. Five years after that, Peter Gerard Stuyvesant drowned in an accident at Niagara Falls. His will ordered that the bulk of his $4 million fortune go to his nephew, Lewis and Margaret's eldest child, but only if he abided by a provision in the document and swapped his first and last names to become Rutherfurd Stuyvesant, which he did that same year.

The Stuyvesant-Rutherfurd family's papers at the New-York Historical Society shed no light on an oft-repeated claim that at some point Peter Gerard and Helena Stuyvesant had adopted the boy. Regardless, as an heir to Peter Gerard, owner of real estate up and down what would become New York's East Village and Stuyvesant Town, Rutherfurd Stuyvesant, who was known as Stuyvie in the family, inherited remarkably valuable property.*

Stuyvie Stuyvesant had four younger siblings. One of his sisters died young and unmarried; the other married an American ambassador to Italy and France. Though it's often said that an aversion to the spotlight is an inbred characteristic of American patricians, the two younger Rutherfurd brothers emerged as well-known society figures during Theodore Roosevelt's Progressive Era and found themselves under constant public scrutiny. The middle brother, Lewis Morris Rutherfurd Jr., known as Lewy, "was the beau ideal, combining wealth, extravagant good looks, charm and athletic prowess."[3] In 1890, at age thirty-two, he married Anne Harriman Sands, two years his junior and already a widow, a daughter of Oliver Harriman, a wealthy dry-goods merchant. She and Lewy lived in a mansion on the Stuyvesant estate at East 15th Street and Second Avenue, and at Tranquility in New Jersey, where all three brothers had country homes. Together, the two younger brothers managed Stuyvie Stuyvesant's inherited Manhattan real estate. Their "jobs" as Stuyvie's rent collectors let the younger brothers pursue their real avocations as sportsmen and gentlemen; Lewy liked fast cars, and his brother Winthrop, aka Winty, collected medieval armor (which he would later give to the

---

* The remainder of the estate was split between Peter Gerard's nephews Hamilton Fish and Gerard Stuyvesant.

Metropolitan Museum) and bred fox terriers.[4] Lewis Sr. died in 1892, leaving most of his estate to Winty and Lewy, as Stuyvie didn't need more money. Lewy barely got a chance to enjoy it.

After his daughter was born in 1891, Lewy was diagnosed with tuberculosis, and he spent a decade seeking cures before dying of the disease in Davos, Switzerland, in 1901. In the interim, brother Winty became the odd man out in international society's most compelling Gilded Age love triangle, when he and Great Britain's Duke of Marlborough competed for the hand of a Vanderbilt. When the titled Briton won the contest, the resulting wedding was the most famous, if least felicitous, marital merger in a brief burst of extreme upward mobility that saw five hundred American Gilded Age heiresses marry titled Europeans.

Tiaras and titles are, perhaps, their own reward, but there were also psychosocial causes for what one observer estimated as a $220 million transfer of wealth from American fortunes to impecunious European nobles in the Gilded Age. The decline of the Puritan ethic in secular American society was a factor in this marriage market, alongside the rise of American worldliness and the general retreat of the European upper class after the Revolutions of 1848 against the monarchies of Sicily, France, Germany, Italy, and Austria. Though those revolts mostly failed, the aristocracy never really recovered. So not only was American money attractive to bride-seeking bachelors across the Atlantic, but so was the relative innocence, fizziness, and novelty of young American brides. And for the Americans, a dose of Europe's gravitas and seasoning was welcome. Just as America's newly enriched magnates were buying art and backing museums to prove their equality with their Old World counterparts, ambitious American mothers guided their daughters toward marriageable European men to ensure their own status back home. Their social insecurity met its match in the financial neediness of Europe's land-rich, cash-poor top tier.

One of the first such matches was the marriage of Betsy Patterson, daughter of a wealthy Baltimore merchant, to Jerome Bonaparte, Napoleon's youngest brother, in 1803. He promptly left her on Napoleon's orders, and before her death, she was said to have remarked that her life's motivations were love, ambition, and avarice. In 1874, Jennie Jerome, daughter of a New York banker, married Lord Randolph Churchill and gave birth to their son Winston. Two years later, the eighth Duke of Manchester married Consuelo Yznaga, a Cuban beauty popular in New York society. But the year 1895 was the high point of mercenary marriages: nine American heiresses caught titled Europeans that year. And no bride got more attention than Willie K. and Alva Vanderbilt's daughter Consuelo, mostly because she married the Duke of Marlborough, who happened to be Winston Churchill's cousin. More crucially, perhaps, he owned the most valuable country house in the world, Blenheim Palace in Oxfordshire, England, an 11,500-acre estate given to John Churchill, the first Duke, by Queen Anne after he beat French and Bavarian troops in a crucial battle in 1704. Almost two centuries later, the cost of its upkeep threatened to ruin the reigning duke.

Born Alva Erskine Smith, Consuelo Vanderbilt's mother came from a southern family, itself ruined by the Civil War. After a brief interregnum in Paris, the Smiths ended up in New York, where Alva's father traded cotton and her mother ran a boardinghouse. Alva's friend Consuelo Yznaga introduced her to Willie, and Alva later named their daughter in her honor. Alva's ambition—for prestige and power for herself and her daughter—was boundless, and she was fierce in fulfilling it. Within the Vanderbilt family, she had been in a constant, bitter competition for social superiority with her sister-in-law Alice, Willie's older brother Cornelius's wife, ever since William H. Vanderbilt's death and the revelation of his decision to split the bulk of his estate between his two eldest sons.

A Sunday school teacher who went to church daily, sometimes twice a day, but became quite grand, Alice resented Alva, condemning the two women to an ongoing and expensive battle for social supremacy that drove Alva half mad.[5] To please his demanding spouse, Willie bought the world's largest yacht and named it the *Alva* in 1886, and then bankrolled a "cottage" called Marble House in Newport, both designed as launch pads for daughter Consuelo.[6] Alva's goal was to marry her off spectacularly. Thanks to Alva's parallel war with Lina Astor, society knew all of that, but had even more reason to be riveted by Alva's machinations: Alva and Willie K.'s marriage was on the rocks, and Consuelo was in love with another man, Winthrop Rutherfurd.

The *Alva* sank in 1892 and was replaced by the *Valiant*, which, on its maiden cruise—a voyage of several months to India and the south of France—carried Winthrop Rutherfurd as well as Alva's lover and Winty's best friend, Oliver Belmont, August's son. Belmont, younger than Alva, half Jewish and divorced, was another reason Alva insisted her daughter marry a title. She feared she would be ostracized when, inevitably, she divorced Willie to marry him. Alva and Willie stopped speaking at sea.

"The News Produces a Big Sensation," cried a front-page headline in the *New York Tribune* on March 6, 1895, reporting on the ensuing scandal. In spring 1894, the yachting party had all gone to Paris, where Willie was also having an affair, and Alva sued him for divorce. With Consuelo, then seventeen, she went on to London, where they met the Duke of Marlborough, Charles Richard John Spencer-Churchill, who allegedly had been rejected after proposing to Gertrude Vanderbilt, a great-granddaughter of the commodore. Back in New York, Winty Rutherfurd proposed to Consuelo first—and she secretly accepted.[7] When the women went back to Paris, Winty followed, but Alva banished him, and mother and daughter went to Blenheim Palace, Marlborough's family seat, where Consuelo realized the Duke was broke and doubled her resolve to marry Winty. Back in Newport, she revealed that plan to Alva, who pitched a fit and threatened to murder Rutherfurd, to be hanged for the crime, and to commit suicide—and also faked a heart attack—all as the impecunious Marlborough was en route to join them in Rhode Island.[8]

"My mother tore from me the influence of my sweetheart," Consuelo would tell a 1926 Vatican tribunal that annulled her marriage to Marlborough six years after their civil divorce. "She made me leave the country. She intercepted all letters my sweetheart wrote and all of mine to him. She caused continuous scenes. She said I must obey."[9]

On August 28, 1895, Alva gave a ball for the Duke; she had separated from Vanderbilt just before the party. On the last day of Marlborough's visit, he proposed, Consuelo relented under pressure, and Alva announced her coup the next day. Lina Astor attended the November 1895 wedding, which Alva ensured would take place by placing a guard outside Consuelo's door; the bride nonetheless arrived at St. Thomas, an Episcopal church on Fifth Avenue, twenty minutes late and "seemed much troubled."[10] The day ended with the signing of a $25 million marriage contract, sweetened with additional $100,000-a-year payments to Marlborough.[11] Consuelo's new title of duchess didn't come cheap.

Alva married Belmont the next year, and Willie moved to Paris, where Consuelo often visited, returning with more money for Blenheim, even as she and her husband both took lovers. Hers was Jacques Balsan, nine years older and one of her father's best pals. Though she had two boys with Marlborough (giving the duke the requisite heir and a spare), the marriage would end in a 1905 separation, divorce in 1920, and six years later, after she married Balsan, that official annulment by the Holy Tribunal of the Roman Catholic Church on grounds of intimidation and coercion, even though the wedding had been performed by a Protestant minister. Consuelo testified she had never loved the Duke. "The arrogance of his character created in me a sentiment of hostility," she told the tribunal. "He seemed to despise anything that was not British."[12] Winty Rutherfurd's role in the scandal was only then revealed in headlines calling him her "hapless suitor."

The Rutherfurds produced delicious gossip for years, titillating the public with voyeuristic glimpses into the complex and messy lives of the WASP elite, a storyline that would continue to amuse the masses for decades to come. Shortly after Anne Harriman Sands Rutherfurd lost her husband, Lewy, her mother also died, and her father, Oliver Harriman, was declared legally insane, his fortune put under his children's control. A year later, Willie K., then fifty-two and still in Paris, was linked to Anne in gossip among the Americans in Paris, and he sought to change the terms of his divorce, which forbade his remarriage while Alva was alive.[13] In April 1903, he got permission and, in what the *New York Times* would later term "a peculiar coincidence," given Winty Rutherfurd's love for Willie's daughter, Vanderbilt married Winty's brother's widow.[14]

At forty-four, Anne became one of the wealthiest women in the world, "her quiet, exquisite, and very expensive tastes . . . gratified to the boundless limits of honeyed prodigality."[15] She quickly blossomed as a social leader and progressive philanthropist, but unfortunately, neither Vanderbilt's wealth nor her close—some said intimate— friendship with J. P. Morgan's daughter, another Anne, could buy happiness for her and Lewy's daughters.[16] Mother and children fell under the spell of dubious self-help gurus, all had multiple marriages, and daughter Barbara suffered numerous breakdowns, was institutionalized, and predeceased her mother. All of it was fodder for the popular press, which profited from schadenfreude, the delight felt by many in the misfortunes of the fortunate few.

The cast of characters was quite irresistible. Winty Rutherfurd was a catch, with huge dark eyes over a handlebar mustache, social connections, English style, and enormous wealth. Ava Astor, wife of John Jacob Astor IV, was among his rumored conquests, and Edith Wharton said he was "the prototype of my first novels," though one wag sniped that at "six feet two in his golf stockings, he was no match for five feet six in a cornet."[17] Two years after his first marriage in 1902, Winty had built the Brick House, an eighteen-thousand-square-foot three-story Tudor-style manor house (with thirty-three-rooms and seventeen bathrooms) on his family's five-thousand-acre Allamuchy, New Jersey, estate. He spent his summers there, breeding Jersey, Guernsey, and Holstein cows, Dorset sheep, and his beloved fox terriers, and running a profitable farm, albeit one where everyone dressed for dinner, even when the house had no guests, as was often the case. A dozen servants worked inside, and more on the grounds, which included a 1,000-acre fenced park for hunting, stocked with elk, deer, and pheasants.

Winty's wife was Alice Morton, the youngest daughter of Levi P. Morton, New York's governor, who had previously served as the U.S. minister to France and Benjamin Harrison's vice president. Alice was tall, blond, chic, and "a great society belle," according to the *Times,* which called her new husband "perhaps one of the best-known men in New York society . . . a capital shot, a well-known yachtsman, and a daring rider to the hounds" in an engagement announcement.[18]

Lina Astor's name appeared first on the list of guests at their Grace Church wedding. They had six children before Alice died after surgery in 1917. Two years later, Lucy Mercer, a descendant of a signer of the

Declaration of Independence, entered Winty's home. She needed an income, and he needed someone to care for his children. But Lucy was also fleeing an affair with another man who had been found out by his wife. He was Franklin Delano Roosevelt, then Woodrow Wilson's assistant secretary of the navy, a job his distant relation Theodore Roosevelt had once held. In 1905, Franklin had married his fifth cousin Eleanor Roosevelt, two weeks after her uncle T.R.'s second inauguration as the twenty-sixth president.

Eleanor, in need of a social secretary, hired Lucy Mercer. Franklin couldn't help but notice his wife's stunning new assistant and began calling her "the lovely Lucy."[19] It wasn't long before gossip about them started. Gently Eleanor fired Lucy, and five days later Franklin arranged for her to be hired by his office.[20] Their fling was facilitated by friends, including another daughter of Levi Morton who invited them to her elaborate dinners and weekends. Among her circle was Winty, widower of her sister Alice. Casual adultery had become as common among WASPs as stern piety was for the Puritans. Clearly, times had changed.

In summer 1918, Franklin fell ill en route home from a trip to Europe. Fearing he had contracted the Spanish flu, Eleanor met his boat with an ambulance, and while unpacking his bags she discovered love letters from Lucy. Eleanor told him she would never share his bed again—and that Lucy had to go. Early in 1920, Lucy and Winty married. He was exactly twice her age but, unable to marry the man she loved, the twenty-nine-year-old Lucy rebounded into a more than acceptable life. For Franklin, the end of the affair meant an unhindered path to a brilliant political career. Not even Guillain-Barré syndrome, which a 2003 study in the *Journal of Medical Biography* found he'd contracted in 1921, leaving his legs paralyzed, would stop him.[21] But neither would he stop caring for Lucy Rutherfurd, even as she added a daughter to Winty's brood and ran his five homes (including the estate in New Jersey and another in posh Aiken, South Carolina).

Lucy never stopped thinking about FDR, either. Letters suggest they kept seeing each other in the mid-1920s. In 1932, Winty voted against FDR when he ran for president, but Lucy went to Washington for his inauguration, chauffeured in a car FDR sent. They kept in touch afterward; White House operators were instructed to put her straight through when she called the president. Meanwhile, Winty's health was failing. By Roosevelt's third inauguration in 1941, Rutherfurd, at seventy-nine, was debilitated by strokes that left him in a wheelchair, one arm useless. Roosevelt helped with doctors and advised Winty's sons on life decisions, including, at Lucy's urging, guiding them into the service during World War II. He and Lucy continued to see each other on the sly.

Lucy stopped visiting, though, as Winty declined, dying in March 1944 at eighty-two. His widow was just fifty-two, an age that showed only in wisps of gray in her hair. But FDR was a shadow of his former self, for his health was failing, too. Still, in 1944, with the world at war, FDR decided to seek a fourth term—and en route to a last quiet weekend in Hyde Park before the campaign, he stopped at Allamuchy, telling reporters on his train he was seeing an old friend whose husband had recently died. In fact, he visited the whole Rutherfurd clan, taking the children for a ride in his car with its siren-shrieking motorcycle escort before a seated lunch. Then, at Thanksgiving, the president went to Warm Springs, a Georgia spa where he had long been treated for paralysis, and Lucy joined him from Aiken. The clandestine visits continued into 1945.

When FDR went back to Warm Springs that March, Lucy called eight times in his ten days there, and arrived for an extended visit on April 9. On the twelfth, though, his health clearly perilous, FDR was sitting for a watercolor portrait when he slumped back in his chair, one arm jerking, and then collapsed. One of his secretaries shooed Lucy and the artist from the house with the excuse that their bedrooms would be needed for the Roosevelt family, and they fled in the artist's car.[22] But en route to Aiken, Lucy insisted on stopping to call and check on FDR. Her premonition proved correct. The president had already died of a cerebral hemorrhage.[23]

All concerned kept up their WASP dignity and behaved admirably in the years that followed. Early in 1948, Lucy was diagnosed with leukemia; she died at fifty-seven and was buried next to her husband at Allamuchy. Among her possessions at her death was a painting of the president by that same artist, sent to her just after FDR's death by Eleanor, a gesture Lucy thought generous. Writing in a thank-you note to Eleanor that she would treasure it, she added, "I send you—as I find it impossible not to, my love and deep sympathy."[24]

25

Cleveland Amory, in his 1960 classic *Who Killed Society?*, considered the Astors, Vanderbilts, and Whitneys the three leading families in American society, but the Whitneys were the last of them to achieve great wealth and stake a claim to all it commanded. Under the sponsorship of the New York governor and failed presidential candidate Samuel Tilden, William Collins Whitney, descendent of William Bradford of Plymouth through marriage, had established himself in Democratic politics and New York City government in the 1870s. But only in 1882 did his wife Flora's bachelor brother Oliver Payne—a founder, director, and longtime treasurer of Standard Oil—lift his in-laws into the ranks of New York's exquisites when he gave Flora a birthday gift of $1.5 million in Standard shares.

Whitney resigned his job as New York City's corporation counsel, though he had two years left in his term, and returned to private practice as a lawyer. He was named to the board of a railroad recently acquired by Willie Vanderbilt, and he became a homeowner when Oliver staked Flora to the $600,000 purchase price for a mansion at the newly fashionable intersection of 57th Street and Fifth Avenue. The site would years later be occupied by the headquarters of Tiffany & Co.

Politicians, especially reform-minded Democrats like Whitney, were generally persona non grata among the bon ton. But Whitney and Flora followed the path cleared by August Belmont, who, alongside Whitney, had been enlisted by Flora's father, Henry Payne, an Ohioan, to promote Tilden as a presidential candidate in 1876. The Whitneys were immediately accepted because they added charm and their *Mayflower* connection to the alluring wealth and business connections that had paved the way into society for Belmont.

The social neophytes adapted easily to their new milieu. They attended Alva Vanderbilt's 1883 housewarming ball dressed as symbols of post-Revolution Parisian social life, and they joined an Episcopal church. William frequented fashionable clubs like the Knickerbocker and the Union, and Flora—by then, thanks to Oliver, considered the richest woman in America—began supporting fashionable charities and giving parties in their private ballroom, said to be the largest in the city. William also signed on as a founding sponsor of the Metropolitan Opera, alongside several Vanderbilt relations, George Peabody, J. P. Morgan, and James Roosevelt, and was assigned box no. 63 when it opened that fall.[25]

The next year, Whitney reengaged with politics on behalf of Henry Payne, who sought an Ohio Senate seat and still hoped to occupy the White House. Whitney, who had cultivated the antitrust crusader Joseph Pulitzer, the owner of the *St. Louis Post-Dispatch* who'd just bought the *New York World*, lobbied him on Payne's behalf, claiming his father-in-law was an opponent of Standard Oil, though he wasn't (son Oliver was a Standard man and Henry a stockholder). Pulitzer not only spurned the approach but ran a story revealing that Whitney's new house was likely paid for by Oliver and tying Payne to Standard. Payne won election anyway, after Oliver spread $100,000 around the state capital.[26] But Payne once again failed to gain a nod as president. Grover Cleveland ran and won instead, aided by Pulitzer and Whitney. In 1885, shortly after the Whitneys hosted their first party at their new home, William C.'s long alliance with Cleveland paid off when he was named secretary of the navy, and the family moved to Washington, D.C., where they made a noisy arrival, buying a twenty-eight-room Georgetown mansion, spending $45,000 redoing it, and then entertaining grandly.[27] Whitney replaced the navy's wooden fleet, commissioning enough steel ships that he became known as the father of the modern navy.

As his term in the cabinet ended, Whitney was approached to run for Senate from New York, but decided to concentrate on building his wealth. While still in the cabinet, he identified Thomas Fortune Ryan, an orphan who had become a Tammany-connected stockbroker and then founded his own street rail line, as a potential partner; they joined forces with the Wideners, who had electrified Philadelphia's trolley lines, to become the "traction"—or streetcar—kings of New York City. Their Metropolitan Street Railway Company bought up the city's surface rail lines one by one, using Widener's money, Whitney's legal expertise, Ryan's stock market experience, and their deep oligarchical connections as levers, planning to unify the disparate lines, replace horsecars with electric and steam ones, and expand to other cities. Later they would also consolidate several of New York's gas and electric companies.

Simultaneously, troubling rumors first circulated of trouble in the Whitney marriage. William, it was said, had begun to stray. Flora, who was smart, capable, ambitious, and at loose ends, as all but one of their four surviving children were grown (Dorothy was four), set her sights on becoming a queen of society. Despite William's near-total disinterest in social life, Flora was "propelled into a whirl of entertaining" in New York, in Lenox, where they owned a cottage, and in Bar Harbor and Newport, where they rented.[28]

Flora, inevitably, fell in thrall to Ward McAllister.[29] Even as her husband was still in Washington, she began attending balls and inviting others to her home, which was, the *New York Tribune* noted, "especially adapted for entertainments."[30] She became a regular in the social columns, center stage at McAllister's 1890 New Year's ball alongside Alice and Cornelius Vanderbilt, announcing a series of dances at her home in 1891, and a year later sitting at McAllister's table at the Patriarchs' twentieth-anniversary ball. By then, her husband was important enough in business that when Junius Morgan died, he accompanied Pierpont to the funeral on a special train for the financier's friends.

In 1892, Whitney was in the running for the presidency, but many wanted Cleveland back, and Whitney got behind his patron, engineering his selection on the first ballot at the Democratic convention that June. Elected president for a second, nonsequential term, Cleveland stayed with the Whitneys in New York before taking office, enthroning William as a political eminence after "a Democratic conquest that could hardly have occurred had not Whitney called the tune."[31] Flora was similarly crowned one of New York's top hostesses. A December coming-out party for daughter Pauline (attended by the Clevelands, the J. P. Morgans, Vanderbilts, and various Knickerbockers) and another for friends of son Harry, home from Yale for Christmas, were respectively described as notable and brilliant. When Flora had a

sudden heart attack and died at fifty early in February 1893, leaving
her husband more than $3 million, her pallbearers included the pres-
ident and Cornelius Vanderbilt; McAllister was among the
mourners.[32]

The loss of his wife came as Whitney reached the peak of his influence. Cleveland thought his protégé could become governor of New
York in 1894 and president in 1896. Though because of Flora's failing health he had declined another cabinet post as well as an offer
to be Cleveland's minister to the Court of St. James, Whitney had accumulated not just wealth but social and political power. And he was
about to find himself in a love triangle with no less an eminence than
J. Pierpont Morgan.

Morgan had fallen in love with Edith Sybil Randolph, the pale,
tall, slight, and beautiful brunette daughter of the Washington surgeon who had identified the body of Lincoln's assassin John Wilkes
Booth on his death. Just before Junius Morgan's death, *Town Topics*,
run by Colonel William d'Alton Mann, a suave blackmailer who took
payoffs from prominent men to keep their names out of its pages, had
hinted of an affair between Edith, the widow of a British officer in the
Queen's Own Hussars, and first Oliver Payne and then Whitney.

It would emerge years later that at some point both Morgan and
Whitney gave Mann "loans" of $2,500 and $1,000, respectively. The
questions *why* and *when* were never definitively answered. Neither was
it ever specified why brother-in-law Oliver Payne and Whitney grew
estranged. But Whitney no longer needed a financial benefactor, and
rumors of his deepening involvement with Edith surely didn't please
Flora's brother.[33] In 1890, the Whitneys had visited Europe at the
same time as Edith, who was traveling with Morgan and two of his
daughters. Whitney took excursions alone with Edith, upsetting
Flora.[34] Six summers later, done with his mourning for Flora and
again enjoying life and power, Whitney, on a new yacht, *Columbia*,
crossed paths with Morgan on his *Corsair* at Bar Harbor. Edith Randolph was at the resort, too, and *Town Topics* broadly hinted that she
was the focus of Whitney's "devoted attentions," even as she again
went cruising with Morgan.[35]

Whitney never did run for president, and though he stayed involved in Democratic politics, his influence waned. He returned from the 1896 convention, where the populist William Jennings Bryan was nominated over Whitney's objections, to find that Cornelius Vanderbilt II had had a stroke. His daughter Gertrude was by then engaged to Whitney's eldest child, Harry Payne, though their wedding would be delayed while her father recovered. The Vanderbilts had issues with some of their children's romantic choices, but not with Gertrude's. While some still thought the Vanderbilts parvenus, the Whitneys had that magical *Mayflower* connection and Harry was considered the best-looking bachelor in New York. Their wedding took place at the Vanderbilts' Newport mansion, The Breakers, on August 25, with Henry Codman Potter, the Episcopal bishop of New York, presiding. Despite his growing coolness toward the groom's father, Harry's uncle Oliver Payne gave Gertrude pearls worth $200,000.

Ten days later Henry Payne died in Ohio, and a few short days after that Whitney married Edith Randolph in a hurried ceremony at an Episcopal church in Bar Harbor attended by only a handful of friends—and no family. Edith wanted a husband and J. P. Morgan was unavailable. Despite an attack of rheumatism, Whitney had taken his private rail car from Newport to Maine, where their engagement, previously denied, was announced to newspapers one day before their rushed nuptials. Whitney's three elder children disapproved. Oliver Payne was furious, vowed to impoverish his brother-in-law, and promised Flora's kids a fortune if they disowned their father (which Harry wouldn't do but his younger siblings Pauline and Payne did), despite the fact that Flora had apparently forgiven him any indiscretion, as proven by his inheritance, which paid for the "orgy of spending" that followed, aimed "at surrounding [Edith] with suitable splendor."[36]

It's thought that Oliver asked the children to prevent their father from moving his new bride into the Payne-provided 57th Street house. Harry did write to his father and said as much, and Whitney gave the house to him and Gertrude as a wedding present, then bought another at 871 Fifth Avenue at 68th Street, and hired McKim, Mead & White to redo and redecorate it. It emerged, according to the *New York Tribune,* "a Renaissance palace," filled with treasures from the Doria Pamphilj and Barberini palazzos in Rome, stained glass from a baron's chapel in the south of France, boiserie from Bordeaux, and paintings by Van Dyck, Reynolds, and Millet.

Whitney remained friendly with Pierpont Morgan, who was present at the debut of the Whitneys' new house, a dinner for the trustees of the American Museum of Natural History. Whitney regularly ended his day with drinks with Morgan, Edith, and Morgan's lawyer, Lewis Cass Ledyard.*

Whitney kept a hand in politics, too, helping defeat a mayoral candidate, Seth Low, a Republican who favored a city takeover of transit, in 1897.[37] He was happy in both his new marriage and the new life that inspired Lucius Beebe, a gourmand and newspaper columnist, to dub him a "magnifico . . . Mediocrity in Whitney was unthinkable."[38] But that happiness was tragically short-lived. In Aiken in February 1898, Edith struck her head on a low bridge and was thrown from her horse while fox hunting. Paralyzed by a broken neck, she died fifteen agonizing months later.[39]

The loss of a second wife didn't stop Whitney's compulsive spending, often focused on buying and racing thoroughbreds, an enthusiasm he took up that same year. He was even named president of the Saratoga Racing Association, where it was said he revived a sport that had seen better days. And by the time of his death in 1904, he owned a stable and a private track on three hundred acres in Brooklyn; stock farms on Long Island, in upstate New York, and in Kentucky; a house in London; game preserves in Massachusetts and the Adirondacks (where he owned about sixty-eight thousand acres and had one of his two private golf courses); and estates in Aiken, on Long Island, in the Berkshires, in Newport, and in Florida.†

Whitney also kept doing business, as when he made a stock market run against James Duke's American Tobacco, in which Oliver Payne was a partner. "Whitney gave Payne as good as he got," netting millions for Payne, Ryan, and their associates after their American Tobacco Company gained control of 80 percent of that trade in the

---

* A year earlier, Ledyard, Lewis Cass's grandson, was one of the nine founders of the New York Public Library.

† At his death, Whitney was said to be the largest individual landowner in New York State.

United States in 1901.[40] Ten years later, when the Supreme Court ordered it dissolved as a monopoly, J. P. Morgan's lawyer Ledyard drew up the plan for its breakup, ensuring that its owners, the heirs of his drinking buddy Whitney among them, got fair shares of its redistributed assets.[41]

Whitney's family's strife continued, too, which may have inspired a blind item in *Town Topics* in 1900, hinting that Whitney was seeing "a notorious burlesque actress."[42] Whitney's enemies (who included rival streetcar line owners and market savants who conjectured that he was manipulating Metropolitan Railway's stock) were circling. Oliver Payne enlisted the Rockefellers against him. But after Morgan and Willie K. Vanderbilt came to his rescue, Whitney won control of the last independent streetcar line and defeated the Rockefeller/ Payne group that was trying to squeeze him financially.[43]

On New Year's Eve 1901, Whitney hosted his own coming-out-of-mourning party—disguised as the debut of a favorite niece—at his new home. High society, from Lina Astor on down, was present. A few months later, his nemesis Seth Low took office as the first mayor of greater New York after Manhattan and the Bronx were consolidated with Brooklyn, Queens, and Staten Island. Low, who'd previously been mayor of Brooklyn, was elected as an anti-Tammany, anti-corruption, anti-Whitney reformer, and another Whitney antagonist was elected district attorney. After that, Whitney, already out of politics, began to "extricate himself" from his businesses, too, announcing his retirement just before Low took office.[44] It would later be alleged that Whitney and his partners had drained millions from their streetcar lines by reorganizing their parent corporations to avoid responsibility while continuing to profit from them; had watered, speculated in, pumped up the price of, and then dumped their shares; and had bribed politicians by buying stock for them, handing over the winnings and absorbing any losses. A few years later, during a special grand jury investigation, Whitney would be posthumously called "the uncrowned king" and mastermind of these schemes by no less an expert than Jacob Schiff, the head of the Kuhn, Loeb investment bank, which played a part in the deals. But his partners would be exonerated of wrongdoing, despite the grand jury finding "many things deserving severe condemnation."[45]

The onetime reformer was revealed as corrupt, but cocooned in wealth and power, Whitney didn't run or hide from scrutiny. Rather, he began planning a grand debut for Edith's daughter Adelaide that December, which also served notice of Gertrude Vanderbilt Whitney's reemergence from mourning her father. Mrs. Astor again attended, along with Mr. and Mrs. John D. Rockefeller Jr. and, reportedly, Harry's younger brother Payne Whitney, though it was unclear if he was actually present or merely invited.[46]

In 1902, Payne married Helen Hay, his Yale roommate's sister. Her father was secretary of state John Hay, who had started his career as Abraham Lincoln's private secretary; her maternal grandfather was, just like Payne's, a wealthy Ohio luminary. Payne's father was not invited to the pre-wedding dinner, seeing Lina Astor that night instead. The wedding was held at a Presbyterian church and attended by *le tout* Washington, including the president and Gouverneur Morris IV. The elder Whitney and Oliver Payne avoided each other; Oliver, as usual, lavished gifts on the couple, including diamonds, a honeymoon, and a six-story, forty-room Fifth Avenue mansion.[47]

William C. Whitney skipped Mrs. Astor's annual ball early in 1904, allowing the Payne Whitneys to take their place in society. A few weeks later, he fell ill with appendicitis while attending a performance of *Rigoletto,* and died of peritonitis at age sixty-two as he was being prepped for a second surgery to treat it.[48] His pallbearers included Grover Cleveland, Thomas Fortune Ryan, Elihu Root, Colonel William Jay, and H. H. Vreeland representing J. P. Morgan, who was out of the country. Whitney left $23 million, the bulk of it going to Harry, who was named his sole executor. Most of the rest was left in trust for Dorothy, who was also given the use of his Fifth Avenue mansion for two years; considerably smaller sums, though still in seven figures, went to the disloyal Payne and Pauline. Whitney had no Metropolitan Rail stock left.[49]

His frauds were finally revealed in 1907, when Joseph Choate, a noted lawyer who had been a friend of Whitney's, sued to recover losses incurred by an investor, and described the scheme as "debauchery and corruption."[50] The ultimate WASP reformer, Theodore Roosevelt, subsequently expressed his disapproval of Whitney, too, accusing him of "sharp practices" and calling him one of New York's "bad citizens," but hedging that "nothing whatever criminal has been shown."[51]

With William Collins Whitney's death, American WASPs reached their apogee. Already blessed in so many ways, his heirs, like many in their cohort, inherited unfathomable sums along with names rich with history and genealogical advantages that served as a glide path into the twentieth century. The sources of this newfound wealth, ranging from brilliant industrial innovation to outright exploitation, could be celebrated or ignored as required by circumstance and context. Whitney's offspring demonstrated the wildly different ways heirs can respond to sudden wealth.

Though Payne Whitney was said to have gone into business after his marriage, he "avoided the limelight . . . produced nothing, manufactured nothing, grew nothing, but took money and, by selection and investment, watched it grow . . . living and entertaining on a Lucullian scale . . . with no hint of publicity"—at least none outside of the sports pages, where he had been known as an athlete ever since his days rowing crew and playing tackle on Yale's football team.[52] Wife Helen Hay Whitney was a horse-racing enthusiast, and after buying a seventy-five-acre estate in equestrian country on the north shore of Long Island and naming it Greentree, she established a stable for thoroughbreds there.

Payne, to whom his uncle Oliver Payne had already given $20 million after his father's relatively small bequest, saw his fortunes grow even more when Oliver died in June 1917, leaving him almost $200 million. Pauline got an equal share. Dorothy Whitney got nothing, Harry Whitney got a portrait of Oliver by J. M. W. Turner, and Oliver's personal lawyer and close friend Lewis Cass Ledyard got $100,000. Payne also got all his uncle's remaining belongings, his real estate, and his yacht. This descendent of ascetic Puritans had hit the material jackpot.

Payne and Helen Hay Whitney's equestrian activities ramped up, and Payne began giving away large sums of money—quietly, as was his wont. As much as $100 million went to causes like the New York Public Library, Yale, a high-society psychiatric clinic that would later be renamed Payne Whitney in his honor, and local hospitals, but his spending and giving never caught up with the appreciation of his stocks and real estate. In 1924, he paid more than $2 million in income tax; only John D. Rockefeller and Henry Ford paid more.[53] The announcement of that tax bill was one of the rare times his name made the newspapers for anything other than having his house burglarized or winning horse races.

But Payne Whitney's life was cut tragically short when he fell ill with what he thought was indigestion while playing tennis on his estate in May 1927, and he died of a heart attack at age fifty-one less than half an hour later. Turfmen, as racing aficionados were called, mourned him as the greatest man in their field since August Belmont. The broader public was simply fascinated upon learning that a man they had hardly heard of had left an estate worth almost $180 million, the largest ever appraised in America at the time. Of that sum, $45 million was earmarked for charity. Inheritance taxes totaled more than $15 million.*

Compared to his brother, whose good fortune was amplified by his uncle Oliver, Harry Payne Whitney ended up relatively poor, with only a $63 million fortune when he died, but he was married to a Vanderbilt, so no one felt very sorry for him. Also an athlete at Yale, Harry had gone on to Columbia University's law school, and studied further under Elihu Root, the former secretary of both state and war, senator, and attorney for banks, railroads, and the wealthy. But Harry decided not to pursue a legal career, instead working for his father and then setting out on his own, buying mines worth $10 million with Daniel Guggenheim and others when he was just twenty-nine years

---

* Within two years, the estate grew to $239 million, though its final value was hard to determine, as some of his holdings were sold before the 1929 stock market crash and the start of the Depression. On paper, the portfolio lost almost $53 million by late 1931—but some of that was offset by a $17 million tax refund that year, also the largest ever on record.

old. Three years later, he inherited the bulk of his father's estate, estimated at $24 million, along with a dozen directorships of corporations and banks, and all of William C. Whitney's real estate. Like his brother, he eschewed publicity, preferring private clubs and rich men's sports to making a spectacle of himself. "Harry was a man who all his life would take the small protected world of Society to be *the* world," wrote the author Barbara Goldsmith.[54]

"Tall, with the broad shoulders slightly sloping which so often indicate easy muscular power; a wide, frank mouth; a shrewd expression about the eyes; wears a soft grey hat and loose fitting, double-breasted sacks with trousers rumpling willfully over shoes," as the *New Yorker* described him in 1925, Harry "would be taken anywhere for a banker of the quietly sagacious, unassuming type."[55]

Surrounded by luxury, attended by servants, traveling in yachts and private rail cars, able to buy whatever they wanted, both Whitneys surely took their advantages for granted. Harry's inheritance financed a brawny lifestyle that inspired the *New York Sun* to call him "the greatest all around sportsman in America."[56] In 1909, as a member of a celebrated polo team known as the Big Four, Whitney, a ten-goal player, brought that sport's most prestigious championship trophy back to America after years in England. Polo, yachting, hunting—whether big game in India or quail on his thousands of acres in Georgia—and (like father and brother) breeding and racing thoroughbreds were his passions. In 1924, his two-hundred-plus horses finished first in 272 races, winning $500,000, a record haul for an American stable.

Off the sporting fields, Harry was an invisible man. Though he invested in Mammoth Oil, a company at the center of the Teapot Dome bribery and oil-leasing scandal in 1924, after testifying in court he walked away unscathed. He also paid no price for taking a cut of a deal made by Thomas Fortune Ryan after William C. Whitney's death. Ryan, who had won the nickname "the great opportunist," agreed to develop mining operations and diamond fields for Belgium's King Leopold II in the Congo just before it would be ceded to Belgium—unlike Henry Sanford, he profited from the relationship.

Harry's wife, Gertrude, became a sculptor, and established an artist's club that evolved into the Whitney Museum, showcasing modern American art, which remains her greatest lasting achievement. Harry collected, too, but he wasn't known as a collector or connoisseur. Though he sat on the Metropolitan Opera board, he rarely attended. In one of his few publicized adventures in affluence, in 1926, he bought out a performance of the musical comedy *No, No, Nanette* and brought its cast from Augusta, Georgia, to his horse farm in Aiken to perform for a few of the fortunate friends invited to indulge in his legendary generosity at his homes and on his yacht.

Like his parents, after having three children, Harry and his wife grew politely estranged. While Harry kept his troubles to himself, Gertrude acted out. Though she was upset by Harry's "repeated infidelities . . . [she] did not desert her husband or the world of her birth," wrote Goldsmith in a book on Gertrude's niece Gloria Vanderbilt. "She simply bought herself another world," immersed herself in art, acquired lovers of her own, bought three 1838 buildings in the center of Greenwich Village, and in 1931, had them reconfigured as a private house and art studio and built another studio on their estate on Long Island, all in service of a bohemian life, "where every form of pleasure was available . . . Gertrude was to lead a dual existence for the rest of her life."[57] She also did admirable things like financing and opening a 225-bed hospital, staffed by seventy-five mostly American doctors and nurses, in an old seminary in war-torn France early in World War I.

After pledging $750,000 to the Museum of Natural History in 1929 for a new ornithology wing, Harry survived the stock market crash that fall, even making a little money thanks to his mining interests, but he was a drinker and his alcoholism was exacerbated by Gertrude's long absences and, possibly, his awareness that she, too, had found consolations outside their marriage. In fall 1930, Harry caught a cold he couldn't shake that turned into pneumonia, and within a few days it killed him at age fifty-eight. His funeral, at St. Bartholomew's Episcopal Church, was conducted by Endicott Peabody. His $72 million estate, the second-largest ever probated in New York State after his brother's (despite its shrinking by $10 million during the Depression), was mostly left to the one son among their three children, Cornelius Vanderbilt Whitney, better known as Sonny, with the remainder held in trust for his grandchildren. Harry's Long Island estate and all his possession went to Gertrude, along with the right to live out her days in their New York mansion.

At the will's direction, Harry Whitney's New York City home at Fifth Avenue and 68th Street, inherited from his father, was emptied and razed after Gertrude's death in 1942.* In fact, she had rarely lived there, spending her time in her Village mews house and at her Long Island estate instead. Before the end, the Fifth Avenue mansion was opened to the public to sell off the last furnishings that hadn't gone to family or museums. "Look at that thing," a visitor, described as a housewife from Brooklyn, said, pointing. "They advertise the beautiful furnishings and they're all worn out. Just look at that chair. It's all patched up." The reporter she was speaking to checked the auction catalogue. It was a Louis XIV gilded and carved sofa, upholstered in seventeenth-century crimson velvet from Genoa.[58]

The youngest of William C. Whitney's children, Dorothy, had grown up in her childhood home on 57th Street, where she was groomed for marriage. While no beauty, she was a sparkling catch. Already living independently with her own servants at seventeen, after her father died she took classes at Columbia, volunteered at a settlement house, inherited $7 million at twenty-one, and promptly started giving it away. Influenced by the older Daisy Harriman, a social crusader and suffragist, she also led a campaign for working girls, advocated for the vote for women, and served as the Junior League's president.[59] Her money "led me to feel," she once said, "that wealth entailed social responsibility."[60] Walter Lippmann later wrote that Dorothy "had a strong feeling of conscience that the money she'd inherited from her father was tainted and that she must devote it to public purposes."[61]

Independent and admiring achievement more than lineage or wealth, she had already been pursued by a number of well-born young men when, dining at the home of Daisy's uncle E. H. Harriman, she

* Eight years earlier, Gertrude had played a central role in one of the Depression's great scandals when she went to court seeking to take custody of her ten-year-old niece, Gloria Vanderbilt, from her beautiful, penniless, dissolute widowed mother, the second wife of Gertrude's alcoholic brother, Reggie.

met Willard Straight, twenty-six, a State Department employee just
back from six years in Asia.[62] Dorothy encountered Straight again
in early 1909 at Washington dinners. The son of upstate New York
schoolteachers, partly raised in Japan, Straight had been orphaned
at ten and was impulsive, disruptive, romantic, and highly intelligent—a combination that greatly appealed to Dorothy Whitney.

After college at Cornell, Straight bounced around Asia and became a vice consul in Seoul, where he met Harriman, who wanted to
connect his Trans-Siberian Railroad with a Chinese line. Though he
hoped to work for Harriman (whose daughter Mary attracted him),
he went to Havana instead, when his diplomat boss was named minister to Cuba. There he arranged President Theodore Roosevelt's
daughter Alice Longworth's honeymoon. In thanks, Roosevelt made
him consul general in a Manchurian rail hub, where he could help
Harriman.[63]

In June 1909, Straight resigned from the diplomatic corps to
represent a group of American bankers in China, pursuing the policy that would be formalized as Dollar Diplomacy under Roosevelt's
successor, William Howard Taft. After renewing his acquaintance with
Dorothy in New York, Straight traveled to Peking, where he learned
E. H. Harriman had died. Dorothy, on a world tour, followed, and
they fell in love, despite Straight's lack of wealth or social position.[64]
Their engagement was announced in summer 1911, and they married in Geneva before heading back to Peking, just in time to see the
Qing dynasty collapse. Back in London, Straight worked for J. P. Morgan, and soon they took a cruise on the *Corsair* with Pierpont himself.[65] Straight eventually became a Morgan bank partner.

But his interests and ambition, though broad, diverted him
from the beaten tracks of WASP careers—diplomacy, finance, the
law—and toward a trajectory set by his relationship with Herbert Croly,
an author and reformer with a notion of how to revitalize America
with a program of dynamic reform. Croly had influenced Theodore
Roosevelt, and Straight dreamed of running a publication to promote
progressive ideas like those Roosevelt had championed. After T.R.'s loss
in his last campaign, Straight and Croly began discussing a weekly
magazine, which, conveniently, Dorothy offered to bankroll.[66] The
first issue of *The New Republic* appeared in 1914.

Straight was commissioned as a major in the army in spring 1917. Sent to Paris, he continued supervising *The New Republic,* which caused a breach with Theodore Roosevelt, who disdained its "parlor Bolshevism."[67] The couple were also founders of New York's New School for Social Research in 1918, just before Straight fell ill. He had stayed in France as part of the team negotiating the World War I armistice, but his condition worsened and he died at thirty-eight on December 1, 1918, a few weeks after the armistice was signed, likely a victim of that year's worldwide flu pandemic. T.R. followed him to the grave five weeks later.

Seven years after that, Dorothy was remarried to a penniless but well-born Englishman studying at Cornell University and soon bought a 2,000-acre estate called Dartington Hall in Devon, England, where they started a progressive school and cultural center—effectively a utopian community for democratic idealists like Dorothy—that became a haven for refugees of the Nazis during World War II. Among its lecturers were Bertrand Russell and Aldous Huxley. *The New Republic* was sold in 1953 after costing her $3.7 million over thirty-nine years.[68] She lived quietly for fifteen more years, and her 1968 death attracted a fraction of the attention that was paid to the passing of her brothers, who reveled in their wealth and fruitlessly sought the privacy that came naturally to their sister Pauline, who'd lived in England for almost a decade before her 1916 death, and Dorothy, with her dedication to good works that harkened back to earlier American Protestant virtues. The next wave of WASPs would be neither admirable nor interested in making amends for their privileged existence. Indeed, they'd feel their most compelling duty was to themselves.

Part Eight

MALEVOLENCE

1900–1937
HENRY FAIRFIELD OSBORN

26

In 1916, Madison Grant, the wealthy heir to a colonial New York family, a graduate of Yale and Columbia, a hunter and science hobbyist, published his first book. The preface to *The Passing of the Great Race* was penned by Grant's closest friend, Henry Fairfield Osborn. He was, after Albert Einstein, the most celebrated scientist of his time, often called Charles Darwin's successor. A scion of another old American family, son of a railroad magnate, and the president of the American Museum of Natural History, Osborn not only praised his friend's work but helped place it with the publisher Charles Scribner's Sons not-yet-superstar editor Maxwell Perkins, three years before he signed F. Scott Fitzgerald as an author.

The Passing of the Great Race, a tribute to the two men's shared heritage, hailed WASPs as members of a superior Nordic race. It was also a warning. Irish and German immigrants had rushed to America in the 1840s. An Asian influx began with the 1849 Gold Rush. In 1881, Jewish immigration rose by a factor of seven after the assassination of Russia's czar Alexander II set off anti-Semitic pogroms. Between 1877 and 1887, Italian, Polish, and Hungarian immigration also soared. "It was as if all of eastern Europe was emptying out," observed author Daniel Okrent.[1] Between 1900 and 1910, 7.6 million European immigrants joined the 3.7 million who had arrived in the previous decade.[2] The promises, some real, some illusory, that the

WASPs who invented America had made were the draw. Living up to those promises had proved to be as great a challenge as integrating the latest immigrants.

In 1790, the American population, Native Americans excepted, had been 48 percent English, 19 percent of African ancestry, 12 percent Scots, and 10 percent German, with smaller numbers of French, Irish, and Welsh. Between 1841 and 1890, a wave of 15 million immigrants arrived, 4 million of them German, 3 million Irish, 3 million English, and 1 million Scandanavian. In the second great wave of immigration in the early twentieth century, 4 million arrivals were Italian, 3.6 million were from the Austro-Hungarian Empire, and another 3 million were from Russia, almost all of them Slavs or Jews. It's no exaggeration to say that thereafter, because of influential WASPs like Grant and Osborn, immigration slowed to a crawl until passage of the Immigration Act of 1965; in the next thirty years, the vast majority of arrivals came from Latin America, the Caribbean, and Asia, with only 12 percent from Europe.[3]

Members of America's founding WASP families—Osborn and the younger, less wealthy Grant among them—were proud that America was so attractive to outsiders, but panicked by the millions of new arrivals. Three years earlier in 1913, the Seventeenth Amendment had taken away one of the oligarchy's most potent sources of power when it mandated that the U.S. Senate, conceived by the founders as a U.S. version of England's hereditary House of Lords, be directly elected by voters instead of state legislators who were often in thrall—and debt—to their local gentry.* Immigrant voters were an unwanted wild card.

"The Anglo-Saxon branch of the Nordic race" is "that upon which the nation must chiefly depend," Osborn wrote in a second preface to a 1917 reprint of Grant's tome. "In no other human stock which has come to this country is there displayed the unanimity of heart, mind and action which is now being displayed by the descendants of the blue-eyed fair-haired peoples of the north of Europe."[4] The book and its endorsement by an eminence like Osborn outraged the editors of

---

* That the Senate would come to be greatly influenced if not controlled by corporations demonstrates how money came to trump blood in the American hierarchy.

Dorothy Whitney Straight's *The New Republic,* who deemed it dangerous.[5] The future Nazi dictator Adolf Hitler would read a German translation in prison while writing his own *Mein Kampf,* and in a fan letter to the author he would call *The Passing of the Great Race* his bible.

In summer 1934, in the same month Hitler declared himself Germany's Führer, Osborn, nearing the end of his museum career, sailed there to collect an honorary degree from Goethe University in Frankfurt. Osborn was in essential agreement with Hitler on the subject of race, and his Nazi Party eagerly sought the American's approval of its policies. Osborn couldn't help but be impressed by the discipline of the German students and flattered by the attention of their professors, who had already survived a purge of those who disagreed with Hitler's positions, and upon his return to America he issued fulsome praise of Germany's racial restrictions.

Criticized, Osborn called negative press coverage of the Nazis misguided and a one-sided reflection of the biases of Jews, who, he insisted, controlled the media. Germans could teach America a thing or two, he proclaimed, adding prophetically, "To observe the spirit of the young Germans is to realize that the world will have much to deal with in the not-too-distant future."[6]

Before those words proved all too true, Osborn would die after a life of good fortune and an extraordinary career propelled by erudition and showmanship. He began his career hunting fossils but ended it in disgraceful irrelevance due to his virulent prejudice, dismissed as "beyond the pale" by a longtime museum colleague. His fall marked the abrupt start of the decline of the American patriciate in the twentieth century.

⌁

"My boyhood and youth were similar to those of almost any other boy," wrote Henry Osborn, who would later be known as Fairfield.[7] He was born in 1857, his parents' second child. On the maternal side, his roots went back to Revolutionary-era figures Nathan Gold and Andrew Ward and to Rev. Ebenezer Pemberton, a founder of Princeton. His maternal grandfather, Jonathan Sturges, a merchant, founder of the Illinois Central Railroad, a founder of the Metropolitan Museum of Art, and a president of the New York Chamber of Commerce, was another of the reformers who brought down Boss Tweed.

Fairfield's paternal side sprang from Puritan Salem, Massachusetts. His father, William Henry Osborn, had left his family farm there at thirteen in 1837 to work for an East India trading company that sent him to Manila and made him a partner at twenty-one. By 1850, he was wealthy and owned his own firm when he returned to America and promptly met and fell for Virginia Sturges.

They married, and her father gave Osborn a job reorganizing his railroad; Osborn was so successful at that he was named the Illinois Central's president. He then went west seeking new opportunities for the line, and attracted European financing for an expansion fueled by his efforts to attract homesteaders to the west and create a civilization that grew in tandem with the railroad.* Virginia and William bought a country home in Buttermilk Falls, New York, where one-year-old Fairfield met J. P. Morgan, a frequent guest in the summers before the Civil War. In 1859, the Osborns moved to Garrison, where Fairfield's father bought hundreds of acres and built a new house he called Castle Rock.

In 1861, Morgan married Virginia's sister Amelia and became Fairfield's uncle. Despite Amelia's quick death, the financier stayed close to the Osborns and built his own country home near theirs. They were all part of a newly blended industrial-mercantile elite. Oliver Harriman's nephew E.H. started his career working for the Illinois Central. The Vanderbilts and Jay Gould were competitors. Fairfield's younger brother Frederick was best boyhood friends with Theodore Roosevelt. Morgan, of course, had his railroad investments. Exemplars of WASP clannishness, they belonged to the same clubs, lived in the same neighborhoods, worshiped in the same churches, and shared cultural and philanthropic interests.

Religion and obligation were constants in Osborn's upbringing. His parents were strict Scottish Presbyterians who read the Bible at home and regularly attended church. Fairfield would eventually

---

* Abraham Lincoln became the Illinois Central's lawyer and the Civil War generals Ambrose Burnside and George McClellan were, respectively, its treasurer, and its chief engineer and vice president. During the war, they all worked together to move troops and supplies on the line.

migrate to Morgan's St. George's Episcopal, but he retained the belief his parents had instilled in him that his advantages entailed moral, social, and religious obligations. Fairfield's mother wrestled with questions about salvation, the meaning of life, and the afterlife. In 1875, when both his sister and a brother, a budding naturalist, died, Virginia Osborn framed the twin tragedies as God's challenge to the survivors. She believed that wealth wasn't enough, and considered adversity and struggle positives. She sent Fairfield regular religious encouragement and money to give to charity to inculcate that habit, and he later fondly recalled the era's "pioneer spirit of Christian education and civilization."[8]

At sixteen, Fairfield joined the class of 1877 at the College of New Jersey (the future Princeton), co-founded by his maternal great-uncle. A bit of a dandy, nicknamed "Polly" for his girlish appearance, he was an unexceptional student, but there he formed a lifelong friendship with the slightly older Charles Scribner Jr. after Osborn triumphed in a traditional "spree" in which undergraduates beat each other with canes. His humorless mother hectored him in letters demanding he be a student leader and not fall in with "worthless" elements.

A Calvinist institution run by an evangelical Scottish Protestant president, Princeton reinforced her devout message, but it also delivered a competing one to the directionless young Fairfield. A banker had subsidized a new natural history museum at Princeton, and its director, Arnold Guyot, a pious geology professor, filled it with specimens, including fossils and displays of reconstructed dinosaurs. Osborn and a classmate took courses from him and were riveted.

Like Princeton's president, Guyot believed that the natural world didn't conflict with religion but was brimming with evidence of divine intelligence.[9] The duo managed to reconcile religion and science, seeing Charles Darwin's theory of evolution, published sixteen years earlier, as part of God's design, not a rejection of religion. Perhaps recalling his mother's philosophy, Osborn embraced Darwin's idea of struggle as key to the formation and survival of a species, as it was to individuals, but was less sure about natural selection, and was wrestling with all that when, at the end of junior year, he and some classmates proposed to spend a summer in the West, hunting fossils and camping out. Osborn suggested a preliminary trip to the Catskills, where they could stay at his family home. After graduation in 1877, the first Princeton Scientific Expedition of eighteen students and two professors set off, armed and dressed like cowboys, to collect fossils in Colorado, Utah, and Wyoming.

The summer after they graduated, Fairfield, twenty-one, inherited the considerable sum of $30,000 from his Sturges grandfather, and his mother urged him to use it to do good. It also appears to have boosted his independence. Back at Princeton as one of its first graduate students, he rejected a preordained career working for his father in railroads to pursue science, took anatomy classes at a medical school, and then followed one of his classmates to England and Germany. In London, he studied comparative anatomy with Thomas Huxley, Darwin's friend and advocate, who took a shine to him, though they parted company on philosophy and theology; Osborn's metaphysical beliefs were not shared by the eminent scientist. Huxley also introduced Osborn to Darwin, leaving the young fan speechless.

After winning a fellowship and earning a doctorate in 1881, Henry, as he was then still known, succumbed to parental pressure and went to work for his father, who had just bought the Chicago, Nashville, and New Orleans Railroad. But his preference for nature was clear; he would disappear to hunt for alligator fossils in Louisiana and amphibian embryos in Texas, the latter quest a failure that led him to focus on paleontology, the study of evolution through fossils.

His father, urged on by Princeton's president, who believed in his young protégé, built him a private library at Castle Rock in Garrison, in the hope he would turn his enthusiasm into a scientific business empire. But when Fairfield returned to Princeton, where his surviving little brother, William Church Osborn, was completing his own undergraduate studies, and joined the faculty as an assistant professor of science and anatomy, his father's objections were finally overcome, and he even gave money to Princeton. However, unsatisfied with Fairfield being a teacher or scientist, Osborn père continued urging him to do something more useful and prestigious.[10]

Fairfield married Lucretia "Loulou" Thatcher Perry, who was related to his mother as well as to the Belmonts, in an Episcopal church on Governor's Island, where her brigadier general father was

stationed.* After their honeymoon, they lived in Princeton. With his
father in decline, Fairfield began to play a larger role in his younger
brother's life, nudging him toward politics and away from business after
he graduated from law school at Harvard. Fairfield also blossomed into
a workaholic, researching the development of organisms, teaching em-
bryology and psychology, boosting Princeton's broader ambitions in
science, and chairing a committee on Princeton athletics, as well as
starting several clubs before returning to England for a lengthy visit
in 1886 to study Mesozoic mammals.

Osborn's new fossil fascination soon led him to Edward Drinker
Cope, a wealthy Philadelphia Quaker who had studied at the University of Pennsylvania under Joseph Leidy, the first American paleontologist superstar. Cope was behind the first of the very public feuds
that marred Osborn's career.[11] Cope had worked on family farms as a
boy, kindling an interest in the natural world, then studied anatomy
at the University of Pennsylvania. After the Civil War, he ended up at
Haverford teaching zoology to support his passion, fossil-hunting.

Cope had colonial roots; his stepmother was a Biddle. Similarly,
the family of an older man who would become Cope's rival and bête
noir, Othneil Charles Marsh, had come to America in 1634. Marsh's
late mother was a Peabody, the sister of the financier George, who paid
the dowry that bought the farm where O.C., as he was called, was born.
Inspired by the widening of the Erie Canal near their home, which
brought to the surface a wealth of fossils embedded in the region's
shale, Marsh began collecting them. But his Erie idyll ended when his
mother died young and O.C.'s father lost almost everything, including
most of the money George Peabody had given their family. Neither
Cope nor Marsh got along with their fathers, but Cope had a mother
to lean on. Marsh left home, using what remained of his mother's
dowry to enroll in Phillips Academy in Andover, Massachusetts.

Peabody approved of his nephew's ambition to teach natural science, monitored his academic progress from London, and subsidized his matriculation at Yale and a trip to England and Germany

---

* Lucretia's sister was married to a nephew of Pierpont Morgan.

for postgraduate studies. Peabody then agreed to sponsor Marsh for a professorship at Yale, giving the school a $150,000 gift that not only encouraged the faculty to create and give Marsh a chair in geology and paleontology—the first in America and second in the world— but paid for a building to house the relatively new scientific discipline (it later became the first home of the Peabody Museum). As the post was unpaid, Peabody gave Marsh an allowance and paid, too, for him to acquire a two-and-a-half-ton fossil collection for the school. In years to come, subsidized by a $150,000 inheritance after his uncle's 1869 death, Marsh amassed large collections of skeletons, fossils, and archaeological and ethnological artifacts for Yale. Then, with further backing from the U.S. War Department, he planned his first trip West, following the Union Pacific railroad line, using army posts as bases while seeking fossils. A Darwinian, he hoped to find proof of the great man's theories.

Marsh and Cope had first met in Berlin in 1864, where the former was studying and the nine-years-younger Cope was on a grand tour. Inevitably, Marsh came to see the less-educated Cope as a patrician dilettante, and they became bitter rivals, as they both sought nothing less than to discover and explain the development of life on earth. In 1870, Marsh publicly humiliated Cope, revealing he had put together his latest skeleton incorrectly, mounting the skull of an extinct creature on its tail instead of its neck. Though they both started off as well-to-do entrants in the new discipline of paleontology, over time Marsh's Yale ties would give him distinct advantages, both financial and social. Thomas Huxley, visiting New Haven in 1876, was awed by Marsh's collection of horse fossils and stayed in an apartment that greatly impressed him; it had once been George Peabody's.

Cope and Marsh were obsessed with each other, and neither was above poaching—literally digging in marshes and bogs first opened by the other, and hiring away workers. Their fights, at the cutting edge of science, were epic but often petty; they even gave the same fossils different genus and species names. Each had triumphs, but Cope, who discovered the second significant dinosaur skeleton in America in 1866, published promiscuously and sometimes too quickly, which led him to make mistakes that hurt his reputation, while Marsh's rose. But then, Cope got a financial windfall; his father died in 1875, and an inheritance reinvigorated Cope's activities, while Marsh made his own mistakes, most notably in 1883 when he combined bones from various sites and ancient creatures to complete his first restored skeleton, which he declared a brontosaurus; it proved to be an animal that had never existed.[12] Their ever-escalating rivalry was as uncommon in scientific circles as it was unfortunate.[13]

Neither man was initially welcoming to Osborn. A Cope associate at Princeton had inspired Fairfield's first fossil-hunting expedition after graduation, but when he approached Cope for advice, he met a "wary and cagey" response.[14] For his part, Marsh treated Osborn and a fossil-hunting friend with overt hostility, wearing carpet slippers so that he could silently stalk them when they visited his Peabody collection.

Cope warmed up when he realized Osborn and his friend weren't Marsh agents, and he turned them into "staunch enemies of Marsh" in the growing conflict.[15] Osborn was also drawn to Cope's take on Darwin's natural selection theory, which Cope rejected as it "seemed to harbor terrible religious, moral, and social implications." Cope and Osborn leaned toward an earlier construct of evolution, named for Jean-Baptiste Lamarck, a French naturalist who gave "spirituality and morality" a place in "a kinder, gentler evolution," allowing science to "simultaneously deal with the emerging fossil record and still shelter some of Victorian society's most cherished tenets."[16]

As far as the mechanism of evolution is concerned, Lamarck believed that individual living things could adapt to their environment, transforming themselves to meet the needs of survival, like giraffes whose necks stretched to reach food in high trees, and then passing those adaptations to their offspring. Darwin theorized that existing individual characteristics just made some organisms better suited to compete and pass their advantages on to their offspring, like hawks whose sharp eyesight improved their chances for survival. Remaining gaps in the fossil record allowed the argument to continue for years, despite Marsh's discoveries of what he felt was physical proof of Darwin's theory.

Cope's star fell when he got in over his head financially after taking control of a science journal while simultaneously trying to prepare and illustrate the scores of fossils he had already gathered. By 1879, with Marsh ensconced in a cushy job at the U.S. Geological Survey, collecting fossils as a subsidized government official, Cope fell behind and never recovered, reduced to collecting an opposition research file he called "Marshiana . . . which at some future time I may be tempted to publish."[17] His peers increasingly saw him as bitter and eccentric.[18]

In 1884, Congress started to investigate government scientific bureaus like the U.S. Geological Survey, and Cope saw an opening to move against Marsh. Osborn helped gather evidence, and though Cope sometimes felt Fairfield was too diplomatic, the Princeton biology professor had great acumen, financial resources, and powerful connections just as Marsh did. Combined, they would make Osborn a formidable opponent to Marsh in years to come, as the feud festered.[19] Osborn even joined Cope's backers in reviving his journal, *American Naturalist*, in 1888. A year later, Cope got a further boost when he was named a professor at the University of Pennsylvania. Around the same time, an argument arose as to whether Marsh's fossil collection was federal property. Sensing opportunity, Cope turned to a newspaper hatchet man he hoped would finally cut Marsh down to size.

In January 1890, the *New York Sunday Herald* (the same paper that had sent Henry Stanley to Africa in search of the missing missionary David Livingston) ran an exposé on the Marsh-Cope feud. A reporter sought out Osborn to comment on the contretemps, and he said carefully that he had read the *Herald*'s story with real interest and was "glad the matter has at last come out. It will clear the atmosphere." After hailing Cope as "a scientist of high attainments and one of the most powerful and original thinkers alive," Osborn sent the reporter away: "I don't think I want to say another word."

His reticence was repaid when the reporter suggested that Osborn was being considered as a possible successor to Professor Marsh when he retired from Yale. Marsh asked for a refutation, but Osborn deftly sidestepped the demand, wiring that he hadn't "seen or authorized" the article. The issue then faded away in the face of the fledgling American science community's disinterest in airing dirty laundry and utter indifference on the part of the public.

As Osborn's upward trajectory continued, he took Cope's place as a thorn in Marsh's side, while the older man's career declined in the 1890s. In another congressional investigation that caused Marsh's government funding to be curtailed, Osborn declared the U.S. Geological Survey's Marsh-led paleontology efforts "error-filled, high-handed . . . [and] inaccurate" and noted that the government's fossils were hidden from public view in the museum of a private institution.[20] Marsh's annual appropriation was cut, damaging both his lab and field work. And in years to come, when Osborn became the head of one of the museums that would henceforth rule the fossil field, he continued to support Cope, raise money to buy his fossils, help him win election to the presidency of the American Association for the Advancement of Science, and when Cope fell ill in 1897 arrange for a top surgeon to operate on him.

When Cope died later that year, Osborn served as co-executor of his estate, the value of which he increased considerably when the American Museum of Natural History bought two more Cope specimen collections. In a final irony, in 1924 Osborn would take both Marsh's place as the vertebrate paleontologist of the U.S. Geological Survey and custody of his unfinished work. He even gained access to the Peabody collections that Marsh had kept off-limits to others. In that, he helped birth the culture of inter-museum cooperation that sometimes exists today, repairing some of the damage done by the epic Cope-Marsh feud.

27

In his mid-thirties, Osborn dedicated himself to advancing his career and reputation. By 1890, he had developed his own theory of evolution, moving away from Lamarck and toward, if not yet into, the natural selection camp. He posited an immortal, ancestral set of racial characteristics, superior to acquired ones, that guided an organism's evolution. "I am not a Darwinian," he would say. "I do not think we have solved the evolution problem. Perhaps we shall never, but survival of the fittest . . . is a law as well-demonstrated as the laws of gravity and this is the essence of Darwinian teaching."[21] Evolution was thus consistent with science and religion, both built in and predetermined.

To support his have-it-both-ways thesis, Osborn adopted a notion developed by British and German scientists of immutable, racially determined "germ plasm," their term for inheritable genetic information, "impervious to environmental influences," an idea that would strengthen the foundation of Osborn's later vocal opposition to race mixing.[22] Developing his own theory suited the ambitious young scientist, fulfilling his parents' hope he would be prestigious and socially useful. It also allowed him, however awkwardly, to fashion an artful synthesis of his religious beliefs and science.[23] Germ plasm, "the most incomprehensible phenomena which has yet been discovered in the universe," became his scientific stand-in for the hand of God, while still allowing some evolutionary change through individual struggle.[24] Faith would have to camouflage the contradictions.

That year, Seth Low, just named Columbia College president, sounded Osborn out about joining its faculty, and he did so in 1891 after he and Low planned a new biology discipline that would morph into a zoology department and enhance both Columbia's and Osborn's scientific reputations.* Simultaneously, Fairfield was offered a job at the American Museum of Natural History. His connections to that institution, which was conceived in 1869 and opened in 1877, were many. Among its founders were Theodore Roosevelt Sr. and Pierpont Morgan. In 1886, Osborn's brother, known as Church (after his father's artist friend Frederic Church), had married Alice Dodge, whose family were also museum founders; her father, an heir to the Phelps-Dodge mining fortune, was a trustee, and he knew two of her brothers from Princeton. So both Osborn brothers were well placed at the intersection of family, influence, culture, finance, and science.

While their motivations were diverse, the museum's trustees, many of whom had helped bring down the Tweed Ring, were almost exclusively WASPs, and deeply committed to philanthropy that supported the established social order and the civil leadership of their caste. But they were enthusiasts—merchants, industrialists, and bank-

---

* Osborn's teaching career ended in 1910, though he remained a research professor of zoology.

ers like the museum's first president, Morris K. Jesup—not men of science like Osborn.

Jesup, who hired Osborn, was a visionary who began an expansion effort, hiring more scientists and initiating the sort of research that would enhance the collections donated or paid for by his fellow capitalists. Believing scientific education could uplift the population, both mentally and spiritually, he considered fossils not just a popular attraction but a way to demonstrate "nature's laws and lessons."[25] Few WASPs doubted that their superiority was one of those natural laws. That all made the paleontologist Osborn an ideal hire to head a new department. He shared its trustees' "desires for social order and stability," the promotion of science, and the moral ideals science was thought to impart.[26] Even before Osborn formally accepted both jobs, he began planning as soon as Low and Jesup agreed to share the fruits of his labors, integrating Columbia's teaching with the museum's collecting and research.

Osborn joined the museum staff in fall 1890, and the next spring, just after he started at Columbia, was named a curator. He moved to Manhattan that year, buying a townhouse at the corner of Madison Avenue and 70th Street. He immediately started using his connections in the overlapping worlds of dinosaur-hunters and the wealthy, setting up a network of informants to tell him when mining or railroad excavations uncovered fossils, and continuing to dabble in the fossil-hunting field work that had first attracted him, joining museum expeditions in 1893, 1897, 1903, and annually from 1906 to 1910, becoming a scientific celebrity in the process.

Osborn had evolved from laboratory biologist at Princeton to a champion of fieldwork and direct observation of nature. This dovetailed with the agenda of supporters like Theodore Roosevelt Jr., who advocated modern men confronting and preserving nature, reflecting a larger ambition to preserve a status quo that upheld the social sovereignty of wealthy white men.[27] Faced with an ever more urban, industrial world and the rabble it produced, the wealthy WASP trustees perceived a threat to their dominance of "the established order."[28]

That was the context of Osborn's friendship with Madison Grant, the virulent white supremacist whose dominant characteristic was pride in his Nordic ancestry, which he alternately called Anglo-Saxon and Aryan. They first bonded after Osborn joined the museum, which celebrated Grant's boyhood hobby, natural history; though untrained and really more of a hunter/explorer, Grant considered himself a scientist. Born into the same milieu, they had also crossed paths at Columbia, where Grant got a law degree in 1890, and were fellow members of several private clubs, including the Boone and Crockett Club, a group dedicated to the preservation of game animals founded by Theodore Roosevelt Jr., in 1887, and named for two of his heroes, legendary American backwoodsmen. It was at that club, in 1894, that Grant, Osborn, and others dreamed up the New York Zoological Society as a first step toward bringing a zoological park to New York, a promise kept when today's Bronx Zoo opened in 1899.* Osborn would serve the society as an executive for years. Grant, in turn, sat on numerous museum committees, including the powerful nominating committee that chose new trustees, and in 1926 followed Osborn as the zoo's president.

Zoos, like museums, were about preserving more than merely fauna. The Boone and Crockett Club, and the society and zoo it spawned, were also dikes holding back the erosion of traditional values and institutions and the decline of the WASP social class that depended on and profited from them or, as Grant put it, kept hold of "some remnant of the heritage which was our fathers'."[29] Like their industrialist friends fighting unionization, Osborn and Grant wore paternalism as a velvet glove over their fierce desire to suppress the ambitions of all they thought inferior and, Grant said, "save as much as possible of the old America."[30] They also used their zoo to promote their notions of racial disparities; in 1906, the zoo stuck a twenty-three-year-old Mbuti (pygmy) man from the Congo named Ota Benga in an empty cage in its Primate House, inadvertently infuriating a number of Christian clergymen with both "the implication that Negroes were the missing link between apes and humans" and what they perceived as "a direct endorsement of evolution."[31] Thanks to the intercession of a group of African American ministers and the superintendent of an orphan's asylum, Benga was released after being caged for three weeks.

---

* Three years later, the society took over the New York Aquarium as well. Osborn and Grant were also co-founders of the Save the Redwoods League after a visit to California's Humboldt County in 1917.

⌇

Fairfield Osborn described his life's work as "the systematic research and description and comparison of the fossil mammals of North America."[32] His highest joy was the discovery of "an entirely new animal" and relationships between animals "new or previously undiscovered."[33] But while continuing as a professor at Columbia, his focus for forty-four years was his job at the American Museum of Natural History; his goal was to make the museum preeminent, supporting his personal desire to dominate paleontology and promote his broader social agenda. That coincided with the interests of the museum's trustees and benefactors like William Collins Whitney, who, like Osborn, had a personal interest in horses, for example, but in terms of breeding, riding, and racing them rather than using their fossils to prove theories of evolution.*

In pursuit of his goal, Osborn guided the museum's accumulation of one of the world's finest vertebrate fossil collections and championed innovative techniques in museum display that were entertaining, educational, and wildly popular: dramatic presentations of reconstructed and mounted fossils, habitat groups, and, later, realistic dioramas populated with taxidermy animals. The American Museum had 10,000 specimens from 483 species bought from Cope in 1895 that raised both its and Osborn's public profile. After it opened a Hall of Fossil Reptiles in 1905, confirming the wild popularity of dinosaurs, Osborn returned to fossil hunting at forty-nine, heading to the Nebraska Badlands and the Egyptian desert, trips that earned an invitation to visit President Roosevelt at the White House. Then, during a 1907 expedition to Libya, discoveries crucial to understanding the evolution of elephants were made, and proved Osborn's notion that their homeland was Africa.

Powerful friends aided Osborn's ascent. Jesup appointed him to administrative positions as he expanded the building and staff, made him a museum trustee and officer, raised his department's bud-

---

* Another example of the shared interests of benefactors and scientists was the 1928–1929 expedition to today's Ethiopia, paid for and run by Henry Sanford's granddaughter Gertrude Sanford and her future husband, Stanley Legendre, which brought the American Museum samples of 267 mammals, 63 birds, and 12 reptiles.

gets, and groomed him to become its fourth president, even before his uncle J. P. Morgan promised him the job. Long a museum backer, Morgan had subsidized Osborn's activities, contributed to the purchase of Cope's fossils, arranged free shipping for them, and in 1906 established a research fund for Osborn's personal use after the Smithsonian Institution tried to lure him away to Washington, D.C. Not only did Osborn succeed Jesup—in a ceremony held in Morgan's library—on his predecessor's death in 1908, but he got the use of millions Jesup left to the museum in his will. And in years to come, Morgan would continue to subsidize the research behind Osborn's prolific writing. By his own count, his bibliography had more than nine hundred entries, though most were actually produced by cadres of subordinates, which is likely how he fit it all in between his museum and educational duties. Through the first three decades of the twentieth century, he continued to enlarge the museum, too, more than doubling its space, adding buildings, wings, and the Theodore Roosevelt Memorial, which encompassed the museum's entrance hall, grand rotunda, and several exhibition spaces, while tripling its staff, increasing its endowment by a factor of seven, and growing membership by 400 percent.

As difficult as he was successful, Osborn was "insufferably haughty even to those who were his superiors . . . condescending at best and impatiently dismissive at worst, to those he deemed beneath him," with whom he communicated exclusively by hand-delivered letter or even telegram.[34] Highly ambitious, he used his status and connections without compunction.[35] His field work was well publicized but generally only supervisory; at digs, he dressed in formal clothes or colonial-style safari jackets and pith helmets, and he often brought family members with him. He was typically supercilious toward the underlings who did the nitty-gritty finding, collecting, cleaning, and preparing of specimens for the museum, though he gladly took credit for their work, inevitably causing friction. Privately, the museum staff responded to his vanity with bitter, contemptuous disdain.[36] "Never blot the signature of a great man," he once snapped at an employee after autographing a book for him.[37] He was also mocked behind his back as his professional byline evolved from H. F. Osborn to Henry F. Osborn to the full Henry Fairfield Osborn.

Osborn thought of himself as the heir to Darwin and Huxley, if not quite their equal. But though his pretensions caused some snickering behind the scenes at the museum, his connections and access to wealth made him untouchable, and those who got along with him, or whom he considered his social and intellectual peers, prospered.[38] One was Roy Chapman Andrews, who joined the museum's taxidermy department as an assistant out of college, become an Osborn acolyte, and was soon taking expeditions to Alaska, the East Indies, and Asia to study whales, dolphins, and porpoises. By 1915, the same year Osborn put the museum's iconic *Tyrannosaurus rex* fossil on display, Andrews was the museum's chief of exploration in Asia (and an inspiration for countless real and fictional explorers, such as Egypt's Zahi Hawass and the movie character Indiana Jones). His glamor and stature helped him win approval for the first of a series of multidisciplinary expeditions to Mongolia that became an obsession for Osborn. At the turn of the century the museum head had decided, pretty much out of the blue, that Central Asia was the birthplace of humankind, and he hoped Andrews would prove that theory.[39] Morgan donated $100,000 to the effort and the Whitney, Rockefeller, Colgate, and Frick families also contributed.

Within a few years, the museum's dinosaur display hall was expanded to house Andrews's Asia finds, among them the first dinosaur eggs ever unearthed; a skull from the largest land mammal, resembling a giant rhinoceros without a horn; other previously unknown mammal and reptile fossils, and what was called compelling proof that Central Asia was home to prehistoric humans.[40] But Fairfield Osborn's desire for a breakthrough discovery in Asia was thwarted when, in 1924, remains of a human who walked on two legs—called the Taung child, of the species *Australopithecus africanus*—were found in Africa, arguing against Osborn's out-of-Asia theory. That find, and the now generally accepted out-of-Africa theory of humankind's origin, were only slowly acknowledged, though, so the source of humanity remained in question, and Osborn's backers persisted in believing that his work "served as a model of individual achievement and racial fulfillment."[41]

Before it was named anthropogeny in the nineteenth century, the study of the origins of humankind began with myth and later, pseudoscientific guesswork. In 1775, Johann Friedrich Blumenbach, a German naturalist, made race part of that conversation. Another German, poet Dietrich Eckart, coined the term "Aryan" for an Indian/Germanic race, and French scholar Abraham-Hyacinthe Anquetil-Duperron proposed that a mythical, superior Aryan race was the beginning of humanity, arguing against biblical (i.e., Jewish) origins. Elaborate evolution fantasies, like a notion of apelike protohumans spreading from a lost continent in the Indian Ocean, were constructed to support a racial hierarchy with Aryans at the top and Jews, incapable of understanding German greatness, toward the bottom. A mythology grew up among romantics and idealists (as well as supporters of slavery) to counter the mechanistic spirit of the Enlightenment and support a claim of European and Caucasian superiority. That was particularly important in a fragmented Germany seeking a unifying doctrine apart from religion. The British had a more unified culture, so were less inclined to such speculation. But they were also fixated on class, so discussions of civil versus savage and inferior versus superior races appealed there as well.

Darwin saw the origins of humans in African primates, but as Africans and Asians were said to more closely resemble dark apes than Nordics did, some feared making any connection. "Keeping [early primates] in their place grew problematic. . . . The fascination with brutes, both real and imagined, grew steadily" after the publication of *On the Origin of Species*. Evolution became a target of ridicule, satire, and condemnation, and racial conclusions were inevitably drawn. Any connection to wild animals was a threat to the highly cultivated, civilized self-image of white Europeans.[42] So Fairfield Osborn couldn't bring himself to consider the notion that humans had descended from apes.[43]

Geology had introduced the scientific method into the study of human origins. The first fossil accepted as an early human was discovered in 1856 by lime quarry workers at the Feldhofer Cave in the Neander Valley, near Dusseldorf, Germany. Named Neanderthal (or *Homo neanderthalensis*), it sparked a debate that coincided with the 1859 release of Darwin's *On the Origin of Species* over whether it was a modern human or a member of a distinct species. More obviously human skeletons found in a French cave in 1868 were called Cro-Magnon, and in 1891, Java (or Trinil) Man was discovered in Indonesia and proclaimed as evidence that humans had sprung from Asia, but the Dutch army surgeon, anatomist, and geologist who found the fossil wouldn't let other scientists examine it for decades. Though it was indeed an example of the human precursor *Homo erectus,* some dismissed it as a fraud. Another fossil found in Germany in 1907 was named Heidelberg Man, and scientists have argued ever since whether it is an example of *Homo erectus* or something else.

After the discovery of painted caves in southern France in 1908, followed by that of a nearly complete Neanderthal skeleton, and the unveiling of fossil fragments of what was touted as a new prehistoric species, dubbed Piltdown Man, in England in 1912, Osborn started collecting casts of human fossils and touring Paleolithic (Old Stone Age) sites, refocusing his and his institution's interest on human evolution. Piltdown Man was not universally accepted, and more than forty years later it would finally be revealed as a hoax—an amalgam of human, orangutan, and chimp bones—but in the years after its discovery it became a cornerstone of Osborn's developing theory of human evolution.

In his hugely popular 1915 book *Men of the Old Stone Age,* a summary of scientific knowledge of Paleolithic humanity, Osborn proposed that animal migration patterns proved Asia was the source of human life. Piltdown Man, he argued, disproved the notion of man's African ancestry; it supported his contention that Darwin had erred and evolutionary change was predetermined, even if it was influenced by individual struggle. Over the next decade, he refined his notion that "man belongs to a family of his own . . . entirely independent of all other families"—those of apes and monkeys—and that on the tree of life, different branches sprouted over "an incalculable period of time," separating tree-dwelling primates from men, and then some men from others, with Piltdown Man marking the ancient and epochal moment of separation of highly intelligent Caucasians like Osborn's fellow WASPs from the less well-developed and less intelligent races he called Chinese (Mongolian), Mediterranean, Hottentot (Negroid or Black), and Australian.[44]

Another argument pitted plurality (multiple origins for multiple races) against unity (a single human origin). Plurality, at least in America, greatly appealed to those who denigrated Indians and Blacks. Craniology—the study of the size and shape of skulls—developed to "prove" that slavery had been a natural condition. The range of theories about Native American origins was vast, including the theologian Roger Williams's seventeenth-century contention they had descended from the Jews.

Early humans had developed, Osborn decided, as separate races along parallel lines but with no connections among them, a "series of replacements" rather than products of descent and commingling. Physical differences were outward manifestations of polygenesis, the notion that the human races had different origins and were separate species. As time went by, his obsession with race grew. Family background and racial heritage became all-important for science as well as social standing.[45]

Despite skepticism about its authenticity that began within a few years of its public debut, Piltdown Man was featured prominently in the American Museum's Hall of the Age of Man, opened in 1921, which depicted what were thought to be the earliest humans, Neanderthals, as tough, dark brutes. In an article at the time, Osborn hinted at the racist underpinnings and twisted logic of his theories when he wrote that the later, lighter-skinned Cro-Magnons, also on display, were "people like ourselves . . . and the characters of the head and cranium reflect their moral and spiritual potentialities, while the body skeleton points to a physically perfect race." Nearby finds from Campigny, France, dating to the later Neolithic period—the era of early farming societies—represented a "northern fair-haired race" that "if of Nordic affinity . . . was courageous, warlike, hardy, and probably of lower intelligence than the Cro-Magnons," though it remained unclear to "what primary branch of European stock" Campignian Man belonged.[46]

For Osborn, evolution was "a continuous, directed process," and nature "the visible expression of the divine order of things" that "begins and ends the purposes of God."[47] God caused and guided evolution, and therefore, evolution supported rather than undermined religion. He tied himself into theoretical and linguistic knots to maintain his belief in God as the prime mover behind evolution.

In 1922, a Nebraska rancher sent Osborn a worn tooth found there five years earlier that seemed to be from an advanced primate, an ape-man of sorts, and Osborn declared that early humans, a species distinct from Neanderthals, had come to America over a land bridge from Asia. But a Smithsonian scientist threw cold water on the claim, calling the newly discovered "Nebraska Man" low and savage and likely merely a Native American Indian; most human remains found in the nineteenth century were indeed misidentified modern skeletons.[48] Osborn insisted it was neither ape nor human. Finally it was identified as the tooth of an extinct piglike creature. Nonetheless, the search for a so-called missing link between animals and humans intensified, which made Osborn all the more determined to prove Asia was the unique source of humanity, white humans in particular. So the Osborns joined Roy Chapman Andrews on his latest trip to China, seeking proof of the humans who had left apes behind. Despite coming up empty, those Gobi Desert expeditions made Osborn more broadly famous, and he began to use his celebrity as a soapbox for social commentary. Unfortunately for him, the outbreak of civil war in China in 1927 threw the country into anarchy, and the Central Asiatic Expedition was a casualty.

The end of the expedition was a crushing blow for Osborn, yet he grew ever more creative in advancing his theories. That same year, to rid human evolution of any association with savage apes, he proposed the notion of Dawn Man, a hypothetical thirty-million-year-old ancestor whose existence Osborn inferred from recent discoveries in England of flint and stone implements "shaped by human agency."[49] Scientists were unimpressed, but Osborn continued to elaborate his theory that modern humans had descended from human ancestors unconnected to apes, ancestors who lived not in the calm arboreal Eden of the tree-dwelling simians but in a hard, brutish realm like the high plateaus of Central Asia, where the basic needs of survival forced their evolution, fueled by their advanced germ plasm. One biographer concluded, "He was here to search for the first humans, but in a way, Osborn was looking for himself."[50]

Osborn was motivated as much by fear for the future of his caste as by pride in its success in distancing itself from brutish antecedents. He was convinced that as ancient humans moved toward civilization, they became divorced from nature and its struggles, threatening continued progress. This dovetailed with Osborn's and his WASP allies' belief that the social and demographic changes triggered by immigration were "morally repugnant as well as biologically and socially debilitating."[51] As Grant put it, after the Civil War "careless, wealthy, and hospitable America" had welcomed "hordes of immigrants of inferior racial value," including "the weak, the broken, and the mentally crippled of all races drawn from the lowest stratum of the Mediterranean basin and the Balkans, together with hordes of the wretched, submerged populations of the Polish Ghettos."[52] The fear was that despite the alleged superiority of the white Christian race, it was in spiritual, intellectual, social, and moral peril and would be swept aside by uncontrolled breeding in a world that favored more people over better people. His work inexorably led to the neo-Nazi pseudoscience of eugenics—and the corrosion of Osborn's shiny reputation.

Eugenics organizations were some of the most nefarious byproducts of the Progressive Era, springing from agricultural research into genetics as well as the Country Life movement, which sought to bolster and improve rural communities and ran parallel to the preservationist ideology championed by Theodore Roosevelt. Springing from the American Breeders Association and the American Genetics Association early in the twentieth century, eugenics, the study of evolution and genetics, took a dark turn with the formation of the Eugenics Research Association in 1913, which openly promoted what was called racial anthropology. Their emergence was partly a reaction to the growing influence of Franz Boas, a German Jewish anthropology professor at Columbia who championed nurture over nature, directly challenging the views of his faculty colleague Fairfield Osborn.

In the 1910s, Osborn promoted the most repugnant goal of the pseudoscience: the removal of the unfit from the breeding population. He joined the Immigration Restriction League, started in 1894 (the year immigration from southeastern Europe first surpassed that from northwestern regions) by the Harvard-educated blue bloods

Charles Warren, Robert DeCourcy Ward, and Prescott Farnsworth Hall. They believed social ills were caused by immigrants with inferior, degenerate blood and supported limiting their entry with intelligence and literacy testing. Then in 1918, with eugenicist Madison Grant, the league's vice president, and another prominent eugenics proponent, Osborn co-founded the Galton Society, named for Charles Darwin's cousin and acolyte Francis Galton, who proposed that both genius and mental deficiency tend to be inherited, and that marriage and child-rearing could be manipulated to improve mankind.[53] Galton coined the term "eugenics" from the Greek *eugenes*, or "good in stock."[54]

Grant decreed the society would be "aristocratic in structure and governed by a self-elected and self-perpetuating oligarchy," its membership "confined to native Americans" (meaning, presumably, his fellow WASPs) "who are anthropologically, socially, and politically sound."[55] The Galton Society promoted the notion of birth selection, or micromanaged breeding by the best and brightest, because Osborn feared that the "purest of New England stock is not holding its own," and society's decline was inevitable without racial purity.*[56] In fact, as the anthropologist Ashley Montagu wrote in 1946, "Two mediocrities may produce a genius," and "Selective breeding is inbreeding and that is a notoriously dangerous process."[57] Nonetheless, the museum gave its president a powerful bully pulpit to promote his view that racial purity was a natural state, and that the preservation of pure Nordic bloodlines—English, Scottish, and Scandinavian ones—was the only way to halt an otherwise inevitable descent into extinction. The alternative was tantamount to suicide for his beloved WASPs.[58]

Some of the lesser-known scientists at the museum, and some museum supporters like the German Jewish American banker Felix Warburg, a museum trustee, pushed back against Osborn's promotion of these prejudices. They took cold comfort from the fact that the messages on race, class, and nature flew right over the heads of most visitors, and for some, at least, promoted the notion of evolution and the importance of science.†

---

* Osborn opposed birth control, asserting that its adoption would accelerate the decline of the superior Nordic race.
† To his credit, Osborn also encouraged scientists who disagreed with him, viewing their work as an affirmation of his broader policies of promoting research and public education.

Fairfield Osborn might have chosen a different path. In 1906, he boasted that he had invited "people of all classes" from his neighborhood to his daughter Josephine's first-communion party. His brother, Church, whom he had nudged into politics, delved much further into inclusivity and became a champion of civic reform. Though J. P. Morgan wrote to a friend when Church was born that he doubted the child would grow up to be as fine a citizen as his older brother, the siblings were both quite accomplished, if differently so. Over the years, Church was hailed for his patience, tolerance, simplicity, "deep sense of humanity," "attractive, aristocratic personality of no little charm," and advocacy for "the advancement of man's humanity to man."[59] He was his brother's polar opposite.

A Harvard-trained lawyer, Church was admitted to the bar in 1889 and began a career in corporate and railroad law. The next year, he took on his most prominent public role as a trustee of the Children's Aid Society, dedicated to the protection and welfare of precisely the sort of underprivileged youngsters his brother feared; in 1901, Church became its fourth president, a role he occupied for forty-eight years before becoming the society's chairman. One of his proudest achievements was opening a center in the Black neighborhood of Harlem in 1929.

Aside from serving on the boards of Princeton, the Hudson Valley Conservation Society, and various railroad and family corporations, and as a warden of the Episcopal church in Garrison, early in his career Church Osborn was a legal advisor to both Franklin Delano Roosevelt when he first ran for the state senate in 1910 and the then-governor of New York, a Republican.[60] Though he failed in several early runs for office himself, he chaired New York's Democratic State Committee for several years before World War I, and ran for office again, this time for governor, in 1918, with Roosevelt's endorsement. He lost that race to Al Smith, who would become an ally and go on to become the first Catholic candidate for president of the United States. The younger Osborn also fought corrupt politicians, collected art, and served on the board of the Metropolitan Museum of Art for forty-five years beginning in 1904 and as its president throughout World War II.

If joint appearances in the press are any indication, Church had little public interaction with Fairfield, though the latter did appear with his brother at the dedication of a miniature natural history museum at a Children's Aid Society summer camp in 1935. Two years later, shortly after his brother's death, the liberal and unostentatious Church would display their vast differences when he pointed at the Statue of Liberty while being interviewed for an article on his seventy-fifth birthday. The statue "lights the way for all foreigners who enter here," he told the reporter, describing the immigrants his brother had tried to bar as "sincere, honest people."[61]

Though he sometimes spoke out against hate and prejudice, and had long sought to educate the masses and end ignorance and want, immigration had hardened Fairfield Osborn's racialist views. Anglo-Saxon whites had seen and decried New York's changing population since before the Civil War. By 1910, that trend had greatly intensified, and the lower and middle classes felt threatened as more and different types competed for jobs, space, and resources. Blacks, Catholics, and later Jews became the focus of hatred as the city's population shifted until, in 1910, about 40 percent were foreign-born. New ideas like socialism added to the perceived threat. World War I amplified those fears. Osborn worried that as Nordics killed each other in Europe, they would be outnumbered and overrun, and courage, honor, and duty would die off with them.

Initially, Osborn felt immigration policy had to be reasonable and selective. While some, like Church, turned to philanthropy to help the poor, or hoped that assimilation would close the gap with earlier Americans, Osborn and his allies, claiming science backed them up, became willing to consider bureaucratic solutions like sterilization and "cleansing" of those who, simply by virtue of being different, were thought to carry inferior traits; immigrants were often referred to as feeble-minded, criminal, and addicted. Naturally clannish, these American aristocrats believed that great men bred great men and that the tendency of lesser men to breed more constituted an existential threat to them. Keeping them from breeding—or, worse, mixing—would safeguard the WASP majority.

In the early twentieth century, immigration bills banned anarchists, epileptics, lunatics, polygamists, people with "poor physique," carriers of everything from tuberculosis to syphilis and leprosy, the impoverished, and the incompetent.[62] The third Galton Society cofounder, Charles Davenport, ran the Eugenics Record Office on Long Island, where Mary Harriman, E.H.'s daughter and a founder of the Junior League, had studied in summer 1906 after she discovered eugenics in a biology class at Barnard taught by Fairfield.[63] Davenport needed money to support his extensive effort to gather data proving eugenics theory, so when E.H. died, Davenport turned to his widow, also named Mary. Another fan of thoroughbred racehorses, her guiding philanthropic impulse was to halt what she perceived as the decline of white Protestant America.[64] Over the next seven years, she provided 95 percent of the funding for Davenport and his wildly flawed research into what he deemed "defectives," the "insane, feeble-minded, epileptic, criminal, incorrigible and blind."[65] Another backer was John Harvey Kellogg, the breakfast-cereal maker. Davenport's ideas were sadly ascendant.

The most extreme expression of the pro-eugenics, anti-immigration position was *The Right to Be Well Born* by William Earl Dodge Stokes, a distant relative of Church Osborn's wife. A litigious real-estate developer, horse breeder, and prolific seducer of young women, Stokes, the wealthy heir to a mercantile and mining fortune, railed against "rotten, foreign diseased blood" and praised Jews for marrying their own kind to ensure that their devious, grasping financial acumen would not be diluted by cross-breeding.[66]

⌐

A year after Francis Galton died, at the First International Eugenics Conference, held in London in 1912, sterilization and the elimination of "inferior blood" and "defective inheritance" topped the agenda.[67] Involuntary sterilization laws had already been enacted in seven American states. Eugenics even entered the curriculum of prestigious universities.

When World War I began, a second eugenics conference headed by Fairfield Osborn was postponed, but interest kept growing. At early meetings of the Galton Society in 1918 at Osborn's home, and then the American Museum of Natural History, he said he was convinced that "racial characteristics" determined an individual's "spiritual, physical, moral and intellectual structure."[68] In the meantime, unionism, radicalism, bombings, housing and job shortages, and fear of foreign influence whipped up a xenophobic anti-immigration frenzy—and the popularity of eugenics even spread into fiction, name-checked in F. Scott Fitzgerald's classic *The Great Gatsby*.* Calvin Coolidge, then governor of Massachusetts, promoted the notion of racial separatism in *Good Housekeeping* in 1920.[69] "Biological laws tell us that certain divergent people will not mix or blend," the future president wrote. "The dead weight of alien accretion stifles national progress."[70] That March, the National Research Council, created by President Woodrow Wilson to coordinate scientific research, authorized a second eugenics conference to be run by Osborn and Grant at the American Museum of Natural History.

This eugenics moment was rooted in the Half Moon Club, another collaboration between Grant and Osborn. Formed in 1906 and named for Henry Hudson's ship, it gave semiannual white-tie dinners for a small band of adventurous New York aristocrats with interests in exploration and ideas. A lecture in 1908 on the history of racial migration in Europe and its implications for American society as it embraced the role of international melting pot caught Grant's imagination, and he was inspired to write his book on the subject. He refocused eugenic attention on racial groups instead of "defective" individuals by revising Western history as the story of northern European (Nordic or Aryan) superiority over middle (or Alpine) and southern (or Mediterranean) Europeans.

Less than a decade earlier, Georges Vacher de Lapouge, a French anthropologist, had hailed the northerners he credited with European and American enterprise and love of liberty.[71] Osborn felt that "what we call the lowest races" also had positive traits worth encouraging, but the imprimatur of his sponsorship made Grant's "scientific racism" respectable when *The Passing of the Great Race* was

---

* Fitzgerald and Madison Grant shared a publisher, Scribner's, and an editor there, Maxwell Perkins.

published a year after Scribner's had released Osborn's latest book.* Grant fed the worst in Osborn's character at the very moment his focus turned from dinosaur bones to those of humans. Both men worried that the WASP might go the way of the American bison. They were a matched set, having spoken almost daily for decades, dined together regularly, and met every Saturday at their zoo. Grant helped Osborn find what he described, in a 1910 letter to a museum trustee, as "an agreeable Hebrew," Felix Warburg, to sit on his museum's board.[72] Osborn fought to get Grant a position there, too, and together they stage-managed the second immigration conference in fall 1921, right down to insisting on white tie for Fairfield's welcome address at the opening reception. Alexander Graham Bell, John Harvey Kellogg, Herbert Hoover, and Mary Harriman financed the congress, and Mrs. Harry Payne Whitney served on the reception committee. The museum's Forestry Hall was renamed Eugenics Hall for the occasion; among the exhibits, one showed fetal skulls to prove that Negro brains were smaller than those of white people, and another retailed the notion that immigrants bred like rabbits.[73]

In his welcome speech, Osborn dismissed as "political sophistry" the notion that "all men are born with equal character and ability to govern themselves" and "the educational sophistry that education and environment will offset the handicap of heredity."[74] He described a "serious struggle to maintain our historic republican institutions through barring the entrance of those who are unfit," and claimed there was "incontestable evidence that other countries, aided by foreign steamship agencies, are endeavoring to do the selection, to send us the people they believe they can spare, and retain the people they believe they need."[75]

Osborn saw the conferences as another way to protect the white race, and henceforth penned regular, outspoken articles and letters that claimed European science and culture were the realm of superior Nordics, including Leonardo, Dante, Cervantes, Giotto, Galileo, Petrarch, and Columbus—never mind their national origins—the last of whom carried their bloodlines to the Western Hemisphere. While other races could and did produce great men, it was up to WASPs to

---

* Theodore Roosevelt endorsed *The Passing* as "a capital book" by a "gentleman."

celebrate their own exemplars.[76] When his Columbia colleague Franz
Boas attacked his ideas as fallacious, Osborn flinched, assuring the
columnist Walter Lippmann he wanted to "keep good-humored"
when it came to the subject of race. He often claimed no special
knowledge and cut his prescriptions finer than Grant and Davenport,
whose views he considered narrow, but he fully endorsed their
opposition to miscegenation and was unafraid of wild conspiracy
theories. "The cavemen knew," he said, and so should modern men,
that Neanderthals and Cro-Magnons shouldn't mix.[77] Osborn was as
emphatic on this point as he was wrong (later research would indicate that in fact, the two species did mix). In 1927, a newspaper reporter summed up his views: "Purity of race must be preserved at all
costs so that promiscuous mingling of higher and lower strains"
wouldn't breed "an inferior type of man."[78]

Others were dubious about the perils of miscegenation, and
Grant, furious that scientists didn't embrace his book, sometimes
asked Osborn to intervene. He did, now and then, even taking up
Grant's claim that Giotto, Pulaski, Lafayette, Bonaparte, Racine, and
Richelieu were Nordics.[79] But his defenses of his friend could sometimes seem halfhearted, as privately he considered Grant's willy-nilly
blend of anthropology, paleontology, conservationism, and racism less
than scholarly. At least once Osborn even wrote to Grant that his book
needed "rewriting from beginning to end."[80] Yet the popularity of
eugenics doctrine—local eugenics societies popped up across America; tens of thousands of forced sterilizations of mental patients,
many of them poor and African American, were performed; Theodore
Roosevelt, Alexander Graham Bell, and John D. Rockefeller Jr. were
supporters; and Margaret Sanger, leader of a movement encouraging birth control, used eugenics and the need to guard against defective offspring to argue for it—clearly enabled Osborn's wallowing
in his own anti-Semitism and paranoia about white Christian race
suicide.

Grant, Osborn, Davenport, and three other leading eugenicists
convened a self-appointed Eugenics Committee of the United States
at the museum in 1922. They quickly began raising funds and recruiting a council of ninety-nine prominent advisors, most of them progressive Republican WASPs, seeking to make their movement both

powerful and permanent.[81] In 1926, an offshoot, the American Eugenics Society, would be officially incorporated. In the meantime, they succeeded in extending emergency immigration quotas that favored Nordics; then the Immigration Restriction Act of 1924 severely curtailed the human flow to America, except, of course, from northern Europe. That effort won Mary Harriman a medal and Fairfield Osborn's endorsement for supporting "the selection of the best, the exclusion of the worst."[82]

"In cold-blooded, scientific language, our best stock is threatened with extinction," Osborn warned in a 1923 speech to a conference of corporate executives, advocating a policy banning from America unassimilable Asians and Blacks, while allowing "desirable types" from "healthy, sound families" in Italy and the Balkans.[83] With the immigration pipeline plugged, the public lost interest in the eugenics advocates' cause. But that didn't stop the zealots. Another Princeton eugenicist, Carl Campbell Brigham, published *A Study of American Intelligence* in 1923, arguing that Nordic Caucasians were smarter than southern and eastern Europeans and Africans, and subsequently invented the Scholastic Aptitude Test. Though designed to ensure the continued dominance of white Christians, the SAT would, ironically, become a crowbar that would pry open the doors of elite institutions of higher learning like Harvard, Yale, and Princeton, helping to admit precisely those it was designed to exclude, becoming a foundational element of the meritocracy that replaced the native-born oligarchy after World War II.

Simultaneously, a new religious movement, Protestant fundamentalism, was on the rise and chose the teaching of evolution in schools as its wedge issue. Five states soon banned it. When the Nebraska Democratic politician and thrice-defeated presidential candidate William Jennings Bryan, known as "the Great Commoner" for his professed faith in the common man, wrote a fundamentalist anti-evolution opinion essay, Osborn replied, defending science as "divinely inspired," claiming that acceptance of evolution was a tentpole of Christianity dating back to St. Augustine, and coincidentally demonstrating that Christians were not monolithic.[84] Protestant fundamentalists piled on, and Bryan escalated his attacks in his book *In His Image,* calling Osborn a "tree man," effectively a monkey.[85] That

argument likely inspired Osborn's theory of a Dawn Man unconnected to apes, and surely forced an uncomfortable balancing act
for a true believer in both science and religion.

The debate grew even more heated after Tennessee passed an
anti-evolution bill in 1923 and the American Civil Liberties Union
recruited a science teacher named John Scopes to violate it and give
them a test case. In 1925, Osborn met Scopes's defense lawyer, Clarence Darrow, a radical agnostic opposed to eugenics; despite that,
Osborn offered advice and financial support to Scopes as a fellow
man of science. But he didn't attend or testify at what newspapers
termed the Monkey Trial, despite what must have been a great temp-
tation to take on a prosecution team headed by Bryan. Instead, Osborn disappeared, claiming to be too busy to appear as a scientific
witness. But he did publish a slim book, *The Earth Speaks to Bryan,*
preaching his gospel that the study of divinely inspired nature wasn't
inimical to faith.

Behind that claim was an anti-Darwinian theory called creative
evolution, first proposed early in the century by Henri Bergson, a
French philosopher who won the Nobel Prize in Literature in 1927,
in part thanks to his notion that an *elán vital,* or vital impulse comparable to gravity or electromagnetism, guided creation. Osborn would
use the term at the dedication of Yale's Peabody Museum of Natural
History in 1925, placing it at "the critical point in modern biology
where we pass from the rational . . . to the super-rational."[86]

Religious leaders who pushed back included Boston's Cardinal
William O'Connell, who correctly diagnosed Piltdown Man as a fake,
and John Roach Straton, pastor of Calvary Baptist Church in New
York, who accused Osborn of poisoning the minds of schoolchildren
with bestial theories, and demanded the museum give the Bible equal
standing with its fossils, a false equivalence. Osborn dismissed the pastor as a bigot and called for public schools to teach "a simplified religion" unified with "reverent science."[87] He also seemed to endorse
the fundamentalist anti-evolution, anti-ape position.[88] The Monkey
Trial put arguments about humankind's descent from apes into the
headlines, where they remained well into the Depression, and Osborn, with his love of struggle, his desperate desire to save his theories and his reputation, and as always his craving for attention and

adulation, was at the center of all of them, never once wavering from the notion that "the ape-human theory [was] totally false and misleading."[89]

By 1927, he was incredibly specific, dating the origin of modern humans to "16,000,000 years ago" in his latest book, *Man Rises from Parnassus*, dedicated to his brother Church.[90] It's possible he was right; by the 1960s, a primate called *Ramapithecus*, which resembled a human, was identified as fourteen to sixteen million years old, but other recent theories date the human-chimp missing link to six to eight million years ago, and there is still no consensus on what is now referred to as the last common ancestor between humans and their sister species.[91]

28

New York in the Roaring Twenties was a far cry from the city Osborn knew as a young man—and a source of outrage. The rise of Harlem, Prohibition, gangsterism, and the Nineteenth Amendment (giving women the vote) were to him evidence of society's decline into decadence and individualism, leading to "racial deterioration" due to "care for the individual, neglect for the race," he wrote in 1927.[92] He had sold his Madison Avenue townhouse where his four children grew up and in 1920, with Loulou, moved to a twelve-room duplex on Fifth Avenue, where Levi Morton also lived. The Osborn townhouse was torn down for an apartment building, another sign of the times.

In 1922, his prejudices were put to a personal test when his youngest child, Josephine, then thirty-two, married Jay Coogan, the Irish Catholic stockbroker son of James Jay Coogan, a Tammany-connected former Manhattan borough president close to Franklin Roosevelt. He was the namesake of Coogan's Bluff, a promontory in upper Manhattan inherited by his wife, a descendent of the Gardiners, founders of the first English settlement in New York in 1639. Coogan's Bluff towered over more family property, including the Polo Grounds, the stadium where baseball's New York Giants played for almost seventy years before the team's move to San Francisco.

A small crowd attended the wedding at Osborn's home. Though he gave his daughter away, Osborn was upset and effectively disowned her.[93] The Coogans were not elite. And Josephine was never a happy person, even in her glamorous life before marriage, when she traveled the world with her father. She grew even more depressed afterward.

The 1926 announcement that remains of an early *Homo erectus* had been found near Beijing, and the subsequent discovery of a skull there in 1929, no doubt cheered the Asia-obsessed Osborn, but good news was then the exception: the Depression had hurt him and his museum, though he remained wealthy. Then Loulou's health deteriorated, and she died in summer 1930, just after their forty-ninth anniversary. Osborn never really recovered. Only work distracted him. On indefinite leave to finish another book on elephants, he began contemplating retirement, and in spring 1931, he announced he would leave his job on the first day of 1933.

Early in 1932, Osborn took what he hoped would be a restorative one-hundred-day around-the-world cruise, visiting museum exploration parties in the field—many of which were about to be shut down due to the ongoing Great Depression. On his return he said visible signs of the Depression—unemployed workers, idled ships and trains, empty warehouses and wharfs—proved the necessity of eugenic programs.[94] Back at Castle Rock in Garrison, he began having health problems, but he continued to advocate for selective breeding.

At the time, Madison Grant was finishing his second book for Max Perkins at Scribner's, *The Conquest of a Continent*, an attack on the inferior, unfit, and undesirable that argued for sterilization. Osborn disliked an early draft but kept that to himself, telling his friend it was great and writing another introduction. The text he provided wasn't great and neither Perkins nor Grant wanted to include it, but they acceded, and an oblivious Osborn remained a Grant supporter. The book failed miserably.*

---

* Grant made sure to send a complimentary copy to Alfred Rosenberg, the Nazi Party's chief ideologist, and his French fascist counterpart praised it as very interesting, according to Osborn biographer Brian Regal. In America, the Anti-Defamation League considered it anti-Jewish and sought to stifle press attention and reviews.

A third eugenics congress was convened at the museum in 1932. Progressives had mostly departed, leaving behind reactionaries on the verge of collaborating with the rising Nazis in Germany. Osborn was heading in that direction, too: the 1934 trip to pick up his honorary degree from Goethe University in Frankfurt would forever stain his legacy by widely publicizing his agreement with Adolf Hitler. The following year, at the 1935 annual meeting of the Eugenics Society, he said urban Blacks could grow smarter than southern rural whites, but in a side-by-side comparison, "adjacent whites" would always come out on top.[95] By then he had left the museum, where those who had long considered him out of date, out of step, and even cringeworthy had finally outlasted him and prevailed as the societal threat posed by Nazism became inescapable. That said, Osborn kept an office at the museum until his death.[96]

His final attempts to salvage his theories were ignored by the scientific community even as it kept him "on the dais." But die-hard eugenicists stuck by him, and it's not entirely surprising that, cocooned in their support, he saw the rise of the Nazis as a positive.[97] His final days were spent at Castle Rock in Garrison. Alarmed by his deteriorating health, his doctors sedated him, but he left his bed and kept writing, railing against a fellow WASP, the Democratic president and detested class traitor Franklin Roosevelt, and advocating for eugenics until he died at his desk in fall 1935 of a heart attack at seventy-eight.

Fairfield Osborn's legacy is mixed. He created a powerful scientific institution, gave his team great opportunities, and expanded the reach of American science, but he also weaponized the pseudoscience of eugenics to support the ambitions of the elite that supported him and to expand WASP influence and social and economic power. Afterward, his imperial regime was replaced, and a new generation rejected his theories and priorities, diminishing his reputation and raising that of the American Museum of Natural History. Though he saw the future, he was too tied to old ideas to fully inhabit it, even as he supported programs to educate the children of immigrants whom he considered inferior.[98]

The desire to reconcile science and religion faded, though it, like creationism, persists. So does the museum, where in 2020, after years of protests, and in the wake of the police murder of George Floyd in Minneapolis, the equestrian statue of Theodore Roosevelt at its entrance, with its mounted subject towering over figures of an Indian and an African, was removed. "Simply put, the time has come to move it," the museum's longtime president, Ellen V. Futter, said. As an Osborn biographer had already noted, "The museum is no longer a bastion of white male superiority."[99] Osborn embodied that obsolete notion.

Ironically, the first hint of the future came just before Osborn's death, when America's growing and disparate non-WASP population united to elect the patrician WASP Franklin Delano Roosevelt to the presidency. He was at the end of his second term when the Eugenics Record Office met its end and a eugenics archive was refused as "thoroughly unscientific" by the former Eugenics Research Association, renamed the Association for Research in Human Heredity.[100] It was headed by Osborn's nephew, Church's son Frederick, who linked the families of the two siblings but did more to restore the reputation of eugenics than the opinions of his uncle.

After graduating from Princeton in 1910 and spending five years rising to the presidency of the Detroit, Toledo and Ironton Railroad, Frederick Osborn joined the Red Cross and drove an ambulance in France during World War I after he was rejected as too tall—at six foot ten—for the army. He referred to Fairfield's relatives in Castle Rock as "those people," but, encouraged by his uncle, he was also a founder of the American Eugenics Society in 1926. Shortly afterward he sold his railroad and in 1928, joined the Galton Society and retired from business to become what his grandson calls "a science dilettante" and an unpaid research associate in anthropology at his uncle's museum, which made him a trustee in 1932.[101] Through that decade, Frederick Osborn was also an advisor to his Hudson Valley neighbor, President Franklin Roosevelt, and in World War II he served as a brigadier general and chief of the Morale Branch of the War Department.

After taking over the American Eugenics Society, he became "the respectable face of eugenic research," according to a note on his background that accompanies the American Philosophical Society Library's record of his papers, which credits him with rejecting "race- and class-consciousness."[102] Under Frederick Osborn, the society "was no longer thinking in terms of 'superior' individuals, 'superior' family stocks, or even of the social conditions which would bring about a 'better' distribution of births," he wrote in a 1971 history of the society. "It was thinking in terms of the importance of diversity."[103] Later, he represented the United States on the United Nations Atomic Energy Commission, co-founded the Population Council, and actively opposed the Vietnam War. He died at ninety-two in 1981.

He had seemed the clichéd chip off the old block. But after his uncle's death, he began moving eugenics away from its formative prejudices and toward a more scientific approach, with a new focus on population issues and the medical aspects of heredity. "Early eugenicists placed a false and distasteful emphasis on race and social class," he wrote in that history, adding that "Hitler's excesses and misuse of the word 'eugenics'" also led to the group's decline from 1,260 members in 1930—"a veritable blue book of prominent and wealthy men and women," with very few men of science among them—to under 400 in 1960, almost all science and medical professionals. Though he didn't openly criticize his uncle, his history thoroughly rejected Fairfield Osborn's thinking.

For that matter, neither does Princeton University embrace Henry Fairfield Osborn. Its Osborn Clubhouse, a training facility for athletes that he donated in 1892, was renamed in 1971, becoming the Third World Center, promoting ethnic diversity.[104] The center was given another new name in 2002 and is now the Carl A. Fields Center for Equality and Cultural Understanding, honoring a former Princeton dean who was the first African American to hold such a high-ranking post at an Ivy League school. The former Osborn Clubhouse building was demolished in 2011.

The American Museum of Natural History barely mentions Fairfield Osborn on its website. But it does feature a page on which it addresses his worst excesses. "One hundred years ago, Henry Fairfield Osborn, the then-President of the American Museum of Natural History, welcomed participants to the Museum for the Second International Eugenics Congress. Today, the Museum welcomes the opportunity to acknowledge, confront, and apologize for its role in the eugenics movement," it says, referring to the discipline as a "pseudo-science" aimed at "vulnerable populations," and states that it now sees such ideas as "antithetical to the values, mission, and ongoing work of this Museum."

The statement goes on to note that in fall 2021, the museum's then-president, Ellen Futter, took part in a virtual "anti-centennial" during the COVID-19 pandemic, marking the anniversary of that second eugenics congress as part of its "reckoning with its history" and its determination "to confront modern attempts to distort science to achieve nonscientific social outcomes. We hear echoes of eugenics in today's anti-immigration rhetoric, continuing racism, anti-Semitism and other forms of religious discrimination, and gender bias. And we see the ways in which science has been manipulated to foster distrust in efforts to combat the pandemic. Untruths and misinformation, like eugenics itself, are a pernicious force that undercuts the trust in legitimate science and also undermines society at large."[105]

Aside from that passing reference to Osborn, the specific part the museum's WASP founders, its leader, and their circles played in supporting and promoting eugenics and the politics of exclusion goes unaddressed.

~

Part Nine

DECADENCE

1936–1995

MICHAEL BUTLER

29

It's tempting to see the cancellation of Henry Fairfield Osborn as a signpost; a decade or two after Osborn's death, following the end of World War II and the defeat of Nazism, the notion of WASP superiority would gradually start to become as untenable as that of Nordic supremacy was abhorrent. In the years that followed, other ethnic groups—Catholics and Jews, Irish and Latinos, Blacks and Asians, some of them the targets of imperial Japan and Nazi Germany's repudiated ideology of racial superiority—renewed their efforts to claim what the Constitution had promised them. And though only incrementally successful, that would bring down the curtain on the WASPs' long reign of unearned privilege and begin to upend the American status quo.

Some WASPs, entrenched in the highest echelons of government, corporate culture, and elite social life, were able to live out their lives in a state of blissful entitlement despite the erosion of their cultural dominance. Others took flight, withdrawing from public life and the civic arena into the insular world of school ties, posh suburbs, restrictive clubs, elite charities, and the powerful financial sinecures that still cocooned them. But a few in their cohort saw the future and, consciously or not, began adapting its outlook, expectations, ambitions, and behavior in order to better align with it. Some of them even managed to hang on to the speeding train of America's rapidly changing culture, even as it left most of their ilk behind. They found continued relevance by embracing what still seemed to be nonconformity, embodying the notion that if you can't beat 'em, you might as well join 'em. One such man was Michael Butler, best known as the producer of Broadway's hippie musical, *Hair*.

Born in 1926, the same year the American Eugenics Association was incorporated, and raised just outside Chicago in the village of Oak Brook, which his family had created on land it long owned, Butler might have been a poster child for twentieth-century WASP exceptionalism were it not for the fact that, as he once said, "our family affairs have always been a mess."[1] Despite that, and the fact that at age ninety-two in 2019, he was broke and living with his son in the San Fernando Valley outside Los Angeles instead of on one of the lavish estates he owned in his heyday, he portrayed himself in several long conversations that year as still busy, proud, and rich with privilege.

"I wouldn't change my life for anybody's," he said.[2]

The Butler family's messy saga—its members were famous as much for their multiple marriages and sexual and legal entanglements as their entrepreneurial achievement—isn't unique; indeed, it illustrates the precipitous decline of high WASPs into a state of decadence. But Michael Butler, the second of four youngsters raised as full and half-siblings, managed the neat trick of offsetting his caste's dissipation with a surprising capacity for reinvention after he bought the rights to *Hair*, an off-Broadway musical, in 1968 at age forty-two. Always, he reflected his times—even if they no longer cared very much about people like him.

❧

After World War II, and even as affluence spread, a backlash against both Theodore Roosevelt's Square Deal and his cousin Franklin's New Deal progressivism set in among WASPs. Hidebound, and furious over New Deal initiatives like the Wealth Tax, introduced in 1935, and progressive reforms that followed in 1937 and beyond, which tightened loopholes used by the oligarchy and effectively redistributed its wealth, its members reinforced the walls that still stood around their prerogatives and barricaded the doors of their corporations and private clubs. Even as outsiders sacked some WASP citadels, others, like white-shoe law firms and top investment banks, remained redoubts for American aristocrats. Within, attitudes hardened. Anyone different—women, people of color—was kept at arm's length. What is now called political incorrectness was common currency. Aside from trading anti-monarchism for anti-communism, WASP politics would have seemed familiar to Randolph of Roanoke. George Santayana made a distinction between "polite" East Coast aristocrats and "the crude but vital" upstart self-made Americans.[3] But enlightened WASPs like Henry Cabot Lodge, Nelson Rockefeller, and John V. Lindsay, who embodied liberal Republicanism, were the exceptions. They might have spoken up for outsiders and the oppressed, but their clubs—where speaking your mind without shame was protected, even encouraged—still wouldn't let those others in.

Another Protestant religious revival was under way, with church membership growing, but it was driven by the heirs of backwoods revivalists and born-agains, not mainstream WASPs. The World War II general Dwight David Eisenhower, raised a Mennonite, converted to Presbyterianism and, as the first president baptized in the White House, started the traditions of national prayer breakfasts and pandering to the religious right. As southern and western states grew in wealth and population, power shifted away from an eastern WASP elite already isolated by tradition and inclination.

Once, patricians with distinguished forebears and bearing, New England accents, tailored suits, educations from St. Grottlesex (the collective nickname of the prep schools Groton, St. Paul's, and Middlesex) and the Ivy League, sailing and polo trophies on their bookshelves, and exclusive club memberships "not only tended to uphold the status quo; they *were* the status quo."[4] They began as protégés of "wise men" like the politician and diplomat Averill Harriman, a son of E.H., or got jobs in law, business, or the executive branch. With perfectly pitched WASP understatement, Elliot Richardson, a Boston Brahmin whose career in public service spanned three decades, called his cohort "one of the smaller minority groups making up our multicultural society," but with "an open path to further advantages and the possibility of power."[5]

They ruled as if by divine right, believing they had been put on earth to follow a tradition of good works in the service of their fellow citizens that began before the American Revolution and continued unbroken into the present. The Brahmin academic turned political operative McGeorge Bundy (a Lowell and a Putnam) felt that responsibility rested "where legitimacy has placed it."[6] But as Paul Moore Jr., an idealistic Episcopal priest who later headed that church in Washington and New York, gently put it, after the 1960s "the domination of society by old established institutions was being resisted."[7] Suddenly merit mattered more than lineage.

The Depression, Franklin Roosevelt's presidency, and the war he waged "had broken the promise of self-perpetuating privilege," as one recipient of it, Kingman Brewster, put it.[8] An eleventh-generation lineal descendent of Plymouth's Elder Brewster, Kingman Brewster taught law at Harvard before becoming provost and then president of Yale in 1963. He was one of those who managed to hold on to position and advantage into the 1960s. Many of his peers and friends served and some rose to positions of great power during John F. Kennedy's administration, when they bucked the prevailing tide and tightened their hold on the reins of government, again via institutions they created or controlled or that simply paid them deference—the State Department, the Central Intelligence Agency, the National Security Council, and the North Atlantic Treaty Organization.

Michael Butler's roots were in that milieu—indeed, he was personal friends with JFK—but he was raised in suburban Illinois and in international society, not on the East Coast, and would eventually embrace and even come to symbolize the liberation agenda that flowered after the WASP-in-Catholic-clothing took the White House. After Kennedy's assassination, Lyndon Baines Johnson, a member of the Disciples of Christ Church (which emerged in the West in the early nineteenth century) though married to an Episcopalian, presided over the last great gasp of classic American liberalism, a time when upper-class progressives, rooted in the Roosevelts and newly emboldened by Kennedy, had their last hurrah.* Brewster's law school

---

* East Coast patricians would still play in presidential politics, but the Bush family, though now considered moderate, were conservative Republicans, and John Forbes Kerry was, unfortunately for him, a loser. George Romney and his son Mitt, though wealthy, were Republicans, too, but also Mormons, so are rarely described as WASPs even though an ancestor, Anne Hutchinson, was a Puritan reformer who arrived in Massachusetts in 1634.

classmate Endicott "Chub" Peabody, grandson of Groton's rector, said that "everyone has a duty to participate in public affairs," and thought himself both a Brahmin and a Democrat.[9]

The impulse to engage ran in Peabody's family. In March 1964, when he was midway through a one-term, two-year tenure as governor of Massachusetts, Peabody's mother was arrested at a Southern Christian Leadership Conference civil rights protest. A member of their church had invited Mary Peabody along, and without telling son Chub her plans, she sat with a Black woman in a segregated St. Augustine restaurant, hoping to be arrested; a return trip was required before she succeeded. Mary, then seventy-two, was finally jailed, charged with trespassing, conspiracy, and being an "undesirable" guest in a motel dining room. Florida's governor called his counterpart to say, "Hey Chub, I got your mom in the slammer."[10] The charges against her and about four hundred others were dropped a year later by federal court order.

But the Kennedy-Johnson interregnum was an anomaly that couldn't halt the loosening of the liberal WASP establishment's grip on power or the rise of a new conservativism in the South and West. Barry Goldwater's defeat by Johnson in the 1964 election would turn out to have been an inflection point; Johnson became so unpopular in the next four years that he had just announced he wouldn't run for reelection when the curtain rose on Michael Butler's spiffed-up Broadway version of *Hair,* billed as "the tribal love-rock musical," on April 29, 1968. Its impact was so great that fifty-four years later, when the show had its latest revival, *Los Angeles* magazine would note that "nudity was only one of its many firsts: long before Lin-Manuel Miranda, a Black female actor donned a top hat every night as Abe Lincoln and recited a mock Gettysburg Address while a blond, white girl shined her shoes. *Hair*'s actors played openly gay and lesbian characters while transgender and bisexuality were portrayed as equally 'normal.'"[11] Soon, perhaps inevitably, given how fast the world was changing, Richard Nixon, campaigning on a promise to restore law and order—the status quo ante before the rise of liberation movements, civil disruption, and progressive politics—would be elected president.

Still, the success of the musical on the Great White Way was evidence of an epochal cultural change, demonstrating the nation could take two steps forward while simultaneously lurching backward. The civil rights, anti-war, and American Indian movements, and a feminist protest outside the Miss America pageant in Atlantic City just over four months after *Hair* arrived on Broadway, reflected the same shift; issues like the rights of Indians, Latinos, Blacks, and women would never be ignored again, notwithstanding the politics of division perfected by Nixon and exploited by Republicans ever since.

All those disparate causes brought together a new coalition of Catholics, evangelical Christians, and southern whites to oppose them. Progressive Protestants pushed back, and through the 1970s many churches would remain on the social justice side of the political divide, particularly on issues like the environment and arms control. But thanks to the poisonous, centuries-old compromises over slavery that gave the Constitution the three-fifths rule and the electoral college, clever opportunists would link arms with the religious right to create a new, conservative voter base. Technocrats, urbanites, and liberals would remain an electoral-vote minority into the twenty-first century, when the patrician Yale graduate George W. Bush won the presidency by playing a retrograde Western bumpkin for public consumption.[12]

The Butlers, though not bumpkins, owned ranches, played at being farmers, and were genuinely intimate with the odor of manure; one of their number, Butler's uncle Julius, even stopped paying taxes in 1968, was arrested and fined in 1973, and became a founding member of his local chapter of the ultra-right militia Posse Comitatus. But Julius Butler was an exception to the family rule. They were members in good standing, if not always good behavior, of what was then called the establishment. And while Michael Butler cherished his ability to have it both ways, he was their prodigal black sheep, and would become a symbol, depending on your point of view, of either his family's and his caste's descent or its liberation from restrictive upper-class expectations.

In 2019, Michael Butler's sister, Jorie, and her daughter, Reute, gave a talk to the Colonial Dames of America, of which both are members. Their family research had led them to Lieutenant William Butler of

Ipswich, Massachusetts, the first of their family born in America. He was "said to be descended" from Theobold "le Boteler" FitzWalter, who was made the first Chief Butler, or ruler, of Ireland in 1177 by Henry II of England, allegedly the source of the family's surname. "Originally, the family had come over with William the Conqueror," Michael Butler added of what he called his "heavy family background," before admitting that family claims of descent from the Plantagenet dynasty of the Middle Ages and the Irish Dukes of Ormond and a blood relationship to Anne Boleyn, the second wife of Henry VIII, are apocryphal.

Genealogy resources place the first Butler on American soil in 1637, when a Nicholas Butler, his wife, three children, and five servants arrived in Massachusetts on the *Hercules* and settled in Dorchester. Four generations later, a great-grandson, Thomas Butler Jr., married into a family that had arrived in Massachusetts on one of the ships led by the future Governor Winthrop. Two generations after that, Zebediah Butler Jr. brought the Butlers into the paper-making trade in which they would prosper, and his older son, Oliver, followed him, working for, and perhaps earning a small interest in, one of the first American paper mills in Vermont in 1827. Oliver headed to Illinois in 1845, settling in a town west of Chicago, where he partnered with the owner of what was said to be America's only paper mill west of Pittsburgh, increasing its production and adding newsprint to its product line, and bringing new customers across three states to its client list. In 1846, Oliver's younger brother Julius joined the firm, opening a paper store and warehouse in Chicago, where they collected the rags that were their raw material. The then-new *Chicago Tribune* was printed on Butler paper, delivered by wheelbarrow—and other newspapers followed.

The Civil War increased demand for newsprint, and the Butlers survived a fire that destroyed one of their plants in 1867; later, after the company fell victim to the Great Chicago Fire of 1871, Julius bought out his brother. By 1878, his sons Frank Osgood Butler and Julius Frederick Butler had joined the firm, and the Butlers began acquiring subsidiaries. They eventually owned eleven paper companies, stretching from the Midwest to the West Coast, and in the twentieth century served six thousand customers in all forty-eight states and parts of Mexico. Julius became a bank director and officer of his local Congregational church.

The Butler brothers moved their families to Hinsdale, a town conveniently located between their paper mill and their Chicago operation, where Frank Osgood Butler's elder son, Paul, was born in 1892. As Butler Paper's revenues soared into eight figures, Frank began buying up the nearby countryside, built a farm and stables, added a working dairy farm with hundreds of acres to his holdings, and then bought 134 more acres, on which he built a golf course to indulge in the newly popular sport. But horses were his real preoccupation. When Julius died, F.O., as he was known, inherited a ranch in Montana and bought others in Wyoming and in Hot Springs, South Dakota, at the foot of the Black Hills, where he spent months every year. He built a race track, bred cattle and horses, and used his sprawling Illinois property to fatten up his cows, en route to Chicago's stockyards, and the horses he supplied to the U.S. Army Remount Service in World War I.

His son Paul first gained public attention in 1917, when Hinsdale neighbors snitched to federal authorities that he and younger brother Julius had failed to register for military service in the war. But the commander of a Chicago-based army hospital unit stepped in to defend them, and Paul would end up in France in 1918, where he became a cavalry lieutenant. Some of his men, family histories have it, had trained for combat on the Butler ranches, where they also indulged in a game they called cowboy polo, a version of the ancient sport first brought to America in 1876. Also in the war, Butler learned to fly when the army cavalry began using planes for reconnaissance, the start of a lifelong love affair with aviation, despite his father's objections to flying's cost.

After the war, the Butler properties outside Chicago began to attract others, including the owner of one of the largest coal companies in America, Francis Stuyvesant Peabody, a seventh-generation descendant of Francis Pabodie and a Butler relation through marriage. F.O. sold him land on which he built an estate that still stands and is listed on the National Register of Historic Places. In 1921, F.O. donated land near his dairy farm to build a schoolhouse for his neighbors, and also staked out the family's first polo field. The next year, back from France, his son Paul formed a polo club there, named it Oak Brook, and began expanding its stables and fields. F.O., who was breeding polo ponies at his South Dakota ranch, passed management of the paper company to Paul in 1930 and retired, dying in Palm Beach in 1955. Though F.O.'s wife, Fanny, also rode, she preferred society to her husband's steeds. When she died at eighty-four in 1959, the *Chicago Tribune* noted she "was known . . . for her love of lavish costume parties" and for spending winters in Palm Beach and summers in Chicago's Palmer House, a luxury hotel that doubled as the city's social center.[13]

By then, Paul was an established business and social leader, putting a series of youthful scandals behind him. His first marriage, in 1918, was hushed up for years, and was only publicly revealed when the former Josephine Roonely of County Mayo, Ireland, and their son, Norman, sued him in 1960. They asked the court to void the couple's divorce, put Butler's businesses into receivership, and restrain him from diluting assets.

Josephine's story was a knotty one. She was eighteen and Fanny Butler's paid traveling companion when Paul married her. Their son was born later that year. In 1922, Paul was named as the other man in a divorce action filed by an artist's husband, who alleged his wife had deserted him a month after their wedding and moved in with the married Butler, who had courted her with gifts of clothing, jewelry, and cash. Paul didn't divorce Josephine until 1924. In her 1960 lawsuit, she claimed he first sought a divorce in 1922, fraudulently filing the action in a county where he didn't live. Then, she said, he dropped the divorce suit and instead personally put her and their son Norman on a ship to France, but not before plopping a box of chocolates and some more legal papers in her lap. In those papers he claimed she deserted him.

In Josephine's version of the events, Butler had already identified his next wife, Marjorie Stresenreuter, whom Josephine's lawsuit described as a "sub-deb, the daughter of so-called society people." When Josephine assented to a divorce, she charged, Butler's father gave her a $200,000 trust and $1,000 a month to support Norman. But that wasn't the whole story. Rather, it was concocted to protect F.O., who had actually impregnated Josephine and was Norman's father. Paul Butler agreed to marry her and get her and the child out of America. In return, his father gave Paul "everything, without taxes, for getting F.O. off the hook," said a family intimate. That cut out Paul's brother, Julius, but he had "had a motorcycle accident and was never the same." And no one was the wiser until Norman appeared in Hot Springs, South Dakota, during World War II to reveal his existence to the family. Apparently, Josephine wasn't satisfied with the truth coming out, and her lawsuit followed fifteen years later. But after six months of legal squabbling, she lost her case.

In the years between his parents' divorce and his mother's lawsuit, Norman Butler had marital adventures of his own, apparently funded by Butler largesse. Educated in England, he joined the U.S. Navy at thirty-three and was a decorated bomber pilot in the South Atlantic during World War II. Back in England, he worked for Butler Paper, and was married in 1948 to a divorcée named Pauline Winn. Her mother, Olive Cecilia Paget, was the daughter of Lord Queensborough, a British industrialist, yachtsman, politician, and founder of a corps of massage therapists who treated wounded soldiers during World War I. More important, in the small world of American WASPs, Olive Paget's mother was the former Pauline Payne Whitney, elder daughter of William Collins and Flora Whitney, and an heiress to Oliver Payne's fortune. That marriage linked the Butlers, through the Paynes and the Whitneys, to Plymouth's governor William Bradford.

Norman and Pauline had two children before separating in 1956 and divorcing two years later after an acrimonious courtroom battle described as "sordid" by the presiding judge; testimony included, but wasn't limited to, charges that Norman had hit his wife at a party in 1952, thrown a telephone book at her a month later, and between summer 1957 and early 1958 committed "about 40 adulteries" at his apartment in London's swank Ritz Hotel, all witnessed by an elevator operator spying on him for private detectives hired by his soon-to-be ex-wife. Butler's lawyer later sued him for legal fees.*

---

* Besides his residence at the Ritz, Butler also kept an apartment in London's Mayfair district, where he was also said to have romanced a seventeen-year-old stable girl who worked for a

That same year, Norman, then forty, took another British lord's twenty-two-year-old niece on a six-month jaunt to America, but sent her home, pregnant, when their affair concluded. She thought they would remain friends, at least until their child was born and Butler introduced her to his latest girlfriend, twenty-three-year-old Penelope Dewar, in St. Moritz. Within days, he vanished, taking Penelope to America to meet his parents in advance of his next planned wedding. Hearing that, the new mother sued him for paternity, which Butler deemed blackmail before the case was dropped.

Even more upset was Penelope's father, Baron Forteviot, chairman of Dewar Whiskey, maker of an acclaimed brand of Scotch. He had tried to talk his daughter out of the trip, but she persisted, and from Paul Butler's estate, by then named Oak Brook after his polo team, she coldly complained to the press about her predecessor in Norman's affections, "I think it is disgusting the way she brings out everything in public. I cannot imagine any nice person doing something like that. . . . It is entirely her own fault anyway."[14] Simultaneously she demonstrated WASP reticence and its obsolescence.

Their engagement was announced in June 1959 after Norman spent hours with a Catholic bishop in Edinburgh, Scotland, her hometown, to ensure that the wedding, at least, would go smoothly, as it did that December. Six months later, a son was born and named Paul Butler III; the first Paul Butler was Norman's not-quite father, and Paul Butler II was the man who in the future would be known as Michael Butler.*

Paul Butler II was Norman's younger not-quite brother, a son of the first Paul and his "sub-deb" second wife. But in 1947, at age twenty-one, he would change his name to Michael, evidence, he said, of mixed feelings about a father once described as "quiet, icy, and somewhat distant," which succinctly sums up the clichéd characteristics of WASP parenting.[15] Michael Butler was torn about the stern,

polo-playing British lord, breaking up with her after his father objected to his offering her a job in Chicago.
* Norman and Penelope had two more children before divorcing.

autocratic father he alternately rebelled against and desperately sought to prove himself to. His opinion of his mother is more negative, for good reason. Marjorie Stresenreuter, a German American real estate developer's daughter, met her first husband in 1922, when she was only fourteen years old and he was twenty-six. When she died in 2004, her death notice added a "von" between her and her father's first and last names, an upgrade to noble patrilineality, and described her mother, born Laurietta Ford, as Countess Filipponi, though her second husband's blue blood was dubious at best.

Like Alva Vanderbilt, Laurietta wanted her two daughters to marry up, and though Paul Butler was not a prince, he was a prize. The Stresenreuters, on the other hand, were something of an embarrassment. The future Michael Butler was born just before his maternal grandmother's second husband, Filipponi, was arrested in Chicago after a street fight with his best man, who would be accused of check-kiting. Within days, the "count's" title and claims of aristocracy were debunked.

Michael, then still Paul Jr., was seven, his brother Frank Osgood Butler II was five, and their sister Marjorie Maxine, known as Jorie, was three when their parents divorced in 1933. Mother Marjorie, twenty-four, charged their father, forty-one, with extreme and repeated cruelty, and got two cars, $535 a month for a decade, and the promise of a lump sum of $100,000 thereafter. It was agreed that the children would stay in Hinsdale while their parents alternated living with them.[16]

Precisely ten years later, Marjorie and Paul were at odds again. He charged that after three more brief marriages, two of which ended in divorce, Marjorie was morally unfit to have custody of Jorie, whom she had recently snatched and taken to Florida, where she asked a court to grant her sole custody. Paul claimed she had also taken their sons on a long road trip in the company of a professional boxer, with whom she spent nights in tourist camps and cheap hotels. Early in 1944, the brothers testified against their mother, and Paul Jr. (not yet renamed Michael) said his mother had slept with both of his stepfathers before marriage, drank heavily, fed her dogs better than her children, and when he complained, she had him tied to a tree and beaten with a dog's leash. He also said she spoke glowingly of Adolf

Hitler, and his brother said she had asked them to call her Marge, not Mother, so no one would think she had children.[17] Within days the warring exes had reached a secret settlement and the boys' testimony was stricken from the court record—but lived on in the press. Marjorie would marry three more times and outlived all seven of her husbands. In the meantime, Butler married a third time, in 1940, to a twenty-four-year-old art student and *Vogue* model, but divorced again in 1948, just after Paul Jr. became Michael.

The children's father never married again, but he still had a lot of living to do. By 1962, Paul Butler, restrained and private to the point of introversion, had turned his inherited family company into a conglomerate with sixty-five divisions and annual revenues of $100 million. But he was more interested in the wealthy WASP sport of polo than he was in his own paper products. When the lean, mean, and tall Paul wasn't commanding his polo club, the Black Horse Troop, named for and consisting of former members of his cavalry unit, he was monomaniacally focused on his Oak Brook lands, which grew steadily to thirty-six hundred acres. In 1942, Oak Brook residents, many of them polo players to whom he rented his sixteen farmhouses at favorable rates, created the Oak Brook Civic Association to organize local World War II defenses in case of attack. After World War II, they incorporated as a quasi-governmental operation for the three hundred residents.

Butler hired an equestrian to run Oak Brook's sports facilities. Two years later, he initiated the Oak Brook Hounds fox hunt, which ran for decades until land grew scarce. In 1946, Butler combined several polo fields into an airport with three runways to handle the small prop planes that ferried in his wealthy, horse-crazy friends. He formalized his aviation interests two years later when he founded Butler Aviation to service private planes. It would grow into America's largest "general aviation" company, providing fuel and maintenance services for corporate, private, and government and military aircraft at twenty-nine airports; at one time it pumped more fuel than the U.S. Air Force. Butler sold it in 1967; it ceased to exist after a 1992 merger with a competitor.

In years to come, Butler would methodically subdivide his land and seek to attract corporations engaged in, as an aide put it, "strictly think projects—i.e., no factories."[18] Marshall Field and McDonald's Hamburger University settled in, with affluent executives following. Butler used his influence to divert highways that might have divided his holdings, and added a fire department, a utilities company, a shopping mall, a hotel, the nondenominational Christ Church of Oak Brook, a game preserve where he raised and shot ducks and pheasants, thirty-six miles of riding trails, and what he called a Sports Core that eventually included tennis, swimming, archery, soccer, trap shooting, duck blinds, a lake for fishing, and banquet facilities, as well as two golf courses, one public, the other a championship-caliber invitation-only club. The original one-square-mile village had only 103 residents; the area now boasts a population of about 8,000.

A crucial turning point came in 1953. The Meadowbrook Polo Club in Old Westbury, on Long Island, had been the center of American polo since it was established in 1881 by a group of wealthy, mostly WASP founders that included August Belmont Jr. and Tommy Hitchcock Jr., whose New York mercantile family fortune had been enlarged when he married an oil-rich Mellon from Pittsburgh. The annual U.S. Open, held at Meadowbrook for thirty years, attracted crowds as large as thirty thousand to cheer much-lauded, socially prominent riders like Laddie Sanford, a descendant of Henry Sanford, and Butler, a four-goal polo player (ten goals is the highest ranking). After Meadowbrook was sold to developers that year, Oak Brook's polo club, with its airstrip, stables for four hundred horses, thirteen polo fields, and matches that attracted British royals, King Hussein of Jordan, the maharaja of Jaipur, and Hollywood and Broadway stars, as well as run-of-the-mill millionaires, became the sport's new American hub.

30

Paul Butler also bred cattle and made canny investments in Broadway musicals; among his successes were *Peter Pan* (1951), *Kismet* (1953), and *The Music Man* (1957). But he preferred to be a player, as he was in polo, not a passive investor or spectator. He even learned to fly jets in his sixties. So perhaps Michael Butler changed his name because his father was a tough act to follow. Indeed, initially he seemed to be on a glide path to living the life his father wanted for him.

He was too young to be affected by his parents' divorce, he said, though he later came to think his mother was "a very bad scene." He said as much in court during the 1940s custody fight. "I was talked into it by the lawyers," he recalled. "It was a pretty ruthless situation." Years later, his sister, Jorie, tried to effect a reconciliation over dinner, but instead they fought after Marjorie asked Michael for a look at Paul Butler's will, "and I was not very diplomatic. I said, 'Mother, you're married to your sixth husband. Why would I talk to Father about his will? I've never talked to Father about it.' That ended our relationship."

Butler also managed to overcome a childhood handicap that could have crippled his entire life. At age seven or so, he was given a bay pony named Do It for Christmas that he rode around a large courtyard outside the Oak Brook stables. "And I went galloping past a basement door," he recalled, "and I hit the wood part and went down into rotten wood. I got a lot of rusty nails in my right arm." At Hinsdale's hospital, doctors wanted to amputate, but they were overruled by Paul and Marjorie, who demanded a repair job requiring three months in bed. "In many ways I have to thank them," said Michael, "except I have a crippled arm," withered and bent after he refused the prescribed therapy of carrying weights. "So the arm stayed that way."

For years it was felt Butler couldn't play polo, despite it being "the dominating conversation" at family meals, but he rode nonetheless, and learned show-jumping; he once said he felt closer to his instructor than his father. He learned well enough that he spent his first prize money on a red four-door Buick convertible. "Father said, 'Get it out of the garage.' It was so gaudy. We had Dusenbergs and sixteen-cylinder Cadillacs."

His upbringing reflected a complex family as much as the times. He never went to church, joking later that he had been raised a pagan, and had a peripatetic education. He attended multiple schools and was sometimes driven by a bodyguard carrying a sawed-off shotgun for fear of kidnapping. He finally left the local schools because "every child, their parents worked for us, so that was a very bad situation." A classmate once called him "typically rich, pampered and spoiled."[19] Butler has said his childhood "was miserable."[20]

Then, around the time of his father's last marriage, like many children of the establishment, Butler was sent to boarding schools. The first was in Tucson, Arizona—"according to Father, the most expensive school in the United States." Next, as World War II began, he chose Culver, a military academy in Indiana, where "Father had enough influence to get me in."

There he started a history and debate society, and was made assistant coach of the jumping team, the only cadet ever so honored, "even though I was a terrible student," he said. "I had one demerit after another. I was smoking at the time, which was illegal." Finally he incited a riot that he recalls as a political protest against the school superintendent. Culver's officers had all gone to war, and "there was nothing military about it," he said. "I became really disgusted. I wanted to quit and my father wouldn't let me. Finally I was thrown out." But not before his first solo jet-set adventure.

His class went on a trip to Mexico City, where the tall, handsome fifteen-year-old with dark hair and piercing eyes made a break for it and took a bus to Acapulco, then a bolt-hole for millionaires and celebrities. "I got down there, ran out of money pretty quickly, wound up sleeping on a beach." Despite his handicap, he was hired as a boat boy by Bono Batani, who ran a water-ski school catering to the likes of Ava Gardner. Though it was illegal to hire foreigners, Butler's looks and savoir-faire were worth the risk, and Batani's mother, who ran a boardinghouse, gave him a room until the season heated up and "I wound up sleeping on a canvas cot in the laundry." At least, until his father ordered the head of Butler Paper to find him and bring him back to Culver. To get him to stay in school, Paul Butler agreed to let Junior return to Acapulco and Batani's ski school for the next three summers, where he was befriended by the son of Mexico's new president, Miguel Alemán, who had a beach house nearby.

After dropping out of college in 1948, Butler managed parts of Oak Brook and then spent nine months in Africa, "driving from Capetown to Khartoum in a wooden station wagon." After that his father agreed to let him into what he called Butler Paper School, working as a salesman. A stroke of luck accelerated his career. Gussie Busch, then the CEO of Anheuser-Busch of St. Louis, the Budweiser beer brewery, also indulged in show-jumping, but he wouldn't fly, so when the bus he took to a horse show in Illinois broke down, Butler offered to drive him home. En route, Busch said, "You're in the paper business, would you help me out?"

The beer mogul thought his brewery's purchasing agent was cheating him, and when Butler found proof of that, Busch gave Butler Paper a contract to produce shipping boxes. His father rewarded Butler with the title of vice president of sales at $25,000 a year, a spacious office, and a board seat, but the last thrust him into corporate politics, and he soon quit. "There was a lot of fighting, family fighting. . . . One of the ways Father kept control of the company was by pitting characters against one another, in very unscrupulous ways." That's when he changed his name and became Michael Butler, for several reasons. "I hated being called Junior," he said, adding that his maternal grandmother "did not like the name Paul and always called me Michael," and "probably" disliked his father, too.

The early 1950s were a blur for Butler, as vague about his twenties as he was consistent in signaling that his father gave him as much agita as advantages. Equestrian sports and polo, the avocations Paul Butler turned into a business, were the greatest edge of all, even before he began playing himself fifteen years later; the most sophisticated people in the world flocked to Oak Brook. Michael was still tied to his father, doing odd jobs between horse shows and fox hunts, and while he couldn't cut the golden cords that tied him to his family just yet, his exposure to the postwar jet set seeded dreams of bolting.

Since 1949, Michael Butler had hosted a Hunt Ball at Oak Brook each December on his birthday, and in 1952 he celebrated his twenty-sixth by initiating what's been described as a ménage à trois with the bisexual Hollywood idol Tyrone Power and his then-wife, starlet Linda Christian.[21]

In Butler's telling, his involvement with the couple began with a surprising sexual liaison. Hunt Ball weekends were a round of polo matches, cocktail parties, and meals, climaxing at the ball, where the men wore scarlet tailcoats and the women beautiful gowns. That year, at a cocktail party at the Racquet Club in Chicago given by two Chicago bon vivants, Butler was introduced to a beautiful actress named

Linda, and after the party he took her and his mother to a private club for dinner. There, Linda whispered, "Let's get out of here," and though he didn't even know her last name, they spent the weekend in bed before parting company.

Not long afterward Linda called and asked Butler to meet her at the Ambassador East Hotel, where he found her sitting at the top table in its famous Pump Room with the movie star Tyrone Power, "a god, probably the most attractive man who ever walked," and also Linda Christian's husband. Whether she knew that her lover and her husband would shortly be lovers, too, is unclear, but after their meal, she was clearly playing with matches when she announced to the two men, "Michael has a house in the Bahamas; we're going to go there for Christmas."

Christian had unlocked the box in which Butler kept an important secret—his bisexuality. He had realized in prep school that he "had different feelings" about sex. "Or it could have been earlier, because of my arm. I figured no girl would have any interest. I thought women couldn't stand me. I only realized it was a different story when I wound up with Linda." Yet it was only natural that he and Power, also a closeted bisexual, would click, and "the upshot of it was that Ty and I became closer than Linda and I," he said. "It's impossible to describe what a lovely person he was, a real sweetheart."

Butler didn't advertise his preferences. Though he was hardly the first WASP to enjoy same-sex encounters, he knew enough to honor his caste's prime directive—"Don't scare the horses"—and mostly kept them to himself. But Butler was hardly alone among WASPs of his generation and social class—one in which all forms of unorthodoxy, eccentricity, and iconoclasm were tolerated, if not actively encouraged—in discovering a taste for rule-breaking. Nonconformists were no longer seen as outliers. Naughty could be nice. And while WASPs in Butler's set were not yet openly embracing Bohemianism à la Kerouac and Ginsberg, espousing liberation or revolution, they were evolving, feeling tugged toward an undefined something else, seeking wider experience than their constricted circle offered and an as yet amorphous relevance. By admitting his bisexuality, Butler took his first step toward becoming a man a step ahead of his caste.

Like the promiscuous and brilliant bisexual writer Gore Vidal, one year older than he and also descended from a colonial family with roots in Great Britain, Butler was part of the avant-garde, a sort of spiritual godfather of the crowd of maverick WASPs who followed in the early 1960s, inspiring arguments over whether they were well-born rebels or just spoiled brats. Among them were Tommy Hitchcock's grandson William Mellon "Billy" Hitchcock, who would, like Michael Butler, refuse to conform to patrician expectations. Instead, he became another significant figure in the 1960s counterculture as part of a conspiracy to manufacture and sell the drug LSD.* Others included acolytes of the artist Andy Warhol like Brigid "Polk" Berlin and Edie Sedgwick, the artist and fashion designer Gloria Vanderbilt, and the debutante Fernanda Wanamaker Wetherill, whose 1963 debut featured guests swinging from chandeliers, splintering furniture, smashing china and windows, shooting bottles with air rifles, dancing on a mantelpiece, and dangling from the rafters of the Southampton, Long Island, beach house where an all-night after-party led to a grand jury charging fourteen guests (five of them listed in the *Social Register*) with willful destruction of property. When no convictions resulted, the *New York Times* ran a page-one story reporting that neighbors in Suffolk County were convinced "that the rich and well-born are more immune to the penalties of the law than rank-and-file residents."[22]

Michael Butler's rebellion emerged only after a romantically inspired detour into religion. Tyrone Power was a Roman Catholic. Sargent

---

* Billy Hitchcock, whose wealth came from the Irish Presbyterian Mellon family, provided the LSD chemist Augustus Owsley Stanley III, a descendant of several governors of Kentucky, with financial advice and set up offshore bank accounts for him before, in 1963, renting his family's 2,500-acre estate in Millbrook, New York, for $500 a month to the notorious LSD advocate Timothy Leary. When Leary was arrested at the Texas-Mexico border late in 1965 and sentenced to thirty years in prison for drug possession, Hitchcock created a legal defense fund for him and became its primary contributor. Seven years later, after an intergovernmental task force investigated his role in drug dealing, Hitchcock was charged in a separate case with tax evasion and violation of stock market rules for trading stock worth $40 million, entirely on credit, and would eventually receive immunity and testify against the distributors of Stanley's LSD. He also paid nearly $850,000 in fraud penalties and taxes as well as a $20,000 fine, received a suspended five-year sentence, and was required to consult a psychiatrist.

Shriver, a descendent of a signer of Maryland's Constitution and Bill of Rights, who had come to Chicago in the late 1940s as the manager of the Merchandise Mart, owned by Joseph P. Kennedy, and married his boss's daughter Eunice, arranged for Butler to take instruction from his priest. Butler was christened at New York's St. Patrick's Cathedral with Power standing as his godfather. Sadly, Power would die in Spain just a few years later, shortly after Butler bought the right to Gore Vidal's novel *Messiah*, a story about the collapse of Christianity and rise of a new, cultish, death-worshipping religion, as a starring vehicle for the actor. Butler last saw Power at a lunch with Vidal to discuss the project.

Despite his flirtation with Power, Butler was neither done with women nor ready to leave his comfortable nest. Ambivalence—or perhaps a desire to have it both ways—would become a defining feature of his life. In 1953, he met Audrey Hepburn at another Hunt Ball and followed her to New York, where, he claims, he suggested her to producer Roger Stevens for the lead role in a Jean Giraudoux play, *Ondine*, on Broadway. His father had invested in plays produced by Stevens and offered to split any profits with Michael if he got involved with the theater. But once again, his father's manipulations turned opportunity into a source of resentment. A pattern was established. Paul would dangle the possibility of support and then yank it away at the last minute, leaving Michael befuddled and angry.

In 1954, as Hepburn vied for the part of a water nymph in love with a human, she and Butler had liaisons at Long Island's Creek Club and, later, in California and Mexico, but it was more a fling than a great romance. "I was, behind the skin, a middle western boy and she was a very, very sophisticated woman. I wasn't intellectually up to her," Butler said. And after Stevens gave her the part, she fell for the male lead, Mel Ferrer, "who was sort of a Svengali type, so I lost her. It was way too bad."

He may have lost Hepburn, but, following his father's lead while desperately seeking to impress him, Butler networked his way into impressive connections of his own. Before his death, Tyrone Power had introduced him to Edmund Goulding, who had directed films like *Grand Hotel*, *Dark Victory*, and several with Power, including the classic *The Razor's Edge.* Though his hopes that Goulding might direct Vidal's *Messiah* were dashed when Power died, the older man became a friend and mentor, often taking him to Greta Garbo's apartment on the East River in Manhattan to "sit in the kitchen and tell stories."

Goulding also brought Butler to visit friends in Hyannisport, Massachusetts, on Cape Cod: Joseph Kennedy, the former American ambassador to Great Britain, and Serge Semenenko, a secretive Russian American Boston banker with deep ties to the entertainment business. Butler unabashedly related that he was recruited as a procurer of young women for the trio of wealthy older men—and enjoyed the role. At dinners with Kennedy, he was introduced to his son Jack, who in 1953 had just entered the Senate for the state of Massachusetts and the state of matrimony with the former Jacqueline Bouvier.

"I liked Joe a tremendous amount and he liked me," said Butler, "but I met Jack and fell in love, so Jack and I used to go out quite a bit. I was not on Jackie's favorite list." His role was clear to the senator's wife. "If I'd ever seen a Peck's Bad Boy, it was Jack," Butler said. "I never introduced him to any girl I wasn't ready to share."

Butler, who had done a lot of small-boat sailing, bought a 120-foot schooner, the *Coradina,* that he took between the Caribbean and Nova Scotia, and lived on it between trips. He kept it at anchor in Oyster Bay on Long Island, where he parked his Mercedes-Benz gullwing two-seat sports car at a marina. After work in New York on Fridays, he took a seaplane from an aerodrome on the East River to fly over Long Island Sound to his boat, often with Kennedy.

Though he enjoyed their shenanigans, Butler decided to get married in April 1954 to the first of the three wives he would accumulate in just under a decade. She was Marti Stevens, twenty-three, a singer and actress whose father was Nicholas Schenck, the Russian-born president of Loew's, Inc. and a movie business pioneer. Tellingly, Marti had also changed her last name when she launched her career in 1949. A regular performer at Hollywood's Mocambo and New York's Blue Angel nightclubs, soon after she and Michael met, they rushed to Mexico "for a hasty marriage."[23] "Marti and I wanted to get away from our families, frankly, so we decided to get married, and we did get married in Mexico at Dolores Del Rio's house," Butler said. His friend Miguel Alemán Jr. arranged the paperwork, and they honeymooned at a bullfighter's Acapulco home. But within a year, they "agreed to disagree," according to a gossip column, blaming the split on "conflicting careers." The breakup was amicable enough that among Butler's exes, she remained the only friend.

They broke up at the Venice Film Festival, and Marti fled to Paris, leaving Butler behind with Betty Estevez, the wife of a bisexual costume designer, who introduced him to a young actor, Rock Hudson, "because she felt so sorry for me." The two young men embarked on a romance and left Venice for Florence and Rome in a gold-trimmed black Rolls-Royce convertible, planning to sail back home on the *Queen Mary* and move in together, but Hudson's agent, Henry Willson, and Universal, the studio that was grooming Hudson as a leading man, intervened. Aghast at the closeted actor's indiscretion, they ordered him home at once—alone—and then arranged for Hudson to marry the agent's secretary. While his relationship with Tyrone Power had been secret and sweet, the revelation of Butler's trysts with Rock Hudson had set off alarm bells in Hollywood, where, as was the case across much of America in the 1950s, homosexuality was still considered loathsome.

The breakup devastated Butler, who never saw or spoke to Hudson again. Butler fled to Deauville with the producer Mike Todd, then making his film *Around the World in 80 Days* while seeking financing (from Butler, among others) to complete it. There Butler met another woman, whom he took to the Hotel du Cap on the Riviera, where John Kennedy, touring Europe with his wife while recovering from back surgery, snuck away to meet his friend and the woman on the *Coradina*, which had come to fetch him.[24] Said Butler, "You can imagine what happened. It was a scene."

His relationship with Kennedy would only deepen through the late 1950s. And an episode in Newport, Rhode Island, when the *Coradina* was fogged in for several days, led to what Butler has referred to as "our rumored reputation for carousing," which so annoyed Jackie Kennedy. "She felt that I was leading Jack astray. But years later," he wrote in an online diary, they managed to renew their

acquaintance because "I think she had realized that I was the acolyte, not the master."[25]

~

Butler's rental house in the Bahamas was on Hog Island (now called
Paradise Island), then owned by the richest man in Sweden, Axel
Wenner-Gren, who had made a fortune in vacuum cleaners and diversified into newspapers, munitions, and finance. He was reportedly
friendly with the Nazi official Hermann Göring, who was married to
a Swede, as well as with the Duke of Windsor, England's former King
Edward VIII and a Nazi sympathizer. That led to Wenner-Gren's appearance on an economic blacklist during World War II, despite his
saving more than three hundred survivors of a Nazi attack on an
ocean liner on the first day of the war when his yacht, the world's largest, happened by. Continuing on its way, the yacht passed Hog Island, and Wenner-Gren, enthralled, bought it. Years later, Butler
sought him out there because "Ty and Linda wanted to meet him."

With Wenner-Gren, Butler would start three trading and finance
businesses, one of which was eventually renamed Butler Overseas;
they built coal-washing plants in India and planned the reconstruction
of the Hejaz Railroad, which Islamic pilgrims rode from Damascus to
Mecca. "I was competing against the British to sell military aircraft to
the Shah and the British won," Butler once said.[26]

Butler then was living most of the time in a villa on the Bosporus
near Istanbul and traveled the region to tend to interests in Egypt, Iran,
Saudi Arabia, and Iraq, hobnobbing with prime ministers, princesses,
and King Faisal II of Iraq and his cousin King Hussein of Jordan. His
newish friend Senator Kennedy would sometimes ask him to be "a
source of information. I would be told before I left on my trips, 'This is
what we want to know.' Nothing to do with military or security or anything like that. He wanted political and commercial information.
American embassies had an attitude that if you hang out with the lo-
cals, you'll go native, [but] the type of information that Jack wanted
really came out of the souk, and out of the type of work that I did,
which was selling paper or planes or engineering. So I would get an-
swers and send them back. This caused me to have increasing respect
for the scope of his mind and intelligence. He became a hero to me."

A less powerful but equally glamorous new connection was the Duke of Windsor, who had assumed that title after abdicating his throne in 1936 in order to marry American commoner and divorcée Wallis Simpson. They were also then residents of Nassau, but Butler met them early in 1955 at their home in exile in Paris's Bois du Boulogne, thanks to C. Z. Guest, the wife of a polo champion and Butler family friend. Michael was staying with the Dominican diplomat and playboy polo player Porfirio Rubirosa when Guest called to ask if Butler would escort her to a dinner party at the Windsors' fourteen-room mansion. Though immediately bored by the Duke, he fell under the spell of the duchess and they became sufficiently close that he was rumored to be one of her lovers. That put him in the sights of gossip columnists, who introduced him to their readers as a new character in their chronicle of society, calling him her aide-de-camp and wingman, which made him highly sought-after in New York society, a status for which he was well prepared. The warm welcome and heated attention he received in New York seemed, for a time, to keep him from straying back into unconventional behavior.

That said, New York society allowed its initiates considerable leeway. When the Windsors visited Long Island, they stayed with Florence Baker, the widow of a prominent banker. Soon Butler was in a romance with Mrs. Baker's beautiful granddaughter, Fern Tailer Gimbel, who was divorcing her department-store-heir husband. When all concerned attended a party at the Bakers' for the Windsors, the duchess seemed inseparable from Butler because "she loved the fact that I was having an affair with Peter Gimbel's wife and she was becoming the beard to the whole thing." Unfortunately, that night ended in bloodshed when another guest, Ann Woodward, left the party and shot to death her husband, William Woodward Jr., in a murder that would fascinate society for decades. C. Z. Guest and Butler, standing under the house's porte cochere having cigarettes, were, according to Butler, the last two people to see the Woodwards before the murder.

Under cover of rumors of impending nuptials with the former Mrs. Gimbel that persisted into 1957, Butler was actually romancing Robin Boyer, a product of Philadelphia's Main Line and Vassar then studying art at Barnard College. He married the beautiful, vivacious blond daughter of the head of the pharmaceutical house Smith, Kline & French, in a Presbyterian church in September 1957. Their marriage "was a creation of her mother and my mother," Butler said. "They were best friends and they thought we should get married and put the pressure on for many years. What I should have done with Robin, who was an incredibly beautiful gal and a very lovely human being . . . we should have lived together a while, but instead we went into a very pretentious wedding in Philadelphia without really knowing what we were doing."

Though they started their connubial life in Turkey, Butler soon switched gears and began developing luxury real estate projects in New York and Vermont with Olivier Coquelin, a French expatriate he met on the island of Capri. Though their project was aimed at the elite, Butler and Robin moved to a bohemian apartment above P. J. Clarke's tavern on Third Avenue in midtown Manhattan, where they entertained the likes of King Hussein, who had become a friend when Butler worked on the Hejaz Railway, and Soraya Pahlevi, second wife and queen consort of the shah of Iran.

But there was a serious issue with Robin, though he didn't see it as a problem at the time. "The night we were married, I told her I was bisexual," Butler continued. "I felt out of respect I should tell her this." As a result, he added, his ex-wife "doesn't like me very much." That's quite true. "You don't do that," she agreed, still angry after sixty-five years. "How can you get to your honeymoon suite and say, 'Really, I'm gay'?"

Yet they stayed together for about two years, eventually moving into a grand duplex apartment with a double-height living room on East 57th Street, next door to Coquelin's home. But the two men's collaboration, the Islands in the Sun Club, crashed and burned even before Butler's marriage did. Its first project was Talisman, a private community of twenty-four homes, a marina, and a clubhouse, designed, Butler said in a 1958 interview, to "bring the *Social Register* to Fire Island," a New York barrier beach reachable only by boat or seaplane.[27] Their next project was Sugarbush, a resort in Vermont, where they optioned about two thousand acres and opened a members-only ski resort for a similar crowd, including Igor Cassini and his fashion designer brother Oleg, George Baker Jr., and Stavros Niarchos, the shipping tycoon. Butler and Coquelin hoped to build similar communities in the Bahamas, in the Balearic, Ionic, and Windward Islands, and on the Côte d'Azur. Butler would take a mid-six-figures loss when Talisman collapsed in 1964.* He and Coquelin had exited Sugarbush by then, too, and Butler's father refused a request for a bailout.

Life magazine would later spotlight Butler's ability to "turn assets into deficits." "I failed many times and it tore me to pieces," he told the magazine. "I lost a lot of money. I wasn't living up to what was expected of me."[28] He claimed the failure of Islands in the Sun broke up his marriage, and fifty years later his regret was still tangible. "I was so blown away, so embarrassed, so destroyed by this that I left New York," he said. "So that's the reason I left Robin. We broke up because of [my] being destroyed."

The breakup devastated Robin, too; she came home one day and Butler was gone. "You cannot walk out on someone and not say where you've gone," she recalled of her reaction to her husband having bolted. "It's one thing to say you're bisexual; he should have said that before. But you don't leave someone in a huge house with enormous bills. Why didn't he say, 'I'm in trouble'? I was a kid! You must be a very weak person to marry and then push off, leaving them with shit in their hands. Why was he so morally thin? He really undid me. It's second-rate."[29]

Fifty-five years later, Butler acknowledged and was still grieved by his behavior. "It was inexcusable. I did a terrible thing to her. But my world had come to an end." Unbeknownst to Robin, Michael had fled to Miami and then crept home to Oak Brook, where he would run the family's polo operations until *Hair* intervened.

It was left to gossip columnist Cholly Knickerbocker to announce that Michael and Robin had "agreed to disagree."[30] Though they made one last appearance together at the El Morocco nightclub in fall 1961, they shortly divorced. Told that Butler owned up to how badly he behaved, Robin said, "I'm pleased he has the spirit to acknowledge what he did." But she scoffed at a suggestion that his

---

* Talisman was taken over by the National Park Service and incorporated into its Fire Island National Seashore. Its buildings now house park rangers and a visitors' center.

upbringing might have been his undoing. "Oh, come on," she said. "Everyone's family is a bloody mess if you really delve into it."[31]

In the meantime, John Kennedy had run for president and won with a little help from Michael, who gave the candidate money and use of Butler Aviation planes and services during the campaign. But Kennedy's right-hand man, his brother Bobby, felt the Butlers didn't do enough, and let Butler know he was as disappointed in him as Butler's father was. His relationship with the president ended.

Like Hudson, Kennedy was irreplaceable, but Butler didn't wait long before finding a new wife. Loyce Stinson Hand had been a member of the Island in the Sun club—and, like Butler, came from a family of aviation buffs; they had founded an aircraft company in 1913. Butler's father objected to his marrying Loyce, who had just divorced her second husband, but that didn't stop him from becoming her third spouse and she his late in 1962, their wedding taking place in Paul Butler's home with only family and a few friends in attendance. Within a few months, Michael and Loyce settled into a nearby farmhouse, snug in his family's Oak Brook embrace.

Butler had finally begun playing polo himself, despite his crippled arm. His first game was his father's last—Paul Butler retired from active competition at seventy-two—and son replaced father on the Oak Brook team, playing alongside professionals. Polo immediately became "the major addiction of my life. It's a very difficult sport. It's a very dangerous sport. It's like dope. It's so demanding that you're just totally turned on. It's very addictive. Not only for me." Selling the *Coradina,* he seemed, briefly, to settle down, running the polo club for his father.

In mid-1963, Loyce announced she was pregnant. A son, Adam, was born in New York in January 1964. But Butler and his wife had separated just before their son was born, "based on her insecurity and her realization that I was bisexual," he said. Then, early in 1964, as the couple attempted to reconcile in Acapulco, the phone rang. Butler's former antagonist, Robert Kennedy, was calling. Though his brother had been assassinated a few months earlier, Kennedy was still attorney general of the United States. "We need some help in Illinois," he said. Otto Kerner Jr., the state's Democratic governor, was in a tough reelection battle against Charles Percy, a corporate executive. His feud with Kennedy over, Butler went to work for Kerner, and it was "another love affair, really," he said. "He'd been my father's commanding officer in the cavalry, so I put my producer's hat on to see what I could put together to improve his position," and Kerner won. Butler was rewarded with the title of commissioner of the Port of Chicago and posts running Kerner projects in sports and in cultural and economic development, as well as the Lincoln Academy, which honored Illinois achievers.

The breakup of Butler's third marriage was a slow-motion affair narrated, of course, by gossip columnists. In spring 1965, Cholly Knickerbocker's successor, Aileen Mehle, writing under the nom de plume Suzy Knickerbocker, reported that Loyce was "about to shake loose" from Butler "to try again with big three-time loser, burly Bruce Norris, the multi-millionaire. This is one of the great all-time stories," she teased, adding portentously, "Remind me to tell it to you."[32] She never did.

Five months later, the same column reported Butler fighting the divorce, Loyce seeking an annulment, and Butler threatening a $500,000 lawsuit against Norris, a much-married grain farmer and cattle rancher who had inherited the Detroit Red Wings ice hockey team. According to Suzy, "the big puzzle" was "why" Butler was resisting a divorce. Six days later, the details of his legal action were revealed in Chicago: it turned out to be a $2 million suit charging Norris with adultery in three states and on a yacht off Florida, and with alienation of affection. Loyce's initial response was succinct: "If I'm going to be auctioned off, I think I'm worth more than that."[33] A formal response followed in court charging that an "unscrupulous" Butler was engaging in "blackmail" for his "unjust enrichment." Butler said Loyce also threatened to expose an affair he claims he had with the young actress Catherine Deneuve.

In June 1965, a New York court granted Loyce an annulment, later gave her $200 a week to support their son, Adam, and sealed the paperwork to keep the grounds confidential, but the fighting would continue far longer than Loyce's affair with Norris, who married someone else in 1967. In January 1968, Butler sued Loyce for divorce, charging she had obtained the annulment through fraud. Two years later, he demanded the return of all his child support payments, while Loyce's lawyers insisted he had paid nothing for a year and demanded alimony. In 1971, Loyce showed up in court, tan, "with three strands of marble-sized pearls, and a two-strand gold choker" in a full-length mink coat to complain that Michael had stolen and ruined all her other fur coats and to beg for more money for their son, including $150 a month for water sports in Acapulco. Butler still won a divorce on grounds of desertion and reached a confidential settlement of all their disputes. Suzy Knickerbocker would have the last word on the matter a few days later when she revealed that Loyce, then staying with Paul Butler in Oak Brook, got $1.5 million "in money and property."[34] Butler's bisexuality remained a closely held secret.

But that wasn't the end of Loyce's marital disputes. Fifteen months later, she married Thomas Milbank, a much older man who was a descendant of the founders of both Borden, the dairy company, and the Milbank Tweed law firm, with eight-year-old Adam serving as best man—and Milbank bought Butler's Acapulco house in the bargain. A year later, he sued Loyce for divorce, charged that she had taken over their lavish apartment at 834 Fifth Avenue "by covert means," and claimed she was hiding $100,000 in securities from him. He would soon be bounced from the *Social Register* when it emerged that she had been his fourth wife, not his second, a disqualifying fact in the eyes of the arbiters at what was sometimes called society's "stud book."[35] Less than a year later, he died of a heart attack at age sixty, still married to Loyce. In Acapulco, where she remained on the social scene for years, it was said Milbank had died while hammering on her door, trying to serve her with divorce papers. She promptly demanded half of his $7 million estate, though he had disinherited her months earlier, adding a codicil to his will stating "that she has abandoned me."[36]

31

At the same time he was shedding his final wife, the ever busy Michael Butler launched a discothèque, Le Bison, in Chicago, and two new careers. One was a failure, the other an astonishing success that turned him from wealthy curiosity into international celebrity. His rapprochement with Bobby Kennedy and work for Governor Kerner led Butler to take a stab at politics; he hoped to one day follow Kerner into Illinois's governor's mansion in Springfield. But in 1966, he started small and ran for state senate, buying billboards that showed him lounging in a turtleneck sweater over the slogan "Michael Butler likes polo ponies. Parties. And Pop Art. Does that make him a bad guy?" But he also countered that image with campaign buttons reading, "We all have the same problems."[37] And a two-page ad in the *Chicago Tribune* said in part, "He's made, quite frankly, some mistakes. (What man hasn't?) But he's become wiser, deeper for them." However, the district surrounding Oak Brook was "notoriously Republican," he recalled, and though he lost, he could boast that he won more votes there than any Democrat ever had.

He then returned to New York and the entertainment business for the first time since leaving Robin. In 1965, he was one of the baker's dozen original investors in Ondine, a nightclub run by the fashion photographer Jerry Schatzberg and Olivier Coquelin. In 1970, Butler invested in another Coquelin club, Hippopotamus.

In the summer of 1967, Butler joined Governor Kerner in New York for meetings of a body formed after race riots swept America. Created by Lyndon Johnson, the National Advisory Commission on Civil Disorders, also called the Kerner Commission, had come to see John Lindsay, mayor of New York and the commission's vice chairman. Leafing through the *New York Times* while in the city, Butler spied an ad for an off-Broadway show called *Hair* at the New York Shakespeare Festival Public Theater, illustrated with a picture of three American Indians and two members of a more recent American tribe, hippies. "I did not notice that two of the braves were white-faced," said Butler. "They were the authors. But I thought, 'My God, the Indians have got a show together.' Indians were a major cause to me because of my grandfather's story." In the shadow of the Black Hills, F. O. Butler had told young Michael tales of the mistreatment of Native Americans. Theirs was, he said, a cause that engaged him.

Together with Coquelin and Nancy Friday, a young journalist he hired to edit a magazine for Islands in the Sun, he saw a preview— and discovered the play was not about Indians, "but the strongest anti-war statement going," an early indicator of rising anger among the young over America's increasingly controversial involvement in the war in Vietnam.

Butler had already decided to run for the U.S. Senate in Illinois and said he had the backing of both Kerner and Chicago's all-powerful Democratic mayor, Richard Daley. He saw *Hair* as a way to refine his message and make opposition to the war central to his campaign. Then the show took over his life and politics fell by the wayside. "I called the governor and mayor and told them I was not going to run for the Senate," Butler later said. "They thought I was absolutely crazy, they really did." A few years later, Senator Charles Percy told Butler, "You made the best decision of your life when you decided to do *Hair* instead."[38]

Roger Stevens introduced Butler to *Hair* producer Joseph Papp, and Butler talked him into giving it a second production late in 1967 at Coquelin's latest discothèque, Cheetah. Afterward Papp wanted to move on, so Butler raised $225,000, including $90,000 in family money and more from Tommy Smothers of the Smothers Brothers, and Rebecca Harkness, an arts patron married to a Standard Oil heir, to buy the rights. He hired Tom O'Horgan to rework the show, which he felt was more "a put-down, rather than a put-on," removing three songs and adding a dozen more, as well as an unprecedented nude scene staged in semi-darkness that became both a provocation and a promotional bonanza, and a happy ending, all in service of what he had come to think of as his creed: "If you're not living on the edge, you're taking up too much room."[39] He even stripped down and appeared in the nude scene a few times himself, albeit at the back of the throng onstage. Papp disapproved. Butler didn't care.

Though he eventually fought with the musical's authors, James Rado and Gerome Ragni, and briefly fired them, *Hair* gave Butler the chance to outdo his father on the world stage of Broadway and introduced him to a new world—the counterculture.[40] He threw himself into it with a fervor he had previously only felt for polo. He wasn't the only haute WASP in hippiedom, but he became one of its most prominent acolytes.

In February 1968, he was in Palm Beach, his old milieu, "sputtering up and down [Worth] Avenue on his motorbike," wrote Suzy.[41]

By April, he had grown his own hair long, sported a drooping walrus mustache, and was dressing like the cast of the musical—though, of course, his leather jackets came from pricey designer boutiques, and his "love beads" consisted of a coral necklace with a mother-of-pearl Islamic star and crescent (a gift from Jordan's King Hussein), a medieval Crusader's medallion (a gift from the shah of Iran), and a simpler chain he got from the maharaja of Jaipur. He was already familiar with other accoutrements of the era. "I did smoke marijuana," he said, "but I was in a totally different lifestyle than hippies. It changed my life. It withdrew me from a great number of my friends. I was so involved I didn't have time for anything else."

At first his father helped him, pulling strings on Broadway so Michael could book a theater, but then, typically, on opening night he demanded back his investment in the production.[42] "He sent his hatchet man with orders to sell his interest," Michael said, but he waited until *Hair* was a huge success to buy out his father's share.[43] He no doubt glowed with pride when Roger Stevens rebuked Paul Butler: "You made a mistake on this one, didn't you?" he said.

His son finally earned financial independence, making an estimated $10 million, but then squandered it almost as quickly on an entourage with whom he shared private planes, parties, and a 1936 Rolls-Royce. He also tried to leverage his one success. While *Hair* would play on Broadway for years, Butler only succeeded in generating fizzles and failures with other productions: rock musicals (*Frankenstein, Boris Gudonov, Reggae*), a five-film production deal (*You Are What You Eat* was the first and only one actually made), a record deal, managing a rock band, a magazine, fashion lines, a "*Hair* and horses" development called Shangri-La in Ojai, California, an entertainment complex in partnership with United Artists Theaters, and boutiques and restaurants. His sister, Jorie, took over operating Oak Brook, even as *Life* magazine profiled Michael as Paul Butler's heir apparent.

In public, Butler demonstrated a convert's passion: he championed drug use, anti-materialism, and the hippies, and echoed their rudimentary philosophy. "The hippies ask searching questions," he said to the *Los Angeles Times*, "like, 'If the tenets of the American Revolution are beautiful, why don't we follow them? If we're all created equal, why are some of us more equal than others?'"[44] His public battles mirrored private conflicts: "You know, there's a frightening thing happening in this country," he observed to *Newsday.* "There's an estrangement between the younger and older generations."[45]

Propelled by hit songs derived from the score of *Hair,* "Aquarius/Let the Sunshine In" by the 5th Dimension, "Good Morning, Starshine" by Oliver, and the title track by the Cowsills, *Hair*'s success made Butler, at forty-two, an unlikely and inconsistent spokesman for the trending cult of youth and its heartfelt if often muddled revolt against the American establishment. Though he never carried a wallet and spoke of "questioning all the establishment values and . . . rejecting all the hypocrisies," Butler still got his own hair cut at the posh Kenneth salon in the Waldorf-Astoria Hotel, drove around New York in his Rolls, and enjoyed the family properties in Montana, outside Palm Beach, and in Oak Brook, where paintings by Van Dyck, Tintoretto, and Gainsborough hung on the walls.

"I know too many rich people—including members of my own family—who don't have an easy time of it when they look in the mirror," he whined to *Life.* "I love a good life, but it hasn't been that much fun being rich."[46] And getting rich on his own proved less than satisfying. "The Protestant ethic doesn't work," he pronounced. "Making money is not the purpose of my existence. It's the badge you get, the carrot after you've galloped a good course. The purpose is accomplishment. . . . [Money] should be used to make more money or to have fun."[47]

Fun he had, his losses and protests notwithstanding. He also kept up his promiscuous pursuit of women, even though, like his father before him, he had finally soured on marriage. One weekend when he "was taking the tribe to Fire Island," including a Black cast member in *Hair* whom he was dating, he shared a car to the ferry with a fashion photographer and a girl he'd brought along, Minnie Cushing, then the wife of another photographer and heir to great wealth, Peter Beard, great-grandson of a railroad founder and business ally of Pierpont Morgan.

Beard had met Minnie on safari in Africa, and they lived in Kenya, but their marriage was brief and troubled, and when Michael met Minnie, "I fell in love for the first time in my life," he said. Before his death in 2020, the outspoken Beard recalled that Michael Butler caused "huge difficulty" with his wife. Their dalliance was significant enough to lead a Suzy social column early in 1969. And despite Beard's disdain, Minnie and Michael were "on and off for years," Butler said. In 1985, when Beard was arrested and jailed for beating a poacher on his Kenyan ranch, Butler even came to Beard's rescue and helped free him, at Minnie's request.

"I'm still in love with her," he said, "since I first set eyes on her."

Butler and his father were on and off, too. In 1969, Michael expanded *Hair*'s reach with touring companies, and let his father, who had seen the light, "put all the money up for the Chicago production" that opened that October. He felt liberated, independent, yet still bent his knee to the reigning lord of Oak Brook. "I pledge my fealty to him as a free man—and he knows it," Butler would soon say. "I walk always a little behind him. When he comes into a room, I always get out of my chair."[48]

He decided to buck Broadway's standard operating procedures and brought the show to other cities quickly, "taking business from New York, because I wanted to get the story out as far as possible. I was totally at home with what I was doing and why. I believed . . . that *Hair* was a gift from God." Thirty different road companies would bring the show to twenty-plus countries, where it would be seen by some twelve million people by 1972. Butler often accompanied them.

A favorite stop was England, where Butler played polo in the summer and *Hair* was more popular than in New York, playing 1,997 performances through summer 1973, as opposed to its 1,742-show run in New York. In 1971, Helen Lawrenson, an editor and writer for chic magazines, visited Butler at an estate he rented in Ascot to write a profile for *Esquire*. She was driven in one of two 1939 Bentleys Butler had added to his automotive collection, and the car deposited her at the estate, with its twelve-bedroom mansion, polo field, tennis court, pool, and vast acreage, which Butler used to house his "tribe" of fifteen-plus camp followers—an entourage that included several secretaries, a diet and exercise counselor, a cook, a chauffeur, three polo teammates, a groom, a veterinarian, and a new girlfriend, "Boo Brassey, English, with short, straight, black hair and bangs, narrow black eyes, and an odd little catlike face," wrote Lawrenson.[49]

"This is the Inner Tribe," Butler told her. "I am the chief." He added, "It's sort of a tribal camping ground here. Not anybody can come, but damn near." He did not mean the WASP tribe into which he had been born. Asked whom he admired, he cited Winston Churchill, William Randolph Hearst, and Genghis Khan. "I admire achievement in any field," he said. "It has nothing to do with content or moral judgment. . . . I'm interested in power. . . . My trip is a power trip. . . . It's a heavy trip."

Lawrenson noted a post-*Hair* success: the Broadway play *Lenny*, about the comedian Lenny Bruce. "I don't deserve any credit except for putting up the money," Butler said. "I haven't seen the show; I didn't read the script." She catalogued ventures simmering in Butler's pot, including a movie set in Morocco, and revealed his plan "to go into politics in a heavy way . . . in a behind-the-scenes role."

He had sold some paintings and his New York duplex during his divorce from Loyce but returned to the landed class when he bought Warfield Hall, a historic country house on 150 acres in Berkshire, England, and flew eighteen polo ponies and eight grooms there in a chartered Boeing 707, with seven more horses following by ship, to compete at Windsor Great Park for the prestigious Queen's Cup. "They didn't win," Lawrenson added, noting that his loss was witnessed by the Queen of England, her consort, Prince Philip, and their son Charles, both of whom would remain Butler polo pals long after he abandoned Berkshire.

⌒

As Michael established his own, separate identity, Paul Butler turned to his daughter, Jorie, the closest of the children to their father. In 1963, he started selling off his businesses in order to focus on Oak Brook, and he had rid himself of them by 1967. Jorie Butler had been comptroller of the aviation company and executive vice president of the parent Butler Companies, and was as promiscuous in marriage as her father and older brother. "In those days, nice girls were supposed to get married," said novelist Sugar Rautbord, a Chicago social figure and friend of Jorie's. "She took it to the limit. She's an over-achiever."[50]

Jorie's first husband, Edward Shober Jr., was from a family of well-born Pennsylvanians that included a governor, a general, and the founder of the Wharton School of Business. An equestrian, of course, he was an infantry lieutenant, and became a newsprint exporter after their 1951 marriage at St. Bartholomew's Episcopal Church. By the end of the decade, she was on her second husband, Messmore Kendall Jr., son of a lawyer, entrepreneur, movie theater owner, and Broadway producer of plays by Somerset Maugham, who was president of the National Society of the Sons of the American Revolution and a noted collector of George Washington memorabilia. Messmore Sr. died the day they wed.

Her third husband, Henry F. Richardson, was a widower and longtime mayor of Northport, on Long Island. Michael Butler hosted their wedding party at Oak Brook in 1965, and the newlyweds lived in a farmhouse there, but within a year, Jorie and Henry would divorce and she would take back her maiden name. Five years later, Jorie was painting portraits of polo players on china plates she sold as part of what she described as "a whole new trend" of wealthy women taking on creative work for profit.[51] In 1972, the polo club, briefly closed after a fire, was being rebuilt to accommodate a clubhouse for the new Butler National Golf Course. It reopened that fall, in time for Michael to return with his polo ponies and compete against a British team that included Major Ronald Ferguson, whose daughter Sarah would marry Britain's Prince Andrew and become the Duchess of York.

By then, Jorie had gone into business with Geoffrey Kent, a former British guards officer, who would become her fourth husband. In the mid-1970s, as the last of Butler's Oak Brook land was developed and control began to shift to its residents, Jorie split her time between Oak Brook, where she ran the Sports Core; Sun Ranch, her twenty-four-thousand-acre cattle and horse operation in Montana; Sun South, a subsidiary horse-training farm and estate in Lake Worth, Florida, near the Palm Beach Polo and Country Club; and Kenya, where she ran a photo safari business for her soon-to-be husband's family business, Abercrombie & Kent, providing luxe travel services to clients with names like Rockefeller, Firestone, and Butler. "If Ayn Rand had been interested in Polo," a Chicago columnist wrote, "she would have invented Jorie Ford Butler."[52]

In 1972, Jorie bought Geoffrey Kent's parents out of Abercrombie & Kent, and she married him in 1979, just as British Airways granted Abercrombie & Kent exclusive rights to its African holiday packages and the business exploded. They proved to be a good team. By 2003, A&K would own cruise boats, sailboats and yachts, trains, and safari camps and lodges, and have exclusive rights to some of Africa's best game-viewing camps and the sort of staffed, private villas that rented for upward of $25,000 a week. Its forty offices and three thousand employees arranged both prepackaged and customized trips to about a hundred countries for clients like Bill Gates, Warren Buffett, Henry Kissinger, and Barbra Streisand. In 2003, the company was valued at $375 million by the *Sunday Times* of London, which ranked Geoffrey Kent no. 133 on its annual list of the richest Britons.[53]

～

Jorie and Michael's brother Frank was quite another story, though he, too, had unfortunate romantic adventures. Frank Osgood "Boo" Butler II was at an extreme disadvantage in an equestrian family: he was allergic to horses, a discovery he made at age eighteen while attending bullfights in Spain in between high school at Michael's alma mater, Culver, and the Virginia Military Institute. In 1957, he was working with Jorie running Butler Aviation in Palm Beach when he married Gloria Franceschini, a Stanford graduate. The marriage ended six months later amid reports that his estranged wife "kept a diary" that threatened "a rash of headlines even more irritating to the clan" than Norman's simultaneous bust-up with Penelope Dewar in London.[54]

Frank moved to Portugal, where he was a real estate developer. Then, in 1964, simultaneous with Jorie Butler's latest engagement, Suzy reported Frank's plan to marry again, to a descendant of a signer of the Declaration of Independence. No wedding followed; instead, he moved to Aspen, Colorado, where he worked in real estate again until a 1980s return to Palm Beach.

Frank was gay, said Michael, who had a troubled relationship with his brother. They shared a summer on a yacht in the Mediterranean one year when Michael decided Frank was ambivalent about his sexuality, and blamed their father, whose disapproval of Frank was tangible. "Father would really put Frank down. They had a love-hate relationship. My mother would manipulate him. She'd say to his face, 'I love you,' and then anytime he'd try to do anything, she'd put him down." A skier, Frank once got the chance to buy a ski school in Aspen, and Michael not only encouraged him but asked their father to subsidize the purchase. "He wouldn't do it." On another occasion, when Frank tried to become a New York realtor, his mother told him it was a good idea, but then told their father, who said, "I don't want him to do that." Paul was proud, however, that Frank had worked on communications for the Eisenhower-Nixon presidential ticket in the 1950s.

In 1970, Frank, then forty-two, was captured by *Women's Wear Daily,* the catty fashion trade newspaper, "surrounded by the high school set" at the Oak Brook Bath and Tennis Club, "with a teenage boy he says is his godson and assistant and his equally young girlfriend in tow." Contradicting a report that he "really doesn't do anything," Butler told the newspaper he was busy customizing a "Butler blue" Corvette Stingray with a laser and a smokescreen, and then described his five Portuguese tailors and the shaved raccoon maxi-coat Christian Dior was making for him. "I wanted mink, but I decided I was too old," he said. From Oak Brook, the paper reported, "Frank flits . . . to Palm Beach and Portugal," swimming, skydiving, collecting expensive cars, and fiddling with electronics. His political views differed markedly from his brothers'. "*Social Register* society—the conservative society—is the only thing that's holding America together," he told *Women's Wear Daily,* that "godson" by his side.[55]

❧

As Frank Butler cavorted with teenage boys in Ohio, his brother Michael flitted, too, in his case between England, Ireland (where another real estate deal proved a fantasy), Paris (where he dated Brigitte Bardot), a house in Los Angeles with sweeping views above Sunset Boulevard (where he met and befriended Mick Jagger when the Rolling

Stones borrowed it before Butler even moved in; Butler was trying to get a film of *Hair* off the ground), and Santa Barbara (where he hoped to buy and expand the local polo club). Once again, though, his reach exceeded his grasp. The *Hair* film was delayed because Rado and Ragni still controlled the rights and "were using a tarot card reader to decide who would do the film," Butler said. "So, I made a deal and I bought them out" for a million dollars, which he had to borrow.

Butler signed with Paramount and brought on a hot director, Hal Ashby, to develop the movie, but Ashby had a bad cocaine habit, and after a regime change at Paramount, the deal died, only to be revived by the producer and rock music impresario Robert Stigwood, who was making the disco musical *Saturday Night Fever* at the time. But Stigwood "had a drinking problem," said Butler, and handed the project to another producer, who sold it to United Artists, hired Milos Forman to direct, and developed a script Butler didn't like. Neither did he like the way United Artists marketed the resulting film, released in 1979, long enough after the original to seem dated, but far too early to have nostalgic appeal. It didn't perform well, making only $15 million, barely covering its $11 million budget. It was a huge financial setback for Butler, who needed the film to succeed, in part because a Broadway revival of the musical had flopped, closing in only a month in fall 1977, and his musical *Reggae* was having trouble finding backers. He sold his Los Angeles house to the director John Schlesinger (it would later belong to Richard Gere and Cindy Crawford) and offloaded his spread in Santa Barbara, too.

In 1978, at fifty-one, Butler was back in Oak Brook, anticipating the opening of the *Hair* film and the eventual theatrical debut of *Reggae*, too. "Deep in my heart, I know I'm a winner," he told the *Chicago Tribune*.[56] But *Reggae* would close after twenty-one performances in spring 1980.

32

In late June 1981, a day after his eighty-ninth birthday, Paul Butler was standing in front of his home in Oak Brook taking night photographs when he was mowed down and killed by a passing motorist under the influence. The accident would set off a dozen years of legal and familial strife, end the Butlers' reign in Oak Brook, and drive Michael Butler into bankruptcy.

At the time, Paul's estate was estimated at between $50 million and $125 million. Those figures would prove to be wildly inflated. Paul's will divided his holdings equally among Jorie, Frank, and Michael, and named them co-executors. However, the estate no longer owned some of the properties in the various bequests, and an assessment was required before an equal division could be made. They quickly paid Norman the $250,000 Paul left him, "to have our hands washed of him," they said in a deposition.[57] Then the arguments began.

According to Michael, Jorie refused to help with the estate, preferring to remain at the successful Abercrombie & Kent. Frank was the wrong man for the job. So Michael became president of what remained of the Butler Company, which amounted to 225 remaining undeveloped acres. But he claims he made money, and he certainly kept living large; in 1983, he hired twenty-one identical white Cadillac Seville sedans to drive around Chicago and confuse anyone trying to track the movements of Mick Jagger, girlfriend Jerry Hall, and director Donald Cammell as they visited Oak Brook to discuss a movie they would never make. But despite his roots there, the village of Oak Brook considered Michael an outsider and turned his life into "a series of frustrations, trying to sort through fact and fantasy about the founder's relationships with the village," Michael told the *Chicago Tribune*.[58]

Later that year, after Butler failed to make a land swap with Oak Brook so he could build an office and shopping complex, and refused an offer for the land he still controlled, the village sued to condemn and take it. Two years after that, he and Jorie formed a joint venture with the retailer Carson Pirie Scott to develop a grand, multiuse project there, including retail (which Oak Brook lacked), offices, a resort, entertainment and sports facilities, and a convention center, but McDonald's, which had once owned the land and swapped it to Paul for its Hamburger University property, sued, claiming that delays in developing it gave it the right to buy the land back.

Meanwhile, the Butler siblings had gone to war with each other. Michael filed an action in probate court to oust Frank and Jorie from their roles as co-administrators of their father's estate, claiming they had mismanaged it and taken illegal payments from the Butler Company. They countersued. A settlement was reached, but it promptly unraveled after Frank objected, with the judge commenting tartly that they couldn't "even agree on the time of day."[59] Adding insult to the familial insanity, Oak Brook rejected a proposal to rename a street after its founder. And a judge ordered Michael to move his home, which sat on the disputed tract of land. "Today," the *Chicago Tribune* concluded, instead of an "oligarchy of civility," the Butlers had become "synonymous with litigation."[60]

In summer 1986, the Butlers announced they had reached another settlement. "Jorie and I finally decided that we couldn't work with Frank," said Michael, and decided to pay their brother off after they won their battle over the threatened condemnation and a judgment of $17 million. Finally able to develop a small shopping center for the village on that land, they "decided we'd pay Frank more than his share and do it ourselves." Frank may have been pleased, but their mother wasn't, and issued a statement praising him and blaming Jorie and Michael for the estate's problems. Michael cut Frank off forever. He and Jorie wouldn't speak again for about twenty-five years. The shopping center would never be built.

For a while the good times at Oak Brook continued, regardless. Prince Charles, who played polo in Palm Beach in 1980, returned with his new wife, Diana, Princess of Wales, in 1985 and stayed with the Kents, who owned a ranch in a nearby town, where they kept dozens of ponies. The royals visited Oak Brook at the end of summer 1986 to play a chukker of polo and attend Butler's annual ball. In 1988, *Hair* was again revived in Chicago. Michael had, in the meantime, moved into his father's house in Oak Brook after the land under his was sold, moving his eclectic belongings with him—Moroccan saddlebags, Mexican church doors, an Apache peyote fan, an Indian war bonnet, old Vuitton trunks, a Van Dyck portrait, a Delacroix study, and a Tintoretto painting—with him. And he kept giving interviews as the elder statesman of the Age of Aquarius. But a crisis of insolvent savings and loan associations was rolling across America and would shortly knock him down for good.

~

Frank Butler had problems of his own. He was living in Palm Beach at La Claridad, a villa his father had bought and split into two separate homes in the 1940s. He filled its four-story foyer with a floor-to-ceiling Christmas tree each year, above the basement Frank sometimes referred to as his dungeon, which featured a heavy, medieval-style portcullis he designed. "It was a joke," said a female friend. "He showed it to everyone," feeding the tales of his outré sex life, well known to many in the posh resort. "He was a dark and dirty character," one neighbor said. "A roaring queen," said his niece Reute Butler, in a brief interview. "It was no secret," said the woman friend. "He liked to be outrageous. He liked young men. He never denied it. I said, 'I do, too.'" But business was more problematic for him than fulfilling his sexual desires was. In 1981, in a deal initiated by his father just before his death, Frank, Dan Walker, a former governor of Illinois, and Walker's wife, a management expert, started a company to operate quick-oil-change garages around Chicago, which they sold to Jiffy Lube four years later, retaining five of them as franchisees.

Many of the garages sat on land belonging to a Walker-owned savings and loan association in Oak Brook, which was declared insolvent and seized by federal regulators in 1986. They soon charged that the S&L's loans to the oil-change shops had been "unsafe and unsound," and the next year Walker pleaded guilty on charges of receiving improper loans and spending some of his ill-gotten gains on personal expenses, including an $850,000, eighty-foot yacht he called the *Governor's Lady*.[61]

The partnership ended in mutual recrimination, with Butler accusing Walker of misappropriating business funds and Walker describing, "in some detail, the personal and social style of Frank Butler, which, he claims, didn't help business any," according to a Chicago newspaper.[62] Walker ended up in jail.

Frank wasn't implicated, but he continued to trip over his own shoelaces. In 1988, he gave an indiscreet interview to a British society magazine covering Palm Beach. Described, dubiously, as the fourteenth richest man in America, Frank was quoted disparaging the "café people and a lot of kikes, very rich people, but not in the real world," who had lately invaded the resort town.[63] A year later, he made a deal with his siblings to sell them his share of the parcel Oak Brook had tried to condemn. When they failed to secure sufficient financing and backed out, he sued them, and they countersued, claiming he sabotaged them.

By the time a judge ruled that they were required to buy Frank out, it was too late; his victory was pyrrhic, as the property had been foreclosed two months earlier and his share was worthless.[64] And then in 2006, at age seventy-eight, he was sued in Palm Beach by a twenty-two-year-old man from Oak Brook who alleged that Butler, described as his godfather and an "ever-present figure" in his childhood, had sexually molested him.[65] Butler denied it, and this latest godson's case was dropped two years later.

Shortly afterward Frank and Jorie briefly reconciled after he fell and broke his thigh. A few years later, Frank was suffering from cancer when Glorvina Schwartz, a Palm Beach neighbor, accompanied him on a Ugandan safari, arranged by Jorie after Schwartz encouraged Frank to again put their differences aside. "I was one of his harem; he collected single women who adored him," she said. They had met in 1952, when she was seventeen and briefly engaged to Michael Butler before his marriage to Robin. A friendship with Frank resulted. "We were like brother and sister," she said. Frank was "very spoiled and knew how to spoil himself. He had to have the best of everything and be treated as if he was a king, and he had a very high opinion of himself." On that trip to Africa, when he said he felt too weak to join Schwartz on a walk through the jungle to see gorillas, "Jorie had a chair strapped to a platform and four very strong young men carried him like a maharaja."

"He was charming, fun, polite, and a very bad boy," a friend of his observed. "But he was a pedophile, too. I had a problem with that. The whole town knew."[66]

⌐

Jorie appeared to be the most successful Butler sibling at the turn of the millennium, still a Palm Beach social leader and, with husband

Geoffrey Kent, running Abercrombie & Kent, the bespoke travel service. In 1982, she had launched a philanthropic venture for the brand that became deeply involved in conservation; community assistance in health, education, ecology, and the protection of endangered species; rescue efforts after natural disasters; and providing seed money for schools, orphanages, and hospitals in Asia, Africa, the Middle East, South America, and New Zealand.

But appearances can deceive. In 1988, Geoffrey Kent found a girl-friend via an ad in the *International Herald Tribune* in which she called herself a dead ringer for the actress Victoria Principal and offered herself up as an escort. Kent, who brought her with him when he traveled and installed her in rented apartments while he stayed with Jorie in luxury hotels, would describe himself as the luckiest man in the world. "I have two wives," he'd say. "One indoor and one outdoor."

Then, in August 2002, London's *Daily Mail* revealed that Kent had dyed his hair "a strange orange colour," left his wife, and taken up with a much younger Egyptian woman, a former beauty queen, the niece of the governor of Cairo, and editor of a travel magazine. She denied the *Mail*'s report, but he had left both Jorie and his mistress simultaneously. Even after they sold two-thirds of their travel company to a resort operator, he and Jorie stayed business partners, with each holding 16.5 percent of the business. Jorie would remain a director of Abercrombie & Kent until 2016, and retained that position at Abercrombie & Kent Philanthropy as recently as 2021.

If the American aristocracy was in decline, the Butlers had become its exemplar. In fall 1990, Michael, sixty-four, filed for protection from creditors under Chapter 11 of the federal bankruptcy code, listing unsecured debts of more than $4 million against assets of just over $7 million, most of it in illiquid real estate—a fraction of the $33 million or more many assumed he had inherited from his father. He also announced plans to take the Butler polo company into Chapter 7 liquidation. The real estate market was suffering one of its cyclical downturns; the developments they had managed to finish were burdened with debt; Butler had been subsidizing Oak Brook's money-losing polo operations out of his own pocket, and its revenues had been decimated by rainy weather that summer; his latest *Hair* revival had been a flop; and as a family intimate put it, the fights among the Butler siblings had ensured that "attorneys walked away with the family fortune." It emerged that the three siblings had been left only about $300,000 each when their father's estate was finally distributed.

Frank Butler, who would soon file claims totaling $6.3 million for his interest in shared assets, described it as "terribly embarrassing" that it had taken Michael "nine years to do everything wrong." Michael acknowledged his failure as a financial steward but still blamed his father for failing to follow the family tradition of financially supporting his children and for selling off the Butler companies and putting all his eggs in his ego-driven Oak Brook basket. "It was a mess," Michael said of what followed. "I won the fight and lost the war." About the schadenfreude that accompanied his surrender to reality, Butler acknowledged in 1990, "I have never stinted in having a good time. But a lot of people in Chicago, where the Puritan ethic is strong, don't understand."[67] Ancient expectations still held sway for some.

Still living in the family homestead and driving a Range Rover, Michael Butler admitted friends were helping him financially. He tried several maneuvers to survive, including bidding to lease back the polo field and presenting a plan to swap stock with his sister in an attempt to recover still-undeveloped Oak Brook land. But after Frank and the bank holding an eight-figure mortgage on the property objected, Michael was forced to move out of his house and into an adjoining cottage, liquidate his assets, and make partial payment to his creditors via an auction sale in June 1991. Among the lots were framed photographs of Mick Jagger, vinyl LPs by Bob Marley and the Wailers, signed *Hair* posters, paintings now "attributed to" Van Dyck and Tintoretto, a table "probably" designed by Mies van der Rohe, his Indian headdress, and a wedding portrait of him and Robin. "It's strange, like facing surgery," he said at the time.[68]

Frank and Marjorie Childress (his, Jorie, and Michael's mother) arrived at the auction in a Rolls-Royce.[69]

~~~~

A year later, Michael Butler would be reduced to selling options on the Chicago Mercantile Exchange and trying to launch a new polo club in a vacant lot in downtown Chicago. A year after that, at a dinner dance at his sister's latest home in Lake Worth, Florida, he admitted to a *New York Times* reporter that he was broke.[70] But he still hadn't hit bottom; that came when Oak Brook more than doubled his rent and he chose to move into an apartment in Chicago, where he claimed he felt liberated and, at sixty-nine, sought to reinvent himself yet again as a rainmaker, helping his many acquaintances make deals. He produced another musical, *Pope Joan,* in a local theater in 1996, but it wasn't well received, and he flinched at "the ugliness of the criticism, the personal attacks."[71]

In about 2016, he moved to the San Fernando Valley, north of Los Angeles, to live with his son, Adam, and his wife and child, while Adam managed what little was left of his share of the family fortune. Frank Butler died of cancer in 2014, after his own financial reverses caused him to sell off his Rolls and Palm Beach mansion. In a death notice, sister Jorie, the only sibling who was still wealthy, called Frank "an American aristocrat."[72]

Suffering from neuropathy, macular degeneration, and circulation problems, Michael Butler was still managing, as late as 2019, to go to Polo Association meetings, a memorial for Tyrone Power, and long visits to a polo pal in Hawaii, and he owned a production company, albeit one without active projects, and an eponymous website, last updated in 2016, featuring his recollections, personal photos, and memorabilia, and observations on subjects from politics to nutrition.

Butler was far happier revisiting his past than he was considering the present or future, "because the biggest problems are beyond us. Beyond anybody," he said in 2019, ticking off a litany of vexations—climate change, overpopulation, "billionaires and millionaires coming out the ears," and the degradation of manners and morals—that worry many senior citizens, not just aging WASPs in diminished circumstances. By mid-2022, he had moved to a nursing home in Reseda, outside Los Angeles, called the Jewish Home. "It's the best place to be," he said, a few months before he died there in November 2022.

"Failure, then, is the WASP's epitaph," Michael Knox Beran wrote in *WASPs,* his mournful 2021 study of, and the latest literary death knell for, the cohort.[73] But white Christian Americans have not just a past but a present and a future, and while they have all presumably had their fair share of failure, they have also, to channel Butler's *Hair,* found ways to let the sun shine in on the twilight of what the political columnist Joseph Alsop once called the WASP Ascendancy.

Part Ten

✐

ADAPTATION

Today

33

It is unfair, even dangerous, to generalize. All WASPs are not alike. Most are not from wealthy and established elite clans like those featured in the preceding pages. Yet many, if not all, look at those families as role models, exemplars to be either honored and emulated or, in some cases, rejected as the sort of reprobates Calvinists might have assigned to damnation. Neither is it always clear who deserves celebration and who condemnation. Honor is only determined in the heart of each observer.

Living members of the Bradford and Whitney, Morris and Rutherfurd, Cass, Biddle, Sanford, Peabody, and Osborn families may have more in common than their names and legacies, but they are also individuals, too numerous, too distinct to be summed up simply. Living family members who have made a mark on the world have developed three general approaches to managing their WASP inheritance (short of crime or suicide). Michael Butler embodied each at different times of his life, which may be part of what makes him so fascinating, whether one liked him or not.

One method of coping is self-indulgence: wallowing in one's advantages, seeking fun and frivolity, and applying the principle of compound interest to life. As Benjamin Franklin once wrote, "Money makes money and the money that money makes more money." It also greases the path to more possessions and more experience. Unless, like Michael Butler, you fritter away your principal and find yourself left with nothing but your family and yourself. But the notion that a WASP Descendancy, personified by Butler in his later years, has inevitably and irreversibly followed the clan's ascent is also worthy of critical examination.

Another approach is escape, an alluring choice for those who can't cope with the responsibilities of inheritance. In the twentieth century, drinking, drugs, and sex were often means to that end. The quest for self-actualization could be an isolating intoxicant, too.

Engagement is a third way forward, and WASPs in the forefront use their financial, intellectual, and spiritual resources to do good, face the future, or just reach for relevance, like Michael Butler did with *Hair*.

On younger branches of the WASP family tree, the challenge has been living up to a name and, rich or not, doing more than resting on the soft pillow of inheritance. Some have sought to meet the expectations imposed by generations of family history, a few by leveraging their advantages to keep trying to better the world; others have chosen pragmatism, eccentricity, libertinism. In the present day, particularly the late twentieth and early twenty-first centuries, members of the families in the preceding pages have taken all three paths—self-indulgence, escape, and engagement—into the future, sometimes staying on one, sometimes changing direction. Not surprisingly, the results have varied.

Bokara "Bobo" Legendre, Henry Shelton Sanford's great-granddaughter, once called herself a "stiff upper lip WASP," in what was described as a "splendid whiskey voice" full of "money and breeding."[1] She certainly experienced adversity: she was ignored by a pampered, entitled mother. But stiff as Bobo's top lip might have been, it reflected neither self-restraint nor stoicism. She and her mother both inherited Henry Sanford's knack for frittering away opportunity.

Bobo's grandmother, Henry's daughter Ethel, married a second cousin, John, from the moneymaking carpet-factory side of the family. John's father, Stephen Stanford, bred racehorses, and John was among America's first polo players. John and Ethel had three children: Stephen or "Laddie," who'd become a polo champion; Jane; and another Gertrude, called Gertie, who would become

Bobo's mother. When Gertie was eleven in 1913, their father inherited $40 million, and after World War I he moved his family into a mansion on Manhattan's East 72nd Street. Gertie and Jane were chauffeured around in a Rolls-Royce by their own driver, and the family's butler, "a perfectly cheerful Jeeves," would buy theater tickets daily, just in case anyone in the family was so inclined.[2]

"I knew that I wasn't going to be like most girls," Gertie later wrote in a memoir.[3] She discovered hunting at twelve. At eighteen, in 1920, after coming out at a debutante party, she headed to the Grand Tetons in sheepskin chaps, lumberjack shirt, and a ten-gallon Stetson cowboy hat, where she shot an elk through the heart, which "filled [her] with pride."[4] In 1927, Gertie and Laddie were invited on an African safari where they shot zebras for fur coats, three lions, and a rhino, then went on to Uganda to hunt elephant. She would later rationalize the carnage by killing only for museums, Fairfield Osborn's American Museum of Natural History among them.

In summer 1928, the Sanfords rented another mansion in London, where Morris and Sidney Legendre, former Princeton football players from New Orleans, were their guests. Tall and athletic, they had been raised by their sister Katharine Legendre Biddle. The Legendres had once been French émigrés to Saint-Domingue, today's Haiti, and later, after slave revolts began there in 1791, joined a mass exodus to New Orleans when Louisiana was still a French colony. Among the Creole refugees "who brought a well-developed taste for luxury" was Georges Legendre, a coffee plantation owner, and his brother Emile, a merchant.[5] Emile is said to have had fifteen children with three families; he had a Caucasian wife and both a white mistress and one of color.

The last, Marie Laveau, gave the family a special notoriety. Multiple accounts name her and her mother, also Marie, as successive reigning voodoo queens of New Orleans, practitioners of a religion of the African diaspora that evolved in Haiti and then Louisiana. Voodoo queens were celebrities who used secret rituals and sex to manipulate lovers and punish enemies.[6] Their family ties to voodoo gave the handsome Legendre brothers a provocative edge. Gertie was smitten.

That summer in Europe, Janie and Gertie went on to visit the wealthy expatriates Gerald and Sara Murphy at Antibes, France.

"There was a lot of posing and posturing among the social set. I never thought of myself as one of them," Gertie observed, unimpressed by the Jazz Age Americans. Fellow guests Ernest Hemingway and Scott Fitzgerald "were drunk most of the time," and while the Murphys were "incomparable hosts . . . [t]he Riviera didn't mean as much to me as it did to those who lived there."[7] Yet she joined in with enthusiasm, inveigling the Legendre brothers to come along as the entourage moved to King Leopold II's Villa Les Cèdres, where Harpo Marx would play his harp for them and Gertie's noisy antics with the Legendres drew the ire of the playwright Somerset Maugham. "Now, there's nothing I liked better at that age than to show off and be the center of attention," she recalled. "Our antics by night were probably more contemptible than those by day."[8]

Back at home, after Gertie pointed out the cost of some polo ponies he had given to her brother, their father pledged $30,000 to Fairfield Osborn for her next expedition. The Legendres signed on, and that winter they were off to Abyssinia, today's Ethiopia, where they dined with Emperor Haile Selassie.[9] When Sidney Legendre returned alone to Addis Ababa with their trophies—three hundred dead mammals, one hundred living birds, and a live cheetah—Gertie realized she had fallen in love with him.[10] In fall 1929, they were married at New York's St. James Episcopal Church, and bought Medway, a plantation outside Charleston that boasted a 1686 brick house, the oldest in the Carolinas, once home to the governor of the colony and 120 slaves. Gertie's father paid the $100,000 purchase price.[11] The Legendres turned it into a 7,600-acre rider's and hunter's paradise, teeming with deer, quail, turkey, and other animals.

In summer 1930, Gertie and Sidney returned to France. "Who would have thought that the Great Depression was just beginning?" Gertie later recalled in a memoir. "Fortunately, father had very little money in stocks. The misery of much of the world was unknown to us."[12] Their next trip in spring 1932, again for the American Museum of Natural History, was to Indochina. In a book about the expedition. Sidney was caustic and racist, calling the Vietnamese "cringing, lying, thieving, sneering." Gertie wasn't immune from prejudice; in a letter to Sidney years later she suggested they move west because America's East Coast was "too full of jews."[13]

Their first daughter, Landine, was born in 1933. But Gertie wasn't going to be tied down by children and was soon off to Africa in 1936 and Iran in 1938. Traveling became more difficult with the outbreak of war in Europe, and by the time Germany invaded Poland in 1939, Gertie was burdened with another pregnancy, producing Bokara on their eleventh wedding anniversary in 1940. She was named for a city in Uzbekistan; they spun a globe while drinking to pick a name for their younger daughter.

Their lives inspired the Broadway show and film *Holiday;* Katharine Hepburn played a character based on Gertie. From an early age the girls lived with nannies, separated from their parents and each other.[14] "My mother didn't much like children around and brought us up in the style of the British aristocracy," Bobo later recalled, "shuttled between various rented cottages and apartments, generally in towns my parents didn't frequent." Most of Bobo's time was spent with her caretaker, Mamie.[15]

In 1942, Sidney joined the navy and shipped out to Hawaii as an officer and Gertie got a job with what would become the Office of Strategic Services (OSS), managing its cable desk in Washington. A security review noted that her family was rich and that sister Landine had married an Italian big-game hunter and diplomat who was a link to Italian society and thus potentially Italy's dictator, Benito Mussolini. The Legendres and their daughters were separated for the next two years. Bokara alternated between New Orleans and Sidney's sister and surrogate mother Katharine Biddle in Philadelphia.

Gertie wasn't one to let war cramp her style. Transferred to London in 1943, she went golfing and shooting on weekends at the great houses of England. After D-Day in 1944, she was transferred to Paris to run the OSS communications office. A few days after arriving, she had a vague notion of visiting the front "to actually feel the urgency of war."[16] Another OSS officer, who had a Jeep and an OSS driver, offered to help, "so the lady could hear some gunfire."[17] But just over the German border, a sniper killed their driver. Cowering, they and a third officer burned their OSS identification and raised a handkerchief to surrender.[18] The Germans promptly broadcast their first capture of an American woman—and a wealthy one at that.

At the OSS, concerns ran rampant over what Gertie and the two men might reveal, but the three captives stayed mum as they were moved among prisons, at first together, then separately. Gertie ended up in a castle used to house "special interest" prisoners, where she was interrogated by a German who had lived in America for years and probed her wealth and connections.[19] It was likely no coincidence that Hitler then ordered her into Gestapo custody in Berlin.[20] En route, she stayed in a hotel where "special and honored" prisoners, including King Leopold II of Belgium, were housed.[21]

Her next stop was a private residence—the home of an executive who treated her as his guest and toasted her with champagne. Then a Gestapo agent with a British accent arrived and inexplicably announced she would be set free at the Swiss border.[22] In March 1945, the Nazi regime was collapsing when she arrived at the home of the head of the OSS in Switzerland, Allen Dulles, who found her contrite—a suitable reaction to the fury and concern inspired by her madcap-heiress jaunt to wartime Germany. He would later write a memo to the head of the OSS, calling her penitent regarding "her escapades," but also impressively resourceful.[23] Dulles sent her on to Paris with a warning to lie low, but she celebrated her forty-third birthday with friends instead. Five days later, when she got home, her daughter Bobo greeted her as a stranger.[24]

Sidney and Gertie resumed their nomadic life until 1948, when Sidney's heart gave out and he died at age forty-five. Gertie would continue traveling and hunting, and in Kathmandu she met Richard Mack, a young Yale graduate and outdoorsman. Mack remained a presence long enough to meet the preteen Bobo at Medway before Gertie married a just-divorced surgeon whose nickname was "Piggy" due to his penchant for spending other people's money. Bobo thought him "a poseur, drinking expensive wines and listening to Caruso in the big beige chair in the living room at Medway."[25] He was also a morphine addict.

The couple would divorce in 1956 after an American Museum of Natural History trip to French Equatorial Africa. Back at Medway, Bobo would later relate in her memoir, Piggy had tried to poison Gertie and flew into a rage when she refused a spiked drink. Bobo reported, "Mummy immediately called a powerful friend who flew down that night in his private plane and mysteriously whisked Piggy . . . away."[26] Gertrude hied off to Nepal.

After the war, the six-year-old Bobo and her mother moved to horsey Aiken, South Carolina, where they were surrounded by "golfers clad in linen trousers and alligator shirts and polo players in white jodhpurs." Gertie was an exotic in comparison, wrapped in Indian brocades, silks, and jewels, accessorized with a turban and a long black-and-gold cigarette holder. "Who is this woman?" Bobo later told the *New York Times* she had asked herself.[27] Sidney's 1948 funeral had been the first time Bobo had ever felt a part of her family.[28] Gertie sent her husband off with a shotgun blast, and then went "for a horseback ride all alone on her favorite mount, Divorcee."[29] Six years later Bobo followed Landine to Foxcroft, "less a girls' academy than a military camp for rich and social girls.[30] After graduation she "was afflicted with two" coming-out parties.[31]

Briefly Bobo studied acting in New York, a career that sputtered into the late sixties. She also flitted through the New York art scene, met painters Willem de Kooning, Robert Rauschenberg, and Larry Rivers, smoked pot with Frank Stella, and was put down by Andy Warhol, who thought her "a phony baloney . . . carpet heiress." She admits, "Warhol was right . . . I was afraid I was a fraud, a shadow trying to find a form."[32]

Moving to Washington, D.C., she got jobs in Senator Claiborne Pell's office, with the Associated Press, and as a radio show booker, and had the revelation that, her family's conservative background notwithstanding, she was a progressive liberal.[33] By 1964, age twenty-four, she was living with her uncle Laddie in Palm Beach, where she created her own local TV show, *Bobo in the Celebrity Room.*[34] A year later, back in New York, she wrote stories for the *Charleston News and Courier,* owned by Landine's then-husband.

None of it curbed her self-indulgence. In the early seventies she fell in love with Morocco, "a country where permission for total abandonment and the freedom to be oneself was inherently part of the culture. What appealed to me was the possibility of throwing off the traces, so to speak, of my WASP upbringing and allowing my huge, soft inner self to bask in the sun and find complete acceptance."[35] But after attending the coronation of the king of Nepal, she was back in New York when she got a call from Gertie's onetime traveling companion, Richard Mack, who had been married three times. He invited Bobo—fifteen years his junior—to his ranch in Carmel, and after he swept her off her feet and into a suite at the Beverly Wilshire Hotel, he proposed to her. Though he was still married and she had only known him five days, she agreed. It's unclear if the mother of the bride bothered to attend their 1971 wedding. "I just want you to know that I never went to bed with him," Gertie insisted, though Bobo would come to think that was a lie.[36]

Five years of fights over money later (Mack didn't have as much as the Legendres), Bobo was living in a rental apartment in San Francisco, seeing her husband only on weekends, and taking lessons in Transcendental Meditation. By 1976, she was divorced and back in Washington, where she took another television job, was feted by the head of the National Gallery, and was profiled by the *New York Times* as a new *saloniste* in the capital, albeit one sometimes ridiculed as a dilettante.

Then, in summer 1978, on the WASP resort Fisher's Island, she met Arthur Patterson, a venture capitalist out of St. Mark's and Harvard, whose father, as the chairman of J. P. Morgan in the 1970s, had helped avert the bankruptcy of New York City. Patterson's mother was the second president of the Girl Scouts of America and the grandniece of Joseph H. Choate, the renowned lawyer, diplomat and friend of William C. Whitney. Patterson "suited my taste in many ways," Bobo recalled. "As Mummy said, he was an 'old shoe,' the ultimate WASP compliment ... He had charm, manners, and a lovely sense of humor."[37]

They married, but Bobo wasn't much of a wife. In March 1979, she took off for Sikkim and became a Tibetan Buddhist, "the true beginning of a lifetime of spiritual pilgrimages—journeys to find out who I was, and my place and purpose in life."[38] Four years later, after Arthur started Accel, a venture capital firm in Silicon Valley, Bobo found a new enthusiasm when she joined a group of wealthy heirs who met to learn about and practice philanthropy under the tutelage of a progressive investor who called his disciples the Donuts— that is, "the nuts with dough."[39] Patterson was "somewhat mystified by my need to go on these endless searches for enlightenment ...

or new shores . . . or whatever they were."[40] But she was inspired. She sold a Matisse inherited from an aunt, and with the $1 million it fetched she created a foundation that she named Tara, after a female Buddhist deity, with a mission as unfocused as she was. Gertie, furious, snapped: "I could have used that money! Why would you give it away?"

Arthur and Bobo spent so little time together that in 1989 he asked if they should remain married—and they split up just after her fiftieth birthday. Bobo "gave in to my desire for youth, sex and shiny boyfriends" while also suffering from chronic back pain and frequent illness, which worsened in the wake of the divorce.[41] She took up with a thirty-two-year-old hippie type named Skye, moved to a cottage on the sea in Mill Valley, and divided her time between there and her comfortable Park Avenue life in New York. Friends say that later she bitterly regretted leaving Patterson.*

〜

As Gertrude Legendre aged, she gave up hunting and travel and reinvented herself as a conservationist. She also started using her plantation as a tool to manipulate her offspring. Saving Medway as a memorial to her life became an obsession, that caused further fissures in an already dysfunctional family. Who would inherit the property? Bobo found herself a pawn in her mother's chess game against death, with Medway as Gertie's hedge against mortality.[42] When its small timber business petered out after a 1989 hurricane, Gertie sold part of the property, placed binding conservation easements on both what she sold and what she kept, and used the proceeds to endow a nonprofit to which she gave title to Medway. That turbocharged Bobo's need for attention and her thirst for revenge for Gertie's decades of neglect. Her family felt she was flailing to forestall any further emotional damage.

Bobo managed to have Gertie name her the Medway Environmental Foundation's sole trustee, and she negotiated a foothold there for her Tara Foundation; guided by such notables as Laurance

---

* Patterson's Accel would eventually invest in Facebook, Dropbox, Spotify, Etsy, GoFundMe, and other internet start-ups.

Rockefeller and George Plimpton, she began holding conferences on the plantation, beginning with one on extraterrestrial life, followed by others on the environment, arts, and spirituality.[43] She could never rest easy, though. "In the last years of her life, [Gertie] lay in bed and redid her will every day," Bobo told an interviewer.[44]

Gertrude Legendre died on March 8, 2000. Landine refused to attend her mother's funeral.[45] Bobo hired spiritual singers to perform "I Got Plenty of Nothing" from *Porgy and Bess* at Gertie's grave, "a sort of joke," she recalled.[46] Medway's staff promptly shrank from twenty-two employees to seven. Bobo had more than nothing left, but far less than she was used to.

Gertie's father had put his fortune into trusts in the 1920s, but at the end of Gertie's life the trusts terminated, and Bobo "spent like a drunken sailor." In fall 2004 she sold her New York apartment, put Medway on the market for $25 million, and bought a house on Mount Tamalpais, just north of San Francisco, where she continued to host dinner parties attended by writers, doctors, and ecologists as well as shamans and meditation teachers.[47] She launched a satellite television show, began declaiming monologues about her life at performance venues, and started writing a memoir. Medway was finally sold in 2012 for $11 million, to a Greek shipping tycoon, and Bobo's memoir, *Not What I Expected,* was published in 2017, five months before her death at age seventy-seven from thyroid cancer.

"If I knew dying was so much fun, I would have done it more often," a friend quoted Bobo in her *San Francisco Chronicle* obituary.[48] Certainly, she'd inherited her taste for a carefree life from her mother, but their legacy also included a troubled love life and a propensity for "squandered fortune" that traced back to Bobo's great-grandfather Henry Shelton Sanford.[49] In an earlier era, Gertrude Shelton Legendre had been considered a quintessential WASP for her self-indulgence and passionate escapism, but by the time her daughter came of age, similar behavior had come to seem the quintessence of presumption and pretension.

Bobo's saving grace was her persistent eccentricity, which allowed her to see and portray herself as a rebel and seeker of esoteric truths for whom life was an amusement park ride. But in vulnerable moments her façade slipped, revealing the emptiness that had come to define so many elite WASP lives. "I do realize that I'm terribly lucky," she had told an interviewer in 1976, describing her many projects and comparing herself favorably to "people who have money, and can do things, but don't." She had to be doing something, always. Otherwise, "I would die of boredom."

That her shadow never found a form seemed to elude her, but she instinctively understood that going nowhere in style, as she and her mother had long done, could distract from their utter absence of achievement. "I mean, it's that terrible Protestant ethic in us all that raises its ugly head," she said.[50]

34

The Whitneys were among America's highest-profile heirs of the Gilded Age. Harry Payne Whitney and Gertrude Vanderbilt had three children, Flora (b. 1897); Cornelius Vanderbilt Whitney, who was also known as both C.V. and Sonny (b. 1899); and Barbara (b. 1903); they inherited fortunes from both their father and their grandfather William C. Whitney. The fortune of Oliver Payne, William C.'s estranged Yale roommate and brother-in-law, passed through Harry's brother Payne to his wife Helen Hay Whitney's children, Joan Whitney Payson and John Hay "Jock" Whitney, born, respectively, in 1903 and 1904.

Barbara Whitney led a quiet life, married three times, raised two children, ran a small art gallery, and raced thoroughbreds. But with their inherited fortunes left relatively undiminished by taxes, and an obvious delight in taking full advantage of them, Flora, Sonny, Jock, and Joan all loomed large in twentieth-century America. Though each of them worked and was quite successful on their own, their primary occupation seemed to be living life to the outer limit, taking full advantage of their inherited wealth.

When Jock wasn't playing polo or collecting art (he owned two Rembrandts, two Michelangelos, three Picassos, and works by Monet, Degas, Cézanne, and Renoir, among others) and real estate (over the years, his holdings included a Manhattan townhouse and Beekman Place duplex, inherited acreage in the Adirondacks, a five-hundred-acre estate on Long Island, two thousand acres in South Carolina, a similar-sized estate in Virginia, ten thousand acres in Massachusetts, a beach house on Fisher's Island off Connecticut, and homes in Saratoga Springs, New York, Augusta, Georgia, and London, as well as a nineteen-thousand-acre Georgia hunting plantation), he was increasing the huge fortune he inherited.

Jock was successful in business, owning the *New York Herald Tribune*, and in sports, playing polo and raising and racing thoroughbreds. He also invested in Broadway productions and movies; with his cousin Sonny he made millions just from 1939's *Gone with the Wind*. He served as ambassador to the Court of St. James from 1957 to 1961, was chairman of the board of the Museum of Modern Art and president of New York Hospital, and started an eponymous $10 million foundation to focus on aiding the underprivileged; its chief consultant was the president of Fisk University, a historically Black college in Nashville. The last was begun the same year Jock requested that his name and that of his wife, Betsey Cushing (who had divorced Franklin Roosevelt's son James a few years earlier; Whitney adopted their two children), be stricken from the *Social Register*, which he deemed "a travesty of democracy."[51] Jock died at seventy-seven in 1982.

Jock's older sister, Joan, led a slightly simpler life, if such is possible after inheriting $100 million. In 1924, she married Charles Shipman Payson, who "multiplied the money he married" with investments in sugar and steel.[52] After Helen Hay Whitney's 1944 death, Jock and Joan merged what had been three family stables into one under their mother's Greentree salmon pink and black colors, and made it one of the most successful family-owned breeding and horse-racing concerns in America. A minority owner of baseball's New York Giants, Joan had her heart broken when the team moved to San Francisco in 1957, so four years later, when the National League expanded to ten teams, she financed the New York Mets. From the team's hapless beginnings in 1962 she saw them morph into the Miracle Mets, winning the World Series in 1969.

Joan, too, enjoyed the trappings of American wealth: a personal Pullman car; multiple homes (on the family property in Manhasset, a Fifth Avenue apartment, in Kentucky horse country, in Portland, Maine, on Florida's Jupiter Island, and an inherited mansion in

Saratoga Springs); seats on the boards of the Metropolitan Museum of Art, the Museum of Modern Art, and several hospitals; and ownership of two art galleries and a priceless painting collection. At her death in 1975, an inventory of her art ran ten pages, studded with names like Degas, Matisse, Cezanne, Wyeth, and Manet. But her *New York Times* obituary also highlighted her lack of pretension, which was evident in both her bequest of most of her fortune to her not-always-faithful husband, Charles Shipman Payson, and the playing of "Take Me Out to the Ball Game" at her funeral.

Sonny Whitney inherited less but still lived large. During World War I, and still a teenager, he enlisted in the fledgling U.S. air force and after a mere one hundred minutes of training took his first solo flight. He then taught combat and acrobatic flying to fighter pilots heading into World War I, and served again in World War II. Between the wars, he went to Yale, where he developed a playboy reputation when a Ziegfield Follies dancer sued him for breach of promise. Several years later he was exonerated, and she was forced to pay him $131 in legal costs and enjoined from further litigation.[53] He emerged from the scandal determined to prove himself. "I always thank my father. . . . He sent me out to the mines," where he dug ore at the deepest levels of Nevada's Comstock mines, rose to assistant foreman, and then joined his father's Metal Exploration Company, where he and its chief engineer figured out how to make a profit from operations his father had written off as a total loss.[54] Within six years, he was running mining operations that threw off $7 million at the height of the Great Depression.[55]

Sonny and a Yale classmate, Juan Trippe, were fascinated with the prospect of commercial aviation, and with Sonny's profits from an investment in Mexican farmland and more funds from Jock and a Vanderbilt cousin they launched Pan American Airways in 1927; by 1941, it operated in fifty-five countries. Sonny would eventually inherit $20 million, but his ambitions went beyond money. In 1932, he narrowly lost a race for Congress as a Democrat in his Long Island district. "In times like these, I felt that it was the duty of young men to take interest in public life," he explained.[56]

After World War II, Sonny was named Harry Truman's first assistant secretary of the Air Force, then an undersecretary of commerce.

The last of his four wives, Marylou, a former actress and divorcée, inherited his $100 million fortune when he died at ninety-three in 1992, and it financed her reign as a social leader in the elite horse racing circles of Saratoga Springs and Lexington, Kentucky. When she died, also at ninety-three, she left almost everything to John Hendrickson, her third husband, a former tennis pro and aide to a governor of his native Alaska, who was almost four decades Marylou's junior.

━━

Sonny's sister Flora was educated—sporadically—at Brearley and Foxcroft, and through travels with her mother (she had her own apartment in Paris at age fourteen). She was engaged to Theodore Roosevelt's youngest son before he was shot down behind enemy lines in World War I. At twenty-three she married a friend of young Roosevelt, Roderick Tower, a Philadelphia stockbroker whose grandfather and father, both named Charlemagne, were respectively a coal, rail, and mining executive and America's ambassador to Austria, Germany, and Russia.

The marriage lasted four years and produced two children before Flora divorced Tower in Paris for desertion. A sculptor like her mother, Flora remarried, had two more children, and lived a very social life in Aiken, South Carolina. After Gertrude Vanderbilt Whitney died, Flora struggled to preserve her mother's Whitney Museum; she tried but failed to merge it into the Metropolitan Museum of Art, but then revived it with the help of her siblings, and ran it until 1974, at one point even selling at auction a J. M. W. Turner painting she inherited for a then-record price of $6.4 million, and giving her museum a portion of the proceeds. A daughter, also named Flora, would later run the Whitney Museum.*

Flora's son Whitney Tower was a Harvard graduate who, mirroring his uncle, flew reconnaissance missions for the Army Air Force in World War II. In 1948, newly married to Frances Drexel Cheston

---

* Flora married Sydney Francis Biddle, a lawyer turned artist from the Philadelphia Biddles, in 1979 and stepped down from the museum's chair in 1995. Though it's no longer controlled by the family, a great-granddaughter of Gertrude Vanderbilt Whitney still sits on the Whitney Museum's board today.

and hoping to write about horse racing, he took a job as a sports reporter at the *Cincinnati Enquirer,* remaining there until 1954. By then
the father of a two-year-old son, Whitney Jr., he returned to New York
to become horse racing editor of a new weekly magazine, *Sports Illustrated,* a post he held for twenty-two years. He later ran the National
Museum of Racing in Saratoga Springs.

After an infancy in Cincinnati, Whitney Jr. grew up in Old Westbury on Long Island, where his grandmother ruled over an eight-
hundred-acre farm on what's still called Whitney Lane. The family
spent summers at Whitney Park, where they owned a quarter of his
great-great-grandfather's sixty-eight-thousand-acre tract of virgin for-
est in the Adirondack Mountains.

When Whitney was seven, most of the original Long Island
property—which had once encompassed a thirty-room copy of a
French château, a nineteen-room colonial manor house, two stables,
six cow barns, cottages for 150 employees, and other outbuildings—
was sold for development. The Towers had a home of their own a half
mile away. Whitney was sent to the forty-acre campus of the Green
Vale School at the end of Whitney Lane in Old Brookville, which his
father and an aunt had attended before him. He knew his father
was in "the horse business," he said in a lengthy interview in 2020.
"I was at every racetrack in the world." But he claimed he didn't
know his family had been rich. WASP reticence ruled the day. "There
was no talking about money."[57]

At thirteen he was thrown out of Green Vale after he was caught
selling fireworks in a bathroom at recess. He went next to a boarding school in Massachusetts, where a history class focused on the
Gilded Age robber barons. When William C. Whitney's name came
up and he said he thought they were related, he recalled that his
teacher responded, "If Whitney is your last name, you've got it made."

In tenth grade, Whitney was sent to another boarding school in
Colorado Springs while his parents prepared to divorce. His father
had multiple mistresses. "There was a girl behind a counter wherever
there was a race track. My mother was devastated. I'd say my prayers,
'I wish they'd stop arguing.'" He was flying to Colorado with his
parents when his father deplaned in Chicago. "My mother was cry-
ing, my father was, 'Bye.'" Whitney says his father was then having a

fling with Michael Butler's horsey sister, Jorie. Two girlfriends later, that same year, Whitney Sr. married the second of his three wives. Back at school, caught with a girl in his room, Whitney Jr. was asked to leave.

Whitney was sixteen and in public school in Bedford, a wealthy New York suburb, in 1977 when his mother married another journalist.* At the same time his father finally answered his question, "Why are people so nice to me?" He swears he only then learned that his family was still rich. "Not many kids had 160,000 acres. There were so many things about my family in the newspapers, everyone thought Whitney had money." But as a trust fund kid, he didn't, not yet. "I was on a strict allowance. I was probably the poorest person in my class. I was always borrowing money."

Having learned to drink in Colorado, Whitney graduated to drugs in public school. "All my friends did [drugs]; I was the addict who loved it." He first took cocaine at seventeen. "Not daily. When people had it. It was so innocent, until it innocently blew up." That happened a year after he enrolled in the University of Colorado. He was halfway through his sophomore year and friendly with brand-name heirs to the Merck pharmaceutical and General Foods fortunes ("We were the little rascals of the jet set") when this latest school asked him to leave. He recalls, "They said, 'You can't have all Fs.' I said, 'Why not?' 'You'll understand when your parents talk to you.' They never talked about that stuff."

Fascinated by the movies, Whitney Jr. enrolled at the Neighborhood Playhouse, a prestigious New York acting school, and then moved to Hollywood in 1972. He made a few commercials, but also made trouble, and ended up in drug rehabilitation. Afterward he would bounce from coast to coast, and by the late 1970s he was enmeshed in New York's late-night scene. One new friend, John Phillips, former leader of the Mamas and the Papas, was a notorious drug

---

* Tower's stepfather, John Train, was a writer, financial advisor, and likely an unofficial operative of American espionage agencies, as well as a co-founder of *The Paris Review*. When he died, a *New York Times* obituary published on September 23, 2022, said he "exemplified the attitudes and values of the exalted class he was born into: the white Anglo-Saxon Protestants of the postwar era. He was globe-bestriding but also self-effacing, erudite but also pragmatic, cosmopolitan but also nationalistic, solemn at one moment and droll the next."

user. One night Whitney responded to a summons to Phillips's East Side townhouse, where the Rolling Stones frontman Mick Jagger opened the door; the two became fast friends. Jagger had an ulterior motive. "I did ask, Why me? Mick wanted to befriend the A-list. He knew the names. He was very much socially minded. Andy [Warhol], too. They were insatiable about being invited to the best parties by socialites. I never had so much fun. I never got so high." More stints at rehab ensued, but "they didn't take." He shot up at a family funeral, where he asked First Lady Nancy Reagan what inspired her Just Say No to Drugs campaign. Sometimes, he said, "I thought I was gonna die."

In the early 1980s, Tower was a fixture on the Reagan-era young social scene, appearing regularly in the party pages of *Women's Wear Daily* as one of the era's pretty young things, bouncing from Studio 54 to Xenon to Regine's. In 1985, Tower fell for a girl at a party; Pamela Franzheim's father, a Texas oil man and breeder of thoroughbreds, had been a Nixon-era ambassador. The couple married and together descended into addiction. A son, a third Whitney Tower, was born in 1987. A family intervention and another rehab stint followed. Then in the early 1990s, Whitney said, his wife walked out, but not before calling his mother to say her son was "a hard-core addict."

Confirming these events, Franzheim says she was engaged when a mutual friend took her to Tower's apartment, where she found him in a giant Victorian bed with pneumonia—and "it was love at first sight." She noticed but ignored the multiple pill bottles on his bedside table, and soon "blew off" her fiancé, and after a "huge" wedding, she and Tower went to Bangkok, Thailand, for their honeymoon. An expat friend of her new husband's arrived before their luggage did, and she was introduced to "chasing the dragon"—smoking heroin. "I'm not saying I was a perfect girl," says Franzheim, now living in Corpus Christi, Texas, "but I didn't know opiates—or that there was an issue. We never left the hotel. It was a bad beginning."

A few good years followed, living near Whitney's mother in Bedford, New York, but after Whitney III, who she calls Little Peanut, was born, "Whitney started again." Franzheim calls his behavior self-sabotage but admits she joined in, and they alternated stints in drug rehab clinics like Hazelden, in Minnesota. Eventually, her weight dropped to 89 pounds, she was riddled with infections, and "I couldn't take it anymore," she says, admitting she called her mother-in-law to say, "We both needed help." A tortured, years-long custody battle ensued, with their boy bouncing back and forth between them. "It was heartbreaking," she allows.

Finally, Franzheim says, she cleaned herself up, got a PhD in Psychology, and started a company in Houston, Texas, specializing in crisis counseling, working with drug addicts, battered women, and others in distress, who were referred to her by local Texas courts. Today, she is an artist, while continuing her counseling career. "We're all good now," she concludes, adding of her ex-husband, "He's managed to survive and maintain his essense. That's why he's Whitney; he's witty."

While getting divorced, Whitney had lived alone in a tiny New York apartment and worked as a gofer for a music manager. He later moved to Bedford and stayed with his mother, then got a house of his own there with bedrooms for his son and the child's nanny. He can't recall each recovery and relapse but estimates he submitted to drug rehabilitation more than ten times. "I took jobs when I needed money and I always needed money. I went through $1.5 million," part of his share of a $25 million trust fund. But then his trustees cut him off, telling him, "If you're gonna continue this lifestyle, we'll give you an allowance. Don't ask for more."

Tower had already traded away a sofa that had belonged to his Vanderbilt grandmother to pay for his portrait by Warhol, and then sold that for drug money. "I stole from my mother. Silver. A first edition of *Tom Sawyer*. That didn't go over very well. My brothers and sisters hardly speak to me, still." He was in rehab again in 1998 when his father had a stroke after bypass surgery. He thought about leaving rehab and finding some drugs, but his father begged him to stay in the program. So instead of quitting and relapsing, he checked into a halfway house, stayed a year, returned to Bedford, and signed a contract promising he wouldn't get high again. "I said, I won't, and of course, I did it all."

After his father died in 1999, Tower relapsed again, ending up in rehab in Delray Beach, Florida, a town where "sober homes" for ex-addicts are a cottage industry. It was the start of his longest stretch of sobriety in thirty years. He didn't return to New York—"the scene of so many crimes," he would later write in a magazine confessional—for years.[58] Six months later he got a place of his own in Palm Beach, and in 2003, he married his second wife, a decorator.

They met at an Alcoholics Anonymous meeting. "She was more of an addict than I was. She started to want this and that. She thought I could get a lot of money." He refused. Then, in 2005, out of the blue, he had a heart attack. Told his drug abuse had damaged his heart, he took it as a warning. Another came when his wife ended up back in rehab in 2006. Whitney called a local lawyer, one who advertised on matchbooks. "He got me a divorce in eight hours," for a mere $750.

During that marriage, ironically, Tower had begun to work as an assistant drug counselor. He was amused by his friends' reactions to his new career. "I'm sure you know a bit about that!" he quoted them, laughing. "It all adds up to a great story that can help other people." But though he completed most of the required training, he never earned his final credentials. Having survived that heart attack at age fifty-one ("I died. My heart stopped. I coded. They had to bring me back"), at sixty-six he ended up in an assisted- and independent-living community in West Palm Beach, Florida, after another car hit his, flipping it over at an intersection in nearby Delray Beach, breaking his back.

"I could have managed my life in a better way," he said, showing off the scar to a visitor while acknowledging other, mostly invisible scars from a half century of addiction to "alcohol, pot, cocaine, heroin." Raised to be superior, he had a long way to fall—and did with a fierce, thoughtless enthusiasm. Though he spent decades as a leading exemplar of WASP irresponsibility, entitlement, and moral decay, he still feels the tug of his family's legacy of achievement, however tainted it might be, and the irony of his wasted advantages.

Tower leaned forward in his wheelchair with the impish grin that had always drawn others to him. "The doctors here are like a tribe in Africa with a drum," he said. Aware of his past, they refused him pain medication. Somehow he was still able to laugh at himself. Which he did, thinking about his great-uncle Payne Whitney, who "decided his relatives were crazy enough to need their own mental institution," the Upper East Side New York psychiatric clinic that still bears his name.

"I can't believe we don't have family reunions there."

35

Like Michael Butler, Penelope Tree, an offspring of the Peabody family, became a sixties icon—in her case, as a fashion model. But instead of being tied to her parents she, like Bobo Legendre, was neglected by them. Born late in 1949, she became a latchkey kid while attending New York's elite private school Dalton before she was even a teenager. "I was always down in the Village with friends when I was 11 or 12, playing guitar," she recalled in a 2019 interview.[59] At least, until about 1964, when "somebody found out that we were going to nightclubs and I got busted." She was sent to Concord Academy, a strict all-girls Massachusetts prep school—a disaster from her point of view, after the freedom she experienced at Dalton, where the education was progressive and freeform. "I did have great friends there, but I was very depressed," a depression that led to anorexia and the school administration's realization that she didn't belong there. Her mother, Marietta Tree, was unsympathetic.

Marietta was a grandchild of Groton's rector Endicott Peabody and his wife, Frances. Their only son, Marietta's father, Malcolm, followed in his father's footsteps as an ordained minister, and made an auspicious marriage to Mary Elizabeth Parkman, another Boston Brahmin. Their eldest child, Mary Endicott Peabody, nicknamed Marietta, was born in 1917, and four brothers followed: Endicott (aka Chub) in 1920, George in 1922, Sam in 1925, and Malcolm Jr. (known as Mike) in 1928. They all went to boarding schools and spent summers in Northeast Harbor, Maine, and Easter in Locust Valley, New York, with in-laws.

The Peabodys, known for their devotion to discipline, reserve, ritual, and rectitude, taught their children that they would find "redemption through duty."[60] While the Peabody kids grew up in wealthy environments, they didn't feel they were of them. They were the minister's children, the rich folks' poor relatives, even after Malcolm

was named Episcopal bishop of central New York. The chilliness of
their family life likely didn't help them. As the writer Holly Brubach
later put it, "The God of the Peabodys was, it seems, remote and
joyless, punitive, without compassion—not unlike the Peabodys
themselves."[61]

Marietta tried to slip that leash. In 1939, she married Desmond
FitzGerald, an Irish Protestant lawyer, and after their first daughter,
Frances, known as Frankie, was born in October 1940 and Desmond
went to war, Marietta went to work, beginning a career in public
service—and an affair with the film director John Huston. When
FitzGerald returned home, he barely knew his wife.

Soon Marietta met and fell in love with an Anglo-American diplomat and member of Britain's Parliament, Ronald Tree, a grandson
of the wealthy retailer and publisher Marshall Field. When both Marietta and Tree sought to divorce their spouses, Marietta's parents
and some of her siblings were aghast.[62] It's unclear if they knew that
Tree was bisexual. Ronnie and Marietta married the day after her divorce from FitzGerald. After her second daughter, Penelope, arrived, that marriage turned chilly, too, and Marietta found another
interest when she got involved with New York's Democrats—and grew
close to Adlai Stevenson when he ran for president in 1952. By 1954
she was a state committeeperson, a volunteer for Averell Harriman's
campaign for governor of New York, and only an occasional visitor
to her husband's home in Barbados.

Marietta had used Penelope as an excuse to stay in New York
while Tree remained in Barbados, where he would head a group of
investors turning Sandy Lane, a Barbados plantation, into a lavish resort. "Not to be too hard on my parents," said Penelope, "but I grew
up in benign neglect. By the time I came along, my mother was off
having her very interesting political life. So, she really was not around
very much. And my father lived in the West Indies, and came back
for holidays. They had separate lives."

In 1956, their marital breach widened after Marietta was named
New York co-chair of Adlai Stevenson's second campaign for the presidency, became the divorced politician's wife replacement, and
then, after he lost a second time, "something happened between Adlai and Marietta."[63] They were presumed to be lovers as Marietta

continued in politics. First she won a spot on what became the New York City Human Rights Commission. Then, after Stevenson's last attempt to gain the presidency failed at the Democratic convention in 1960, she campaigned for the party's young nominee, John F. Kennedy. In 1961, he named Stevenson as his United Nations ambassador and Marietta as U.S. commissioner for human rights there, a post originally held by Eleanor Roosevelt. In 1964, Stevenson promoted her to an ambassadorial position, in which she displayed the sort of substance and dedication that would have made her long-dead grandfather proud.

Marietta's father, Malcolm, the Episcopal bishop, had recently retired, and with his wife, Mary, moved back to Cambridge, where she, too, had gotten involved in civil rights and made headlines—and a public impact—when she was arrested at a civil rights protest. Three of Marietta's brothers were also prominent in public life in the sixties. Chub served in the Harry Truman administration and as the governor of Massachusetts from 1962 to 1964; George followed their father into the Episcopal ministry and played a prominent role in the national Episcopal Church; Mike shuffled in and out of government, fighting for civil rights, charter schools, and campaign finance reform. The youngest, Sam, taught school, but also waved the Peabody family flag. With his wife, the former Judith Dunnington, Sam became a highly regarded, hands-on philanthropist, as well as a beloved, high-profile social figure in New York.

～

Adlai Stevenson died in 1965. "We were together," Marietta told her diary succinctly.[64] She remained at the United Nations after Stevenson's replacement dismissed her, moving to secretary general U Thant's staff as a United Nations School fundraiser—which was not her strong suit. Neither was motherhood, though in 1966, she brought Penelope home, enrolling her in the UN school. Just after Thanksgiving, they both attended Truman Capote's Black and White Ball at the Plaza Hotel, where Penelope was discovered and turned into a fashion model.

Just seventeen, she was spotted by the photographer Richard Avedon, who called *Vogue*'s then-editor, Diana Vreeland, "the next morning, and then she rang me and I went to lunch with her," said Tree, who was booked for a job with Avedon about a week later. It wasn't clear which she loved more, him or the attention she got. "I think I really needed to show my mother up."

The gangly, big-eyed, five-foot-ten Tree quickly became a top model even though she didn't work steadily; her looks were too exotic to be broadly appealing, and she was pulled in multiple directions, also taking a job reading manuscripts for a London publisher. There she met Vreeland's *British Vogue* counterpart, who introduced her to Avedon's younger competitor, photographer David Bailey, "in one of those fateful moments. So then I did some work with him, and there was this incredible vibe between us. But he was married to Catherine Deneuve." She knew she shouldn't get involved with a married man, but a few months later, when she was alternating between student life at Sarah Lawrence College and modeling, Bailey showed up at a shoot she was doing in Paris with Avedon, "and there was a bit of a struggle with Dick."

Avedon was bisexual, married, and lived a tony lifestyle, whereas Bailey was notoriously heterosexual and had had affairs with models like Jean Shrimpton and Sue Murray. Bailey's style was street rather than Avedon's penthouse—and Tree felt the American photographer was horrified by the notion she might sleep with Bailey, and tried to stop that from happening. But it was too late. "I was a goner, really, unfortunately, or fortunately." Though she returned to Sarah Lawrence, after finishing that term she quit because she was making money as a model and, thinking "this might be my last chance" to succeed in fashion, "I went to live with [Bailey] and that was it."

Marietta didn't approve, and even tried to slam the door of her Manhattan mansion in Bailey's face when he came to sweep Penelope off to London. "I jammed my foot in and said to her, 'Don't worry, it could be worse. I could be a Rolling Stone,'" Bailey wrote in his memoir, in which he called Marietta "the biggest bitch."[65]

Penelope would not be denied and moved in with Bailey, whose Cockney charm was undeniable, though he was a dozen years older. Tree explained in that 2019 interview, "It was also showing my mother that I could live a so-called independent life. But, of course, I just went from being dependent on my parents to being dependent on Bailey.

Six years later . . ." She paused. "It was a very long university education. Higher education."

Their life was a nonstop party, with cameo appearances by Tibetan monks and Black Panthers—but also a constant, blatant parade of other women. "The way I was brought up was to never confront any big issue. So I just let things slide. And I went out and I got my own life. I sort of rebelled against Bailey as well. He became a parental figure in some ways. I started taking too many drugs. We were painfully separating, but it took quite a long time."

Along the way, Tree was arrested for drug possession by London's Flying Squad, which focused on organized and major crime. She had just bought a gram of cocaine when her dealer was arrested. "So they thought that there was a lot of coke in the house where I was. Eight plainclothes policemen burst into this room where I was sitting with my friend and my friend's baby. It was really terrifying."

Tree had developed a skin condition, severe late-onset acne, and the police, not believing she was a model or that she could possibly be the daughter of a wealthy former member of Parliament, held her incommunicado overnight. She was traumatized, feeling stripped of her identity. "But it was probably quite a good thing that it happened. It woke me up." And just in time. While she had managed to keep her anorexia and later bulimia under control, never letting her weight drop below a hundred pounds, her skin condition had derailed her career, and suddenly she was forced "to go to the police station every week, and sit there with a whole lot of other people who were getting busted for very minor things, mostly Black people getting arrested for this thing called loitering with intent to commit an arrestable crime. My bubble was burst. This bubble of narcissistic self-obsession, this life that we led, which was very rarified. It was an eye-opener."

It was also oddly good timing, as her arrest ended her relationship with David Bailey. Though she was claiming her independence, she was depressed by the breakup, turning to dance classes and analysis for relief, and traveling—through the Caribbean and Central and South America—for a change of scene, at least until her father had a stroke, after which she spent time with him. It was a full life, but still somehow insufficient. "Bailey was the first time I'd ever really been in love, and

I just assumed that would go on forever. And the fact that it didn't and it was so painful, was quite devastating. I had no confidence whatsoever after that, with my skin and the fact that I went from being a sought-after model to being somebody that nobody really wanted to look at. But it was quite salutary, quite an interesting experience from, you know, fifty years on."

A new love affair changed her perspective. She met Ricky Fataar, a South African musician who had just left the Beach Boys after several years as the surf-rock band's drummer. Moving from London to Los Angeles, they had a daughter and, in 1980, married, but Tree hated L.A., where "everybody was taking a lot of coke, and it was not a place where you felt like you could bring up children." An Australian friend suggested they move to Sydney, where she remained for seventeen years, even after breaking up with Fataar. Tree then got involved with a Jungian analyst and had her second child, a son, nine years after her daughter. But following a move to London, she realized her analyst made David Bailey look faithful.

She wanted no sympathy. "I've been very, very lucky with my children. And my friends." And she kept busy studying and practicing Buddhism, which led her to volunteer for Lotus Outreach, a Southeast Asian organization combatting sex trafficking, and work with a foundation promoting Buddhist scholarship. She even returned to modeling now and then, and a renewed friendship with David Bailey.

In an interview with a British newspaper in 2008, Tree reflected on her distant, emotionally unavailable mother, "this rather annoying person who came back every so often to lay down the law." Though they shared a love of fashion, they had little else in common. "I can genuinely say without any bullshit that I have inherited her strength," Penelope said of Marietta, who survived a bout with cancer in 1981, five years after Ronald Tree's death, before finally succumbing in 1991. Thirty years later, Penelope Tree wondered "what it would have been like to have a loving mother . . . or even a mother."[66]

In her mid-seventies, her children grown, Tree remained in England, on the board of Lotus Outreach, and represented the Khyentse Foundation in the United Kingdom. "I've been a dharma student for thirty years, but am very much still in Buddhist kindergarten," she said in that 2019 interview. "It's not that I disavowed the Episcopalian church, more that I could not relate to it." Discovering that one of her relatives, the nineteenth-century educator and Transcendentalist Lizzie Peabody, had translated Buddhism's Lotus Sutra into English from French, reminded her that after living in England and Australia since age eighteen, she knew very little about her Peabody ancestors. "Most likely my loss," she lamented.

Tree's half-sister Frankie FitzGerald also had a distant relationship with their mother, who fit her elder daughter "into her schedule . . . but only just."[67] But she took after her mother and her uncles in one vital respect: trying to stay seriously engaged and play a positive role in the world, carrying forward the legacy of Peabodys from George to Lizzie to the rector of Groton.

Frankie attended Foxcroft, where she crossed paths with Bobo Legendre, and spent summers in Maine with her distant, strict Peabody grandparents. But while Penelope sank in such cold water, Frankie, despite loneliness, worked hard to stay close to her mother, and found ways to thrive, perhaps because she developed her own friendship with Adlai Stevenson, becoming pen pals when she was still a child and later working on his campaigns. She even joined him, Marietta, and Ronnie Tree on a trip to Africa in 1957, where the sixteen-year-old decided her mother and Stevenson were sexually involved.[68]

Frankie initially imagined herself a novelist. After graduating magna cum laude from Radcliffe in 1962, she went to Paris, spending two years working for the CIA-funded Congress for Cultural Freedom while she tried to write, but "I didn't know what I was doing," she said in a telephone interview for this book.[69] Back in New York, she met Clay Felker, editor of *New York*, a Sunday magazine distributed with the *New York Herald Tribune*, then owned by Jock Whitney. Felker didn't pay much, but he was happy to teach the ropes to talented neophytes in journalism.

In Vietnam, a simmering conflict had been heating up for half a decade, and by the end of 1966, more than four hundred thousand American servicemen were in harm's way. Frankie's father had served in Southeast Asia in World War II, and she wanted to see it, so she went on her own, as a freelancer, "because no one would send me. I ended up in Saigon, thought I'd write a piece and leave, but I couldn't leave. I got stuck. I stuck myself." She focused on how the war was perceived by the Vietnamese people, rather than on the fighting. "The United States was deeply involved yet it didn't understand the Vietnamese at all."

In 1968, a year after her father's premature death, Frankie, back in America, signed a contract to write *Fire in the Lake,* a book about Vietnam that was excerpted in the *New Yorker,* published in 1972, and won a Pulitzer Prize the following year. FitzGerald returned to Vietnam several times and gave speeches for the Indochina Peace Campaign before publishing more books on history, society, and the evangelical movement in America. In the meantime, she was photographed by Patrick Lichfield for a *Vogue* feature on her "great American family," which lauded her as "gay, amusing, handsome, marvelously frank, worldly even in blue jeans and a careless shirt." Tellingly, she had chosen not to have her photo on the jacket of *Fire in the Lake,* fearing it would require a reference to her family. "And who exactly wasn't there to live up to in my family?" she asked an interviewer who questioned that omission.

36

Like the Peabodys, many Biddles would distinguish themselves in public life, and serve as an exceptional rebuke to the rule of the inevitable diminishment of great families. Among the better-known Biddles in the twentieth century were Francis, attorney general under Franklin Delano Roosevelt and a judge in the Nuremberg trial of Nazi war criminals, and his brother George, an artist of note, whose call for relief for visual artists during the Great Depression inspired the creation of arts programs that produced some of the most enduring public monuments of Roosevelt's New Deal. Working for Senator Claiborne Pell, a school chum, Livingston Ludlow Biddle Jr. drafted legislation to create the National Endowment for the Arts (NEA), served as deputy to its first chairman, was later named its third chairman, and was credited by many with saving it from "budgetary death" during the presidency of Ronald Reagan.[70]

Francis and George descended from Clement Biddle, a great-grandson of the first Biddle in America; Livingston descended from Charles Biddle, the father of Nicholas, the banker. Those in the Clement Biddle line were considered the family's aristocrats, especially after the Biddles and Drexels merged in 1872. But as a boy, Anthony Joseph Drexel Biddle Sr., born in 1874 in Philadelphia, was often bullied due to his privileged upbringing, small stature, and asthma, becoming both eccentric and pugilistic in response.[71] After marrying and having three children, he shocked his fellow well-born Philadelphians by taking a job as a waterfront reporter for a local newspaper; kept alligators he caught in the Everglades as house pets; carried suitcases of bricks to build up his muscles; and installed a boxing ring in the stable behind his Rittenhouse Square home and regularly fought bouts there and in public settings with professionals like Jack Johnson and Gene Tunney, seeking to promote boxing as a "smart" sport.

In 1907, searching for deeper meaning in life, he wandered into his local Episcopal house of worship, the Church of the Holy Trinity, and was inspired to start the Drexel Biddle Bible Classes, which combined religion and fisticuffs. They would evolve to offer military training to twenty thousand World War I noncommissioned officers, and after enlisting in the Marines as a forty-one-year-old, Biddle emerged a captain and the corps' reigning expert on hand-to-hand combat.

His elder children were riveting characters, too. Early in 1915, three weeks after her debut, seventeen-year-old Cordelia Biddle was engaged to Angier Buchanan Duke, a nouveau riche descendant of a North Carolina tenant farmer and a grandson of Washington Duke, the founder of the American Tobacco Company. Just after their wedding, Angie's sister Mary Duke, also a teenager, accepted a marriage proposal from Cordelia's brother Anthony Jr. The pair of brides would only briefly reign as Mrs. Biddle Duke and Mrs. Duke Biddle, though. Cordelia separated from Angier in 1918, and he died in 1923, drowning when he stepped out of a motorboat into Long Island Sound after a party. Anthony Jr.'s marriage lasted longer but was dissolved in 1931.

Anthony Jr.'s life to that point had lacked purpose. But as 1934 ended, the Democratic Party and its head, President Franklin Delano

Roosevelt, offered him an opportunity. Nudged into politics by his second wife, Margaret Thompson Schulze, heiress to an $85 million copper mining fortune, he had made contributions to various Democrats, inspiring the party to float his name as a potential ambassador; he had the required money, manners, and social skills to head an embassy. Roosevelt named him minister to Norway.

Transferred to Poland in 1937, Anthony Jr. rented a Warsaw palace and a country estate where, at one of his parties, 897 bottles of champagne were consumed.[72] But then, on September 1, 1939, Nazi Germany attacked Poland, and when the Polish government fled and urged diplomats to follow, Biddle, chased by machine-gun fire from German planes as Nazi radio broadcast his progress across Poland, made a mad dash into today's Ukraine. Twelve days later, he telegrammed Washington to reveal that five thousand German planes were attacking civilians. "Population terrorized," he wrote.[73]

In response to his reports, Germany issued a statement charging him with trying to drag America into war: "We can give Mr. Biddle the comforting assurance that our air force has objectives of greater military value than a young man rolling in millions who outlines his life's history by counting twenty-two feudal clubs to which he belongs."[74] By September 24 he reached France, where he learned that German troops had carried off about $250,000 in property from his Warsaw palace. By then, Biddle had been named envoy extraordinary to France and had followed the French government to Bordeaux, fleeing the Nazis. There he and his wife slept in style—when bombs didn't wake them—in the Château La Mission Haut-Brion.

In March 1941, Biddle was transferred to London, where he added the exiled governments of Belgium, Yugoslavia, Czechoslovakia, and the Netherlands to his ministerial portfolio. In 1942, he took on Greece, and the next year he traded Yugoslavia for Luxembourg. "What are you making—a collection?" friends asked about the position that, reportedly, he alone would accept.[75]

He had found his forte as a dashing diplomat. No longer seen as a rich flit, he was praised for his energy, tact, courage, social skills, and capacity to learn. Described as perpetually buoyant and energetic, the urbane Biddle had an "old boy," "old sport" argot and dry humor he used when dismissing a minor official as "a rimless zero" and the king of Yugoslavia as "a sort of owl in short pants."[76]

In 1944, Biddle joined Supreme Commander Dwight D. Eisenhower's staff as a lieutenant colonel and chief liaison with America's European allies just before their June invasion of France turned the tide of the war. In 1946, at forty-eight, he was put in charge of liaison with foreign military at Allied Supreme Headquarters in Frankfurt, where he remained until 1955, when he returned to Philadelphia as adjutant general of the state's National Guard and a major general in the army reserves. Six years later, even though the lifelong smoker was suffering from lung cancer, new president John F. Kennedy swore him in as ambassador to Spain. But he held the post only a few months before contracting pneumonia and dying of a heart attack at sixty-four.

<hr />

Cordelia Biddle Duke's sons Angier Biddle Duke and Anthony Drexel Duke were in awe of their uncle Tony Biddle.* Tony Duke went to Princeton and Angie to Yale in the midst of the Depression. Hitler was already rising to power in Germany, and in 1932, traveling together in Europe, Angie and Tony Duke were at the Munich Opera when the music suddenly stopped and, Tony recalled in an interview in 2004, "Hitler and 20 stormtroopers walked in" and sat right in front of them. "Half the crowd applauded, the other half sat quiet with bowed heads."[77] Then, in 1934, while on another visit to Europe accompanied by their uncle, Austria's chancellor was assassinated by Nazis in a brief uprising. The young brothers decided to attend his Vienna funeral, "because history was happening," Tony Duke recalled. They had heard the uprising was put down, "but it hadn't been. There were pockets of Nazis, wearing armbands, and we were suddenly set upon by twenty young men. They fired a bullet through the windshield, smashed the windows, pulled us out of the car, and the leader said, 'If they're Jewish, kill them.' They shoved us in a cellar jail in a bakery."

---

* Angie's mother changed his middle name from Buchanan to Biddle after her divorce.

Three hours later, Austrian troops arrived and shot their guard, and the Nazis left. "We banged on the window, waved a shirt, a captain took our story, put a U.S. flag on our car, and sent us on our way. Angie was nineteen. I was sixteen. Our uncle became his role model because he let us go and we experienced something we would always remember. I shudder to think of it."

Angie dropped out of Yale in 1936 after the announcement of his engagement to a relative of Franklin D. Roosevelt. They married in 1937 in the Episcopal church in wealthy Tuxedo Park, where her parents lived. The marriage lasted three and a half years, during which Angie was arrested several times for speeding and driving while intoxicated. It also produced a son, St. George Biddle "Pony" Duke, before it was terminated in Reno on the standard grounds of cruelty. Three months later, Angie married again. Margaret Screven White Tuck was descended from a signer of the Declaration of Independence and from the Confederate commander of the Civil War iron-clad vessel *Merrimack*. Angie would shortly join the Army Air Corps and emerge a major after V-J Day. He bought a gentleman's farm in social Southampton, New York, had a *Vogue*-caliber Park Avenue New York apartment filled with antiques and family portraits, and briefly seemed set on a social trajectory, but "Angie's heart wasn't in it," his brother said. "It was a stopgap between the military and doing what he wanted: diplomacy."

Inspired by Franklin Roosevelt, Angie Duke became a Democrat, and in 1949 President Harry Truman named him an assistant to the U.S. ambassador to Argentina. When the ambassador was transferred to Madrid two years later, he followed. His second marriage ended after he was appointed the youngest ambassador in American history in March 1952, representing the United States in El Salvador at age thirty-six. Two months later, after converting to Roman Catholicism, he married Maria Luisa de Arana, the granddaughter of an impoverished Basque marqués whom he had met in Madrid. When he then took up his new post in San Salvador, a social wag quipped, "From El Morocco to El Salvador."[78]

Tony Duke, meanwhile, had left Princeton for the navy, where he commanded a tank landing ship on D-Day in 1944. His uncle Tony introduced him to Eisenhower. After earning three battle stars and a Bronze Star in the war, Tony returned to Boys Harbor, a summer camp for underprivileged children that he started in 1937. He revived it, added girls, expanded it into social services, and ran it until 2005.* He also played a vital role in saving his older brother's career after Eisenhower was elected president as a Republican in 1952 and began to move the pieces on America's diplomatic chess board. Democrat Angie's job in El Salvador seemed doomed until he called his brother. "I called the White House," Tony recalled, "and to my utter amazement, Eisenhower gets on the phone."

"What can I do for you?" asked the president, who allowed Angie to stay another six months before he finally yielded to political pressure to replace him. But Angie Duke had found his calling. Asked to take over the International Rescue Committee, which had been formed in the 1930s to aid refugees and victims of dictatorships, Angie expanded the humanitarian aid group's activities behind the Iron Curtain. He also stayed involved with the Democrats, chairing conventions and committees and evaluating diplomacy in Central and South America for John F. Kennedy's 1960 campaign.

That New Year's Eve, just before Kennedy was inaugurated, the president-elect, a friend of long standing, asked Duke to be his chief of protocol, essentially the government's concierge for the diplomatic community and eminent foreign visitors, but also a linchpin in the conduct of foreign relations. Though he hoped for another embassy, when Kennedy agreed to give him ambassadorial rank, he accepted, and immediately resigned, quite publicly, alongside attorney general–designate Robert F. Kennedy, from a Washington club that refused to admit Black diplomats. Then he pressured local businesses to serve Black and brown clients, and helped nonwhite envoys find suitable housing in Washington.

Duke lost his third wife in a plane crash a few months later, but he soldiered on. When President Kennedy was assassinated in Texas in November 1963, Angie guarded Jacqueline Kennedy from the crowd that greeted Air Force One on its return, and she asked him to assemble a dossier on the funerals of Presidents Washington,

---

* Its New York City arm, based in Harlem and also serving the South Bronx, continues, offering before- and after-school youth services programs and arts classes.

Lincoln, Grant, Theodore Roosevelt, and Harding and of King Edward VII. Library of Congress researchers worked all night, and at dawn Duke handed the First Lady a report, then pivoted to organize the team that oversaw the huge number of world leaders who attended the funeral, putting together the seating plan inside St. Matthew's Cathedral, and coping with the ripple effect of world leaders ignoring it.

After he was elected for his own full term in 1964, Lyndon Johnson named Duke, then forty-nine, ambassador to Spain. In 1967, he returned to America as Johnson's protocol chief, then briefly served as ambassador to Denmark, and ended his diplomatic career as Jimmy Carter's ambassador to Morocco.

Angie retired in 1981, but barely slowed down. He served on boards and councils until 1995, when he was hit by a car while rollerblading near his home in Southampton. He was listening to a Sousa march when he died. His brother, Tony, retired to emeritus status at Boys and Girls Harbor a few years later, and lived to age ninety-five. A mourner's comment on Angie applied to them both: they died as they lived, "at full speed ahead."[79]

The life of their uncle Tony Biddle's son was just as dramatic and significant. He was born Anthony Joseph Drexel Biddle III in 1921. Shortly after his parents divorced when he was twelve years old, he and his mother petitioned to change his name to Nicholas Benjamin Duke Biddle. Nicky, as his friends would call him, took his parents' split hard, and developed a mind of his own early on, demanding to change boarding schools, doing the same later on in college, and then leaving Harvard before graduation in order to enlist after Pearl Harbor.

His wartime experience was extraordinary, though he never talked about it, even to his family. Only when his army record was discovered in family storage were his children able to reconstruct what he barely acknowledged. Biddle was a member of the 460th Parachute Field Artillery Battalion, trained as a paratrooper, and won his Silver Wings in 1943. In May 1944, the 460th left Newport News, Virginia, bound for Naples, Italy. The battalion first engaged the enemy outside Rome a few weeks later, and then joined Operation Dragoon, the invasion of southern France by almost six thousand paratroopers that followed the Allied landing on the beaches of Normandy.

Twenty planes dropped the first wave of soldiers, including the 460th, near Fréjus (between Cannes and St.-Tropez), where they assembled their guns and returned to combat that August. They pushed the German military into the Alps, where they fought for three months before loading onto trains for northern France to join the bloody Battle of the Bulge in occupied Belgium and Luxembourg. There, for more than a month, they engaged German SS, Panzer, and airborne troops in combat every day before the battle ended in victory.

That wasn't the end of Biddle's service, as intense combat continued for days before his unit was briefly sent to the German border. Its last assignment, to join the crossing of the Rhine River, was called off, and the Airborne Division, which included the 460th, was slated to ship out to Japan. But then President Truman authorized the use of the two nuclear weapons that ended the Pacific War. Asked once by a relative what he thought of the atomic bomb, Biddle said it was hard to be impartial, as he felt sure he would have died had the bombs not dropped.[80]

In 1947, Biddle married a fashion editor, Anne Bullitt, the once-divorced daughter of the American ambassador to France whom Biddle's father had briefly served as a deputy early in the war. Biddle then enrolled in Columbia Law School, but dropped out before getting a degree. The retired Bullitt, who had previously been America's first ambassador to the Soviet Union, had told Biddle about an exciting opportunity at a new government agency being formed out of the wartime Office of Strategic Services, called the Central Intelligence Agency. Fluent in both Spanish and French, Biddle was made an agent and sent to Madrid under cover as a foreign service officer. By the early 1950s, he had officially left the CIA to become a businessman in Spain, but his family believed he remained in the intelligence community for most of the rest of his life.

After a divorce, he moved to Biarritz, France, got married again to Paula Denckla, the granddaughter of a steel tycoon, and had a daughter before that marriage failed. By 1960, he was often back in New York, where his cousin Angie asked him to run a Caribbean branch of the International Rescue Committee. Late that year, Nicholas Biddle married for the third time, and then, when he wasn't working on behalf of refugees from Fidel Castro's Cuba, traveled to France, Spain, and Central America, where he invested in a range of businesses (agriculture, ports, mining, film stock production); his partners included numerous American businessmen and several controversial foreign leaders, including former presidents Fulgencio Batista of Cuba, Miguel Alemán of Mexico, and the Nicaraguan military's Anastasio Somoza. "It was all very vague," said a relative. "He never talked."

—

"We had tremendous privilege," said George Biddle, Nicholas's son by his third wife, Nancy Preston.[81] At Harvard, he studied government and international relations, focusing on Latin America, where the Reagan administration was then recruiting and arming a rebel army to fight the new leftist government in Nicaragua, which had overthrown the Somoza regime in 1979. In 1982, George worked in neighboring Costa Rica, his first exposure to a developing country, and returned to write a thesis on the threats to its democracy. His first job was assistant to the president of the Institute for East-West Security Studies, a think tank that brought together scholars from NATO and the Warsaw Pact, hoping to bridge the East-West divide. He earned a master's degree in international affairs from Johns Hopkins, and then in 1989, at twenty-eight, he founded the Institute for Central American Studies, which sought, he said, "to use U.S. power for good."

The following year, a trip to war-torn El Salvador with his uncle Angie for the International Rescue Committee was a revelation that confirmed his life path. The next year, he met a Salvadoran land reformer seeking to "create dialogue between guerillas and the government" and worked with him for seven years, organizing in the region and seeking "reconciliation and change" throughout Central America as it struggled with endemic violence. Finally, though, his private funding ran out.

Biddle became vice president of the International Crisis Group in 1997, running its Washington office. It had been formed two years earlier by a former UN official and a mentor, diplomat Morton Abramowitz, and was chaired by U.S. senator George Mitchell, all of them driven by frustration over the international community's failure to anticipate and address crises in Somalia, Rwanda, and Bosnia. But in 2000, the International Rescue Committee made Biddle an offer he couldn't refuse, to serve as its executive vice president. Eighteen months later, at thirty-eight, he became the group's acting president, a job he held for fifteen-plus years, through many trips to dangerous places.

In 2011, Biddle took on the chairmanship of a Massachusetts-based nonprofit that was evolving from a focus on mothers and children in the Caribbean and Latin America to the broader goals of economic opportunity, environmental protection, and funding community-based microprojects in health and education, especially for girls. World Connect, as it is now called, seeks to be "a model for how grass-roots development should be done, one based on trust and confidence in local leaders' capacity and ingenuity." Ever a student, his work in poor countries was "an amazing way to understand cultures and countries," he said in an interview for this book.

Biddle dedicated himself to service. "You recognize you got a break. And I was fortunate to create my own institute. But yeah, there's a sense of family responsibility." The same forces operated on Ambassador Anthony Joseph Drexel Biddle Jr.'s daughter Meg, though her focus was more local. "I took a lot from both of my parents," she said. "My family were public servants, always helping, saving, inspiring."[82]

As a child, Meg, like many Biddle cousins her age, volunteered at Tony Duke's Boys and Girls Harbor. "It was our training program. I grew up with, 'What are we doing here? Well, be useful.'" Exhausted by anti-war activism at the end of the 1960s, Meg dropped out of college and moved to California. An illustrator, cartoonist, painter, and watercolorist, Biddle came out as gay and married her wife, Marcia Perry, also an artist, in the early 1980s. "Coming out was a little testy, but we had no drama, which was unusual," said Meg. "We're out and outspoken." The women had a daughter together, about whom Meg observed, "As she was growing up, the last thing you want is to be different, but, in fact, everyone is."

In 2000, Meg and Marcia funded a nonprofit after-school arts school and mentoring program for high school and college students in Monterey, California, where they lived for several years. It answered the question of what her purpose was: "To mentor, in my case," which encompassed art, but also emotional health and professional guidance, in relationships that could last as long as six years. "We have their backs for a long time," Meg said. "They're kids from all walks of life. They have no idea what's possible. We just expect them to be genuine—and we are, too. This is the most meaningful thing I've ever done."

37

One of the last direct descendants of Gouverneur Morris, Betty Bonsal personified a constructive use of a family's inheritance of experience and tradition, if not wealth, by championing a fundamental right long refused to a large cohort of Americans. In 2008, Connecticut became the third American state to legalize gay marriage. After that, Bonsal, then a justice of the peace in the town of Greenwich, is said to have married more same-sex couples—254 of them—than anyone else in her state. The 246th couple she married was her daughter and her longtime partner.

"I'm looking at a picture of Gouverneur Morris," said Betty's daughter, Liz Bonsal, at the start of a telephone interview for this book. She traced her descent from Gouverneur Morris III's daughter Henrietta, whose brother, Gouverneur IV, a screenwriter for silent films, was the penultimate Morris to bear that name. Betty Bonsal and her husband, Stephen, started dating when he was a Harvard student. They married and, after having three kids, moved to Greenwich, Connecticut, a Republican town where Betty became chair of the local Democratic Party. Being a Democrat in conservative Greenwich wasn't easy, but she managed to be named one of twelve justices of the peace in the wealthy town. Her daughter, Liz, graduated from college and came out in 1990, in her early twenties. Though she had known she was gay "since I was five," and protested for gay rights with Queer Nation and ACT UP, she had kept her family in the dark. But, freshly broken up with a girlfriend and "holding so much in, I needed to share," she told her mother she had a secret to reveal. "Mom's a talker, but she just listened. It was a first. I talked and talked and talked and talked and got a little smile."

Her mother's first words were a question: "How do lesbians do it?" Her next question was who would tell Liz's father, and her mother immediately volunteered to do it. Her father called Liz immediately afterward, offering "love and support," Liz reported.

Liz and her wife were together seventeen years before they married in 2016. A committed progressive, Liz said her convictions were based in her family heritage: "You think more and more about what the Founding Fathers tried to do. Especially now, when you look at the state of the nation. The first Gouverneur Morris would be appalled. We are so polarized now into immovable camps. I hope, as I know he would, that we can see our way out of this and the experiment continues another two hundred years."

38

As it was with Penelope Tree, family history was a bit of a mystery to Frederick Henry Osborn III, the great-great-grandson of Fairfield Osborn's brother William Church Osborn. Fred was aware of Fairfield's dark side, and his branch of the Osborns inherited Fairfield's interest in breeding and genetics, albeit "in a totally different way, nothing to do with race," he said in an interview for this book, adding that while Fairfield was a visionary museum leader and brilliant academic, "all the good seems overshadowed."[83]

Fred III's education began at Episcopal Academy in Merion, Pennsylvania, which was "about as WASPy as you could get," he acknowledged. Admitted to Princeton at sixteen, he hated it, left during his sophomore year, and in 1966 was drafted and sent to Vietnam, returning to Maine's Colby College after his discharge. In 1971, he married Anne de Peyster Todd, a descendant of Lewis

Morris and of Jacobus Van Cortlandt, John Jay's grandfather. By then, Fred III was making medical devices, but at twenty-five he sold an innovative patent for shrinking integrated circuits and retired.

After he and Anne attended an Episcopal encounter weekend for couples—"a very moving religious experience"—he became, as he put it, "a serious WASP." For the next quarter century he pursued an "unplanned career in the religion business," managing the finances of and fundraising for the Episcopal Church in Boston, Portland, and Hartford before returning to New York and the national church organization.

Fred also kept up his family's philanthropy. When he was a college freshman, his grandfather had told him, "'You're going to be a leader of society'—this sort of pompous pronouncement," but he took that inheritance seriously. "As a teenager, I'd resisted, rebelled against everything my parents stood for: wealth, prestige, and WASPiness, but of course, I began to embrace it, and I now feel that I'm living in their shadow."

After a second retirement in 2006, he gave up his seat on half of the fourteen boards on which he served. "I still get to spend a lot of time with a lot of interesting people doing interesting things. What a privilege it is," he said, embracing a fraught word that is now often seen as a negative. "I've become the person that I wanted to be."

39

Defiance of his privilege and guilt over the inheritance that turbocharged it made George Pillsbury who he wanted to be, but his family legacy, which traces back to the Plymouth Colony's Governor Bradford, played an even larger part in making him one of America's pivotal agents of change in the last half century.

Pillsbury never wavered from the commitment he saw embodied in the legacies of his mother's Whitney family and his father's Pillsbury clan. In his age of innocence at Yale, as a bit of a nut with dough, in 1969 he left $200 in cash in a paper bag on the porch of the headquarters of the local Black Panthers branch. He then became a pioneer of progressive philanthropy in the 1970s, continuing that work into the early 2020s, when he could be found advocating for the right of all Americans to vote and their duty to do so.

The Pillsburys came from England in about 1640 in the person of William Pillsbury Jr., who rose from indentured servant to owner of forty acres in Newbury, Massachusetts, in his first decade in America. That land remained in the family over nine generations. But in 1855, John Sargent Pillsbury, a New Hampshire storekeeper with an entrepreneurial streak, moved to a town on the Mississippi River just north of Minneapolis to seek his fortune. Fourteen years later, he and several relatives created C. A. Pillsbury and Co., named for a nephew who had bought a share in a local flour mill. It turned into a giant food products concern and made the Pillsburys one of Minnesota's wealthiest families. Their company's mascot, the Pillsbury Dough Boy, inspired a derisive nickname that George much later turned into an ironic calling card.

The family record of public service started with three Pillsbury ancestors on Lexington Green at the initial skirmish of the American Revolution. "I think about my ancestors a lot. They were impatient for the world to get better," he said in an interview for this book. John Sargent Pillsbury served in Minnesota's state senate, then as the state's governor, and became a philanthropist after a British syndicate briefly bought control of the flour mills in 1889. He often donated money anonymously, but he was also known as the father of the University of Minnesota, his alma mater, which he rescued from killing debt in its infancy and then supported throughout his life. His credo was said to be "Act; act now; act effectively; act for the greatest good."*

George Sturgis Pillsbury, a great-nephew of John Sargent Pillsbury, spent twenty-four years at the family firm before running for the state senate himself. He married Sally Whitney in 1947. Before the Civil War, her branch of the Whitney family moved to St. Cloud, Minnesota, where her grandfather, Albert Gideon Whitney, prospered in real estate, lending, insurance, and streetcars and by the 1920s held an effective monopoly over St. Cloud's electric supply. Albert's widow, the former Alice Wheelock, whose family founded

---

* Twenty-two years after Pillsbury's death, the family bought back its flour business and kept control of it until 1989.

Dartmouth College and also fought at Lexington, remained one of the city's leading citizens. She donated the land for St. Cloud's airport and once welcomed Marian Anderson to her home when the African American contralto was turned away from a local hotel.

The family's tradition was carried on by Alice and Albert's grandson, Wheelock Whitney Jr. An investment banker, he served as part-time mayor of Wayzata, a wealthy Minneapolis suburb, and as a moderate Republican ran unsuccessfully for the U.S. Senate in 1964 and the Minnesota statehouse in 1982; in between, he supported New York's moderate Republican governor Nelson Rockefeller for president over Richard Nixon. A lifelong friend of George H. W. Bush, he brought baseball's Washington Senators to Minneapolis, where they became the Twins, and was part owner of football's Vikings and hockey's North Stars. Late in life he spoke out for the right of gay people to marry—both a son and a grandson were gay—and women's right to abortion, though his positions were anathema to his party.

Sally and George Pillsbury were also moderate Republicans. Sally opposed the Vietnam War and George broke with his party often, even leading an effort to change his state's party name to Independent-Republican after the Watergate scandal. In 2008, he left the party altogether and backed Barack Obama for president. Among their favored causes was Women Winning, an organization that encourages female candidates who support abortion rights, hardly the stuff of Republican orthodoxy.

Their son George Pillsbury cited supporting Rockefeller over Nixon at the 1968 Republican convention as "my last act as a Republican." At college, he joked in an interview, he became "what people fear"—a political activist. Inspired by his mother's progressive politics, George got involved in the civil rights and peace movements while at Yale. In 1971, he inherited a $500,000 trust and sold most of the stocks it held, considering them unethical. Graduating the next year, he moved to Cambridge, Massachusetts, where he earned a master's degree in working-class history at the brief-lived Goddard-Cambridge Graduate Program in Social Change.

Seeking a socially responsible career, he was inspired by San Francisco's Vanguard Foundation, formed in 1972 by heirs to various fortunes to channel their wealth into social change, "investing well, not just giving it away." George started an East Coast analogue with a small group of wealthy friends and named it Haymarket after a deadly 1886 riot that followed a pro-labor rally in Chicago. He hoped to encourage fundamental, systemic change by funding community-oriented organizations formed by the poor and working class. He also launched a support group where wealthy heirs like him could discuss their lives and the pressures imposed on them by inherited wealth. All of it made him a target for snarky comments. "In short, it would appear, Pillsbury is out to overthrow himself," said the *Boston Globe*.[84] His trust fund was quickly drained.

By the mid-seventies, others had followed Pillsbury's lead, including his younger sister Sarah, who created the Liberty Hill Foundation in Los Angeles, named for the site of an Upton Sinclair speech during a longshoremen's strike in 1923.* By 1975, George was thinking bigger, and he left Haymarket to help similarly minded scions develop the Funding Exchange, a national group offering technical assistance to alternative foundations, and the Film Fund, with documentarian Barbara Kopple, to support films with social justice themes.

Though he had long resisted family entreaties to stop giving away his money—a grandmother stopped giving any to him—Pillsbury's attitude shifted after he got married in 1981, bought a house, and had two children. "My kids also had a stake" in the family trusts, he said in his interview for this book. "My grandkids won't have that kind of wealth."†

In 1987, at age forty, Pillsbury took a full-time job earning about $20,000 a year as the development director of the Jobs with Peace Campaign. It targeted the military-industrial complex and sought to redirect spending from war to needs like housing and transportation. It convinced him that solving social problems required political power, so in 1993, he switched gears and enrolled in a midcareer master's degree program to study public administration for political reform at Harvard's Kennedy School. Voting rights became his new focus, and over the next two decades he worked with the Massachusetts Money

---

* Where George spent his life as a full-time activist, Sarah also made movies. After winning an Oscar for a short film, she teamed with a partner and produced films like *Desperately Seeking Susan* and *River's Edge* and the TV movie *And the Band Played On*, which won an Emmy.
† George Sturgis Pillsbury died in 2012; his wife, Sally, died in 2018.

and Politics Project, where he studied legislative fundraising in the state; MassVOTE, a nonpartisan nonprofit promoting voter participation; and Nonprofit Vote, which urges nonprofit groups to promote voting and civic engagement. "We can't change the world when half the country isn't voting," he said. "These should be nonpartisan issues." After the 2016 election, he focused on reform of the electoral college, one of the lingering constitutional accommodations to America's original slave states.

Pillsbury acknowledged his advantages, the flip side of which is obligation, another aspect of his tribal inheritance. "I do think about the history. I inherited a drive for fairness and justice that was passed down over generations. Not all, but many colonial families fleeing a monarchy saw the benefit of helping their neighbors. There are flaws and bumps along the way, different strains, but there's a powerful tradition of caring. You see it in the Revolution, the Lincoln Republicans, the Civil War. Yes, we were elites, but we were civically involved by necessity."

40

What was once America's ruling class won and freely exercised its power in the late eighteenth century, but over the course of many generations, it husbanded, spent, and then frittered away its capital, both financial and otherwise, until it was considered irretrievably broken, if not entirely broke, at the dawn of the twenty-first. Yet the current sociopolitical moment argues for a renewed appreciation of some white Anglo-Saxon Protestant virtues. The rise of tribalism, anger, emotion, blind loyalty, and a generalized lust for retribution created an opportunity not only for our second Roman Catholic president, Joe Biden, a paragon of decency, but also for the WASPs, that ever-smaller percentage of the citizenry, to remind America of its foundational ideals. There is, in effect, a societal job opening, and it offers WASPs a chance to regain some of their impact and influence on American society. There is a yawning void where the best of WASP culture might make a difference again. The higher core virtues traditionally associated with America's founders have the potential to remind us of what Abraham Lincoln called "the better angels of our nature," what Americans have always aspired to be as a people.

America's ruling class is no longer the homogeneous, incestuous clique of WASP first families and the friends they admitted into their circle. The decline of the WASP ruling class that began during World War II and the diminution of the power and influence of the white Anglo-Saxon Protestants who had ruled America since before its founding seemed irreversible by the late 1960s. By the time America's forty-first president, George H. W. Bush, died in 2018, WASPs seemed entirely irrelevant. Yet, due to the counterexample of the forty-fifth president, Donald J. Trump, then almost two years into his first term in office, Bush's death set off a torrent of WASP nostalgia. In mourning Bush 41, the nation was also mourning the loss of WASP virtues, and giving voice to a yearning for a revival of the ideals of the Enlightenment that were the foundation of their invention, the American national experiment, without the baggage that has always accompanied and ultimately tarnished it. Many people still embody those ideals, but since the peak of WASP power and influence, they've been dispersed, discouraged, and disenfranchised, their voices silenced, their social coherence diluted. So, too, the influence of the elite WASP who once embodied the spirit of the nation.

In 1993, WASPs ceased to be America's majority. By 2014, they accounted for just under a third of the population.[85] White Protestants were in the majority in only six states: South Dakota, Alabama, Arkansas, Tennessee, Kentucky, and West Virginia.[86] In 2020, only 12 percent of young Americans identified as mainstream Protestants, as compared to 20 percent of senior citizens. Two-thirds of Republicans identified as white Christians, compared to 39 percent of Democrats, but only 22 percent of them considered themselves in the Protestant mainstream.[87] It is hardly surprising that those embattled white Anglo-Saxon conservative Protestants were the foot soldiers of the populist army that has transformed American politics in the last quarter century.

Yet despite the elite WASPs themselves, their manifest weaknesses, and their multitude of sins, the ideals of humility, responsibility, simple civility, and the rest that they long represented could and perhaps should remain crucial to the American enterprise, even if they are no longer central to it. While wiser, quieter voices are drowned out by the cacophony that has replaced constructive civic debate in America, that WASP ideal—still not achieved, but still a touchstone—can again serve as a common aspiration. It's what this country ought to be.

This sociopolitical moment begs for a new appreciation of what WASPs did best, despite their myriad failures; it provides an opportunity for this ever-smaller percentage of the citizenry to remind America of its foundational ideals. Today, in matters large and small—standards of civic and corporate behavior, identity and equality, technology, the environment, investing, and simple quotidian existence—the values traditionally associated with WASP culture matter again as a necessary component of what we aspire to be as a people. They are what Michael Butler, Penelope Tree, Frankie FitzGerald, Whitney Tower Jr., Betty and Liz Bonsal, George Biddle, George Pillsbury, and many others, in their vastly different ways, still seek to honor.

WASPs, integral to America's DNA as the founders of this national experiment four hundred years ago, could also be vital to its future. They are more likely to return to relevance than to renewed dominance. But instead of injecting more poison into the body politic, the sting of the WASP could now serve as an antidote, reminding us that there is an alternative to our present selfish, narcissistic, tribal, atomized condition, a possibility of restoring America's civic conscience, collective purpose, and national community.

ACKNOWLEDGMENTS

The idea of this book came to me in 2003, inspired by the mother of my friend Christine Biddle, Katherine Mortimer Blaine, who died that year. Years earlier, I'd read her unpublished family memoir, "The Sting of the WASP," and the notion of telling the story of a colonial American family stuck with me, even after I turned instead to another book. But it wasn't until fifteen years later, in January 2018, at a lunch with Grove Atlantic's owner, Morgan Entrekin, that I mentioned the never-executed idea, and his enthusiasm for it revived and then refined the notion. Over the next year, after reading shelves of books on white Anglo-Saxon Protestants and having several more long conversations with Morgan and Grove Atlantic's executive editor, George Gibson, the idea evolved into the volume you are now reading, focusing on about a dozen families, all across America, over the more than four hundred years since the *Mayflower* reached Cape Cod, Massachusetts. My first thanks go to Morgan and George; they represent everything that book publishing should be. And George's deft, incisive editing is the best I've encountered in my career. Sue Warga's copyediting saved me from numerous embarrassments. Also at Grove Atlantic, I thank Deb Seager, Brenna McDuffie, Emily Burns, Julia Berner-Tobin, Becca Fox, Gretchen Mergenthaler, Erica Nuñez, Cassie McSorley, Judy Hottensen, Natalie Church, Rachel Gilman, and Ian Dreiblatt.

I continued reading in 2019, as I started reaching out to members of interesting families and digging in archives, seeking the most interesting characters within them. I was also fortunate enough to be granted a desk that summer in the Frederick Lewis Allen Room at the New York Public Library's Main Building, an extraordinary research resource for authors. At NYPL, I thank Melanie Locay for welcoming and helping me.

After a few months, though, the COVID-19 pandemic shut down the NYPL and all the other libraries, repositories, and archives I'd hoped to visit. So I continued to do interviews by phone, placed more emphasis on secondary sources, and began to write, a process that seemed more urgent and fraught after the May 2020 death of George Floyd made Americans ask searching questions about their origins and identity. My next debt of gratitude is to the authors and researchers who preceded me in studying the individuals and families I'd decided to include. Their books are all in the bibliography and endnotes that follow, and anyone who wants to dig deeper into these families would do well to start there.

I am fortunate to have a group of personal friends and publishing professionals whom I depend on. My wife, Barbara Hodes, shared an office with me throughout the COVID lockdown and the creation of this book. My debt to her is enormous. I've been represented by my agent, Dan Strone at Trident Media Group, since 2003, and he has been a constant source of encouragement and wisdom. I thank his assistants Tess Weitzner and Claire Romine, too.

Flight of the WASP is dedicated to Barbara, to Christine Biddle and her mother, and to a handful of other WASPs who have been friends for many years—and in several cases are members of families discussed in these pages. They all inspired and helped me to write the book. Though he is mentioned only in passing, Sam Peabody and his wife, Judy, both of whom died before this project began, were also inspirations. They have been described as a couple that epitomized noblesse oblige—an aristocratic sense of obligation—but Sam and Judy's goodness and loyalty stemmed not from any class-based obligation but from a voluntary and ennobling decency. Their story, like dozens of others, was left on the cutting room floor, not because they weren't interesting, but to serve the interests of narrative economy, and keep this book from growing to 1,000 pages.

For support and help over my many years covering the social set, as well as with this book, I also thank David Patrick Columbia, the founder and editor of New York Social Diary, the late Michael M. Thomas, Earle and Carol Mack, Gene and Christine Pressman, Sharon Sondes and Geoffrey Thomas, H. Woody Brock, Nannette and George Herrick, and Steve Cooper of Reed Smith. For advice on explaining the economic aspects of this story, I thank William D. Cohan and Liaquat Ahamed. For personal services rendered during the writing and companionship during the COVID-19 pandemic, I am grateful to Lavinia Snyder, Alison Spear and Alexander Reese, Jeff Blick, Andrew and Leslie Siben, John and Sara Cassis, Hari and Himayani Ramanan, Elizabeth Eilender and David Jaroslawicz, Steven Lamm, Graeme Whyte, Nirmal Tejwani, and Barry Kieselstein-Cord and Sara Nesbitt. I also thank David Schalk, Professor Emeritus of History at Vassar College, for sparking my interest in the past.

I have always depended on student researchers while writing books. This time, I commend Jason Sheldon, Nataleah Joy (and the staff of the Dolph Briscoe Center for American History in Austin, Texas), Katherine Leister, and Kedar Berntson for helping with research tasks large and small. Ted Panken transcribed my interviews with precision. And Melissa Wilde at the University of Pennsylvania was generous with statistics.

Several members of the families in the book shared memories with me in lengthy interviews. For that, I must single out the late Michael Butler, Whitney Tower Jr., Penelope Tree, Frankie FitzGerald, Liz Bonsal, George Pillsbury, Frederick Osborn III, and the late Tony Duke.

I am grateful to Professor Patrick Allitt at Emory University for help with the pages on colonial religion. The pages on the Morris and Rutherfurd families could not have been written without the help of Winthrop Rutherfurd Jr., Kristen Jean Block, Chappy Morris, Bonnie Osler, Dudley Bonsal, the late Deering Howe, the reference librarians at the New-York Historical Society, Sarah Jacobs at New York's Racquet & Tennis Club, Sarah King, and Sargent M. McCormick. Aaron Crawford at the University of Tennessee in Knoxville and Taylor Stoermer at Johns Hopkins University assisted me with the pages on the Randolphs of Virginia. Among the Biddles who were particularly generous with their time were Biddle Duke, Cordelia Biddle, Daisy Biddle Eiman, Ed Biddle, George Biddle, Meg Biddle, George Craig

Biddle, Karen Biddle, Stark Biddle, and Sydney Biddle Barrows. Connie S. Griffith Houchins, executive director of the Andalusia Foundation, Asher Edelman, Carla Kaplan, and Laurie Cielo at St. Peter's Church in Philadelphia also helped with those pages.

I thank Catherine, David Ledyard and Michael Mortimer Ledyard Sr. and Jr., respectively the ninth and tenth generations of Ledyard family lawyers, for bringing the family of Lewis Cass into the present, and for assistance with the story of the Sanfords and Legendres. I thank James Armstrong, Sarita Hixon, Peter "Sandy" Wood, Savannah Poole, Seth Bramson, Alicia Clarke, and Brigitte Stephenson at the Sanford Museum, and Harlan Greene, Samuel Stewart, and Mary Jo Fairchild at the College of Charleston's Addlestone Library.

The Peabody pages come alive thanks to Elizabeth Peabody, Bill Endicott, Teddy Sanford, Jim Sterba, Robert Caravaggi, Charlene Marshall, Gail Friedman at the Groton School, Linda Lapp and Andrea Schwartz at Bloomsburg University's Andruss Library, and Jessica Hanson at the Phillips Library of the Peabody Essex Museum. Alida Morgan pointed me to contemporary members of the Whitney family. Jay Coogan and Daniel Okrent were invaluable in writing the pages on Fairfield Osborn. And my tales of the Butler family were made infinitely more informative and entertaining thanks to Alexander Gaudieri, Sugar Rautbord, Edward Lee Cave, Anita Feick, Glorvina Schwartz, Jerry Schatzberg, Caroline Graham, Reute Butler, Robin Hambro, Emily Moseley, and Robert Bonanno. Thanks to Leith Rutherfurd Talamo, and to Erik Maza and Darrick Harris of *Town & Country* for help with photo research.

I also thank all those who asked not to be thanked. You know who you are.

Finally, I am grateful to Aaron Woodin, Reiner Evangelista, and Nicole Calyk for various IT services, and Agrippina, Barbara's and my West Highland terrier, for keeping me sane during COVID and keeping me company during long days and nights of research, writing, and editing.

NOTES

INTRODUCTION

1 David G. Savage, "Thomas' Church a Center of Anti-Abortion Activity," *Los Angeles Times*, July 11, 1991.

2 Sarah Pulliam Bailey, "The Post-Protestant Supreme Court," *Christianity Today*, April 9, 2010, https://www.christianitytoday.com/news/2010/april/24-53.0.html.

3 Brookings Institution, "Vital Statistics on Congress," updated February 2021, https://www.brookings.edu/multi-chapter-report/vital-statistics-on-congress/.

4 Melissa Wilde, Tessa Huttenlocher, Joan Ryan, and Elena van Stee, "Religious Inequality in America: The View from 1916," paper presented at the American Academy of Religion annual meeting, November 20, 2021.

5 Melissa Wilde, Patricia Tevington, and Wensong Shen, "Religious Inequality in America," *Social Inclusion* 6, no. 2 (2018): 107–126.

6 Justin Davidson, Ralph Pyle, and David Reyes, "Persistence and Change in the Protestant Establishment, 1930–1992," *Social Forces* 74, no. 1 (September 1995): 157–175.

7 PRRI (Public Religion Research Institute), "The 2020 Census of American Religion," 2020.

8 E. Digby Baltzell, *The Protestant Establishment: Aristocracy and Caste in America* (New York: Vintage, 1964), 380–381.

9 Joseph W. Alsop with Adam Platt, *"I've Seen the Best of It": Memoirs* (New York: Norton, 1992), 17–33.

10 Richard Brookhiser, *The Way of the WASP* (New York: Free Press, 1991), 123.

11 Christopher Lehmann-Haupt, "The Decline of a Class and a Country's Fortunes," *New York Times*, January 17, 1991.

12 David Brooks, *Bobos in Paradise* (New York: Simon & Schuster, 2000), 20, 40.

13 Ben Schreckinger, "The Death of the WASP," *Politico*, April 1, 2014.

14 Rich Lowry, "A Farewell to the WASPs," *National Review*, April 24, 2018.

15 Alsop, *"I've Seen the Best of It,"* 33–38.

16 Frederic Cople Jaher, *The Rich, the Wellborn, and the Powerful: Elites and Upper Classes in History* (Urbana: University of Illinois Press, 1973), 258

17 Baltzell, *The Protestant Establishment*, 72.

18 E. Digby Baltzell, "The Protestant Establishment Revisited," *The American Scholar* 45, no. 4 (Autumn 1976): 503.

PART ONE

1 Dixon Wecter, *The Saga of American Society* (New York: Scribner's, 1937), 37.

2 Samuel Eliot Morison, "The Plymouth Colony and Virginia," *Virginia Magazine of History and Biography* 62, no. 2 (April 1954): 157.

3 Society of Mayflower Descendants in the State of Maryland, "Pilgrim History," https://maryland mayflower.org/pilgrim-history/

4 William Bradford, *Of Plymouth Plantation 1620–1647* (New York: Knopf, 1963), xxv.

5 Olivia B. Waxman, "The First Africans in Virginia Landed in 1619. It Was a Turning Point for Slavery in American History—But Not the Beginning," *Time*, August 20, 2019, https://time.com/5653369 /august-1619-jamestown-history/.

6 Nathaniel Philbrick, *Mayflower* (New York: Viking, 2006), 7.

7 Philbrick, *Mayflower*, 10.

8 Bradford, *Of Plymouth Plantation*, 12.

9 Bradford, *Of Plymouth Plantation*, 17.

10 Rebecca Fraser, *The* Mayflower: *The Families, the Voyage, and the Founding of America* (New York: St. Martin's, 2017), 19, 26.

11 Philbrick, *Mayflower*, 17

12 George F. Willison, *Saints and Strangers: Lives of the Pilgrim Fathers and Their Families* (London: Routledge, 2017), 97.

13 Bradford, *Of Plymouth Plantation*, 23–27.

14 Bradford, *Of Plymouth Plantation*, 29.

15 Morison, "The Plymouth Colony and Virginia," 150

16 Bradford Smith, *Bradford of Plymouth* (Philadelphia: Lippincott, 1951), 109.

17 Fraser, *The* Mayflower, 27–28.

18 Bradford, *Of Plymouth Plantation*, 47

19 Fraser, *The* Mayflower, 52.

20 Philbrick, *Mayflower*, 41.

21 Bradford, *Of Plymouth Plantation*, 75.

22 Fraser, *The* Mayflower, 56.

23 Philbrick, *Mayflower*, 65.

24 Philbrick, *Mayflower*, 71–73.

25 Fraser, *The* Mayflower, 65–67.

26 Bradford, *Of Plymouth Plantation*, 72.

27 Philbrick, *Mayflower*, 76.

28 Bradford, *Of Plymouth Plantation*, 77.

29 Philbrick, *Mayflower*, 85.

30 Smith, *Bradford of Plymouth*, 157.

31 Bradford, *Of Plymouth Plantation*, 88.

32 Fraser, *The* Mayflower, 88–98.

33 Smith, *Bradford of Plymouth*, 10.

34 Smith, *Bradford of Plymouth*, 216.

35 Philbrick, *Mayflower*, 117.

36 Bradford, *Of Plymouth Plantation*, 92.

37 Philbrick, *Mayflower*, 126.

38 Philbrick, *Mayflower*, 135.

39 Philbrick, *Mayflower*, 165.

40 Smith, *Bradford of Plymouth*, 193.

41 Fraser, *The* Mayflower, 104–107.

42 Kim Todt, "Trading Between New Netherland and New England, 1624–1664," *Early American Studies* 9, no. 2 (2011): 366–367.

43 Lucy Mary Kellogg, ed., Mayflower *Families Through Five Generations*, vol. 17 (Plymouth, MA: General Society of Mayflower Descendants, 1975), 1.

44 David Hackett Fischer, *Albion's Seed: Four British Folkways in America* (New York: Oxford University Press, 1989), 16.

45 Fischer, *Albion's Seed*, 21.

46 Fischer, *Albion's Seed*, 25.

47 Fischer, *Albion's Seed,* 27–30.

48 Fischer, *Albion's Seed,* 52–54.

49 Evarts B. Greene and Virginia D. Harrington, *American Population Before the Federal Census of 1790* (Gloucester, MA: Peter Smith, 1966), 61–69; Ira Berlin, *Generations of Captivity: A History of African-American Slaves* (Cambridge, MA: Belknap Press of Harvard University Press, 2003), table I, 272.

50 Fischer, *Albion's Seed,* 152.

51 Smith, *Bradford of Plymouth,* 282.

52 Mark L. Sargent, "William Bradford's 'Dialogue' with History," *New England Quarterly* 65, no. 3 (September 1992): 417.

53 Smith, *Bradford of Plymouth,* 223.

54 Bradford, *Of Plymouth Plantation,* 333–334.

55 Smith, *Bradford of Plymouth,* 259.

56 Bradford, *Of Plymouth Plantation,* xxviii.

57 Smith, *Bradford of Plymouth,* 315.

58 James W. Mathews, "Dr. Gamaliel Bradford (1795–1839), Early Abolitionist," *Historical Journal of Massachusetts* 19, no. 1 (Winter 1991): 5.

59 Mathews, "Dr. Gamaliel Bradford," 7.

60 "Interviews with the Legislative Committee," *The Liberator,* March 26, 1836, 1.

61 "My Election Is Certain," *Boston Daily Globe,* September 26, 1897.

62 "Gamaliel Bradford Passes Away," *Christian Science Monitor,* August 21, 1911.

63 "A Bay State Agitator," *New York Times,* September 8, 1901.

64 "Gamaliel Bradford," *Hartford Courant,* August 30, 1911.

65 "Rejected Lover Slays Himself," *Boston Journal;* "Girl Jilts Young Bradford," *Oregonian;* "Gamaliel Bradford," *Cleveland Plain Dealer;* "Descendent of First Governor Suicides," *Macon Telegraph,* all August 9, 1910, and "Was Found Dead in Bed," *Springfield Sunday,* November 17, 1912.

66 Bruce P. Stark, "Fitch, James," in *American National Biography* (New York: Oxford University Press, 1999).

67 "William C. Whitney," *New York Times,* February 3, 1904, 8.

68 W. A. Swanberg, *Whitney Father, Whitney Heiress* (New York: Scribner's, 1980), 36–38.

69 Swanberg, *Whitney Father, Whitney Heiress,* 41.

70 Swanberg, *Whitney Father, Whitney Heiress,* 44.

71 Swanberg, *Whitney Father, Whitney Heiress,* 46.

72 "Career of Mr. Whitney," *New York Tribune,* February 3, 1904, 3.

73 "Tales of W. C. Whitney," *New York Tribune,* February 7, 1904, A1.

74 Max Weber, *The Protestant Ethic and the Spirit of Capitalism* (New York: Routledge, 2001), xxxix.

75 Weber, *The Protestant Ethic,* 10, 30, 22.

76 Weber, *The Protestant Ethic,* 36.

77 Weber, *The Protestant Ethic,* 119, 104.

PART TWO

1 Alexis de Tocqueville, *Democracy in America,* vol. 1 (London: Longman, Green, Longman & Roberts, 1862), 16.

2 Samuel Stelle Smith, *Lewis Morris: Anglo-American Statesman* (Atlantic Highlands, NJ: Humanities Press, 1983), 56–59.

3 Cleveland Amory, *Who Killed Society?* (New York: Harper & Brothers, 1960), 316.

4 Amory, *Who Killed Society?,* 317.

5 Smith, *Lewis Morris,* 2.

6 Smith, *Lewis Morris,* 3–4.

7 Smith, *Lewis Morris,* 6.

8 Smith, *Lewis Morris,* 7–8.

9 Smith, *Lewis Morris,* 10–11.

10 Smith, *Lewis Morris,* 20.

11   Smith, *Lewis Morris*, 24.

12   Smith, *Lewis Morris*, 27.

13   Smith, *Lewis Morris*, xi.

14   Smith, *Lewis Morris*, 28.

15   Smith, *Lewis Morris*, 29–32.

16   Smith, *Lewis Morris*, 35.

17   James C. Brandow, *Genealogies of Barbados Families* (Baltimore: Clearfield, 1997), 418.

18   Roger G. Kennedy, *Architecture, Men, Women and Money in America 1600–1860* (New York: Random House, 1985), 39.

19   Kristen Block, *Ordinary Lives in the Early Caribbean* (Athens: University of Georgia Press, 2012), 149.

20   Block, *Ordinary Lives in the Early Caribbean*, 153, 174.

21   Block, *Ordinary Lives in the Early Caribbean*, 160.

22   Smith, *Lewis Morris*, 50–52.

23   Block, *Ordinary Lives in the Early Caribbean*, 175–176.

24   Russell Shorto, *The Island at the Center of the World* (New York: Vintage, 2005), 105.

25   Shorto, *The Island at the Center of the World*, 61.

26   Shorto, *The Island at the Center of the World*, 49.

27   Shorto, *The Island at the Center of the World*, 58.

28   Shorto, *The Island at the Center of the World*, 304–5.

29   Block, *Ordinary Lives in the Early Caribbean*, 186.

30   Kristen Block, "Cultivating Inner and Outer Plantations: Property, Industry, and Slavery in Early Quaker Migration to the New World," *Early American Studies* 8, no. 3 (Fall 2010).

31   Smith, *Lewis Morris*, 85–88.

32   Smith, *Lewis Morris*, 89.

33   Smith, *Lewis Morris*, 109–114.

34   Block, *Ordinary Lives in the Early Caribbean*, 187.

35   William Howard Adams, *Gouverneur Morris: An Independent Life* (New Haven, CT: Yale University Press, 2003), 8–9.

36   Martha Morris Lawrence, *The Boundary Line and Other Bits of Biography and History* (Deckertown: Sussex Independent, 1895), 24.

37   Smith, *Lewis Morris*, 98.

38   Stephen Jenkins, *The Story of the Bronx* (New York: Putnam's, 1912), 73.

39   Lawrence, *The Boundary Line*, 26.

40   Lawrence, *The Boundary Line*, 76.

41   "Crown v. John Peter Zenger, 1735," Historical Society of the New York Courts, accessed December 7, 2022, https://history.nycourts.gov/case/crown-v-zenger/.

42   Adams, *Gouverneur Morris*, 10.

43   Dumas Malone, ed., *Dictionary of American Biography* (New York: Scribner's, 1934), 13:214.

44   Adams, *Gouverneur Morris*, 4.

45   Lawrence, *The Boundary Line*, 29–30.

46   Richard Brookhiser, *Gentleman Revolutionary: Gouverneur Morris, the Rake Who Wrote the Constitution* (New York: Free Press, 2003), 1.

47   Max N. Mintz, *Gouverneur Morris and the American Revolution* (Norman: University of Oklahoma Press, 1970), 14.

48   Melanie Randolph Miller, *Envoy to the Terror: Gouverneur Morris and the French Revolution* (Washington, DC: Potomac, 2005), 2.

49   Theodore Roosevelt, *Gouverneur Morris: American Statesman* (Boston: Houghton Mifflin, 1889), 2.

50   Brookhiser, *Gentleman Revolutionary*, 10–11.

51   Mary Elizabeth Springer, *Elizabeth Schuyler: A Story of Old New York* (New York: Blanchard, 1902).

52   Brookhiser, *Gentleman Revolutionary*, 17.

53   Roosevelt, *Gouverneur Morris*, 22, 23.

54   Miller, *Envoy to the Terror*, 3.

55 Frank Monaghan, *John Jay: Defender of Liberty* (Indianapolis: Bobbs-Merrill, 1935), 276.

56 Mintz, *Gouverneur Morris*, 14.

57 Adams, *Gouverneur Morris*, 23.

58 Springer, *Elizabeth Schuyler*, 197.

59 Adams, *Gouverneur Morris*, 44.

60 Adams, *Gouverneur Morris*, 63.

61 Roosevelt, *Gouverneur Morris*, 46.

62 Adams, *Gouverneur Morris*, 57.

63 Brookhiser, *Gentleman Revolutionary*, 28.

64 Lawrence, *The Boundary Line*, 36.

65 Adams, *Gouverneur Morris*, 76.

66 Adams, *Gouverneur Morris*, 82.

67 Brookhiser, *Gentleman Revolutionary*, 37.

68 Adams, *Gouverneur Morris*, 91.

69 Roosevelt, *Gouverneur Morris*, 67.

70 Brookhiser, *Gentleman Revolutionary*, 43–44.

71 Adams, *Gouverneur Morris*, 102.

72 Adams, *Gouverneur Morris*, 107.

73 Brookhiser, *Gentleman Revolutionary*, 51.

74 Brookhiser, *Gentleman Revolutionary*, 53.

75 Roosevelt, *Gouverneur Morris*, 128.

76 Brookhiser, *Gentleman Revolutionary*, 56.

77 John Jay to Gouverneur Morris, April 29, 1778, The Correspondence and Public Papers of John Jay, Vol. 1, 1763–1781, https://oll.libertyfund.org/title/johnston-the-correspondence-and-public-papers-of-john-jay-vol-1-1763-1781?html=true.

78 Brookhiser, *Gentleman Revolutionary*, 58.

79 Brookhiser, *Gentleman Revolutionary*, 58.

80 Roosevelt, *Gouverneur Morris*, 94.

81 Adams, *Gouverneur Morris*, 123.

82 Mintz, *Gouverneur Morris*, 141.

83 Adams, *Gouverneur Morris*, 127

84 Brookhiser, *Gentleman Revolutionary*, 61–62.

85 Roosevelt, *Gouverneur Morris*, 96.

86 Brookhiser, *Gentleman Revolutionary*, 68–69.

87 Brookhiser, *Gentleman Revolutionary*, 71; Roosevelt, *Gouverneur Morris*, 112.

88 Brookhiser, *Gentleman Revolutionary*, 74.

89 Adams, *Gouverneur Morris*, 132.

90 Adams, *Gouverneur Morris*, xii.

91 Brookhiser, *Gentleman Revolutionary*, 76.

92 Brookhiser, *Gentleman Revolutionary*, 74.

93 Adams, *Gouverneur Morris*, 143.

94 Jill Lepore, *These Truths* (New York: Norton, 2018), 120.

95 Brookhiser, *Gentleman Revolutionary*, 82.

96 Brookhiser, *Gentleman Revolutionary*, 86.

97 Adams, *Gouverneur Morris*, 160.

98 Erick Trickey, "Inside the Founding Fathers' Debate over What Constituted an Impeachable Offense," *Smithsonian Magazine*, October 2, 2017, https://www.smithsonianmag.com/history/inside-founding-fathers-debate-over-what-constituted-impeachable-offense-180965083/.

99 Miller, *Envoy to the Terror*, 7.

100 Brookhiser, *Gentleman Revolutionary*, 84.

101 Brookhiser, *Gentleman Revolutionary*, 85.

102   Roosevelt, *Gouverneur Morris,* 131.

103   Roosevelt, *Gouverneur Morris,* 122.

104   Brookhiser, *Gentleman Revolutionary,* 87.

105   Brookhiser, *Gentleman Revolutionary,* xiv.

106   Letter from James Madison to Jared Sparks, April 8, 1831, https://founders.archives.gov/documents /Madison/99-02-02-2323.

107   Brookhiser, *Gentleman Revolutionary,* 91.

108   Brookhiser, *Gentleman Revolutionary,* 92.

109   Miller, *Envoy to the Terror,* 9.

110   Miller, *Envoy to the Terror,* 22.

111   Miller, *Envoy to the Terror,* 18.

112   Miller, *Envoy to the Terror,* 19.

113   Miller, *Envoy to the Terror,* 20.

114   Miller, *Envoy to the Terror,* 16.

115   Adams, *Gouverneur Morris,* 174.

116   Gouverneur Morris, *A Diary of the French Revolution,* ed. Beatrix C. Davenport (Boston: Houghton Mifflin, 1939) 1:23.

117   Miller, *Envoy to the Terror,* 13.

118   Adams, *Gouverneur Morris,* 182.

119   Charles Callan Tansill, *The Secret Loves of the Founding Fathers* (New York: Devin-Adair, 1964), 141.

120   Adams, *Gouverneur Morris,* 189.

121   Roosevelt, *Gouverneur Morris,* 153.

122   Roosevelt, *Gouverneur Morris,* 151.

123   Morris, *A Diary of the French Revolution,* 1:20.

124   Miller, *Envoy to the Terror,* 23, 25.

125   Roosevelt, *Gouverneur Morris,* 196.

126   Brookhiser, *Gentleman Revolutionary,* 110.

127   Tansill, *The Secret Loves of the Founding Fathers,* 144.

128   Adams, *Gouverneur Morris,* 193.

129   Adams, *Gouverneur Morris,* 194.

130   Miller, *Envoy to the Terror,* 32; Brookhiser, *Gentleman Revolutionary,* 111.

131   Roosevelt, *Gouverneur Morris,* 172.

132   Roosevelt, *Gouverneur Morris,* 183.

133   Roosevelt, *Gouverneur Morris,* 192.

134   Brookhiser, *Gentleman Revolutionary,* 106–7.

135   Roosevelt, *Gouverneur Morris,* 179.

136   Adams, *Gouverneur Morris,* 195.

137   Adams, *Gouverneur Morris,* 198.

138   Richard Brookhiser, "The Forgotten Founding Father," *City Journal,* Spring 2002.

139   Roosevelt, *Gouverneur Morris,* 204.

140   Adams, *Gouverneur Morris,* 220.

141   Miller, *Envoy to the Terror,* 50.

142   Morris, *Diary and Letters,* 2:148.

143   Brookhiser, *Gentleman Revolutionary,* 123.

144   Roosevelt, *Gouverneur Morris,* 210–11.

145   Roosevelt, *Gouverneur Morris,* 213.

146   Miller, *Envoy to the Terror,* 138

147   Miller, *Envoy to the Terror,* 86.

148   Miller, *Envoy to the Terror,* 88.

149   Miller, *Envoy to the Terror,* 1.

150   Brookhiser, *Gentleman Revolutionary,* 129.

151 Miller, *Envoy to the Terror,* 120.

152 Miller, *Envoy to the Terror,* 144.

153 Miller, *Envoy to the Terror,* 145.

154 Miller, *Envoy to the Terror,* 157.

155 Adams, *Gouverneur Morris,* 238.

156 Adams, *Gouverneur Morris,* 241.

157 Adams, *Gouverneur Morris,* 243.

158 Miller, *Envoy to the Terror,* 184.

159 Adams, *Gouverneur Morris,* 245.

160 Miller, *Envoy to the Terror,* 133.

161 Roosevelt, *Gouverneur Morris,* 241.

162 Roosevelt, *Gouverneur Morris,* 228.

163 Miller, *Envoy to the Terror,* 218.

164 Miller, *Envoy to the Terror,* 221.

165 Miller, *Envoy to the Terror,* 234.

166 Adams, *Gouverneur Morris,* 254.

167 Miller, *Envoy to the Terror,* 236.

168 Adams, *Gouverneur Morris,* 257.

169 Roosevelt, *Gouverneur Morris,* 256.

170 Meredith Hindley, "Ungoverned Passion," *Humanities* 33, no. 2 (March/April 2012), https://www.neh.gov/humanities/2012/marchapril/feature/ungoverned-passion.

171 Brookhiser, *Gentleman Revolutionary,* 147.

172 Hindley, "Ungoverned Passion"; Brookhiser, *Gentleman Revolutionary,* 149.

173 Hindley, "Ungoverned Passion."

174 Brookhiser, *Gentleman Revolutionary,* 154.

175 Peter M. Kenny, *Honoré Lannuier: Cabinetmaker from Paris* (New York: Metropolitan Museum of Art, 1998), 126.

176 Atwood Manley, "The Little-Known Alexander Macomb," *The Quarterly* (St. Lawrence County Historical Association) IV, no. 1 (January 1959).

177 J. Christopher Herold, *Mistress to an Age: A Life of Madame de Staël* (Indianapolis: Bobbs-Merrill,1958), 279.

178 Roger G. Kennedy, *Orders from France: The Americans and the French in a Revolutionary World, 1780–1820* (New York: Knopf, 1989), 355.

179 Speer Morgan, "Land Fever: The Downfall of Robert Morris," *Missouri Review* 15, no. 3 (1992): 120.

180 William Graham Sumner, *Robert Morris* (New York: Dodd, Mead, 1892), 157–158.

181 Charles Rappleye, *Robert Morris: Financier of the American Revolution* (New York: Simon & Schuster, 2010), 509.

182 Kennedy, *Orders from France,* 35.

183 Morgan, "Land Fever," 121.

184 Brookhiser, *Gentleman Revolutionary,* 161.

185 "Morris Reminiscences," *New York Tribune,* July 23, 1899, A6.

PART THREE

1 Francis Biddle, *A Casual Past* (Garden City, NY: Doubleday, 1961), 20.

2 David Hackett Fischer, *Albion's Seed: Four British Folkways in America* (New York: Oxford University Press, 1989), 210.

3 Fischer, *Albion's Seed,* 214.

4 Author interview with historian Taylor Stoermer.

5 Hugh A. Garland, *The Life of John Randolph of Roanoke* (New York: D. Appleton, 1874), 1.

6 Fischer, *Albion's Seed,* 388.

7 Taylor Stoermer email to author March 19, 2022.

8 Fischer, *Albion's Seed,* 367–368.

9   Fischer, *Albion's Seed*, 411–417.

10 Garland, *The Life of John Randolph of Roanoke*, 5.

11 David Johnson, *John Randolph of Roanoke* (Baton Rouge: Louisiana State University Press, 2012), 11.

12 Garland, *The Life of John Randolph of Roanoke*, 4.

13 Aaron Scott Crawford, "John Randolph of Roanoke and the Politics of Doom: Slavery, Sectionalism, and Self-Deception, 1773–1821," PhD diss., University of Tennessee, 2012, https://trace.tennessee.edu/utk_graddiss/1519.

14 Russell Kirk, *John Randolph of Roanoke: A Study in American Politics* (Chicago: Henry Regnery, 1964), 168.

15 Johnson, *John Randolph of Roanoke*, 10.

16 Garland, *The Life of John Randolph of Roanoke*, 24.

17 Garland, *The Life of John Randolph of Roanoke*, 57.

18 Garland, *The Life of John Randolph of Roanoke*, 58.

19 Cynthia A. Kierner, *Scandal at Bizarre: Rumor and Reputation in Jefferson's America* (New York: Palgrave Macmillan, 2004), 21.

20 Johnson, *John Randolph of Roanoke*, 30.

21 William Howard Adams, *Gouverneur Morris: An Independent Life* (New Haven, CT: Yale University Press, 2003), 286.

22 Kierner, *Scandal at Bizarre*, 60.

23 Christopher L. Doyle, "The Randolph Scandal in Early Virginia, 1792–1815: New Voices in the 'Court of Honor,'" *Journal of Southern History* 69, no. 2 (May 2003).

24 Kierner, *Scandal at Bizarre*, 58.

25 Johnson, *John Randolph of Roanoke*, 32.

26 Johnson, *John Randolph of Roanoke*, 33.

27 Doyle, "The Randolph Scandal in Early Virginia."

28 Andrew Madigan, "The Pair of American Politicians Who Fought the 19th Century's Silliest Duel," *Atlas Obscura*, accessed December 16, 2020, https://www.atlasobscura.com/articles/the-pair-of-american-politicians-who-fought-the-19th-centurys-silliest-duel.

29 Henry Adams, *John Randolph: A Biography* (Armonk, NY: M.E. Sharpe, 1996), 30.

30 Garland, *The Life of John Randolph of Roanoke*, 70.

31 Adams, *John Randolph*, 33.

32 Adams, *John Randolph*, 35.

33 Adams, *John Randolph*, 32.

34 Johnson, *John Randolph of Roanoke*, 4.

35 Adams, *John Randolph*, 39.

36 Garland, *The Life of John Randolph of Roanoke*, 134.

37 Alan Pell Crawford, *Unwise Passions* (New York: Simon & Schuster, 2000), 141.

38 Kirk, *John Randolph of Roanoke*, 28.

39 Crawford, "John Randolph of Roanoke."

40 Adams, *John Randolph*, 69.

41 Adams, *John Randolph*, 95.

42 Adams, *John Randolph*, 91.

43 Johnson, *John Randolph of Roanoke*, 79.

44 Kierner, *Scandal at Bizarre*, 92.

45 Crawford, *Unwise Passions*, 163.

46 Adams, *John Randolph*, 118.

47 Adams, *John Randolph*, 81.

48 Adams, *John Randolph*, 111.

49 Adams, *John Randolph*, 123, 125.

50 Johnson, *John Randolph of Roanoke*, 115.

51 Adams, *John Randolph*, 129.

52 Adams, *John Randolph*, 212.

53   Johnson, *John Randolph of Roanoke*, 127.

54   Adams, *John Randolph*, 157.

55   Adams, *John Randolph*, 140–141.

56   Adams, *John Randolph*, 166.

57   Johnson, *John Randolph of Roanoke*, 129.

58   Johnson, *John Randolph of Roanoke*, 131.

59   Crawford, "John Randolph of Roanoke."

60   Crawford, *Unwise Passions*, 211.

61   Johnson, *John Randolph of Roanoke*, 143.

62   Johnson, *John Randolph of Roanoke*, 144.

63   Johnson, *John Randolph of Roanoke*, 144–146.

64   Johnson, *John Randolph of Roanoke*, 149.

65   Kirk, *John Randolph of Roanoke*, 138.

66   Crawford, "John Randolph of Roanoke."

67   Jared Sparks, *The Life of Gouverneur Morris*, vol. 3 (Boston: Gray & Bowen, 1832), 130.

68   Richard Brookhiser, *Gentleman Revolutionary: Gouverneur Morris, the Rake Who Wrote the Constitution* (New York: Free Press, 2003), 166.

69   Theodore Roosevelt, *Gouverneur Morris: American Statesman* (Boston: Houghton Mifflin, 1889), 288.

70   Adams, *Gouverneur Morris*, 280.

71   Brookhiser, *Gentleman Revolutionary*, 177.

72   Brookhiser, *Gentleman Revolutionary*, 190.

73   Kierner, *Scandal at Bizarre*, 123.

74   Biddle, *A Casual Past*, 42.

75   Kierner, *Scandal at Bizarre*, 124.

76   Adams, *Gouverneur Morris*, 289.

77   Adams, *Gouverneur Morris*, 291.

78   Brookhiser, *Gentleman Revolutionary*, 195.

79   Kierner, *Scandal at Bizarre*, 129.

80   Brookheiser, *Gentleman Revolutionary*, 205.

81   Johnson, *John Randolph of Roanoke*, 162.

82   Johnson, *John Randolph of Roanoke*, 163.

83   Biddle, *A Casual Past*, 45.

84   "An Interview with Melanie Randolph Miller," *Humanities* 40, no. 2 (Spring 2019).

85   Charles Callan Tansill, *The Secret Loves of the Founding Fathers* (New York: Devin-Adair, 1964), 162.

86   Kierner, *Scandal at Bizarre*.

87   Brookhiser, *Gentleman Revolutionary*, 202.

88   Roosevelt, *Gouverneur Morris*, 315.

89   Author correspondence with Sargent M. McCormick Collier, March 24, 2020.

90   Kierner, *Scandal at Bizarre*, 148–151.

91   Kierner, *Scandal at Bizarre*, 152.

92   "Precious Sister—Letters from Euphemia," The Gouverneur Morris Papers, accessed May 15, 2020, http://www.gouverneurmorrispapers.com/2013/.

93   Crawford, "John Randolph of Roanoke."

94   Crawford, "John Randolph of Roanoke."

95   Johnson, *John Randolph of Roanoke*, 174.

96   Crawford, *Unwise Passions*, 259.

97   Kirk, *John Randolph of Roanoke*, 153, 129.

98   Josiah Quincy, *Figures of the Past: Leaves from Old Journals* (Boston: Roberts Brothers, 1888), 213.

99   Johnson, *John Randolph of Roanoke*, 69.

100 Johnson, *John Randolph of Roanoke*, 69–70.

101 Kirk, *John Randolph of Roanoke*, 133.

102   Johnson, *John Randolph of Roanoke*, 70.

103   Johnson, *John Randolph of Roanoke*, 71.

104   Kirk, *John Randolph of Roanoke*, 134.

105   Johnson, *John Randolph of Roanoke*, 72.

106   Kirk, *John Randolph of Roanoke*, 135–136.

107   Kirk, *John Randolph of Roanoke*, 138.

108   Johnson, *John Randolph of Roanoke*, 183.

109   Kirk, *John Randolph of Roanoke*, 153.

110   Johnson, *John Randolph of Roanoke*, 186.

111   Crawford, "John Randolph of Roanoke."

112   Kirk, *John Randolph of Roanoke*, 172.

113   Adams, *John Randolph*, 182.

114   Johnson, *John Randolph of Roanoke*, 205.

115   Johnson, *John Randolph of Roanoke*, 208.

116   Adams, *John Randolph*, 188.

117   Adams, *John Randolph*, 191.

118   Kirk, *John Randolph of Roanoke*, 57.

119   Crawford, *Unwise Passions*, 271.

120   Kirk, *John Randolph of Roanoke*, 151.

121   Jim Humphrey and Rich Wallace, "Randolph Slaves," February 1997, Shelby County Historical Society, https://www.shelbycountyhistory.org/schs/archives/blackhistoryarchives/randolphbhisA.htm.

122   Kirk, *John Randolph of Roanoke*, 8.

PART FOUR

1   Edward Pessen, "Equality and Opportunity in America, 1800–1940," *Wilson Quarterly* 1, no. 5 (Autumn 1977): 136–142.

2   Willard Carl Klunder, *Lewis Cass and the Politics of Moderation* (Kent, OH: Kent State University Press, 1996), 1.

3   Frank B. Woodford, *Lewis Cass: The Last Jeffersonian* (New Brunswick, NJ: Rutgers University Press, 1950), 5.

4   Woodford, *Lewis Cass*, 11.

5   William T. Young, *Sketch of the Life and Public Services of General Lewis Cass with the Pamphlet on the Right of Search and Some of his Speeches on the Great Political Questions of the Day* (Philadelphia: E. H. Butler, 1853), 161.

6   John T. Fierst, "Rationalizing Removal: Anti-Indianism in Lewis Cass's *North American Review* Essays," *Michigan Historical Review* 36, no. 2 (Fall 2010).

7   Lee Soltow, "Wealth Inequality in the United States in 1798 and 1860," *Review of Economics and Statistics* 66, no. 3 (August 1984).

8   Claudio Saunt, *Unworthy Republic: The Dispossession of Native Americans and the Road to Indian Territory* (New York: Norton, 2020), 6–7.

9   C. Miller Biddle, *Willian and Sarah Biddle 1633–1711: Planting a Seed of Democracy in America* (Moorestown, NJ: Privately published, 2012), 1.

10   Biddle, *Willian and Sarah Biddle 1633–1711*, 54.

11   Biddle, *Willian and Sarah Biddle 1633–1711*, 67.

12   David Hackett Fischer, *Albion's Seed: Four British Folkways in America* (New York: Oxford University Press, 1989), 595.

13   Christopher Matthews, "The Black Freedom Struggle in Northern New Jersey, 1613–1860: A Review of the Literature," part 2, "Slavery in Early English East Jersey," Department of Anthropology, Montclair State University, https://www.montclair.edu/anthropology/research/slavery-in-nj/part-2/.

14   Fischer, *Albion's Seed*, 462–464.

15   Biddle, *Willian and Sarah Biddle 1633–1711*, 89.

16   Biddle, *Willian and Sarah Biddle 1633–1711*, 109.

17 Biddle, *Willian and Sarah Biddle 1633–1711*, 199.

18 Biddle, *Willian and Sarah Biddle 1633–1711*, 183.

19 Nathaniel Burt, *The Perennial Philadelphians: The Anatomy of an American Aristocracy* (Philadelphia: University of Pennsylvania Press, 1963), 45.

20 E. Digby Baltzell, *Philadelphia Gentlemen: The Making of a National Upper Class* (Glencoe, IL: Free Press, 1958), 223.

21 Rodney Stark and Roger Finke, "American Religion in 1776: A Statistical Portrait," *Sociological Analysis* 49, no. 1 (Spring 1988).

22 Francis Biddle, *A Casual Past* (Garden City, NY: Doubleday, 1961), 77.

23 Baltzell, *Philadelphia Gentlemen*, 240.

24 Thomas Payne Govan, *Nicholas Biddle: Nationalist and Public Banker 1786–1844* (Chicago: University of Chicago Press, 1959), 2–3.

25 Govan, *Nicholas Biddle*, 4.

26 Govan, *Nicholas Biddle*, 5.

27 Govan, *Nicholas Biddle*, 8.

28 John Clubbe, *Byron, Sully and the Power of Portraiture* (Aldershot, UK: Ashgate, 2005), 138–139.

29 Thomas Payne Govan, "Nicholas Biddle at Princeton, 1799–1801," *Princeton University Library Chronicle* IX, no. 2 (February 1948).

30 Nicholas Biddle, *Nicholas Biddle in Greece: The Journals and Letters of 1806*, ed. R. A. McNeal (University Park: Pennsylvania State University Press, 1993), 179.

31 Govan, *Nicholas Biddle*, 11.

32 Ron Chernow, *Alexander Hamilton* (New York: Penguin, 2004), 717–718.

33 H. W. Brands, *The Money Men: Capitalism, Democracy and the Hundred Years' War over the American Dollar* (New York: Norton, 2006), 59.

34 Anne Felicity Woodhouse, "Nicholas Biddle in Europe, 1804–1807," *Pennsylvania Magazine of History and Biography* 103, no. 1 (January 1979).

35 Clubbe, *Byron, Sully and the Power of Portraiture*, 145–147.

36 Govan, *Nicholas Biddle*, 12–13.

37 Clubbe, *Byron, Sully and the Power of Portraiture*, 139.

38 R. A. McNeal, "Nicholas Biddle, Anarchism, and the Grand Tour," *Pennsylvania Magazine of History and Biography* 120, no. 3 (July 1966).

39 Govan, *Nicholas Biddle*, 17.

40 Govan, *Nicholas Biddle*, 18.

41 Govan, *Nicholas Biddle*, 20–22.

42 Govan, *Nicholas Biddle*, 22.

43 Klunder, *Lewis Cass and the Politics of Moderation*, 9.

44 Klunder, *Lewis Cass and the Politics of Moderation*, 10.

45 Woodford, *Lewis Cass*, 92.

46 Saunt, *Unworthy Republic*, 7.

47 Saunt, *Unworthy Republic*, 11.

48 Klunder, *Lewis Cass and the Politics of Moderation*, 20–21.

49 Woodford, *Lewis Cass*, 114.

50 Saunt, *Unworthy Republic*, 8; Woodford, *Lewis Cass*, 120–121.

51 Klunder, *Lewis Cass and the Politics of Moderation*, 38.

52 Klunder, *Lewis Cass and the Politics of Moderation*, 40.

53 Saunt, *Unworthy Republic*, 32.

54 Saunt, *Unworthy Republic*, 33.

55 Saunt, *Unworthy Republic*, 63–64.

56 Fierst, "Rationalizing Removal."

57 Lewis Cass, "Manners and Customs of Several Indian Tribes . . . ," *North American Review* 22, no. 50 (January 1826).

58 Saunt, *Unworthy Republic*, 68.

59   Saunt, *Unworthy Republic*, 83.

60   Saunt, *Unworthy Republic*, 96.

61   Klunder, *Lewis Cass and the Politics of Moderation*, 47.

62   Matthew Mason, *Apostle of Union: A Political Biography of Edward Everett* (Chapel Hill: University of North Carolina Press, 2016), 53.

63   Klunder, *Lewis Cass and the Politics of Moderation*, 49.

64   Lewis Cass, "Remarks on the Policy and Practice of the United States and Great Britain in Their Treatment of the Indians," *North American Review* 55 (April 1927): 29.

65   Woodford, *Lewis Cass*, 181.

66   Woodford, *Lewis Cass*, 142.

67   Roger G. Kennedy, *Orders from France: The Americans and the French in a Revolutionary World, 1780–1820* (New York: Knopf, 1989), 237–238.

68   Kennedy, *Orders from France*, 246–253.

69   Govan, *Nicholas Biddle*, 25–26.

70   Govan, *Nicholas Biddle*, 35–36.

71   Gunther Barth, "Timeless Journals: Reading Lewis and Clark with Nicholas Biddle's Help," *Pacific Historical Review* 63, no. 4 (November 1994).

72   Govan, *Nicholas Biddle*, 37.

73   Govan, *Nicholas Biddle*, 40.

74   Brands, *The Money Men*, 61.

75   Govan, *Nicholas Biddle*, 45.

76   Thomas Payne Govan, "An Unfinished Novel by Nicholas Biddle," *Princeton University Library Chronicle* 10, no. 3 (1949): 134.

77   Govan, "An Unfinished Novel by Nicholas Biddle," 133.

78   Clubbe, *Byron, Sully and the Power of Portraiture*, 151.

79   Nicholas B. Wainwright, *Andalusia: Country Seat of the Craig Family and of Nicholas Biddle and His Descendants* (Philadelphia: Historical Society of Pennsylvania, 1976), viii–ix.

80   Govan, *Nicholas Biddle*, 81.

81   Bray Hammond, *Banks and Politics in America: From the Revolution to the Civil War* (Princeton, NJ: Princeton University Press, 1957), 301.

82   Govan, *Nicholas Biddle*, 85.

83   Govan, *Nicholas Biddle*, 97.

84   John Jay Smith, *Recollections of John Jay Smith* (Philadelphia: Lippincott, 1892), 206–208.

85   Govan, *Nicholas Biddle*, 104–105.

86   Govan, *Nicholas Biddle*, 107.

87   Jill Lepore, *These Truths* (New York: Norton, 2018), 182–183.

88   Lepore, *These Truths*, 186.

89   Margaret Bayard Smith, "The Inauguration of President Andrew Jackson, 1829," Eyewitness to History, 2007, http://www.eyewitnesstohistory.com/jacksoninauguration.htm.

90   Lepore, *These Truths*, 186.

91   Fischer, *Albion's Seed*, 608.

92   Baltzell, *Philadelphia Gentlemen*, 225–226.

93   Fischer, *Albion's Seed*, 644.

94   Fischer, *Albion's Seed*, 650.

95   Fischer, *Albion's Seed*, 705–707.

96   Fischer, *Albion's Seed*, 778.

97   Fischer, *Albion's Seed*, 842.

98   Fischer, *Albion's Seed*, 847.

99   Lepore, *These Truths*, 199.

100   Govan, *Nicholas Biddle*, 129.

101   Govan, *Nicholas Biddle*, 138.

102   Klunder, *Lewis Cass and the Politics of Moderation*, 68–69.

103 John P. Bowes, "American Indian Removal Beyond the Removal Act," *Native American and Indigenous Studies* 1, no. 1 (Spring 2014).

104 Alfred A. Cave, "Abuse of Power: Andrew Jackson and the Indian Removal Act of 1830," *The Historian* 65, no. 6 (Winter 2003).

105 Klunder, *Lewis Cass and the Politics of Moderation,* 70.

106 Saunt, *Unworthy Republic,* 20–21.

107 Saunt, *Unworthy Republic,* 106–107.

108 Saunt, *Unworthy Republic,* 141.

109 Ethan Davis, "An Administrative Trail of Tears: Indian Removal," *American Journal of Legal History* 50, no. 1 (January 2008–2010).

110 Saunt, *Unworthy Republic,* 220.

111 Saunt, *Unworthy Republic,* 282.

112 Klunder, *Lewis Cass and the Politics of Moderation,* 89.

113 Saunt, *Unworthy Republic,* 309.

114 Clubbe, *Byron, Sully and the Power of Portraiture,* 69.

115 "Dr. Francis West's reminiscences of the last moments of the honorable John Randolph of Roanoke," John Randolph of Roanoke Papers, University of Virginia.

116 Hammond, *Banks and Politics in America,* 295–297.

117 Arlen J. Lange, "History's Two Nicholas Biddles," *We Proceeded On* 16, no. 2 (May 1990).

118 Brands, *The Money Men,* 83.

119 Govan, *Nicholas Biddle,* 202–203.

120 Govan, *Nicholas Biddle,* 213.

121 Govan, *Nicholas Biddle,* 215–216.

122 Sean Wilentz, "Freedoms and Feelings: Taking Politics out of Political History," *New Republic,* April 7, 2003.

123 Govan, *Nicholas Biddle,* 243.

124 Brands, *The Money Men,* 90.

125 Govan, *Nicholas Biddle,* 300.

126 Brands, *The Money Men,* 92.

127 Govan, *Nicholas Biddle,* 1.

128 Govan, *Nicholas Biddle,* 361.

129 Govan, *Nicholas Biddle,* 369.

130 Govan, *Nicholas Biddle,* 350.

131 Dixon Wecter, *The Saga of American Society* (New York: Scribner's, 1937), 102.

132 Govan, *Nicholas Biddle,* 385.

133 Govan, *Nicholas Biddle,* 387.

134 "Suit Against Nicholas Biddle," *Daily Madisonian* (Washington, D.C.), November 4, 1842.

135 John Quincy Adams and Charles Francis Adams, eds., *Memoirs of John Quincy Adams, Comprising Portions of His Diary from 1795 to 1848,* vol. X (Philadelphia: Lippincott, 1876), 361.

136 Wainwright, *Andalusia,* 46.

137 Roger G. Kennedy, *Architecture, Men, Women and Money in America 1600–1860* (New York: Random House, 1985), 247.

138 Clubbe, *Byron, Sully and the Power of Portraiture,* 153.

139 Smith, Recollections of John Jay Smith, 206–208.

140 Baltzell, *Philadelphia Gentlemen,* 188.

141 Klunder, *Lewis Cass and the Politics of Moderation,* 131.

142 Klunder, *Lewis Cass and the Politics of Moderation,* 152.

143 Klunder, *Lewis Cass and the Politics of Moderation,* 165.

144 Klunder, *Lewis Cass and the Politics of Moderation,* 239.

145 Klunder, *Lewis Cass and the Politics of Moderation,* 244.

146 Woodford, *Lewis Cass,* 304.

147 Woodford, *Lewis Cass,* 289.

148 Woodford, *Lewis Cass*, 302.

149 Klunder, *Lewis Cass and the Politics of Moderation*, 286.

150 Klunder, *Lewis Cass and the Politics of Moderation*, 301.

151 *New York Tribune*, June 19, 1866.

152 *Boston Post*, June 21, 1866.

153 Peter Cozzens, *The Earth Is Weeping: The Epic Story of the Indian Wars for the American West* (New York: Knopf, 2016), 82.

154 Cozzens, *The Earth Is Weeping*, 91.

155 Cozzens, *The Earth Is Weeping*, 121.

156 Cozzens, *The Earth Is Weeping*, 200.

157 Cozzens, *The Earth Is Weeping*, 358.

158 Eric P. Kaufmann, "The Decline of the 'WASP' in Canada and the United States," in *Rethinking Ethnicity: Majority Groups and Dominant Minorities* (Abingdon, UK: Routledge, 2004), 61–83.

PART FIVE

1 Joseph A. Fry, "Henry S. Sanford: Diplomacy and Business in Nineteenth Century America," PhD dissertation, University of Nevada, Reno, 1982, 2.

2 Author interview with historian Seth Bramson.

3 Fry, "Henry S. Sanford," 5.

4 Fry, "Henry S. Sanford," 6.

5 Fry, "Henry S. Sanford," 8.

6 Fry, "Henry S. Sanford," 9.

7 Fry, "Henry S. Sanford," 14.

8 Lysle E. Meyer, "Henry S. Sanford and the Congo: A Reassessment," *Africa Historical Studies* 4, no. 1 (1971).

9 Sarah Elizabeth Wiley, "Commerce, Race and Diplomacy: Henry Shelton Sanford and the American Recognition of the International Association of the Congo," PhD diss., University of Montana, 1989, 26.

10 Fry, "Henry S. Sanford," 22.

11 William H. Gray, "The Human Aspect of Aves Diplomacy: An Incident in the Relations Between the United States and Venezuela," *The Americas* 6, no. 1 (July 1949): 72–84.

12 Gertrude Sanford Legendre, *The Time of My Life* (Charleston, SC: Wyrick, 1987), 2.

13 Fry, "Henry S. Sanford," 32–33.

14 Fry, "Henry S. Sanford," 35.

15 Fry, "Henry S. Sanford," 41.

16 Harriet Chappell Owsley, "Henry Shelton Sanford and Federal Surveillance Abroad, 1861–1865," *Mississippi Valley Historical Review* 48, no. 2 (September 1961).

17 Fry, "Henry S. Sanford," 40.

18 Fry, "Henry S. Sanford," 45.

19 Fry, "Henry S. Sanford," 37.

20 Fry, "Henry S. Sanford," 65.

21 Fry, "Henry S. Sanford," 55.

22 Fry, "Henry S. Sanford," 37.

23 Fry, "Henry S. Sanford," 76.

24 Fry, "Henry S. Sanford," 77.

25 Fry, "Henry S. Sanford," 77.

26 Eric Foner, *A Short History of Reconstruction* (New York: Harper & Row, 1990), 61.

27 Foner, *A Short History of Reconstruction*, 63.

28 Fry, "Henry S. Sanford," 85.

29 Fry, "Henry S. Sanford," 68.

30 Fry, "Henry S. Sanford," 93.

31 Fry, "Henry S. Sanford," 97.

32 Fry, "Henry S. Sanford," 125.

33 Henry S. Sanford to Governor Drew, February 18, 1877, State Library and Archives of Florida, Governor Drew Family Papers, 1856–1999, Collection M82-8.

34 Meyer, "Henry S. Sanford and the Congo."

35 Fry, "Henry S. Sanford," 98.

36 Wiley, "Commerce, Race and Diplomacy," 75; Fry, "Henry S. Sanford," 135.

37 Fry, "Henry S. Sanford," 108.

38 Fry, "Henry S. Sanford," 110.

39 Fry, "Henry S. Sanford," 111.

40 "Keep Your Head Above the Financial Waters and Bet on the Growth of the Country," *Manufacturers Record*, January 26, 1922, 60.

41 Fry, "Henry S. Sanford," 131.

42 Adam Hochschild, *King Leopold's Ghost: A Story of Greed, Terror, and Heroism in Colonial Africa* (Boston: Houghton Mifflin, 1998), 59.

43 Hochschild, *King Leopold's Ghost*, 8.

44 Hochschild, *King Leopold's Ghost*, 80.

45 Wiley, "Commerce, Race and Diplomacy," 81.

46 Hochschild, *King Leopold's Ghost*, 65.

47 Fry, "Henry S. Sanford," 140.

48 Hochschild, *King Leopold's Ghost*, 78.

49 Fry, "Henry S. Sanford," 147.

50 Hochschild, *King Leopold's Ghost*, 80–81.

51 Fry, "Henry S. Sanford," 150.

52 Fry, "Henry S. Sanford," 162.

53 Fry, "Henry S. Sanford," 169.

54 Mark Twain, *King Leopold's Soliloquy* (Boston: P. R. Warren, 1905), 26–27.

55 Fry, "Henry S. Sanford," 171.

56 Fry, "Henry S. Sanford," 175.

PART SIX

1 Gore Vidal, *1876* (New York: Vintage, 1976), 186.

2 Edwin P. Hoyt, *The Peabody Influence: How a Great New England Family Helped to Build America* (New York: Dodd, Mead, 1968).

3 Hoyt, *The Peabody Influence*, 15–16.

4 Hoyt, *The Peabody Influence*, 21.

5 Hoyt, *The Peabody Influence*, 59–60.

6 Hoyt, *The Peabody Influence*, 69.

7 Hoyt, *The Peabody Influence*, 98–99.

8 Hoyt, *The Peabody Influence*, 100–101.

9 Hoyt, *The Peabody Influence*, 103–105.

10 Hoyt, *The Peabody Influence*, 106.

11 Hoyt, *The Peabody Influence*, 114.

12 Ron Chernow, *The House of Morgan* (New York: Grove Press, 1990), 6.

13 Hoyt, *The Peabody Influence*, 109.

14 Franklin Parker, *George Peabody: A Biography*, rev. ed. (Nashville, TN: Vanderbilt University Press, 1995), 28.

15 Hoyt, *The Peabody Influence*, 123.

16 Mark Denis Desjardins, "A Muscular Christian in a Secular World," PhD diss., University of Virginia, 1995, 60.

17 Chernow, *House of Morgan*, 13.

18 Hoyt, *The Peabody Influence*, 129–130.

19   Hoyt, *The Peabody Influence*, 134–135.

20   Chernow, *House of Morgan*, 14–15.

21   Hoyt, *The Peabody Influence*, 141–142.

22   Hoyt, *The Peabody Influence*, 143.

23   Hoyt, *The Peabody Influence*, 147.

24   Hoyt, *The Peabody Influence*, 172–173.

25   Hoyt, *The Peabody Influence*, 176–177.

26   Hoyt, *The Peabody Influence*, 181.

27   Paul Johnson, *A History of the American People* (New York: HarperCollins, 1997), 297.

28   Hoyt, *The Peabody Influence*, 185–186.

29   Hoyt, *The Peabody Influence*, 189.

30   Desjardins, "A Muscular Christian," 61.

31   Hoyt, *The Peabody Influence*, 238.

32   Hoyt, *The Peabody Influence*, 239.

33   Hoyt, *The Peabody Influence*, 241.

34   E. Digby Baltzell, *The Protestant Establishment: Aristocracy and Caste in America* (New York: Vintage, 1964), 127.

35   Baltzell, *The Protestant Establishment*, 113.

36   Thomas Jefferson to John Adams, October 28, 1813, *The Adams-Jefferson Letters: The Complete Correspondence Between Thomas Jefferson and Abigail and John Adams*, ed. Lester J. Cappon (Chapel Hill: University of North Carolina Press, 1959).

37   Desjardins, "A Muscular Christian," 36.

38   Desjardins, "A Muscular Christian," 76.

39   Hoyt, *The Peabody Influence*, 245–246.

40   Desjardins, "A Muscular Christian," 7.

41   Desjardins, "A Muscular Christian," 2–3, 85.

42   E. Digby Baltzell, *Philadelphia Gentlemen: The Making of a National Upper Class* (Glencoe, IL: Free Press, 1958), 233.

43   Chernow, *House of Morgan*, 27.

44   Jean Strouse, *Morgan: American Financier* (New York: Random House, 1999), 158.

45   Robert A. Bennett, "No Longer A WASP Preserve," *New York Times,* June 29, 1986.

46   Jay Robert Stiefel, "Francis Martin Drexel, Artist Turned Financier," *Maine Antique Digest*, May 2003.

47   Chernow, *House of Morgan*, 35.

48   Chernow, *House of Morgan*, 38–40.

49   David B. Green, "This Day in Jewish History 1890: A Man Who Ruled Wall Street and Wanted Washington to Buy Cuba Dies," *Haaretz*, November 24, 2015.

50   Moses Yale Beach, *Wealth and Biography of the Wealthy Citizens of New York City*, 6th ed. (New York: The Sun Office, 1845).

51   Cleveland Amory, *Who Killed Society?* (New York: Harper & Brothers, 1960), 446.

52   Roger Finke and Rodney Stark, "Turning Pews into People: Estimating 19th Century Church Membership," *Journal for the Scientific Study of Religion* 25, no. 2 (June 1986).

53   James Thayer Addison, *The Episcopal Church in the United States, 1789–1931* (New York: Scribner's, 1951), 65–73.

54   Cleveland Amory, *The Proper Bostonians* (New York: E. P. Dutton, 1947), 107.

55   Arthur T. Vanderbilt II, *Fortune's Children* (New York: William Morrow, 1989) 79.

56   Dixon Wecter, *The Saga of American Society* (New York: Scribner's, 1937), 199–204.

57   Wecter, *The Saga of American Society*, 209.

58   Alexis Gregory, *Families of Fortune: Life in the Gilded Age* (New York: Rizzoli, 1993), 187.

59   Bray Hammond, *Banks and Politics in America: From the Revolution to the Civil War* (Princeton, NJ: Princeton University, 1957), 292.

60   Eric Homberger, *Mrs. Astor's New York: Money and Social Power in a Gilded Age* (New York: Oxford University Press, 2002), 161.

61 Amory, *Who Killed Society?*, 118.

62 Ward McAllister, *Society as I Have Found It* (New York: Cassell, 1890), 31.

63 McAllister, *Society as I Have Found It*, 34.

64 Homberger, *Mrs. Astor's New York*, 163–171.

65 Wecter, *The Saga of American Society*, 210–211.

66 Homberger, *Mrs. Astor's New York*, 176; Frederick Townsend Martin, *Things I Remember* (London: Eveleigh Nash, 1913), 218.

67 Cleveland Amory, *The Last Resorts* (New York: Harper & Brothers, 1952), 188.

68 Ralph Waldo Emerson, "Napoleon; Man of the World," https://emersoncentral.com/texts/represen tative-men/napoleon-man-of-the-world/.

69 Leo Braudy, *The Frenzy of Renown* (New York: Oxford University Press, 1986), 450.

70 Wecter, *The Saga of American Society*, 271.

71 Abby Patkin, "The Country Club in Brookline: What to Know about the History, Membership, Golf Course," Wickedlocal.com, August 30, 2021, https://www.wickedlocal.com/story/brookline-tab/2021 /08/30/u-s-open-the-country-club-chestnut-hill-history-francis-ouimet-clyde-park-grounds /8211920002/

72 Homberger, *Mrs. Astor's New York*, 156.

73 "The Patriarchs' Ball," *New York Times,* February 10, 1880.

74 Martin, *Things I Remember,* 46.

75 Martin, *Things I Remember,* 69, 70.

76 Homberger, *Mrs. Astor's New York*, 187.

77 "The Family Circle Dancing Club," *New York Times,* January 27, 1880.

78 "Dancing at Delmonico's," *New York Times,* January 4, 1881.

79 McAllister, *Society as I Have Found It,* 72.

80 Homberger, *Mrs. Astor's New York*, 194.

81 Wecter, *The Saga of American Society,* 212, 180.

82 John Foreman and Robbe Pierce Stimson, *The Vanderbilts and the Gilded Age: Architectural Aspirations 1879–1901* (New York: St. Martin's, 1991), 10.

83 Wecter, *The Saga of American Society,* 183.

84 Vanderbilt, *Fortune's Children*, 101.

85 Vanderbilt, *Fortune's Children*, 104–105; Foreman and Stimson, *The Vanderbilts and the Gilded Age*, 27.

86 Alfred Allan Lewis, *Ladies and Not-So-Gentle Women* (New York: Viking, 2000), 96–97.

87 "The Only Four Hundred," *New York Times,* February 16, 1892.

88 Foreman and Stimson, *The Vanderbilts and the Gilded Age*, 50.

89 Martin, *Things I Remember,* 229.

90 Jill Lepore, *These Truths* (New York: Norton, 2018), 335.

91 Lepore, *These Truths*, 347.

92 Lepore, *These Truths*, 365.

93 Elting E. Morison, ed., *The Letters of Theodore Roosevelt*, vol. 3, *The Square Deal 1901–1903* (Cambridge, MA: Harvard University Press, 1951), 107.

94 Joseph Lash, *Eleanor and Franklin* (New York: New American Library, 1973), 173.

PART SEVEN

1 Livingston Rutherfurd, *Family Records and Events, Compiled Principally from the Original Manuscripts in the Rutherfurd Collection* (New York: De Vinne Press, 1894), 140.

2 Rutherfurd, *Family Records and Events*, 145.

3 Alfred Allan Lewis, *Ladies and Not-So-Gentle Women* (New York: Viking, 2000), 129.

4 Lewis, *Ladies and Not-So-Gentle Women*, 128–132.

5 W. A. Swanberg, *Whitney Father, Whitney Heiress* (New York: Scribner's, 1980), 83.

6 Vanderbilt, *Fortune's Children*, 141.

7 Vanderbilt, *Fortune's Children*, 152–153.

8   Vanderbilt, *Fortune's Children*, 155–158.

9   "Rutherfurd Named as Man Ex-Duchess Wanted to Marry," *New York Times*, November 25, 1926.

10   "Rutherfurd Named as Man Ex-Duchess Wanted to Marry."

11   Vanderbilt, *Fortune's Children*, 171–172.

12   "Rutherfurd Named as Man Ex-Duchess Wanted to Marry."

13   Lewis, *Ladies and Not-So-Gentle Women*, 204.

14   "Rutherfurd Named as Man Ex-Duchess Wanted to Marry."

15   Lewis, *Ladies and Not-So-Gentle Women*, 241.

16   Lewis, *Ladies and Not-So-Gentle Women*, 319.

17   Joseph E. Persico, *Franklin and Lucy: President Roosevelt, Mrs. Rutherfurd and the Other Remarkable Women in His Life* (New York: Random House, 2008), 136.

18   "Engagement of Miss Alice Morton," *New York Times*, January 13, 1902.

19   Persico, *Franklin and Lucy*, 85.

20   Persico, *Franklin and Lucy*, 99.

21   Mary Beckman, "Did FDR Have Guillain-Barré? A New Study Suggests the President's Polio Was Misdiagnosed," *Science*, October 31, 2003, https://www.science.org/content/article/did-fdr-have-guillain-barr.

22   Westbrook Pegler, "Mts. Winthrop Rutherfurd and the Death of Roosevelt," *World-Telegram*, December 7, 1949.

23   Persico, *Franklin and Lucy*, 365–366.

24   Peter Carlson, "F.D.R.'s Loyal Mistress," *American History*, December 2010.

25   Swanberg, *Whitney Father, Whitney Heiress*, 61.

26   Swanberg, *Whitney Father, Whitney Heiress*, 68–69.

27   Swanberg, *Whitney Father, Whitney Heiress*, 4.

28   Swanberg, *Whitney Father, Whitney Heiress*, 84.

29   Swanberg, *Whitney Father, Whitney Heiress*, 93.

30   "Tableaus for Charity," *New York Tribune*, February 5, 1885.

31   Swanberg, *Whitney Father, Whitney Heiress*, 103.

32   Swanberg, *Whitney Father, Whitney Heiress*, 105–106.

33   Swanberg, *Whitney Father, Whitney Heiress*, 138.

34   Jean Strouse, *Morgan: American Financier* (New York: Random House, 1999), 288.

35   Strouse, *Morgan*, 326.

36   Swanberg, *Whitney Father, Whitney Heiress*, 150, 152.

37   Swanberg, *Whitney Father, Whitney Heiress*, 156.

38   Lucius Beebe, *The Big Spenders* (New York: Doubleday, 1966), 198.

39   Swanberg, *Whitney Father, Whitney Heiress*, 165.

40   Swanberg, *Whitney Father, Whitney Heiress*, 168.

41   "L. Cass Ledyard, Noted Lawyer, Dies," *New York Times*, January 28, 1932.

42   Swanberg, *Whitney Father, Whitney Heiress*, 170.

43   Swanberg, *Whitney Father, Whitney Heiress*, 176–177.

44   Swanberg, *Whitney Father, Whitney Heiress*, 198.

45   "How Ryan Rose in Wall Street," *New York Times*, November 24, 1928.

46   Swanberg, *Whitney Father, Whitney Heiress*, 196.

47   Swanberg, *Whitney Father, Whitney Heiress*, 204–205.

48   Swanberg, *Whitney Father, Whitney Heiress*, 218.

49   Swanberg, *Whitney Father, Whitney Heiress*, 220–221.

50   Swanberg, *Whitney Father, Whitney Heiress*, 200.

51   Swanberg, *Whitney Father, Whitney Heiress*, 204.

52   Hugh Fullerton, "Pyramided Gold," *Liberty*, November 5, 1927, 42.

53   Fullerton, "Pyramided Gold," 50.

54   Barbara Goldsmith, *Little Gloria . . . Happy at Last* (New York: Knopf, 1980), 213.

55 Jack Frost, "Up From Fifth Avenue," *New Yorker,* July 25, 1925, 9.

56 Karl K. Kitchen, "An Aristocrat of Sport Who Excelled in Every Game He Played," *New York Sun,* October 28, 1930.

57 Goldsmith, *Little Gloria,* 215, 221.

58 "Now This Whitney Mansion: Housewives from Brooklyn, Bronx and Jersey Are Frankly Disappointed," *New York Sun,* April 27, 1942.

59 Swanberg, *Whitney Father, Whitney Heiress,* 225–227, 242.

60 "Dorothy Elmhirst, a Founder of New Republic, Dies," *New York Times,* December 16, 1968.

61 Swanberg, *Whitney Father, Whitney Heiress,* 343.

62 Swanberg, *Whitney Father, Whitney Heiress,* 237.

63 Swanberg, *Whitney Father, Whitney Heiress,* 260.

64 Swanberg, *Whitney Father, Whitney Heiress,* 277–279.

65 Swanberg, *Whitney Father, Whitney Heiress,* 332.

66 Swanberg, *Whitney Father, Whitney Heiress,* 342–343.

67 Swanberg, *Whitney Father, Whitney Heiress,* 397.

68 Swanberg, *Whitney Father, Whitney Heiress,* 470.

PART EIGHT

1 Daniel Okrent, *The Guarded Gate* (New York: Scribner's, 2019), 47.

2 Okrent, *The Guarded Gate,* 142.

3 Melissa Wilde, Tessa Huttenlocher, Joan Ryan, and Elena van Stee, "Religious Inequality in America: The View from 1916," paper presented at the American Academy of Religion Annual Meeting, November 20, 2021.

4 Madison Grant, *The Passing of the Great Race, or the Racial Basis of European History* (New York: Scribner's, 1936), xi.

5 Okrent, *The Guarded Gate,* 217.

6 Jonathan Peter Spiro, *Defending the Master Race: Conservation, Eugenics, and the Legacy of Madison Grant* (Burlington: University of Vermont Press, 2009), 371; *New York Times,* September 14, 1934.

7 Henry Fairfield Osborn and Harriet Ernestine Ripley, *Fifty-Two Years of Research, Observation and Publication 1877–1929: A Life Adventure in Breadth and Depth* (New York: Scribner's, 1930), 151.

8 Brian Regal, *Henry Fairfield Osborn: Race and the Search for the Origins of Man* (Burlington, VT: Ashgate, 2002), 29.

9 Regal, *Henry Fairfield Osborn,* 38.

10 Ronald Rainger, *An Agenda for Antiquity: Henry Fairfield Osborn and Vertebrate Paleontology at the American Museum of Natural History, 1890–1935* (Tuscaloosa: University of Alabama Press, 1991), 30–31.

11 Regal, *Henry Fairfield Osborn,* 49.

12 David Rains Wallace, *The Bonehunters' Revenge: Dinosaurs, Greed, and the Greatest Scientific Feud of the Gilded Age* (New York: Houghton Mifflin, 1999), 159.

13 Mark Jaffe, *The Gilded Dinosaur: The Fossil War Between E. D. Cope and O. C. Marsh and the Rise of American Science* (New York: Crown, 2000), 91.

14 Jaffe, *The Gilded Dinosaur,* 198.

15 Jaffe, *The Gilded Dinosaur,* 274.

16 Jaffe, *The Gilded Dinosaur,* 152–153.

17 Jaffe, *The Gilded Dinosaur,* 306.

18 Regal, *Henry Fairfield Osborn,* 76.

19 Wallace, *The Bonehunters' Revenge,* 200–201.

20 Jaffe, *The Gilded Dinosaur,* 341.

21 Regal, *Henry Fairfield Osborn,* 79.

22 Jonathan Peter Spiro, *Defending the Master Race: Conservation, Eugenics and the Legacy of Madison Grant* (Burlington: University of Vermont Press, 2009), 125.

23 Regal, *Henry Fairfield Osborn,* 82.

24 Regal, *Henry Fairfield Osborn,* 79.

25   Rainger, *An Agenda for Antiquity*, 60.
26   Rainger, *An Agenda for Antiquity*, 71.
27   Rainger, *An Agenda for Antiquity*, 106.
28   Rainger, *An Agenda for Antiquity*, 111.
29   Rainger, *An Agenda for Antiquity*, 118.
30   Spiro, *Defending the Master Race*, xiii.
31   Spiro, *Defending the Master Race*, 47.
32   Osborn, *Fifty-Two Years of Research*, 66.
33   Osborn, *Fifty-Two Years of Research*, 67.
34   Spiro, *Defending the Master Race*, 39.
35   Rainger, *An Agenda for Antiquity*, 66.
36   Rainger, *An Agenda for Antiquity*, 73.
37   Regal, *Henry Fairfield Osborn*, 80.
38   Rainger, *An Agenda for Antiquity*, 77.
39   Geoffrey T. Hellman, "Profiles: The American Museum II," *New Yorker*, December 7, 1968, 88.
40   Hellman, "Profiles," 90.
41   Regal, *Henry Fairfield Osborn*, 104.
42   Regal, *Henry Fairfield Osborn*, 10–11.
43   William K. Gregory, *Biographical Memoir of Henry Fairfield Osborn, 1857–1935* (Washington: National Academy of Sciences, 1938) 75.
44   Henry Fairfield Osborn, *Evolution and Religion in Education* (New York: Scribner's, 1926), 189.
45   Rainger, *An Agenda for Antiquity*, 147–149.
46   Henry Fairfield Osborn, "The Hall of the Age of Man in the American Museum," *Nature*, April 21, 1921, 236.
47   Rainger, *An Agenda for Antiquity*, 131.
48   Regal, *Henry Fairfield Osborn*, 94.
49   Henry Fairfield Osborn, "Facts of the Evolutionists," *Forum* LXXV, no. 6 (June 1926).
50   Regal, *Henry Fairfield Osborn*, xi–xii.
51   Rainger, *An Agenda for Antiquity*, 148.
52   Grant, *The Passing of the Great Race*, 79, 77, 80.
53   Okrent, *The Guarded Gate*, 19.
54   Okrent, *The Guarded Gate*, 19.
55   Spiro, *Defending the Master Race*, 305.
56   Rainger, *An Agenda for Antiquity*, 150.
57   Ashley Montagu, "Eugenics, Genetics and Race," *The Science Teacher* 12, no. 2 (April 1945): 43.
58   Rainger, *An Agenda for Antiquity*, 177.
59   "William Church Osborn," *New York Times*, January 5, 1931; "Eligible for Governor," *New York Sun*, September 18, 1912; [Partial clip from newspaper archive], *New York Sun*, April 13, 1939.
60   "Ex-Roosevelt Aid Supports Willkie," *New York Sun*, October 1, 1924.
61   "A Friend of Children," *New York Times Magazine*, December 19, 1937.
62   Okrent, *The Guarded Gate*, 143.
63   Okrent, *The Guarded Gate*, 120.
64   Okrent, *The Guarded Gate*, 121.
65   Okrent, *The Guarded Gate*, 135.
66   Okrent, *The Guarded Gate*, 244.
67   Okrent, *The Guarded Gate*, 167.
68   Okrent, *The Guarded Gate*, 234.
69   Okrent, *The Guarded Gate*, 270.
70   Calvin Coolidge, "Whose Country Is This?," *Good Housekeeping*, February 1921.
71   Spiro, *Defending the Master Race*, 114–115.
72   Okrent, *The Guarded Gate*, 296–297.

73   Okrent, *The Guarded Gate*, 301–302.

74   "True Love Usually Best, Darwin's View," *New York Herald*, September 26, 1921.

75   "Lo, the Poor Nordic," *New York Times*, April 8, 1924.

76   Regal, *Henry Fairfield Osborn*, 123.

77   Regal, *Henry Fairfield Osborn*, 125.

78   "Modern Man Descendant of 'Down Man,' Not the Ape, Says Osborn in New Book," *Brooklyn Daily Eagle*, December 4, 1927.

79   Okrent, *The Guarded Gate*, 332.

80   Okrent, *The Guarded Gate*, 300.

81   Spiro, *Defending the Master Race*, 181.

82   Okrent, *The Guarded Gate*, 346.

83   National Industrial Conference Board speech, December 14, 1923.

84   Regal, *Henry Fairfield Osborn*, 156.

85   Regal, *Henry Fairfield Osborn*, 158.

86   "Evolution Museum Dedicated at Yale," *New York Times*, December 30, 1925.

87   "Dr. Osborn Asks Public Schools to Teach Religion," *New York Herald*, January 24, 1926.

88   Regal, *Henry Fairfield Osborn*, xvii.

89   "Osborn Surveys Fifty Years of Science," *New York Times*, May 31, 1931.

90   "Man Never an Ape, Dr. Osborn Asserts," *New York Times*, April 30, 1927.

91   Colin Barras, "We Have Still Not Found the Missing Link Between Us and Apes," BBC, May 18, 2017, http://www.bbc.com/earth/story/20170517-we-have-still-not-found-the-missing-link-between -us-and-apes.

92   Henry Fairfield Osborn, *Man Rises to Parnassus* (Princeton, NJ: Princeton University Press, 1927), 186.

93   Author interview with grandson Jay Coogan.

94   "Osborn Advocates 'Birth Selection,'" *New York Times*, May 4, 1932.

95   "Urban Intelligence Excells Rural, Survey of Environment Reveals," *New York Herald Tribune*, May 13, 1933.

96   Okrent, *The Guarded Gate*, 379.

97   Regal, *Henry Fairfield Osborn*, 186.

98   Regal, *Henry Fairfield Osborn*, xviii.

99   Regal, *Henry Fairfield Osborn*, 196.

100   Okrent, *The Guarded Gate*, 378.

101   Author interview with Frederick Osborn III.

102   Frederick Henry Osborne Papers, American Philosophical Society Library, https://search .amphilsoc.org/collections/view?docId=ead/Mss.Ms.Coll.24-ead.xml#bioghist.

103   Frederick Osborn, "History of the American Eugenics Society," January 20, 1971, https://diglib .amphilsoc.org/islandora/object/paper-history-american-eugenics-society#page/1/mode/1up.

104   Okrent, *The Guarded Gate*, 380.

105   American Museum of Natural History, "Museum Statement on Eugenics," September 2021, https:// www.amnh.org/about/eugenics-statement.

PART NINE

1   Josh Greenfield, "The Man Who Gave Us 'Hair,'" *Life*, June 27, 1969.

2   Except where noted, quotations from Butler come from telephone interviews with the author conducted on July 29, November 13, and November 16, 2019.

3   Geoffrey M. Kabaservice, *The Guardians: Kingman Brewster, His Circle, and the Rise of the Liberal Establishment* (New York: Henry Holt, 2004), 47.

4   Kabaservice, *The Guardians*, 10.

5   Kabaservice, *The Guardians*, 34.

6   Kabaservice, *The Guardians*, 6.

7   Kabaservice, *The Guardians*, 7.

8   Kabaservice, *The Guardians*, 60.

9   Kabaservice, *The Guardians*, 118.

10 Kabaservice, *The Guardians*, 204.

11 Zia Wesley, "It's One Final Hair-Raising Show in L.A. for Michael Butler," *Los Angeles Magazine*, December 6, 2021, https://www.lamag.com/culturefiles/its-one-final-hair-raising-show-in-l-a-for-michael-butler/.

12 Jill Lepore, *These Truths* (New York: Norton, 2018), 656.

13 "Fanny Butler Rites Will Be Held Tuesday," *Chicago Daily Tribune*, March 24, 1959.

14 "British Peer Opposes Butler Trip with Heiress," *Chicago Daily Tribune*, June 8, 1959; "Await Butler Son and Heiress Here," *Chicago Daily Tribune*, June 10, 1959; "Names Chicago Heir as Father of British Baby," *Chicago Daily Tribune*, August 3, 1959; "Butler Calls Baby Charge 'A Blackmail,'" *Chicago Daily Tribune*, August 4, 1959; "Norman Butler of Chicago Is Married in London Rites," October 15, 1959.

15 "The Butlers of Oak Brook," *Classic Chicago Magazine*, February 21, 2016.

16 "Judge Awards Divorce to Wife of Paul Butler," *Chicago Daily Tribune*, November 5, 1933.

17 "Mother Unfit. Prefer Father, Say Butler Boys," *Chicago Daily Tribune*, January 11, 1944.

18 William Barry Furlong, "Man with 14 Polo Fields," *Sports Illustrated*, October 22, 1962.

19 Greenfield, "The Man Who Gave Us 'Hair.'"

20 Helen Lawrenson, "A Weekend with Chief Michael Butler and His Inner Tribe," *Esquire*, November 1971.

21 "The Butlers of Oak Brook."

22 "Suffolk Reflects on Wild Party; Asks if Rich Have Immunity," *New York Times*, April 17, 1964.

23 "Marti Waits to Be Mrs.," New York *Daily News*, April 27, 1954.

24 Charles Kaiser, *The Gay Metropolis: The Landmark History of Gay Life in America* (New York: Grove, 2007), 95–96.

25 "How and Why I Got into *Hair*," *Pages from Michael Butler's Journal* (blog), accessed December 7, 2022, http://www.orlok.com/orlok/michael/jfk.html.

26 Lawrenson, "A Weekend with Chief Michael Butler and his Inner Tribe."

27 [Untitled clipping from *New York Sun* Newspaper Morgue Files, 1900–1950, at the New York Public Library], *Journal-American*, July 28, 1958.

28 Greenfield, "The Man Who Gave Us 'Hair.'"

29 Author interview with Robin Hambro, May 27, 2021.

30 Cholly Knickerbocker, [Untitled clipping from *New York Sun* Newspaper Morgue Files, 1900–1950, at the New York Public Library], *Journal-American*, September 18, 1961.

31 Author interview with Robin Hambro, May 27, 2021.

32 Suzy Knickerbocker, *Journal-American*, June 11, 1965.

33 "Michael Butler Files 2 Million Love Suit," *Chicago Tribune*, November 24, 1965.

34 "Suzy Says: Bitter Butlers," *Chicago Tribune*, June 26, 1971.

35 "Divorce Wanted by Social Figure Married a Year," *Hartford Courant*, October 18, 1973; "He's Getting It from Both Barrels," *Hartford Courant*, December 27, 1973.

36 "Scandal Is a-Brewing," *Chicago Tribune*, December 2, 1974.

37 "Underdog Millionaire Making a Lively Race," *Chicago Tribune*, November 6, 1966.

38 "Splitting Hairs," *Polo Player's Edition*, United States Polo Association, October 2020.

39 Murry Frymer, "The Hippie Millionaire," *Newsday*, June 22, 1968.

40 "2 Broadway 'Hair' Writers Out in the Cold," *Chicago Tribune*, April 12, 1969; "Hair Producers Fire Lead Performer," *Globe and Mail*, January 22, 1970.

41 "Suzy Says," *Chicago Tribune*, February 4, 1968.

42 Eugenia Sheppard, "Michael Is Hippiest Millionaire," *Hartford Courant*, October 6, 1968.

43 Lawrenson, "A Weekend with Chief Michael Butler and His Inner Tribe."

44 "Michael Butler: Hippiest Millionaire," *Los Angeles Times*, March 9, 1969.

45 Frymer, "The Hippie Millionaire."

46 Greenfield, "The Man Who Gave Us 'Hair.'"

47 Frymer, "The Hippie Millionaire."

48 Lawrenson, "A Weekend with Chief Michael Butler and His Inner Tribe."

49 Lawrenson, "A Weekend with Chief Michael Butler and His Inner Tribe."

50 Author interview with Sugar Rautbord.

51 "They've Put Their Hobbies to Work," *Chicago Tribune*, October 24, 1971.

52 "The Hippie Millionaire a Decade After 'Hair,'" *Chicago Tribune*, February 26, 1978.

53 Michael Gross, "Abercrombie & Spent: The Rise and Fall of Safari King Geoffrey Kent," *Gotham*, November 2003.

54 "Butler Clan Makes News," *Philadelphia Inquirer*, July 13, 1958.

55 "The Not So Silent Butlers," *Women's Wear Daily*, September 18, 1970.

56 "The Hippie Millionaire a Decade After 'Hair.'"

57 "In Village It Created, Butler Family Feels Loss of Clout," *Chicago Tribune*, July 14, 1986.

58 "Paul Butler's Heirs Settle Feud Over Estate," *Chicago Tribune*, July 16, 1986.

59 "In Village It Created, Butler Family Feels Loss of Clout."

60 "Visions of Oak Brook Split Civic, Family Heirs," *Chicago Tribune*, July 13, 1986.

61 "Ex-Gov. Walker Admits Bank Fraud," *Chicago Tribune*, August 6, 1987.

62 "Walking Tall," *Chicago Tribune*, August 9, 1993.

63 Nicola Shulman, "The Palm Beach Story," *Harpers & Queen*, June 1988.

64 "Judge Set to Close Latest Chapter in Butler Family's Financial Saga," *Chicago Tribune*, January 15, 1993.

65 "Palm Beach Heir Sued by Man Alleging Abuse," *South Florida Sun-Sentinel*, November 12, 2006.

66 Author interview with Ann Copeland.

67 "Money Woes Strip the Mystery from Michael Butler," *Chicago Tribune*, October 28, 1990.

68 "Auctioneer to Host the Last Bash at Butler's Digs," *Chicago Tribune*, June 12, 1991.

69 "Butler Calls Bank Auction a Part of Life," *Chicago Tribune*, June 23, 1991.

70 "Something Will Happen to Bring the Age of Aquarius About," *New York Times*, April 25, 1993.

71 "Butler Did It!" *Chicago Tribune*, June 30, 1996.

72 "Frank Osgood Butler II," *Palm Beach Daily News*, August 28, 2014.

73 Michael Knox Beran, *WASPs: The Splendors and Miseries of an American Aristocracy* (New York: Pegasus, 2021), 434.

PART TEN

1 Bokara Legendre, *Not What I Expected* (Bloomington, IN: Balboa, 2017), 9; *New York Times*, May 2, 1976.

2 Gertrude Sanford Legendre, *The Time of My Life* (Charleston, SC: Wyrick, 1987), 14.

3 Legendre, *The Time of My Life*, 18.

4 Legendre, *The Time of My Life*, 25.

5 "The Legendres of New Orleans," unpublished manuscript, courtesy Sandy Wood.

6 "The Legendres of New Orleans."

7 Legendre, *The Time of My Life*, 53.

8 Legendre, *The Time of My Life*, 50–52.

9 Legendre, *The Time of My Life*, 56–57.

10 Legendre, *Not What I Expected*, 35–36.

11 Peter Finn, *A Guest of the Reich* (New York: Pantheon, 2019), 41.

12 Legendre, *The Time of My Life*, 67–70.

13 Finn, *A Guest of the Reich*, 49.

14 Legendre, *Not What I Expected*, 37–38.

15 Legendre, *Not What I Expected*, 40.

16 Finn, *A Guest of the Reich*, 9.

17 Finn, *A Guest of the Reich*, 15.

18 Finn, *A Guest of the Reich*, 20–21.

19 Finn, *A Guest of the Reich*, 89, 105.

20   Finn, *A Guest of the Reich*, 110.

21   Finn, *A Guest of the Reich*, 133.

22   Finn, *A Guest of the Reich*, 165–166.

23   Finn, *A Guest of the Reich*, 170–173.

24   Finn, *A Guest of the Reich*, 174–175.

25   Legendre, *Not What I Expected*, 65.

26   Legendre, *Not What I Expected*, 65.

27   "Gertie's Ghost," *New York Times*, October 14, 2011.

28   Legendre, *Not What I Expected*, 45.

29   Legendre, *Not What I Expected*, 84.

30   Legendre, *Not What I Expected*, 50.

31   Legendre, *Not What I Expected*, 56–57.

32   Legendre, *Not What I Expected*, 73.

33   Legendre, *Not What I Expected*, 74.

34   Legendre, *Not What I Expected*, 76.

35   Legendre, *Not What I Expected*, 92.

36   Legendre, *Not What I Expected*, 97.

37   Legendre, *Not What I Expected*, 121.

38   Legendre, *Not What I Expected*, 131.

39   Legendre, *Not What I Expected*, 154.

40   Legendre, *Not What I Expected*, 157.

41   Legendre, *Not What I Expected*, 182.

42   Legendre, *Not What I Expected*, 204.

43   Legendre, *Not What I Expected*, 208.

44   *New York Times*, October 16, 2011.

45   Legendre, *Not What I Expected*, 211.

46   Legendre, *Not What I Expected*, 214–215; Finn, *A Guest of the Reich*, 197.

47   Legendre, *Not What I Expected*, 241.

48   "Bokara Legendre: Socialite Transformed into Spiritual Seeker," *San Francisco Chronicle*, December 17, 2017.

49   "Founder's Widow Inherited Legacy of Debt," *Orlando Sentinel*, January 6, 1991.

50   Rudy Maxa, "A Grand Arrival," *Washington Post*, May 2, 1976.

51   E. J. Kahn Jr., "Profiles: Man of Means," *New Yorker*, August 11, 1951.

52   Lisa Gubernick and Alexander Parker, "The Outsider," *Forbes*, October 26, 1987.

53   Geoffrey T. Hellman, "Profiles: The Man Who Is Not His Cousin," *New Yorker*, June 21, 1941.

54   "Business Mogul Cornelius Vanderbilt Whitney Dies," *Washington Post*, December 14, 1992.

55   Ted Ramsay, "Cornelius Vanderbilt Whitney Biographical Sketch," unpublished manuscript, June 2, 1941.

56   "Whitney Picks Hardest Way to Congress Seat," *New York Herald Tribune*, September 16, 1932.

57   Author interview with Whitney Tower Jr., February 24, 2020.

58   Whitney Tower Jr., "Personal History: I Can't Get No Satisfaction," *Town and Country*, August 2012.

59   Author interview with Penelope Tree, October 21, 2019.

60   Author interview with Penelope Tree, October 21, 2019.

61   Holly Brubach, "Running Around in High Circles," *New York Times*, November 9, 1997.

62   Caroline Seebohm, *No Regrets: The Life of Marietta Tree* (New York: Simon & Schuster, 1997), 156.

63   Seebohm, *No Regrets*, 227–230.

64   Seebohm, *No Regrets*, 277.

65   David Bailey, *Look Again* (London: Macmillan, 2020), 213–215.

66   Louise Frank, "People Thought I Was a Freak. I Kind of Liked That," *The Observer*, August 2, 2008.

67   Seebohm, *No Regrets*, 210.

68   Seebohm, *No Regrets*, 235.

69   Author interview with Frances FitzGerald, July 29, 2021.

70   "Livingston Biddle Jr. Dies," *Washington Post,* May 5, 2002.

71   J. P. McEvoy, "Drexel Biddle Gentleman Tough," *American Mercury* 54 (1942).

72   Noel F. Busch, "Ambassador Biddle," *Life,* October 4, 1943.

73   "Biddle Says He Saw Nazis Bomb Open Polish Towns," *New York Herald Tribune,* September 14, 1939.

74   "Nazi Newspaper Raps Biddle for Air Raid Report," *St. Louis Star and Times,* September 16, 1939.

75   A. J. Leibling, "Profiles: The Omnibus Diplomat," *New Yorker,* June 13, 1942.

76   Busch, "Ambassador Biddle," *Life,* October 4, 1943.

77   Author interview with Anthony Drexel Duke, 2004.

78   "Direct Action Envoy, Angier Biddle Duke," *New York Times,* March 9, 1966.

79   "At Angier Biddle Duke's Funeral, Fond Memories," *New York Times,* May 4, 1995.

80   Author interview with George Biddle, Nicholas's son.

81   Author interview with George Biddle.

82   Author interview with Meg Biddle.

83   Author interview with Frederick H. Osborn III.

84   "Radical Foundations? This Pillsbury Says It Best," *Boston Globe,* March 16, 1975.

85   Robert P. Jones, *The End of White Christian America* (New York: Simon & Schuster, 2016), 47.

86   Jones, *The End of White Christian America,* 58.

87   Public Religion Research Institute, "The 2020 Census of American Religion."

Selected Bibliography

Adams, Henry. *John Randolph: A Biography*. Armonk, NY: M. E. Sharpe, 1996.

Adams, John, Thomas Jefferson, and Abigail Adams. *The Adams-Jefferson Letters: The Complete Correspondence Between Thomas Jefferson and Abigail and John Adams*. Edited by Lester J. Cappon. 2 vols. Chapel Hill: University of North Carolina Press, 1959.

Adams, William Howard. *Gouverneur Morris: An Independent Life*. New Haven, CT: Yale University Press, 2003.

Alsop, Joseph W., with Adam Platt. *I've Seen the Best of It: Memoirs*. New York: Norton, 1992.

Amory, Cleveland. *The Last Resorts*. New York: Harper & Brothers, 1952.

Amory, Cleveland. *Who Killed Society?* New York: Harper & Brothers, 1960.

Bailey, David. *Look Again*. London: Macmillan, 2020.

Baltzell, E. Digby. *Philadelphia Gentlemen: The Making of a National Upper Class*. Glencoe, IL: Free Press, 1958.

Baltzell, E. Digby. *The Protestant Establishment: Aristocracy and Caste in America*. New York: Vintage, 1964.

Baltzell, E. Digby. *Puritan Boston and Quaker Philadelphia*. Boston: Beacon Press, 1979.

Beach, Moses Yale. *Wealth and Biography of the Wealthy Citizens of New York City*, 6th ed. New York: The Sun Office, 1845.

Beebe, Lucius. *The Big Spenders*. New York: Doubleday, 1966.

Bender, Marylin. *The Beautiful People*. New York: Coward McCann, 1967.

Beran, Michael Knox. *WASPs: The Splendors and Miseries of an American Aristocracy*. New York: Pegasus, 2021.

Biddle, C. Miller. *William and Sarah Biddle 1633–1711: Planting a Seed of Democracy in America*. Moorestown, NJ: Privately published, 2012.

Biddle, Francis. *A Casual Past*. Garden City, NY: Doubleday, 1961.

Biddle, George. *An American Artist's Story*. Boston: Little, Brown, 1939.

Biddle, Nicholas. *Nicholas Biddle in Greece: The Journals and Letters of 1806*. Edited by R. A. McNeal. University Park: Pennsylvania State University Press, 1993.

Birmingham, Stephen. *America's Secret Aristocracy*. New York: Little, Brown, 1987.

Birmingham, Stephen. *The Right People*. Boston: Little, Brown, 1968.

Block, Kristen. *Ordinary Lives in the Early Caribbean*. Athens: University of Georgia Press, 2012.

Bradford, William. *Of Plymouth Plantation 1620–1647*. New York: Knopf, 1963.

Brandow, James C. *Genealogies of Barbados Families*. Baltimore: Clearfield, 1997.

Brands, H. W. *The Money Men: Capitalism, Democracy and the Hundred Years' War over the American Dollar*. New York: Norton, 2006.

Brookhiser, Richard. *Gentleman Revolutionary: Gouverneur Morris, the Rake Who Wrote the Constitution*. New York: Free Press, 2003.

Brookhiser, Richard. *The Way of the WASP*. New York: Free Press, 1991.

Brooks, David. *Bobos in Paradise*. New York: Simon & Schuster, 2000.

Burt, Nathaniel. *First Families*. Boston: Little, Brown, 1970.

Burt, Nathaniel. *The Perennial Philadelphians: The Anatomy of an American Aristocracy*. Philadelphia: University of Pennsylvania Press, 1963.

Chernow, Ron. *Alexander Hamilton*. New York: Penguin, 2004.

Chernow, Ron. *The House of Morgan*. New York: Grove Press, 1990.

Clubbe, John. *Byron, Sully and the Power of Portraiture.* Aldershot, UK: Ashgate, 2005.

Cozzens, Peter. *The Earth Is Weeping: The Epic Story of the Indian Wars for the American West.* New York: Knopf, 2016.

Crawford, Aaron Scott. "John Randolph of Roanoke and the Politics of Doom: Slavery, Sectionalism, and Self-Deception, 1773–1821." PhD diss., University of Tennessee, 2012. https://trace.tennessee.edu/utk_graddiss/1519.

Crawford, Alan Pell. *Unwise Passions.* New York: Simon & Schuster, 2000.

Desjardins, Mark Denis. "A Muscular Christian in a Secular World." PhD diss., University of Virginia, 1995.

Finn, Peter. *A Guest of the Reich.* New York: Pantheon, 2019.

Fischer, David Hackett. *Albion's Seed: Four British Folkways in America.* New York: Oxford University Press, 1989.

Foner, Eric. *A Short History of Reconstruction.* New York: Harper & Row, 1990.

Foreman, John, and Robbe Pierce Stimson. *The Vanderbilts and the Gilded Age: Architectural Aspirations 1879–1901.* New York: St. Martin's, 1991.

Fraser, Rebecca. *The Mayflower: The Families, the Voyage, and the Founding of America.* New York: St. Martin's, 2017.

Fry, Joseph A. "Henry S. Sanford: Diplomacy and Business in Nineteenth Century America." PhD diss., University of Nevada, Reno, 1982.

Garland, Hugh A. *The Life of John Randolph of Roanoke.* New York: D. Appleton, 1874.

Goldsmith, Barbara. *Little Gloria . . . Happy at Last.* New York: Knopf, 1980.

Govan, Thomas Payne. *Nicholas Biddle: Nationalist and Public Banker 1786–1844.* Chicago: University of Chicago Press, 1959.

Grant, Madison. *The Passing of the Great Race, or the Racial Basis of European History.* New York: Scribner's, 1936.

Gregory, Alexis. *Families of Fortune: Life in the Gilded Age.* New York: Rizzoli, 1993.

Hammond, Bray. *Banks and Politics in America: From the Revolution to the Civil War.* Princeton, NJ: Princeton University Press, 1957.

Herold, J. Christopher. *Mistress to an Age: A Life of Madame de Staël.* Indianapolis: Bobbs-Merrill, 1958.

Hochschild, Adam. *King Leopold's Ghost: A Story of Greed, Terror, and Heroism in Colonial Africa.* Boston: Houghton Mifflin, 1998.

Homberger, Eric. *Mrs. Astor's New York: Money and Social Power in a Gilded Age.* New York: Oxford University Press, 2002.

Hoyt, Edwin P. *The Peabody Influence: How a Great New England Family Helped to Build America.* New York: Dodd, Mead, 1968.

Jaffe, Mark. *The Gilded Dinosaur: The Fossil War Between E. D. Cope and O. C. Marsh and the Rise of American Science.* New York: Crown, 2000.

Jaher, Frederic Cople. *The Rich, the Well Born and the Powerful: Elites and Upper Classes in History.* Urbana: University of Illinois Press, 1973.

Jenkins, Stephen. *The Story of the Bronx.* New York: Putnam's, 1912.

Johnson, David. *John Randolph of Roanoke.* Baton Rouge: Louisiana State University Press, 2012.

Kabaservice, Geoffrey M. *The Guardians: Kingman Brewster, His Circle, and the Rise of the Liberal Establishment.* New York: Henry Holt, 2004.

Kaiser, Charles. *The Gay Metropolis: The Landmark History of Gay Life in America.* New York: Grove, 2007.

Kellogg, Lucy Mary, ed. Mayflower Families Through Five Generations, vol. 17. Plymouth, MA: General Society of Mayflower Descendants, 1975.

Kennedy, Roger G. *Architecture, Men, Women and Money in America 1600–1860.* New York: Random House, 1985.

Kennedy, Roger G. *Orders from France: The Americans and the French in a Revolutionary World, 1780–1820.* New York: Knopf, 1989.

Kierner, Cynthia A. *Scandal at Bizarre: Rumor and Reputation in Jefferson's America.* New York: Palgrave Macmillan, 2004.

Kirk, Russell. *John Randolph of Roanoke: A Study in American Politics.* Chicago: Henry Regnery, 1964.

Kirschke, James J. *Gouverneur Morris: Author, Statesman, and Man of the World.* New York: St. Martin's, 2005.

Klunder, Willard Carl. *Lewis Cass and the Politics of Moderation.* Kent, OH: Kent State University Press, 1996.

Konolige, Kit and Frederica. *The Power of Their Glory: America's Ruling Class, the Episcopalians.* New York: Wyden, 1978.

Lawrence, Martha Morris. *The Boundary Line and Other Bits of Biography and History.* Deckertown: Sussex Independent, 1895.

Legendre, Bokara. *Not What I Expected.* Bloomington, IN: Balboa, 2017.

Legendre, Gertrude Sanford. *The Time of My Life.* Charleston, SC: Wyrick, 1987.

Lepore, Jill. *These Truths.* New York: Norton, 2018.

Lewis, Alfred Allan. *Ladies and Not-So-Gentle Women.* New York: Viking, 2000.

Lundberg, Ferdinand. *America's 60 Families.* New York: Vanguard, 1937.

Martin, Frederick Townsend. *Things I Remember.* London: Eveleigh Nash, 1913.

McAllister, Ward. *Society as I Have Found It.* New York: Cassell, 1890.

Miller, Melanie Randolph. *Envoy to the Terror: Gouverneur Morris and the French Revolution.* Washington, DC: Potomac, 2005.

Mintz, Max N. *Gouverneur Morris and the American Revolution.* Norman: University of Oklahoma Press, 1970.

Monaghan, Frank. *John Jay: Defender of Liberty.* Indianapolis: Bobbs-Merrill, 1935.

Morris, Gouverneur. *The Diary and Letters of Gouverneur Morris, Minister of the United States to France; Member of the Constitutional Convention.* Edited by Anne Cary Morris. 2 vols. New York: Charles Scribner's Sons, 1888. https://oll.libertyfund.org/titles/1170.

Morris, Gouverneur. *A Diary of the French Revolution.* Edited by Beatrix C. Davenport. 2 vols. Boston: Houghton Mifflin, 1939.

Nicholls, Charles Wilbur de Lyon. *The Ultra-Fashionable Peerage of America.* New York: Harjes, 1904.

Okrent, Daniel. *The Guarded Gate.* New York: Scribner's, 2019.

Osborn, Henry Fairfield. *Man Rises to Parnassus.* Princeton, NJ: Princeton University Press, 1927.

Parker, Franklin. *George Peabody: A Biography.* Rev. ed. Nashville, TN: Vanderbilt University Press, 1995.

Persico, Joseph E. *Franklin and Lucy: President Roosevelt, Mrs. Rutherfurd and the Other Remarkable Women in His Life.* New York: Random House, 2008.

Philbrick, Nathaniel. *Mayflower.* New York: Viking, 2006.

Rainger, Ronald. *An Agenda for Antiquity: Henry Fairfield Osborn and Vertebrate Paleontology at the American Museum of Natural History, 1890–1935.* Tuscaloosa: University of Alabama Press, 1991.

Rappleye, Charles. *Robert Morris: Financier of the American Revolution.* New York: Simon & Schuster, 2010.

Regal, Brian. *Henry Fairfield Osborn: Race and the Search for the Origins of Man.* Burlington, VT: Ashgate, 2002.

Roosevelt, Theodore. *Gouverneur Morris: American Statesman.* Boston: Houghton Mifflin, 1889.

Rutherfurd, Livingston. *Family Records and Events, Compiled Principally from the Original Manuscripts in the Rutherfurd Collection.* New York: De Vinne Press, 1894.

Saunt, Claudio. *Unworthy Republic: The Dispossession of Native Americans and the Road to Indian Territory.* New York: Norton, 2020.

Seebohm, Caroline. *No Regrets: The Life of Marietta Tree.* New York: Simon & Schuster, 1997.

Shorto, Russell. *The Island at the Center of the World.* New York: Vintage, 2005.

Smith, Bradford. *Bradford of Plymouth.* Philadelphia: Lippincott, 1951.

Smith, John Jay. *Recollections of John Jay Smith.* Philadelphia: Lippincott, 1892.

Smith, Samuel Stelle. *Lewis Morris: Anglo-American Statesman.* Atlantic Highlands, NJ: Humanities Press, 1983.

Spiro, Jonathan Peter. *Defending the Master Race: Conservation, Eugenics and the Legacy of Madison Grant.* Burlington: University of Vermont Press, 2009.

Springer, Mary Elizabeth. *Elizabeth Schuyler: A Story of Old New York.* New York: Blanchard, 1902.

Strouse, Jean. *Morgan: American Financier.* New York: Random House, 1999.

Sumner, William Graham. *Robert Morris.* New York: Dodd, Mead, 1892.

Swanberg, W. A. *Whitney Father, Whitney Heiress.* New York: Scribner's, 1980.

Tansill, Charles Callan. *The Secret Loves of the Founding Fathers.* New York: Devin-Adair, 1964.

Twain, Mark. *King Leopold's Soliloquy.* Boston: P. R. Warren, 1905.

Vanderbilt, Arthur T., II, *Fortune's Children.* New York: William Morrow, 1989.

Wainwright, Nicholas B. *Andalusia: Country seat of the Craig Family and of Nicholas Biddle and His Descendants.* Philadelphia: Historical Society of Pennsylvania, 1976.

Wallace, David Rains. *The Bonehunters' Revenge: Dinosaurs, Greed, and the Greatest Scientific Feud of the Gilded Age.* New York: Houghton Mifflin, 1999.

Wecter, Dixon. *The Saga of American Society.* New York: Scribner's, 1937.

Wiley, Sarah Elizabeth. "Commerce, Race and Diplomacy: Henry Shelton Sanford and the American Recognition of the International Association of the Congo." PhD diss., University of Montana, 1989.

Willison, George F. *Saints and Strangers: Lives of the Pilgrim Fathers and Their Families.* London: Routledge, 2017.

Woodford, Frank B. *Lewis Cass: The Last Jeffersonian.* New Brunswick, NJ: Rutgers University Press, 1950.

IMAGE CREDITS

Credits for the insert section are as follows: Page 1, image 1 and 2: Wikimedia Commons; image 3: Library of Congress, Prints and Photographs Division. Page 2, image 1: Wikimedia Commons; image 2: Library of Congress, Prints and Photographs Division. Page 3, image 1: Library of Congress, Prints and Photographs Division; image 2: Anne ("Nancy") Cary Randolph Morris (1774–1837), after 1810, unidentified artist, after James Sharples; pastel and gouache on brown paper; overall: 10 x 7 3/4 inches. Gift of Mrs. Gerald Hughes. New-York Historical Society, 1949.72.; image 3: White House Collection/White House Historical Association; image 4: Library of Congress, Historic American Buildings Survey. Page 4, image 1: GRANGER 25 Chapel St. Suite 605 Brooklyn; image 2: Library of Congress, Prints and Photographs Division; image 3: Library of Congress, Prints and Photographs Division. Page 5, image 1: Metropolitan Museum of Art, accession number 37.14.30; image 2: The Morgan Library & Museum / Art Resource, NY; image 3: Library of Congress, Prints and Photographs Division. Page 6, image 1: Courtesy of the Boston Athenaeum; image 2: Wikimedia Commons; image 3: Franklin D. Roosevelt Presidential Library & Museum. Page 7, image 1: Library of Congress, Prints and Photographs Division; image 2: Metropolitan Museum of Art, accession number 49.4; image 3: Wikimedia Commons; image 4: Museum of the City of New York, accession number 40.108.134. Page 8: The Miriam and Ira D. Wallach Division of Art, Prints and Photographs: Print Collection, The New York Public Library. "Ward McAllister." The New York Public

Library Digital Collections. Page 9, image 1: Wikimedia Commons; image 2 and 3: Library of Congress, Prints and Photographs Division; image 4: Bettmann / Getty Images; image 5: Courtesy of Rutherfurd Hall. Page 10, image 1: National Park Service; image 2: Library of Congress, Prints and Photographs Division; image 3: Wikimedia Commons. Page 11, image 1: Photograph by Marina Cicogna, courtesy of Oak Brook Historical Society; image 2 and 3: Courtesy of Adam and Michelle Butler. Page 12, image 1 and 2: Courtesy of Adam and Michelle Butler. Page 13, image 1: Gertrude Sanford Legendre papers, Special Collections, Addlestone Library, College of Charleston; image 2: Wikimedia Commons; image 3: Courtesy of Whitney Tower, Jr. Page 14, image 1: Courtesy of Penelope Tree; image 2: AP Images. Page 15, image 1: Courtesy of George Biddle; image 2: Library of Congress, Prints and Photographs Division. Page 16, image 1: Courtesy of George Biddle; image 2: Courtesy of Liz Bonsal.

INDEX